"The fool that willingly provokes a woman has made himself another evil angel, and a new hell to which all other torments are but mere pastime."

16

Beaumont & Fletcher
"Cupid's Revenge"

John Webster
"The White Devil"

"What do 1612 the dead do, uncle? do they eat, hear music, go a-hunting and be merry, as we that live?"

"No, coz, they sleep."

"Lord, Lord, that I were dead. I have not slept these six nights."

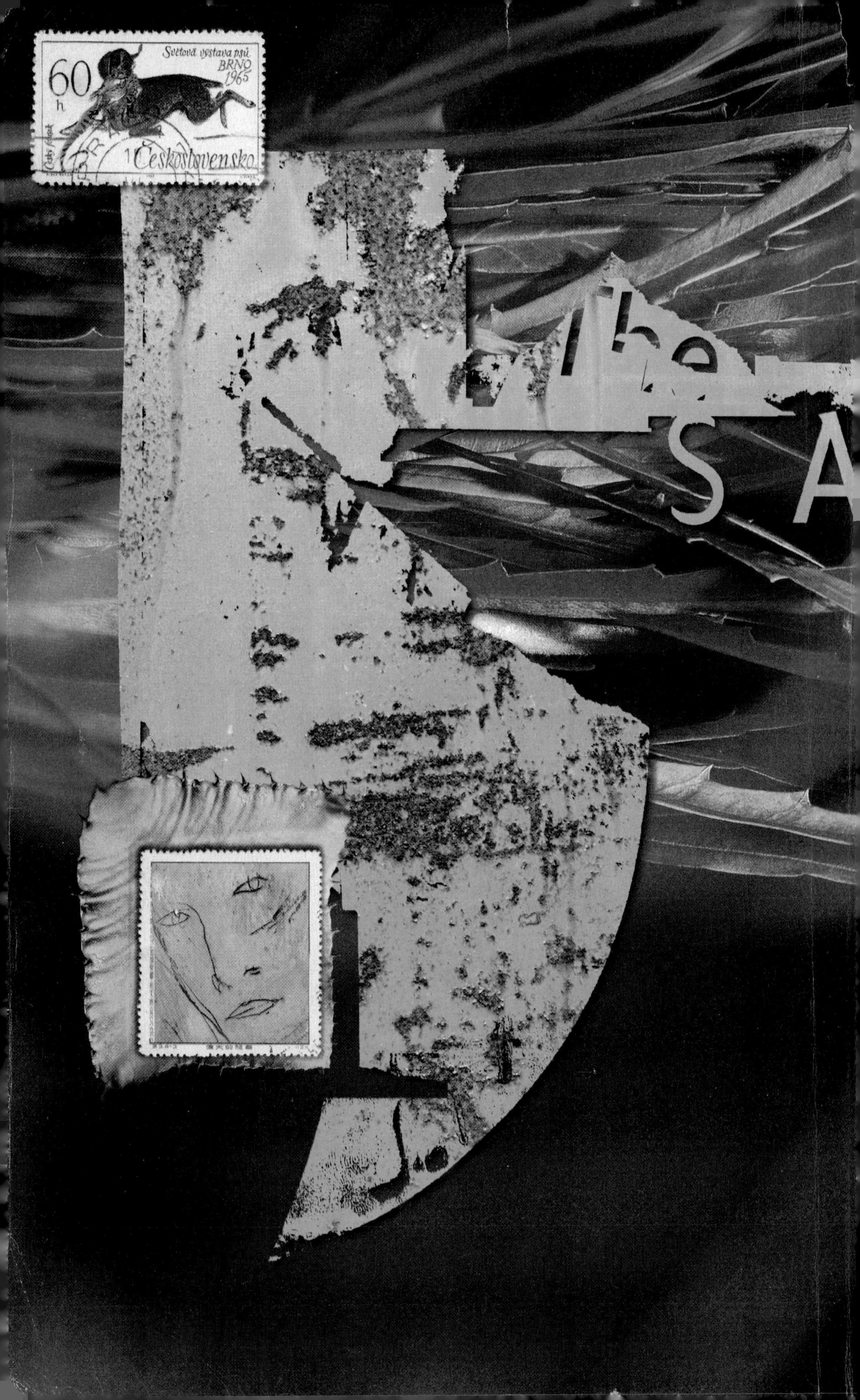
60
h.
Světová výstava psů
BRNO
1965
Československo
S A

The Kindly Ones

Writer:
Neil Gaiman

Artists:
Marc Hempel
Richard Case, D'Israeli,
Teddy Kristiansen, Glyn Dillon,
Charles Vess, Dean Ormston,
Kevin Nowlan

Colorist:
Daniel Vozzo

Separations:
Android Images

Letterers:
Todd Klein
Kevin Nowlan

Covers* and Design:
Dave McKean

*Photo of Ruby on page 72 by permission of **Sheila Metzner**.

Introduction by:
Frank McConnell

THE SANDMAN featuring characters created by
Gaiman, Kieth and **Dringenberg.**

THE

KINDLY

SANDMAN ONES

PUBLISHED BY DC COMICS. COVER AND COMPILATION COPYRIGHT
© 1996 DC COMICS. ALL RIGHTS RESERVED. ORIGINALLY PUBLISHED
IN SINGLE MAGAZINE FORM AS THE SANDMAN 57-69 AND IN
VERTIGO JAM 1. COPYRIGHT © 1993, 1994, 1995 DC COMICS.
ALL RIGHTS RESERVED. ALL CHARACTERS, THEIR DISTINCTIVE
LIKENESSES AND RELATED ELEMENTS FEATURED IN THIS PUBLICATION
ARE TRADEMARKS OF DC COMICS. THE STORIES, CHARACTERS
AND INCIDENTS FEATURED IN THIS PUBLICATION ARE ENTIRELY
FICTIONAL. DC COMICS DOES NOT READ OR ACCEPT UNSOLICITED
SUBMISSIONS OF IDEAS, STORIES OR ARTWORK.
DC COMICS, 1700 BROADWAY, NEW YORK, NY 10019
A WARNER BROS. ENTERTAINMENT COMPANY
PRINTED IN CANADA
ISBN: 1-56389-205-7
COVER AND PUBLICATION DESIGN BY
Dave McKean.
SEVENTH PRINTING.

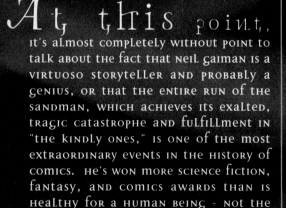

At this point, it's almost completely without point to talk about the fact that neil gaiman is a virtuoso storyteller and probably a genius, or that the entire run of the sandman, which achieves its exalted, tragic catastrophe and fulfillment in "the kindly ones," is one of the most extraordinary events in the history of comics. he's won more science fiction, fantasy, and comics awards than is healthy for a human being - not the least of his accomplishments is that, with all this recognition, he remains a lovely guy - so he doesn't need any new

salaams. and as for the work itself, all you have to do is open any sandman, to any page, and, if you can read at all, you gasp, and when you get your breath back you realize that you're just where all great art is designed to take you: in the presence of the holy.

and that's not a word - "holy" - that i use lightly. amiri baraka, back when he was leroi jones, wrote that art is whatever makes you proud to be human. that is one hell of a good definition of art, and also of the religious impulse, which is after all just the artistic impulse wearing a different hat: the desire to say or see something that convinces us we matter, that our messy, brief lives have a sense, a direction, a clear vector, despite their messiness and brevity. art isn't "order out of chaos": that's god's problem, whoever he/she is. art is the dream of order out of the sense of chaos: the three-cushion shot to the eight ball, the hewn stone that looks like the god apollo, charlie parker improvising on "how high the moon," or fred astaire, even if he's only walking across a room. or "the kindly ones." you hold in your hands one of the most stunning stories of the last half century - in any medium.

peter straub concluded his afterword to an earlier sandman story arc, "brief lives," by writing, "if this isn't literature, nothing is." i couldn't agree more passionately. (i just wish straub hadn't said it first.) as soon as the academic critics get off their famously insensitive butts - i work with them, so trust me, these guys would sleep through the second coming - as soon as they get off their butts and realize it's okay to admire a mere comic book, you'll see dissertations, books, annotations galore on the sandman, and then on the great comics writers - alan moore, frank miller, will eisner, the list is so long - who were his "precursors." gaiman would hate this comparison, being a modest fellow, but he's done for comics what duke ellington did for jazz in the thirties: produced work of such overwhelming magnificence that even the invincibly snobbish and the terminally tone-deaf have to dig it.

dream dies at the end. sorry to bust your bubble, but this is a tragedy - as classically a tragedy as has been written in a long time - so you should know, at the outset, how it's going to end: or do you want hamlet, maybe, to realize it was all just a silly mistake, marry ophelia, and settle down in a nice condo in a really good part of denmark?

dream dies at the end, and part of the wonderfulness of "the kindly ones" is the way it makes that death, in the manner of all great tragedy, seem so inevitable and so finally - not too strong a word - enriching.

dream dies. but how can an anthropomorphic projection of consciousness die, really? well, it can't, although in another way it can. in the last episode, dream of the seven endless, morpheus, the shaper of form, the very principle of storytelling, does indeed die - or possibly commits a complicated form of suicide - only to be replaced by another aspect of himself, a new dream who is himself and yet is not, is subtly and crucially different because humans can no more live without telling themselves stories than you or i can kill ourselves by holding our breath.

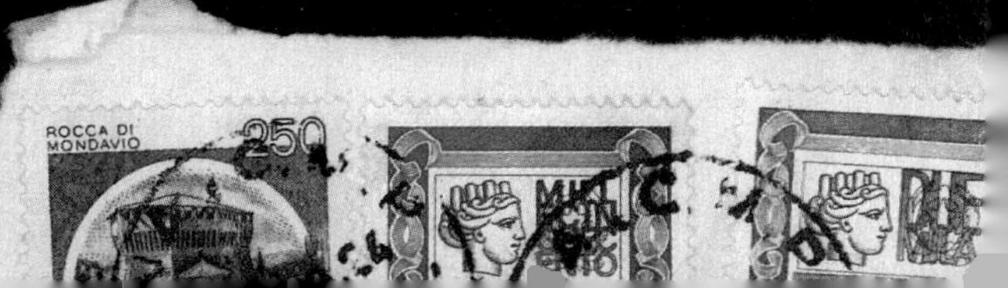
ROCCA DI MONDAVIO
250

gaiman has said repeatedly that the sandman would conclude when the story begun in the first issue was completed. to many who have followed the book through its five-year development, that often seemed a heroic, but rather rash, claim. "the kindly ones" ends with monthly issue #69, and with that issue, he makes good his promise. in the first issue, dream is imprisoned (in 1916) by a black magician in england, only to escape and reclaim his kingdom in 1988, the year, of course, when sandman first appears. one of the endless, one of the seven more-than-gods who are, in fact, the constituents of human consciousness itself, has been trapped by a mere mortal: has been taught painfully that he is not only a transcendent projection of human consciousness, but that he is, after all, dependent upon human consciousness for his existence. and in "the kindly ones," dream, five years after his escape (gaiman is meticulous about time-frames), acknowledges his dependence on the ordinary stuff of human life and accepts - or engineers? - his death and transfiguration into a new dream, into a version of himself more human - the new dream is the exaltation of the child, daniel. - than he thinks he could be.

that's the basic plot of "the kindly ones," and that's the plot of sandman altogether: dream's dawning realization of the poignancy of mortal life, and of his own inescapable implication in that poignancy. the kindly ones, the erinyes, the furies, the eumenides, chase down his life throughout this book because he has killed his son, orpheus: at orpheus's request, to be sure, but nevertheless he has killed him. and with that act dream has entered time, choice, guilt, and regret - has entered the sphere of the human. in chapter eleven, after he has left the security of the dreaming, the fairy nuala, who has summoned him, asks him the question that may be the central secret of the tale. "you . . . you want them to punish you, don't you? you want to be punished for orpheus's death." and the next frame, dream's response, is simply a wordless, tight close-up of his tortured face. (that's an effect, by the way, that neither a novel nor a film could achieve with the same force, since a novel would have to describe his face, and a film could only give us an actor trying to imitate that bleak mask of regret. the comic, in marc hempel's brilliantly reductive drawing style, gives us the thing itself.)

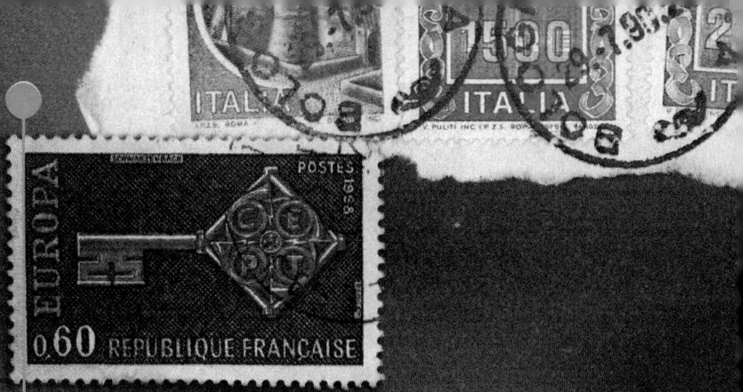
ITALIA
ITALIA
EUROPA
POSTES
1968
0,60 REPUBLIQUE FRANCAISE

i mentioned the inevitability of the tragedy. and inevitable it certainly is. of all gaiman's story arcs, this one has the clearest and most driven momentum of plot. we begin and end with the kindly ones, the furies themselves, but in their aspect not as the furies but as the fates: young clotho, who spins the thread of life, maternal lachesis, who measures it, and old atropos, who cuts it off. this is the archaic triple goddess, who has appeared in sandman from the second issue, and whose power is even greater than that of the endless.

it's absolutely characteristic of gaiman's imagination, though, that these all-powerful goddesses are represented as three women of varying ages, spinning yarn and having tea in a cozy english cottage - even though the oldest does have a dead mouse instead of a cookie with her tea. that layering of the mythic and the everyday is what gives the book its inimitable tone, the tone you also catch in joyce, faulkner, and thomas pynchon.

but there's more. notice that the conversation among the ladies at the opening is deliberately constructed to refer to the act of telling the final major tale in the sandman series. "what are you making him them," asks clotho of lachesis in the third frame of the first chapter. "i can't say that i'm terribly certain, my popsy," she replies. "but it's a fine yarn, and i don't doubt that it'll suit. go with anything, this will." the story begins as a story about storytelling, but also as a story - one of almost mythic simplicity - in its own right: without, sorry for the pun, dropping a stitch.

in fact, eight of the thirteen chapters begin, in the first frame, with a thread of some sort running across the panel, and with a comment that applies equally to the telling of the tale and to the tale itself: "well? how long is it going to take (chapter two)?" "i think it's going to be bigger than i planned (three)." "i wish i could be sure i was doing the right thing (four)." and so on, and so on.

now, this is the kind of writing literary critics like to call "postmodern": letting the reader know you're conscious of what you're doing at the very time you do it. and a writer like gaiman is smart enough to realize that kind of performance is about as "modern" as the odyssey or the divine comedy. the great storytellers have always wanted to tell us as much about the business of storytelling as about the stories themselves. gaiman's opening frames, with their running threads and their comment upon the tale itself, are simply his way of emphasizing that the tale possesses him as much as it does us - and that the thread of story will lead to its inevitable end, however many knots and snags develop in its unraveling.

and knots and snags do develop, thank god. approximately the first forty issues of sandman, brilliant as they are, appeared desultory: stories of genius, but without a clear center, without a clear direction. and then, beginning with "brief lives," the whole thing began to take on an overwhelming speed and shape: the byways and digressions of the early tales began to coalesce into one, stunning, final movement: a comparison to symphonic structure isn't inappropriate here.

and that final movement is the book you're about to read.

gaiman has invented so many characters, so many storylines, over the course of this - okay, i'll say it - epic. he has reintroduced teutonic, greek, egyptian and japanese gods, all of them with absolute accuracy and respect; he has made up delightful characters from the realm of dream, like the prim librarian lucien, the smart-ass pumpkin mervyn; and he has introduced us to fallible human beings, from the feckless rose walker to the arrogant, quasi-immortal hob gadling to the bitter, half-crazed lyta hall. all these, and more, appear in "the kindly ones" - just the way a symphony's fourth movement should include themes from the first three. there's something seriously and a little scarily dickensian in all this. like dickens, who also wrote for serial publication (which means you can't go back and revise your last chapter, because it's already in print), he throws an impossible number of balls in the air, keeps them all aloft during the act, and then gathers them all into his arms as he takes a bow. "what did we make? what was it, in the end?" asks clotho of lachesis, in their cozy home, at the very end. "what it always is," lachesis answers. "a handful of yarn; a little weaving and stitching; some embroidering perhaps. a few loose ends, but that's only to be expected." if there's a more satisfying end to a recent work of fiction - or a better definition of what fiction is - i'm sure i don't know it.

does this mean gaiman is a mind like mozart, who heard every detail of a composition clearly from the first note, or like charlie parker, who would begin to improvise and then weave his random phrases into a perfect pristine whole? i can't get a straight answer out of him on this, and maybe he doesn't know himself. no matter: if you don't realize that wolfie and bird are equally great souls, then you shouldn't be listening to music at all. (try kenny g.)

the point is that this story is a magnificent parable about the humanization of myth; about how the values of regret, responsibility and the awful duties of love outweigh even the power and majesty of the gods we invent and then worship. the very last story arc, "the wake," introduces the new dream (daniel that was, morpheus that is no longer) to the family of the endless: destiny, death, destruction who has left his post, desire, despair, and the wonderful delirium who was once called delight. it is a coda: a graceful, solemn, melancholy farewell to gaiman's astonishingly original blending of myth, folklore, comedy, and human striving and human confusion. we can't talk about its intricacies, its plots-within-plots, its wit, of above all its rich, inexhaustibly allusive language: there's no space.

For the three witches, fates, Norns and graces of sandman, who have midwifed sandman, nurtured it and, issue by issue, put it to bed, this book is for: — the three wired sisters

Shelly Roeberg, Alisa Kwitney & above all, Sandman's fairy godmother, Karen Berger. With gratitude, Neil Gaiman

introduction by Frank McConnell

What we can say is that if this isn't Literature, then nothing is - quoting brother straub - and, more, that this is the stuff of which Literature itself is made: Learned, complex, straightforward, funny, melancholy, and irresistibly humanizing.

frank mcconnell got his ba at notre dame and his ph.d. at yale the year sergeant pepper came out. he taught at cornell when the doors were big; at northwestern between the fall of nixon and the rise of the clash; at uc santa barbara while reagan doodled, bush dawdled and clinton diddled.

(also in east berlin the year before the wall came down - he claims no credit.) has written a lot of books and essays and four detective novels, all better hidden than the secret testament of eliphaz (which, by the bye, doesn't exist). does not, he insists, know what became of the cat halloween night nineteen-eighty-five and can not get neil gaiman to have a brandy and beer chaser before lunch. so far.

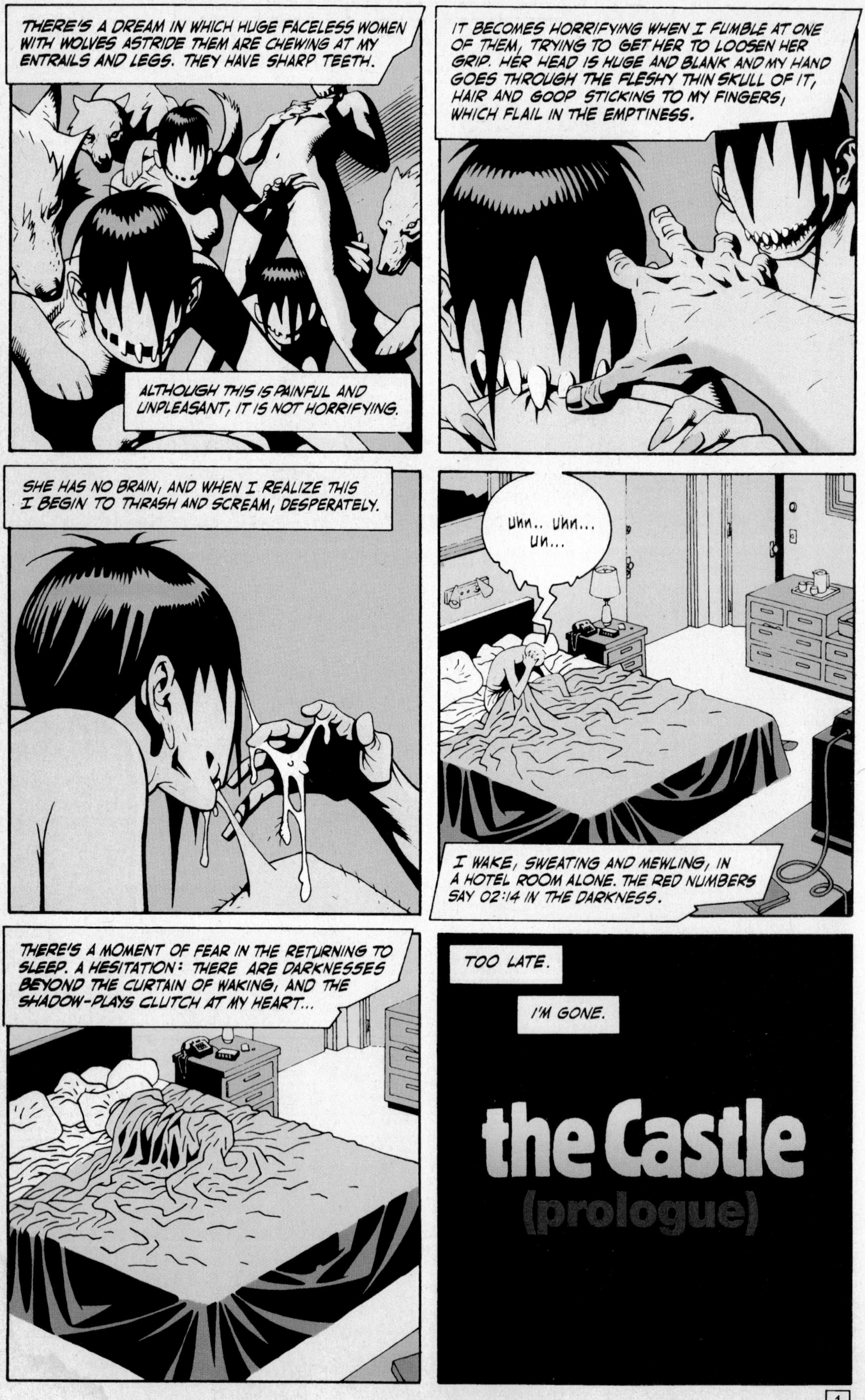

THERE'S A DREAM IN WHICH HUGE FACELESS WOMEN WITH WOLVES ASTRIDE THEM ARE CHEWING AT MY ENTRAILS AND LEGS. THEY HAVE SHARP TEETH.
ALTHOUGH THIS IS PAINFUL AND UNPLEASANT, IT IS NOT HORRIFYING.
IT BECOMES HORRIFYING WHEN I FUMBLE AT ONE OF THEM, TRYING TO GET HER TO LOOSEN HER GRIP. HER HEAD IS HUGE AND BLANK AND MY HAND GOES THROUGH THE FLESHY THIN SKULL OF IT, HAIR AND GOOP STICKING TO MY FINGERS, WHICH FLAIL IN THE EMPTINESS.
SHE HAS NO BRAIN, AND WHEN I REALIZE THIS I BEGIN TO THRASH AND SCREAM, DESPERATELY.
UHN.. UHN... UN...
I WAKE, SWEATING AND MEWLING, IN A HOTEL ROOM ALONE. THE RED NUMBERS SAY 02:14 IN THE DARKNESS.
THERE'S A MOMENT OF FEAR IN THE RETURNING TO SLEEP. A HESITATION: THERE ARE DARKNESSES BEYOND THE CURTAIN OF WAKING, AND THE SHADOW-PLAYS CLUTCH AT MY HEART...
TOO LATE.
I'M GONE.
the Castle
(prologue)

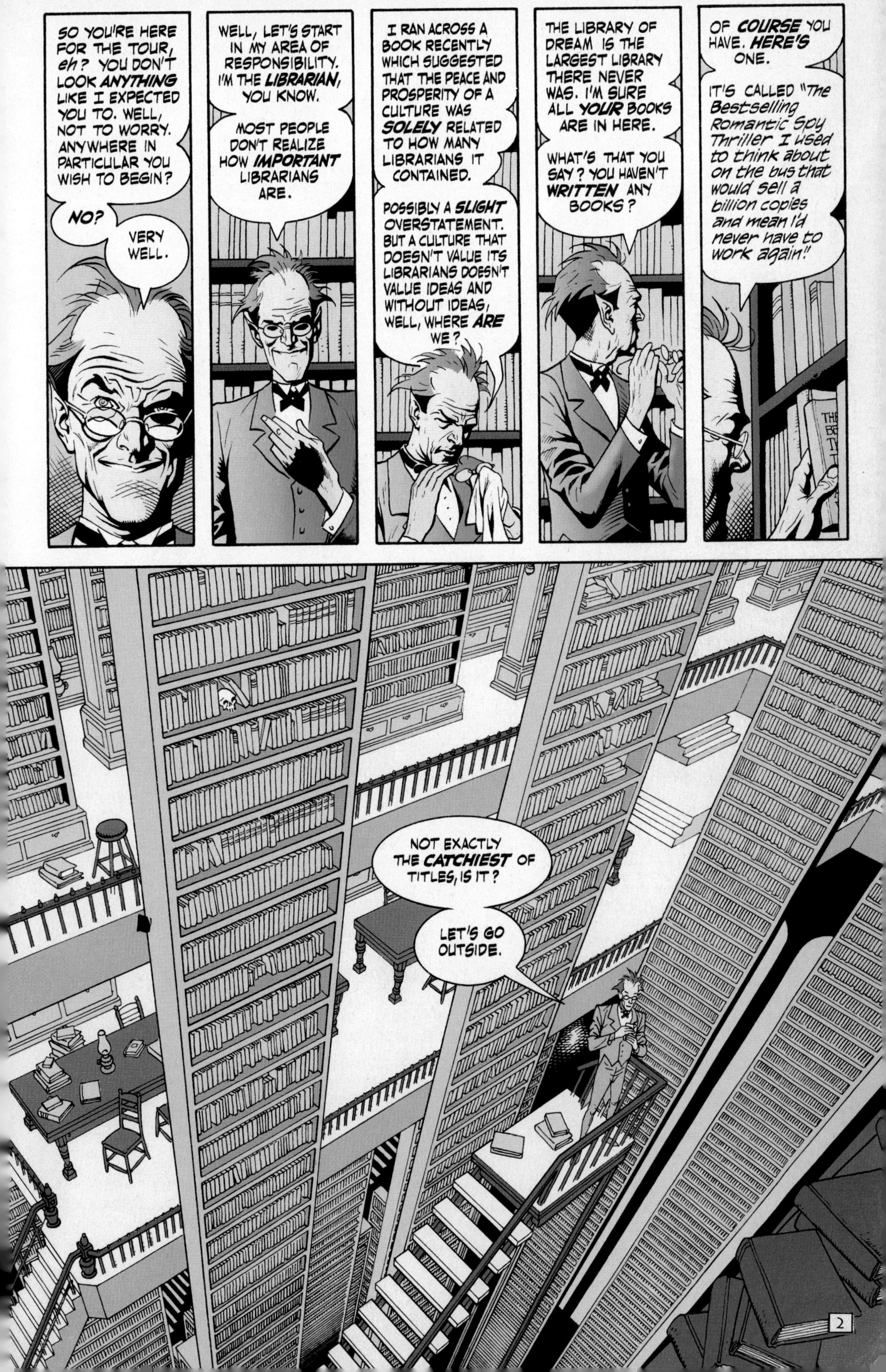
SO YOU'RE HERE FOR THE TOUR, *eh?* YOU DON'T LOOK **ANYTHING** LIKE I EXPECTED YOU TO. WELL, NOT TO WORRY. ANYWHERE IN PARTICULAR YOU WISH TO BEGIN?
NO?
VERY WELL.
WELL, LET'S START IN MY AREA OF RESPONSIBILITY. I'M THE **LIBRARIAN**, YOU KNOW.
MOST PEOPLE DON'T REALIZE HOW **IMPORTANT** LIBRARIANS ARE.
I RAN ACROSS A BOOK RECENTLY WHICH SUGGESTED THAT THE PEACE AND PROSPERITY OF A CULTURE WAS **SOLELY** RELATED TO HOW MANY LIBRARIANS IT CONTAINED.
POSSIBLY A **SLIGHT** OVERSTATEMENT. BUT A CULTURE THAT DOESN'T VALUE ITS LIBRARIANS DOESN'T VALUE IDEAS AND WITHOUT IDEAS, WELL, WHERE **ARE** WE?
THE LIBRARY OF DREAM IS THE LARGEST LIBRARY THERE NEVER WAS. I'M SURE ALL **YOUR** BOOKS ARE IN HERE.
WHAT'S THAT YOU SAY? YOU HAVEN'T **WRITTEN** ANY BOOKS?
OF **COURSE** YOU HAVE. **HERE'S** ONE.
IT'S CALLED "*The Bestselling Romantic Spy Thriller I used to think about on the bus that would sell a billion copies and mean I'd never have to work again.*"
NOT EXACTLY THE **CATCHIEST** OF TITLES, IS IT?
LET'S GO OUTSIDE.

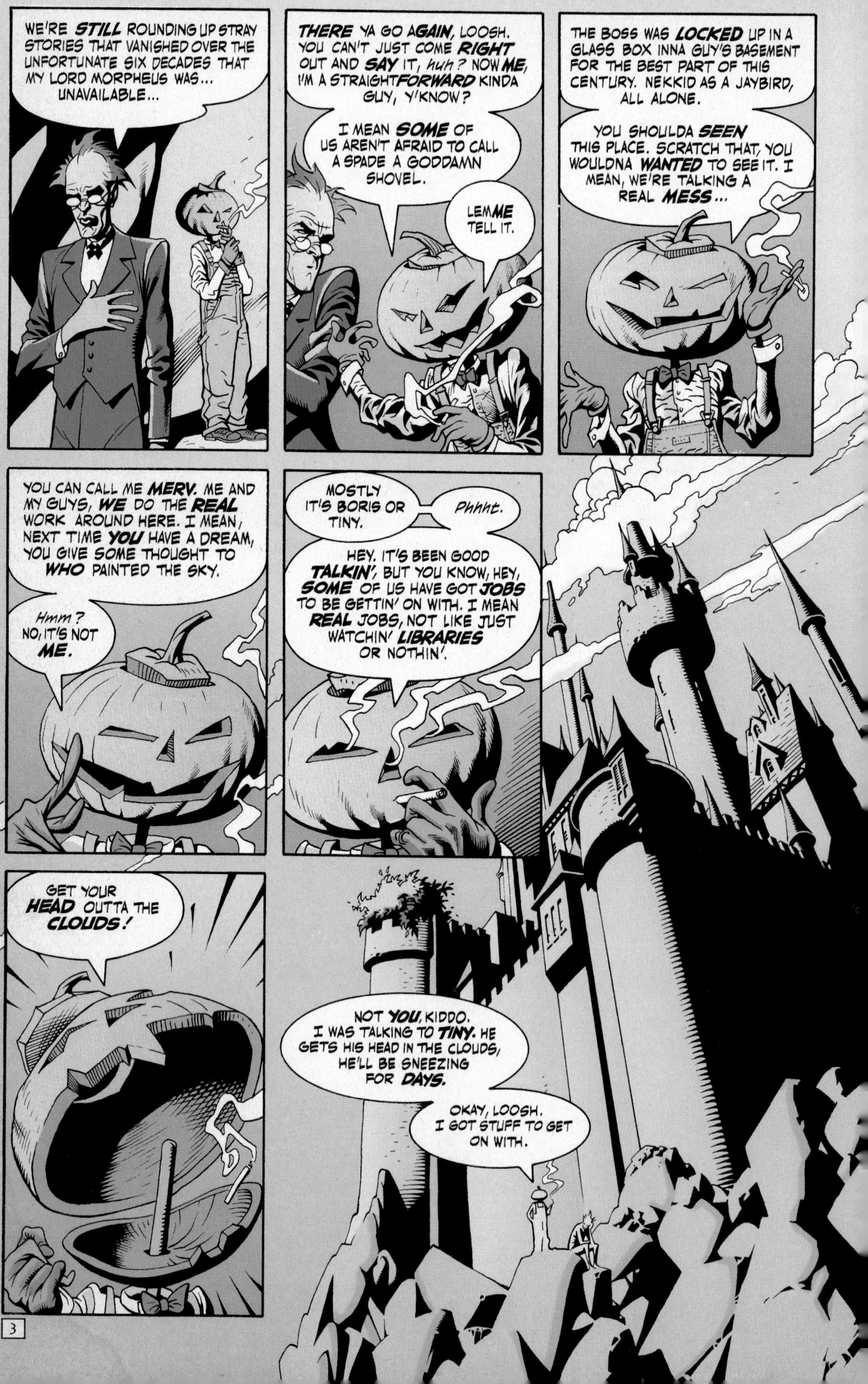
WE'RE STILL ROUNDING UP STRAY STORIES THAT VANISHED OVER THE UNFORTUNATE SIX DECADES THAT MY LORD MORPHEUS WAS... UNAVAILABLE...
THERE YA GO AGAIN, LOOSH. YOU CAN'T JUST COME RIGHT OUT AND SAY IT, huh? NOW ME, I'M A STRAIGHTFORWARD KINDA GUY, Y'KNOW?
I MEAN SOME OF US AREN'T AFRAID TO CALL A SPADE A GODDAMN SHOVEL.
LEMME TELL IT.
THE BOSS WAS LOCKED UP IN A GLASS BOX INNA GUY'S BASEMENT FOR THE BEST PART OF THIS CENTURY. NEKKID AS A JAYBIRD, ALL ALONE.
YOU SHOULDA SEEN THIS PLACE. SCRATCH THAT, YOU WOULDNA WANTED TO SEE IT. I MEAN, WE'RE TALKING A REAL MESS...
YOU CAN CALL ME MERV. ME AND MY GUYS, WE DO THE REAL WORK AROUND HERE. I MEAN, NEXT TIME YOU HAVE A DREAM, YOU GIVE SOME THOUGHT TO WHO PAINTED THE SKY.
Hmm? NO, IT'S NOT ME.
MOSTLY IT'S BORIS OR TINY.
Phhht.
HEY. IT'S BEEN GOOD TALKIN', BUT YOU KNOW, HEY, SOME OF US HAVE GOT JOBS TO BE GETTIN' ON WITH. I MEAN REAL JOBS, NOT LIKE JUST WATCHIN' LIBRARIES OR NOTHIN'.
GET YOUR HEAD OUTTA THE CLOUDS!
NOT YOU, KIDDO. I WAS TALKING TO TINY. HE GETS HIS HEAD IN THE CLOUDS, HE'LL BE SNEEZING FOR DAYS.
OKAY, LOOSH. I GOT STUFF TO GET ON WITH.

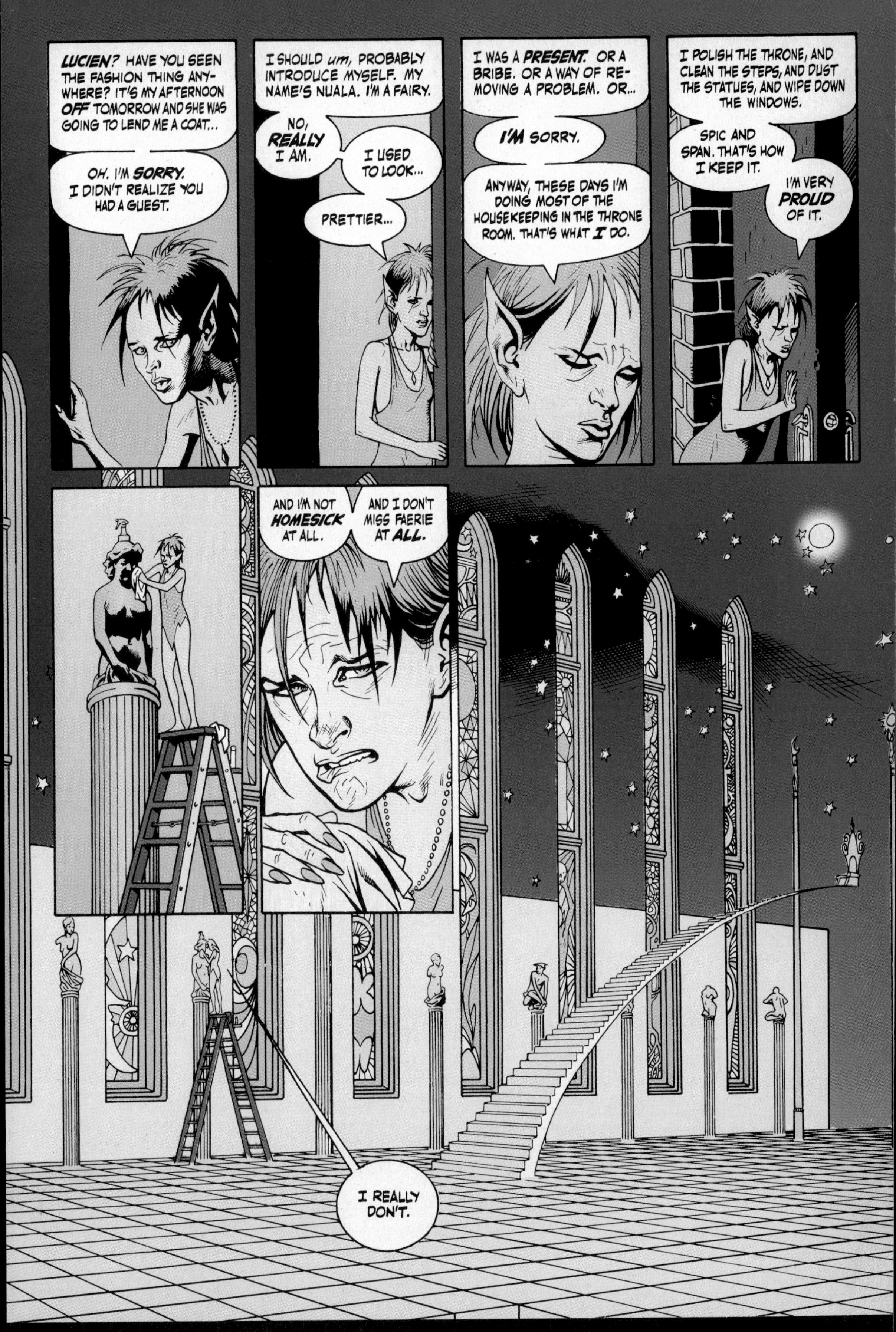
LUCIEN? HAVE YOU SEEN THE FASHION THING ANY-WHERE? IT'S MY AFTERNOON OFF TOMORROW AND SHE WAS GOING TO LEND ME A COAT...
OH. I'M SORRY. I DIDN'T REALIZE YOU HAD A GUEST.
I SHOULD um, PROBABLY INTRODUCE MYSELF. MY NAME'S NUALA. I'M A FAIRY.
NO, REALLY I AM.
I USED TO LOOK...
PRETTIER...
I WAS A PRESENT. OR A BRIBE. OR A WAY OF RE-MOVING A PROBLEM. OR...
I'M SORRY.
ANYWAY, THESE DAYS I'M DOING MOST OF THE HOUSEKEEPING IN THE THRONE ROOM. THAT'S WHAT I DO.
I POLISH THE THRONE, AND CLEAN THE STEPS, AND DUST THE STATUES, AND WIPE DOWN THE WINDOWS.
SPIC AND SPAN. THAT'S HOW I KEEP IT.
I'M VERY PROUD OF IT.
AND I'M NOT HOMESICK AT ALL.
AND I DON'T MISS FAERIE AT ALL.
I REALLY DON'T.

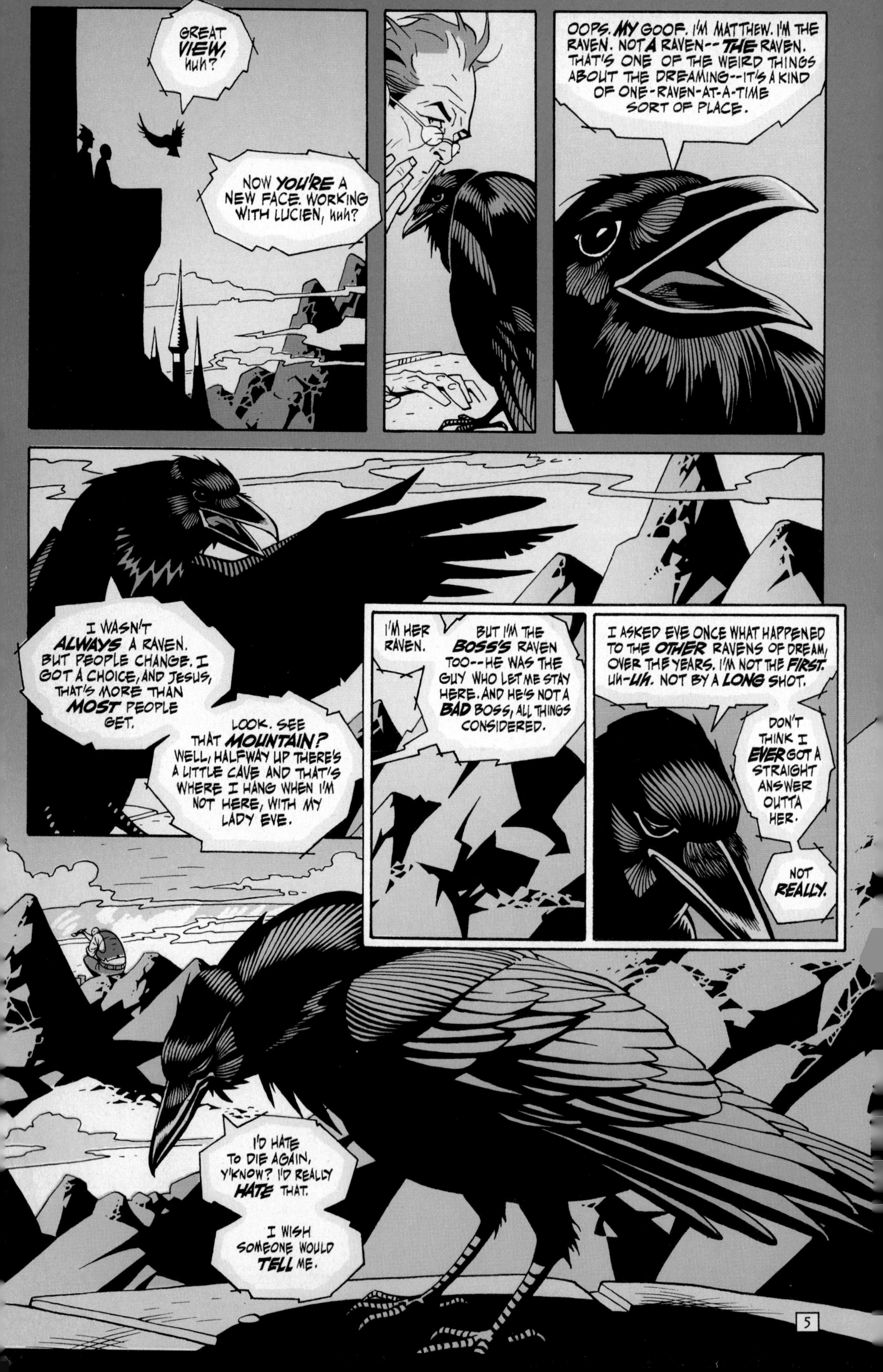
GREAT VIEW, huh?
NOW YOU'RE A NEW FACE. WORKING WITH LUCIEN, huh?
OOPS. MY GOOF. I'M MATTHEW. I'M THE RAVEN. NOT A RAVEN-- THE RAVEN. THAT'S ONE OF THE WEIRD THINGS ABOUT THE DREAMING--IT'S A KIND OF ONE-RAVEN-AT-A-TIME SORT OF PLACE.
I WASN'T ALWAYS A RAVEN. BUT PEOPLE CHANGE. I GOT A CHOICE, AND JESUS, THAT'S MORE THAN MOST PEOPLE GET.
LOOK. SEE THAT MOUNTAIN? WELL, HALFWAY UP THERE'S A LITTLE CAVE AND THAT'S WHERE I HANG WHEN I'M NOT HERE, WITH MY LADY EVE.
I'M HER RAVEN.
BUT I'M THE BOSS'S RAVEN TOO--HE WAS THE GUY WHO LET ME STAY HERE. AND HE'S NOT A BAD BOSS, ALL THINGS CONSIDERED.
I ASKED EVE ONCE WHAT HAPPENED TO THE OTHER RAVENS OF DREAM, OVER THE YEARS. I'M NOT THE FIRST. uh-uh. NOT BY A LONG SHOT.
DON'T THINK I EVER GOT A STRAIGHT ANSWER OUTTA HER.
NOT REALLY.
I'D HATE TO DIE AGAIN, Y'KNOW? I'D REALLY HATE THAT.
I WISH SOMEONE WOULD TELL ME.

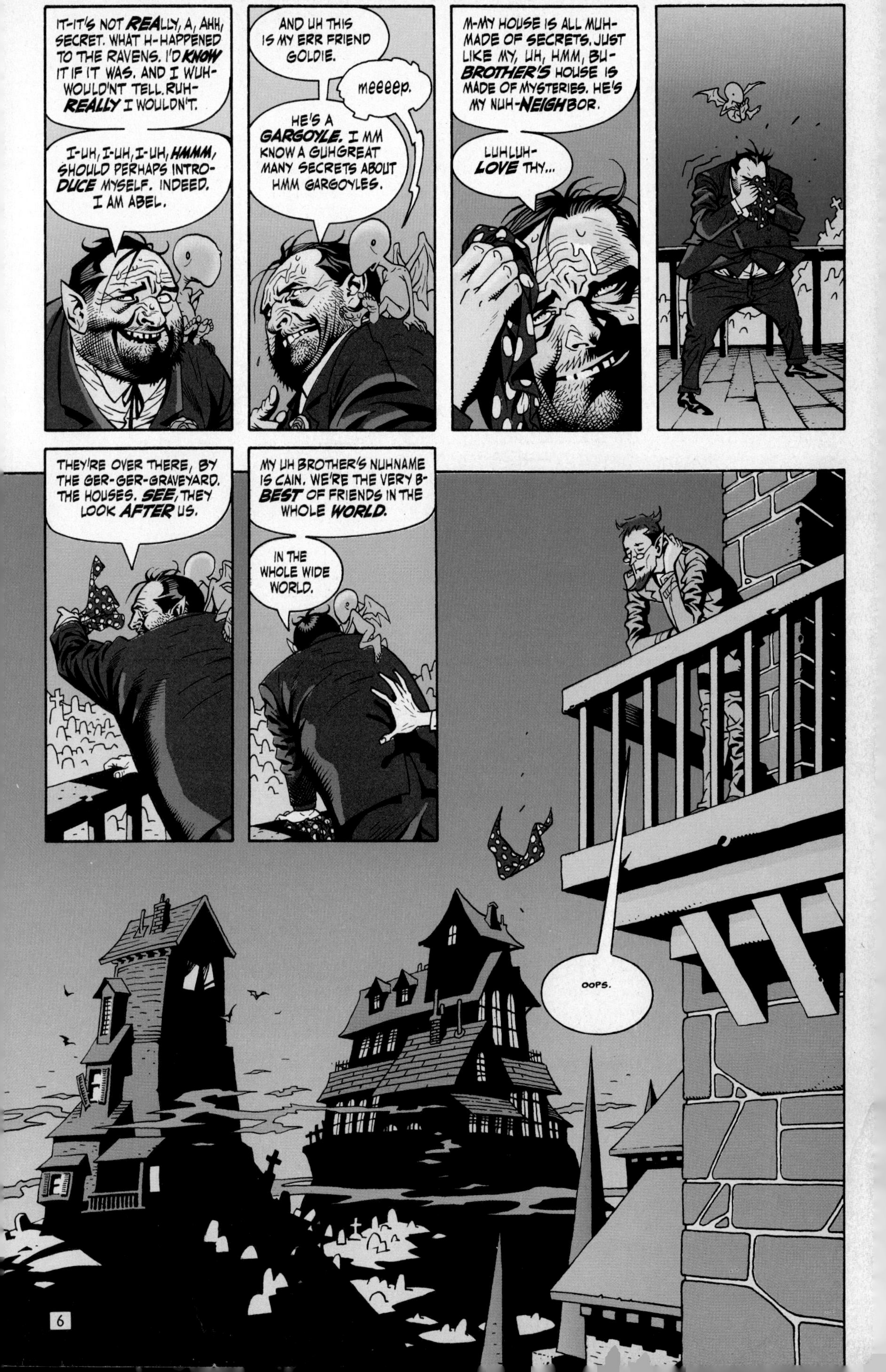
IT-IT'S NOT REALLY, A, AHH, SECRET. WHAT H-HAPPENED TO THE RAVENS. I'D KNOW IT IF IT WAS. AND I WUH-WOULDN'T TELL. RUH-REALLY I WOULDN'T.
I-UH, I-UH, I-UH, HMMM, SHOULD PERHAPS INTRODUCE MYSELF. INDEED. I AM ABEL.
AND UH THIS IS MY ERR FRIEND GOLDIE.
meeeep.
HE'S A GARGOYLE. I MM KNOW A GUHGREAT MANY SECRETS ABOUT HMM GARGOYLES.
M-MY HOUSE IS ALL MUH-MADE OF SECRETS. JUST LIKE MY, UH, HMM, BU-BROTHER'S HOUSE IS MADE OF MYSTERIES. HE'S MY NUH-NEIGHBOR.
LUHLUH-LOVE THY...
THEY'RE OVER THERE, BY THE GER-GER-GRAVEYARD. THE HOUSES. SEE, THEY LOOK AFTER US.
MY UH BROTHER'S NUHNAME IS CAIN. WE'RE THE VERY B-BEST OF FRIENDS IN THE WHOLE WORLD.
IN THE WHOLE WIDE WORLD.
OOPS.

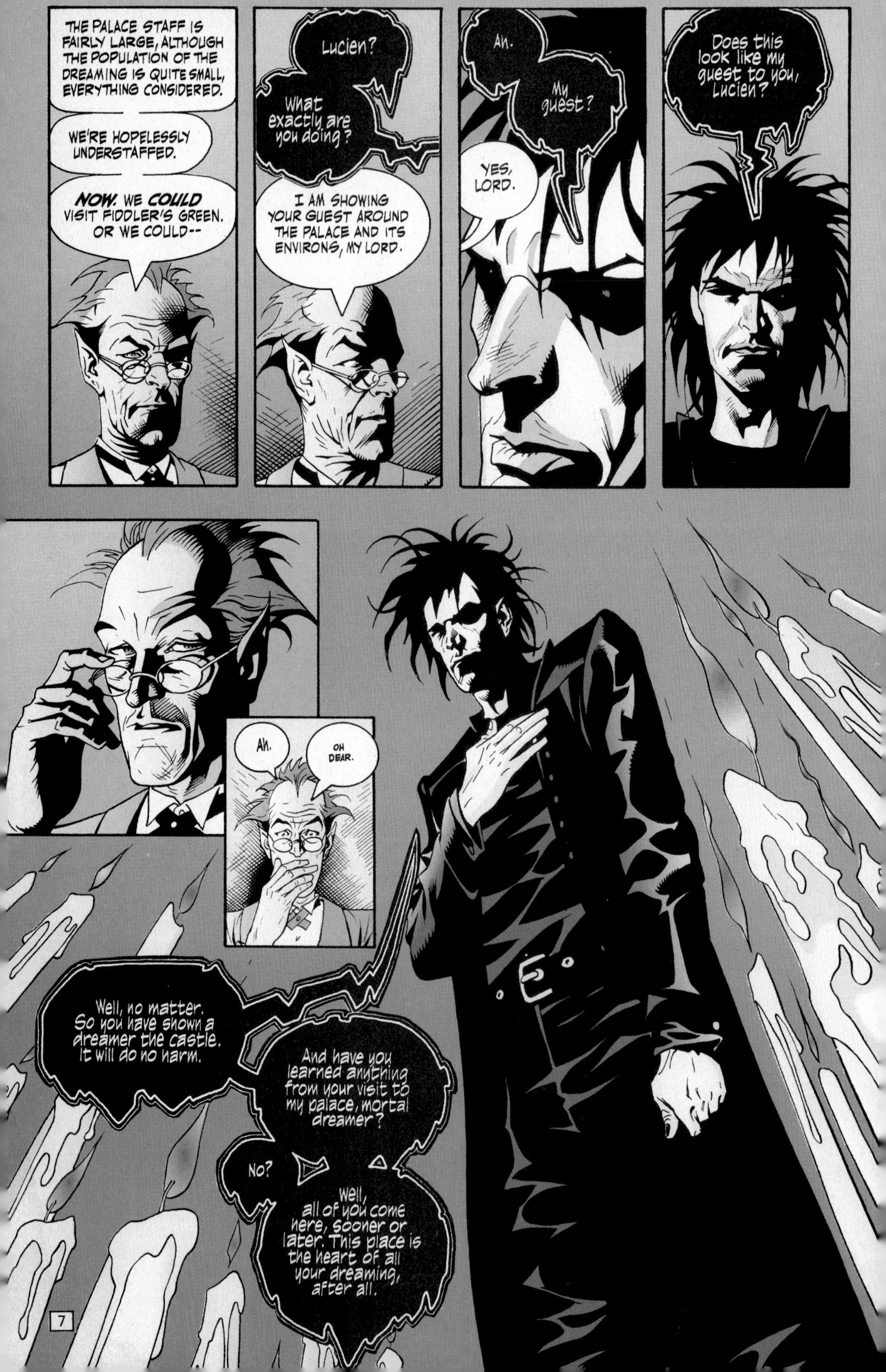
THE PALACE STAFF IS FAIRLY LARGE, ALTHOUGH THE POPULATION OF THE DREAMING IS QUITE SMALL, EVERYTHING CONSIDERED.
WE'RE HOPELESSLY UNDERSTAFFED.
NOW. WE COULD VISIT FIDDLER'S GREEN. OR WE COULD--
Lucien?
What exactly are you doing?
I AM SHOWING YOUR GUEST AROUND THE PALACE AND ITS ENVIRONS, MY LORD.
Ah.
My guest?
YES, LORD.
Does this look like my guest to you, Lucien?
Ah.
OH DEAR.
Well, no matter. So you have shown a dreamer the castle. It will do no harm.
And have you learned anything from your visit to my palace, mortal dreamer?
No?
Well, all of you come here, sooner or later. This place is the heart of all your dreaming, after all.
7

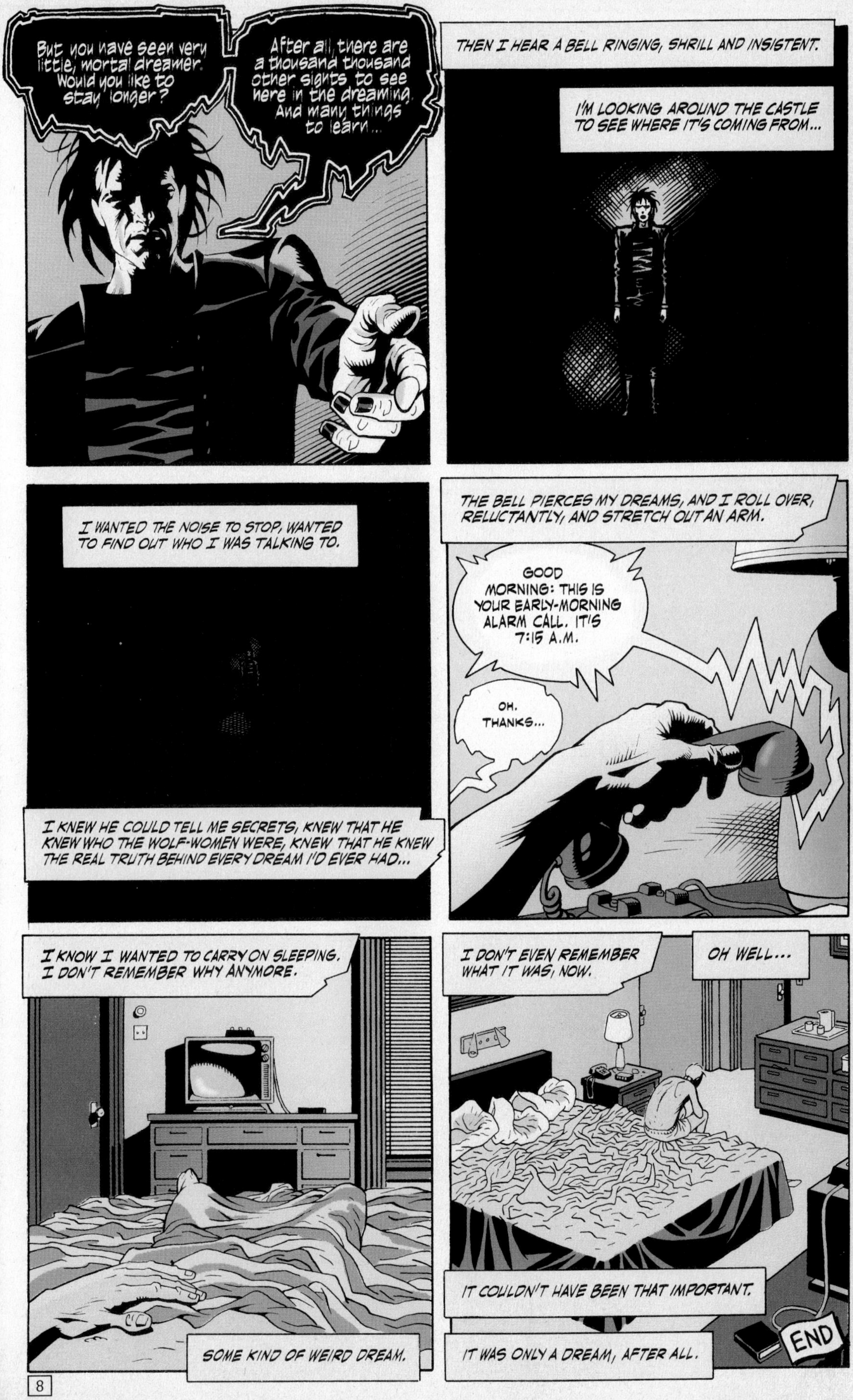
But you have seen very little, mortal dreamer. Would you like to stay longer?
After all, there are a thousand thousand other sights to see here in the dreaming. And many things to learn...
THEN I HEAR A BELL RINGING, SHRILL AND INSISTENT.
I'M LOOKING AROUND THE CASTLE TO SEE WHERE IT'S COMING FROM...
I WANTED THE NOISE TO STOP, WANTED TO FIND OUT WHO I WAS TALKING TO.
I KNEW HE COULD TELL ME SECRETS, KNEW THAT HE KNEW WHO THE WOLF-WOMEN WERE, KNEW THAT HE KNEW THE REAL TRUTH BEHIND EVERY DREAM I'D EVER HAD...
THE BELL PIERCES MY DREAMS, AND I ROLL OVER, RELUCTANTLY, AND STRETCH OUT AN ARM.
GOOD MORNING: THIS IS YOUR EARLY-MORNING ALARM CALL. IT'S 7:15 A.M.
OH. THANKS...
I KNOW I WANTED TO CARRY ON SLEEPING. I DON'T REMEMBER WHY ANYMORE.
SOME KIND OF WEIRD DREAM.
I DON'T EVEN REMEMBER WHAT IT WAS, NOW.
OH WELL...
IT COULDN'T HAVE BEEN THAT IMPORTANT.
IT WAS ONLY A DREAM, AFTER ALL.
END

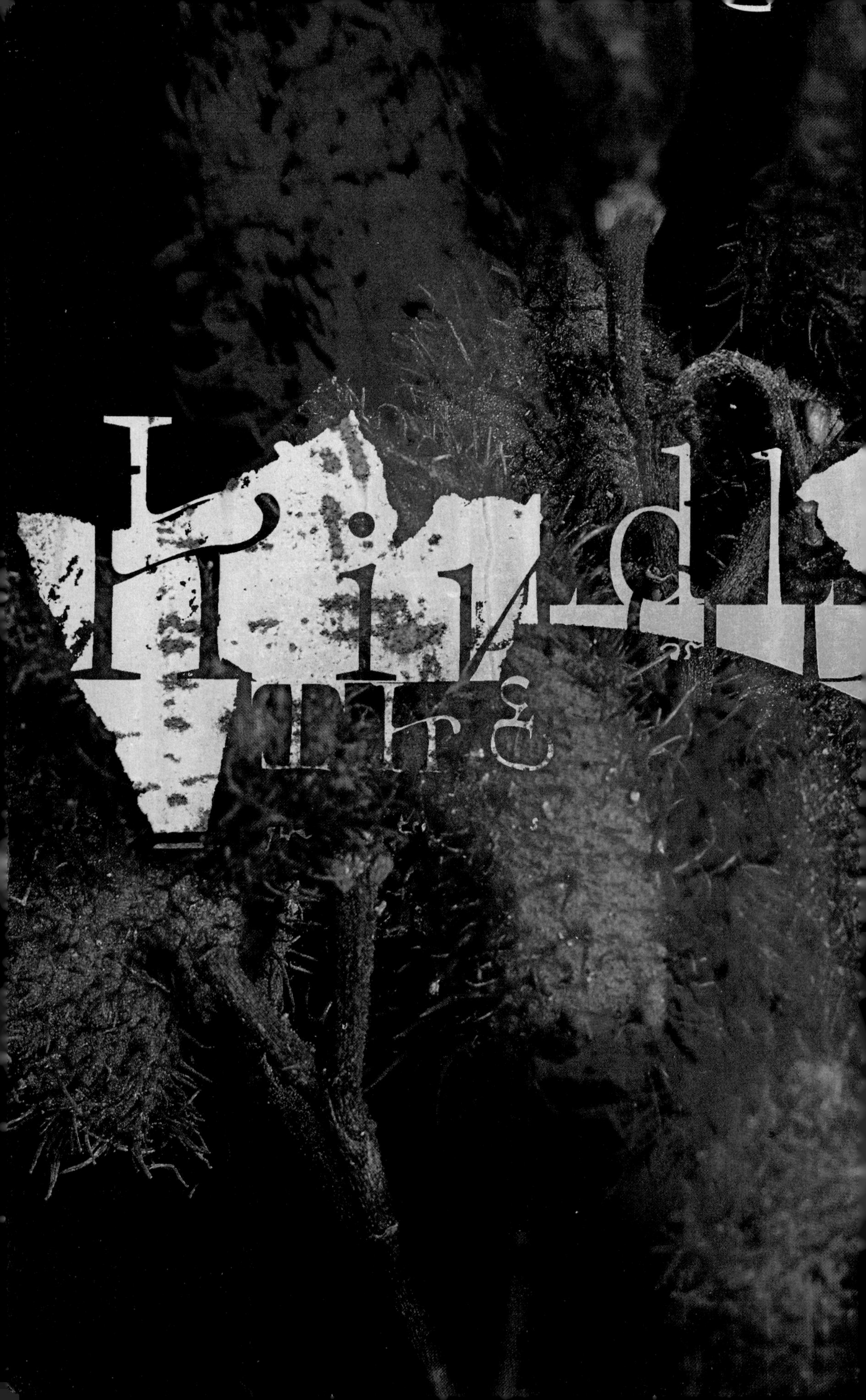

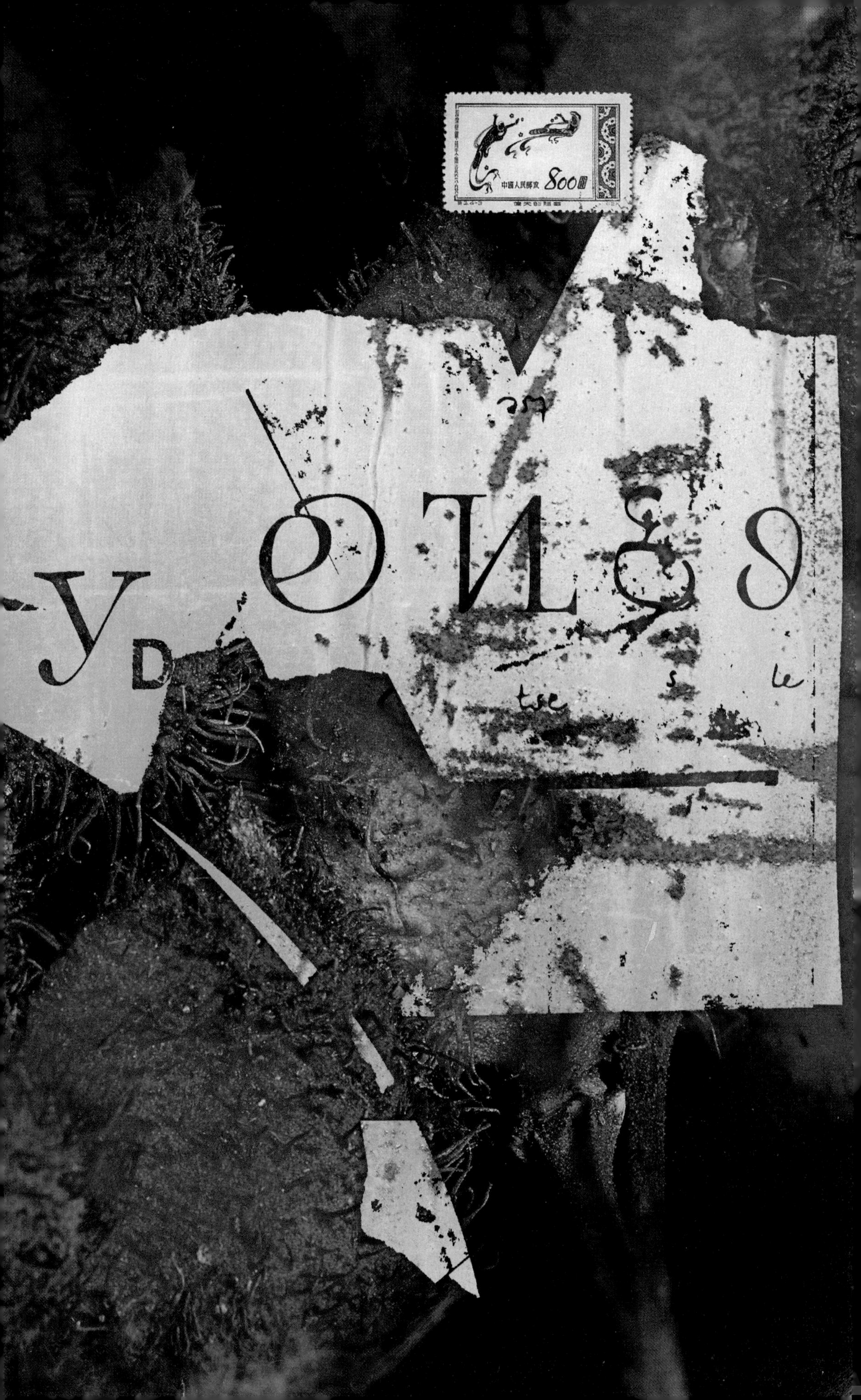

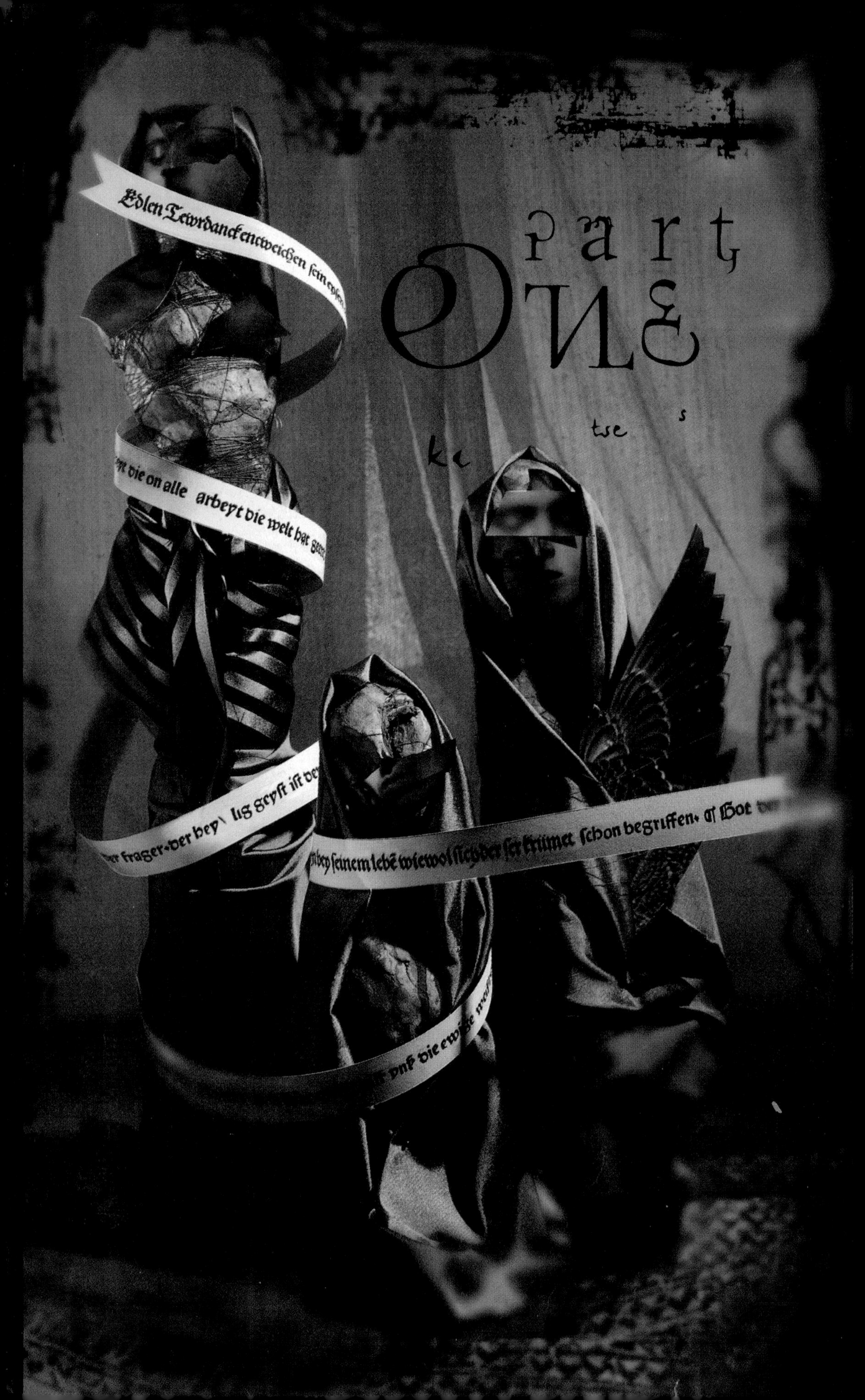
part
ONE

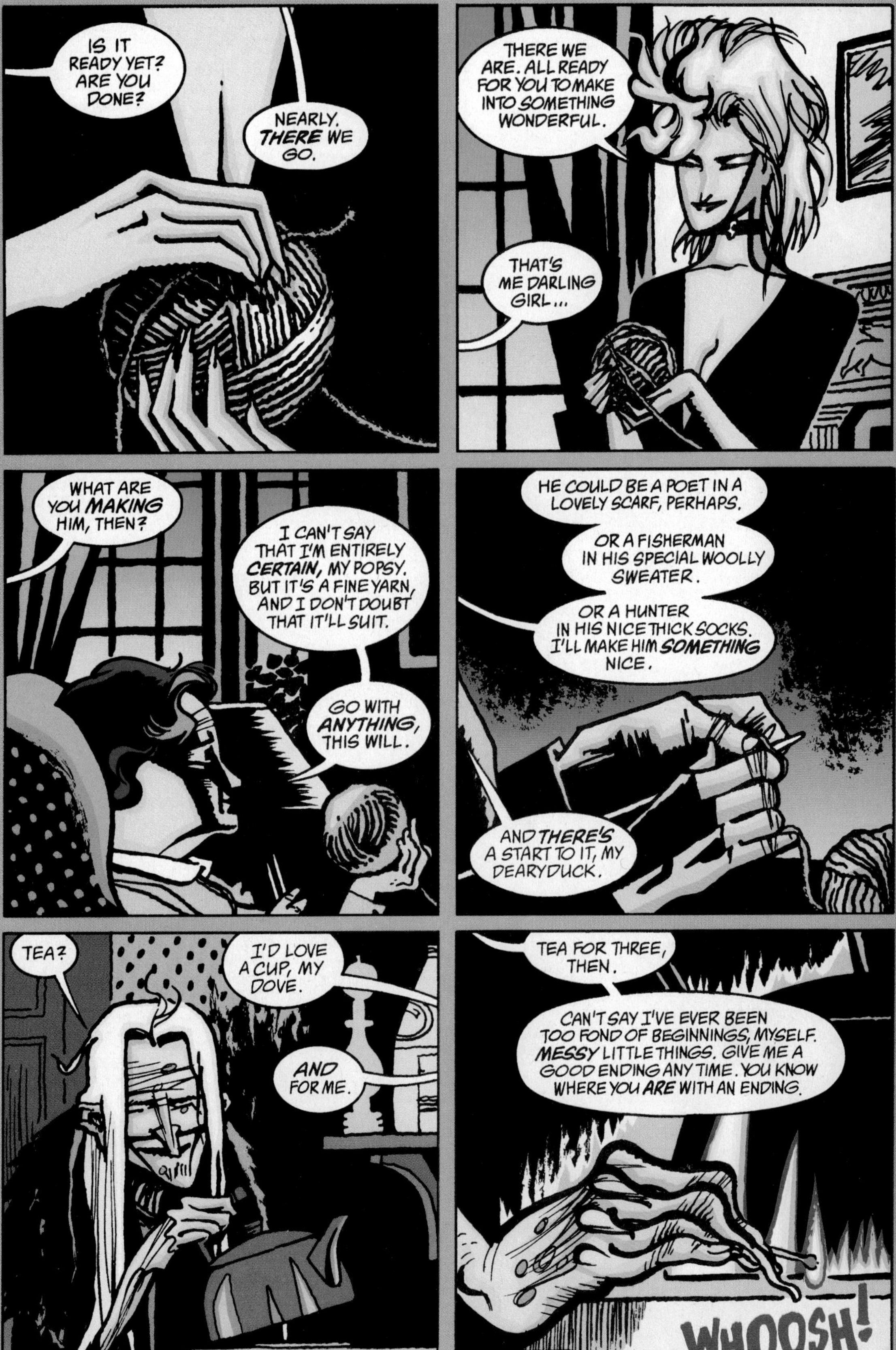
IS IT READY YET? ARE YOU DONE?
NEARLY. THERE WE GO.
THERE WE ARE. ALL READY FOR YOU TO MAKE INTO SOMETHING WONDERFUL.
THAT'S ME DARLING GIRL...
WHAT ARE YOU MAKING HIM, THEN?
I CAN'T SAY THAT I'M ENTIRELY CERTAIN, MY POPSY. BUT IT'S A FINE YARN, AND I DON'T DOUBT THAT IT'LL SUIT.
GO WITH ANYTHING, THIS WILL.
HE COULD BE A POET IN A LOVELY SCARF, PERHAPS.
OR A FISHERMAN IN HIS SPECIAL WOOLLY SWEATER.
OR A HUNTER IN HIS NICE THICK SOCKS. I'LL MAKE HIM SOMETHING NICE.
AND THERE'S A START TO IT, MY DEARYDUCK.
TEA?
I'D LOVE A CUP, MY DOVE.
AND FOR ME.
TEA FOR THREE, THEN.
CAN'T SAY I'VE EVER BEEN TOO FOND OF BEGINNINGS, MYSELF. MESSY LITTLE THINGS. GIVE ME A GOOD ENDING ANY TIME. YOU KNOW WHERE YOU ARE WITH AN ENDING.
WHOOSH!

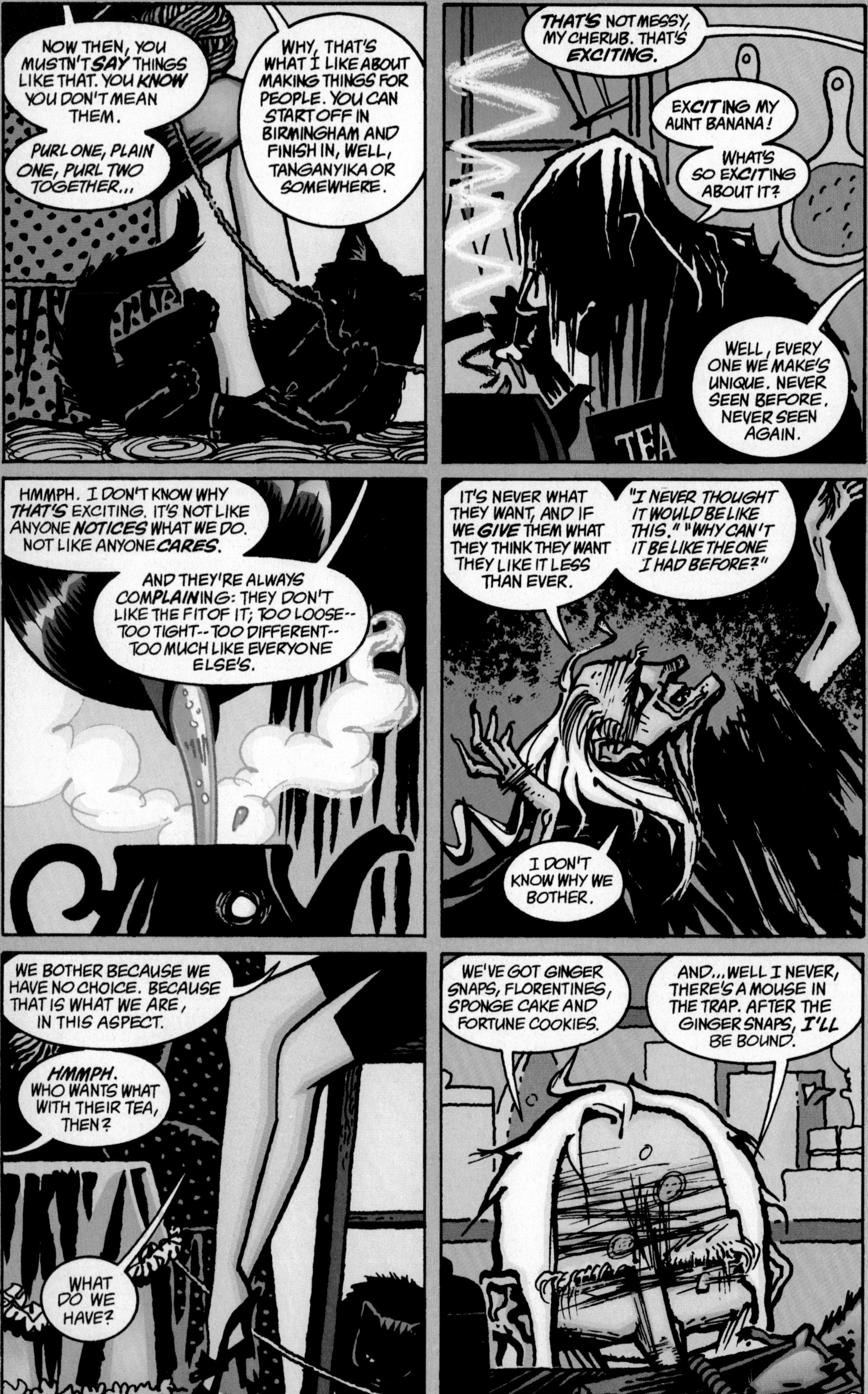
NOW THEN, YOU MUSTN'T SAY THINGS LIKE THAT. YOU KNOW YOU DON'T MEAN THEM.
PURL ONE, PLAIN ONE, PURL TWO TOGETHER...
WHY, THAT'S WHAT I LIKE ABOUT MAKING THINGS FOR PEOPLE. YOU CAN START OFF IN BIRMINGHAM AND FINISH IN, WELL, TANGANYIKA OR SOMEWHERE.
THAT'S NOT MESSY, MY CHERUB. THAT'S EXCITING.
EXCITING MY AUNT BANANA!
WHAT'S SO EXCITING ABOUT IT?
WELL, EVERY ONE WE MAKE'S UNIQUE. NEVER SEEN BEFORE, NEVER SEEN AGAIN.
TEA
HMMPH. I DON'T KNOW WHY THAT'S EXCITING. IT'S NOT LIKE ANYONE NOTICES WHAT WE DO. NOT LIKE ANYONE CARES.
AND THEY'RE ALWAYS COMPLAINING: THEY DON'T LIKE THE FIT OF IT; TOO LOOSE--TOO TIGHT--TOO DIFFERENT--TOO MUCH LIKE EVERYONE ELSE'S.
IT'S NEVER WHAT THEY WANT, AND IF WE GIVE THEM WHAT THEY THINK THEY WANT THEY LIKE IT LESS THAN EVER.
"I NEVER THOUGHT IT WOULD BE LIKE THIS." "WHY CAN'T IT BE LIKE THE ONE I HAD BEFORE?"
I DON'T KNOW WHY WE BOTHER.
WE BOTHER BECAUSE WE HAVE NO CHOICE. BECAUSE THAT IS WHAT WE ARE, IN THIS ASPECT.
HMMPH. WHO WANTS WHAT WITH THEIR TEA, THEN?
WHAT DO WE HAVE?
WE'VE GOT GINGER SNAPS, FLORENTINES, SPONGE CAKE AND FORTUNE COOKIES.
AND... WELL I NEVER, THERE'S A MOUSE IN THE TRAP. AFTER THE GINGER SNAPS, I'LL BE BOUND.

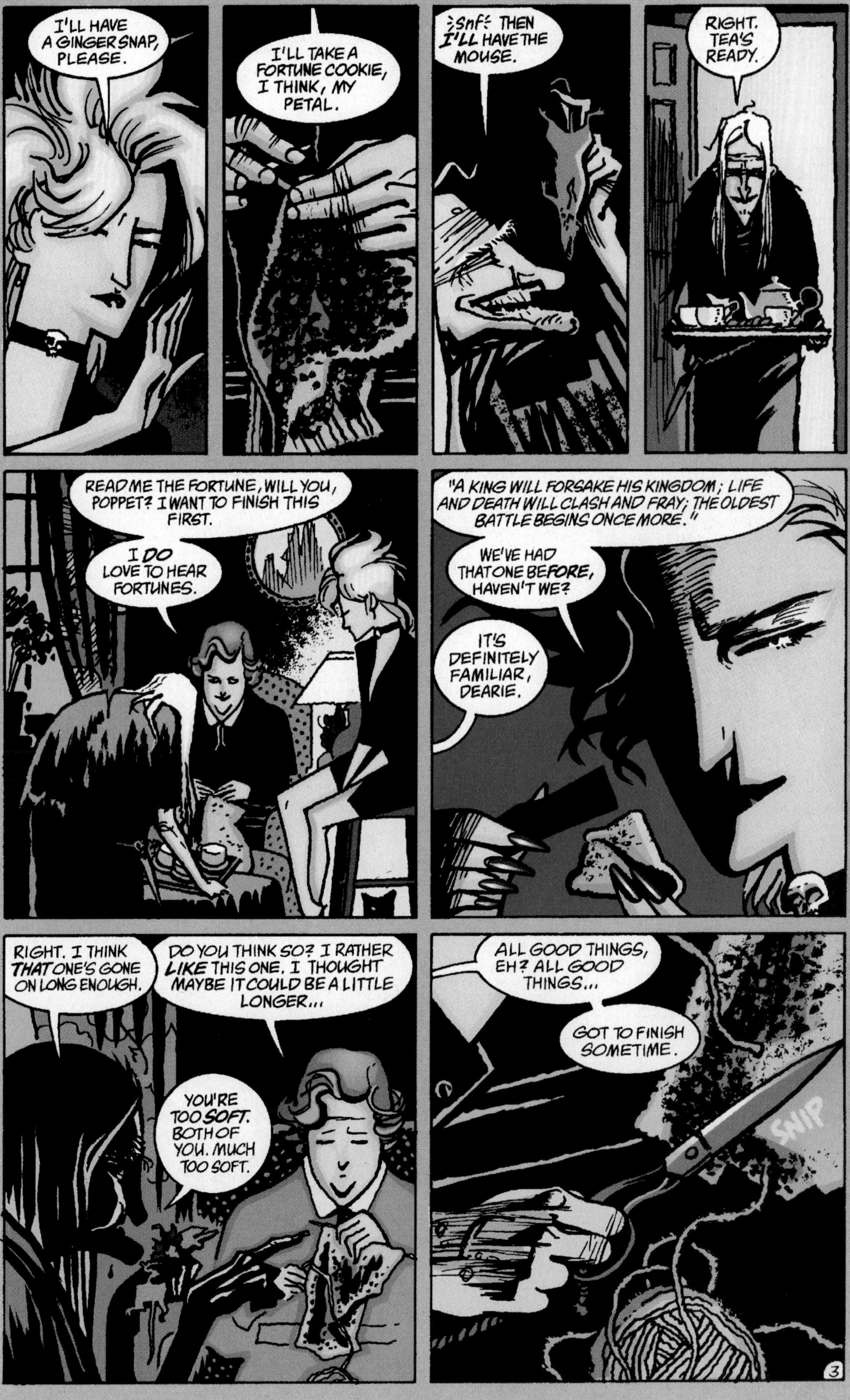
I'LL HAVE A GINGER SNAP, PLEASE.
I'LL TAKE A FORTUNE COOKIE, I THINK, MY PETAL.
Snf THEN I'LL HAVE THE MOUSE.
RIGHT. TEA'S READY.
READ ME THE FORTUNE, WILL YOU, POPPET? I WANT TO FINISH THIS FIRST.
I DO LOVE TO HEAR FORTUNES.
"A KING WILL FORSAKE HIS KINGDOM; LIFE AND DEATH WILL CLASH AND FRAY; THE OLDEST BATTLE BEGINS ONCE MORE."
WE'VE HAD THAT ONE BEFORE, HAVEN'T WE?
IT'S DEFINITELY FAMILIAR, DEARIE.
RIGHT. I THINK THAT ONE'S GONE ON LONG ENOUGH.
DO YOU THINK SO? I RATHER LIKE THIS ONE. I THOUGHT MAYBE IT COULD BE A LITTLE LONGER...
YOU'RE TOO SOFT. BOTH OF YOU. MUCH TOO SOFT.
ALL GOOD THINGS, EH? ALL GOOD THINGS...
GOT TO FINISH SOMETIME.
SNIP
3

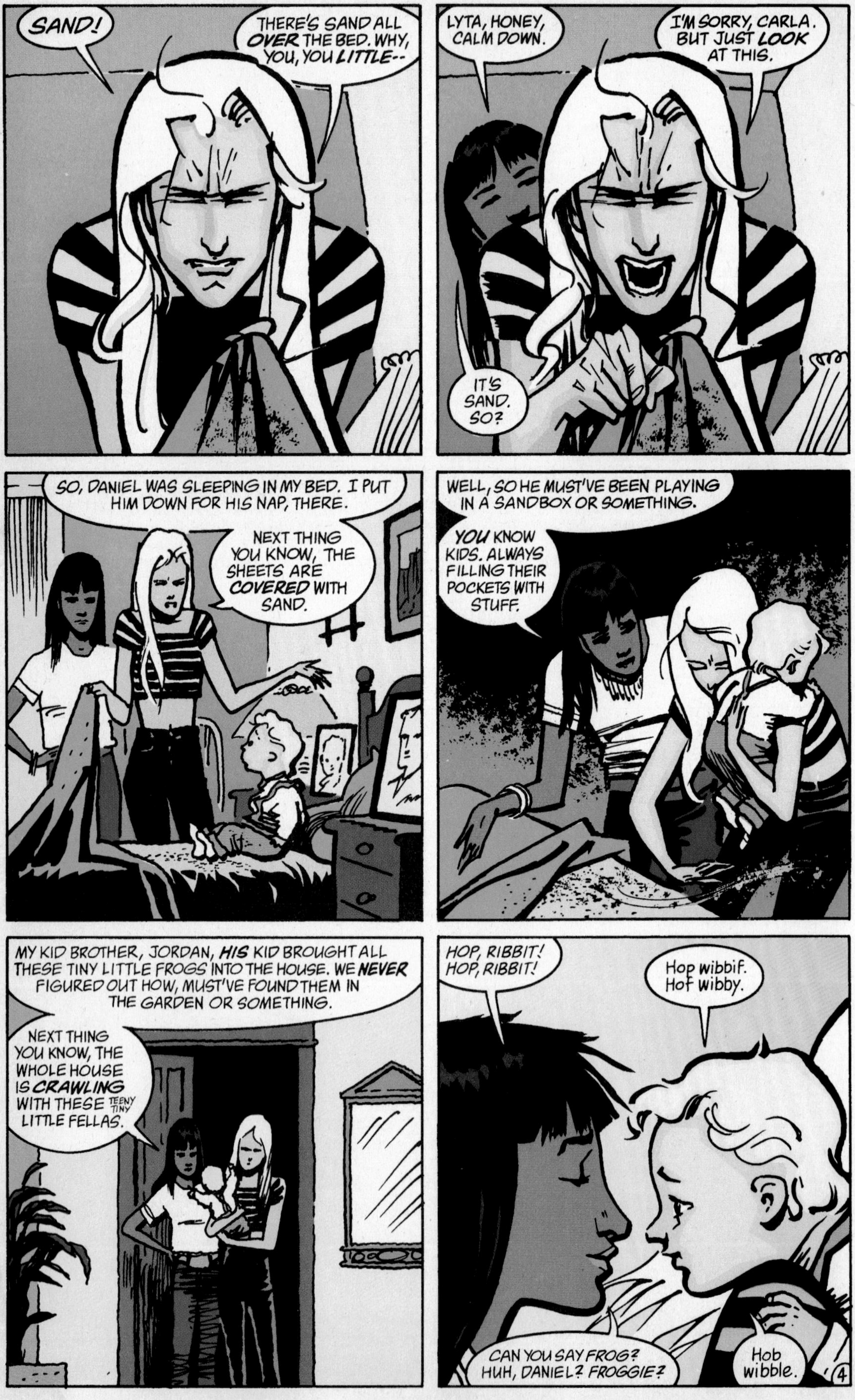
SAND!
THERE'S SAND ALL OVER THE BED. WHY, YOU, YOU LITTLE--
LYTA, HONEY, CALM DOWN.
I'M SORRY, CARLA. BUT JUST LOOK AT THIS.
IT'S SAND. SO?
SO, DANIEL WAS SLEEPING IN MY BED. I PUT HIM DOWN FOR HIS NAP, THERE.
NEXT THING YOU KNOW, THE SHEETS ARE COVERED WITH SAND.
WELL, SO HE MUST'VE BEEN PLAYING IN A SANDBOX OR SOMETHING.
YOU KNOW KIDS. ALWAYS FILLING THEIR POCKETS WITH STUFF.
MY KID BROTHER, JORDAN, HIS KID BROUGHT ALL THESE TINY LITTLE FROGS INTO THE HOUSE. WE NEVER FIGURED OUT HOW, MUST'VE FOUND THEM IN THE GARDEN OR SOMETHING.
NEXT THING YOU KNOW, THE WHOLE HOUSE IS CRAWLING WITH THESE TEENY TINY LITTLE FELLAS.
HOP, RIBBIT! HOP, RIBBIT!
Hop wibbif. Hof wibby.
CAN YOU SAY FROG? HUH, DANIEL? FROGGIE?
Hob wibble.
4

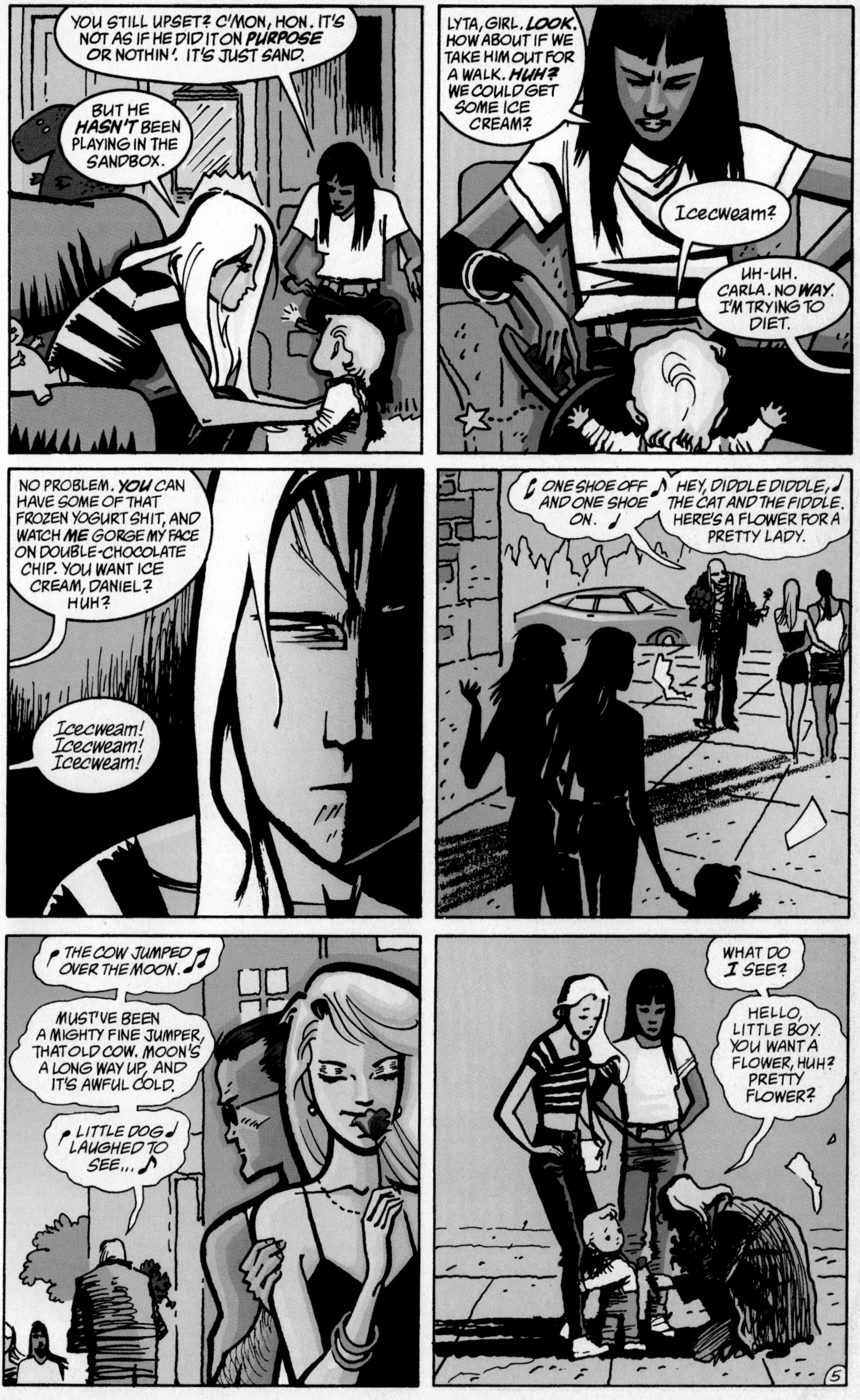
YOU STILL UPSET? C'MON, HON. IT'S NOT AS IF HE DID IT ON PURPOSE OR NOTHIN'. IT'S JUST SAND.
BUT HE HASN'T BEEN PLAYING IN THE SANDBOX.
LYTA, GIRL. LOOK. HOW ABOUT IF WE TAKE HIM OUT FOR A WALK. HUH? WE COULD GET SOME ICE CREAM?
Icecweam?
UH-UH. CARLA. NO WAY. I'M TRYING TO DIET.
NO PROBLEM. YOU CAN HAVE SOME OF THAT FROZEN YOGURT SHIT, AND WATCH ME GORGE MY FACE ON DOUBLE-CHOCOLATE CHIP. YOU WANT ICE CREAM, DANIEL? HUH?
Icecweam! Icecweam! Icecweam!
ONE SHOE OFF AND ONE SHOE ON.
HEY, DIDDLE DIDDLE, THE CAT AND THE FIDDLE. HERE'S A FLOWER FOR A PRETTY LADY.
THE COW JUMPED OVER THE MOON.
MUST'VE BEEN A MIGHTY FINE JUMPER, THAT OLD COW. MOON'S A LONG WAY UP, AND IT'S AWFUL COLD.
LITTLE DOG LAUGHED TO SEE...
WHAT DO I SEE?
HELLO, LITTLE BOY. YOU WANT A FLOWER, HUH? PRETTY FLOWER?

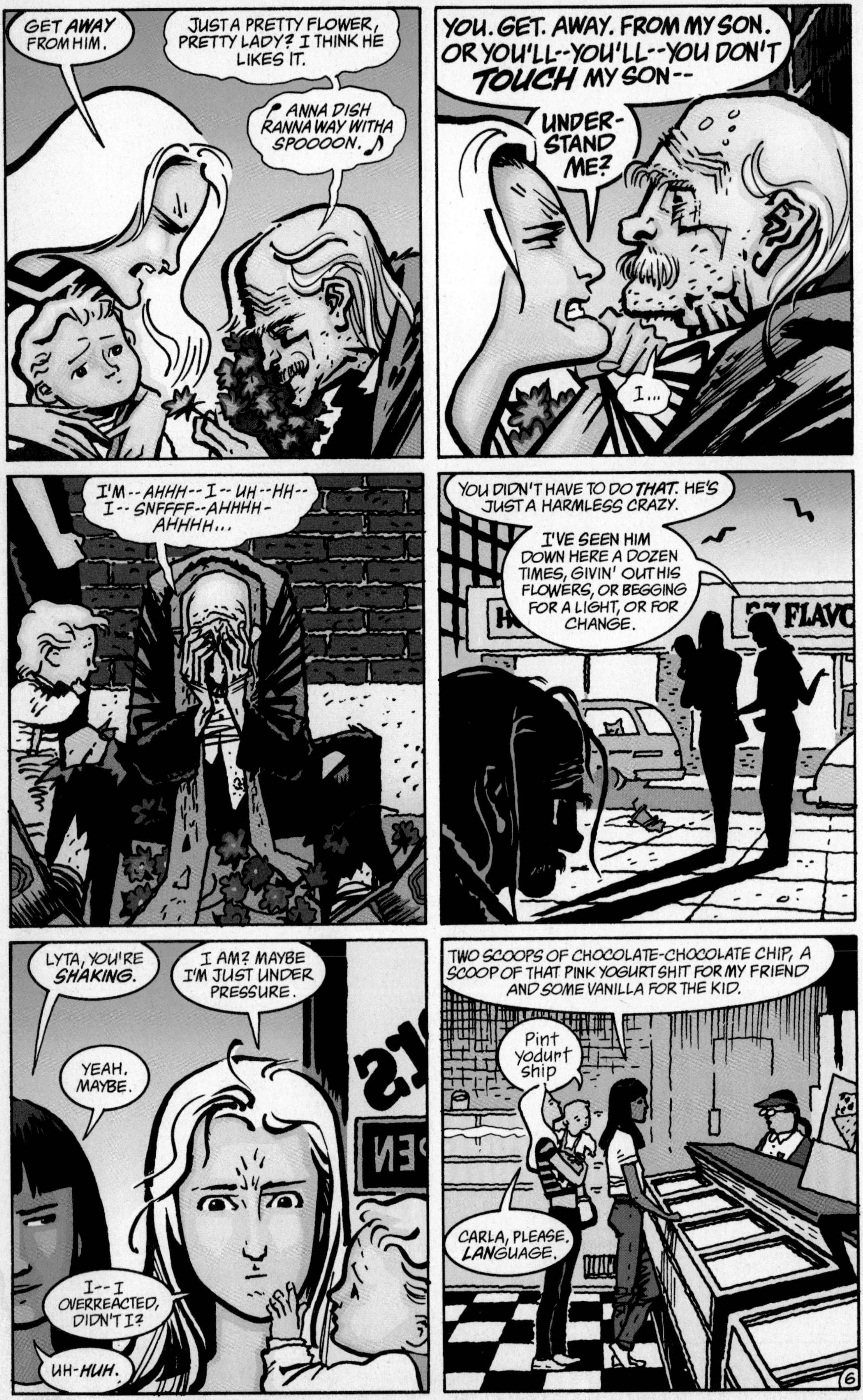
GET AWAY FROM HIM.
JUST A PRETTY FLOWER, PRETTY LADY? I THINK HE LIKES IT.
ANNA DISH RANNA WAY WITHA SPOOOON.
YOU. GET. AWAY. FROM MY SON. OR YOU'LL--YOU'LL--YOU DON'T TOUCH MY SON--
UNDER-STAND ME?
I...
I'M--AHHH--I--UH--HH--I--SNFFFF--AHHHH-AHHHH...
YOU DIDN'T HAVE TO DO THAT. HE'S JUST A HARMLESS CRAZY.
I'VE SEEN HIM DOWN HERE A DOZEN TIMES, GIVIN' OUT HIS FLOWERS, OR BEGGING FOR A LIGHT, OR FOR CHANGE.
FLAVO
LYTA, YOU'RE SHAKING.
I AM? MAYBE I'M JUST UNDER PRESSURE.
YEAH. MAYBE.
I--I OVERREACTED, DIDN'T I?
UH-HUH.
TWO SCOOPS OF CHOCOLATE-CHOCOLATE CHIP, A SCOOP OF THAT PINK YOGURT SHIT FOR MY FRIEND AND SOME VANILLA FOR THE KID.
Pint yodurt ship
CARLA, PLEASE. LANGUAGE.

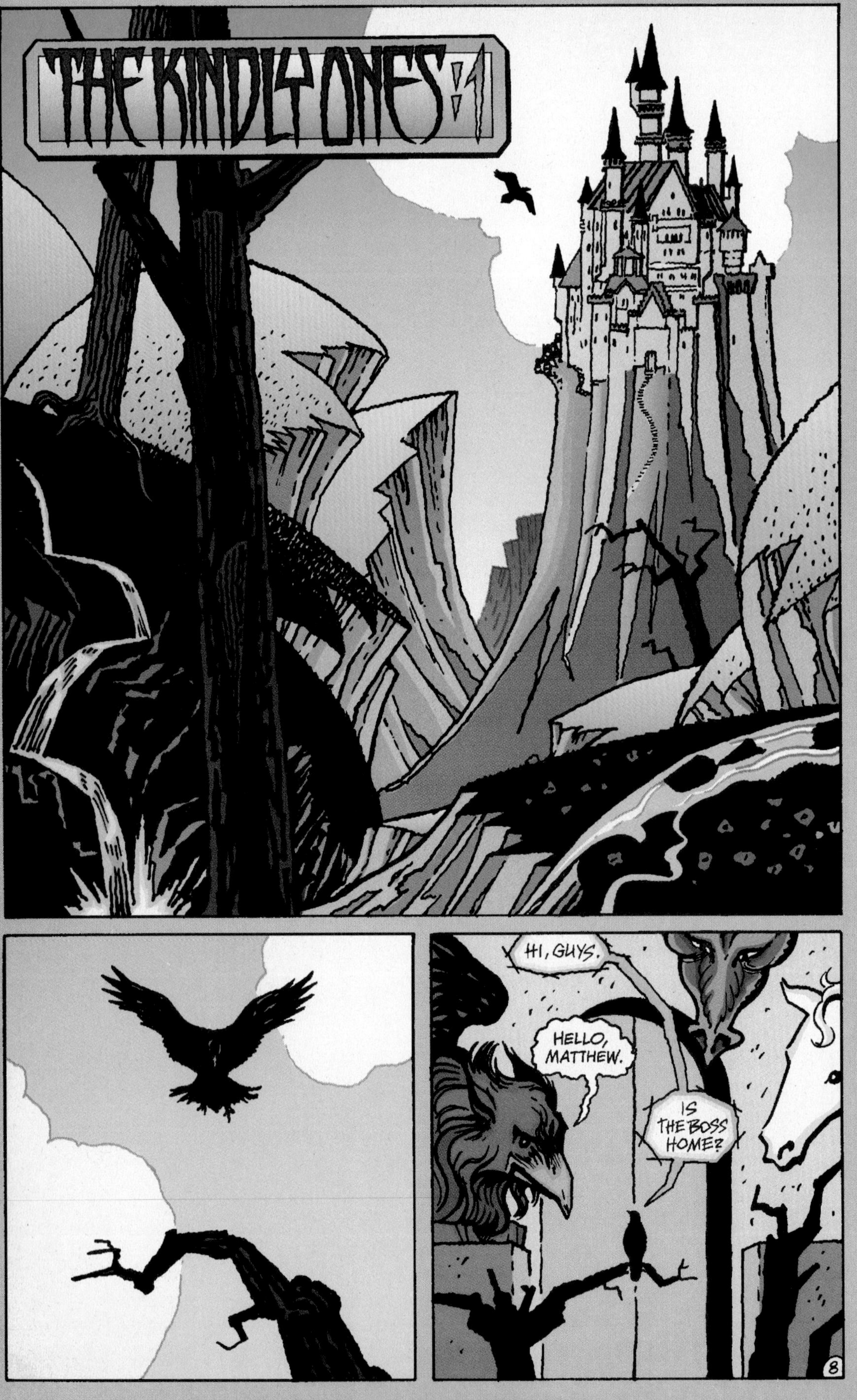
THE KINDLY ONES: 1
HI, GUYS.
HELLO, MATTHEW.
IS THE BOSS HOME?
8

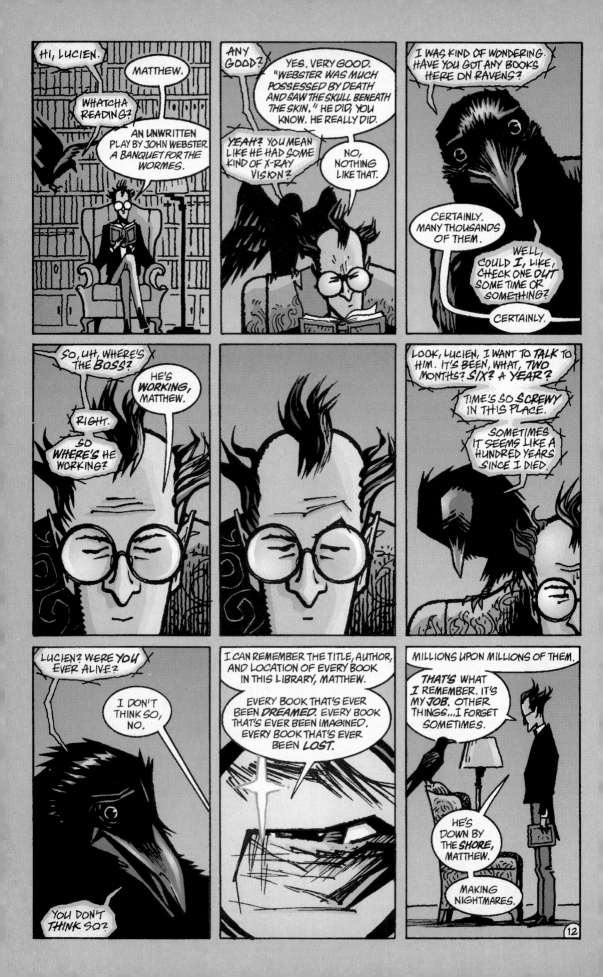

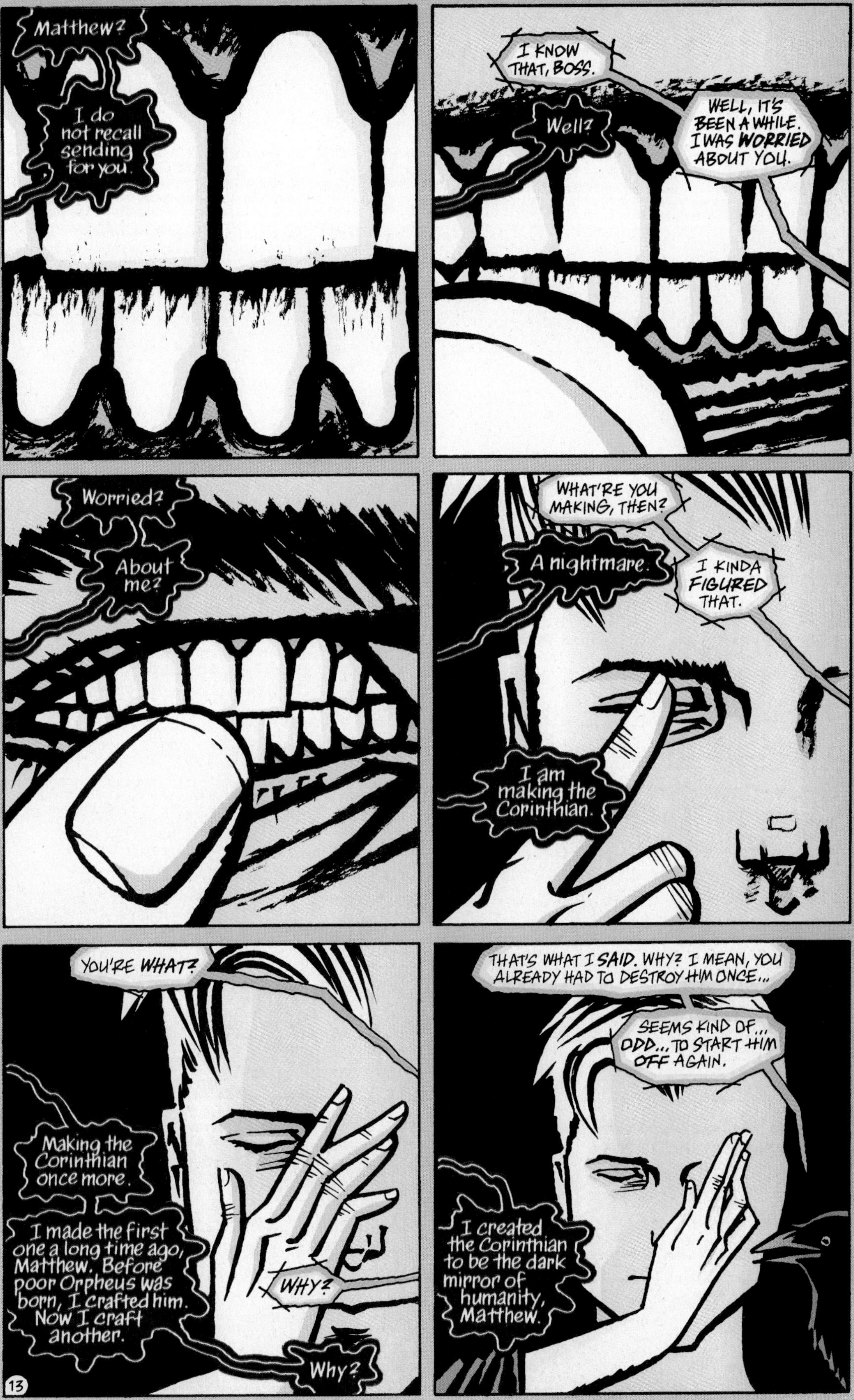
Matthew?
I do not recall sending for you.
I KNOW THAT, BOSS.
Well?
WELL, IT'S BEEN A WHILE. I WAS WORRIED ABOUT YOU.
Worried?
About me?
WHAT'RE YOU MAKING, THEN?
A nightmare.
I KINDA FIGURED THAT.
I am making the Corinthian.
YOU'RE WHAT?
Making the Corinthian once more.
I made the first one a long time ago, Matthew. Before poor Orpheus was born, I crafted him. Now I craft another.
WHY?
Why?
THAT'S WHAT I SAID. WHY? I MEAN, YOU ALREADY HAD TO DESTROY HIM ONCE...
SEEMS KIND OF... ODD... TO START HIM OFF AGAIN.
I created the Corinthian to be the dark mirror of humanity, Matthew.

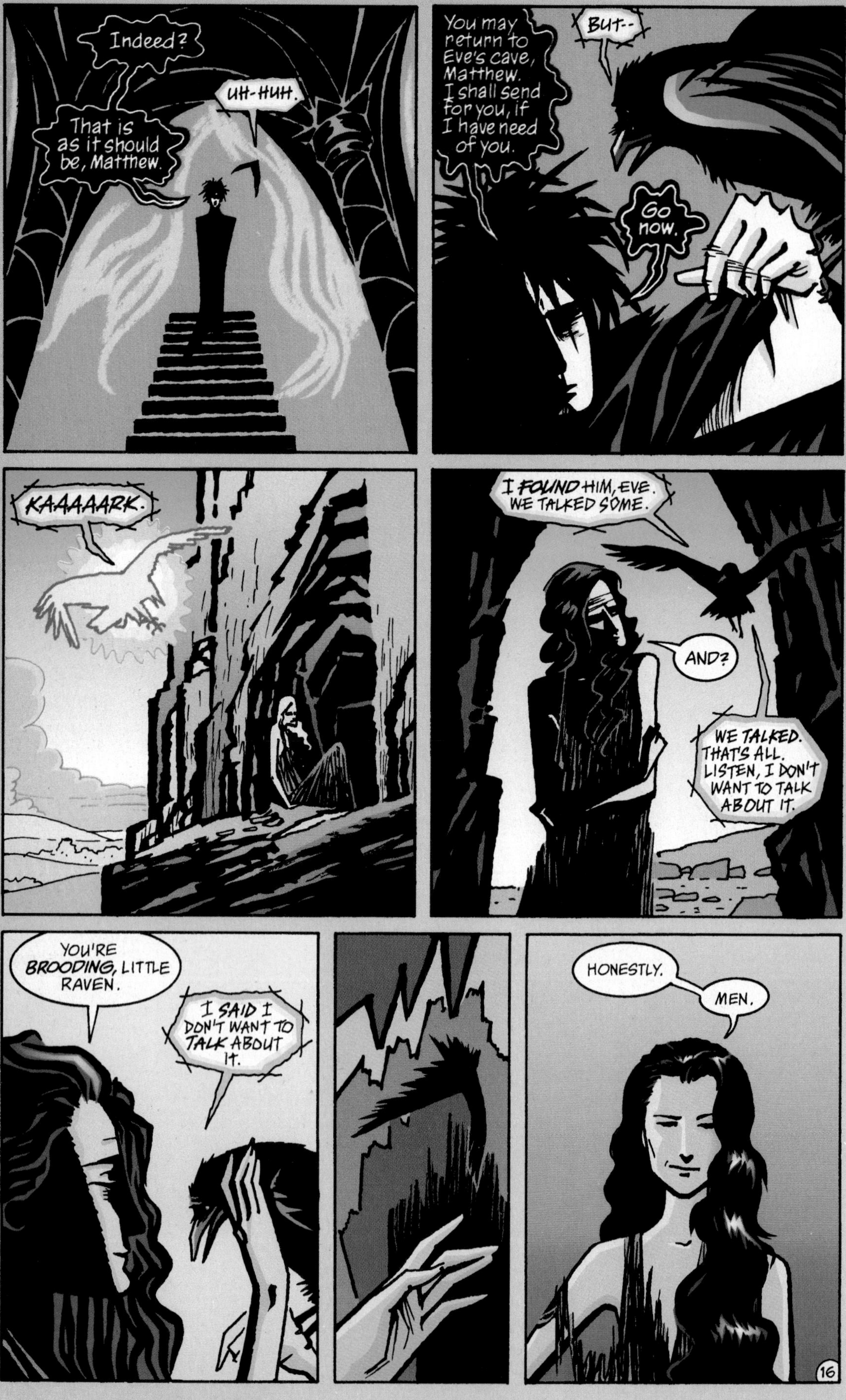
Indeed?
UH-HUH.
That is as it should be, Matthew.
You may return to Eve's cave, Matthew. I shall send for you, if I have need of you.
BUT--
Go now.
KAAAAARK.
I FOUND HIM, EVE. WE TALKED SOME.
AND?
WE TALKED. THAT'S ALL. LISTEN, I DON'T WANT TO TALK ABOUT IT.
YOU'RE BROODING, LITTLE RAVEN.
I SAID I DON'T WANT TO TALK ABOUT IT.
HONESTLY.
MEN.
16

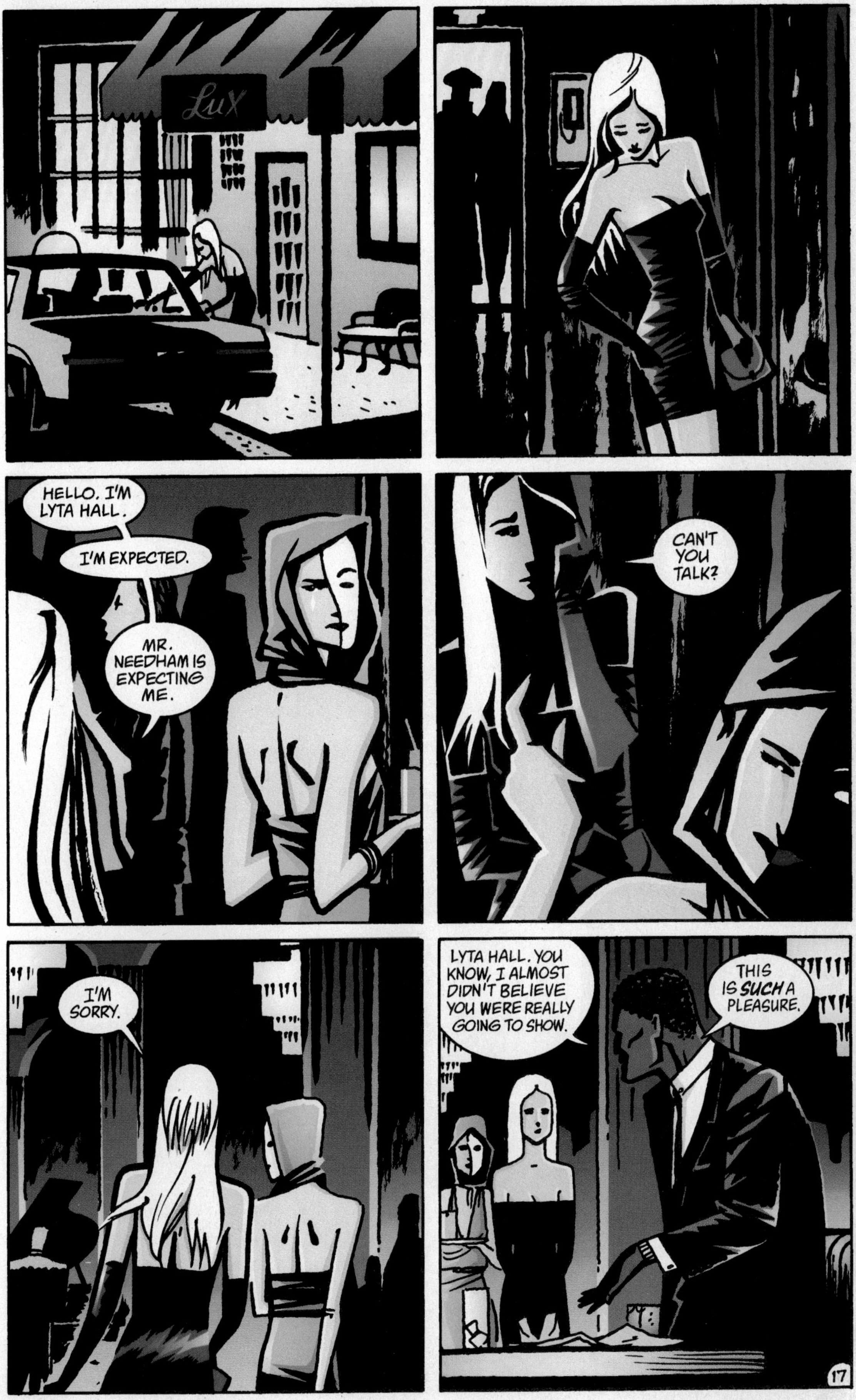
Lux
HELLO. I'M LYTA HALL.
I'M EXPECTED.
MR. NEEDHAM IS EXPECTING ME.
CAN'T YOU TALK?
I'M SORRY.
LYTA HALL. YOU KNOW, I ALMOST DIDN'T BELIEVE YOU WERE REALLY GOING TO SHOW.
THIS IS **SUCH** A PLEASURE.

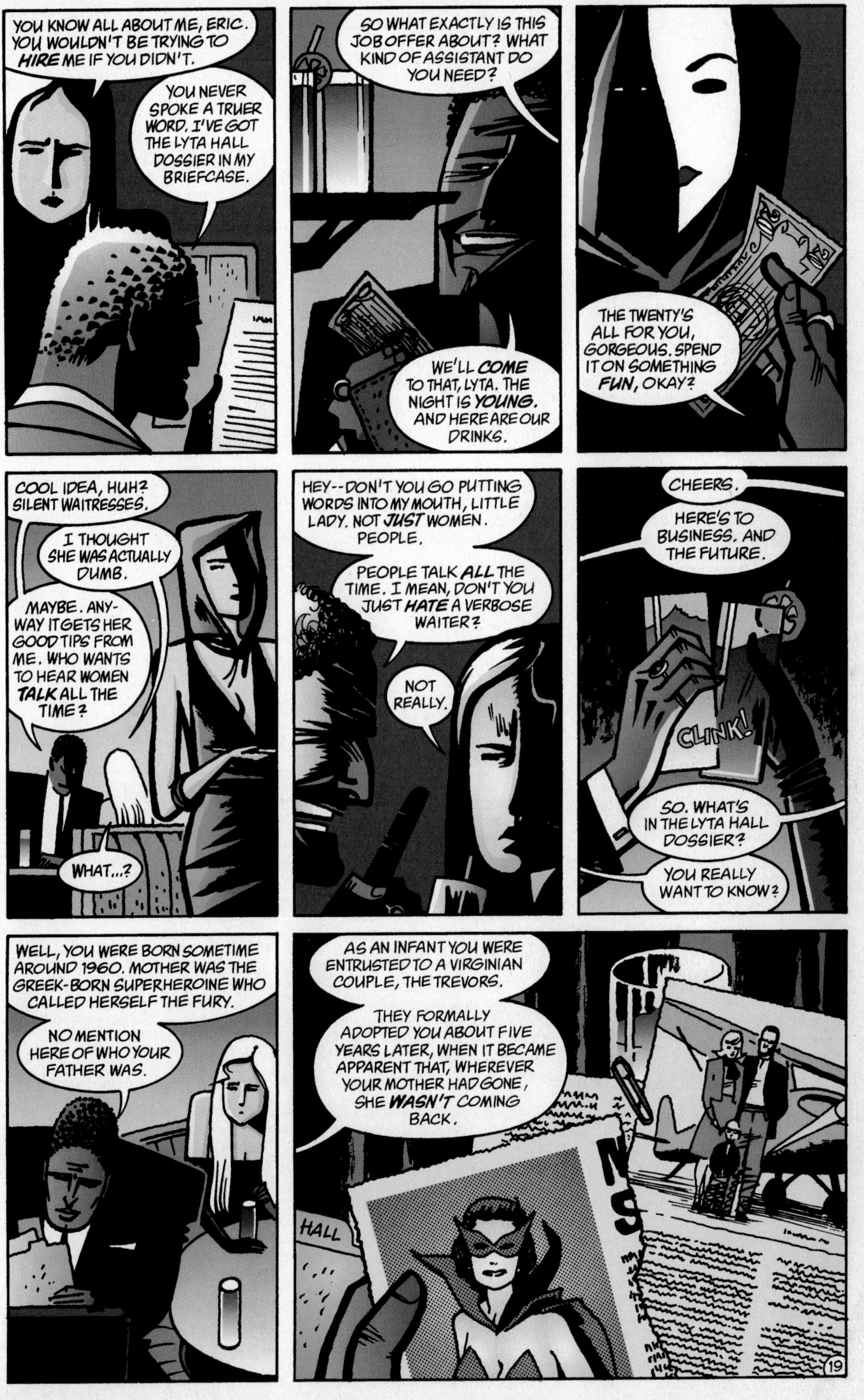
YOU KNOW ALL ABOUT ME, ERIC. YOU WOULDN'T BE TRYING TO HIRE ME IF YOU DIDN'T.
YOU NEVER SPOKE A TRUER WORD. I'VE GOT THE LYTA HALL DOSSIER IN MY BRIEFCASE.
SO WHAT EXACTLY IS THIS JOB OFFER ABOUT? WHAT KIND OF ASSISTANT DO YOU NEED?
WE'LL COME TO THAT, LYTA. THE NIGHT IS YOUNG. AND HERE ARE OUR DRINKS.
THE TWENTY'S ALL FOR YOU, GORGEOUS. SPEND IT ON SOMETHING FUN, OKAY?
COOL IDEA, HUH? SILENT WAITRESSES.
I THOUGHT SHE WAS ACTUALLY DUMB.
MAYBE. ANY-WAY IT GETS HER GOOD TIPS FROM ME. WHO WANTS TO HEAR WOMEN TALK ALL THE TIME?
WHAT...?
HEY--DON'T YOU GO PUTTING WORDS INTO MY MOUTH, LITTLE LADY. NOT JUST WOMEN. PEOPLE.
PEOPLE TALK ALL THE TIME. I MEAN, DON'T YOU JUST HATE A VERBOSE WAITER?
NOT REALLY.
CHEERS.
HERE'S TO BUSINESS. AND THE FUTURE.
CLINK!
SO. WHAT'S IN THE LYTA HALL DOSSIER?
YOU REALLY WANT TO KNOW?
WELL, YOU WERE BORN SOMETIME AROUND 1960. MOTHER WAS THE GREEK-BORN SUPERHEROINE WHO CALLED HERSELF THE FURY.
NO MENTION HERE OF WHO YOUR FATHER WAS.
AS AN INFANT YOU WERE ENTRUSTED TO A VIRGINIAN COUPLE, THE TREVORS.
THEY FORMALLY ADOPTED YOU ABOUT FIVE YEARS LATER, WHEN IT BECAME APPARENT THAT, WHEREVER YOUR MOTHER HAD GONE, SHE WASN'T COMING BACK.
HALL

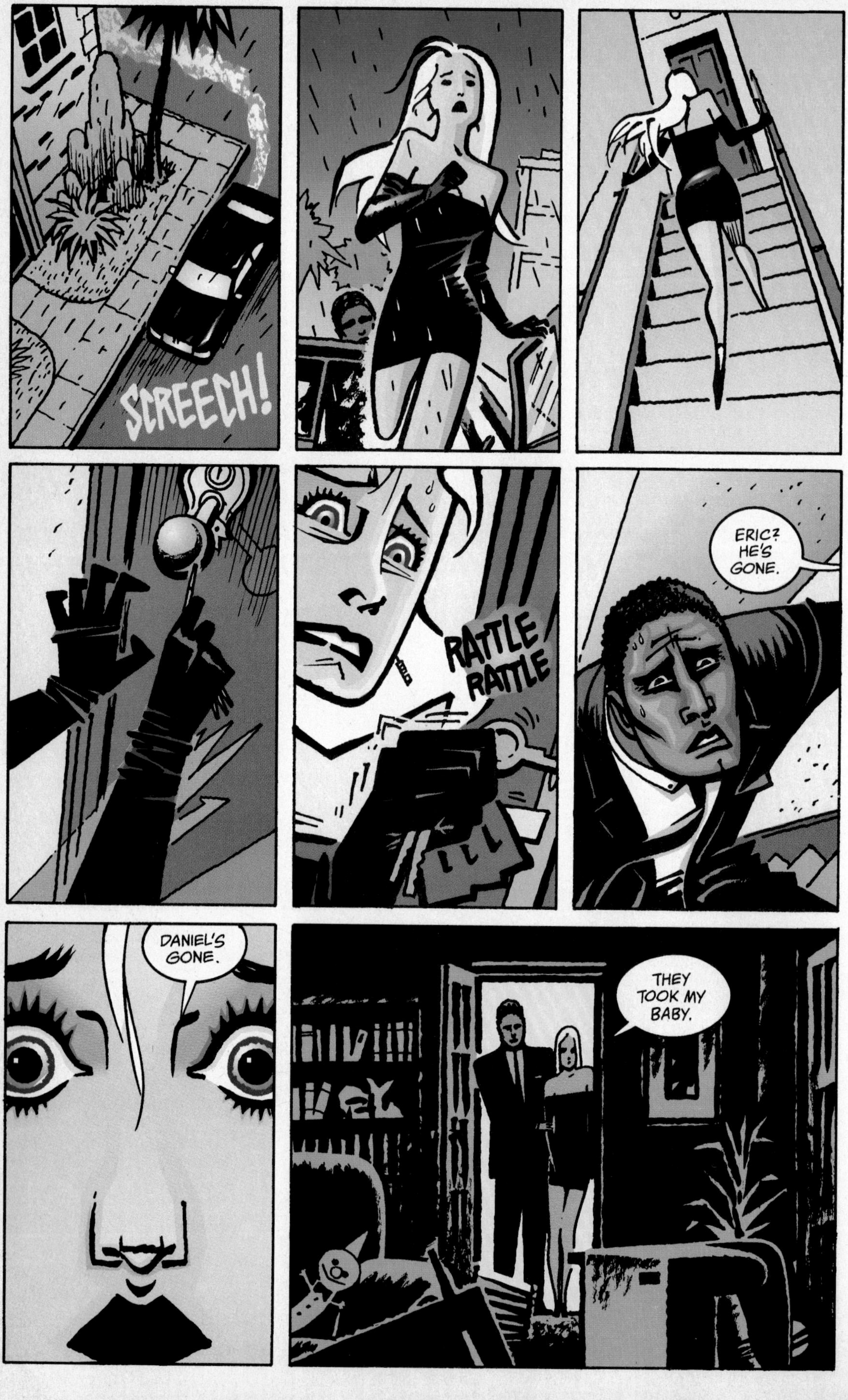
SCREECH!
RATTLE RATTLE
ERIC? HE'S GONE.
DANIEL'S GONE.
THEY TOOK MY BABY.

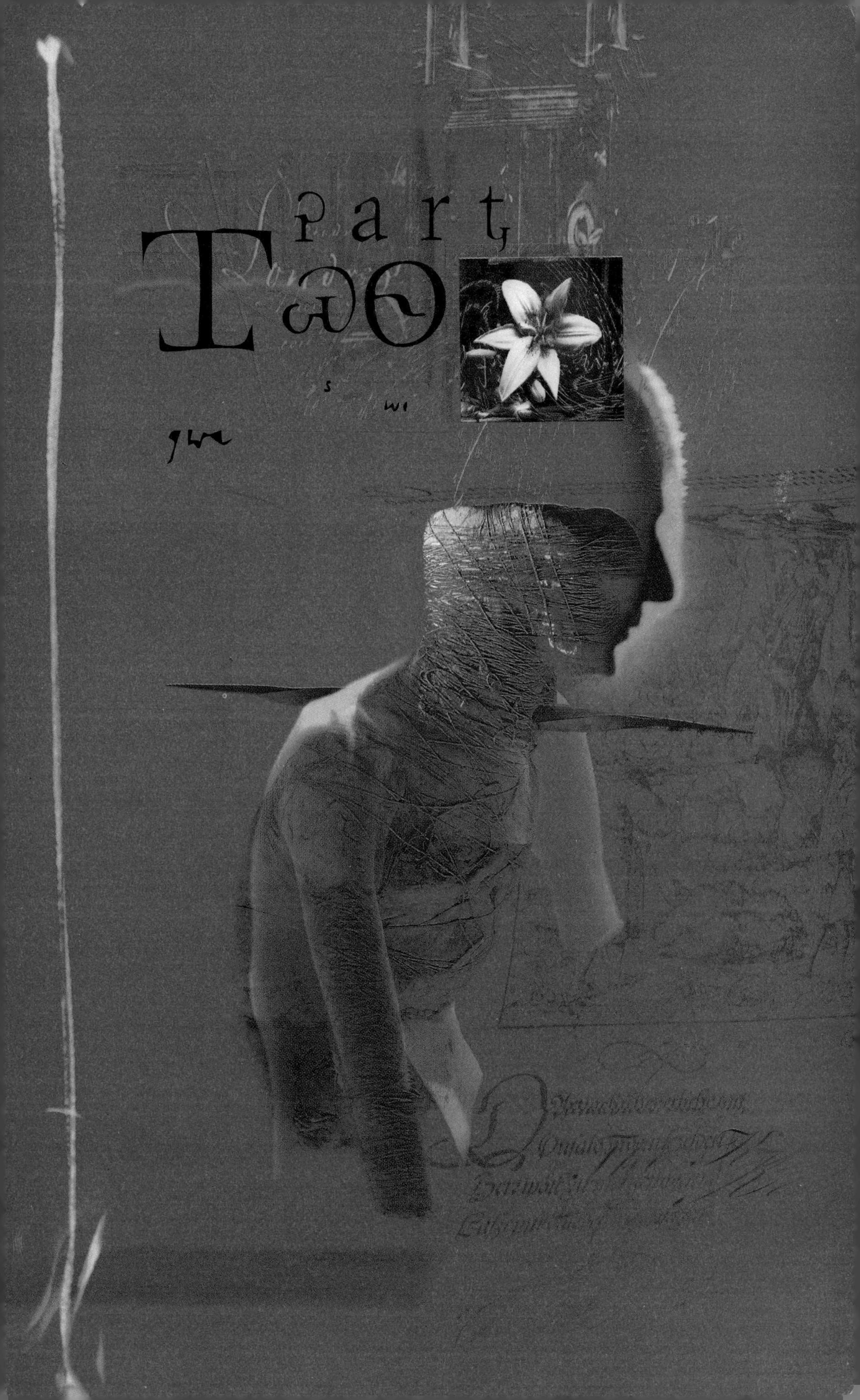
part
Two

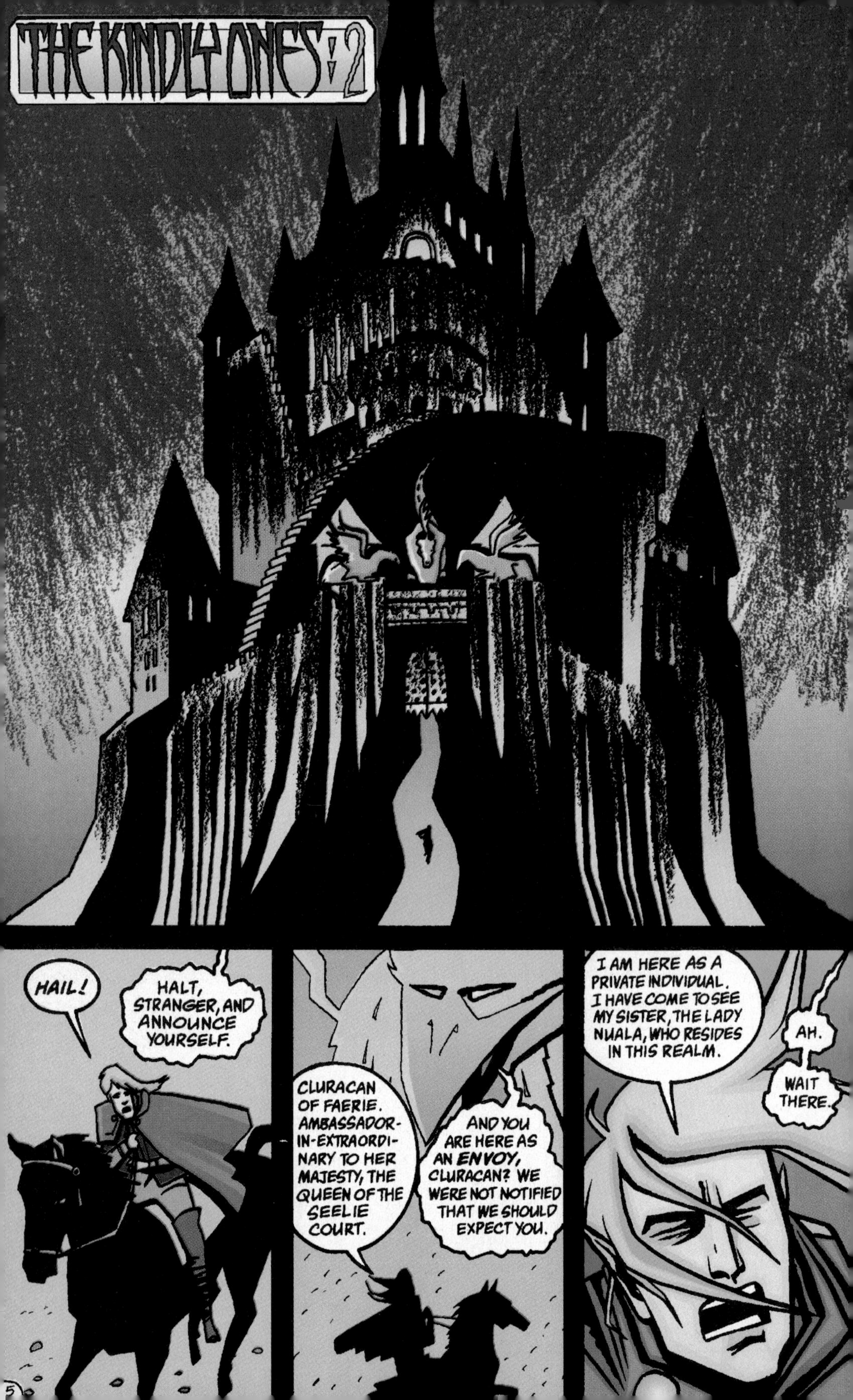
THE KINDLY ONES: 2
HAIL!
HALT, STRANGER, AND ANNOUNCE YOURSELF.
CLURACAN OF FAERIE. AMBASSADOR-IN-EXTRAORDINARY TO HER MAJESTY, THE QUEEN OF THE SEELIE COURT.
AND YOU ARE HERE AS AN *ENVOY*, CLURACAN? WE WERE NOT NOTIFIED THAT WE SHOULD EXPECT YOU.
I AM HERE AS A PRIVATE INDIVIDUAL. I HAVE COME TO SEE MY SISTER, THE LADY NUALA, WHO RESIDES IN THIS REALM.
AH.
WAIT THERE.

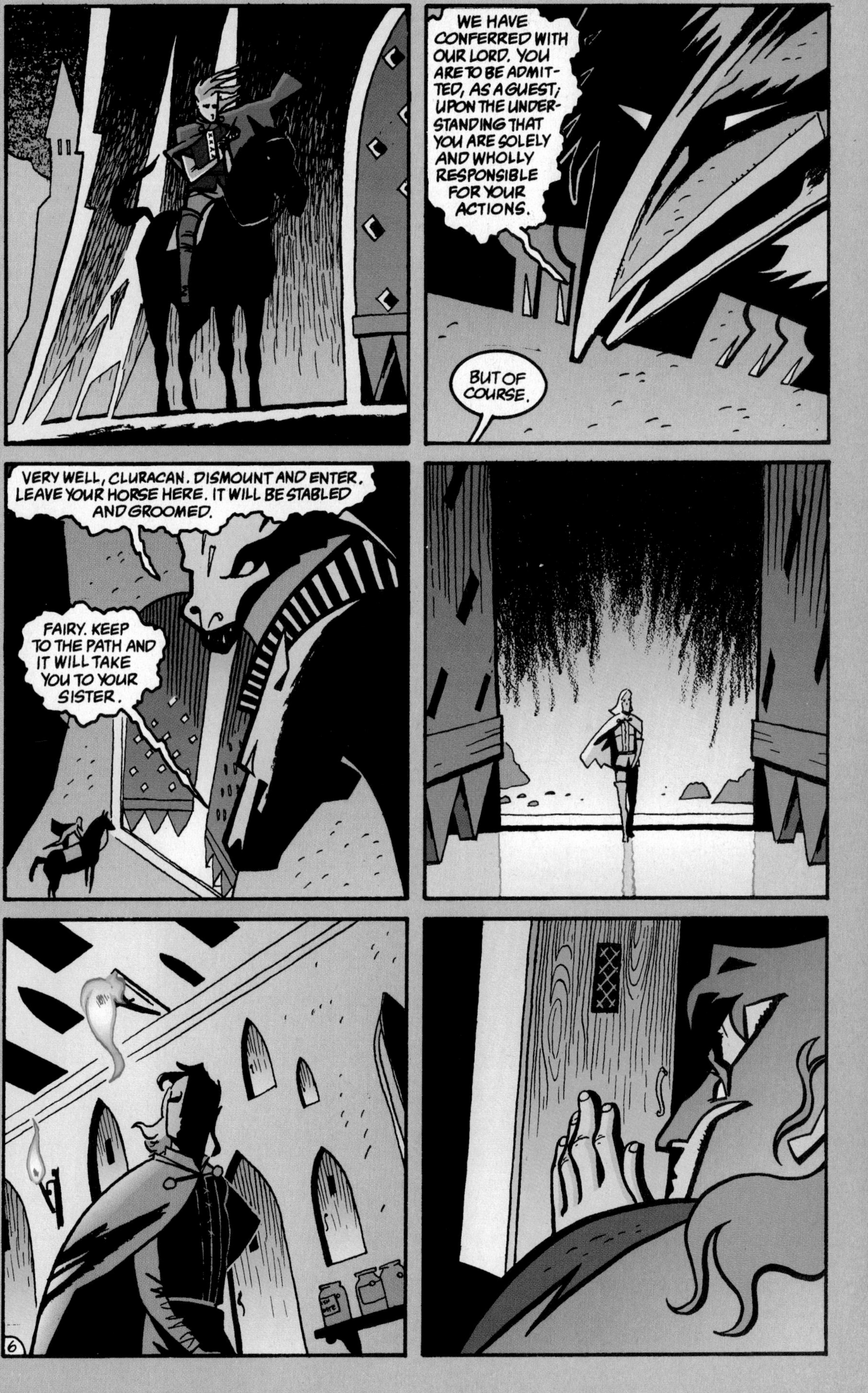
WE HAVE CONFERRED WITH OUR LORD. YOU ARE TO BE ADMITTED, AS A GUEST; UPON THE UNDERSTANDING THAT YOU ARE SOLELY AND WHOLLY RESPONSIBLE FOR YOUR ACTIONS.
BUT OF COURSE.
VERY WELL, CLURACAN. DISMOUNT AND ENTER. LEAVE YOUR HORSE HERE. IT WILL BE STABLED AND GROOMED.
FAIRY. KEEP TO THE PATH AND IT WILL TAKE YOU TO YOUR SISTER.
6

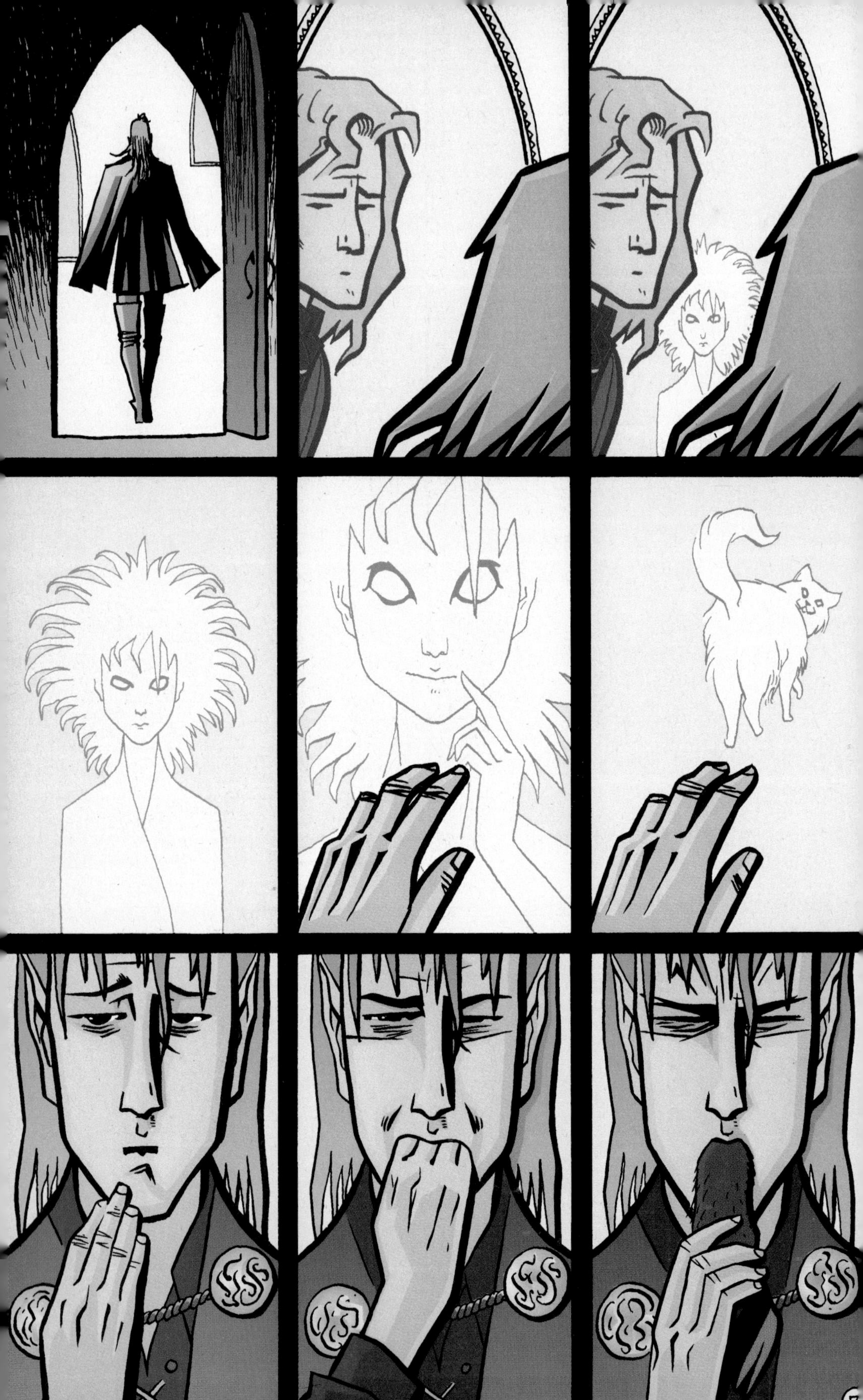

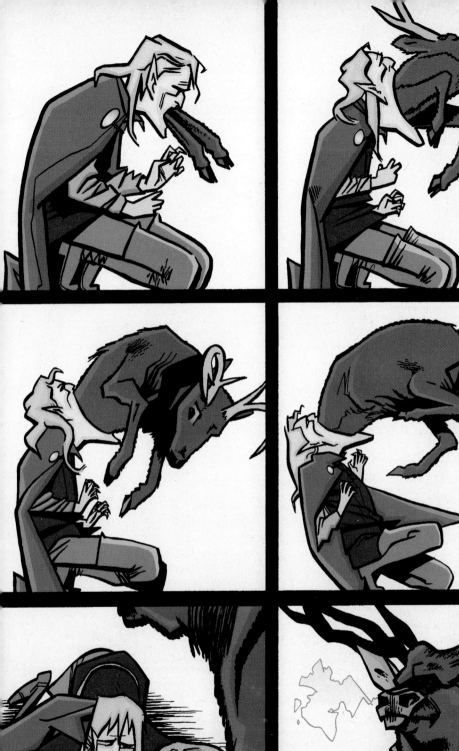

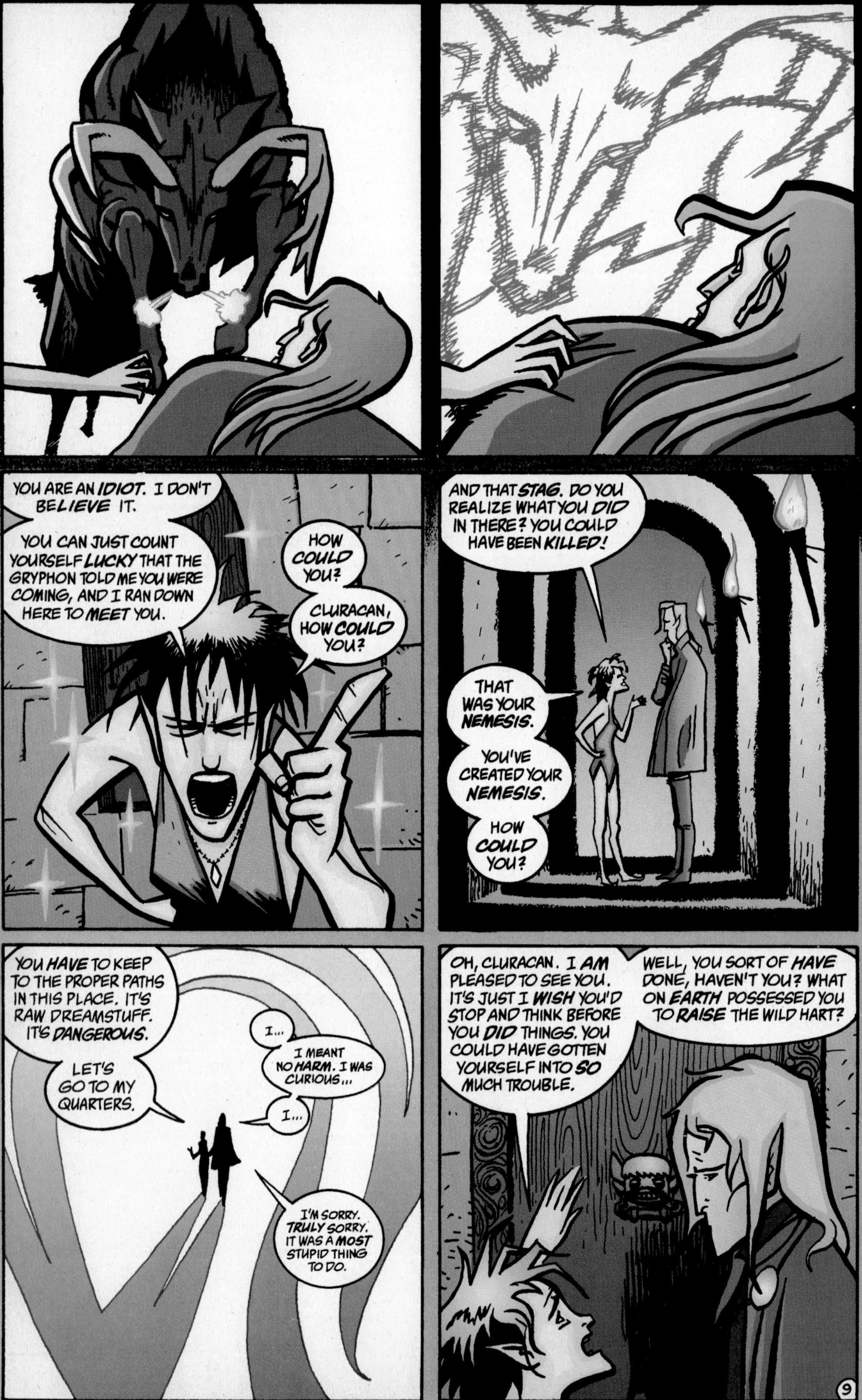
YOU ARE AN IDIOT. I DON'T BELIEVE IT.
YOU CAN JUST COUNT YOURSELF LUCKY THAT THE GRYPHON TOLD ME YOU WERE COMING, AND I RAN DOWN HERE TO MEET YOU.
HOW COULD YOU?
CLURACAN, HOW COULD YOU?
AND THAT STAG. DO YOU REALIZE WHAT YOU DID IN THERE? YOU COULD HAVE BEEN KILLED!
THAT WAS YOUR NEMESIS.
YOU'VE CREATED YOUR NEMESIS.
HOW COULD YOU?
YOU HAVE TO KEEP TO THE PROPER PATHS IN THIS PLACE. IT'S RAW DREAMSTUFF. IT'S DANGEROUS.
LET'S GO TO MY QUARTERS.
I...
I MEANT NO HARM. I WAS CURIOUS...
I...
I'M SORRY. TRULY SORRY. IT WAS A MOST STUPID THING TO DO.
OH, CLURACAN. I AM PLEASED TO SEE YOU. IT'S JUST I WISH YOU'D STOP AND THINK BEFORE YOU DID THINGS. YOU COULD HAVE GOTTEN YOURSELF INTO SO MUCH TROUBLE.
WELL, YOU SORT OF HAVE DONE, HAVEN'T YOU? WHAT ON EARTH POSSESSED YOU TO RAISE THE WILD HART?

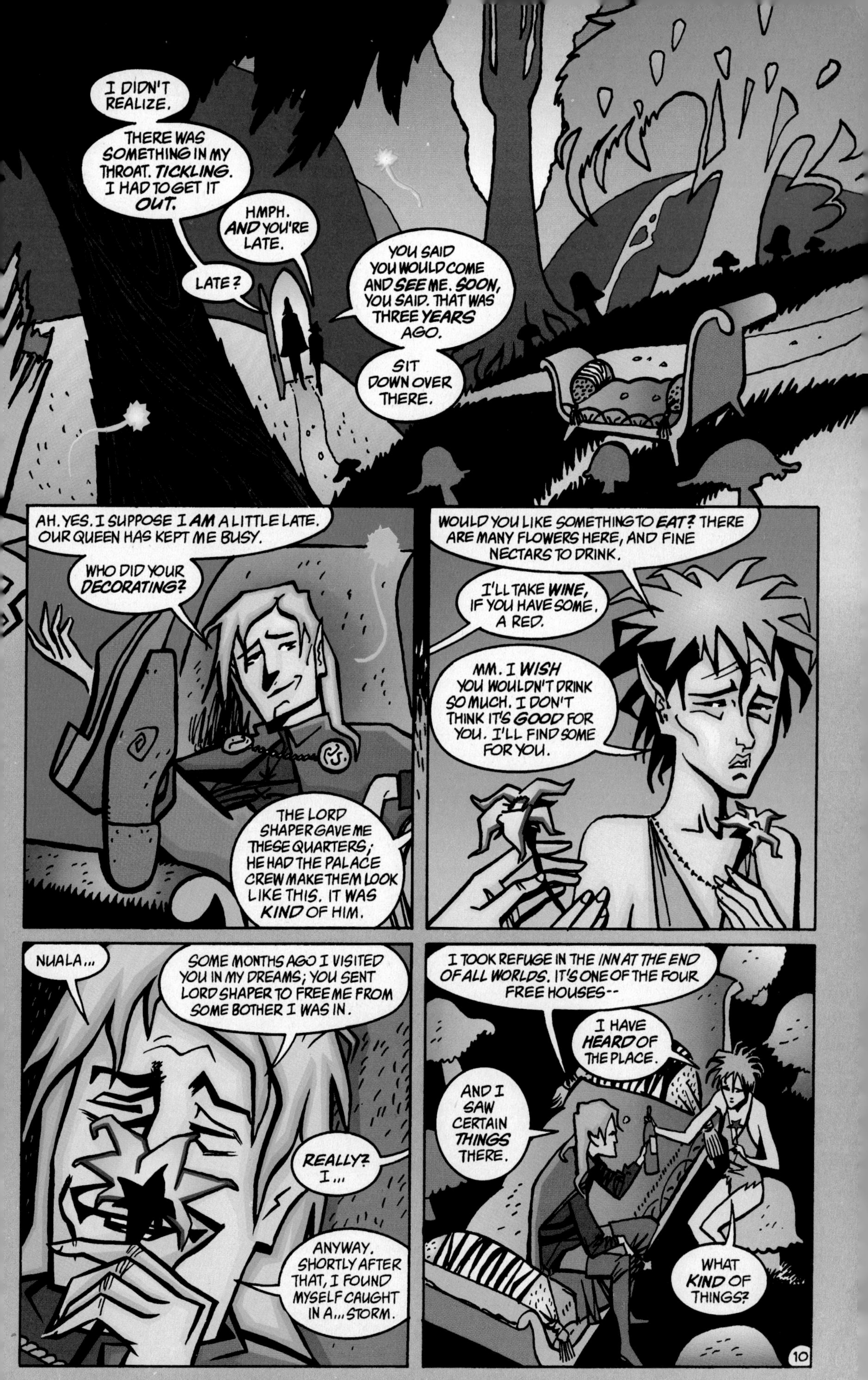
I DIDN'T REALIZE.
THERE WAS SOMETHING IN MY THROAT. TICKLING. I HAD TO GET IT OUT.
HMPH. AND YOU'RE LATE.
LATE?
YOU SAID YOU WOULD COME AND SEE ME. SOON, YOU SAID. THAT WAS THREE YEARS AGO.
SIT DOWN OVER THERE.
AH. YES. I SUPPOSE I AM A LITTLE LATE. OUR QUEEN HAS KEPT ME BUSY.
WHO DID YOUR DECORATING?
THE LORD SHAPER GAVE ME THESE QUARTERS; HE HAD THE PALACE CREW MAKE THEM LOOK LIKE THIS. IT WAS KIND OF HIM.
WOULD YOU LIKE SOMETHING TO EAT? THERE ARE MANY FLOWERS HERE, AND FINE NECTARS TO DRINK.
I'LL TAKE WINE, IF YOU HAVE SOME. A RED.
MM. I WISH YOU WOULDN'T DRINK SO MUCH. I DON'T THINK IT'S GOOD FOR YOU. I'LL FIND SOME FOR YOU.
NUALA...
SOME MONTHS AGO I VISITED YOU IN MY DREAMS; YOU SENT LORD SHAPER TO FREE ME FROM SOME BOTHER I WAS IN.
REALLY? I...
ANYWAY. SHORTLY AFTER THAT, I FOUND MYSELF CAUGHT IN A... STORM.
I TOOK REFUGE IN THE INN AT THE END OF ALL WORLDS. IT'S ONE OF THE FOUR FREE HOUSES--
I HAVE HEARD OF THE PLACE.
AND I SAW CERTAIN THINGS THERE.
WHAT KIND OF THINGS?
10

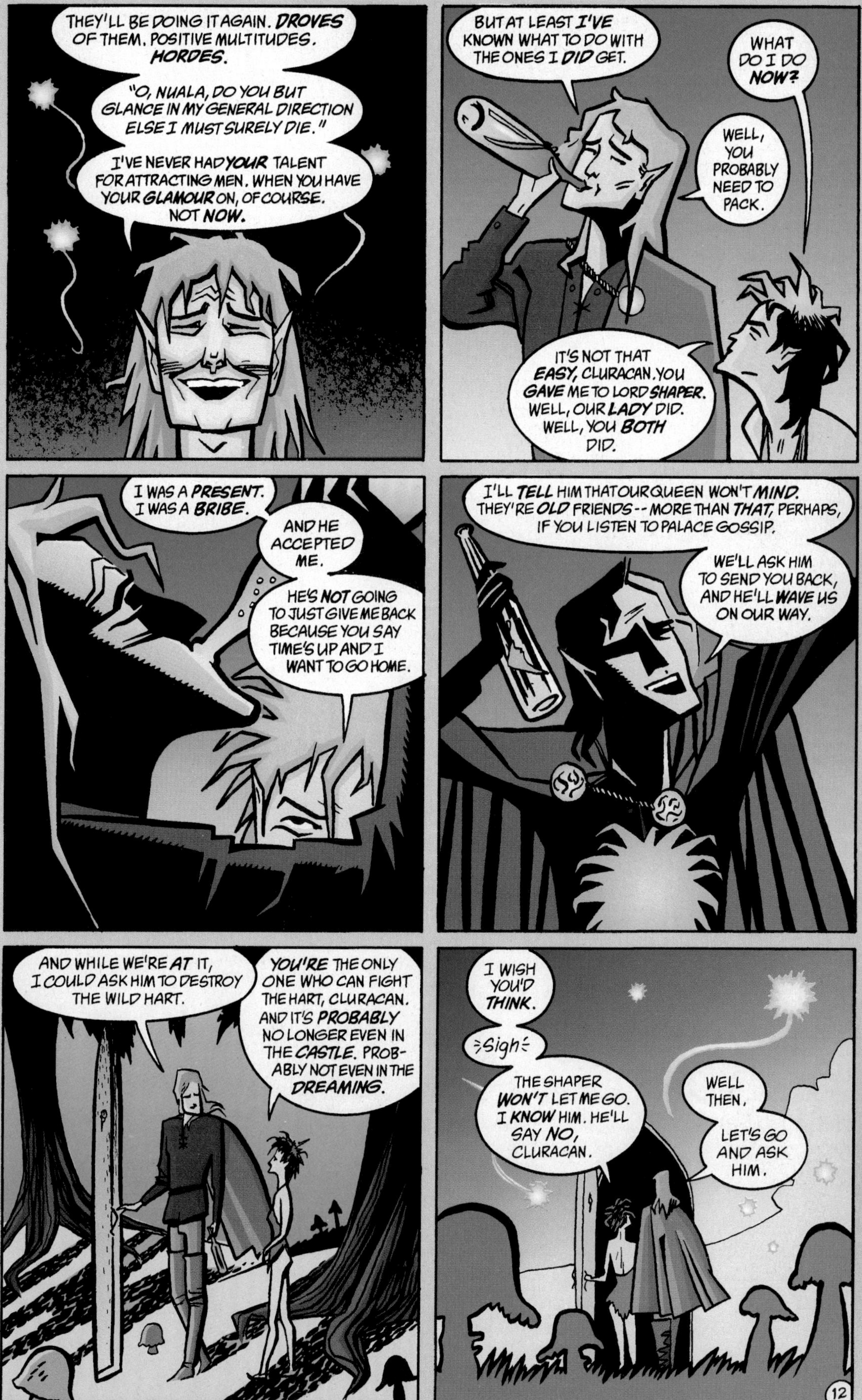
THEY'LL BE DOING IT AGAIN. DROVES OF THEM. POSITIVE MULTITUDES. HORDES.
"O, NUALA, DO YOU BUT GLANCE IN MY GENERAL DIRECTION ELSE I MUST SURELY DIE."
I'VE NEVER HAD YOUR TALENT FOR ATTRACTING MEN. WHEN YOU HAVE YOUR GLAMOUR ON, OF COURSE. NOT NOW.
BUT AT LEAST I'VE KNOWN WHAT TO DO WITH THE ONES I DID GET.
WHAT DO I DO NOW?
WELL, YOU PROBABLY NEED TO PACK.
IT'S NOT THAT EASY, CLURACAN. YOU GAVE ME TO LORD SHAPER. WELL, OUR LADY DID. WELL, YOU BOTH DID.
I WAS A PRESENT. I WAS A BRIBE.
AND HE ACCEPTED ME.
HE'S NOT GOING TO JUST GIVE ME BACK BECAUSE YOU SAY TIME'S UP AND I WANT TO GO HOME.
I'LL TELL HIM THAT OUR QUEEN WON'T MIND. THEY'RE OLD FRIENDS -- MORE THAN THAT, PERHAPS, IF YOU LISTEN TO PALACE GOSSIP.
WE'LL ASK HIM TO SEND YOU BACK, AND HE'LL WAVE US ON OUR WAY.
AND WHILE WE'RE AT IT, I COULD ASK HIM TO DESTROY THE WILD HART.
YOU'RE THE ONLY ONE WHO CAN FIGHT THE HART, CLURACAN. AND IT'S PROBABLY NO LONGER EVEN IN THE CASTLE. PROBABLY NOT EVEN IN THE DREAMING.
I WISH YOU'D THINK.
Sigh
THE SHAPER WON'T LET ME GO. I KNOW HIM. HE'LL SAY NO, CLURACAN.
WELL THEN.
LET'S GO AND ASK HIM.

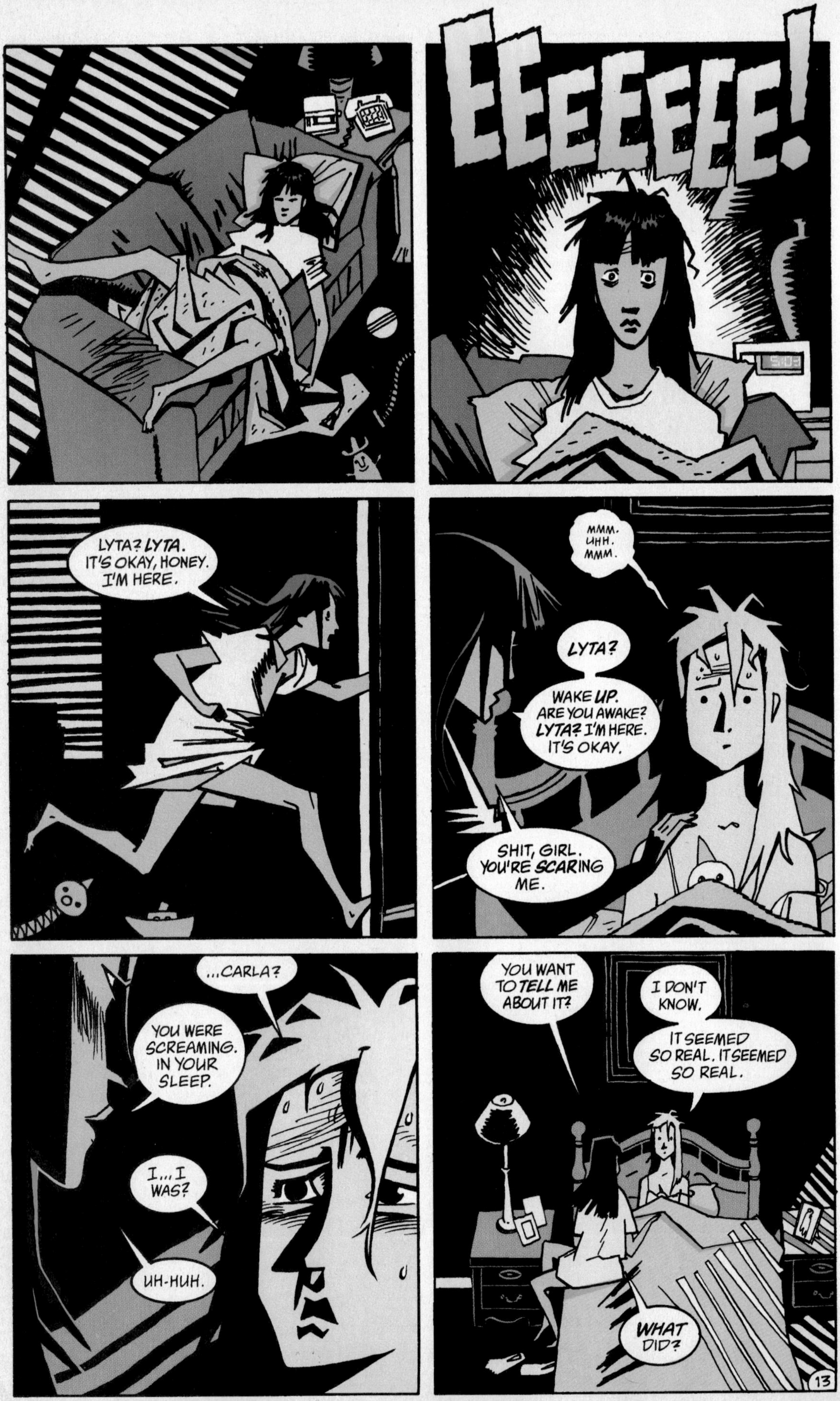
EEEEEEE!
LYTA? LYTA. IT'S OKAY, HONEY. I'M HERE.
MMM. UHH. MMM.
LYTA?
WAKE UP. ARE YOU AWAKE? LYTA? I'M HERE. IT'S OKAY.
SHIT, GIRL. YOU'RE SCARING ME.
...CARLA?
YOU WERE SCREAMING. IN YOUR SLEEP.
I... I WAS?
UH-HUH.
YOU WANT TO TELL ME ABOUT IT?
I DON'T KNOW.
IT SEEMED SO REAL. IT SEEMED SO REAL.
WHAT DID?

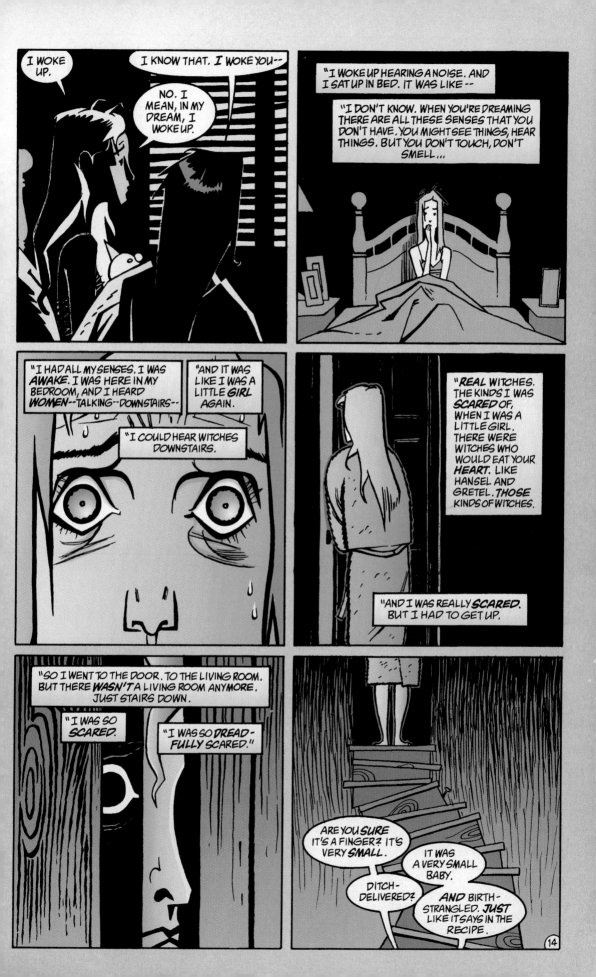

I WOKE UP.

I KNOW THAT. *I* WOKE YOU--

NO. I MEAN, IN MY DREAM, I WOKE UP.

"I WOKE UP HEARING A NOISE. AND I SAT UP IN BED. IT WAS LIKE--

"I DON'T KNOW. WHEN YOU'RE DREAMING THERE ARE ALL THESE SENSES THAT YOU DON'T HAVE. YOU MIGHT SEE THINGS, HEAR THINGS, BUT YOU DON'T TOUCH, DON'T SMELL...

"I HAD ALL MY SENSES, I WAS *AWAKE.* I WAS HERE IN MY BEDROOM, AND I HEARD *WOMEN*--TALKING--DOWNSTAIRS--

"AND IT WAS LIKE I WAS A LITTLE *GIRL* AGAIN.

"I COULD HEAR WITCHES DOWNSTAIRS.

"*REAL* WITCHES. THE KINDS I WAS *SCARED* OF, WHEN I WAS A LITTLE GIRL. THERE WERE WITCHES WHO WOULD EAT YOUR *HEART.* LIKE HANSEL AND GRETEL. *THOSE* KINDS OF WITCHES.

"AND I WAS REALLY *SCARED.* BUT I HAD TO GET UP.

"SO I WENT TO THE DOOR. TO THE LIVING ROOM. BUT THERE *WASN'T* A LIVING ROOM ANYMORE. JUST STAIRS DOWN.

"I WAS SO *SCARED.*

"I WAS SO *DREADFULLY SCARED.*"

ARE YOU *SURE* IT'S A FINGER? IT'S VERY *SMALL.*

IT WAS A VERY SMALL BABY.

DITCH-DELIVERED?

AND BIRTH-STRANGLED. *JUST* LIKE IT SAYS IN THE RECIPE.

14

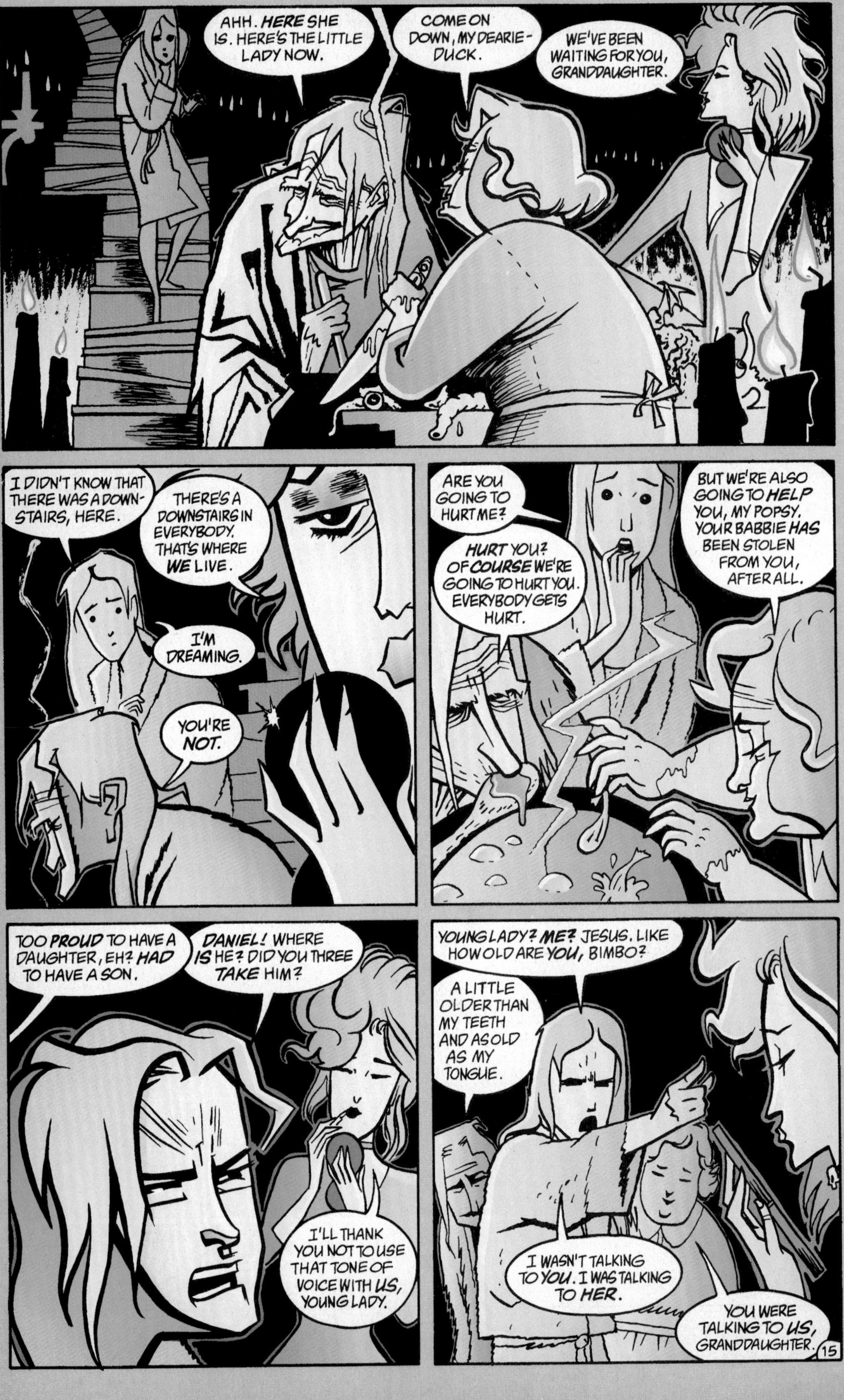
AHH. HERE SHE IS. HERE'S THE LITTLE LADY NOW.
COME ON DOWN, MY DEARIE-DUCK.
WE'VE BEEN WAITING FOR YOU, GRANDDAUGHTER.
I DIDN'T KNOW THAT THERE WAS A DOWN-STAIRS, HERE.
THERE'S A DOWNSTAIRS IN EVERYBODY. THAT'S WHERE WE LIVE.
I'M DREAMING.
YOU'RE NOT.
ARE YOU GOING TO HURT ME?
HURT YOU? OF COURSE WE'RE GOING TO HURT YOU. EVERYBODY GETS HURT.
BUT WE'RE ALSO GOING TO HELP YOU, MY POPSY. YOUR BABBIE HAS BEEN STOLEN FROM YOU, AFTER ALL.
TOO PROUD TO HAVE A DAUGHTER, EH? HAD TO HAVE A SON.
DANIEL! WHERE IS HE? DID YOU THREE TAKE HIM?
I'LL THANK YOU NOT TO USE THAT TONE OF VOICE WITH US, YOUNG LADY.
YOUNG LADY? ME? JESUS. LIKE HOW OLD ARE YOU, BIMBO?
A LITTLE OLDER THAN MY TEETH AND AS OLD AS MY TONGUE.
I WASN'T TALKING TO YOU. I WAS TALKING TO HER.
YOU WERE TALKING TO US, GRANDDAUGHTER.

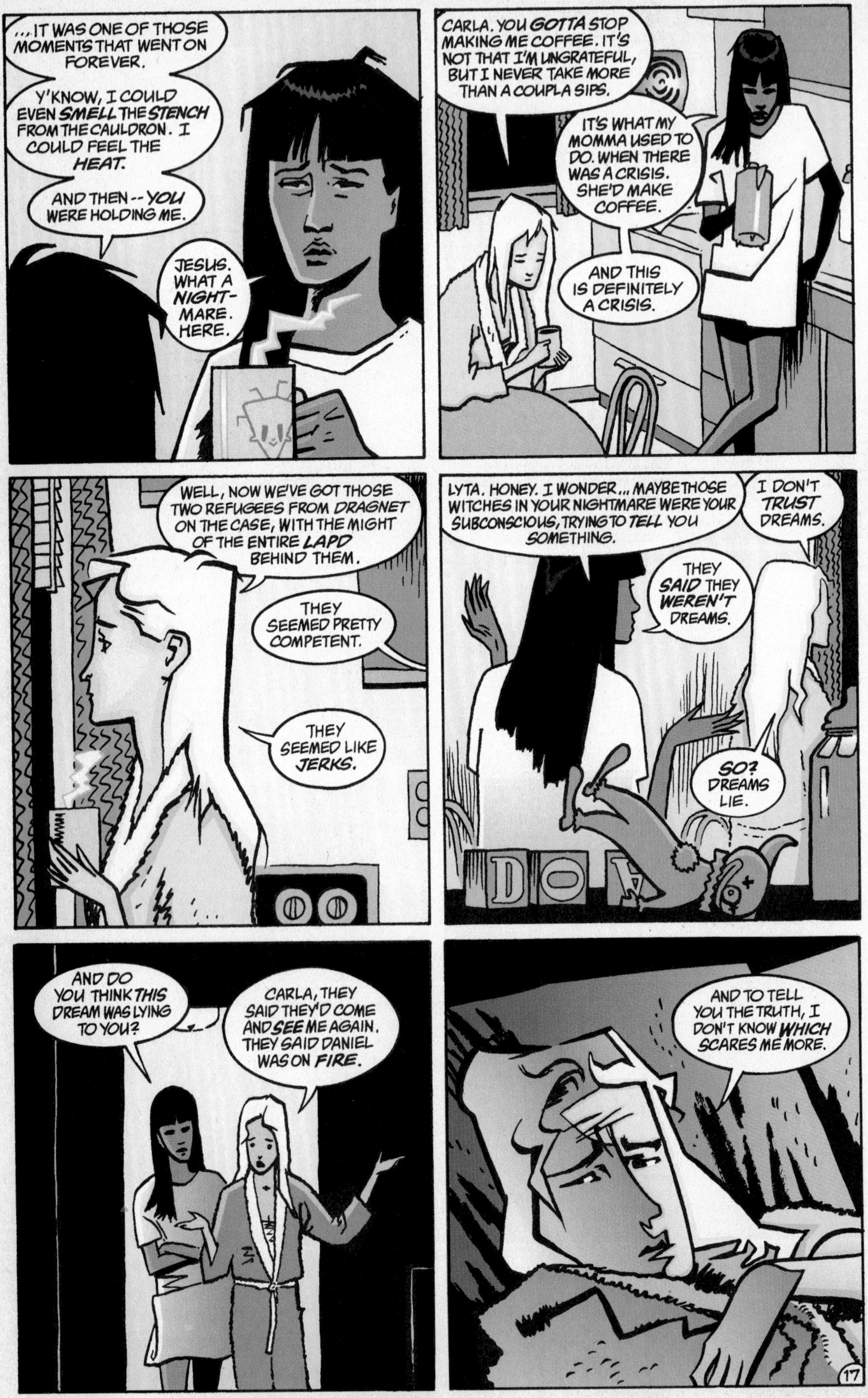
...IT WAS ONE OF THOSE MOMENTS THAT WENT ON FOREVER.
Y'KNOW, I COULD EVEN SMELL THE STENCH FROM THE CAULDRON. I COULD FEEL THE HEAT.
AND THEN -- YOU WERE HOLDING ME.
JESUS. WHAT A NIGHT-MARE. HERE.
CARLA. YOU GOTTA STOP MAKING ME COFFEE. IT'S NOT THAT I'M UNGRATEFUL, BUT I NEVER TAKE MORE THAN A COUPLA SIPS.
IT'S WHAT MY MOMMA USED TO DO. WHEN THERE WAS A CRISIS. SHE'D MAKE COFFEE.
AND THIS IS DEFINITELY A CRISIS.
WELL, NOW WE'VE GOT THOSE TWO REFUGEES FROM DRAGNET ON THE CASE, WITH THE MIGHT OF THE ENTIRE LAPD BEHIND THEM.
THEY SEEMED PRETTY COMPETENT.
THEY SEEMED LIKE JERKS.
LYTA. HONEY. I WONDER... MAYBE THOSE WITCHES IN YOUR NIGHTMARE WERE YOUR SUBCONSCIOUS, TRYING TO TELL YOU SOMETHING.
I DON'T TRUST DREAMS.
THEY SAID THEY WEREN'T DREAMS.
SO? DREAMS LIE.
AND DO YOU THINK THIS DREAM WAS LYING TO YOU?
CARLA, THEY SAID THEY'D COME AND SEE ME AGAIN. THEY SAID DANIEL WAS ON FIRE.
AND TO TELL YOU THE TRUTH, I DON'T KNOW WHICH SCARES ME MORE.
17

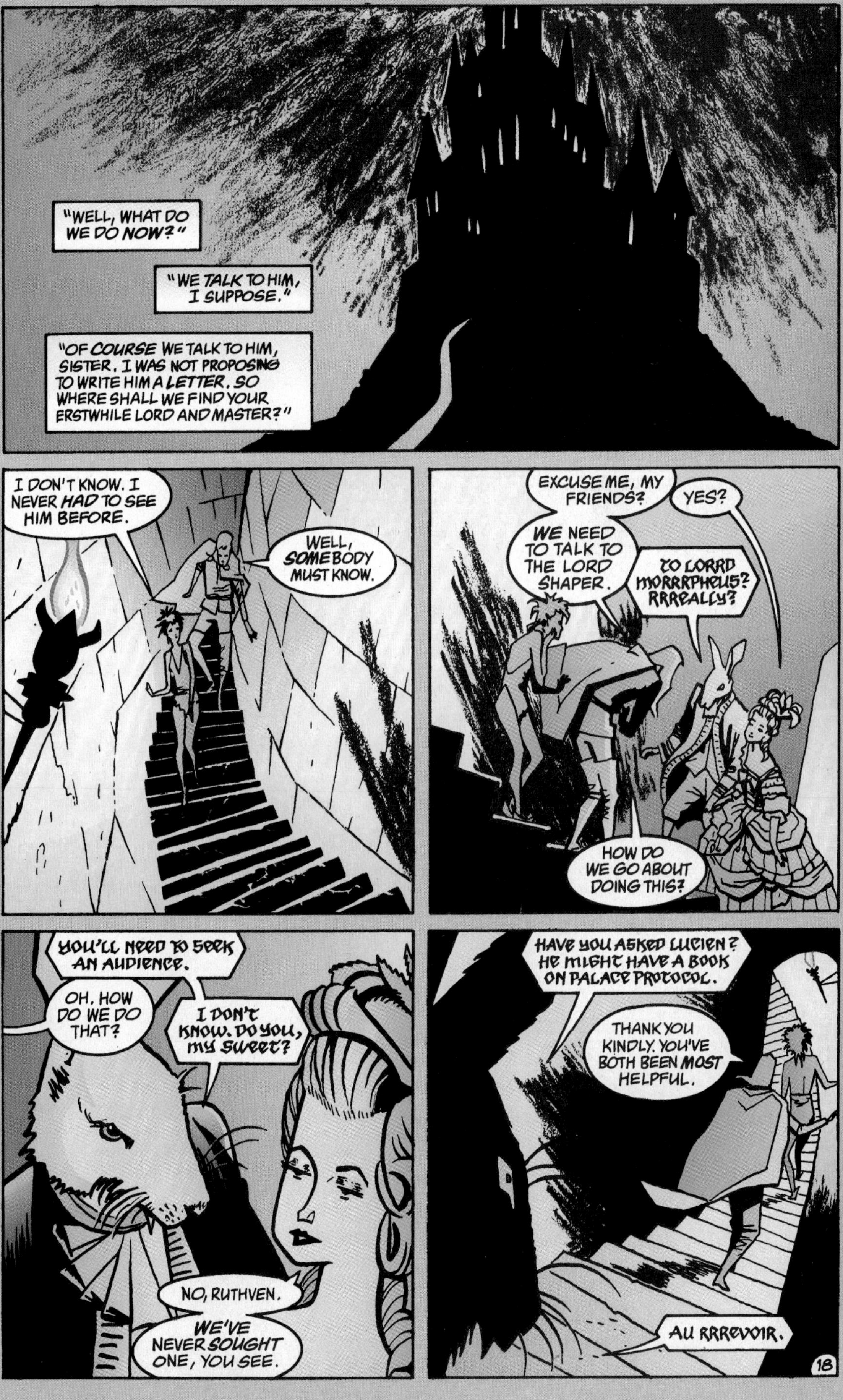
"WELL, WHAT DO WE DO NOW?"
"WE TALK TO HIM, I SUPPOSE."
"OF COURSE WE TALK TO HIM, SISTER. I WAS NOT PROPOSING TO WRITE HIM A LETTER. SO WHERE SHALL WE FIND YOUR ERSTWHILE LORD AND MASTER?"
I DON'T KNOW. I NEVER HAD TO SEE HIM BEFORE.
WELL, SOMEBODY MUST KNOW.
EXCUSE ME, MY FRIENDS?
YES?
WE NEED TO TALK TO THE LORD SHAPER.
TO LORRD MORRRPHEUS? RRREALLY?
HOW DO WE GO ABOUT DOING THIS?
YOU'LL NEED TO SEEK AN AUDIENCE.
OH. HOW DO WE DO THAT?
I DON'T KNOW. DO YOU, MY SWEET?
NO, RUTHVEN.
WE'VE NEVER SOUGHT ONE, YOU SEE.
HAVE YOU ASKED LUCIEN? HE MIGHT HAVE A BOOK ON PALACE PROTOCOL.
THANK YOU KINDLY. YOU'VE BOTH BEEN MOST HELPFUL.
AU RRREVOIR.

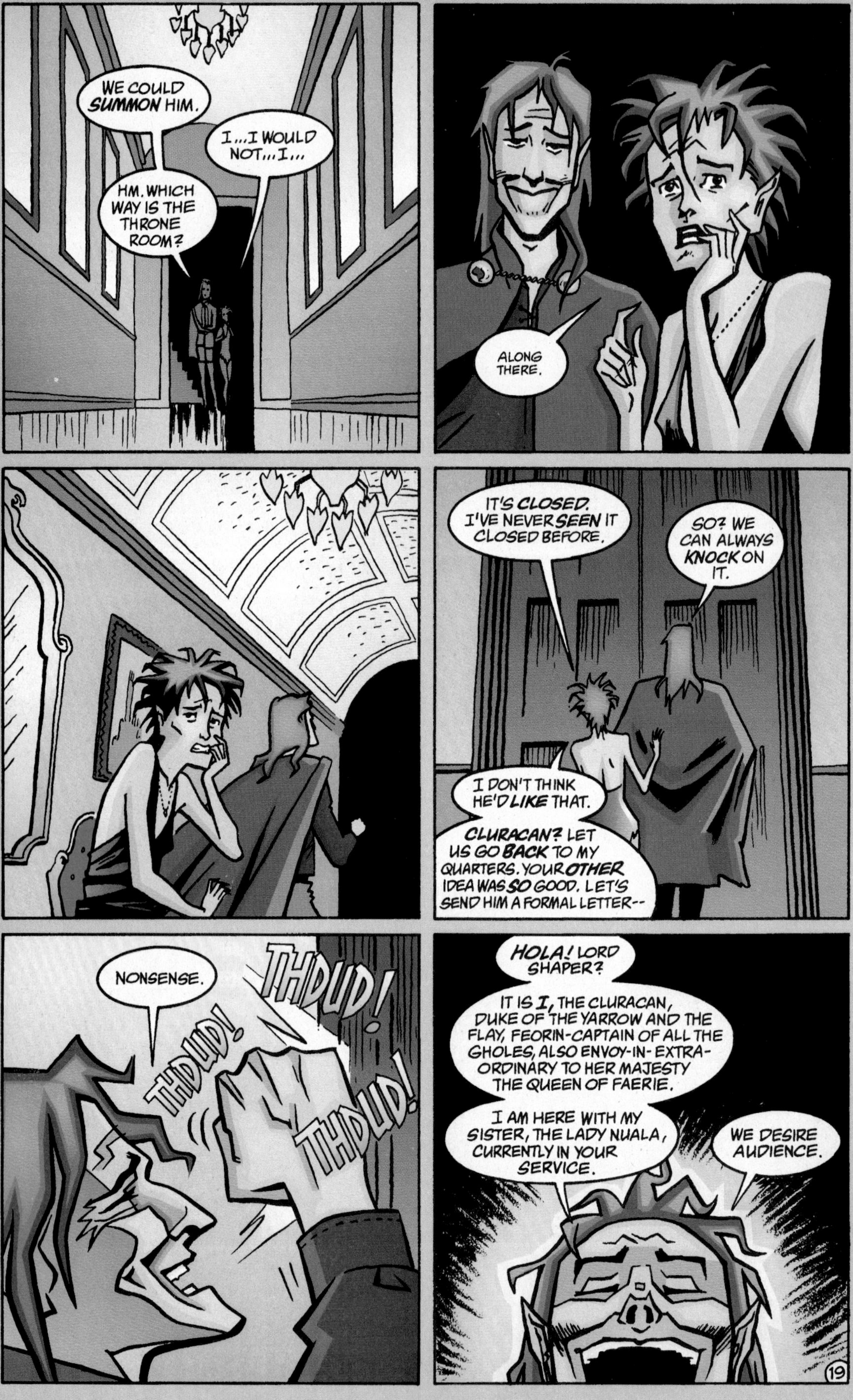
WE COULD SUMMON HIM.
I...I WOULD NOT...I...
HM. WHICH WAY IS THE THRONE ROOM?
ALONG THERE.
IT'S CLOSED. I'VE NEVER SEEN IT CLOSED BEFORE.
SO? WE CAN ALWAYS KNOCK ON IT.
I DON'T THINK HE'D LIKE THAT.
CLURACAN? LET US GO BACK TO MY QUARTERS. YOUR OTHER IDEA WAS SO GOOD. LET'S SEND HIM A FORMAL LETTER--
NONSENSE.
THDUD!
THDUD!
THDUD!
HOLA! LORD SHAPER?
IT IS I, THE CLURACAN, DUKE OF THE YARROW AND THE FLAY, FEORIN-CAPTAIN OF ALL THE GHOLES, ALSO ENVOY-IN-EXTRA-ORDINARY TO HER MAJESTY THE QUEEN OF FAERIE.
I AM HERE WITH MY SISTER, THE LADY NUALA, CURRENTLY IN YOUR SERVICE.
WE DESIRE AUDIENCE.

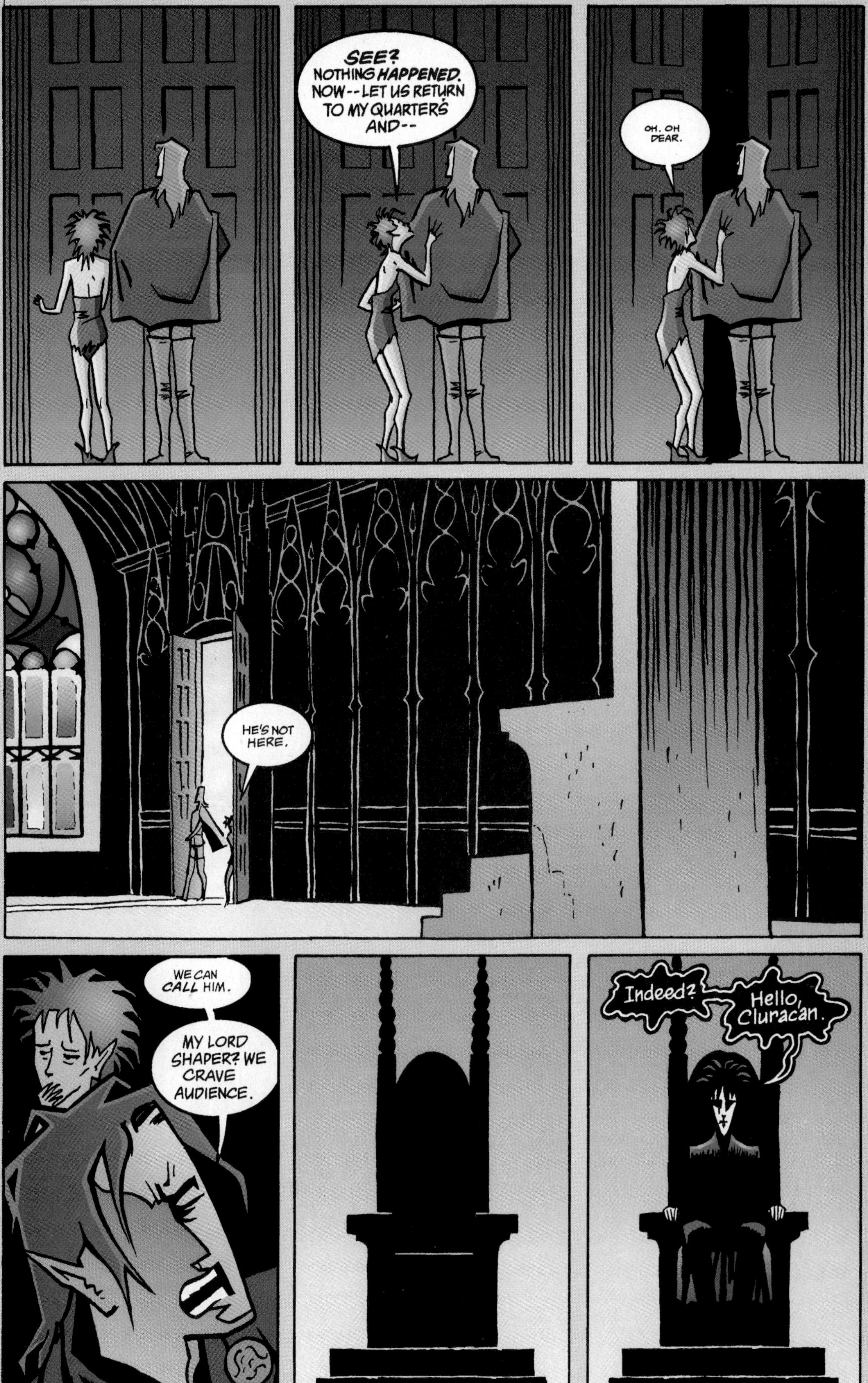
SEE? NOTHING HAPPENED. NOW--LET US RETURN TO MY QUARTERS AND--
OH, OH DEAR.
HE'S NOT HERE.
WE CAN CALL HIM.
MY LORD SHAPER? WE CRAVE AUDIENCE.
Indeed?
Hello, Cluracan.

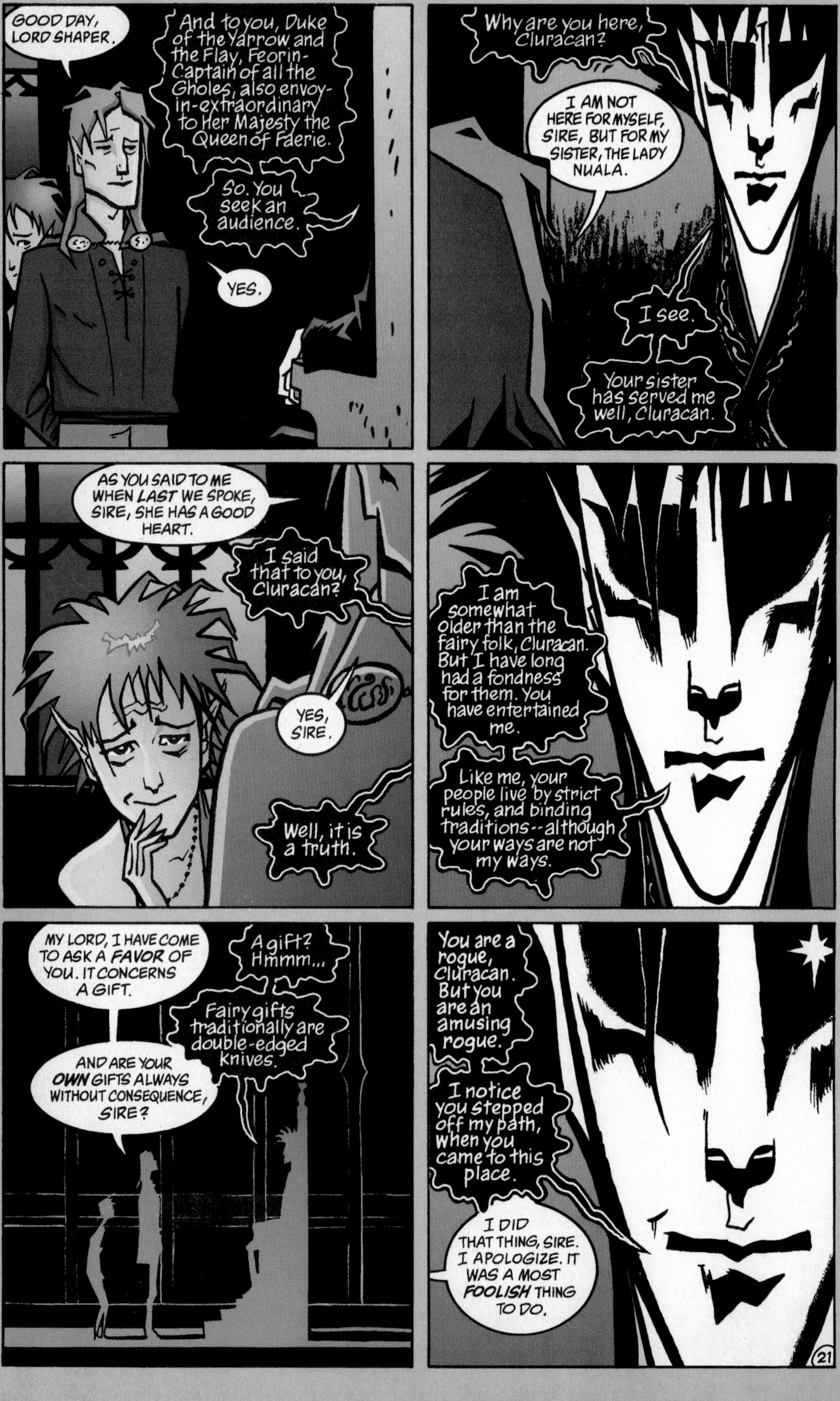
GOOD DAY, LORD SHAPER.
And to you, Duke of the Yarrow and the Flay, Feorin-Captain of all the Gholes, also envoy-in-extraordinary to Her Majesty the Queen of Faerie.
So. You seek an audience.
YES.
Why are you here, Cluracan?
I AM NOT HERE FOR MYSELF, SIRE, BUT FOR MY SISTER, THE LADY NUALA.
I see.
Your sister has served me well, Cluracan.
AS YOU SAID TO ME WHEN LAST WE SPOKE, SIRE, SHE HAS A GOOD HEART.
I said that to you, Cluracan?
YES, SIRE.
Well, it is a truth.
I am somewhat older than the fairy folk, Cluracan. But I have long had a fondness for them. You have entertained me.
Like me, your people live by strict rules, and binding traditions--although your ways are not my ways.
MY LORD, I HAVE COME TO ASK A FAVOR OF YOU. IT CONCERNS A GIFT.
A gift? Hmmm...
Fairy gifts traditionally are double-edged knives.
AND ARE YOUR OWN GIFTS ALWAYS WITHOUT CONSEQUENCE, SIRE?
You are a rogue, Cluracan. But you are an amusing rogue.
I notice you stepped off my path, when you came to this place.
I DID THAT THING, SIRE. I APOLOGIZE. IT WAS A MOST FOOLISH THING TO DO.
21

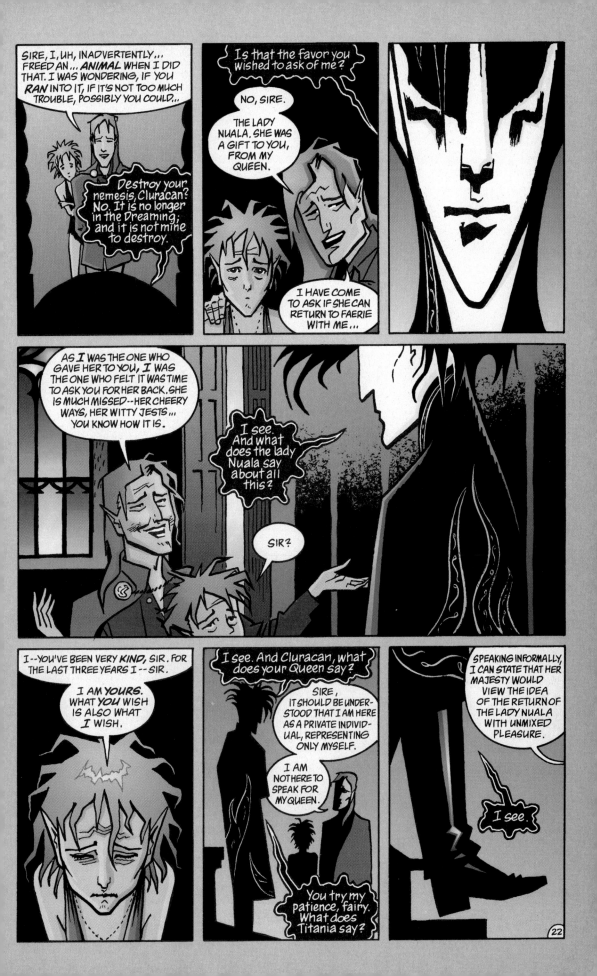

SIRE, I, UH, INADVERTENTLY... FREED AN... *ANIMAL* WHEN I DID THAT. I WAS WONDERING, IF YOU *RAN* INTO IT, IF IT'S NOT TOO MUCH TROUBLE, POSSIBLY YOU COULD...

Destroy your nemesis, Cluracan? No. It is no longer in the Dreaming; and it is not mine to destroy.

Is that the favor you wished to ask of me?

NO, SIRE.

THE LADY NUALA. SHE WAS A GIFT TO YOU, FROM MY QUEEN.

I HAVE COME TO ASK IF SHE CAN RETURN TO FAERIE WITH ME...

AS *I* WAS THE ONE WHO GAVE HER TO YOU, *I* WAS THE ONE WHO FELT IT WAS TIME TO ASK YOU FOR HER BACK. SHE IS MUCH MISSED--HER CHEERY WAYS, HER WITTY JESTS ... YOU KNOW HOW IT IS.

I see. And what does the lady Nuala say about all this?

SIR?

I--YOU'VE BEEN VERY *KIND*, SIR. FOR THE LAST THREE YEARS I -- SIR.

I AM *YOURS*. WHAT *YOU* WISH IS ALSO WHAT I WISH.

I see. And Cluracan, what does your Queen say?

SIRE, IT SHOULD BE UNDERSTOOD THAT I AM HERE AS A PRIVATE INDIVIDUAL, REPRESENTING ONLY MYSELF.

I AM NOT HERE TO SPEAK FOR MY QUEEN.

You try my patience, fairy. What does Titania say?

SPEAKING INFORMALLY, I CAN STATE THAT HER MAJESTY WOULD VIEW THE IDEA OF THE RETURN OF THE LADY NUALA WITH UNMIXED PLEASURE.

I see.

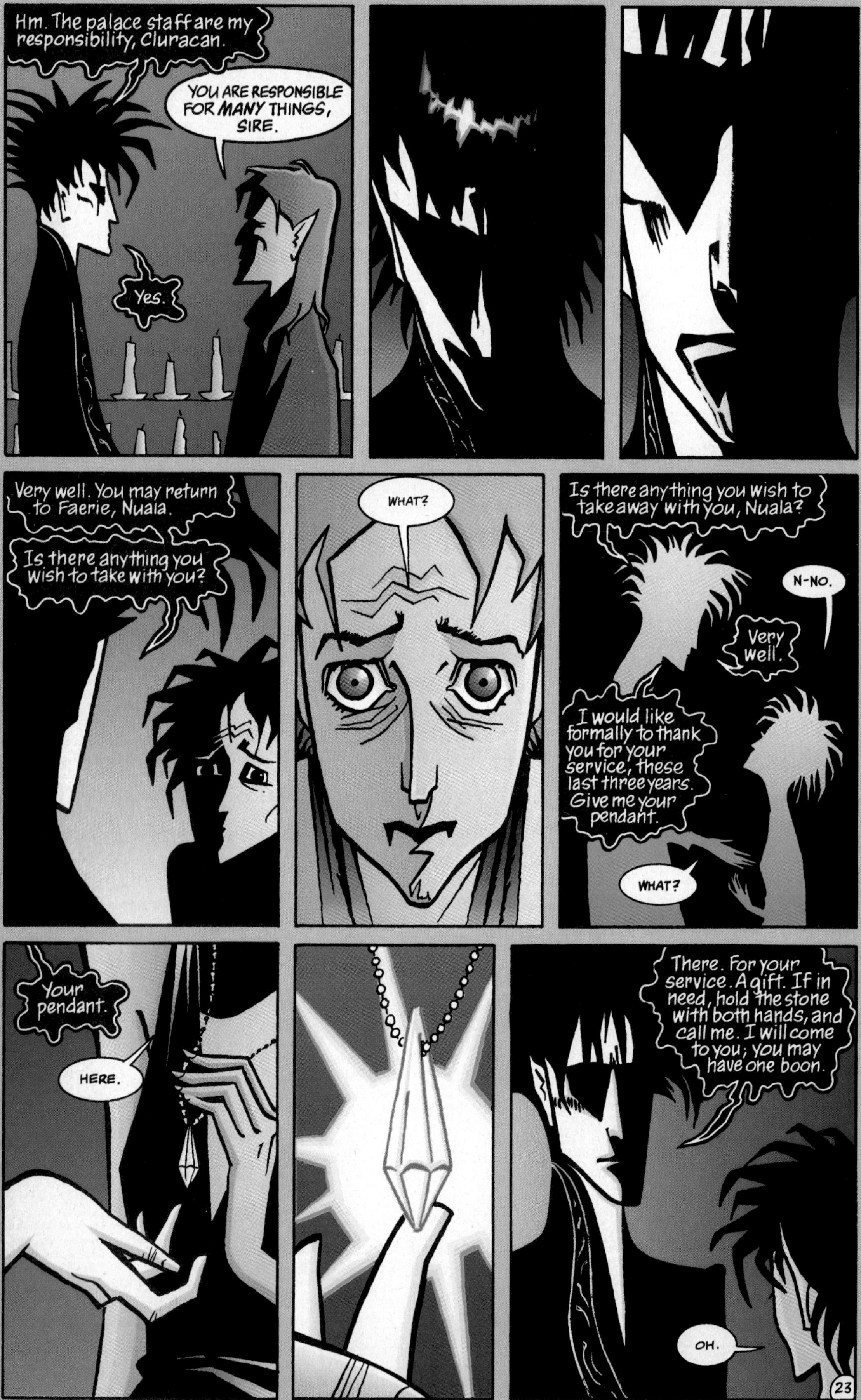

Hm. The palace staff are my responsibility, Cluracan.
YOU ARE RESPONSIBLE FOR MANY THINGS, SIRE.
Yes.
Very well. You may return to Faerie, Nuala.
Is there anything you wish to take with you?
WHAT?
Is there anything you wish to take away with you, Nuala?
N-NO.
Very well.
I would like formally to thank you for your service, these last three years. Give me your pendant.
WHAT?
Your pendant.
HERE.
There. For your service. A gift. If in need, hold the stone with both hands, and call me. I will come to you; you may have one boon.
OH.

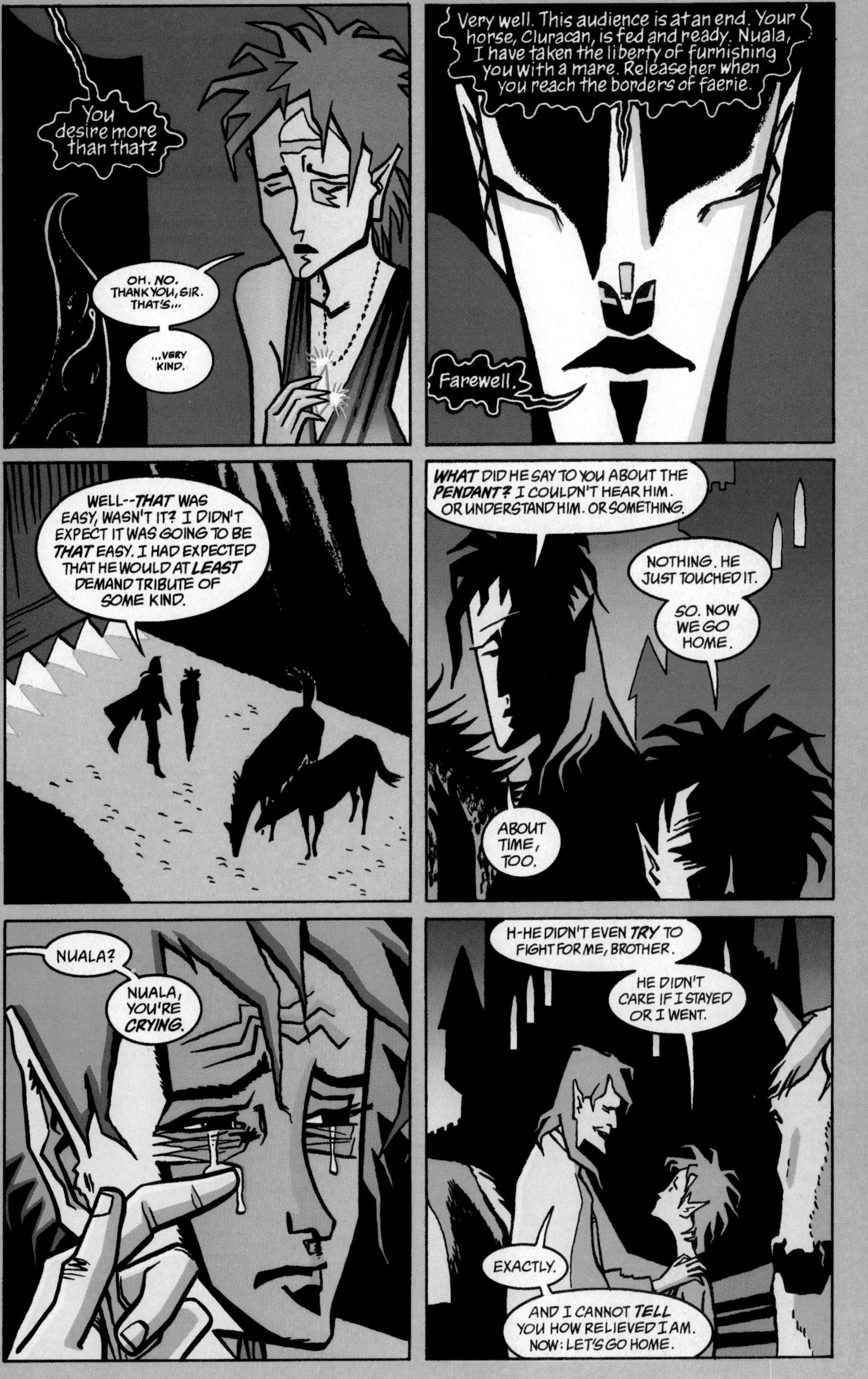

You desire more than that?
OH. NO. THANK YOU, SIR. THAT'S...
...VERY KIND.
Very well. This audience is at an end. Your horse, Cluracan, is fed and ready. Nuala, I have taken the liberty of furnishing you with a mare. Release her when you reach the borders of faerie.
Farewell.
WELL--THAT WAS EASY, WASN'T IT? I DIDN'T EXPECT IT WAS GOING TO BE THAT EASY. I HAD EXPECTED THAT HE WOULD AT LEAST DEMAND TRIBUTE OF SOME KIND.
WHAT DID HE SAY TO YOU ABOUT THE PENDANT? I COULDN'T HEAR HIM. OR UNDERSTAND HIM. OR SOMETHING.
NOTHING. HE JUST TOUCHED IT.
SO. NOW WE GO HOME.
ABOUT TIME, TOO.
NUALA?
NUALA, YOU'RE CRYING.
H-HE DIDN'T EVEN TRY TO FIGHT FOR ME, BROTHER.
HE DIDN'T CARE IF I STAYED OR I WENT.
EXACTLY.
AND I CANNOT TELL YOU HOW RELIEVED I AM. NOW: LET'S GO HOME.

Part Three

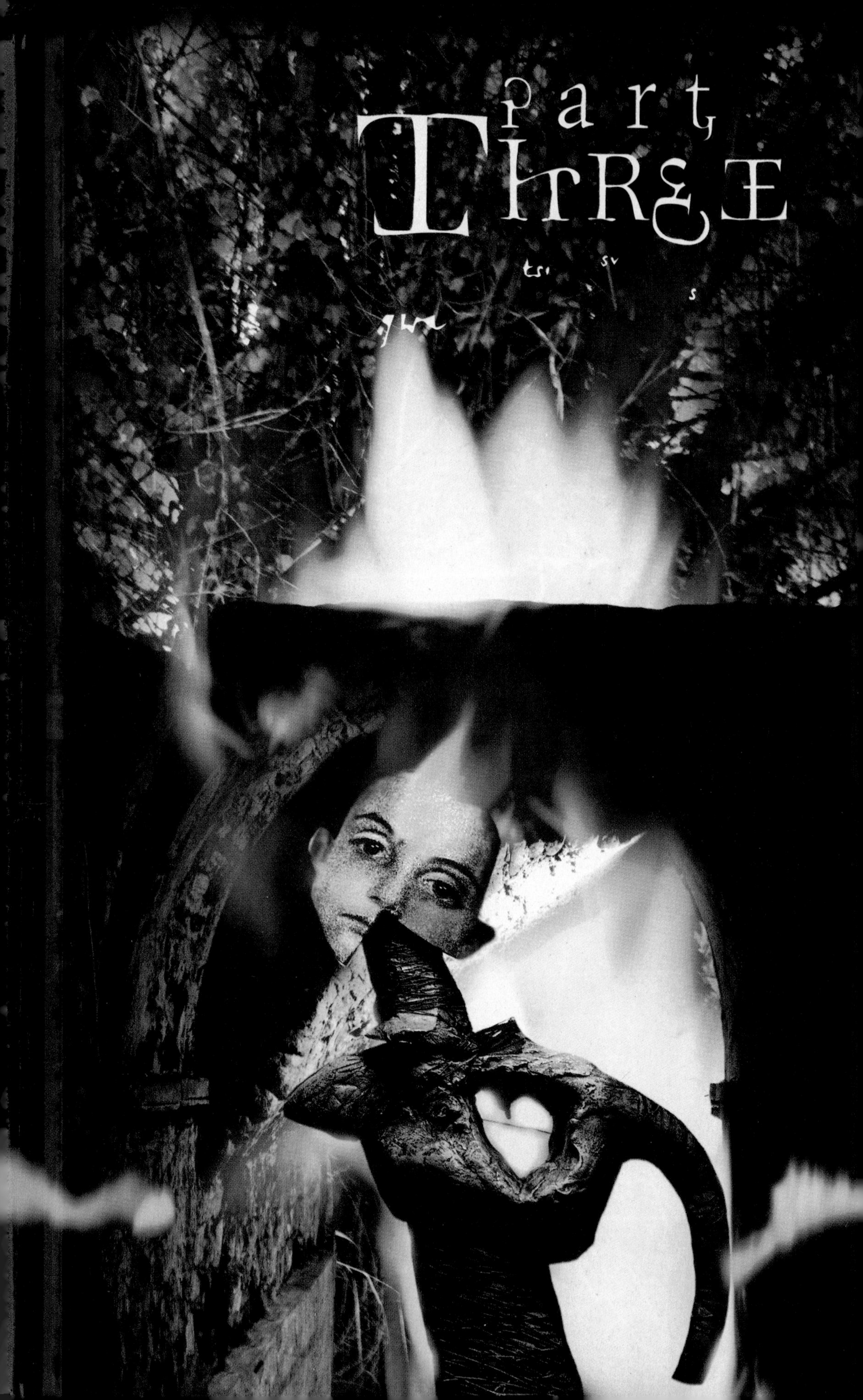

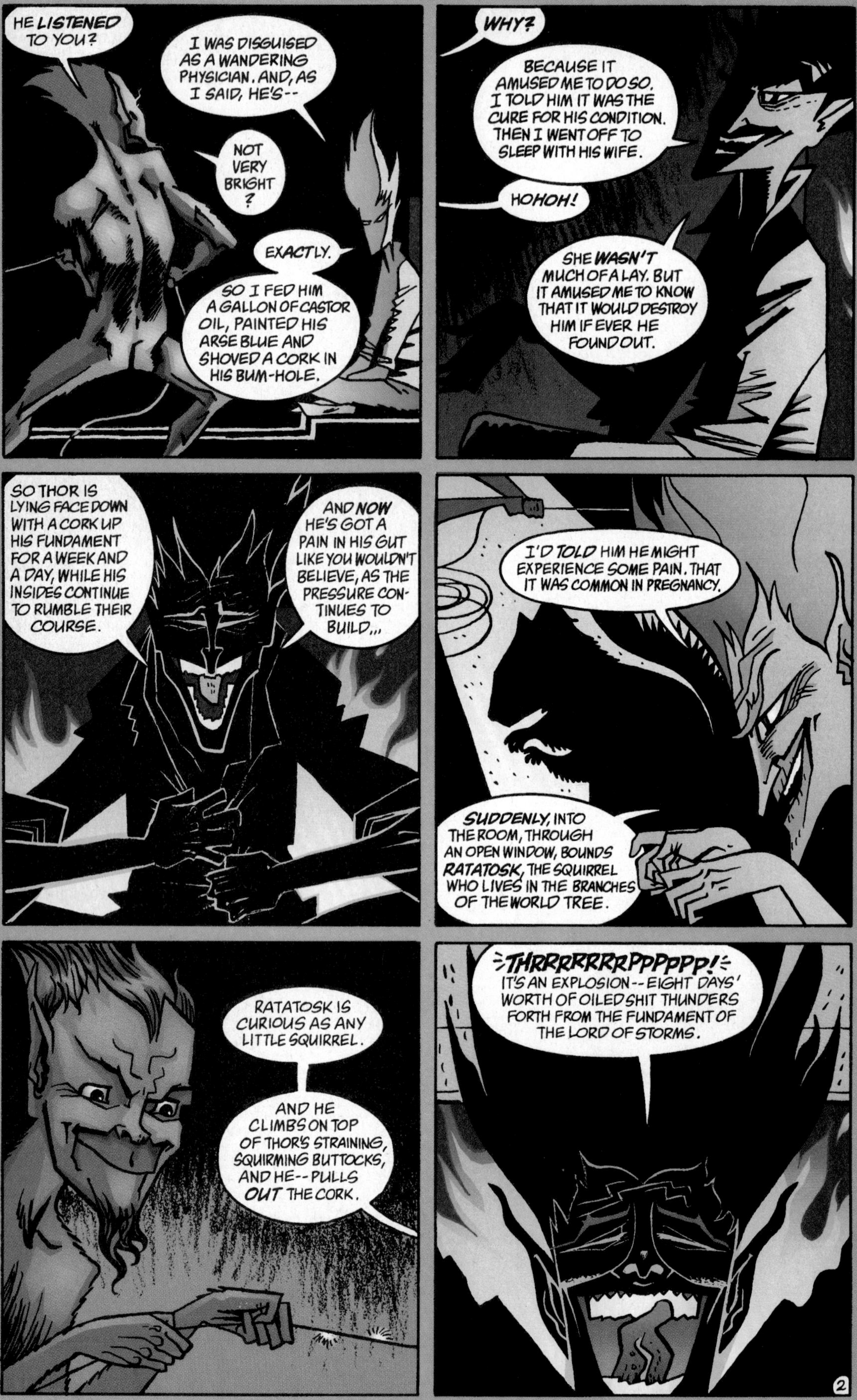

HE LISTENED TO YOU?
I WAS DISGUISED AS A WANDERING PHYSICIAN. AND, AS I SAID, HE'S--
NOT VERY BRIGHT?
EXACTLY.
SO I FED HIM A GALLON OF CASTOR OIL, PAINTED HIS ARSE BLUE AND SHOVED A CORK IN HIS BUM-HOLE.
WHY?
BECAUSE IT AMUSED ME TO DO SO. I TOLD HIM IT WAS THE CURE FOR HIS CONDITION. THEN I WENT OFF TO SLEEP WITH HIS WIFE.
HOHOH!
SHE WASN'T MUCH OF A LAY. BUT IT AMUSED ME TO KNOW THAT IT WOULD DESTROY HIM IF EVER HE FOUND OUT.
SO THOR IS LYING FACE DOWN WITH A CORK UP HIS FUNDAMENT FOR A WEEK AND A DAY, WHILE HIS INSIDES CONTINUE TO RUMBLE THEIR COURSE.
AND NOW HE'S GOT A PAIN IN HIS GUT LIKE YOU WOULDN'T BELIEVE, AS THE PRESSURE CONTINUES TO BUILD...
I'D TOLD HIM HE MIGHT EXPERIENCE SOME PAIN. THAT IT WAS COMMON IN PREGNANCY.
SUDDENLY, INTO THE ROOM, THROUGH AN OPEN WINDOW, BOUNDS RATATOSK, THE SQUIRREL WHO LIVES IN THE BRANCHES OF THE WORLD TREE.
RATATOSK IS CURIOUS AS ANY LITTLE SQUIRREL.
AND HE CLIMBS ON TOP OF THOR'S STRAINING, SQUIRMING BUTTOCKS, AND HE--PULLS OUT THE CORK.
THRRRRRRRPPPPPP!
IT'S AN EXPLOSION--EIGHT DAYS' WORTH OF OILED SHIT THUNDERS FORTH FROM THE FUNDAMENT OF THE LORD OF STORMS.

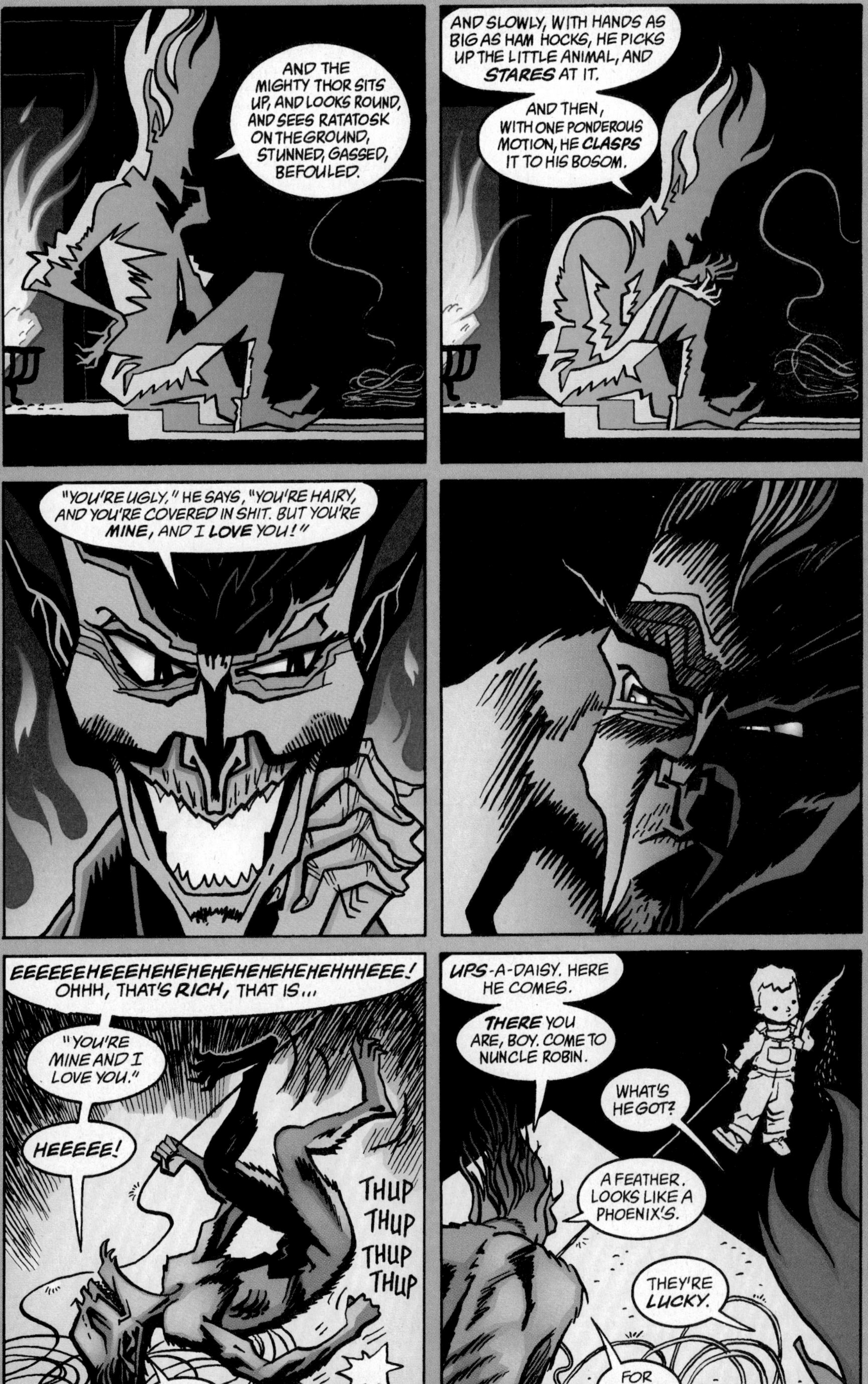

AND THE MIGHTY THOR SITS UP, AND LOOKS ROUND, AND SEES RATATOSK ON THE GROUND, STUNNED, GASSED, BEFOULED.
AND SLOWLY, WITH HANDS AS BIG AS HAM HOCKS, HE PICKS UP THE LITTLE ANIMAL, AND STARES AT IT.
AND THEN, WITH ONE PONDEROUS MOTION, HE CLASPS IT TO HIS BOSOM.
"YOU'RE UGLY," HE SAYS, "YOU'RE HAIRY, AND YOU'RE COVERED IN SHIT. BUT YOU'RE MINE, AND I LOVE YOU!"
EEEEEEHEEEHEHEHEHEHEHEHEHEHEHHHEEE! OHHH, THAT'S RICH, THAT IS...
"YOU'RE MINE AND I LOVE YOU."
HEEEEE!
THUP THUP THUP THUP
OOH...
UPS-A-DAISY. HERE HE COMES.
THERE YOU ARE, BOY. COME TO NUNCLE ROBIN.
WHAT'S HE GOT?
A FEATHER. LOOKS LIKE A PHOENIX'S.
THEY'RE LUCKY.
FOR WHOM?

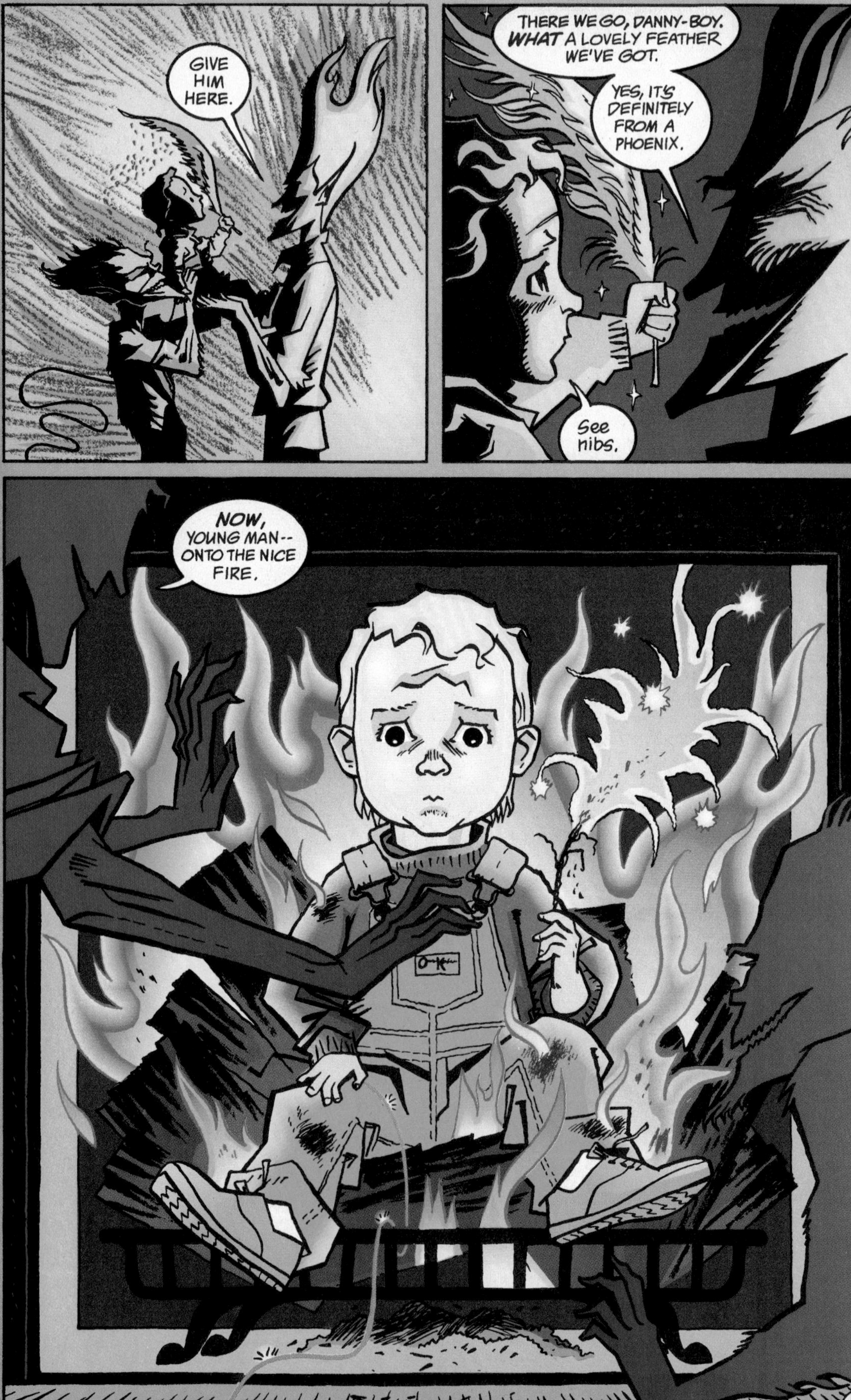
GIVE HIM HERE.
THERE WE GO, DANNY-BOY. *WHAT* A LOVELY FEATHER WE'VE GOT.
YES, IT'S DEFINITELY FROM A PHOENIX.
See nibs.
NOW, YOUNG MAN-- ONTO THE NICE FIRE.
4

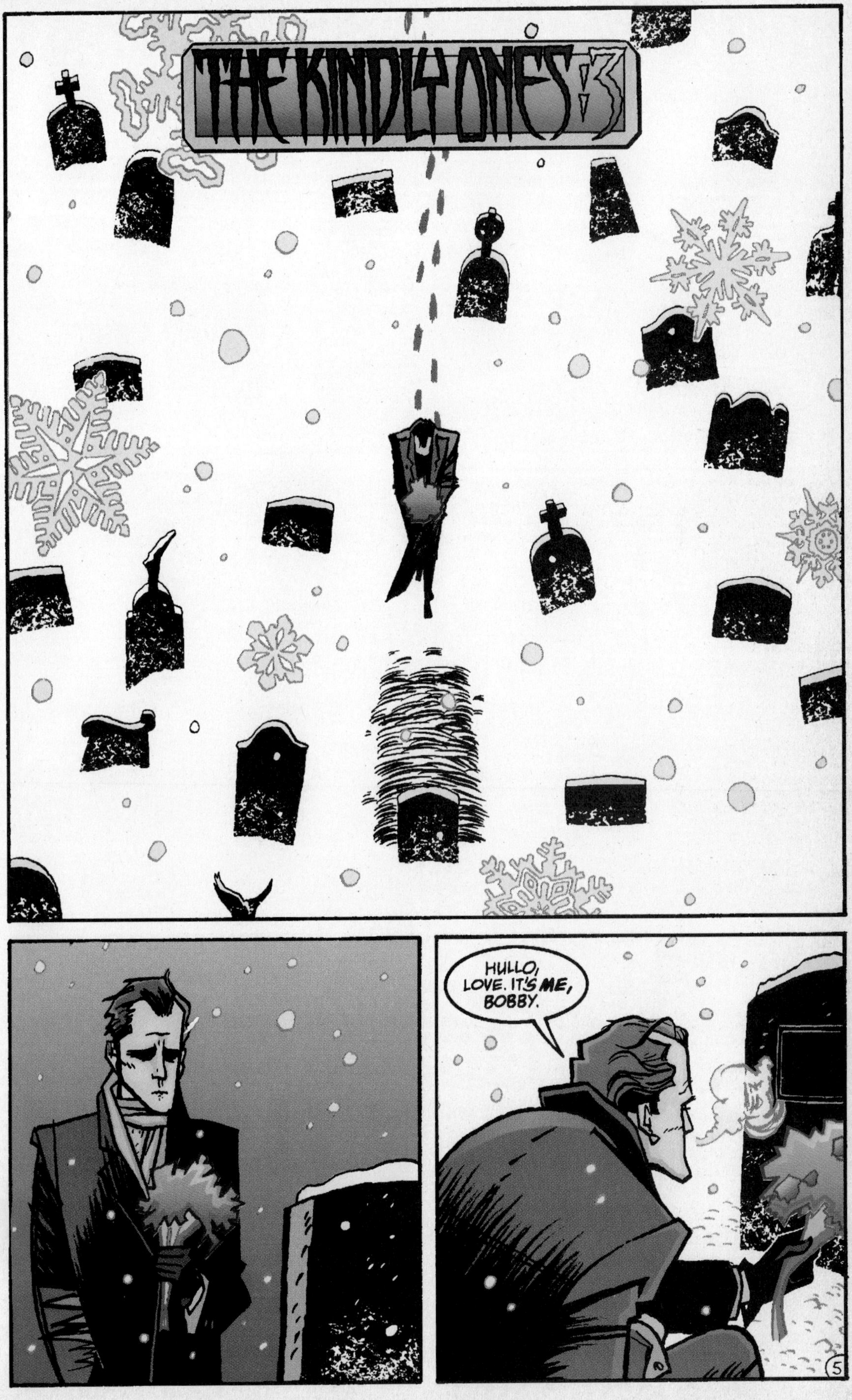

THE KINDLY ONES 13
HULLO, LOVE. IT'S *ME*, BOBBY.

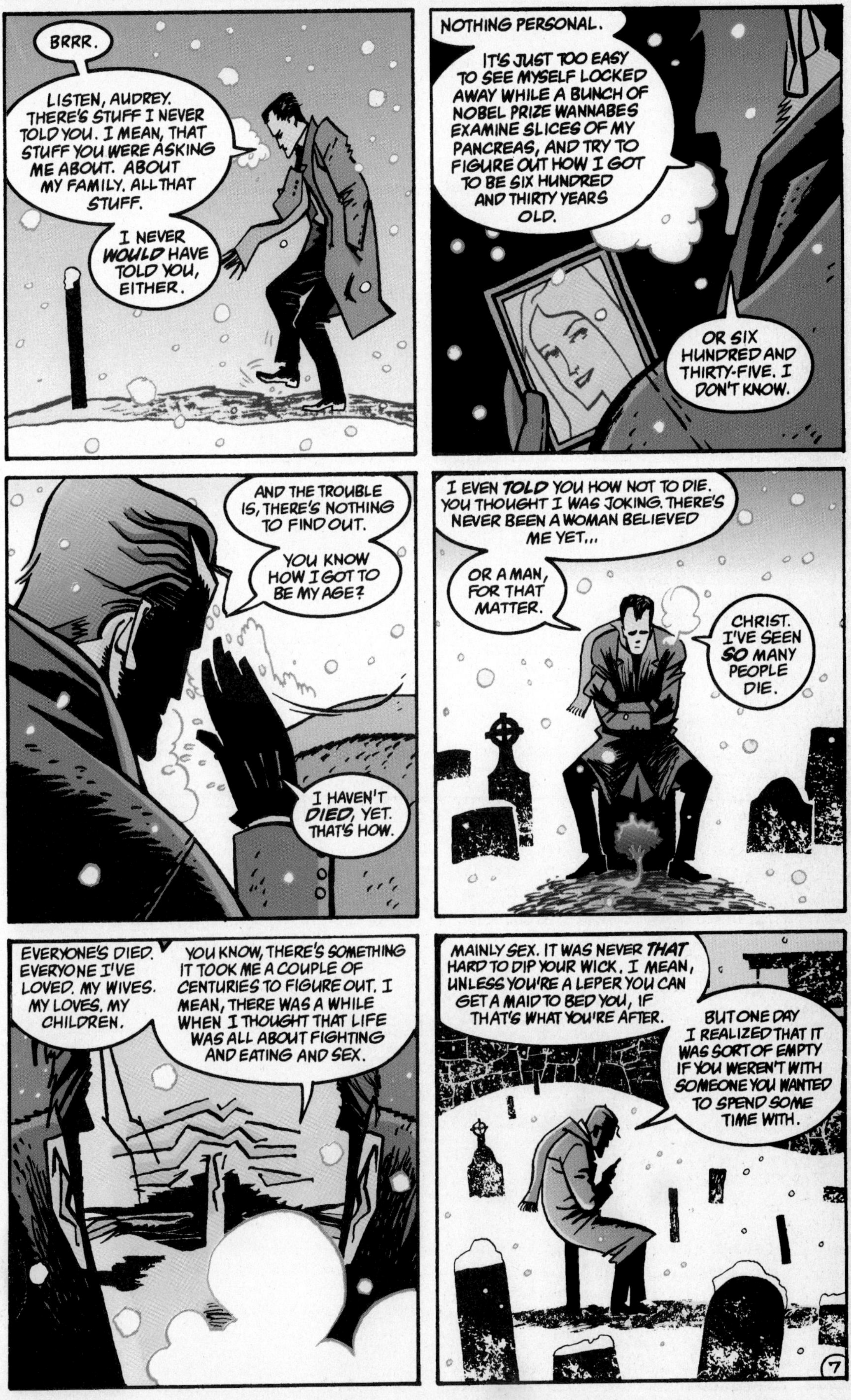
BRRR.
LISTEN, AUDREY. THERE'S STUFF I NEVER TOLD YOU. I MEAN, THAT STUFF YOU WERE ASKING ME ABOUT. ABOUT MY FAMILY. ALL THAT STUFF.
I NEVER WOULD HAVE TOLD YOU, EITHER.
NOTHING PERSONAL.
IT'S JUST TOO EASY TO SEE MYSELF LOCKED AWAY WHILE A BUNCH OF NOBEL PRIZE WANNABES EXAMINE SLICES OF MY PANCREAS, AND TRY TO FIGURE OUT HOW I GOT TO BE SIX HUNDRED AND THIRTY YEARS OLD.
OR SIX HUNDRED AND THIRTY-FIVE. I DON'T KNOW.
AND THE TROUBLE IS, THERE'S NOTHING TO FIND OUT.
YOU KNOW HOW I GOT TO BE MY AGE?
I HAVEN'T DIED, YET. THAT'S HOW.
I EVEN TOLD YOU HOW NOT TO DIE. YOU THOUGHT I WAS JOKING. THERE'S NEVER BEEN A WOMAN BELIEVED ME YET...
OR A MAN, FOR THAT MATTER.
CHRIST. I'VE SEEN SO MANY PEOPLE DIE.
EVERYONE'S DIED. EVERYONE I'VE LOVED. MY WIVES. MY LOVES. MY CHILDREN.
YOU KNOW, THERE'S SOMETHING IT TOOK ME A COUPLE OF CENTURIES TO FIGURE OUT. I MEAN, THERE WAS A WHILE WHEN I THOUGHT THAT LIFE WAS ALL ABOUT FIGHTING AND EATING AND SEX.
MAINLY SEX. IT WAS NEVER THAT HARD TO DIP YOUR WICK. I MEAN, UNLESS YOU'RE A LEPER YOU CAN GET A MAID TO BED YOU, IF THAT'S WHAT YOU'RE AFTER.
BUT ONE DAY I REALIZED THAT IT WAS SORT OF EMPTY IF YOU WEREN'T WITH SOMEONE YOU WANTED TO SPEND SOME TIME WITH.

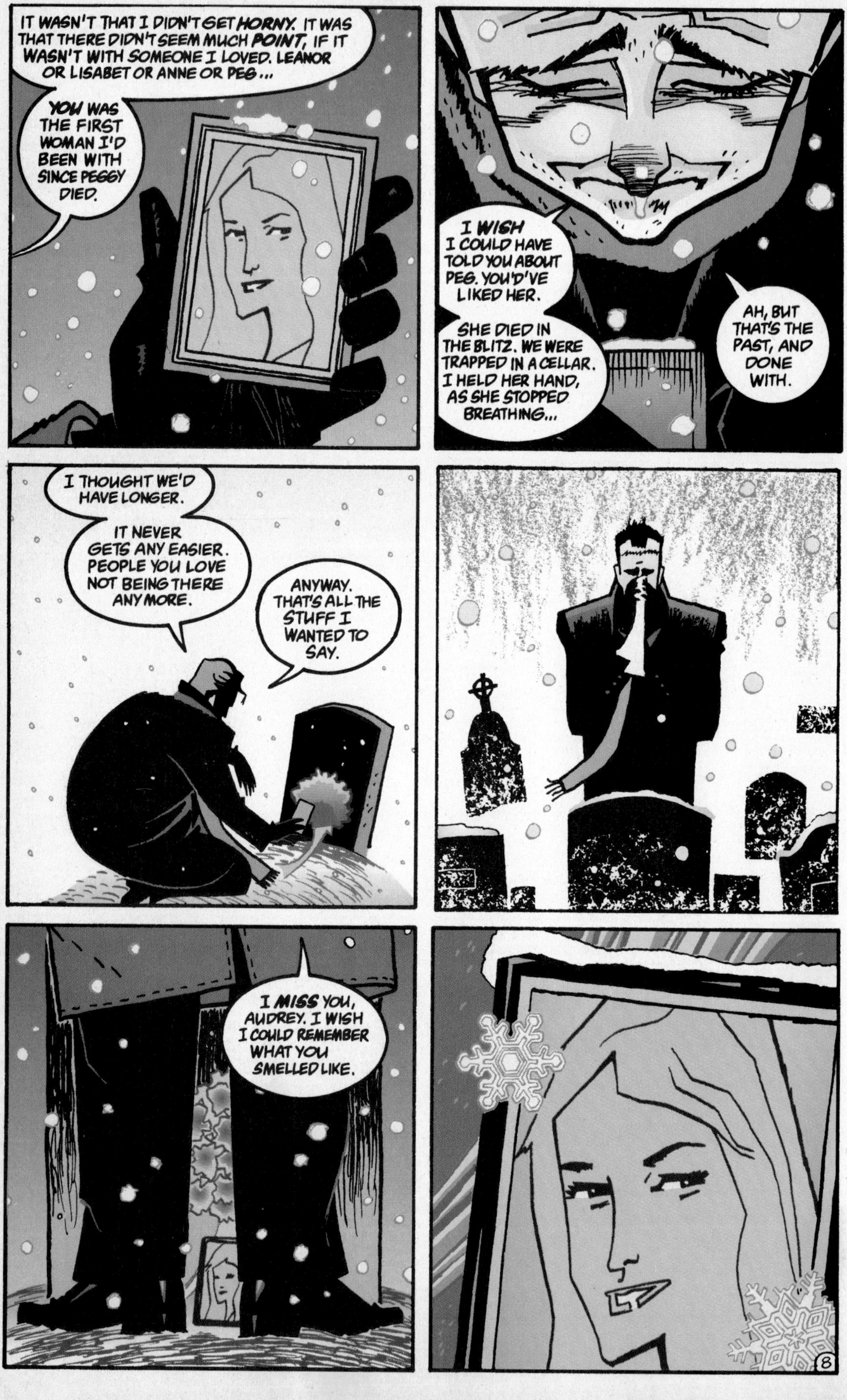
IT WASN'T THAT I DIDN'T GET HORNY. IT WAS THAT THERE DIDN'T SEEM MUCH POINT, IF IT WASN'T WITH SOMEONE I LOVED. LEANOR OR LISABET OR ANNE OR PEG...
YOU WAS THE FIRST WOMAN I'D BEEN WITH SINCE PEGGY DIED.
I WISH I COULD HAVE TOLD YOU ABOUT PEG. YOU'D'VE LIKED HER.
SHE DIED IN THE BLITZ. WE WERE TRAPPED IN A CELLAR. I HELD HER HAND, AS SHE STOPPED BREATHING...
AH, BUT THAT'S THE PAST, AND DONE WITH.
I THOUGHT WE'D HAVE LONGER.
IT NEVER GETS ANY EASIER. PEOPLE YOU LOVE NOT BEING THERE ANY MORE.
ANYWAY. THAT'S ALL THE STUFF I WANTED TO SAY.
I MISS YOU, AUDREY. I WISH I COULD REMEMBER WHAT YOU SMELLED LIKE.
8

9

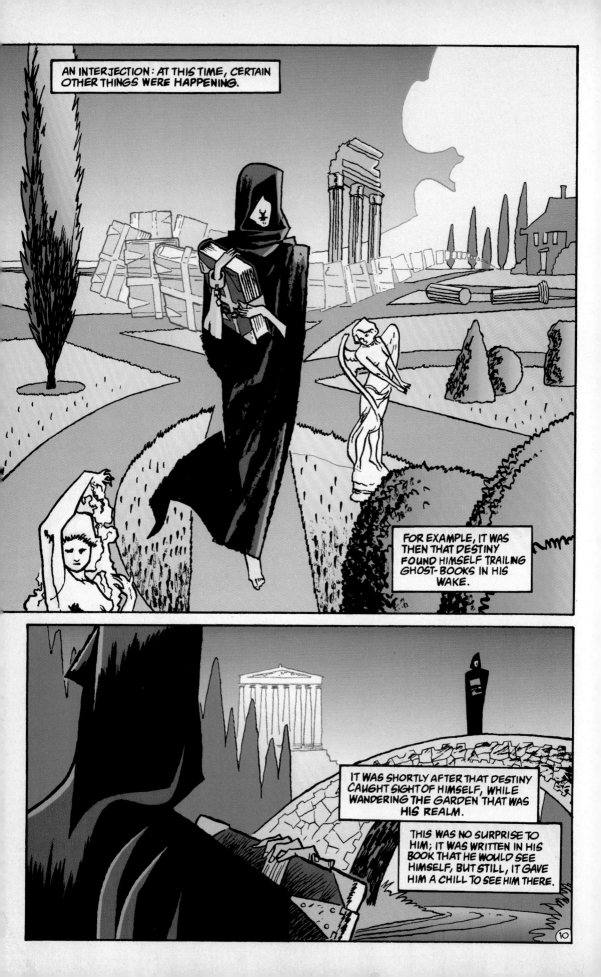

AN INTERJECTION: AT THIS TIME, CERTAIN OTHER THINGS WERE HAPPENING.

FOR EXAMPLE, IT WAS THEN THAT DESTINY FOUND HIMSELF TRAILING GHOST-BOOKS IN HIS WAKE.

IT WAS SHORTLY AFTER THAT DESTINY CAUGHT SIGHT OF HIMSELF, WHILE WANDERING THE GARDEN THAT WAS HIS REALM.

THIS WAS NO SURPRISE TO HIM; IT WAS WRITTEN IN HIS BOOK THAT HE WOULD SEE HIMSELF, BUT STILL, IT GAVE HIM A CHILL TO SEE HIM THERE.

10

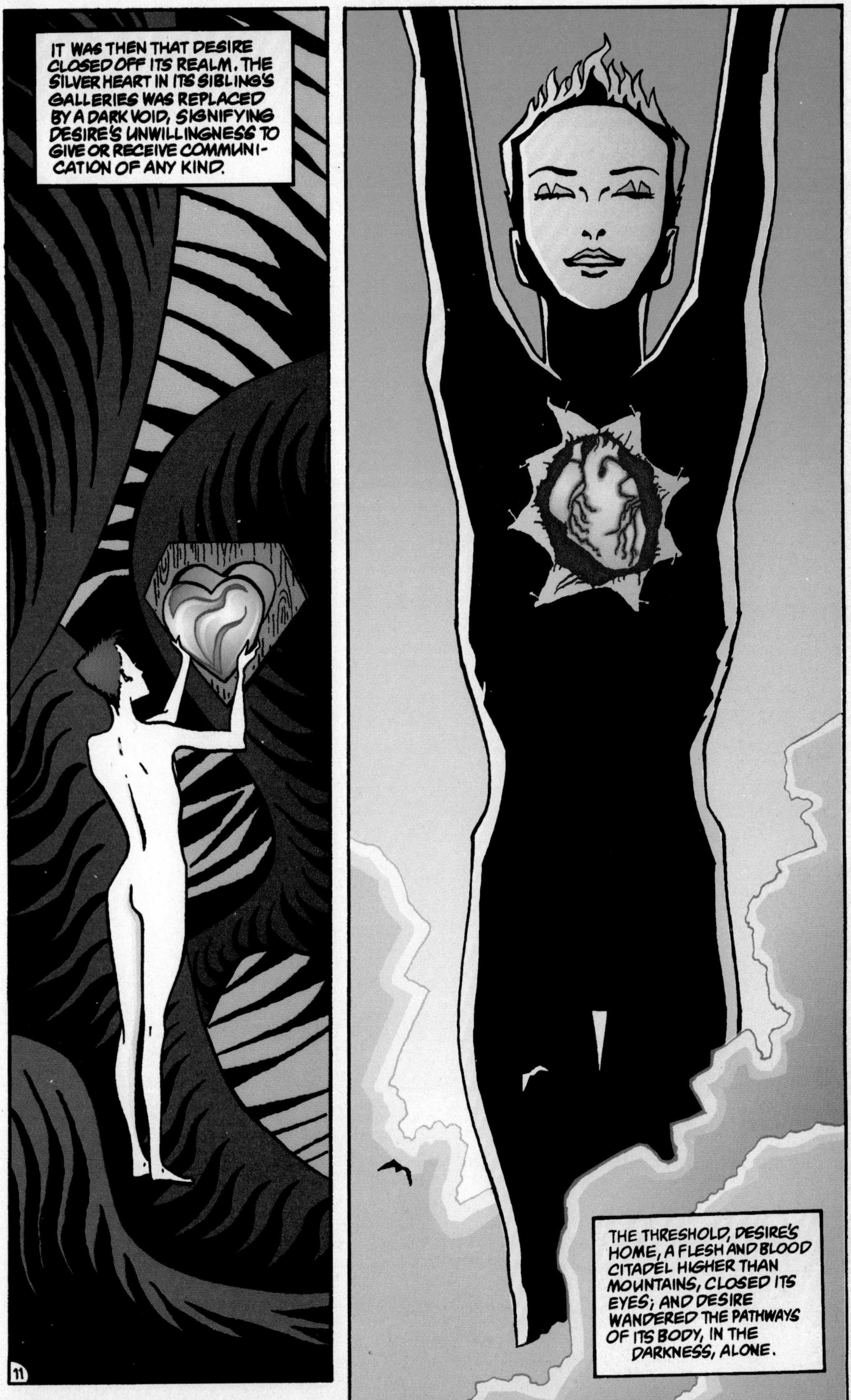
IT WAS THEN THAT DESIRE CLOSED OFF ITS REALM. THE SILVER HEART IN ITS SIBLING'S GALLERIES WAS REPLACED BY A DARK VOID, SIGNIFYING DESIRE'S UNWILLINGNESS TO GIVE OR RECEIVE COMMUNICATION OF ANY KIND.
THE THRESHOLD, DESIRE'S HOME, A FLESH AND BLOOD CITADEL HIGHER THAN MOUNTAINS, CLOSED ITS EYES; AND DESIRE WANDERED THE PATHWAYS OF ITS BODY, IN THE DARKNESS, ALONE.
11

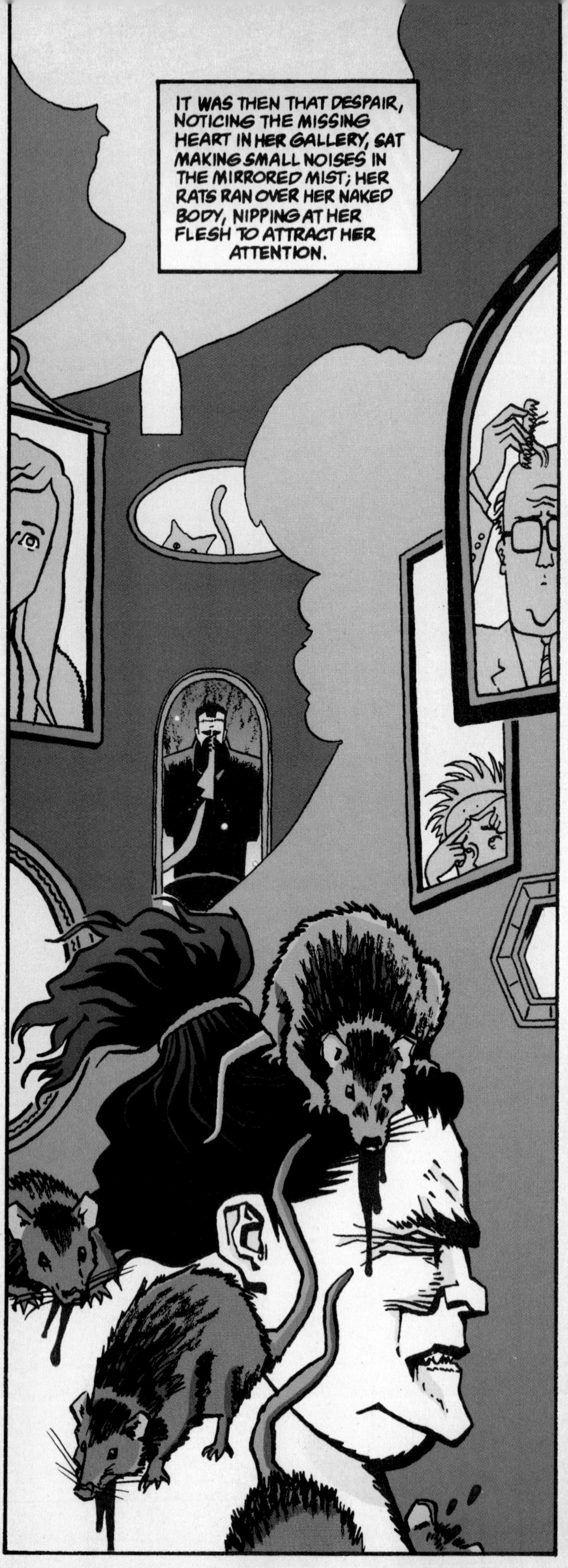
IT WAS THEN THAT DESPAIR, NOTICING THE MISSING HEART IN HER GALLERY, SAT MAKING SMALL NOISES IN THE MIRRORED MIST; HER RATS RAN OVER HER NAKED BODY, NIPPING AT HER FLESH TO ATTRACT HER ATTENTION.

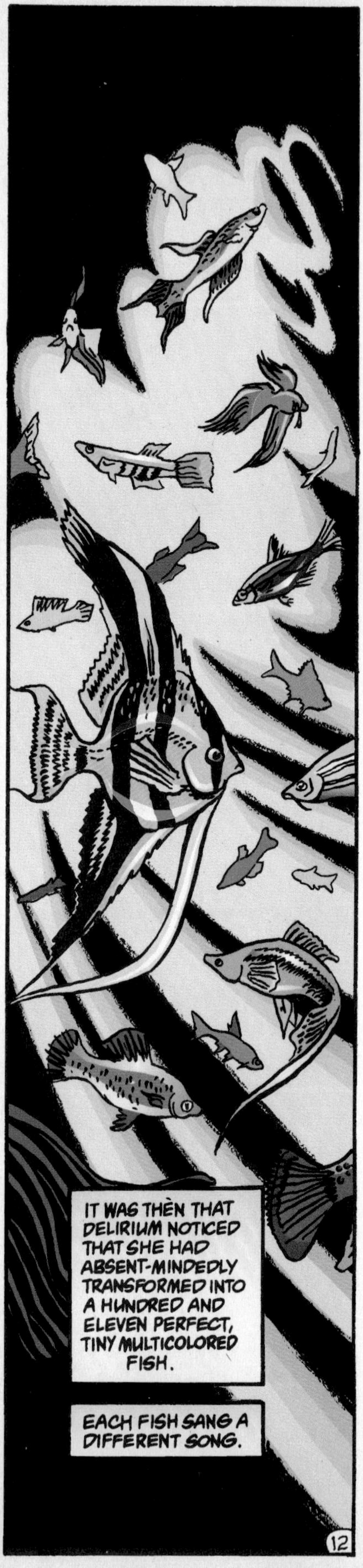
IT WAS THEN THAT DELIRIUM NOTICED THAT SHE HAD ABSENT-MINDEDLY TRANSFORMED INTO A HUNDRED AND ELEVEN PERFECT, TINY MULTICOLORED FISH.
EACH FISH SANG A DIFFERENT SONG.
12

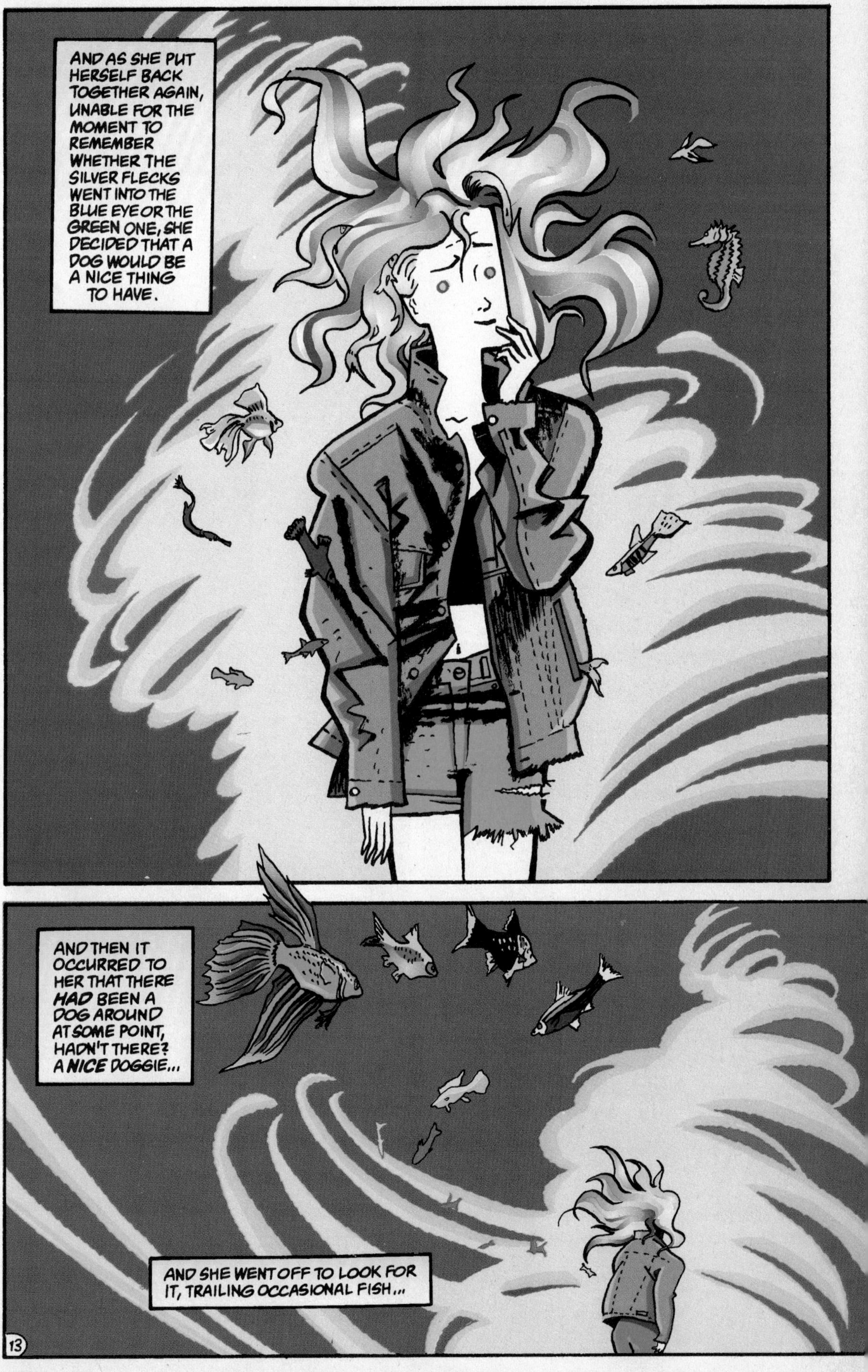
AND AS SHE PUT HERSELF BACK TOGETHER AGAIN, UNABLE FOR THE MOMENT TO REMEMBER WHETHER THE SILVER FLECKS WENT INTO THE BLUE EYE OR THE GREEN ONE, SHE DECIDED THAT A DOG WOULD BE A NICE THING TO HAVE.
AND THEN IT OCCURRED TO HER THAT THERE *HAD* BEEN A DOG AROUND AT SOME POINT, HADN'T THERE? A *NICE* DOGGIE...
AND SHE WENT OFF TO LOOK FOR IT, TRAILING OCCASIONAL FISH...
13

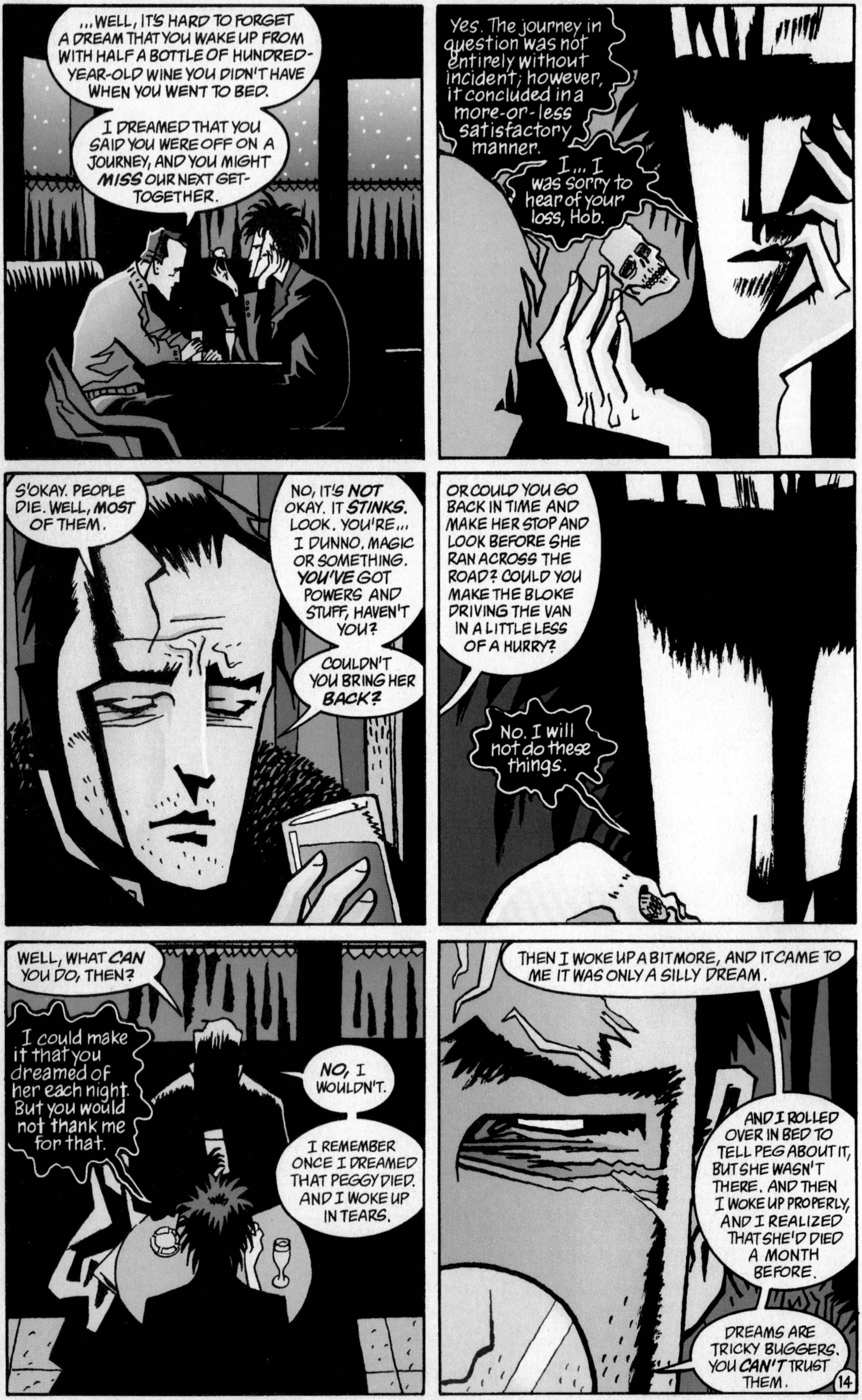
...WELL, IT'S HARD TO FORGET A DREAM THAT YOU WAKE UP FROM WITH HALF A BOTTLE OF HUNDRED-YEAR-OLD WINE YOU DIDN'T HAVE WHEN YOU WENT TO BED.
I DREAMED THAT YOU SAID YOU WERE OFF ON A JOURNEY, AND YOU MIGHT MISS OUR NEXT GET-TOGETHER.
Yes. The journey in question was not entirely without incident; however, it concluded in a more-or-less satisfactory manner.
I... I was sorry to hear of your loss, Hob.
S'OKAY. PEOPLE DIE. WELL, MOST OF THEM.
NO, IT'S NOT OKAY. IT STINKS. LOOK. YOU'RE... I DUNNO. MAGIC OR SOMETHING. YOU'VE GOT POWERS AND STUFF, HAVEN'T YOU?
COULDN'T YOU BRING HER BACK?
OR COULD YOU GO BACK IN TIME AND MAKE HER STOP AND LOOK BEFORE SHE RAN ACROSS THE ROAD? COULD YOU MAKE THE BLOKE DRIVING THE VAN IN A LITTLE LESS OF A HURRY?
No. I will not do these things.
WELL, WHAT CAN YOU DO, THEN?
I could make it that you dreamed of her each night. But you would not thank me for that.
NO, I WOULDN'T.
I REMEMBER ONCE I DREAMED THAT PEGGY DIED. AND I WOKE UP IN TEARS.
THEN I WOKE UP A BIT MORE, AND IT CAME TO ME IT WAS ONLY A SILLY DREAM.
AND I ROLLED OVER IN BED TO TELL PEG ABOUT IT, BUT SHE WASN'T THERE. AND THEN I WOKE UP PROPERLY, AND I REALIZED THAT SHE'D DIED A MONTH BEFORE.
DREAMS ARE TRICKY BUGGERS. YOU CAN'T TRUST THEM.
14

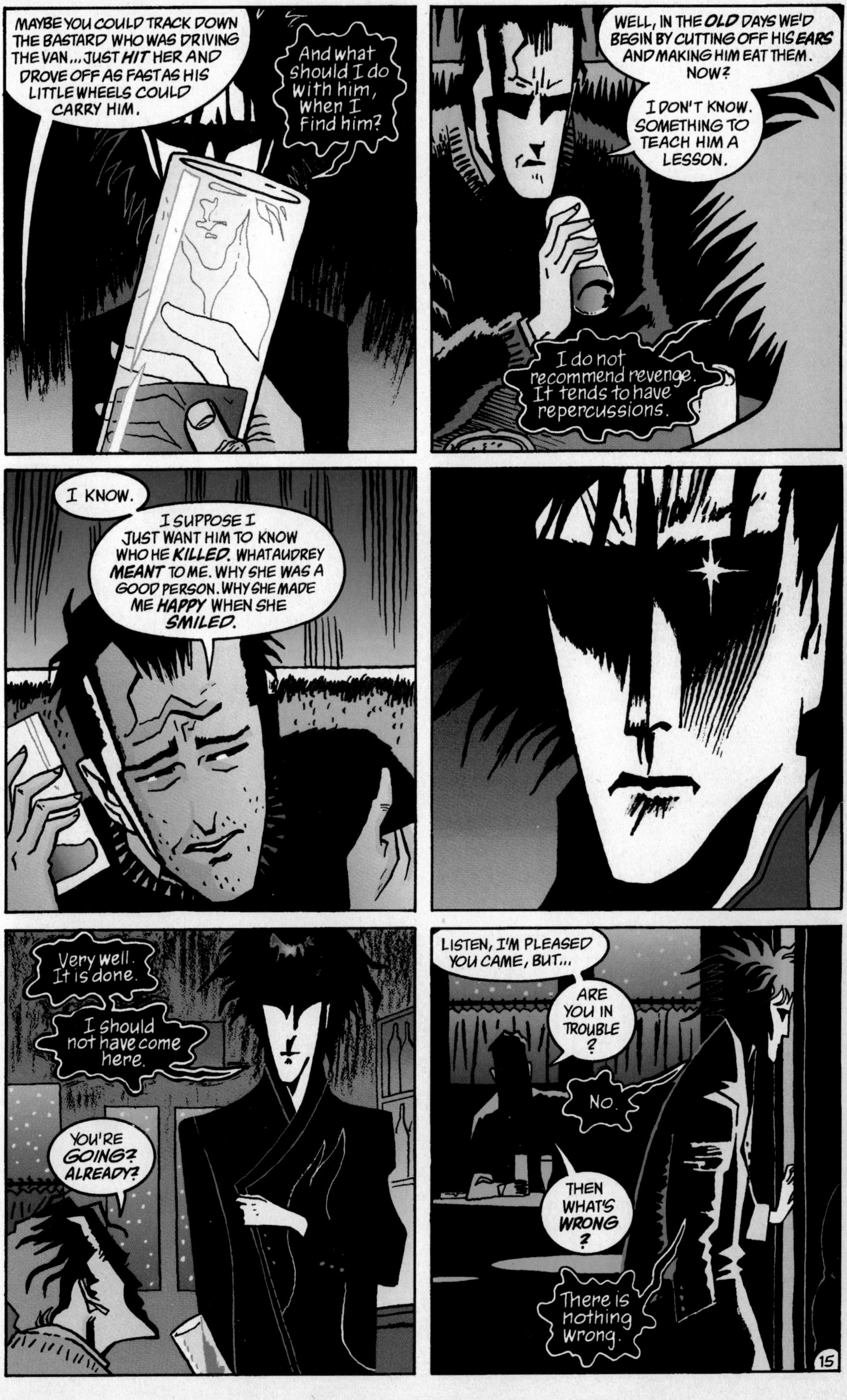

MAYBE YOU COULD TRACK DOWN THE BASTARD WHO WAS DRIVING THE VAN... JUST HIT HER AND DROVE OFF AS FAST AS HIS LITTLE WHEELS COULD CARRY HIM.
And what should I do with him, when I find him?
WELL, IN THE OLD DAYS WE'D BEGIN BY CUTTING OFF HIS EARS AND MAKING HIM EAT THEM. NOW?
I DON'T KNOW. SOMETHING TO TEACH HIM A LESSON.
I do not recommend revenge. It tends to have repercussions.
I KNOW.
I SUPPOSE I JUST WANT HIM TO KNOW WHO HE KILLED. WHAT AUDREY MEANT TO ME. WHY SHE WAS A GOOD PERSON. WHY SHE MADE ME HAPPY WHEN SHE SMILED.
Very well. It is done.
I should not have come here.
YOU'RE GOING? ALREADY?
LISTEN, I'M PLEASED YOU CAME, BUT...
ARE YOU IN TROUBLE?
No.
THEN WHAT'S WRONG?
There is nothing wrong.

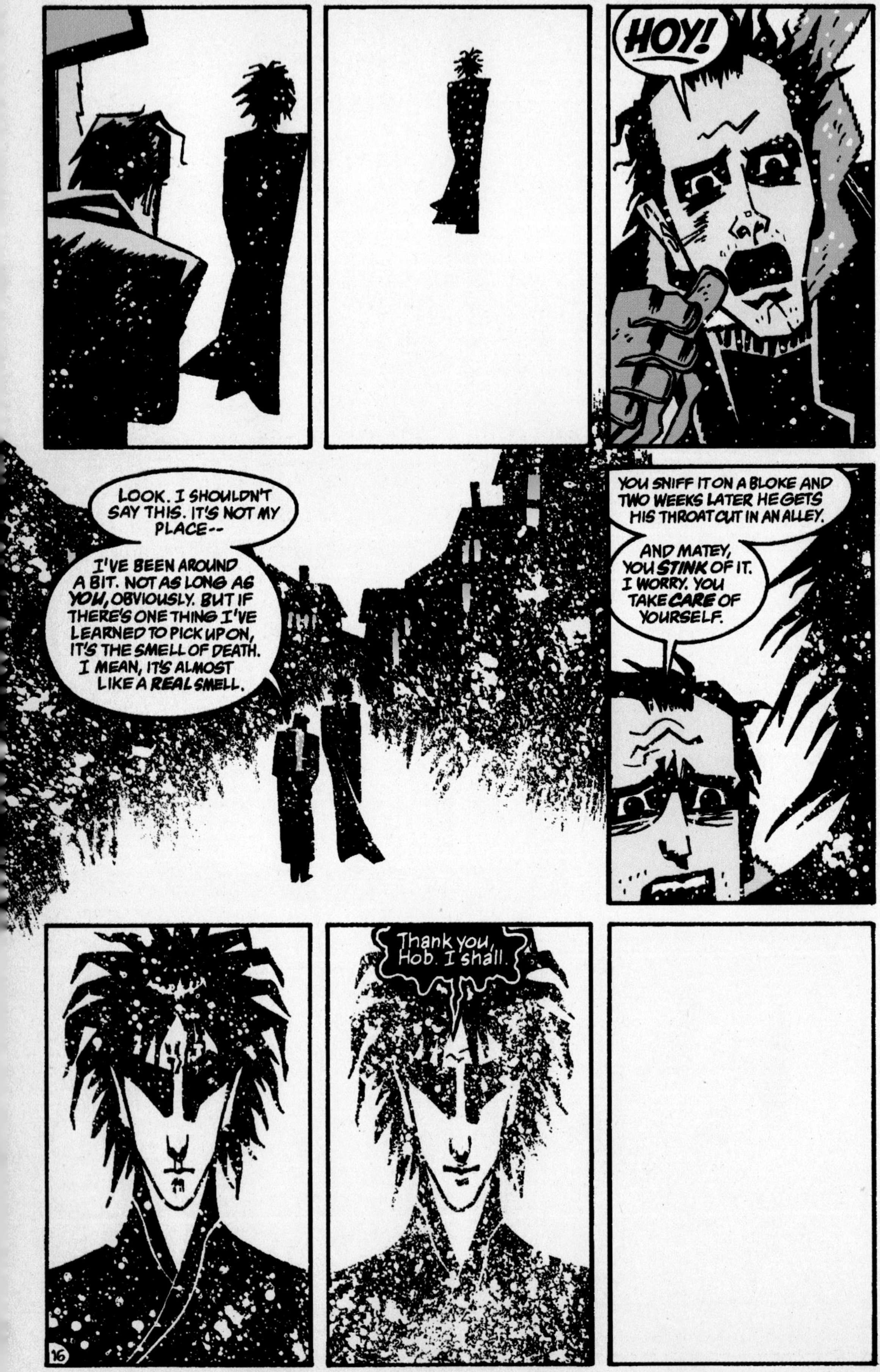
HOY!
LOOK. I SHOULDN'T SAY THIS. IT'S NOT MY PLACE--
I'VE BEEN AROUND A BIT. NOT AS LONG AS YOU, OBVIOUSLY. BUT IF THERE'S ONE THING I'VE LEARNED TO PICK UP ON, IT'S THE SMELL OF DEATH. I MEAN, IT'S ALMOST LIKE A REAL SMELL.
YOU SNIFF IT ON A BLOKE AND TWO WEEKS LATER HE GETS HIS THROAT CUT IN AN ALLEY.
AND MATEY, YOU STINK OF IT. I WORRY. YOU TAKE CARE OF YOURSELF.
Thank you, Hob. I shall.

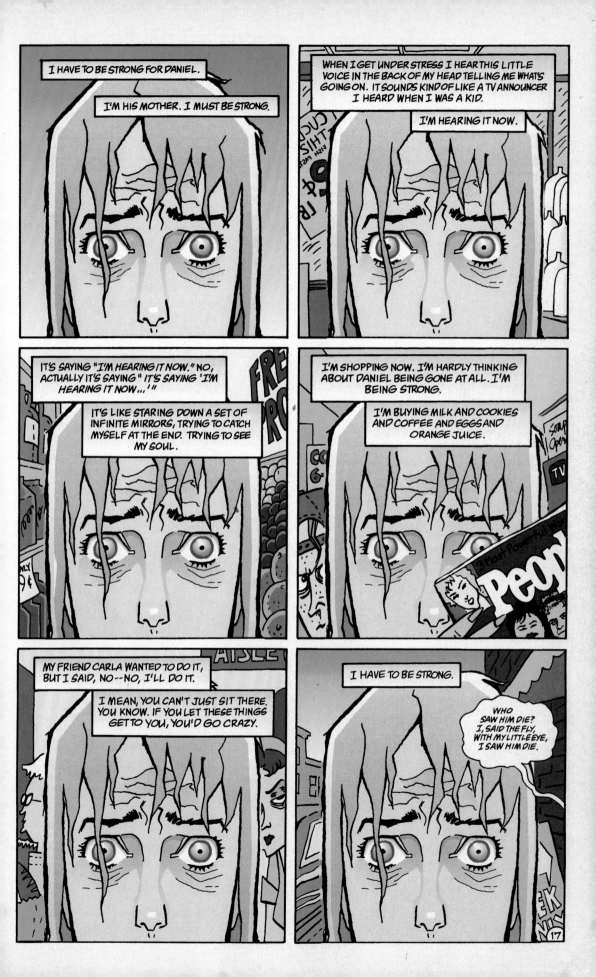

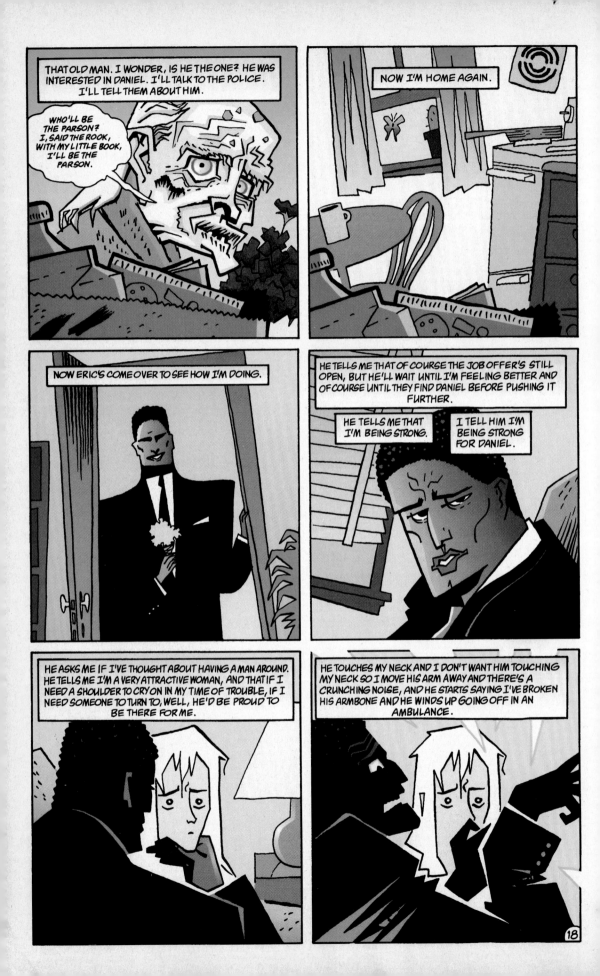

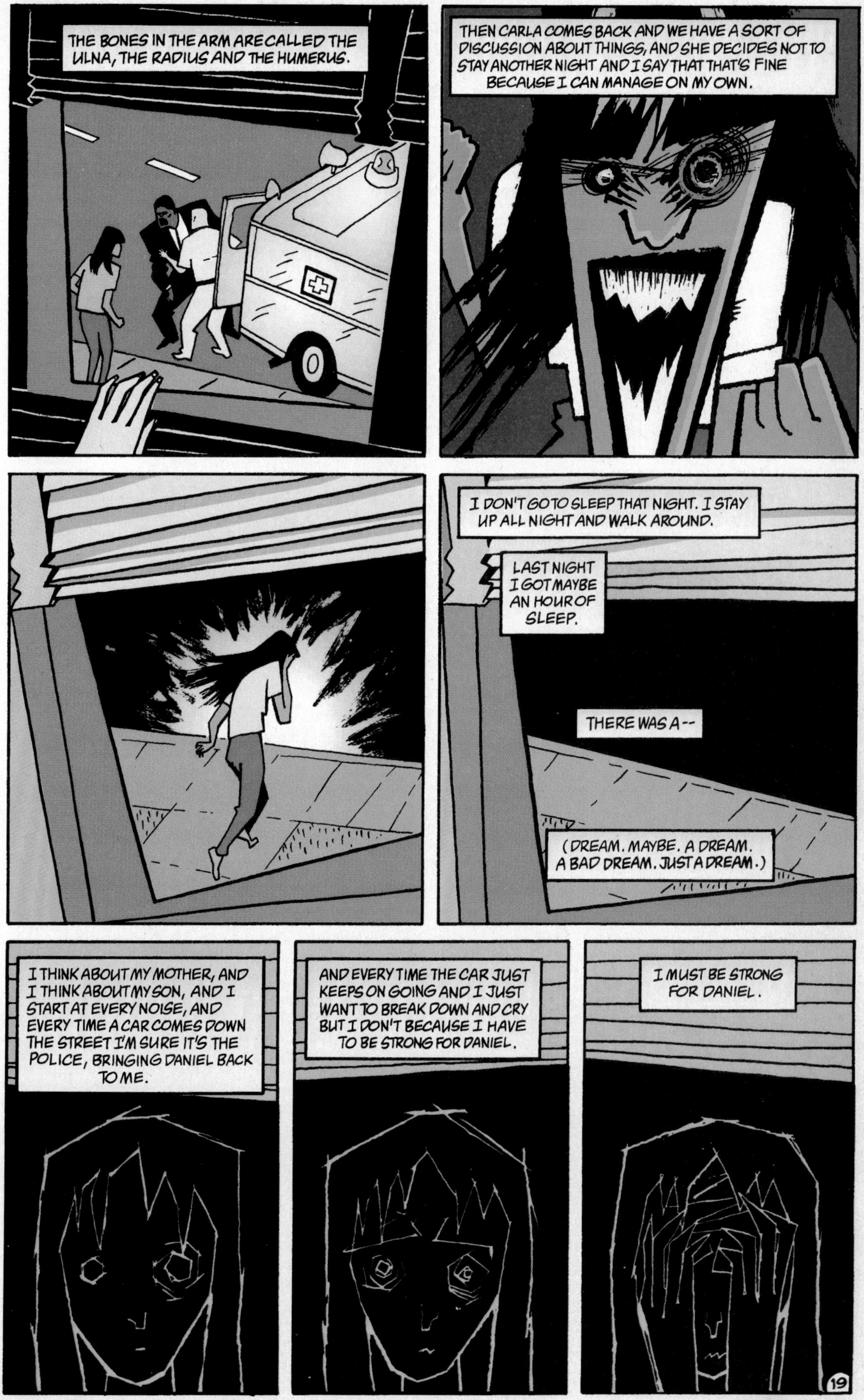
THE BONES IN THE ARM ARE CALLED THE ULNA, THE RADIUS AND THE HUMERUS.
THEN CARLA COMES BACK AND WE HAVE A SORT OF DISCUSSION ABOUT THINGS, AND SHE DECIDES NOT TO STAY ANOTHER NIGHT AND I SAY THAT THAT'S FINE BECAUSE I CAN MANAGE ON MY OWN.
I DON'T GO TO SLEEP THAT NIGHT. I STAY UP ALL NIGHT AND WALK AROUND.
LAST NIGHT I GOT MAYBE AN HOUR OF SLEEP.
THERE WAS A--
(DREAM. MAYBE. A DREAM. A BAD DREAM. JUST A DREAM.)
I THINK ABOUT MY MOTHER, AND I THINK ABOUT MY SON, AND I START AT EVERY NOISE, AND EVERY TIME A CAR COMES DOWN THE STREET I'M SURE IT'S THE POLICE, BRINGING DANIEL BACK TO ME.
AND EVERY TIME THE CAR JUST KEEPS ON GOING AND I JUST WANT TO BREAK DOWN AND CRY BUT I DON'T BECAUSE I HAVE TO BE STRONG FOR DANIEL.
I MUST BE STRONG FOR DANIEL.

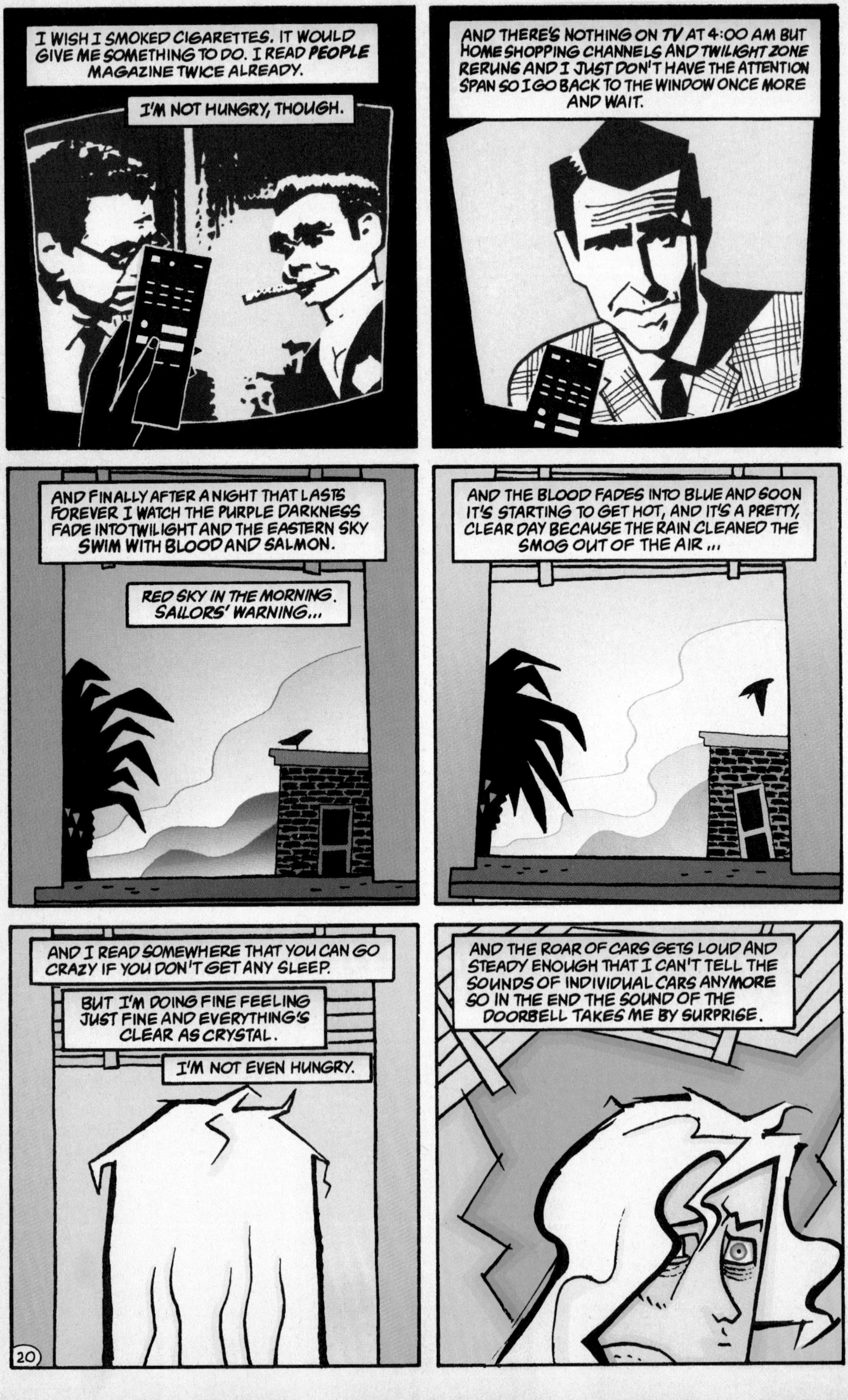

I WISH I SMOKED CIGARETTES. IT WOULD GIVE ME SOMETHING TO DO. I READ PEOPLE MAGAZINE TWICE ALREADY.
I'M NOT HUNGRY, THOUGH.
AND THERE'S NOTHING ON TV AT 4:00 AM BUT HOME SHOPPING CHANNELS AND TWILIGHT ZONE RERUNS AND I JUST DON'T HAVE THE ATTENTION SPAN SO I GO BACK TO THE WINDOW ONCE MORE AND WAIT.
AND FINALLY AFTER A NIGHT THAT LASTS FOREVER I WATCH THE PURPLE DARKNESS FADE INTO TWILIGHT AND THE EASTERN SKY SWIM WITH BLOOD AND SALMON.
RED SKY IN THE MORNING. SAILORS' WARNING...
AND THE BLOOD FADES INTO BLUE AND SOON IT'S STARTING TO GET HOT, AND IT'S A PRETTY, CLEAR DAY BECAUSE THE RAIN CLEANED THE SMOG OUT OF THE AIR ...
AND I READ SOMEWHERE THAT YOU CAN GO CRAZY IF YOU DON'T GET ANY SLEEP.
BUT I'M DOING FINE FEELING JUST FINE AND EVERYTHING'S CLEAR AS CRYSTAL.
I'M NOT EVEN HUNGRY.
AND THE ROAR OF CARS GETS LOUD AND STEADY ENOUGH THAT I CAN'T TELL THE SOUNDS OF INDIVIDUAL CARS ANYMORE SO IN THE END THE SOUND OF THE DOORBELL TAKES ME BY SURPRISE.

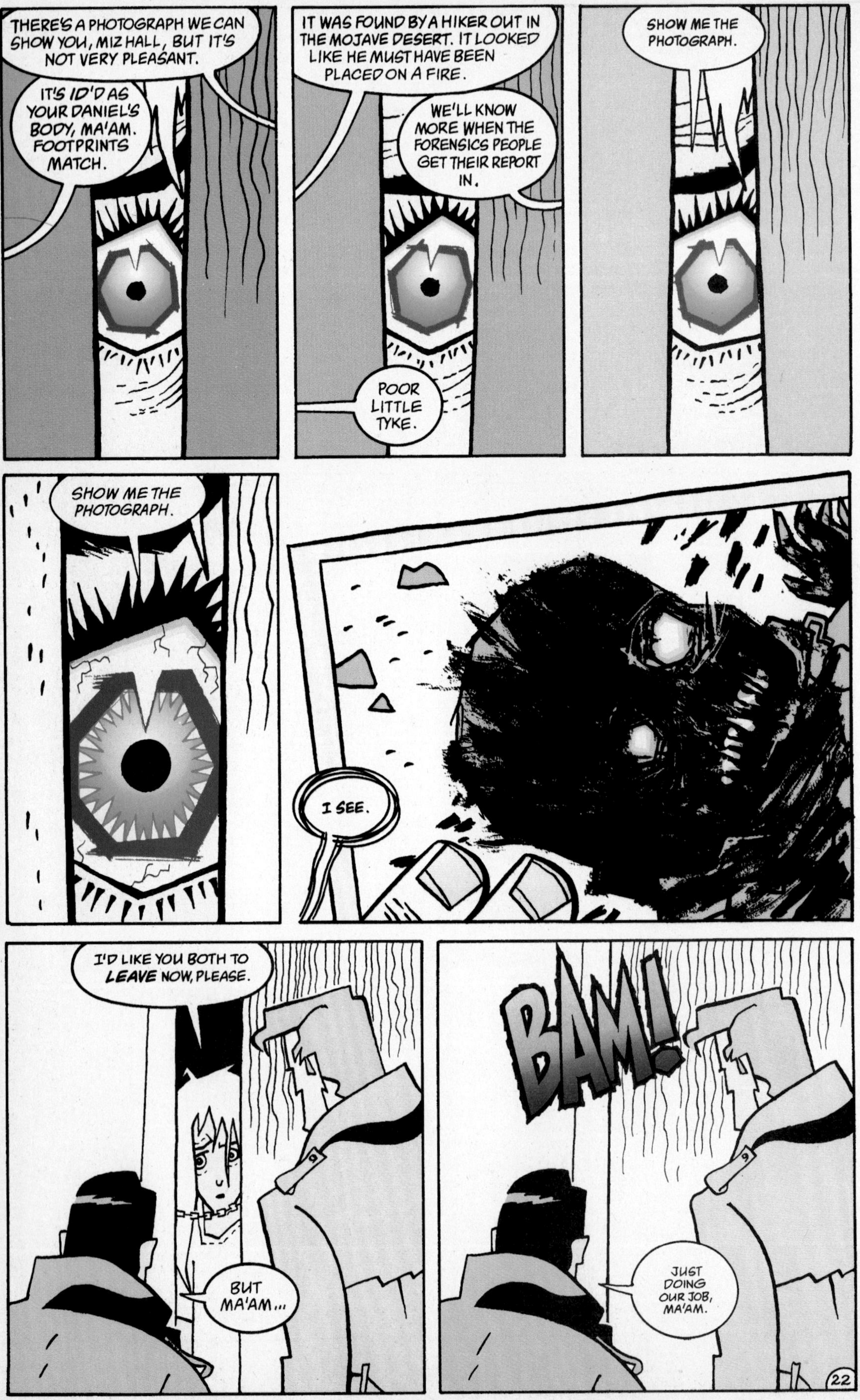
THERE'S A PHOTOGRAPH WE CAN SHOW YOU, MIZ HALL, BUT IT'S NOT VERY PLEASANT.
IT'S ID'D AS YOUR DANIEL'S BODY, MA'AM. FOOTPRINTS MATCH.
IT WAS FOUND BY A HIKER OUT IN THE MOJAVE DESERT. IT LOOKED LIKE HE MUST HAVE BEEN PLACED ON A FIRE.
WE'LL KNOW MORE WHEN THE FORENSICS PEOPLE GET THEIR REPORT IN.
POOR LITTLE TYKE.
SHOW ME THE PHOTOGRAPH.
SHOW ME THE PHOTOGRAPH.
I SEE.
I'D LIKE YOU BOTH TO LEAVE NOW, PLEASE.
BUT MA'AM...
BAM!
JUST DOING OUR JOB, MA'AM.

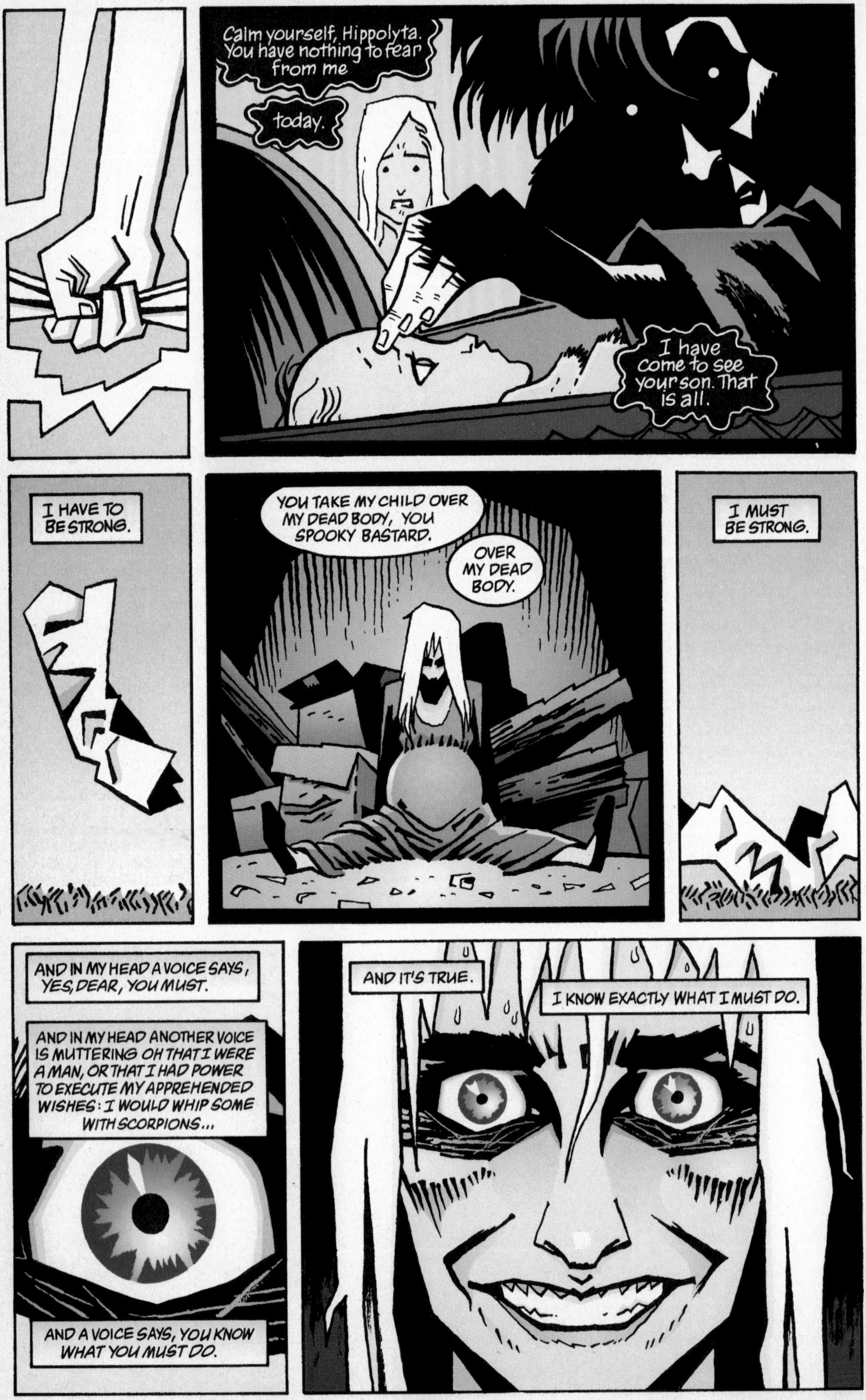
Calm yourself, Hippolyta. You have nothing to fear from me
today.
I have come to see your son. That is all.
I HAVE TO BE STRONG.
YOU TAKE MY CHILD OVER MY DEAD BODY, YOU SPOOKY BASTARD.
OVER MY DEAD BODY.
I MUST BE STRONG.
AND IN MY HEAD A VOICE SAYS, YES, DEAR, YOU MUST.
AND IN MY HEAD ANOTHER VOICE IS MUTTERING OH THAT I WERE A MAN, OR THAT I HAD POWER TO EXECUTE MY APPREHENDED WISHES: I WOULD WHIP SOME WITH SCORPIONS...
AND A VOICE SAYS, YOU KNOW WHAT YOU MUST DO.
AND IT'S TRUE.
I KNOW EXACTLY WHAT I MUST DO.

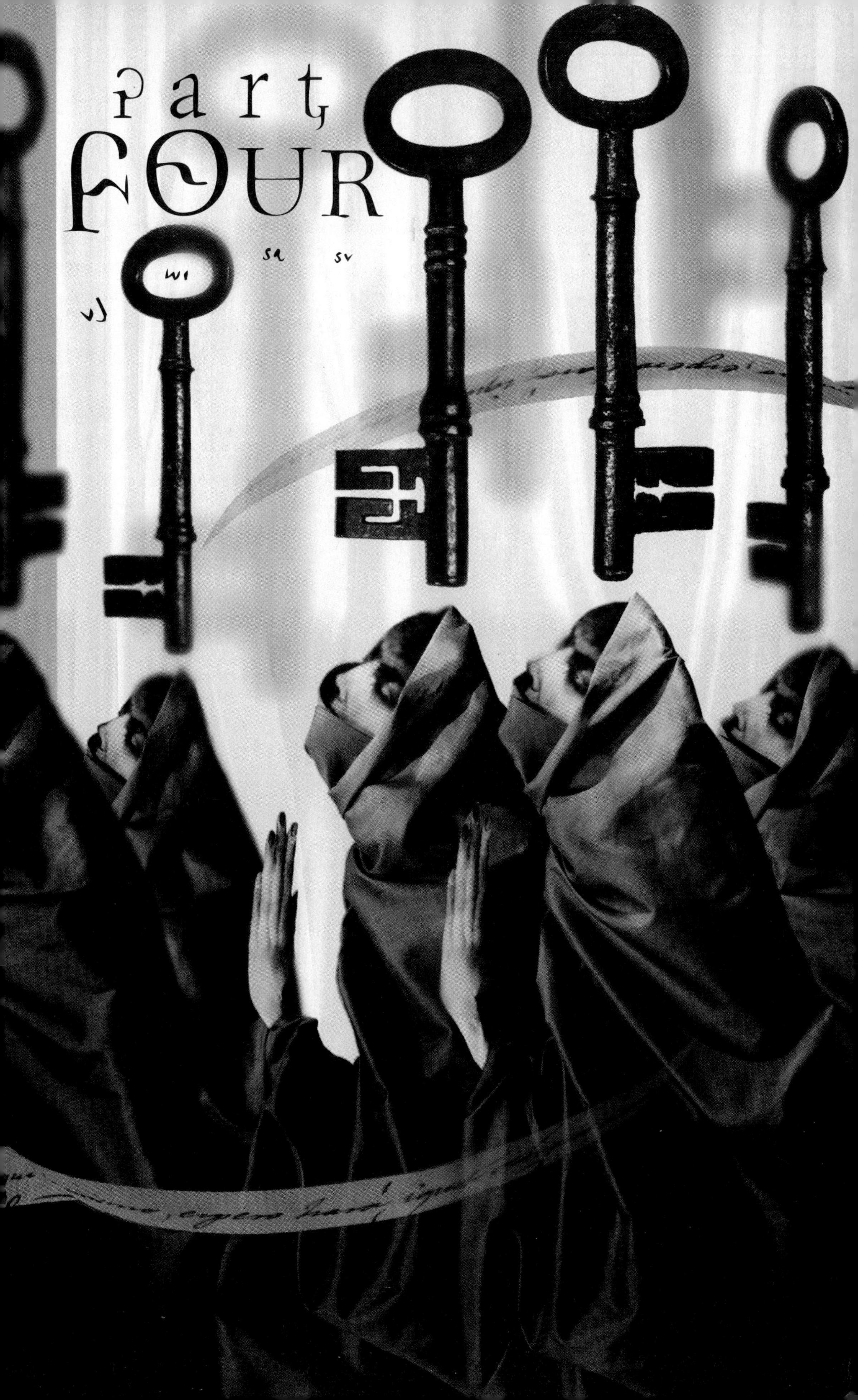
part
FOUR

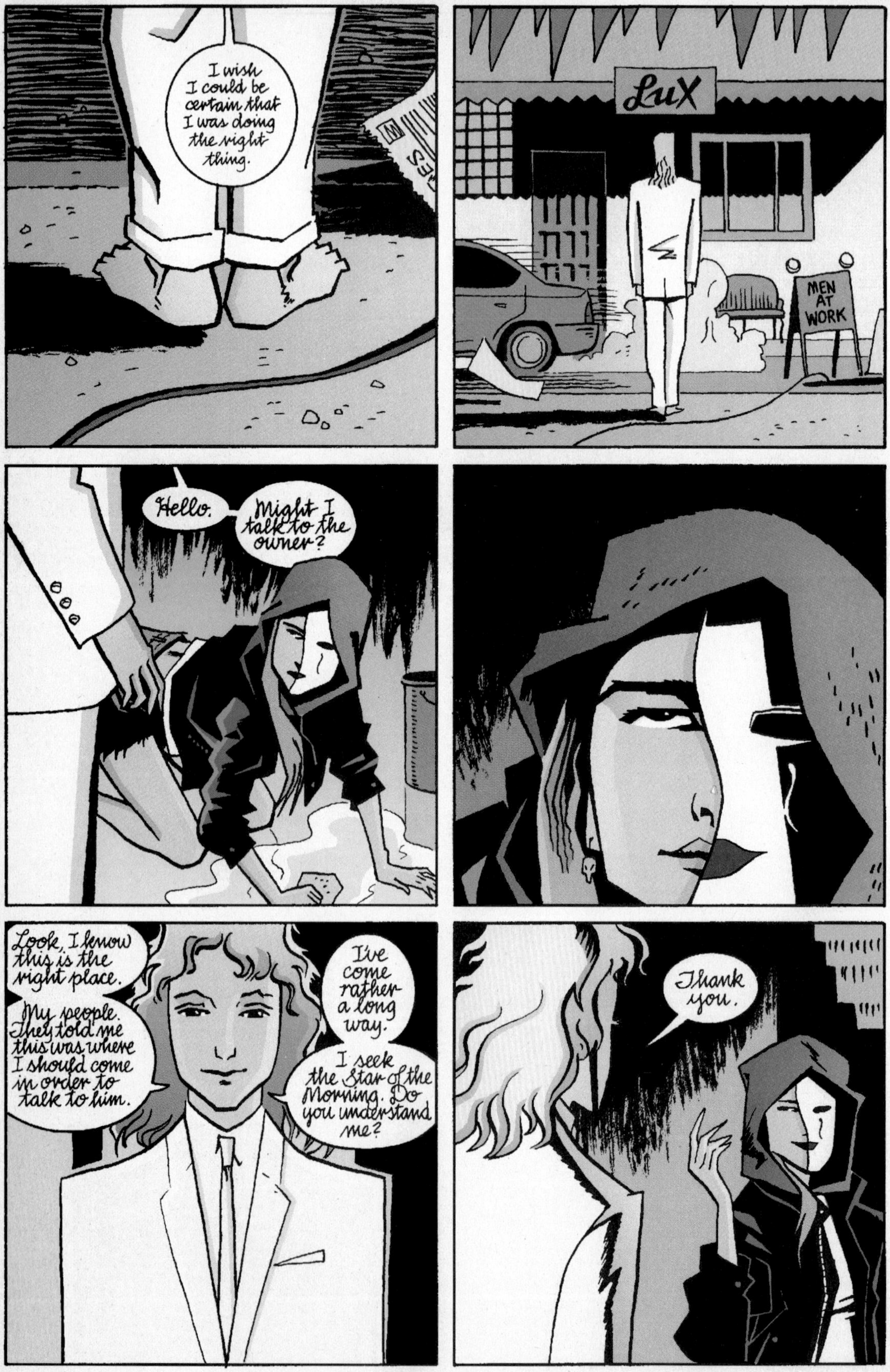
I wish I could be certain that I was doing the right thing.
Lux
MEN AT WORK
Hello.
Might I talk to the owner?
Look, I know this is the right place.
My people. They told me this was where I should come in order to talk to him.
I've come rather a long way.
I seek the Star of the Morning. Do you understand me?
Thank you.

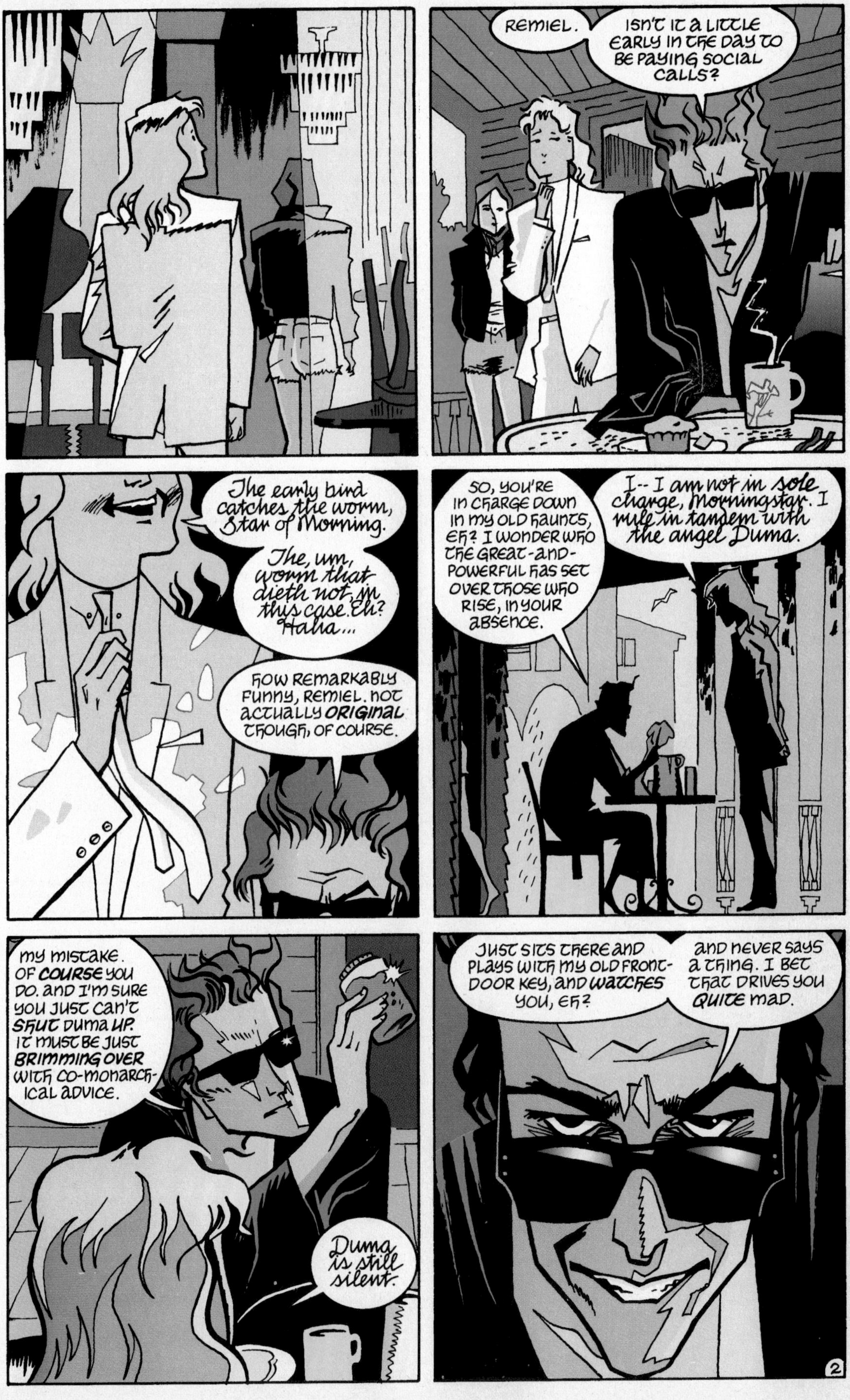
REMIEL.
ISN'T IT A LITTLE EARLY IN THE DAY TO BE PAYING SOCIAL CALLS?
The early bird catches the worm, Star of Morning.
The, um, worm that dieth not, in this case. Eh? Haha...
HOW REMARKABLY FUNNY, REMIEL. NOT ACTUALLY ORIGINAL THOUGH, OF COURSE.
SO, YOU'RE IN CHARGE DOWN IN MY OLD HAUNTS, EH? I WONDER WHO THE GREAT-AND-POWERFUL HAS SET OVER THOSE WHO RISE, IN YOUR ABSENCE.
I-- I am not in sole charge, Morningstar. I rule in tandem with the angel Duma.
MY MISTAKE. OF COURSE YOU DO. AND I'M SURE YOU JUST CAN'T SHUT DUMA UP. IT MUST BE JUST BRIMMING OVER WITH CO-MONARCHICAL ADVICE.
Duma is still silent.
JUST SITS THERE AND PLAYS WITH MY OLD FRONT-DOOR KEY, AND WATCHES YOU, EH?
AND NEVER SAYS A THING. I BET THAT DRIVES YOU QUITE MAD.
2

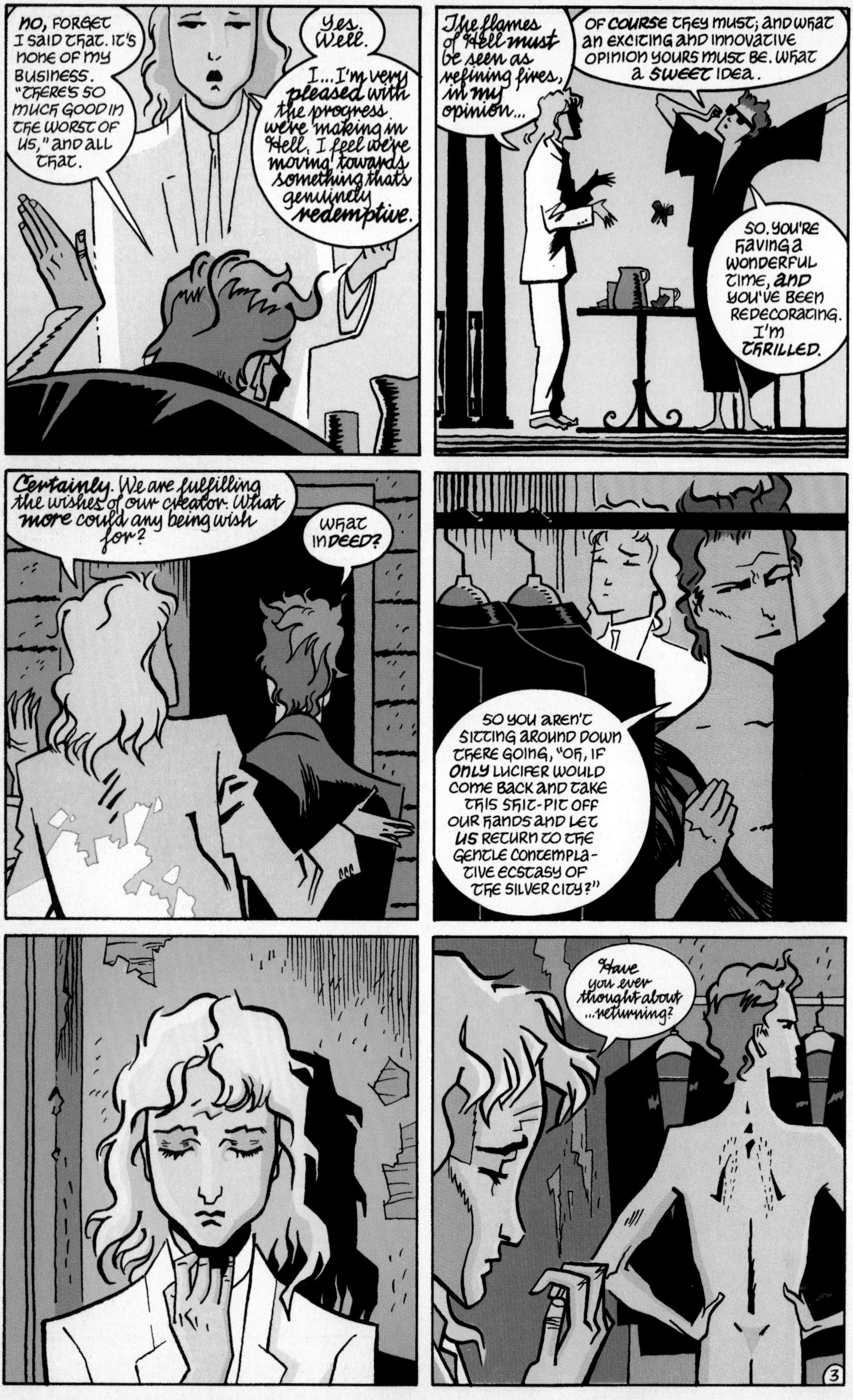
NO, FORGET I SAID THAT. IT'S NONE OF MY BUSINESS. "THERE'S SO MUCH GOOD IN THE WORST OF US," AND ALL THAT.
Yes. Well.
I... I'm very pleased with the progress we're making in Hell. I feel we're moving towards something that's genuinely redemptive.
The flames of Hell must be seen as refining fires, in my opinion...
OF COURSE THEY MUST; AND WHAT AN EXCITING AND INNOVATIVE OPINION YOURS MUST BE. WHAT A SWEET IDEA.
SO. YOU'RE HAVING A WONDERFUL TIME, AND YOU'VE BEEN REDECORATING. I'M THRILLED.
Certainly. We are fulfilling the wishes of our creator. What more could any being wish for?
WHAT INDEED?
SO YOU AREN'T SITTING AROUND DOWN THERE GOING, "OH, IF ONLY LUCIFER WOULD COME BACK AND TAKE THIS SHIT-PIT OFF OUR HANDS AND LET US RETURN TO THE GENTLE CONTEMPLATIVE ECSTASY OF THE SILVER CITY?"
Have you ever thought about ...returning?

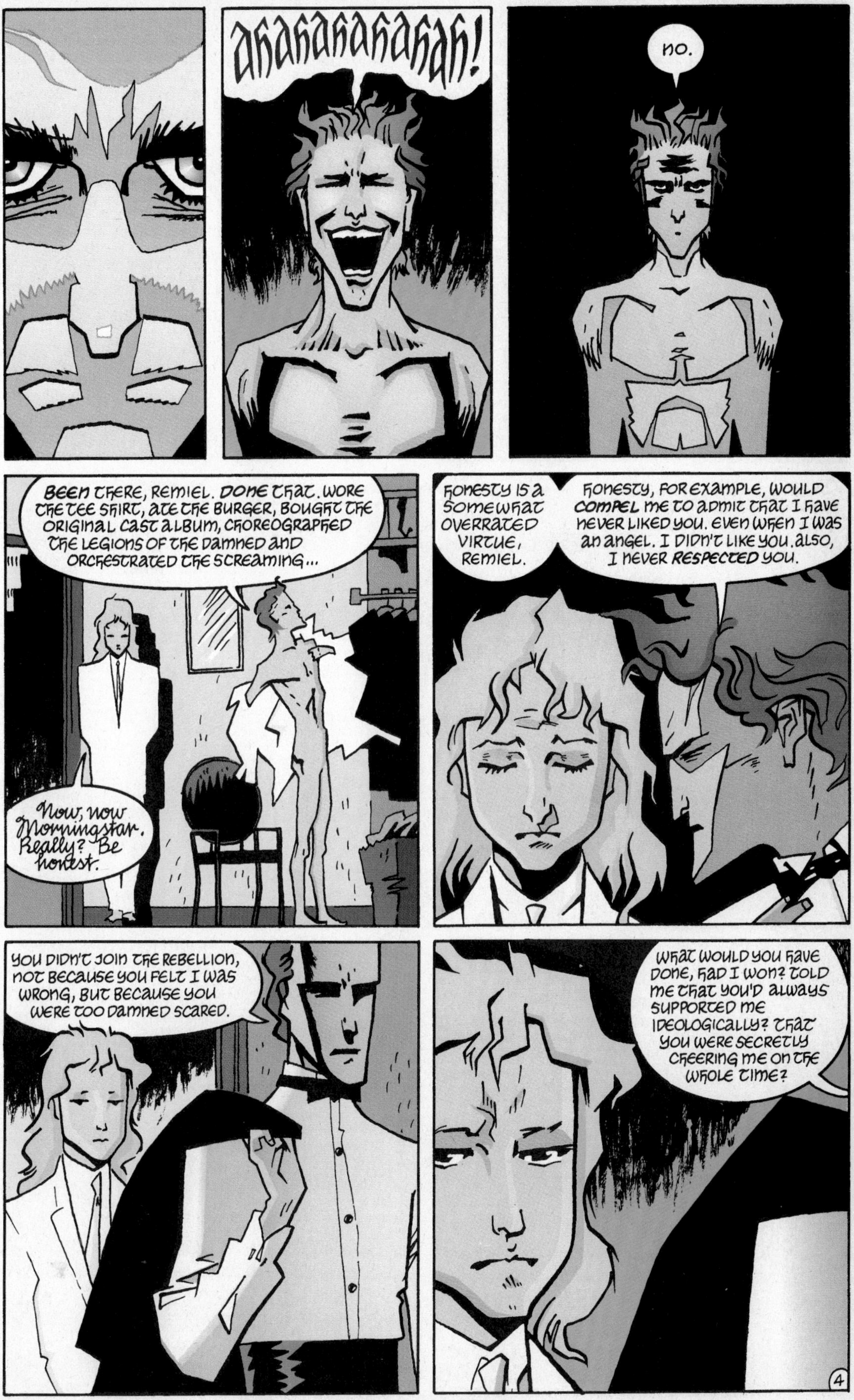
AHAHAHAHAHAH!
NO.
BEEN THERE, REMIEL. DONE THAT. WORE THE TEE SHIRT, ATE THE BURGER, BOUGHT THE ORIGINAL CAST ALBUM, CHOREOGRAPHED THE LEGIONS OF THE DAMNED AND ORCHESTRATED THE SCREAMING...
Now, now Morningstar. Really? Be honest.
HONESTY IS A SOMEWHAT OVERRATED VIRTUE, REMIEL.
HONESTY, FOR EXAMPLE, WOULD COMPEL ME TO ADMIT THAT I HAVE NEVER LIKED YOU. EVEN WHEN I WAS AN ANGEL. I DIDN'T LIKE YOU. ALSO, I NEVER RESPECTED YOU.
YOU DIDN'T JOIN THE REBELLION, NOT BECAUSE YOU FELT I WAS WRONG, BUT BECAUSE YOU WERE TOO DAMNED SCARED.
WHAT WOULD YOU HAVE DONE, HAD I WON? TOLD ME THAT YOU'D ALWAYS SUPPORTED ME IDEOLOGICALLY? THAT YOU WERE SECRETLY CHEERING ME ON THE WHOLE TIME?
4

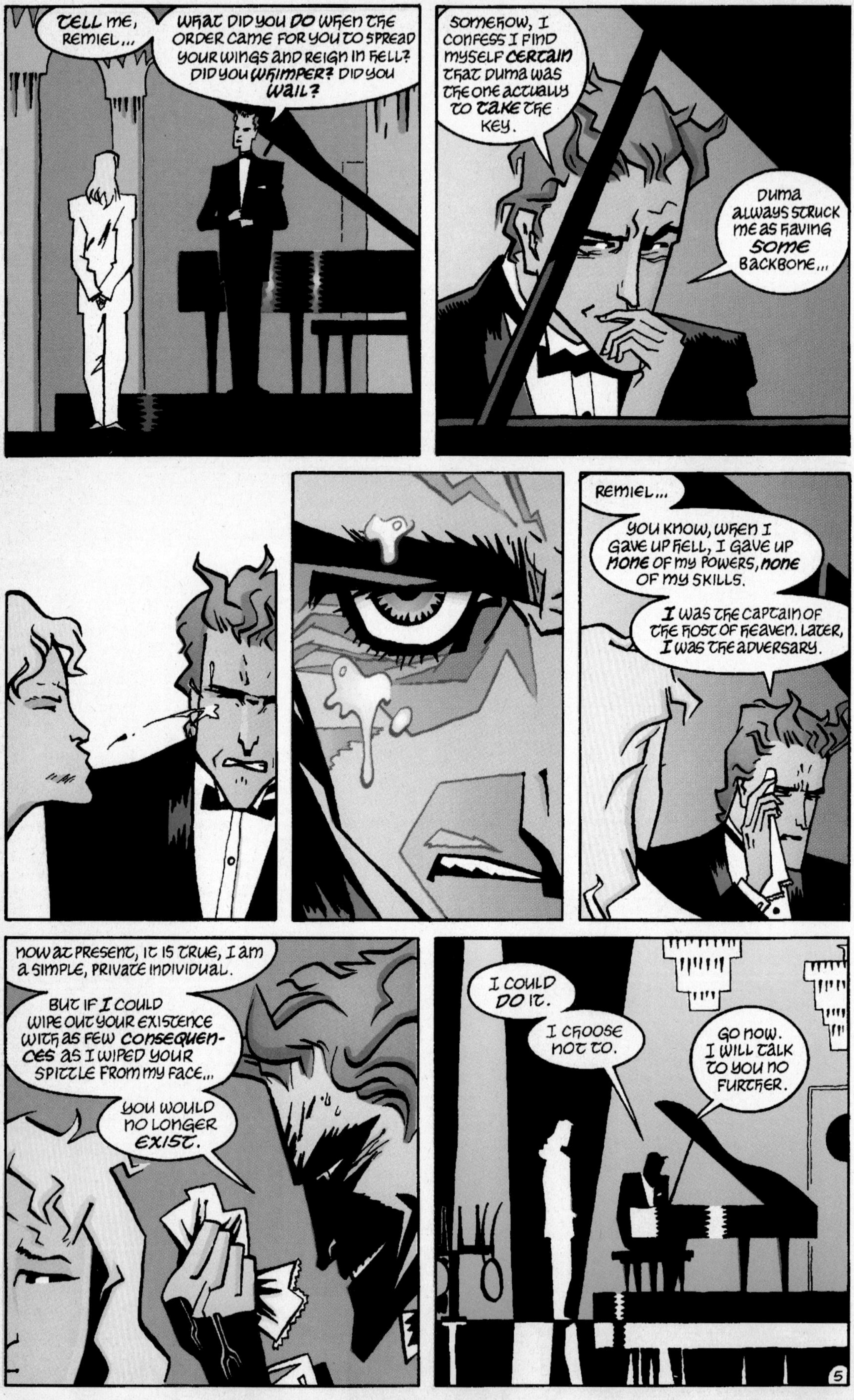
TELL ME, REMIEL...
WHAT DID YOU DO WHEN THE ORDER CAME FOR YOU TO SPREAD YOUR WINGS AND REIGN IN HELL? DID YOU WHIMPER? DID YOU WAIL?
SOMEHOW, I CONFESS I FIND MYSELF CERTAIN THAT DUMA WAS THE ONE ACTUALLY TO TAKE THE KEY.
DUMA ALWAYS STRUCK ME AS HAVING SOME BACKBONE...
REMIEL...
YOU KNOW, WHEN I GAVE UP HELL, I GAVE UP NONE OF MY POWERS, NONE OF MY SKILLS.
I WAS THE CAPTAIN OF THE HOST OF HEAVEN. LATER, I WAS THE ADVERSARY.
NOW AT PRESENT, IT IS TRUE, I AM A SIMPLE, PRIVATE INDIVIDUAL.
BUT IF I COULD WIPE OUT YOUR EXISTENCE WITH AS FEW CONSEQUENCES AS I WIPED YOUR SPITTLE FROM MY FACE...
YOU WOULD NO LONGER EXIST.
I COULD DO IT.
I CHOOSE NOT TO.
GO NOW. I WILL TALK TO YOU NO FURTHER.

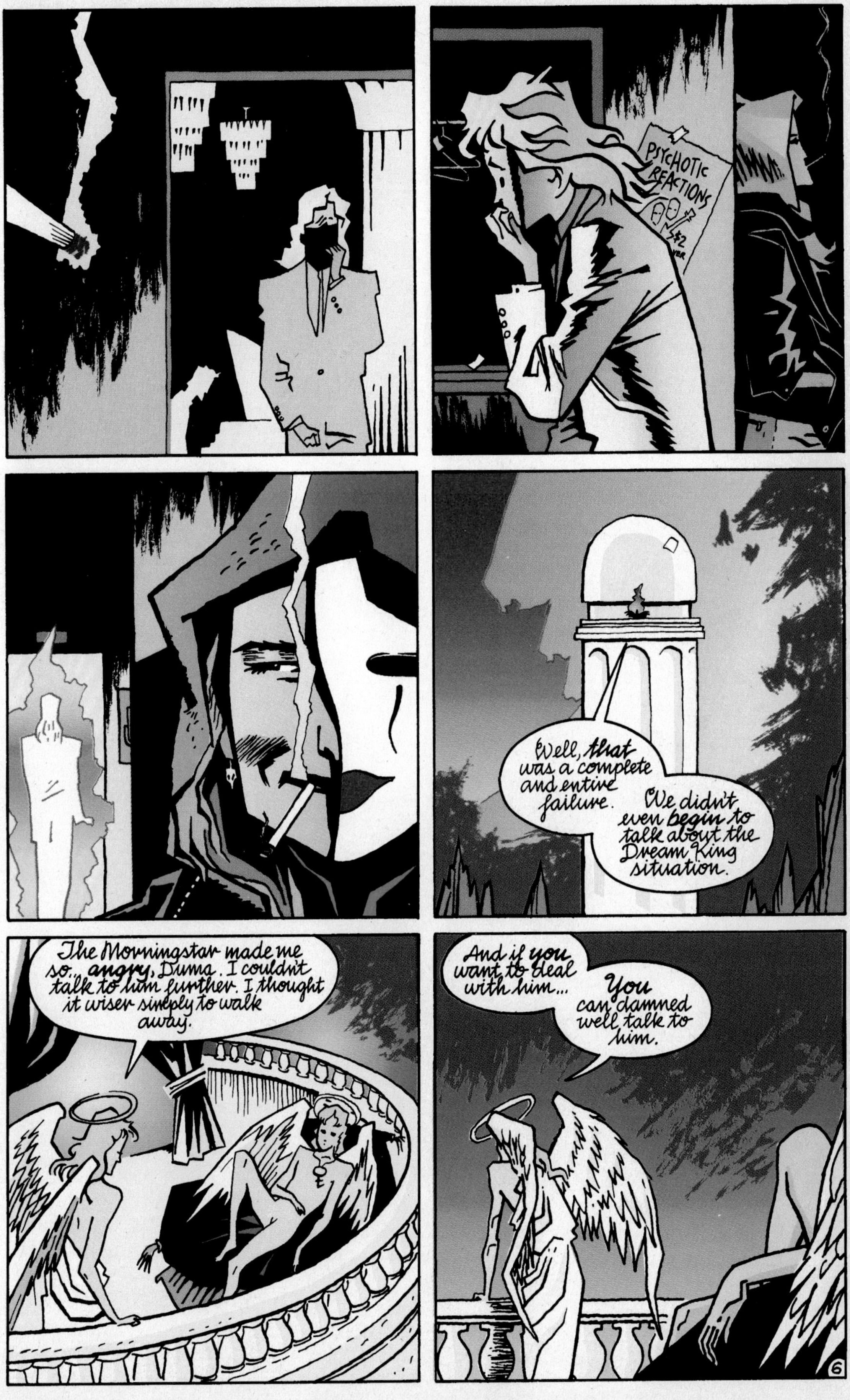

PSYCHOTIC REACTIONS
Well, that was a complete and entire failure.
We didn't even begin to talk about the Dream King situation.
The Morningstar made me so... angry, Duma. I couldn't talk to him further. I thought it wiser simply to walk away.
And if you want to deal with him...
You can damned well talk to him.
6

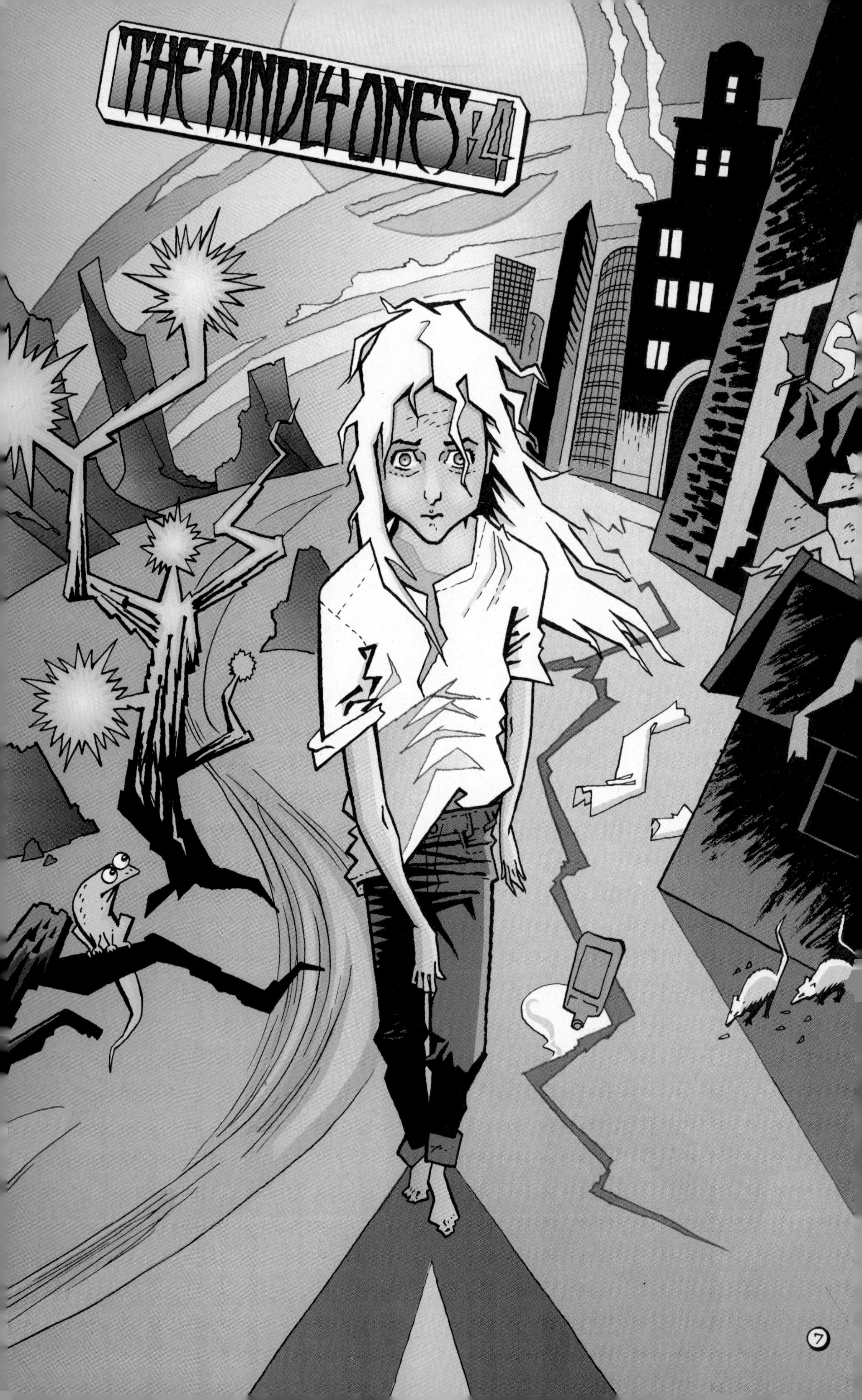
THE KINDLY ONES: 4

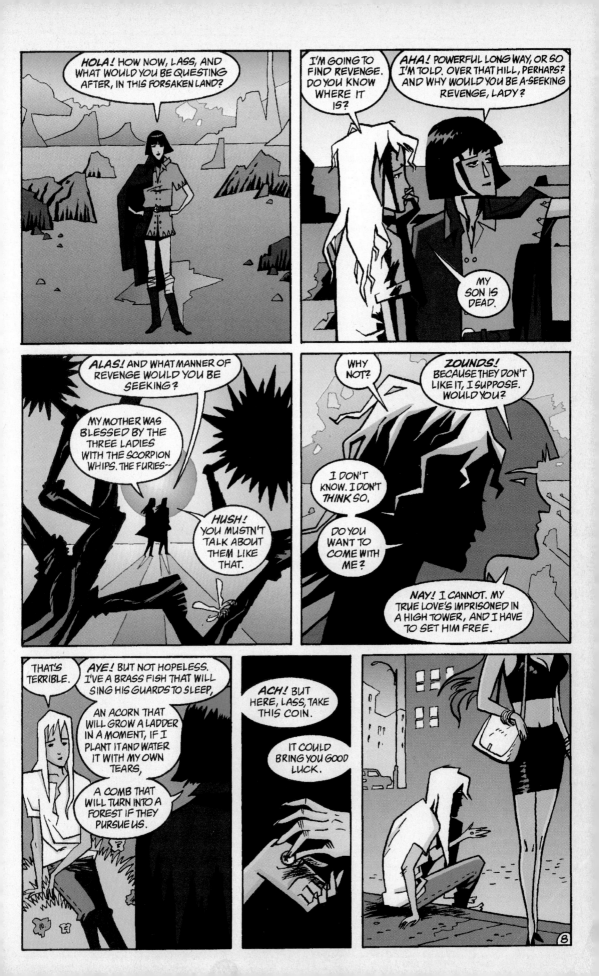

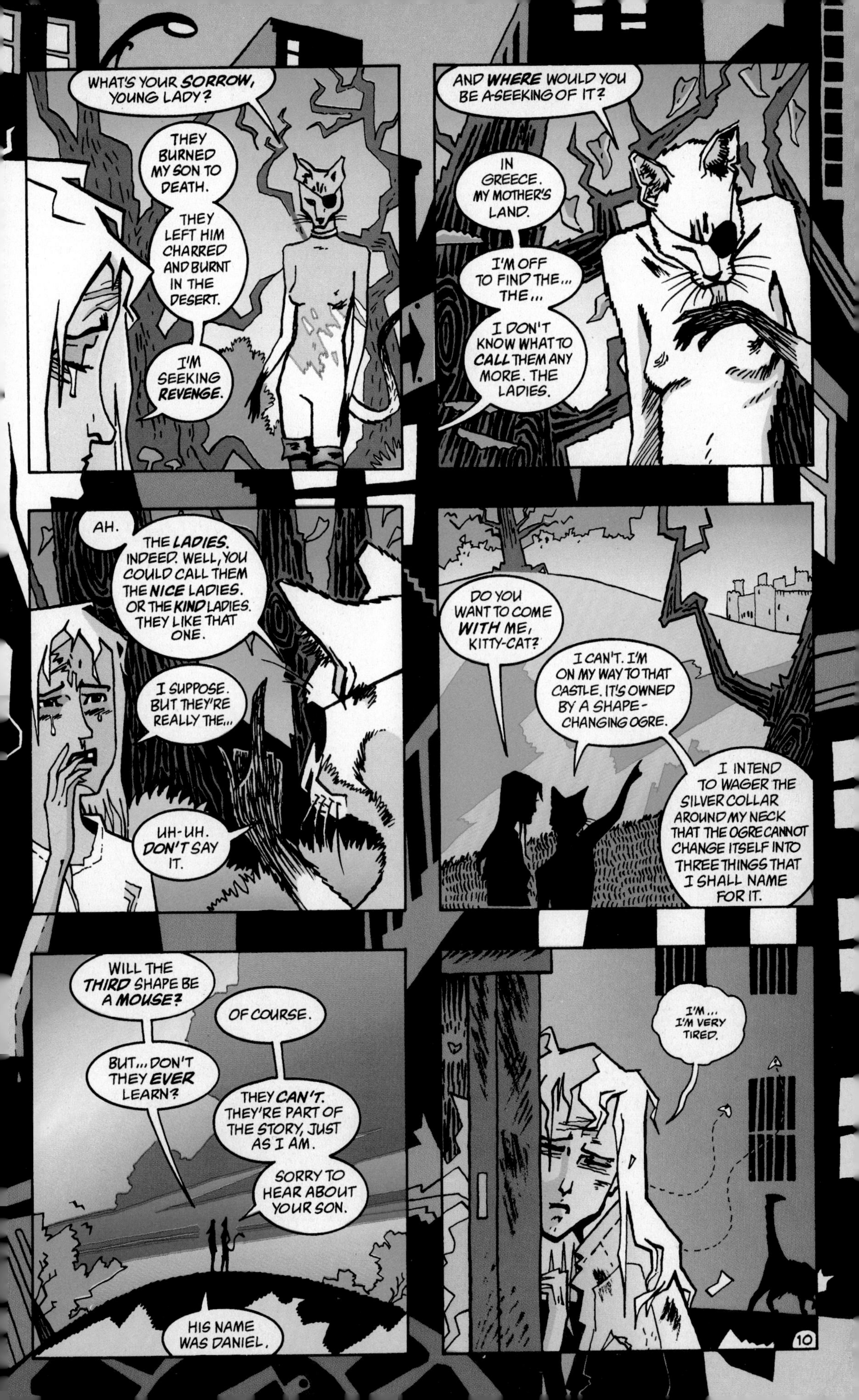
WHAT'S YOUR SORROW, YOUNG LADY?
THEY BURNED MY SON TO DEATH.
THEY LEFT HIM CHARRED AND BURNT IN THE DESERT.
I'M SEEKING REVENGE.
AND WHERE WOULD YOU BE A-SEEKING OF IT?
IN GREECE. MY MOTHER'S LAND.
I'M OFF TO FIND THE... THE...
I DON'T KNOW WHAT TO CALL THEM ANY MORE. THE LADIES.
AH.
THE LADIES. INDEED. WELL, YOU COULD CALL THEM THE NICE LADIES. OR THE KIND LADIES. THEY LIKE THAT ONE.
I SUPPOSE. BUT THEY'RE REALLY THE...
UH-UH. DON'T SAY IT.
DO YOU WANT TO COME WITH ME, KITTY-CAT?
I CAN'T. I'M ON MY WAY TO THAT CASTLE. IT'S OWNED BY A SHAPE-CHANGING OGRE.
I INTEND TO WAGER THE SILVER COLLAR AROUND MY NECK THAT THE OGRE CANNOT CHANGE ITSELF INTO THREE THINGS THAT I SHALL NAME FOR IT.
WILL THE THIRD SHAPE BE A MOUSE?
OF COURSE.
BUT... DON'T THEY EVER LEARN?
THEY CAN'T. THEY'RE PART OF THE STORY, JUST AS I AM.
SORRY TO HEAR ABOUT YOUR SON.
HIS NAME WAS DANIEL.
I'M... I'M VERY TIRED.
10

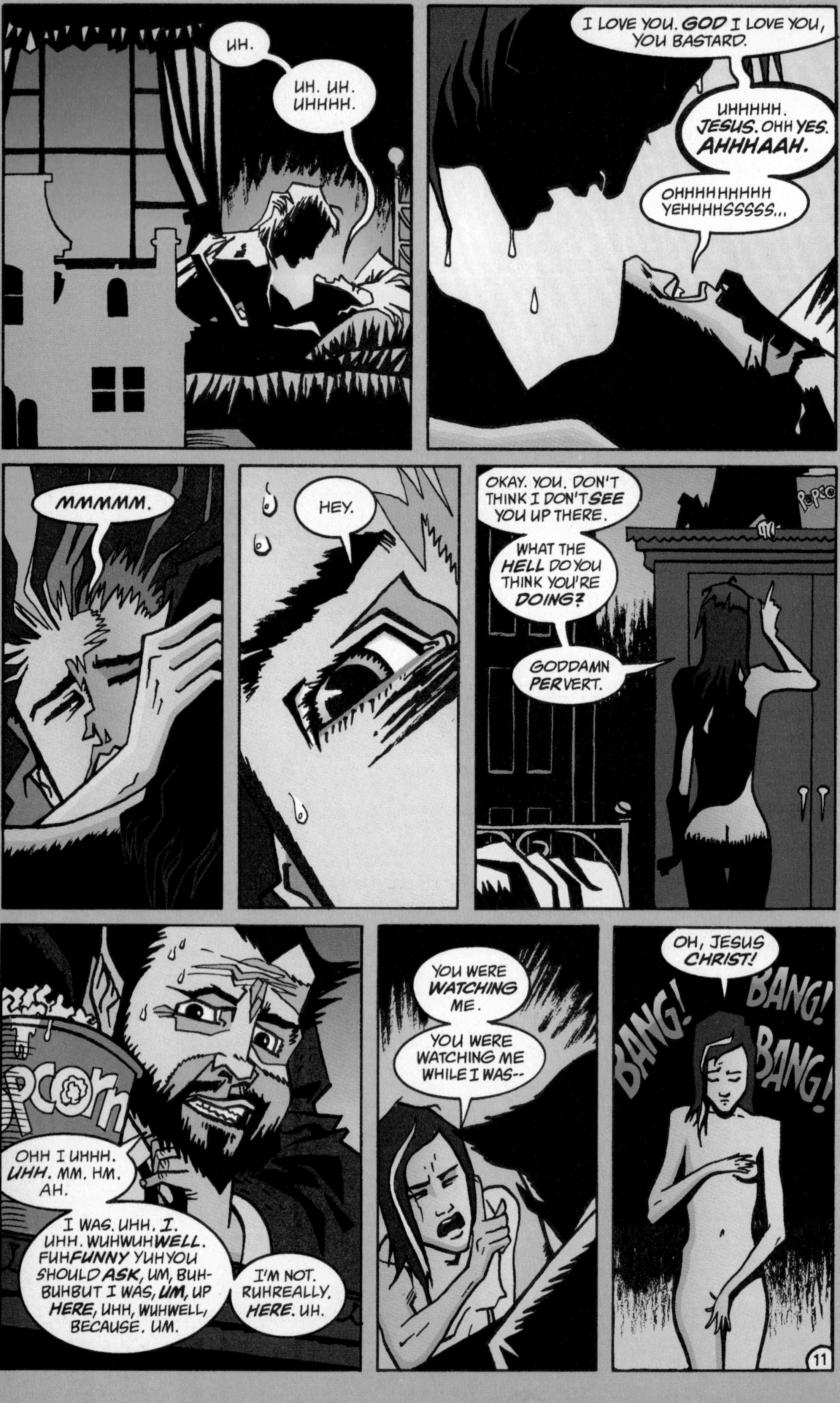

UH.
UH. UH. UHHHHH.
I LOVE YOU. GOD I LOVE YOU, YOU BASTARD.
UHHHHH. JESUS. OHH YES. AHHHAAH.
OHHHHHHHHH YEHHHHSSSSS...
MMMMM.
HEY.
OKAY. YOU. DON'T THINK I DON'T SEE YOU UP THERE.
WHAT THE HELL DO YOU THINK YOU'RE DOING?
GODDAMN PERVERT.
OHH I UHHH. UHH. MM. HM. AH.
I WAS. UHH. I. UHH. WUHWUHWELL. FUHFUNNY YUHYOU SHOULD ASK, UM, BUH-BUHBUT I WAS, UM, UP HERE, UHH, WUHWELL, BECAUSE. UM.
I'M NOT. RUHREALLY. HERE. UH.
YOU WERE WATCHING ME.
YOU WERE WATCHING ME WHILE I WAS--
OH, JESUS CHRIST!
BANG! BANG! BANG!

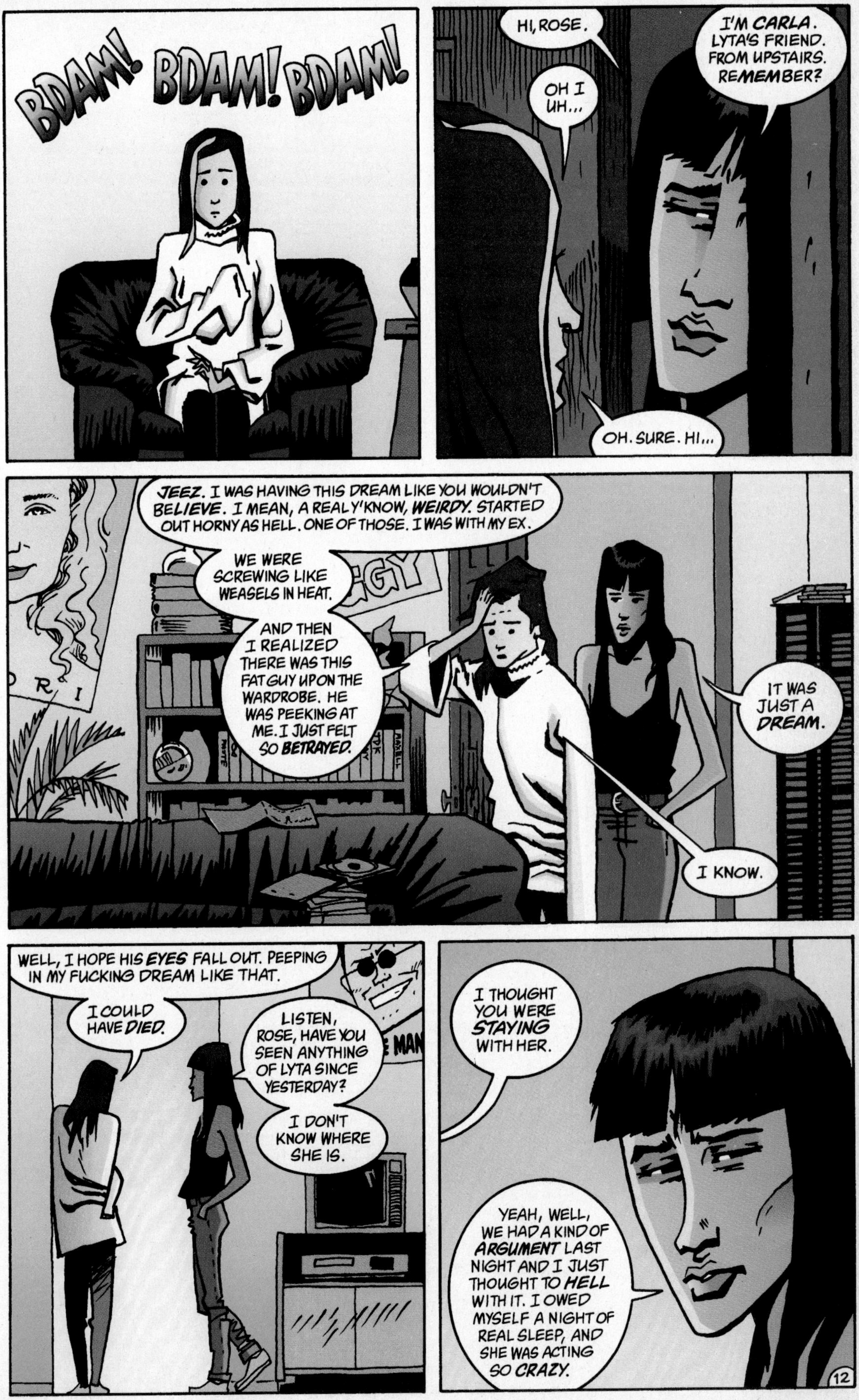
BDAM! BDAM! BDAM!
HI, ROSE.
OH I UH...
I'M CARLA. LYTA'S FRIEND. FROM UPSTAIRS. REMEMBER?
OH. SURE. HI...
JEEZ. I WAS HAVING THIS DREAM LIKE YOU WOULDN'T BELIEVE. I MEAN, A REAL Y'KNOW, WEIRDY. STARTED OUT HORNY AS HELL. ONE OF THOSE. I WAS WITH MY EX.
WE WERE SCREWING LIKE WEASELS IN HEAT.
AND THEN I REALIZED THERE WAS THIS FAT GUY UP ON THE WARDROBE. HE WAS PEEKING AT ME. I JUST FELT SO BETRAYED.
IT WAS JUST A DREAM.
I KNOW.
WELL, I HOPE HIS EYES FALL OUT. PEEPING IN MY FUCKING DREAM LIKE THAT.
I COULD HAVE DIED.
LISTEN, ROSE, HAVE YOU SEEN ANYTHING OF LYTA SINCE YESTERDAY?
I DON'T KNOW WHERE SHE IS.
I THOUGHT YOU WERE STAYING WITH HER.
YEAH, WELL, WE HAD A KIND OF ARGUMENT LAST NIGHT AND I JUST THOUGHT TO HELL WITH IT. I OWED MYSELF A NIGHT OF REAL SLEEP, AND SHE WAS ACTING SO CRAZY.

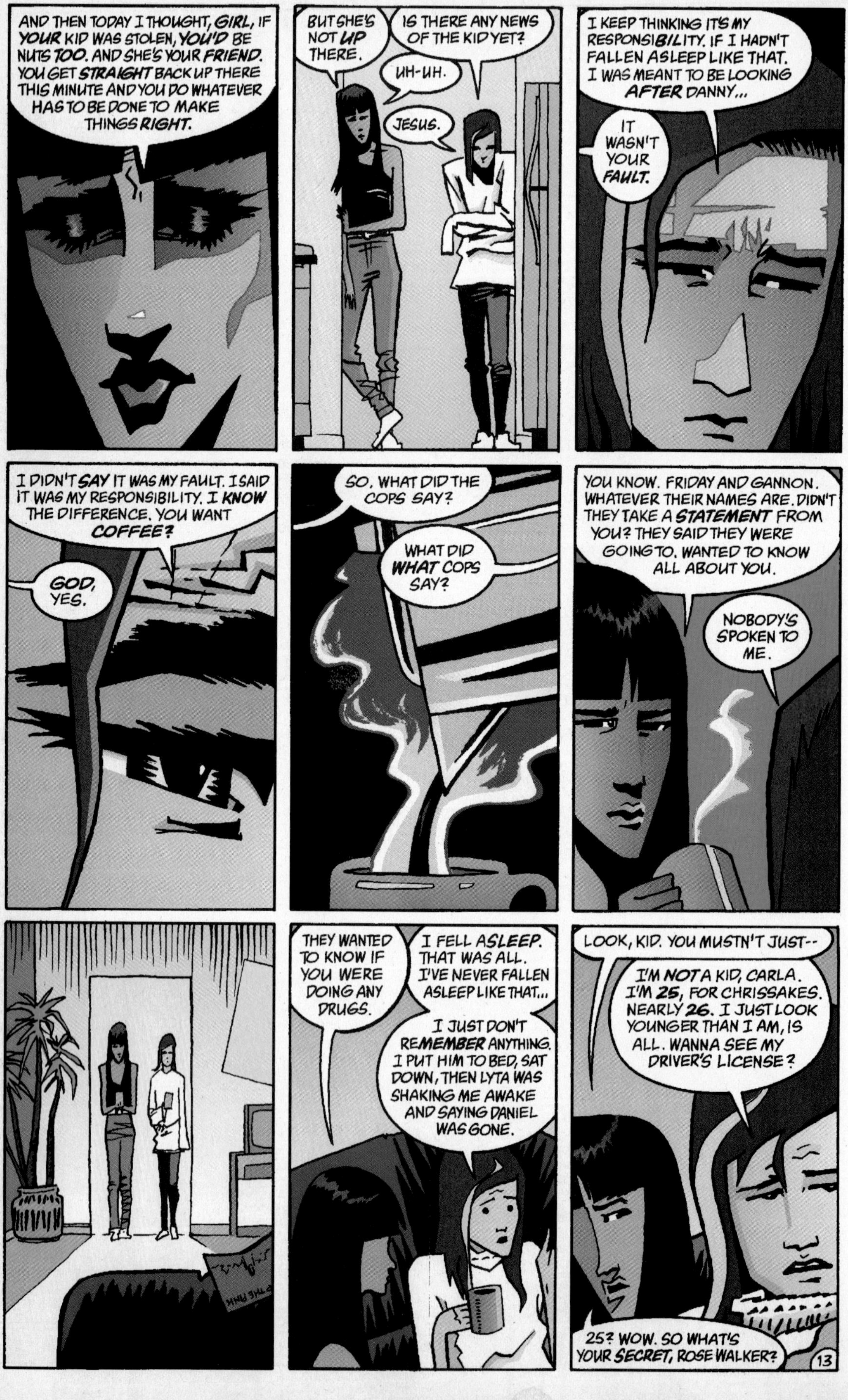
AND THEN TODAY I THOUGHT, GIRL, IF YOUR KID WAS STOLEN, YOU'D BE NUTS TOO. AND SHE'S YOUR FRIEND. YOU GET STRAIGHT BACK UP THERE THIS MINUTE AND YOU DO WHATEVER HAS TO BE DONE TO MAKE THINGS RIGHT.
BUT SHE'S NOT UP THERE.
IS THERE ANY NEWS OF THE KID YET?
UH-UH.
JESUS.
I KEEP THINKING IT'S MY RESPONSIBILITY. IF I HADN'T FALLEN ASLEEP LIKE THAT. I WAS MEANT TO BE LOOKING AFTER DANNY...
IT WASN'T YOUR FAULT.
I DIDN'T SAY IT WAS MY FAULT. I SAID IT WAS MY RESPONSIBILITY. I KNOW THE DIFFERENCE. YOU WANT COFFEE?
GOD, YES.
SO, WHAT DID THE COPS SAY?
WHAT DID WHAT COPS SAY?
YOU KNOW. FRIDAY AND GANNON. WHATEVER THEIR NAMES ARE. DIDN'T THEY TAKE A STATEMENT FROM YOU? THEY SAID THEY WERE GOING TO. WANTED TO KNOW ALL ABOUT YOU.
NOBODY'S SPOKEN TO ME.
THEY WANTED TO KNOW IF YOU WERE DOING ANY DRUGS.
I FELL ASLEEP. THAT WAS ALL. I'VE NEVER FALLEN ASLEEP LIKE THAT...
I JUST DON'T REMEMBER ANYTHING. I PUT HIM TO BED, SAT DOWN, THEN LYTA WAS SHAKING ME AWAKE AND SAYING DANIEL WAS GONE.
LOOK, KID. YOU MUSTN'T JUST--
I'M NOT A KID, CARLA. I'M 25, FOR CHRISSAKES. NEARLY 26. I JUST LOOK YOUNGER THAN I AM, IS ALL. WANNA SEE MY DRIVER'S LICENSE?
25? WOW. SO WHAT'S YOUR SECRET, ROSE WALKER?
13

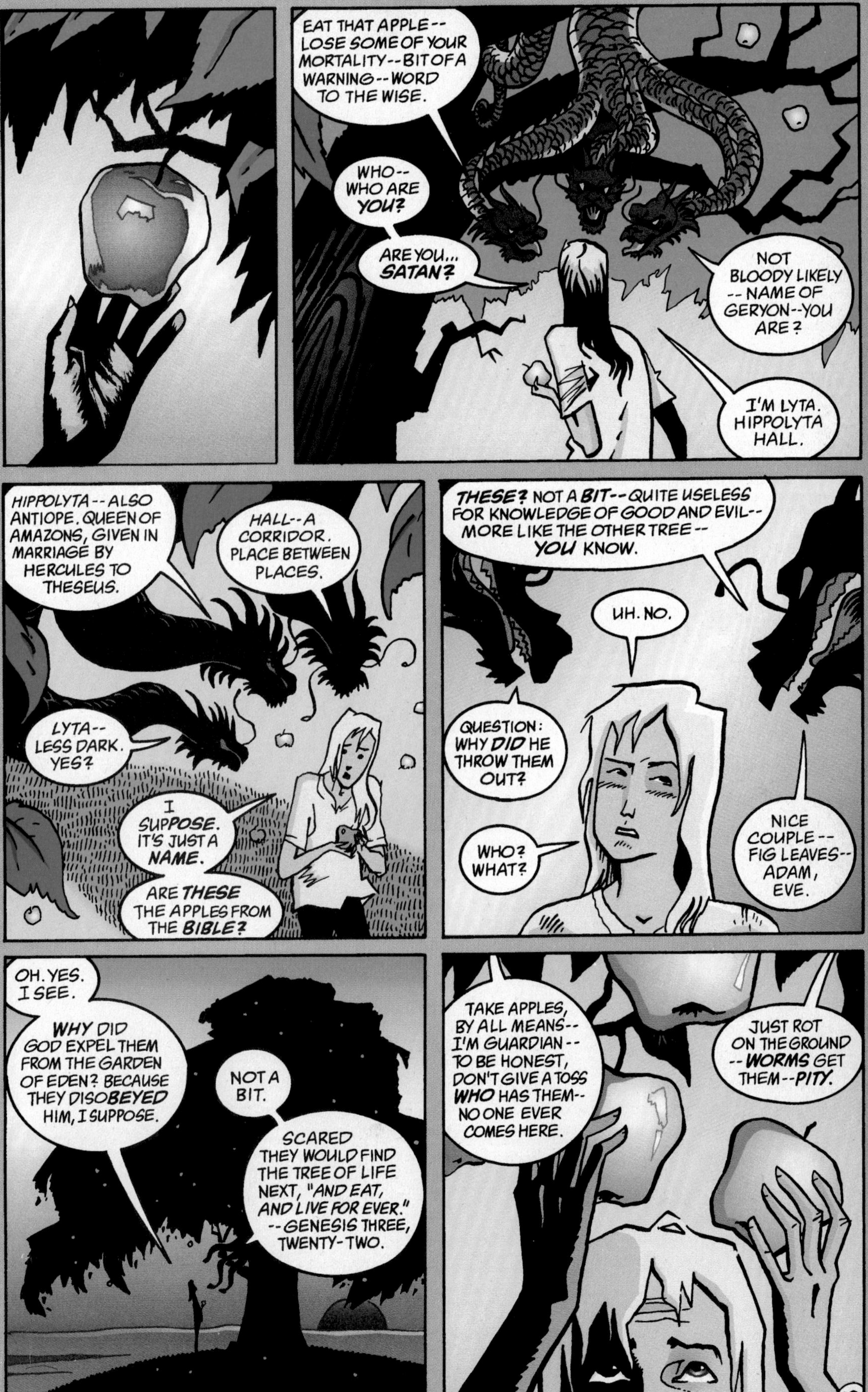
EAT THAT APPLE-- LOSE SOME OF YOUR MORTALITY--BIT OF A WARNING--WORD TO THE WISE.
WHO-- WHO ARE YOU?
ARE YOU... SATAN?
NOT BLOODY LIKELY --NAME OF GERYON--YOU ARE?
I'M LYTA. HIPPOLYTA HALL.
HIPPOLYTA--ALSO ANTIOPE. QUEEN OF AMAZONS, GIVEN IN MARRIAGE BY HERCULES TO THESEUS.
HALL--A CORRIDOR. PLACE BETWEEN PLACES.
LYTA-- LESS DARK. YES?
I SUPPOSE. IT'S JUST A NAME.
ARE THESE THE APPLES FROM THE BIBLE?
THESE? NOT A BIT--QUITE USELESS FOR KNOWLEDGE OF GOOD AND EVIL-- MORE LIKE THE OTHER TREE-- YOU KNOW.
UH. NO.
QUESTION: WHY DID HE THROW THEM OUT?
WHO? WHAT?
NICE COUPLE-- FIG LEAVES-- ADAM, EVE.
OH. YES. I SEE.
WHY DID GOD EXPEL THEM FROM THE GARDEN OF EDEN? BECAUSE THEY DISOBEYED HIM, I SUPPOSE.
NOT A BIT.
SCARED THEY WOULD FIND THE TREE OF LIFE NEXT, "AND EAT, AND LIVE FOR EVER." --GENESIS THREE, TWENTY-TWO.
TAKE APPLES, BY ALL MEANS-- I'M GUARDIAN-- TO BE HONEST, DON'T GIVE A TOSS WHO HAS THEM-- NO ONE EVER COMES HERE.
JUST ROT ON THE GROUND --WORMS GET THEM--PITY.
18

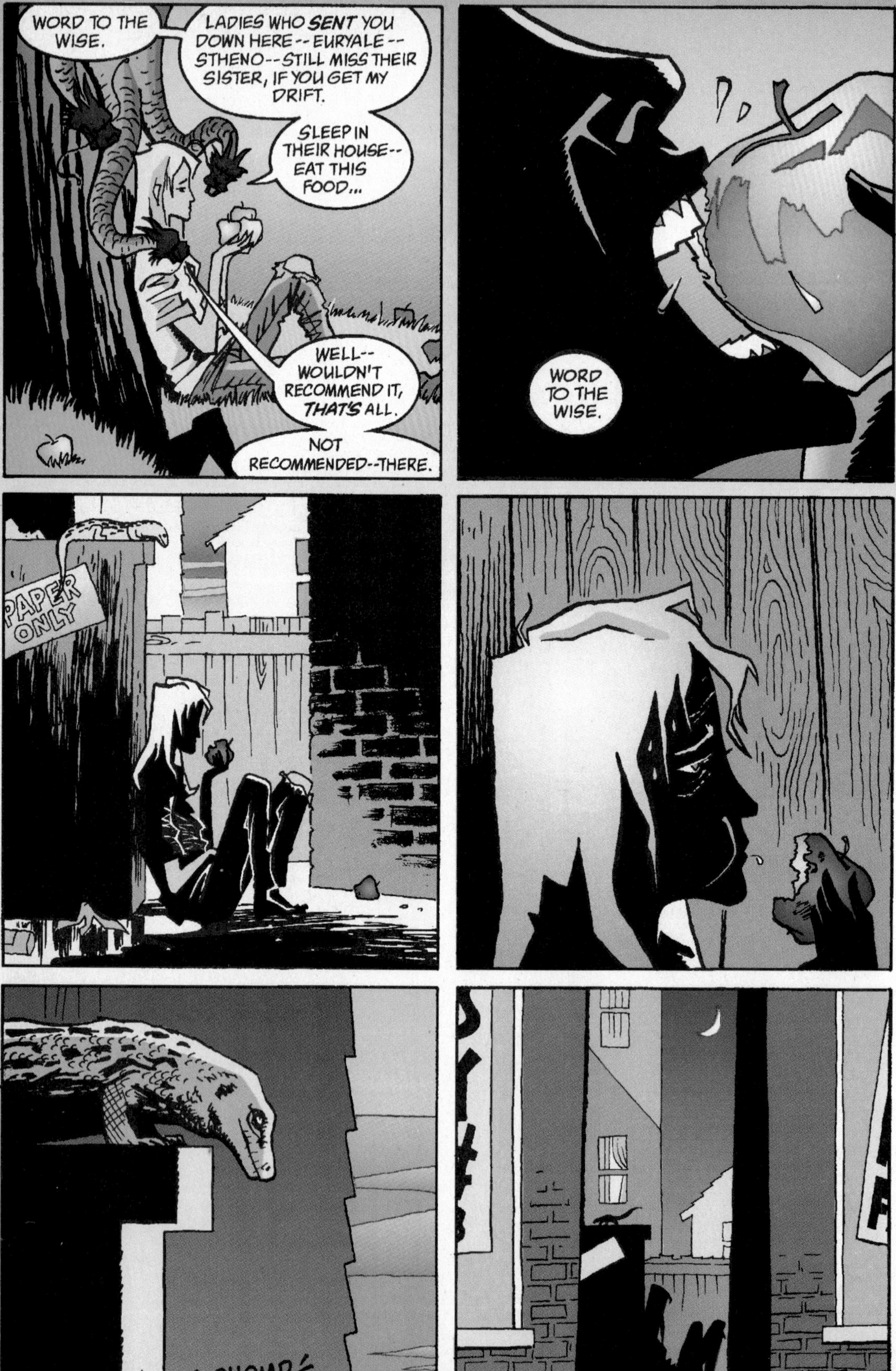
WORD TO THE WISE.
LADIES WHO SENT YOU DOWN HERE -- EURYALE -- STHENO -- STILL MISS THEIR SISTER, IF YOU GET MY DRIFT.
SLEEP IN THEIR HOUSE -- EAT THIS FOOD...
WELL -- WOULDN'T RECOMMEND IT, THAT'S ALL.
NOT RECOMMENDED -- THERE.
WORD TO THE WISE.
PAPER ONLY
CHOMP

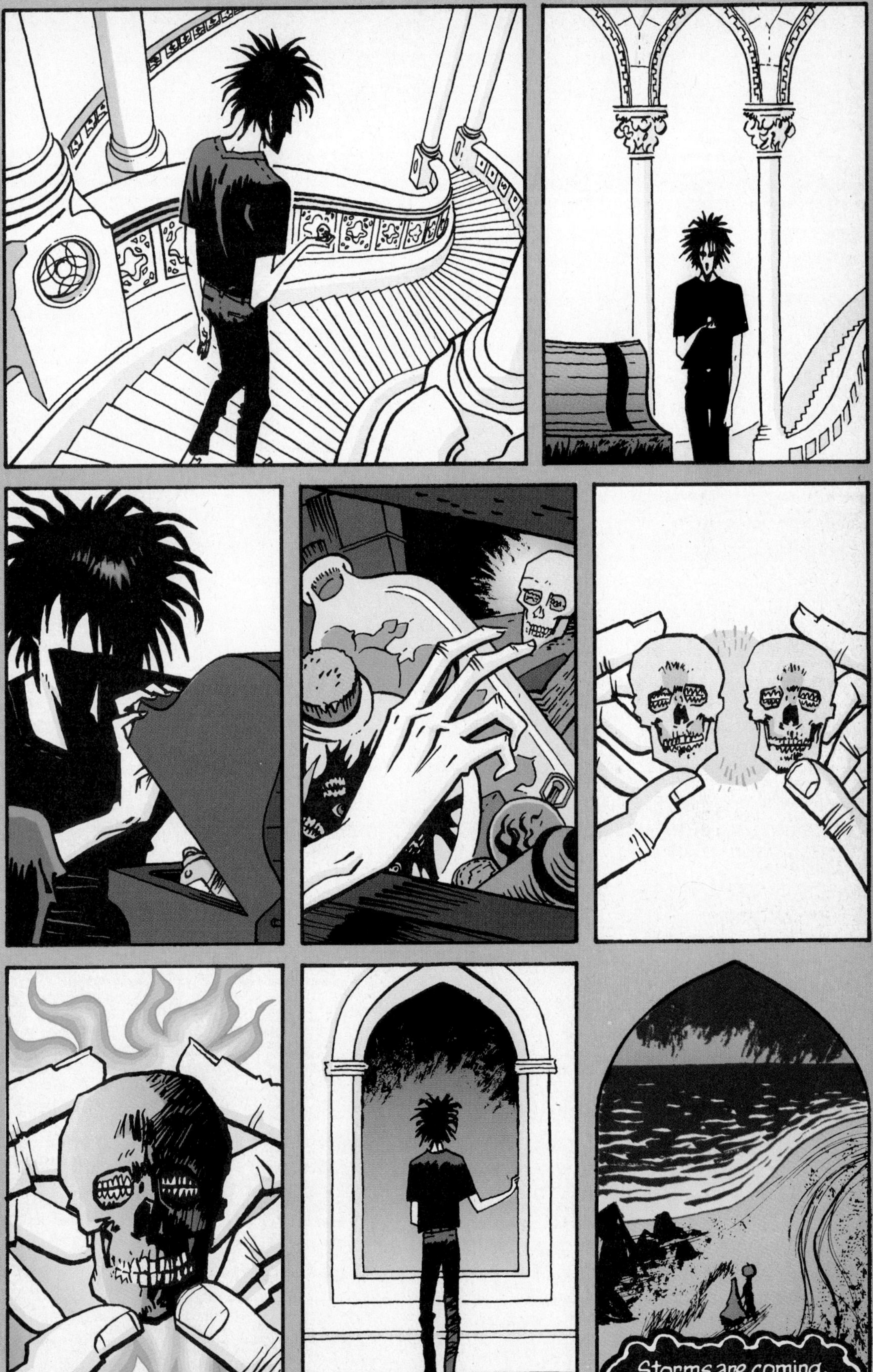
Storms are coming.

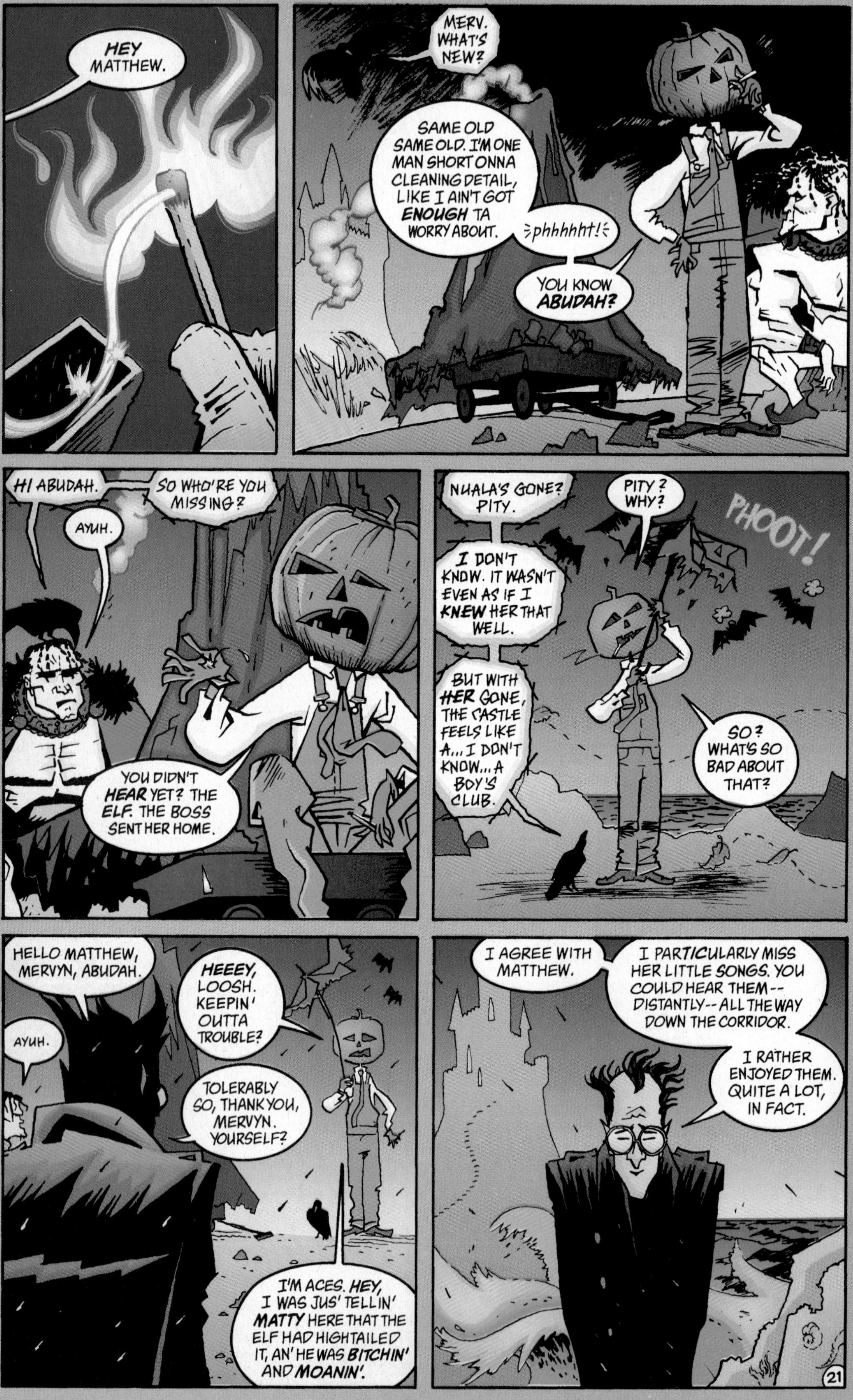

HEY MATTHEW.
MERV. WHAT'S NEW?
SAME OLD SAME OLD. I'M ONE MAN SHORT ONNA CLEANING DETAIL, LIKE I AIN'T GOT ENOUGH TA WORRY ABOUT.
phhhhht!
YOU KNOW ABUDAH?
HI ABUDAH.
SO WHO'RE YOU MISSING?
AYUH.
YOU DIDN'T HEAR YET? THE ELF. THE BOSS SENT HER HOME.
NUALA'S GONE? PITY.
PITY? WHY?
PHOOT!
I DON'T KNOW. IT WASN'T EVEN AS IF I KNEW HER THAT WELL.
BUT WITH HER GONE, THE CASTLE FEELS LIKE A... I DON'T KNOW... A BOY'S CLUB.
SO? WHAT'S SO BAD ABOUT THAT?
HELLO MATTHEW, MERVYN, ABUDAH.
AYUH.
HEEEY, LOOSH. KEEPIN' OUTTA TROUBLE?
TOLERABLY SO, THANK YOU, MERVYN. YOURSELF?
I'M ACES. HEY, I WAS JUS' TELLIN' MATTY HERE THAT THE ELF HAD HIGHTAILED IT, AN' HE WAS BITCHIN' AND MOANIN'.
I AGREE WITH MATTHEW.
I PARTICULARLY MISS HER LITTLE SONGS. YOU COULD HEAR THEM -- DISTANTLY -- ALL THE WAY DOWN THE CORRIDOR.
I RATHER ENJOYED THEM. QUITE A LOT, IN FACT.

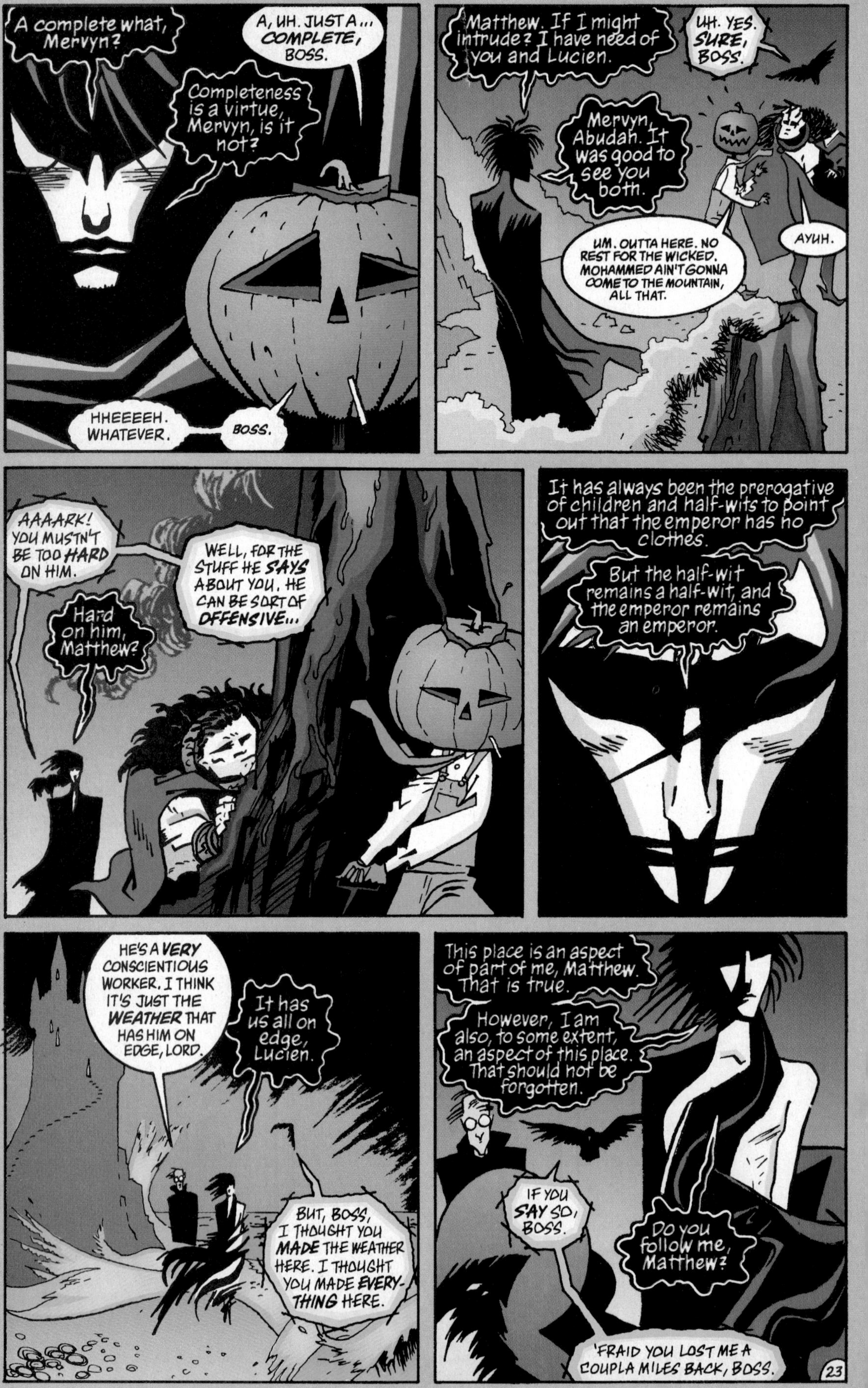
A complete what, Mervyn?
A, UH. JUST A... COMPLETE, BOSS.
Completeness is a virtue, Mervyn, is it not?
HHEEEEH. WHATEVER.
BOSS.
Matthew. If I might intrude? I have need of you and Lucien.
UH. YES. SURE, BOSS.
Mervyn, Abudah. It was good to see you both.
UM. OUTTA HERE. NO REST FOR THE WICKED. MOHAMMED AIN'T GONNA COME TO THE MOUNTAIN, ALL THAT.
AYUH.
AAAARK! YOU MUSTN'T BE TOO HARD ON HIM.
WELL, FOR THE STUFF HE SAYS ABOUT YOU, HE CAN BE SORT OF OFFENSIVE...
Hard on him, Matthew?
It has always been the prerogative of children and half-wits to point out that the emperor has no clothes.
But the half-wit remains a half-wit, and the emperor remains an emperor.
HE'S A VERY CONSCIENTIOUS WORKER. I THINK IT'S JUST THE WEATHER THAT HAS HIM ON EDGE, LORD.
It has us all on edge, Lucien.
BUT, BOSS, I THOUGHT YOU MADE THE WEATHER HERE. I THOUGHT YOU MADE EVERY-THING HERE.
This place is an aspect of part of me, Matthew. That is true.
However, I am also, to some extent, an aspect of this place. That should not be forgotten.
IF YOU SAY SO, BOSS.
Do you follow me, Matthew?
'FRAID YOU LOST ME A COUPLA MILES BACK, BOSS.

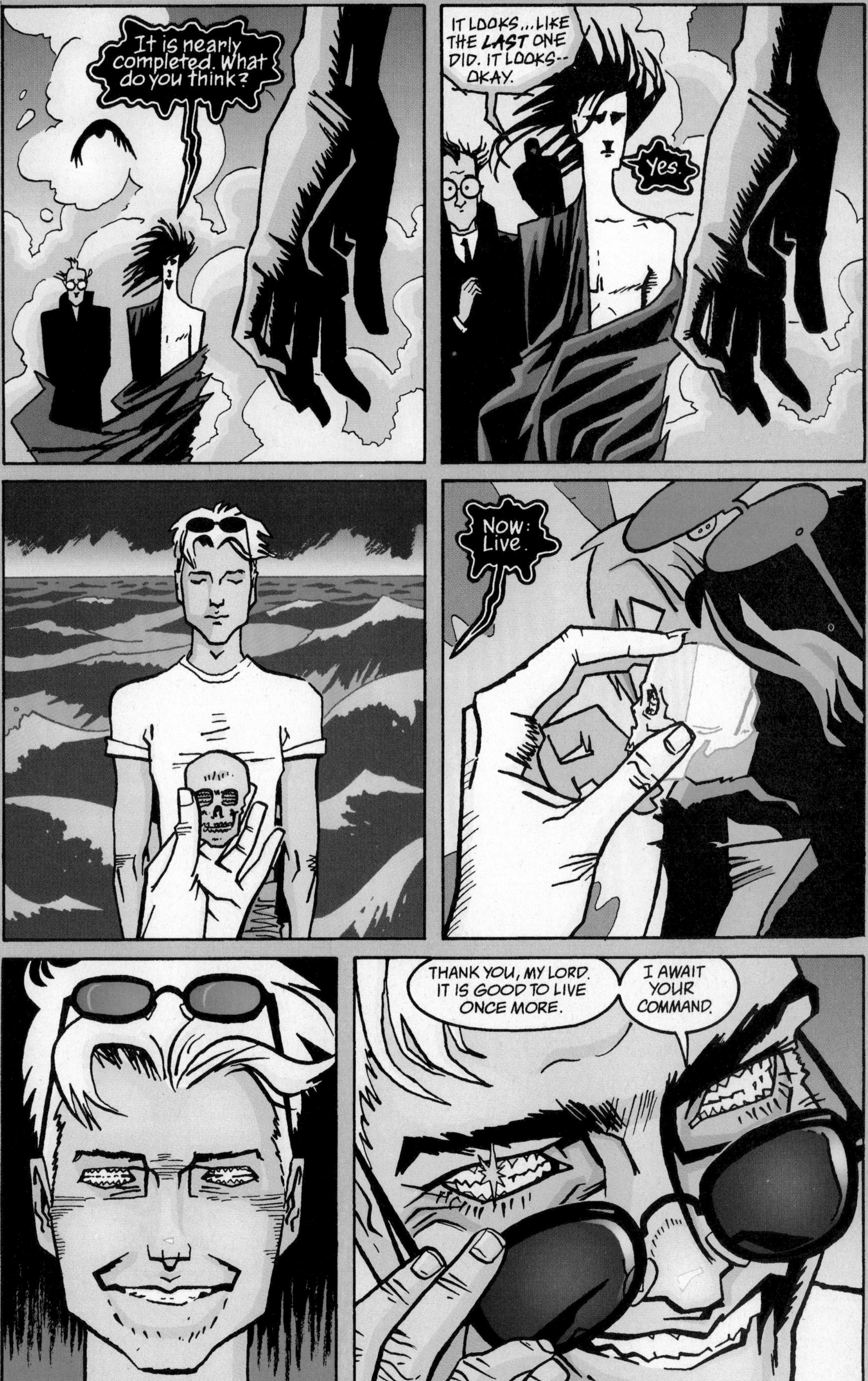
It is nearly completed. What do you think?
IT LOOKS...LIKE THE LAST ONE DID. IT LOOKS--OKAY.
Yes.
Now: Live.
THANK YOU, MY LORD. IT IS GOOD TO LIVE ONCE MORE.
I AWAIT YOUR COMMAND.

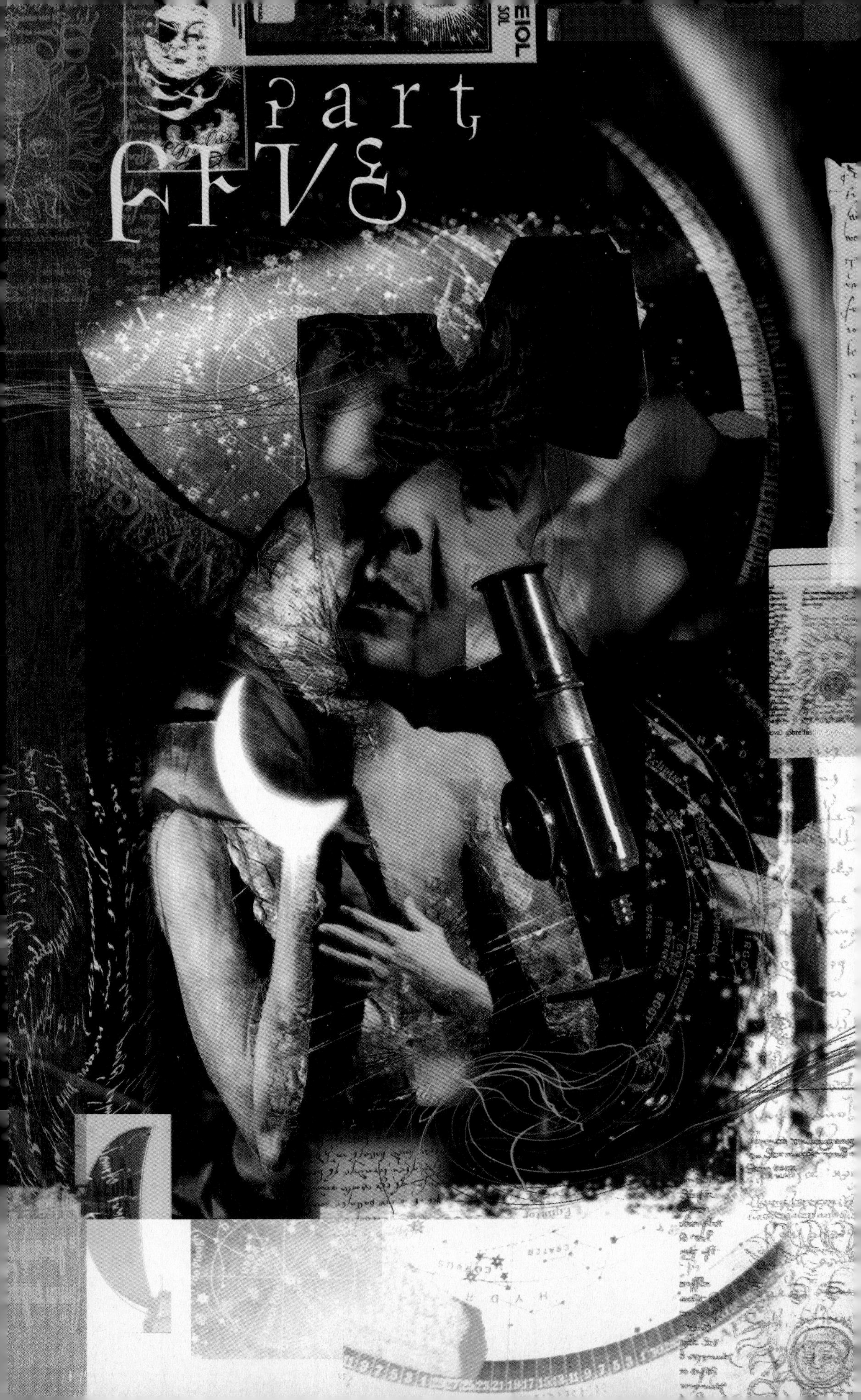

part five

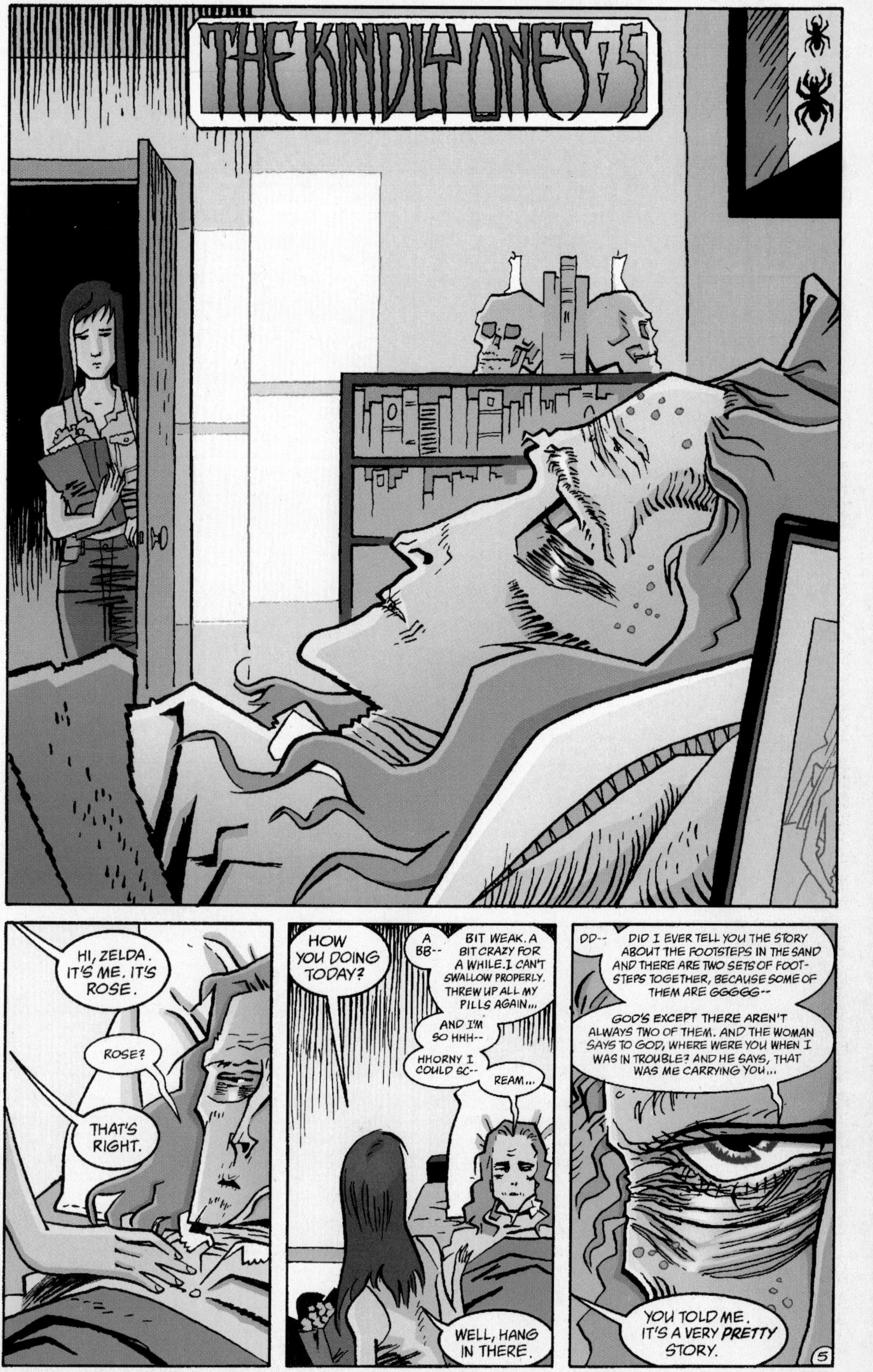
THE KINDLY ONES: 5
HI, ZELDA. IT'S ME. IT'S ROSE.
ROSE?
THAT'S RIGHT.
HOW YOU DOING TODAY?
A BB--
BIT WEAK. A BIT CRAZY FOR A WHILE. I CAN'T SWALLOW PROPERLY. THREW UP ALL MY PILLS AGAIN...
AND I'M SO HHH--
HHORNY I COULD SC--
REAM...
WELL, HANG IN THERE.
DD--
DID I EVER TELL YOU THE STORY ABOUT THE FOOTSTEPS IN THE SAND AND THERE ARE TWO SETS OF FOOT-STEPS TOGETHER, BECAUSE SOME OF THEM ARE GGGGG--
GOD'S EXCEPT THERE AREN'T ALWAYS TWO OF THEM. AND THE WOMAN SAYS TO GOD, WHERE WERE YOU WHEN I WAS IN TROUBLE? AND HE SAYS, THAT WAS ME CARRYING YOU...
YOU TOLD ME. IT'S A VERY PRETTY STORY.
5

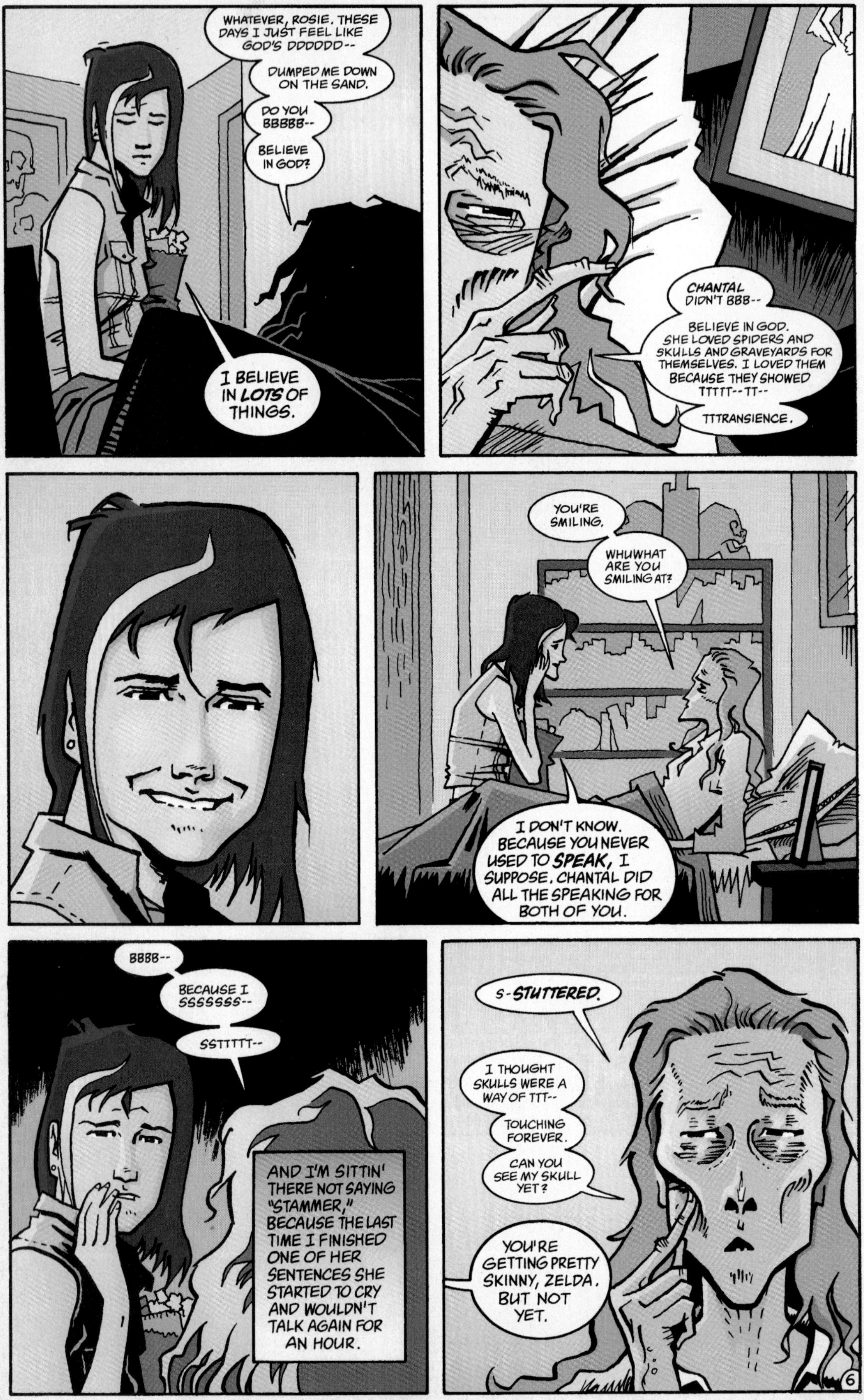
WHATEVER, ROSIE. THESE DAYS I JUST FEEL LIKE GOD'S DDDDDD--
DUMPED ME DOWN ON THE SAND.
DO YOU BBBBB--
BELIEVE IN GOD?
I BELIEVE IN LOTS OF THINGS.
CHANTAL DIDN'T BBB--
BELIEVE IN GOD. SHE LOVED SPIDERS AND SKULLS AND GRAVEYARDS FOR THEMSELVES. I LOVED THEM BECAUSE THEY SHOWED TTTTT--TT--
TTTRANSIENCE.
YOU'RE SMILING.
WHUWHAT ARE YOU SMILING AT?
I DON'T KNOW. BECAUSE YOU NEVER USED TO SPEAK, I SUPPOSE. CHANTAL DID ALL THE SPEAKING FOR BOTH OF YOU.
BBBB--
BECAUSE I SSSSSSS--
SSTTTTT--
AND I'M SITTIN' THERE NOT SAYING "STAMMER," BECAUSE THE LAST TIME I FINISHED ONE OF HER SENTENCES SHE STARTED TO CRY AND WOULDN'T TALK AGAIN FOR AN HOUR.
S-STUTTERED.
I THOUGHT SKULLS WERE A WAY OF TTT--
TOUCHING FOREVER.
CAN YOU SEE MY SKULL YET?
YOU'RE GETTING PRETTY SKINNY, ZELDA. BUT NOT YET.
6

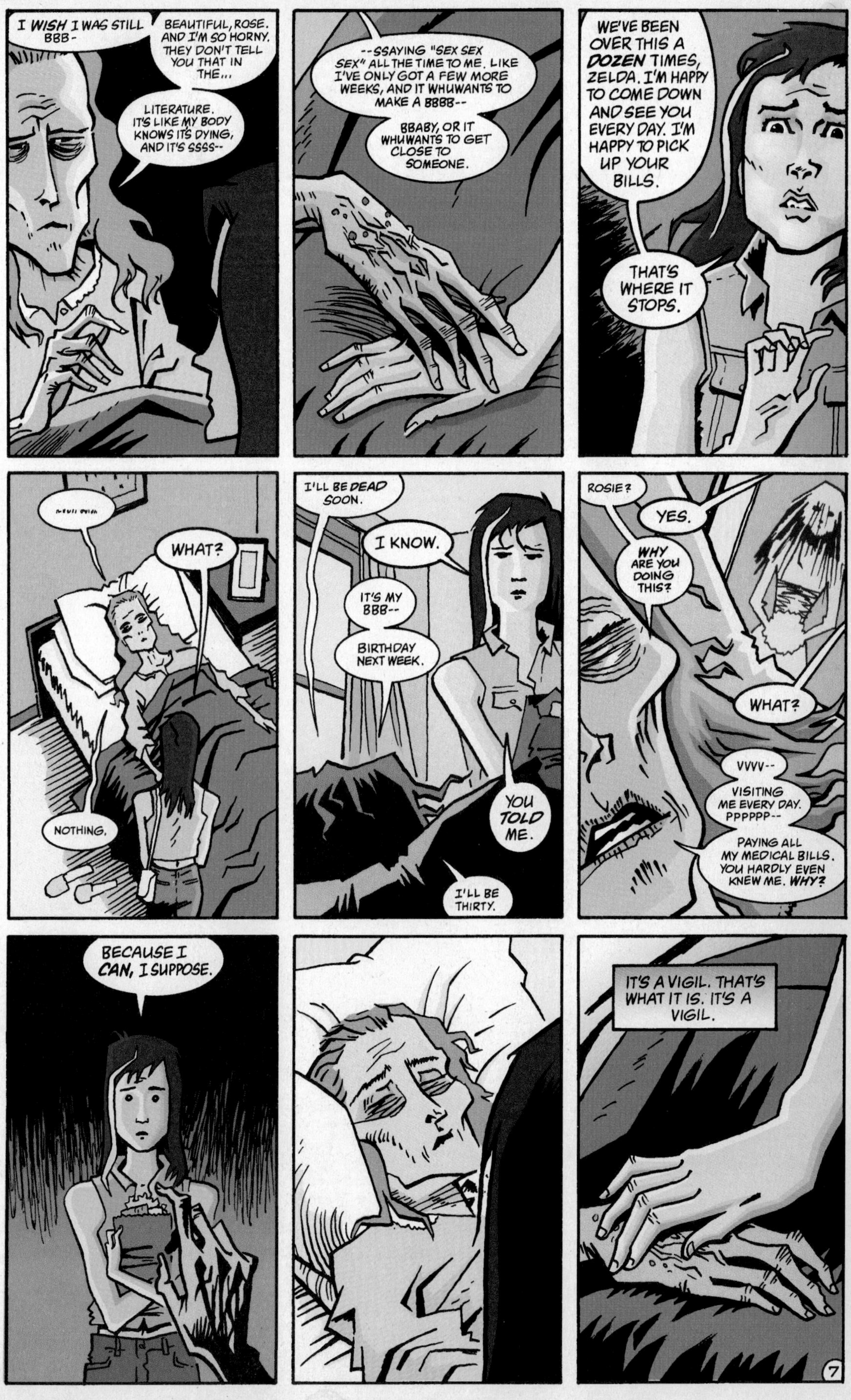

I WISH I WAS STILL BBB-
BEAUTIFUL, ROSE. AND I'M SO HORNY. THEY DON'T TELL YOU THAT IN THE...
LITERATURE. IT'S LIKE MY BODY KNOWS IT'S DYING, AND IT'S SSSS--
--SSAYING "SEX SEX SEX" ALL THE TIME TO ME, LIKE I'VE ONLY GOT A FEW MORE WEEKS, AND IT WHUWANTS TO MAKE A BBBB--
BBABY, OR IT WHUWANTS TO GET CLOSE TO SOMEONE.
WE'VE BEEN OVER THIS A DOZEN TIMES, ZELDA. I'M HAPPY TO COME DOWN AND SEE YOU EVERY DAY. I'M HAPPY TO PICK UP YOUR BILLS.
THAT'S WHERE IT STOPS.
WHAT?
NOTHING.
I'LL BE DEAD SOON.
I KNOW.
IT'S MY BBB--
BIRTHDAY NEXT WEEK.
YOU TOLD ME.
I'LL BE THIRTY.
ROSIE?
YES.
WHY ARE YOU DOING THIS?
WHAT?
VVVV--
VISITING ME EVERY DAY. PPPPPP--
PAYING ALL MY MEDICAL BILLS. YOU HARDLY EVEN KNEW ME. WHY?
BECAUSE I CAN, I SUPPOSE.
IT'S A VIGIL. THAT'S WHAT IT IS. IT'S A VIGIL.
7

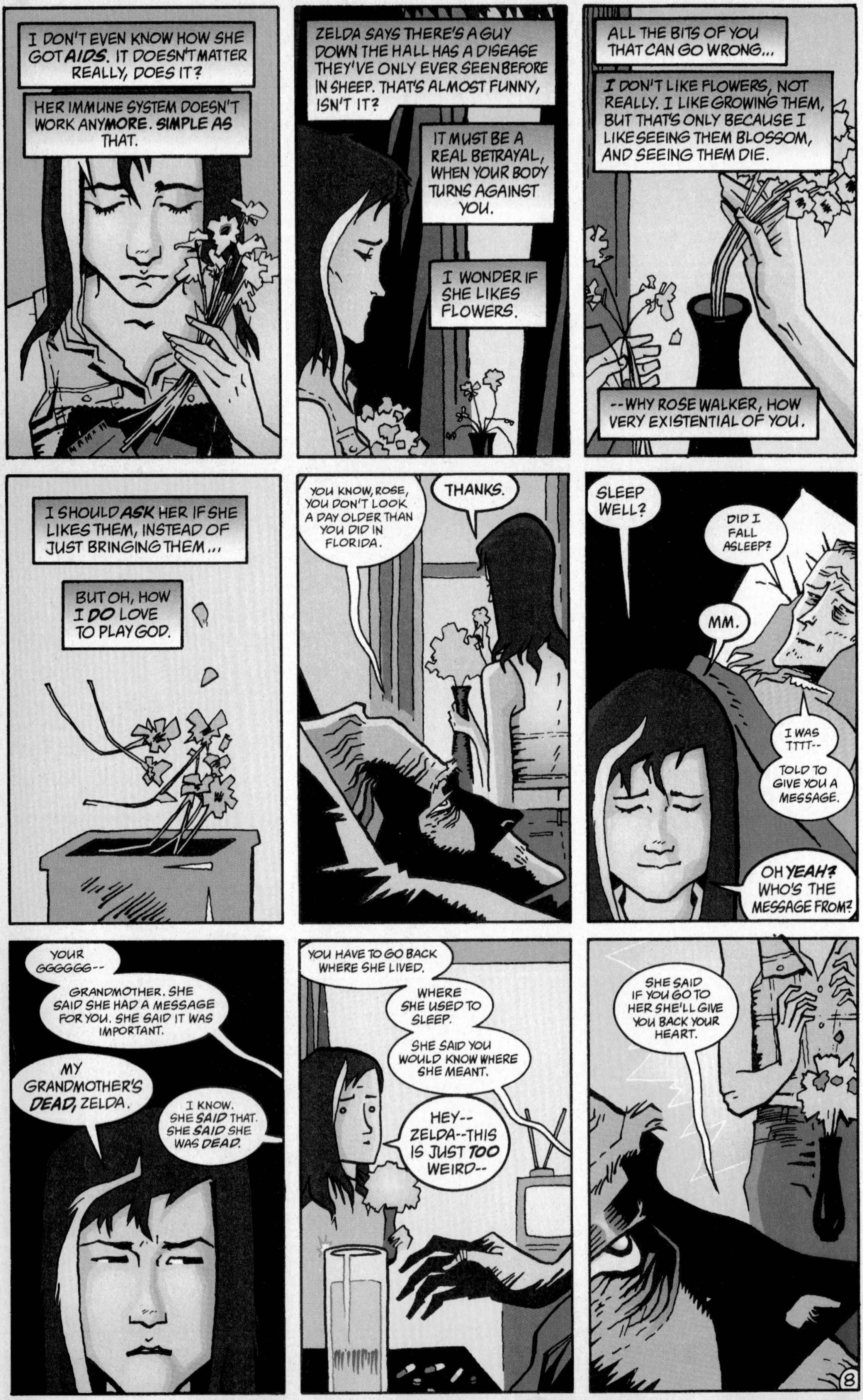

I DON'T EVEN KNOW HOW SHE GOT AIDS. IT DOESN'T MATTER REALLY, DOES IT?
HER IMMUNE SYSTEM DOESN'T WORK ANYMORE. SIMPLE AS THAT.
ZELDA SAYS THERE'S A GUY DOWN THE HALL HAS A DISEASE THEY'VE ONLY EVER SEEN BEFORE IN SHEEP. THAT'S ALMOST FUNNY, ISN'T IT?
IT MUST BE A REAL BETRAYAL, WHEN YOUR BODY TURNS AGAINST YOU.
I WONDER IF SHE LIKES FLOWERS.
ALL THE BITS OF YOU THAT CAN GO WRONG...
I DON'T LIKE FLOWERS, NOT REALLY. I LIKE GROWING THEM, BUT THAT'S ONLY BECAUSE I LIKE SEEING THEM BLOSSOM, AND SEEING THEM DIE.
--WHY ROSE WALKER, HOW VERY EXISTENTIAL OF YOU.
I SHOULD ASK HER IF SHE LIKES THEM, INSTEAD OF JUST BRINGING THEM...
BUT OH, HOW I DO LOVE TO PLAY GOD.
YOU KNOW, ROSE, YOU DON'T LOOK A DAY OLDER THAN YOU DID IN FLORIDA.
THANKS.
SLEEP WELL?
DID I FALL ASLEEP?
MM.
I WAS TTTT--
TOLD TO GIVE YOU A MESSAGE.
OH YEAH? WHO'S THE MESSAGE FROM?
YOUR GGGGGG--
GRANDMOTHER. SHE SAID SHE HAD A MESSAGE FOR YOU. SHE SAID IT WAS IMPORTANT.
MY GRANDMOTHER'S DEAD, ZELDA.
I KNOW. SHE SAID THAT. SHE SAID SHE WAS DEAD.
YOU HAVE TO GO BACK WHERE SHE LIVED.
WHERE SHE USED TO SLEEP.
SHE SAID YOU WOULD KNOW WHERE SHE MEANT.
HEY-- ZELDA--THIS IS JUST TOO WEIRD--
SHE SAID IF YOU GO TO HER SHE'LL GIVE YOU BACK YOUR HEART.

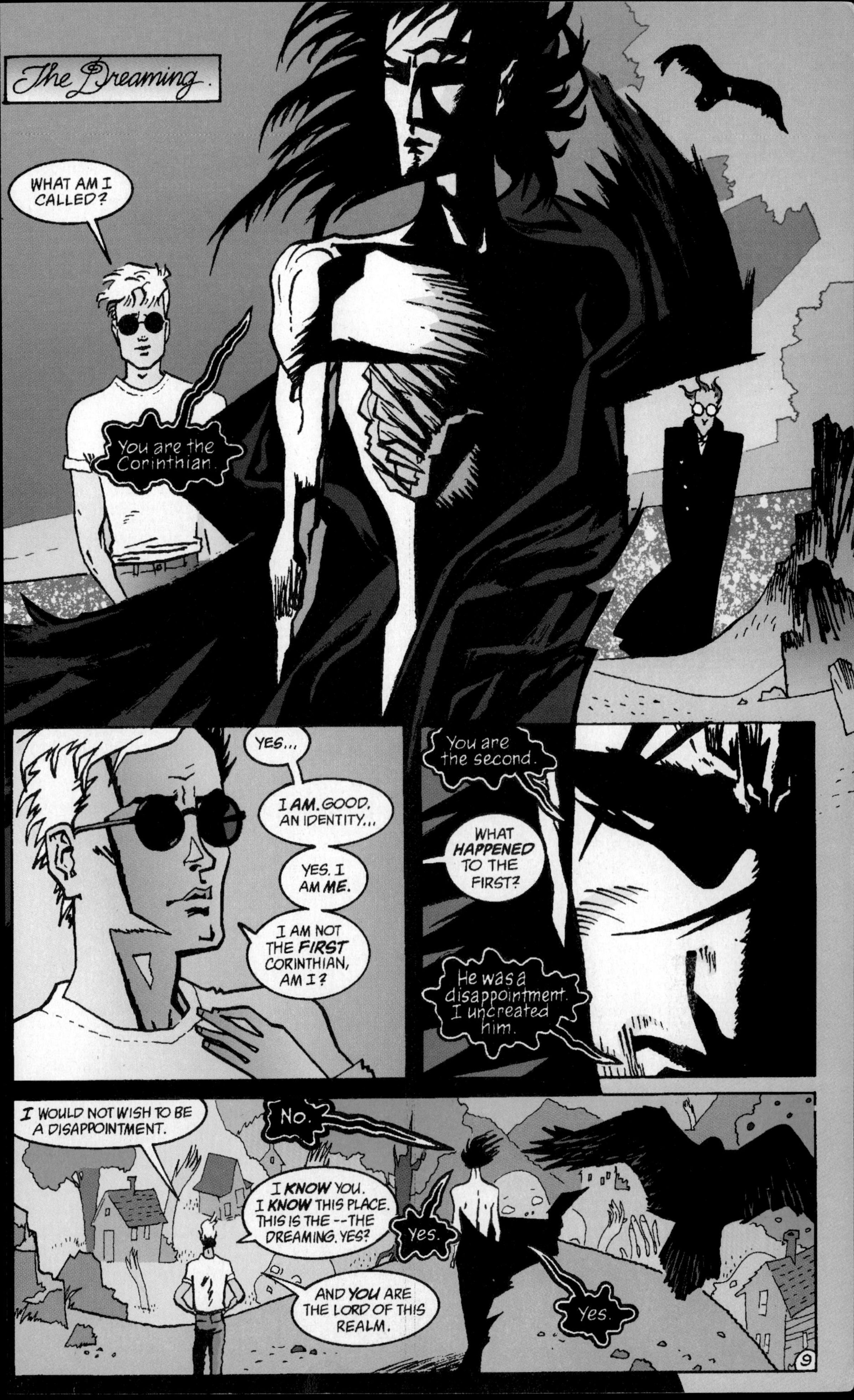
The Dreaming.
WHAT AM I CALLED?
You are the Corinthian.
YES...
I AM. GOOD. AN IDENTITY...
YES. I AM ME.
I AM NOT THE FIRST CORINTHIAN, AM I?
You are the second.
WHAT HAPPENED TO THE FIRST?
He was a disappointment. I uncreated him.
I WOULD NOT WISH TO BE A DISAPPOINTMENT.
No.
I KNOW YOU. I KNOW THIS PLACE. THIS IS THE --THE DREAMING. YES?
Yes.
AND YOU ARE THE LORD OF THIS REALM.
Yes.
9

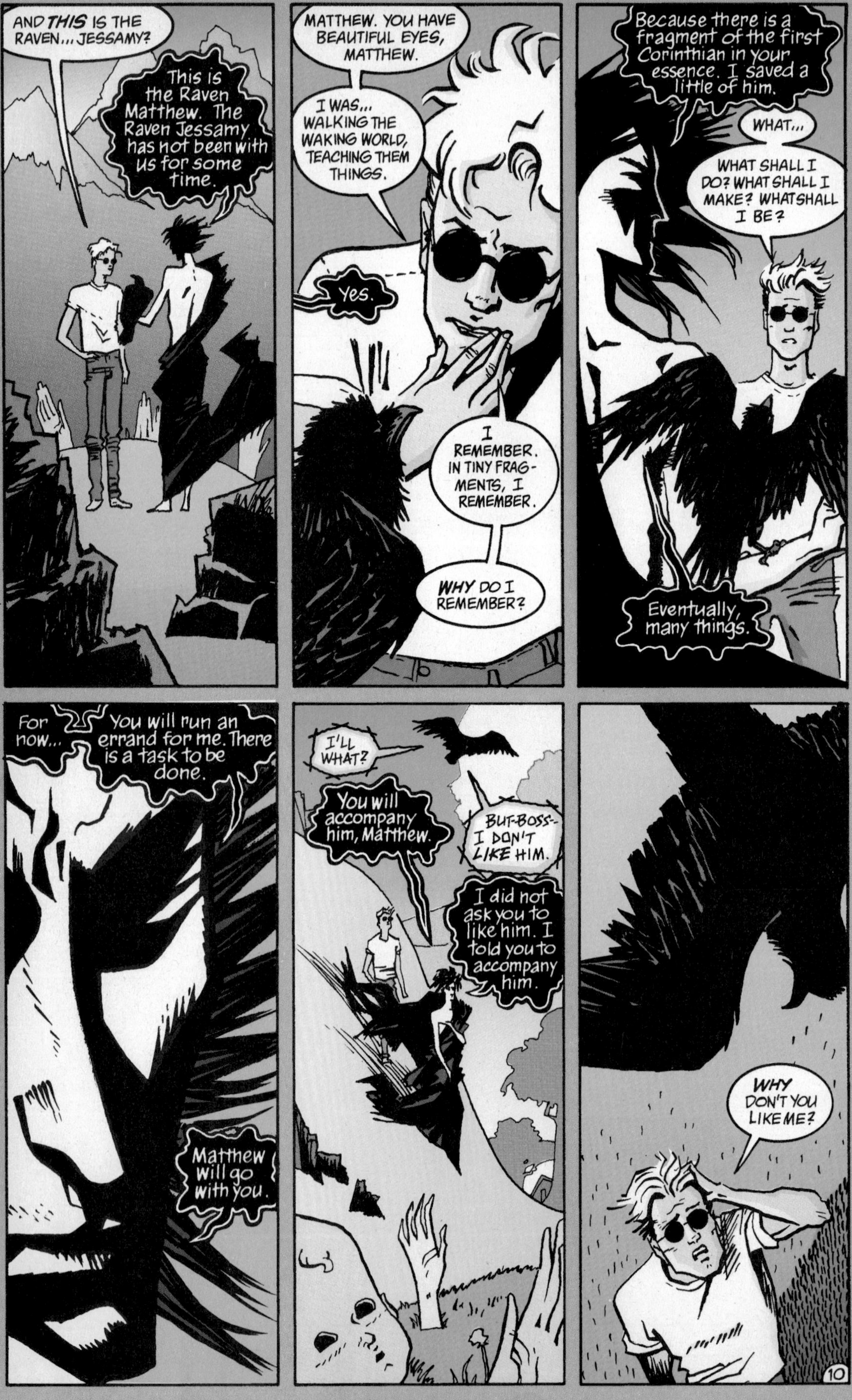
AND THIS IS THE RAVEN... JESSAMY?
This is the Raven Matthew. The Raven Jessamy has not been with us for some time.
MATTHEW. YOU HAVE BEAUTIFUL EYES, MATTHEW.
I WAS... WALKING THE WAKING WORLD, TEACHING THEM THINGS.
Yes.
I REMEMBER. IN TINY FRAGMENTS, I REMEMBER.
WHY DO I REMEMBER?
Because there is a fragment of the first Corinthian in your essence. I saved a little of him.
WHAT...
WHAT SHALL I DO? WHAT SHALL I MAKE? WHAT SHALL I BE?
Eventually, many things.
For now...
You will run an errand for me. There is a task to be done.
Matthew will go with you.
I'LL WHAT?
You will accompany him, Matthew.
BUT-BOSS-I DON'T LIKE HIM.
I did not ask you to like him. I told you to accompany him.
WHY DON'T YOU LIKE ME?
10

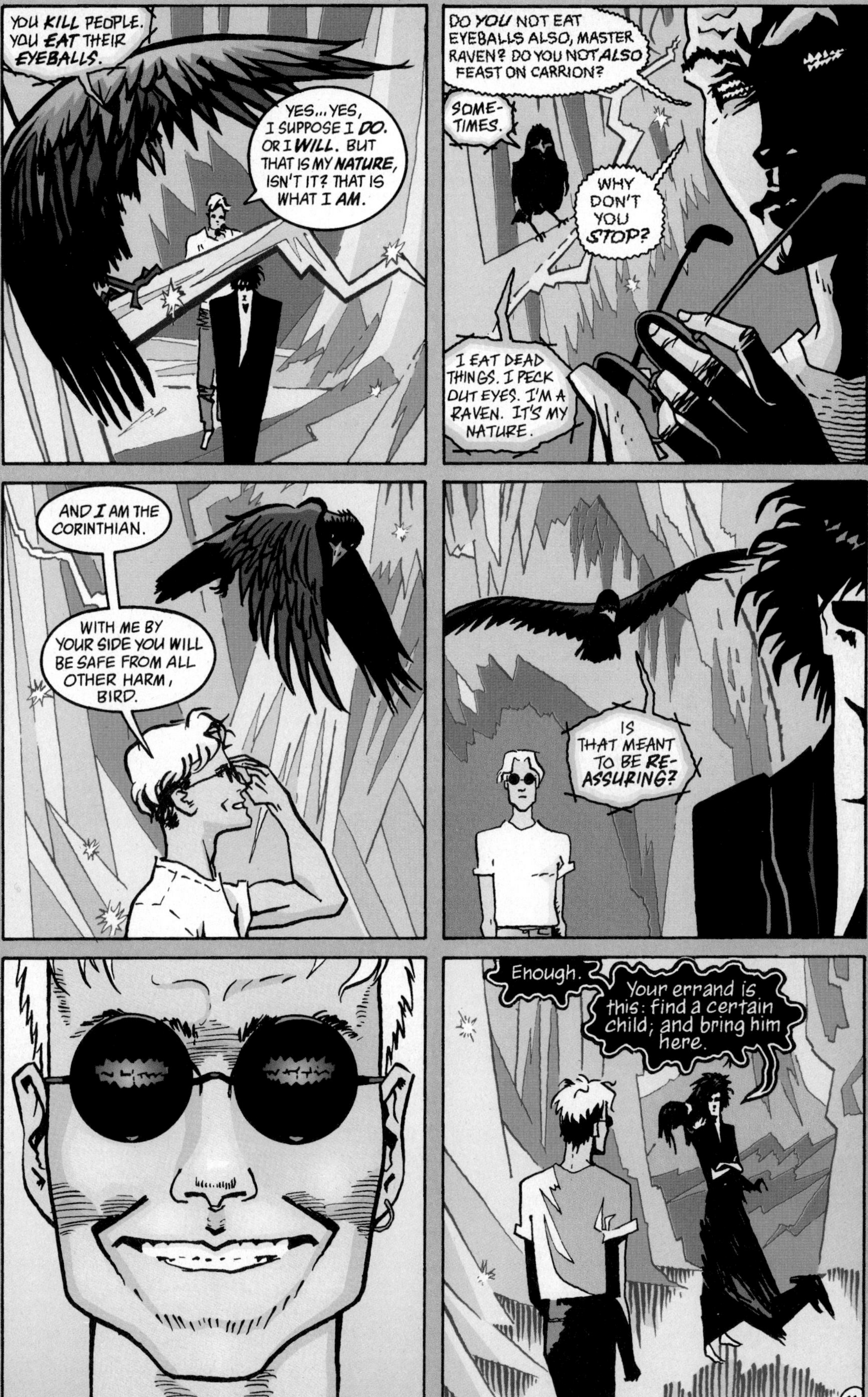
YOU KILL PEOPLE. YOU EAT THEIR EYEBALLS.
YES... YES, I SUPPOSE I DO. OR I WILL. BUT THAT IS MY NATURE, ISN'T IT? THAT IS WHAT I AM.
DO YOU NOT EAT EYEBALLS ALSO, MASTER RAVEN? DO YOU NOT ALSO FEAST ON CARRION?
SOME-TIMES.
WHY DON'T YOU STOP?
I EAT DEAD THINGS. I PECK OUT EYES. I'M A RAVEN. IT'S MY NATURE.
AND I AM THE CORINTHIAN.
WITH ME BY YOUR SIDE YOU WILL BE SAFE FROM ALL OTHER HARM, BIRD.
IS THAT MEANT TO BE RE-ASSURING?
Enough.
Your errand is this: find a certain child; and bring him here.
11

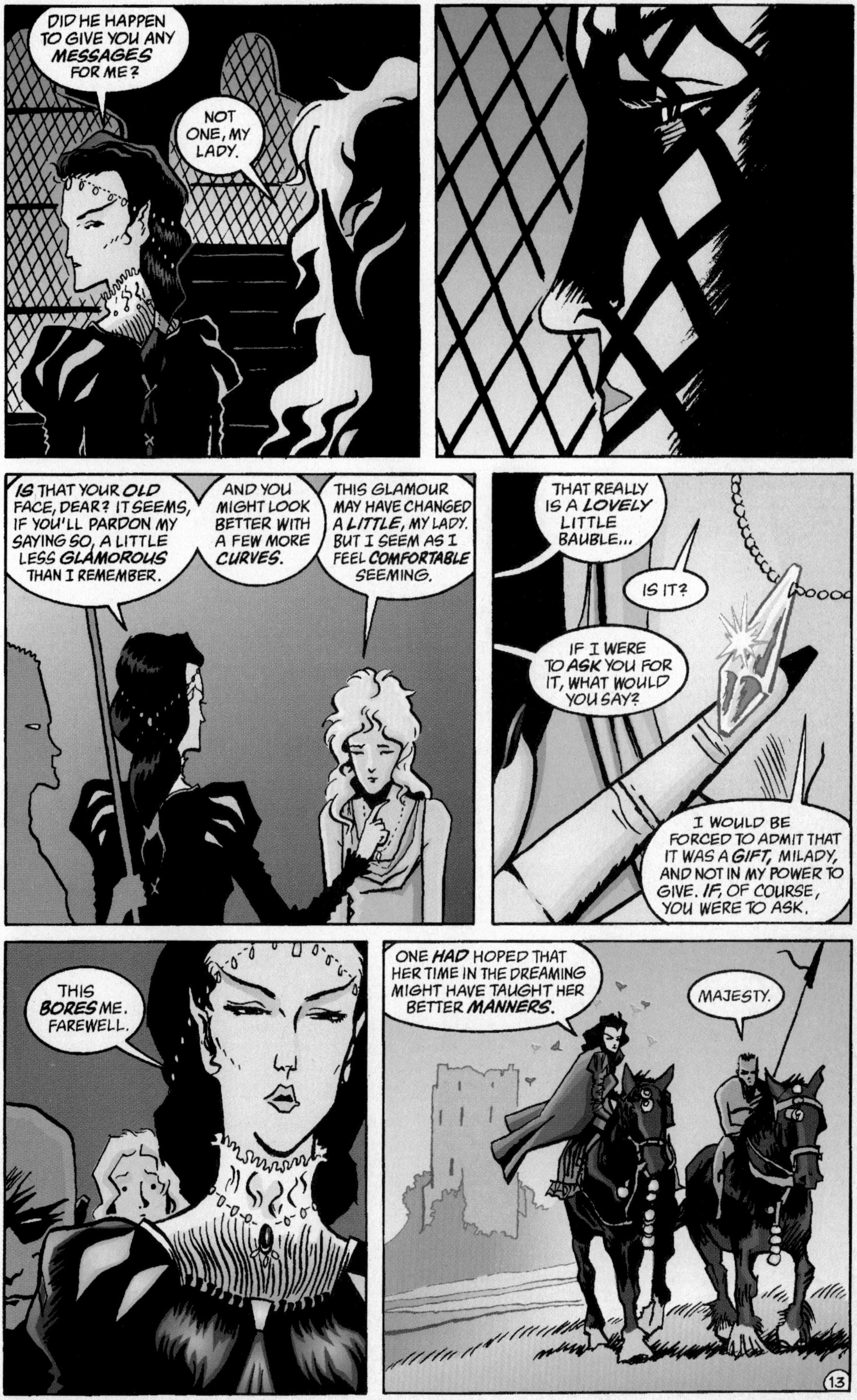
DID HE HAPPEN TO GIVE YOU ANY MESSAGES FOR ME?
NOT ONE, MY LADY.
IS THAT YOUR OLD FACE, DEAR? IT SEEMS, IF YOU'LL PARDON MY SAYING SO, A LITTLE LESS GLAMOROUS THAN I REMEMBER.
AND YOU MIGHT LOOK BETTER WITH A FEW MORE CURVES.
THIS GLAMOUR MAY HAVE CHANGED A LITTLE, MY LADY. BUT I SEEM AS I FEEL COMFORTABLE SEEMING.
THAT REALLY IS A LOVELY LITTLE BAUBLE...
IS IT?
IF I WERE TO ASK YOU FOR IT, WHAT WOULD YOU SAY?
I WOULD BE FORCED TO ADMIT THAT IT WAS A GIFT, MILADY, AND NOT IN MY POWER TO GIVE. IF, OF COURSE, YOU WERE TO ASK.
THIS BORES ME. FAREWELL.
ONE HAD HOPED THAT HER TIME IN THE DREAMING MIGHT HAVE TAUGHT HER BETTER MANNERS.
MAJESTY.

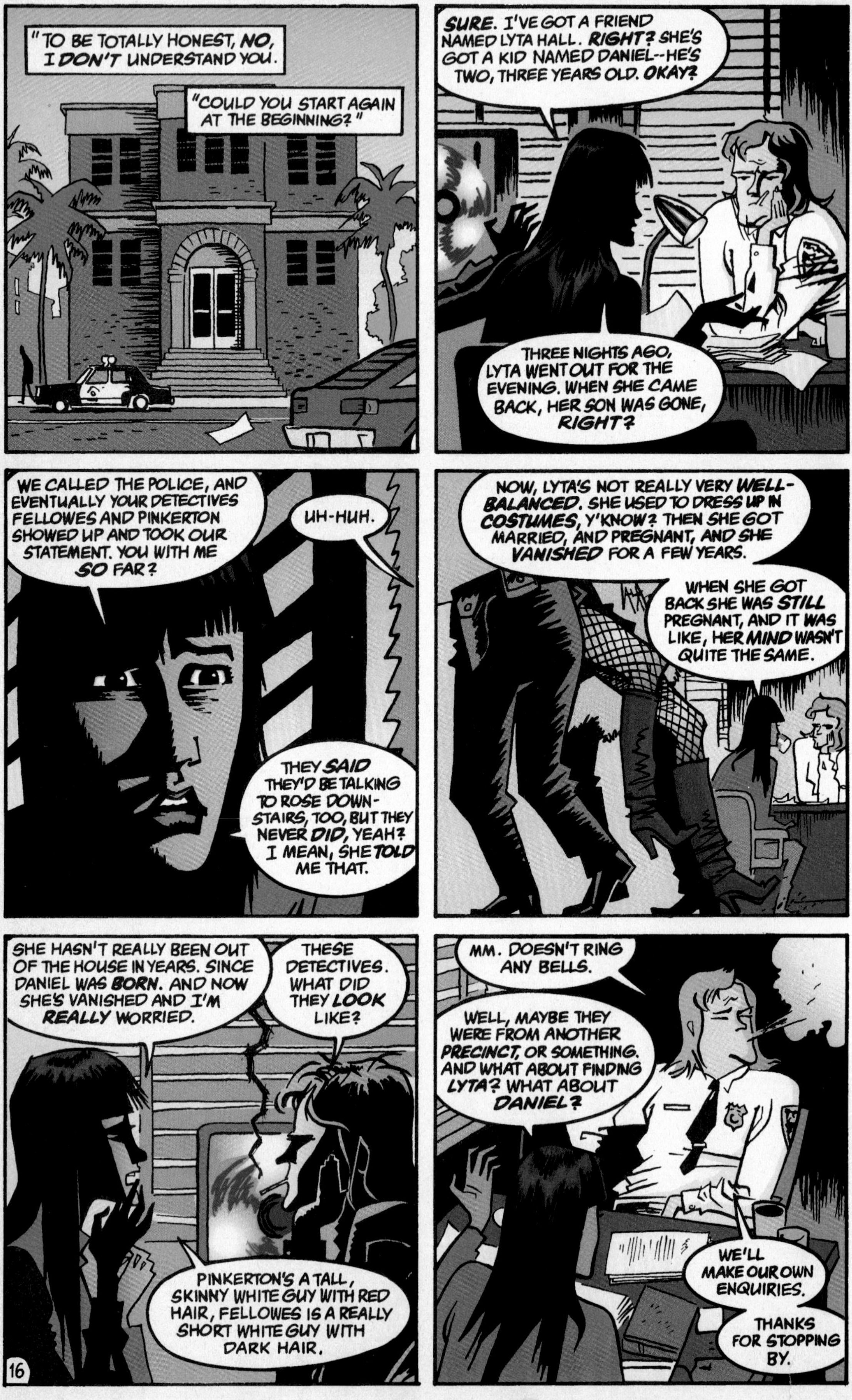
"TO BE TOTALLY HONEST, NO, I DON'T UNDERSTAND YOU.
"COULD YOU START AGAIN AT THE BEGINNING?"
SURE. I'VE GOT A FRIEND NAMED LYTA HALL. RIGHT? SHE'S GOT A KID NAMED DANIEL--HE'S TWO, THREE YEARS OLD. OKAY?
THREE NIGHTS AGO, LYTA WENT OUT FOR THE EVENING. WHEN SHE CAME BACK, HER SON WAS GONE, RIGHT?
WE CALLED THE POLICE, AND EVENTUALLY YOUR DETECTIVES FELLOWES AND PINKERTON SHOWED UP AND TOOK OUR STATEMENT. YOU WITH ME SO FAR?
UH-HUH.
THEY SAID THEY'D BE TALKING TO ROSE DOWN-STAIRS, TOO, BUT THEY NEVER DID, YEAH? I MEAN, SHE TOLD ME THAT.
NOW, LYTA'S NOT REALLY VERY WELL-BALANCED. SHE USED TO DRESS UP IN COSTUMES, Y'KNOW? THEN SHE GOT MARRIED, AND PREGNANT, AND SHE VANISHED FOR A FEW YEARS.
WHEN SHE GOT BACK SHE WAS STILL PREGNANT, AND IT WAS LIKE, HER MIND WASN'T QUITE THE SAME.
SHE HASN'T REALLY BEEN OUT OF THE HOUSE IN YEARS. SINCE DANIEL WAS BORN. AND NOW SHE'S VANISHED AND I'M REALLY WORRIED.
THESE DETECTIVES. WHAT DID THEY LOOK LIKE?
PINKERTON'S A TALL, SKINNY WHITE GUY WITH RED HAIR, FELLOWES IS A REALLY SHORT WHITE GUY WITH DARK HAIR.
MM. DOESN'T RING ANY BELLS.
WELL, MAYBE THEY WERE FROM ANOTHER PRECINCT, OR SOMETHING. AND WHAT ABOUT FINDING LYTA? WHAT ABOUT DANIEL?
WE'LL MAKE OUR OWN ENQUIRIES.
THANKS FOR STOPPING BY.

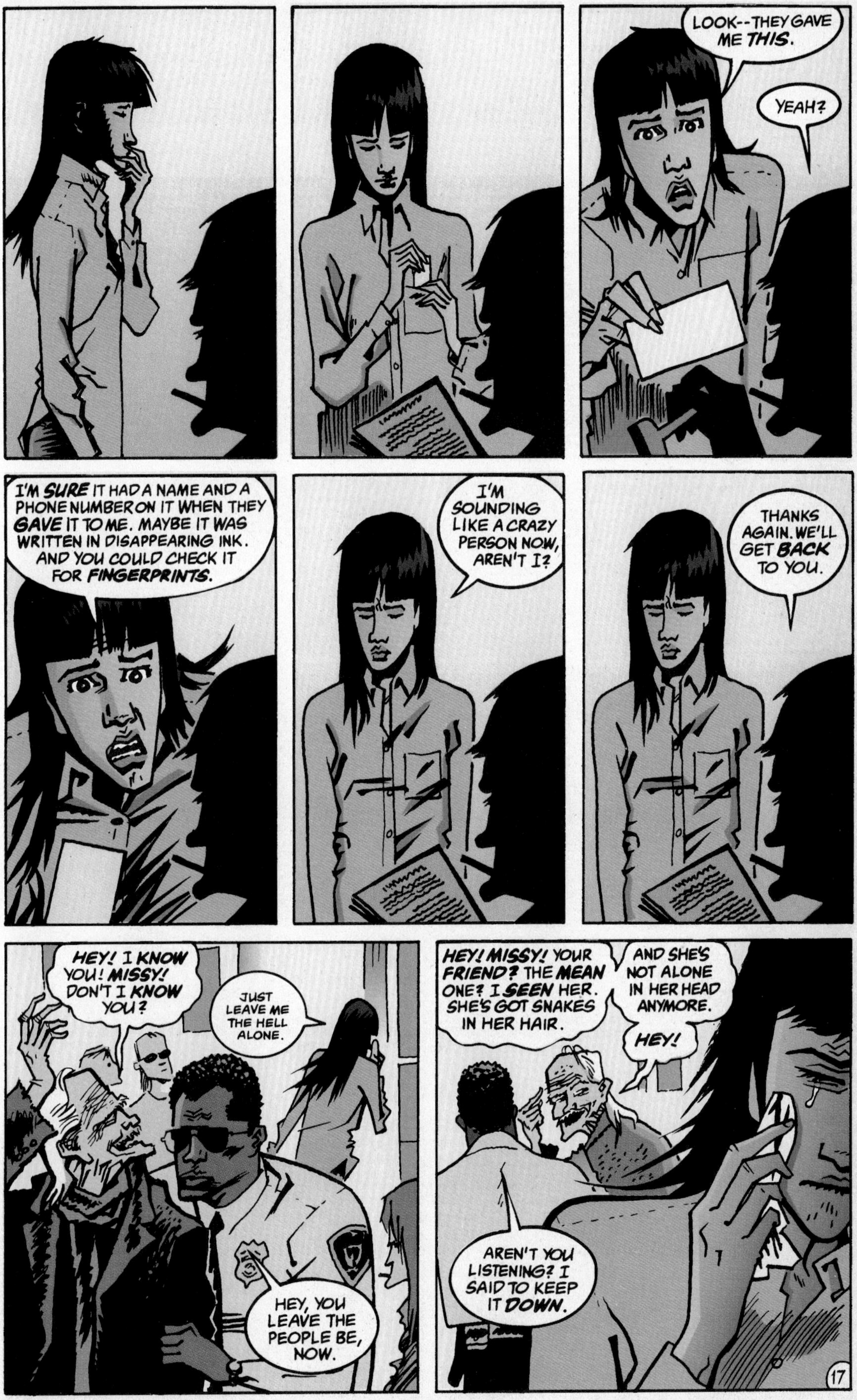
LOOK--THEY GAVE ME THIS.
YEAH?
I'M SURE IT HAD A NAME AND A PHONE NUMBER ON IT WHEN THEY GAVE IT TO ME. MAYBE IT WAS WRITTEN IN DISAPPEARING INK. AND YOU COULD CHECK IT FOR FINGERPRINTS.
I'M SOUNDING LIKE A CRAZY PERSON NOW, AREN'T I?
THANKS AGAIN. WE'LL GET BACK TO YOU.
HEY! I KNOW YOU! MISSY! DON'T I KNOW YOU?
JUST LEAVE ME THE HELL ALONE.
HEY, YOU LEAVE THE PEOPLE BE, NOW.
HEY! MISSY! YOUR FRIEND? THE MEAN ONE? I SEEN HER. SHE'S GOT SNAKES IN HER HAIR.
AND SHE'S NOT ALONE IN HER HEAD ANYMORE.
HEY!
AREN'T YOU LISTENING? I SAID TO KEEP IT DOWN.
17

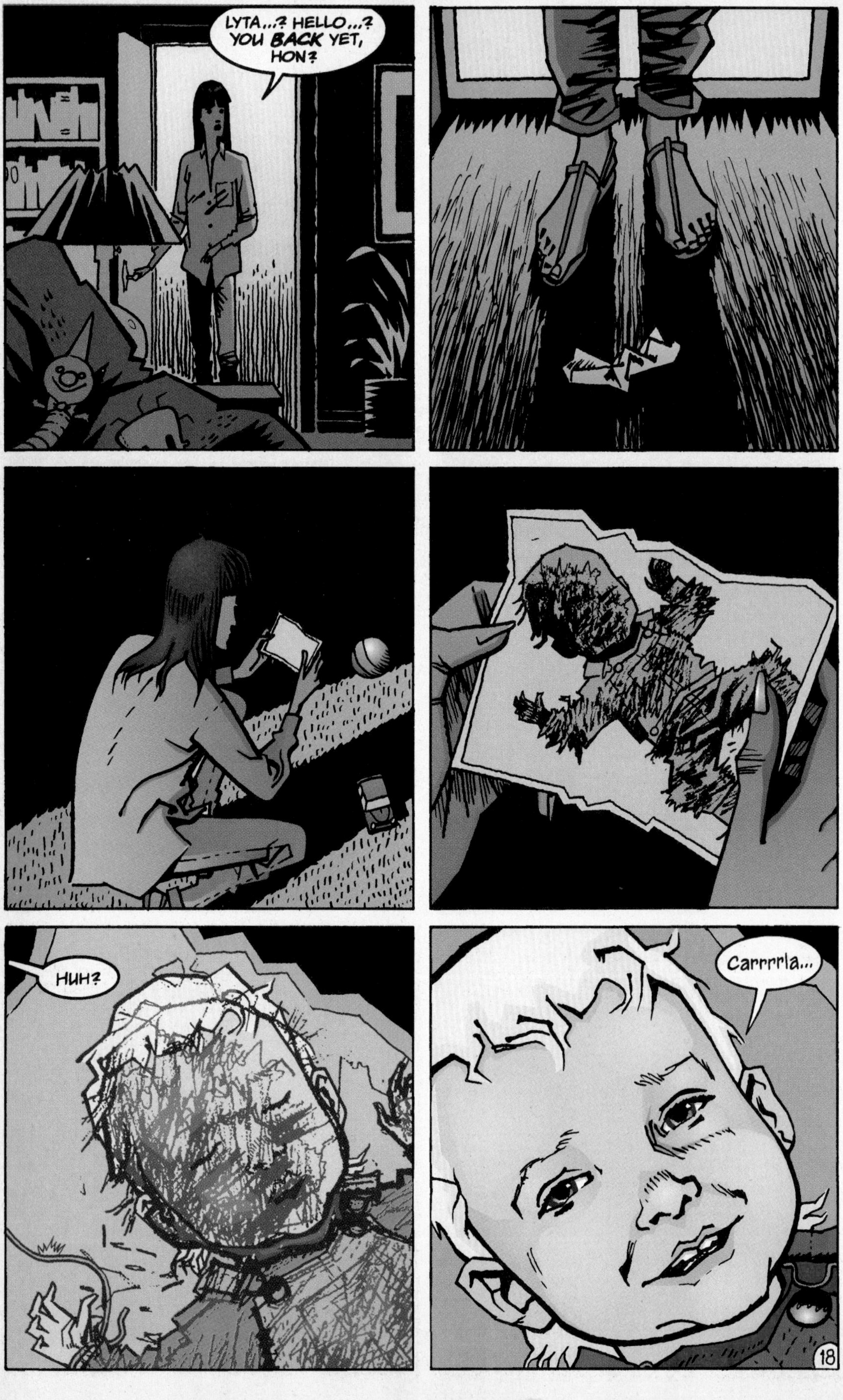
LYTA...? HELLO...? YOU BACK YET, HON?
HUH?
Carrrrla...

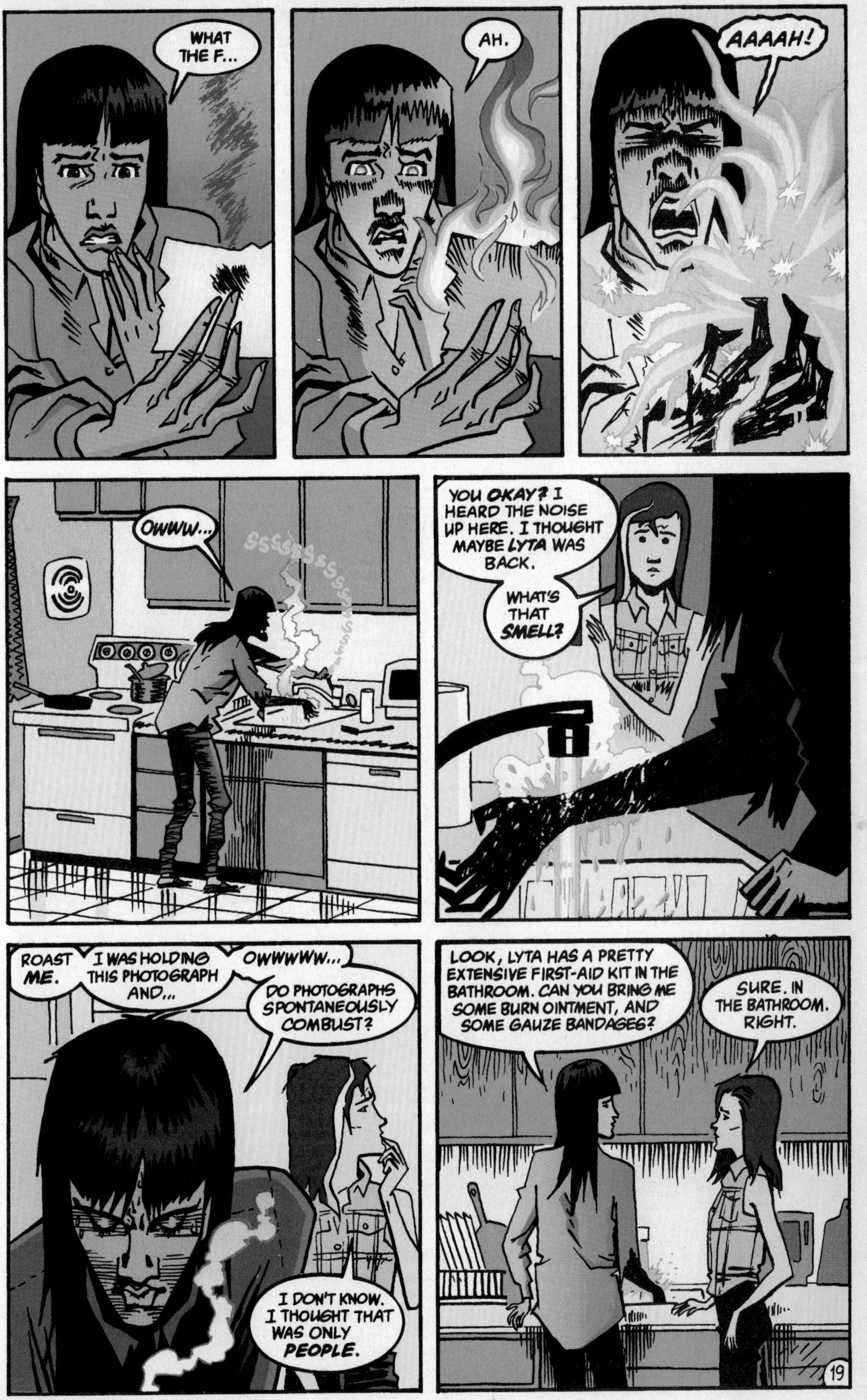
WHAT THE F...
AH.
AAAAH!
OWWW...
SSSSSSSSSSSS
YOU OKAY? I HEARD THE NOISE UP HERE. I THOUGHT MAYBE LYTA WAS BACK.
WHAT'S THAT SMELL?
ROAST ME.
I WAS HOLDING THIS PHOTOGRAPH AND...
OWWWWW...
DO PHOTOGRAPHS SPONTANEOUSLY COMBUST?
I DON'T KNOW. I THOUGHT THAT WAS ONLY PEOPLE.
LOOK, LYTA HAS A PRETTY EXTENSIVE FIRST-AID KIT IN THE BATHROOM. CAN YOU BRING ME SOME BURN OINTMENT, AND SOME GAUZE BANDAGES?
SURE. IN THE BATHROOM. RIGHT.
19

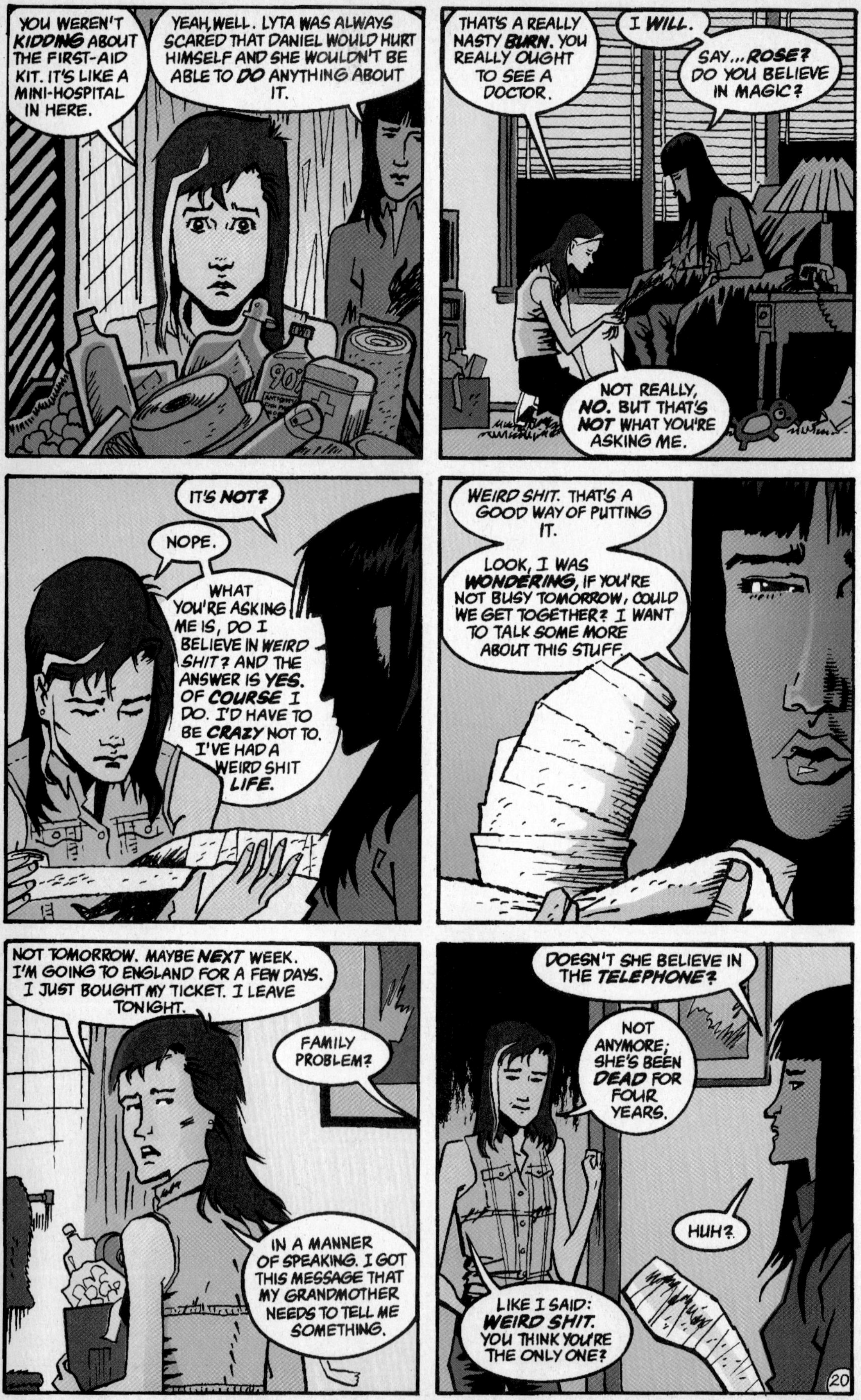
YOU WEREN'T KIDDING ABOUT THE FIRST-AID KIT. IT'S LIKE A MINI-HOSPITAL IN HERE.
YEAH, WELL. LYTA WAS ALWAYS SCARED THAT DANIEL WOULD HURT HIMSELF AND SHE WOULDN'T BE ABLE TO DO ANYTHING ABOUT IT.
THAT'S A REALLY NASTY BURN. YOU REALLY OUGHT TO SEE A DOCTOR.
I WILL.
SAY... ROSE? DO YOU BELIEVE IN MAGIC?
NOT REALLY, NO. BUT THAT'S NOT WHAT YOU'RE ASKING ME.
IT'S NOT?
NOPE.
WHAT YOU'RE ASKING ME IS, DO I BELIEVE IN WEIRD SHIT? AND THE ANSWER IS YES. OF COURSE I DO. I'D HAVE TO BE CRAZY NOT TO. I'VE HAD A WEIRD SHIT LIFE.
WEIRD SHIT. THAT'S A GOOD WAY OF PUTTING IT.
LOOK, I WAS WONDERING, IF YOU'RE NOT BUSY TOMORROW, COULD WE GET TOGETHER? I WANT TO TALK SOME MORE ABOUT THIS STUFF.
NOT TOMORROW. MAYBE NEXT WEEK. I'M GOING TO ENGLAND FOR A FEW DAYS. I JUST BOUGHT MY TICKET. I LEAVE TONIGHT.
FAMILY PROBLEM?
IN A MANNER OF SPEAKING. I GOT THIS MESSAGE THAT MY GRANDMOTHER NEEDS TO TELL ME SOMETHING.
DOESN'T SHE BELIEVE IN THE TELEPHONE?
NOT ANYMORE; SHE'S BEEN DEAD FOR FOUR YEARS.
HUH?
LIKE I SAID: WEIRD SHIT. YOU THINK YOU'RE THE ONLY ONE?
20

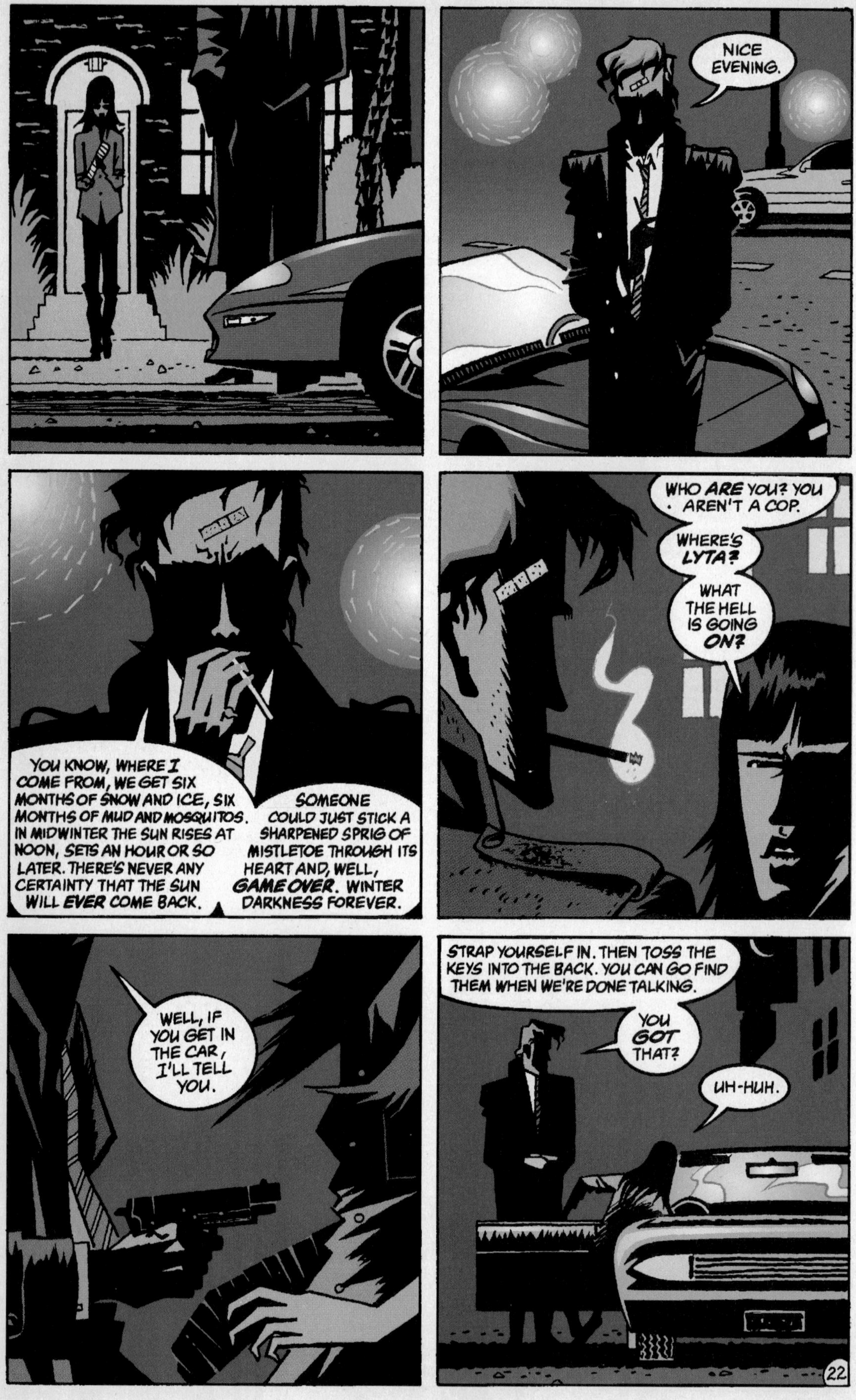

NICE EVENING.
YOU KNOW, WHERE I COME FROM, WE GET SIX MONTHS OF SNOW AND ICE, SIX MONTHS OF MUD AND MOSQUITOS. IN MIDWINTER THE SUN RISES AT NOON, SETS AN HOUR OR SO LATER. THERE'S NEVER ANY CERTAINTY THAT THE SUN WILL EVER COME BACK.
SOMEONE COULD JUST STICK A SHARPENED SPRIG OF MISTLETOE THROUGH ITS HEART AND, WELL, GAME OVER. WINTER DARKNESS FOREVER.
WHO ARE YOU? YOU AREN'T A COP.
WHERE'S LYTA?
WHAT THE HELL IS GOING ON?
WELL, IF YOU GET IN THE CAR, I'LL TELL YOU.
STRAP YOURSELF IN. THEN TOSS THE KEYS INTO THE BACK. YOU CAN GO FIND THEM WHEN WE'RE DONE TALKING.
YOU GOT THAT?
UH-HUH.

part,
Slow

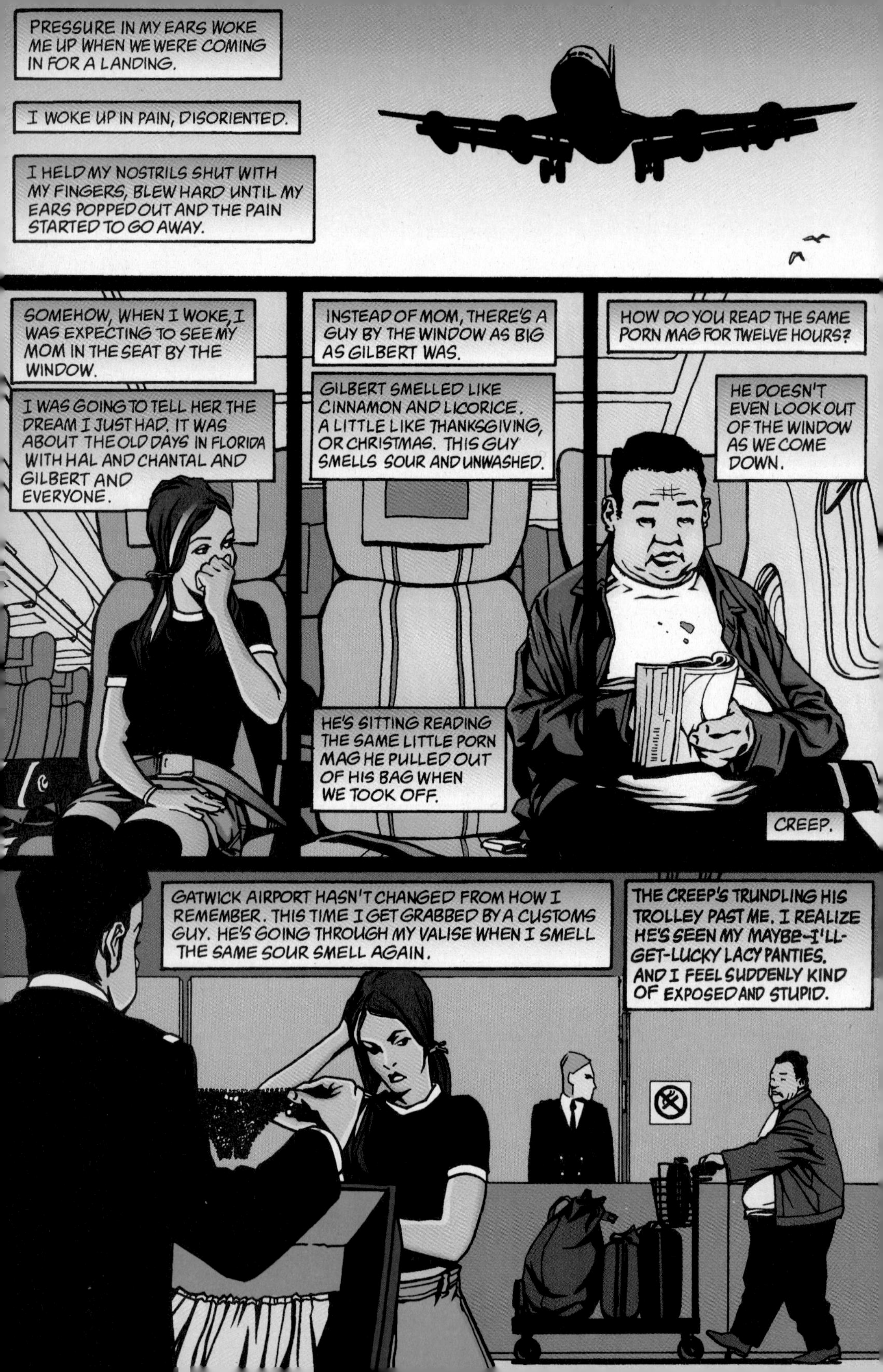
PRESSURE IN MY EARS WOKE ME UP WHEN WE WERE COMING IN FOR A LANDING.
I WOKE UP IN PAIN, DISORIENTED.
I HELD MY NOSTRILS SHUT WITH MY FINGERS, BLEW HARD UNTIL MY EARS POPPED OUT AND THE PAIN STARTED TO GO AWAY.
SOMEHOW, WHEN I WOKE, I WAS EXPECTING TO SEE MY MOM IN THE SEAT BY THE WINDOW.
I WAS GOING TO TELL HER THE DREAM I JUST HAD. IT WAS ABOUT THE OLD DAYS IN FLORIDA WITH HAL AND CHANTAL AND GILBERT AND EVERYONE.
INSTEAD OF MOM, THERE'S A GUY BY THE WINDOW AS BIG AS GILBERT WAS.
GILBERT SMELLED LIKE CINNAMON AND LICORICE. A LITTLE LIKE THANKSGIVING, OR CHRISTMAS. THIS GUY SMELLS SOUR AND UNWASHED.
HE'S SITTING READING THE SAME LITTLE PORN MAG HE PULLED OUT OF HIS BAG WHEN WE TOOK OFF.
HOW DO YOU READ THE SAME PORN MAG FOR TWELVE HOURS?
HE DOESN'T EVEN LOOK OUT OF THE WINDOW AS WE COME DOWN.
CREEP.
GATWICK AIRPORT HASN'T CHANGED FROM HOW I REMEMBER. THIS TIME I GET GRABBED BY A CUSTOMS GUY. HE'S GOING THROUGH MY VALISE WHEN I SMELL THE SAME SOUR SMELL AGAIN.
THE CREEP'S TRUNDLING HIS TROLLEY PAST ME. I REALIZE HE'S SEEN MY MAYBE-I'LL-GET-LUCKY LACY PANTIES. AND I FEEL SUDDENLY KIND OF EXPOSED AND STUPID.

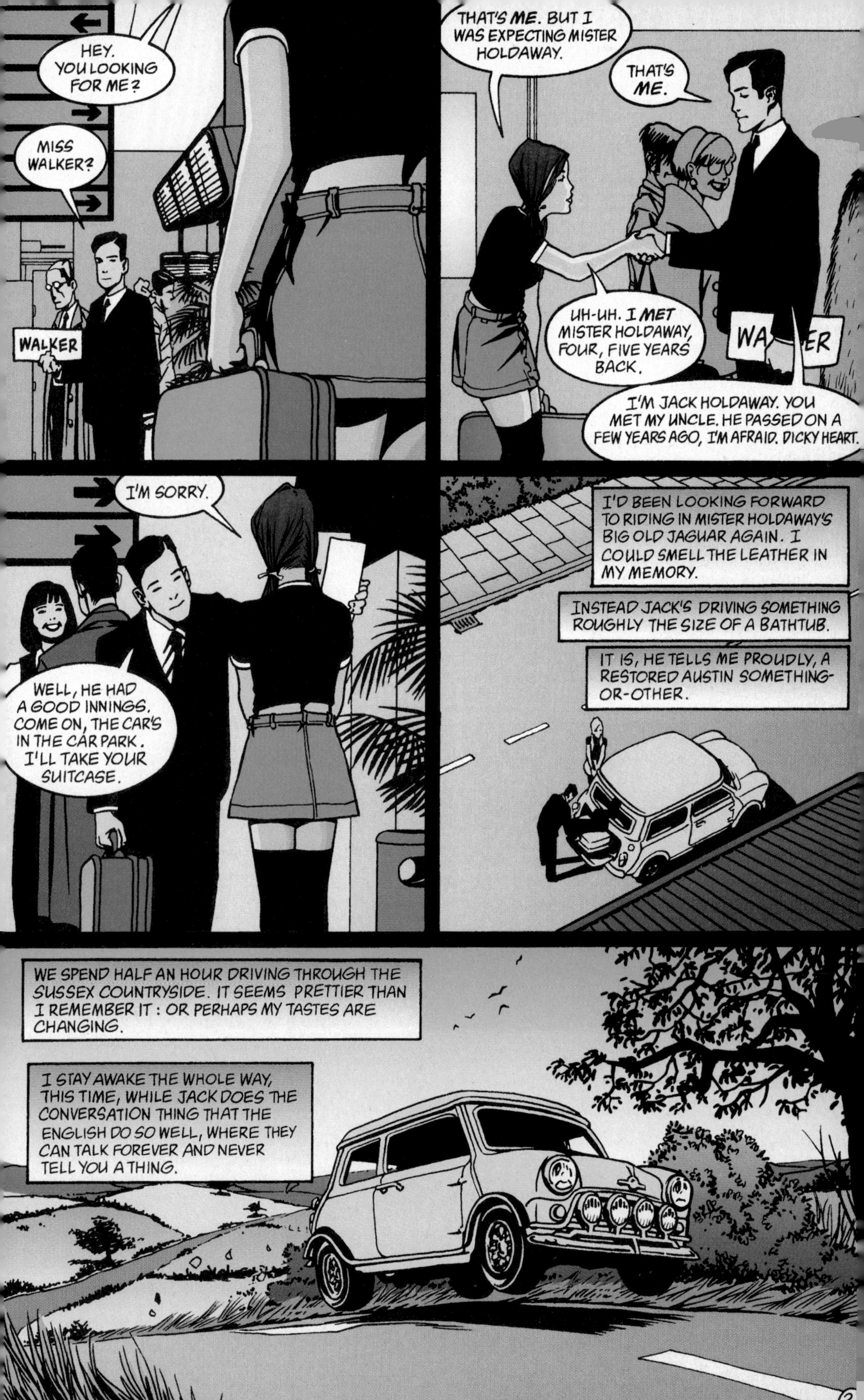
HEY. YOU LOOKING FOR ME?
MISS WALKER?
WALKER
THAT'S ME. BUT I WAS EXPECTING MISTER HOLDAWAY.
THAT'S ME.
UH-UH. I MET MISTER HOLDAWAY, FOUR, FIVE YEARS BACK.
I'M JACK HOLDAWAY. YOU MET MY UNCLE. HE PASSED ON A FEW YEARS AGO, I'M AFRAID. DICKY HEART.
I'M SORRY.
WELL, HE HAD A GOOD INNINGS. COME ON, THE CAR'S IN THE CAR PARK. I'LL TAKE YOUR SUITCASE.
I'D BEEN LOOKING FORWARD TO RIDING IN MISTER HOLDAWAY'S BIG OLD JAGUAR AGAIN. I COULD SMELL THE LEATHER IN MY MEMORY.
INSTEAD JACK'S DRIVING SOMETHING ROUGHLY THE SIZE OF A BATHTUB.
IT IS, HE TELLS ME PROUDLY, A RESTORED AUSTIN SOMETHING-OR-OTHER.
WE SPEND HALF AN HOUR DRIVING THROUGH THE SUSSEX COUNTRYSIDE. IT SEEMS PRETTIER THAN I REMEMBER IT : OR PERHAPS MY TASTES ARE CHANGING.
I STAY AWAKE THE WHOLE WAY, THIS TIME, WHILE JACK DOES THE CONVERSATION THING THAT THE ENGLISH DO SO WELL, WHERE THEY CAN TALK FOREVER AND NEVER TELL YOU A THING.

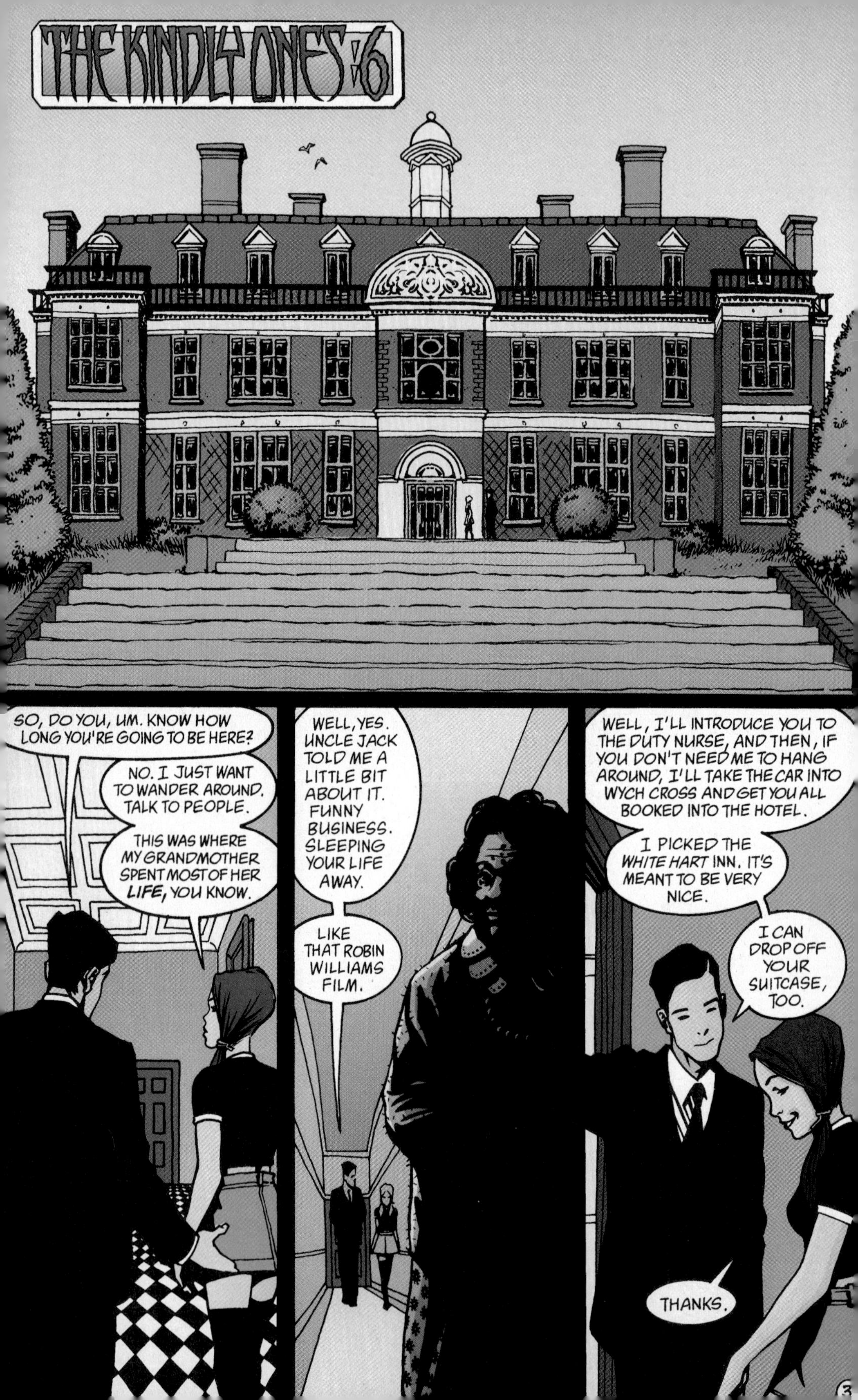
THE KINDLY ONES: 6
SO, DO YOU, UM. KNOW HOW LONG YOU'RE GOING TO BE HERE?
NO. I JUST WANT TO WANDER AROUND. TALK TO PEOPLE.
THIS WAS WHERE MY GRANDMOTHER SPENT MOST OF HER LIFE, YOU KNOW.
WELL, YES. UNCLE JACK TOLD ME A LITTLE BIT ABOUT IT. FUNNY BUSINESS. SLEEPING YOUR LIFE AWAY.
LIKE THAT ROBIN WILLIAMS FILM.
WELL, I'LL INTRODUCE YOU TO THE DUTY NURSE, AND THEN, IF YOU DON'T NEED ME TO HANG AROUND, I'LL TAKE THE CAR INTO WYCH CROSS AND GET YOU ALL BOOKED INTO THE HOTEL.
I PICKED THE WHITE HART INN. IT'S MEANT TO BE VERY NICE.
I CAN DROP OFF YOUR SUITCASE, TOO.
THANKS.
3

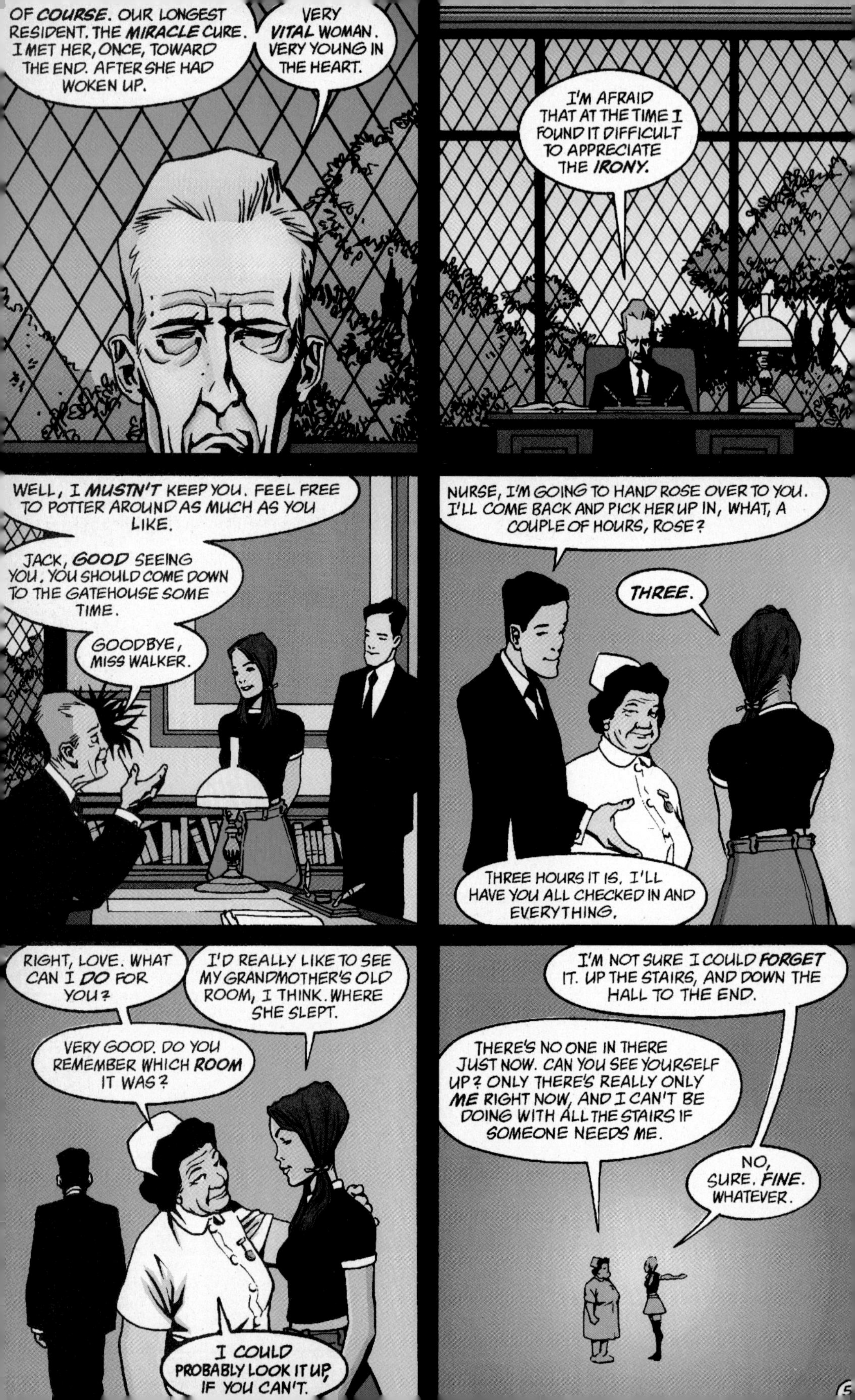
OF COURSE. OUR LONGEST RESIDENT. THE MIRACLE CURE. I MET HER, ONCE, TOWARD THE END. AFTER SHE HAD WOKEN UP.
VERY VITAL WOMAN. VERY YOUNG IN THE HEART.
I'M AFRAID THAT AT THE TIME I FOUND IT DIFFICULT TO APPRECIATE THE IRONY.
WELL, I MUSTN'T KEEP YOU. FEEL FREE TO POTTER AROUND AS MUCH AS YOU LIKE.
JACK, GOOD SEEING YOU. YOU SHOULD COME DOWN TO THE GATEHOUSE SOME TIME.
GOODBYE, MISS WALKER.
NURSE, I'M GOING TO HAND ROSE OVER TO YOU. I'LL COME BACK AND PICK HER UP IN, WHAT, A COUPLE OF HOURS, ROSE?
THREE.
THREE HOURS IT IS. I'LL HAVE YOU ALL CHECKED IN AND EVERYTHING.
RIGHT, LOVE. WHAT CAN I DO FOR YOU?
I'D REALLY LIKE TO SEE MY GRANDMOTHER'S OLD ROOM, I THINK. WHERE SHE SLEPT.
VERY GOOD. DO YOU REMEMBER WHICH ROOM IT WAS?
I COULD PROBABLY LOOK IT UP, IF YOU CAN'T.
I'M NOT SURE I COULD FORGET IT. UP THE STAIRS, AND DOWN THE HALL TO THE END.
THERE'S NO ONE IN THERE JUST NOW. CAN YOU SEE YOURSELF UP? ONLY THERE'S REALLY ONLY ME RIGHT NOW, AND I CAN'T BE DOING WITH ALL THE STAIRS IF SOMEONE NEEDS ME.
NO, SURE. FINE. WHATEVER.

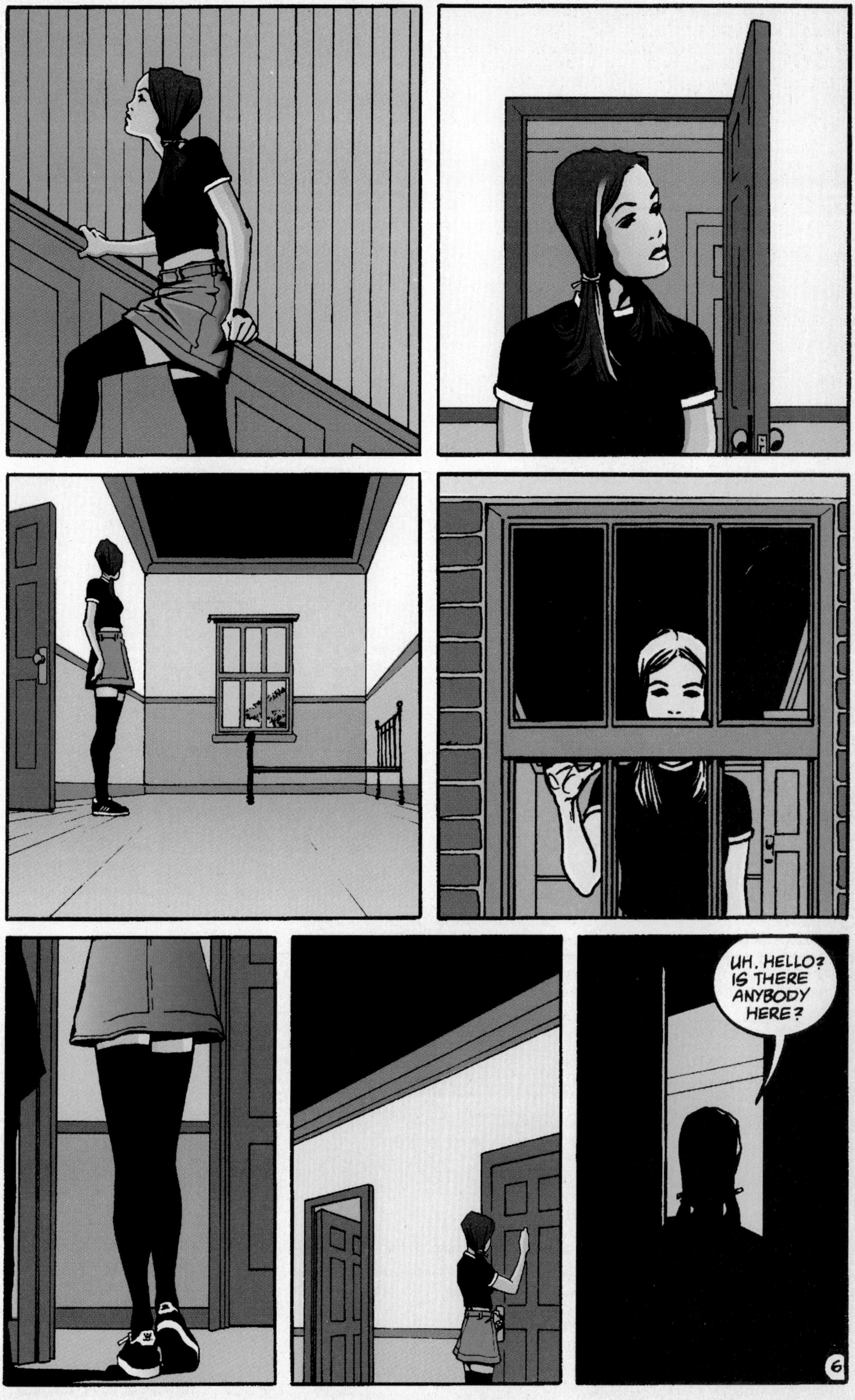
UH. HELLO?
IS THERE
ANYBODY
HERE?

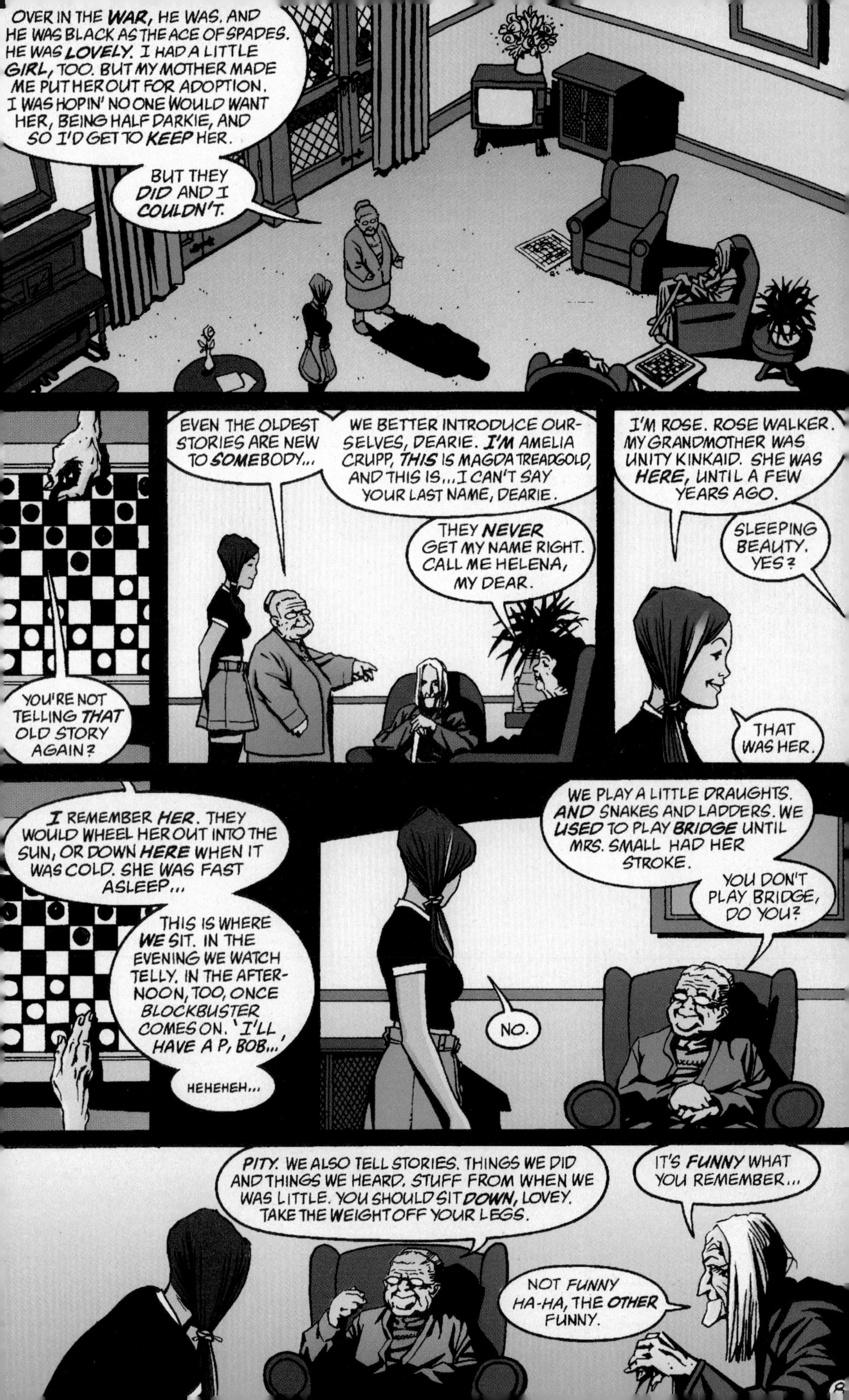
OVER IN THE WAR, HE WAS. AND HE WAS BLACK AS THE ACE OF SPADES. HE WAS LOVELY. I HAD A LITTLE GIRL, TOO. BUT MY MOTHER MADE ME PUT HER OUT FOR ADOPTION. I WAS HOPIN' NO ONE WOULD WANT HER, BEING HALF DARKIE, AND SO I'D GET TO KEEP HER.
BUT THEY DID AND I COULDN'T.
YOU'RE NOT TELLING THAT OLD STORY AGAIN?
EVEN THE OLDEST STORIES ARE NEW TO SOMEBODY...
WE BETTER INTRODUCE OURSELVES, DEARIE. I'M AMELIA CRUPP, THIS IS MAGDA TREADGOLD, AND THIS IS... I CAN'T SAY YOUR LAST NAME, DEARIE.
THEY NEVER GET MY NAME RIGHT. CALL ME HELENA, MY DEAR.
I'M ROSE. ROSE WALKER. MY GRANDMOTHER WAS UNITY KINKAID. SHE WAS HERE, UNTIL A FEW YEARS AGO.
SLEEPING BEAUTY. YES?
THAT WAS HER.
I REMEMBER HER. THEY WOULD WHEEL HER OUT INTO THE SUN, OR DOWN HERE WHEN IT WAS COLD. SHE WAS FAST ASLEEP...
THIS IS WHERE WE SIT. IN THE EVENING WE WATCH TELLY. IN THE AFTERNOON, TOO, ONCE BLOCKBUSTER COMES ON. 'I'LL HAVE A P, BOB...'
HEHEHEH...
WE PLAY A LITTLE DRAUGHTS. AND SNAKES AND LADDERS. WE USED TO PLAY BRIDGE UNTIL MRS. SMALL HAD HER STROKE.
YOU DON'T PLAY BRIDGE, DO YOU?
NO.
PITY. WE ALSO TELL STORIES. THINGS WE DID AND THINGS WE HEARD. STUFF FROM WHEN WE WAS LITTLE. YOU SHOULD SIT DOWN, LOVEY. TAKE THE WEIGHT OFF YOUR LEGS.
IT'S FUNNY WHAT YOU REMEMBER...
NOT FUNNY HA-HA, THE OTHER FUNNY.
8

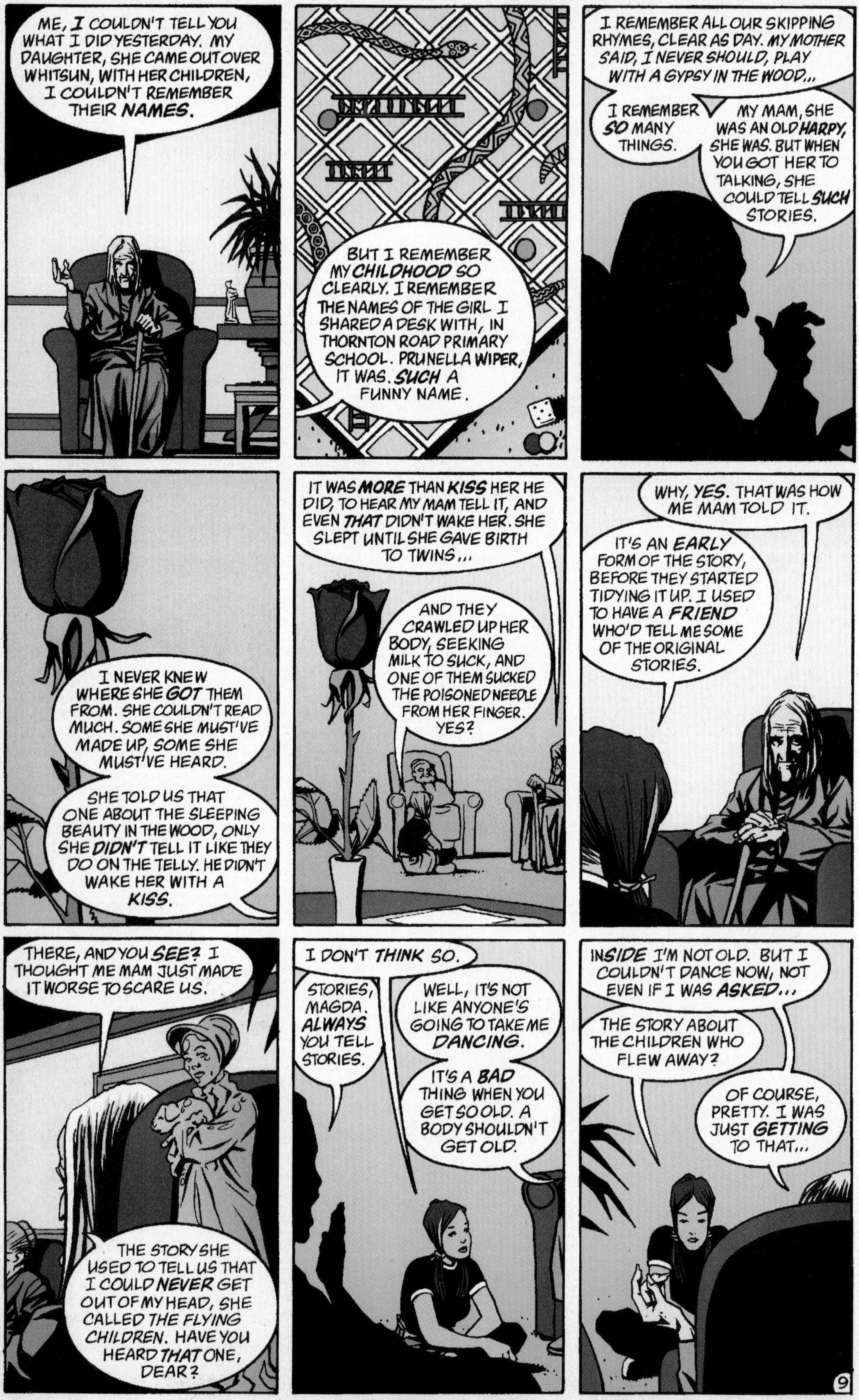

ME, I COULDN'T TELL YOU WHAT I DID YESTERDAY. MY DAUGHTER, SHE CAME OUT OVER WHITSUN, WITH HER CHILDREN, I COULDN'T REMEMBER THEIR NAMES.
BUT I REMEMBER MY CHILDHOOD SO CLEARLY. I REMEMBER THE NAMES OF THE GIRL I SHARED A DESK WITH, IN THORNTON ROAD PRIMARY SCHOOL. PRUNELLA WIPER, IT WAS. SUCH A FUNNY NAME.
I REMEMBER ALL OUR SKIPPING RHYMES, CLEAR AS DAY. MY MOTHER SAID, I NEVER SHOULD, PLAY WITH A GYPSY IN THE WOOD...
I REMEMBER SO MANY THINGS.
MY MAM, SHE WAS AN OLD HARPY, SHE WAS. BUT WHEN YOU GOT HER TO TALKING, SHE COULD TELL SUCH STORIES.
I NEVER KNEW WHERE SHE GOT THEM FROM. SHE COULDN'T READ MUCH. SOME SHE MUST'VE MADE UP, SOME SHE MUST'VE HEARD.
SHE TOLD US THAT ONE ABOUT THE SLEEPING BEAUTY IN THE WOOD, ONLY SHE DIDN'T TELL IT LIKE THEY DO ON THE TELLY. HE DIDN'T WAKE HER WITH A KISS.
IT WAS MORE THAN KISS HER HE DID, TO HEAR MY MAM TELL IT, AND EVEN THAT DIDN'T WAKE HER. SHE SLEPT UNTIL SHE GAVE BIRTH TO TWINS...
AND THEY CRAWLED UP HER BODY, SEEKING MILK TO SUCK, AND ONE OF THEM SUCKED THE POISONED NEEDLE FROM HER FINGER. YES?
WHY, YES. THAT WAS HOW ME MAM TOLD IT.
IT'S AN EARLY FORM OF THE STORY, BEFORE THEY STARTED TIDYING IT UP. I USED TO HAVE A FRIEND WHO'D TELL ME SOME OF THE ORIGINAL STORIES.
THERE, AND YOU SEE? I THOUGHT ME MAM JUST MADE IT WORSE TO SCARE US.
THE STORY SHE USED TO TELL US THAT I COULD NEVER GET OUT OF MY HEAD, SHE CALLED THE FLYING CHILDREN. HAVE YOU HEARD THAT ONE, DEAR?
I DON'T THINK SO.
STORIES, MAGDA. ALWAYS YOU TELL STORIES.
WELL, IT'S NOT LIKE ANYONE'S GOING TO TAKE ME DANCING.
IT'S A BAD THING WHEN YOU GET SO OLD. A BODY SHOULDN'T GET OLD.
INSIDE I'M NOT OLD. BUT I COULDN'T DANCE NOW, NOT EVEN IF I WAS ASKED...
THE STORY ABOUT THE CHILDREN WHO FLEW AWAY?
OF COURSE, PRETTY. I WAS JUST GETTING TO THAT...

Well, the way me mam told it, there was a man who loved the ladies. He was always carrying on with one pretty face after another. Loved 'em, and forgot 'em as he went from town to town.

So one day he spied a gal washing herself in the river, mother-naked and all in her birthday suit. So he hides her clothes. And when she comes out of the river, she sees him.

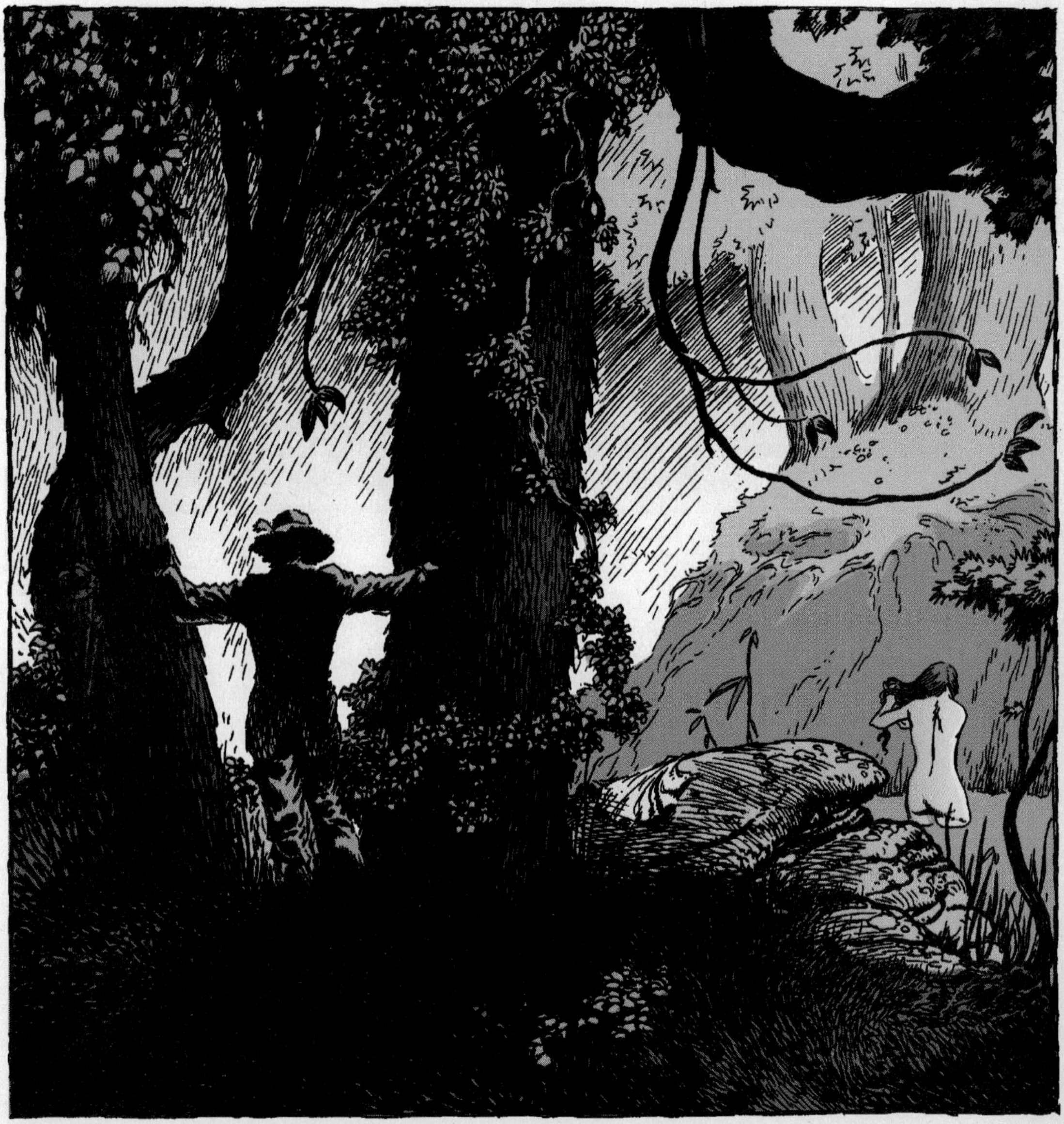

He says he'll give her back her clothes if she'll be his lady-love, but she won't be his lady unless he swears he'll make her his wife--and in the first church they come to, at that.

I swear if I set foot in a church, it'll be to marry you, he said (and the devil he'd step into a church ever again, he swore under his breath).

And what'll you swear, she asks, *if you break the vow?*

f I don't marry you, he said, may that worms shall eat me (for they'll do that anyway, he thought, when my time's over and up), and if I don't marry you, I wish our children might grow wings and fly away (and no great matter if they do, he thought).

So they kissed then and there, and did other things besides, and when they were all done, he gave her her clothes back, and she followed him down the road.

They passed the first church. Let's get married here, she says. Oh, he says, we can't get married here, for the vicar's a sick man, and besides, he's off a-hunting.

She said nothing but she looked at him as if her heart would break.

When they came to the next church, her belly was already beginning to swell.

Let's be married here, she says.

I'm not going into that church, he says, for the vicar's a drunkard, and no better than he should be, and the sexton's no partic'lar friend of mine, neither.

But you SWORE, she said.

I'm not going in the church, he tells her, and he knocks her down.

Her face is bleeding when she gets up.

So THAT'S how it is, she says.

That's how it is, he tells her.

⑪

Well, she says, my belly's big with child. And I want to stop for a while. I can't keep on the road. Isn't there a place where I can rest?

So he has her stop there and sit, at the side of the road, and he goes on ahead.

He gets to a cottage, and he goes into the cottage, for the door's just on the latch, not locked, and in the cottage he sees an old woman fast asleep on the bed.

Now, sometimes the way me mam would tell it, the woman was a witch, and sometimes when she told it, she wasn't. But whichever, she was old and weak, and he held her mouth shut, and held his fingers over her nose until she couldn't breathe no more, and he took her out the back, and buried her in the midden heap.

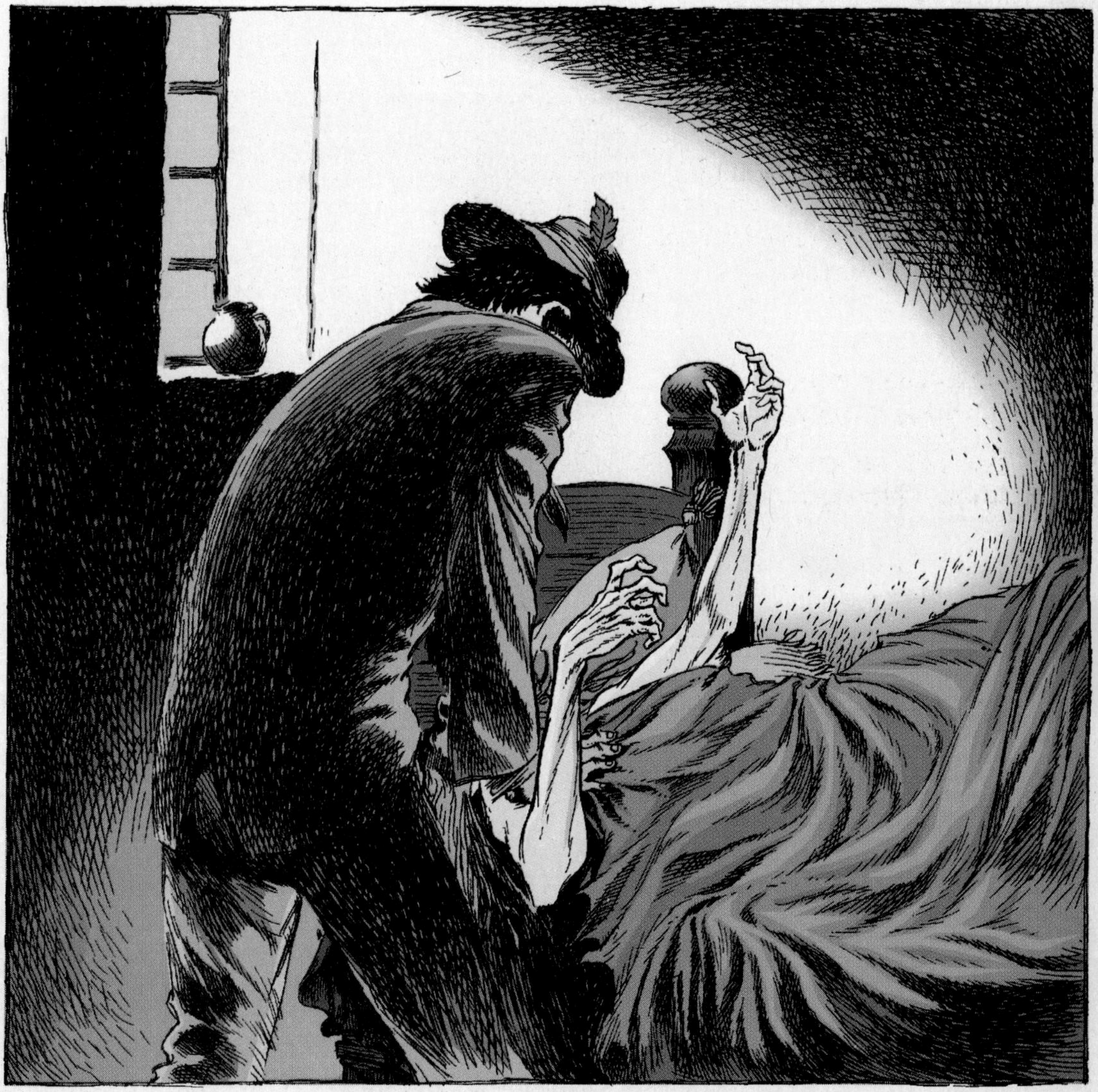

He went back to his wife, and he says *It's a good thing we passed by here, as my old aunt has just died and left us her cottage.*

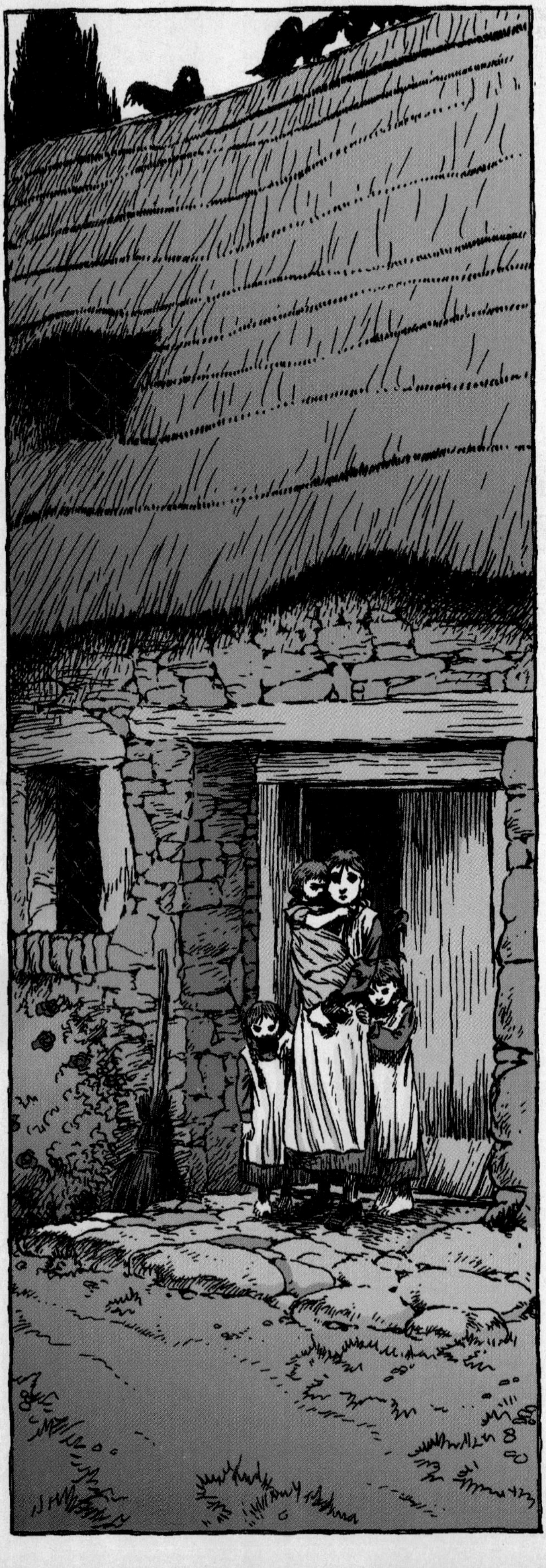

Oh, he was a bad one, that man. So he took her to the cottage...

He was a man. They're all bad.

Not my Danny, he wasn't, God rest him.

So he took her to the cottage...?

Yes, dear, and there he left her. He'd come back every few weeks to make sure she was still there, and to see his children, for she had three lovely girls over the next few years. But he was only home for a day here or there, and then he'd be off tomcatting over the whole countryside again.

It was a deserted part of the country, but there were vegetables in the garden, and now and then he'd bring her back a hen or a pig, so she never starved, and neither did the children.

Only, one day he comes home, and the children are nowhere to be seen. And the little girls are the apples of his eye...

Where are the children? He asks his wife. Gathering berries, she says.

In the spring? He says. (There aren't any berries in the spring, dear. I don't know if they have spring where you come from.)

But she says nothing, and the children don't come home.

So when night comes, he says to her Where's the children? Off fishing, she tells him.

The baby too? he asks her. But she pretended she couldn't hear him.

In the morning he woke her up: Where are the children? WHERE ARE MY GIRLS?

They've flown away, she told him.

Flown away? He shakes her to make her tell him the truth, but she won't change her tale.

So he fetches the axe in from outside, and he chops her up into bits.

There's a noise from outside, so he pushes the lumps and limbs and lights of her under their bed.

And it's his daughters, the oldest, the middle, and the little wee baby, coming down from the sky, each on wings.

They come inside the cottage.

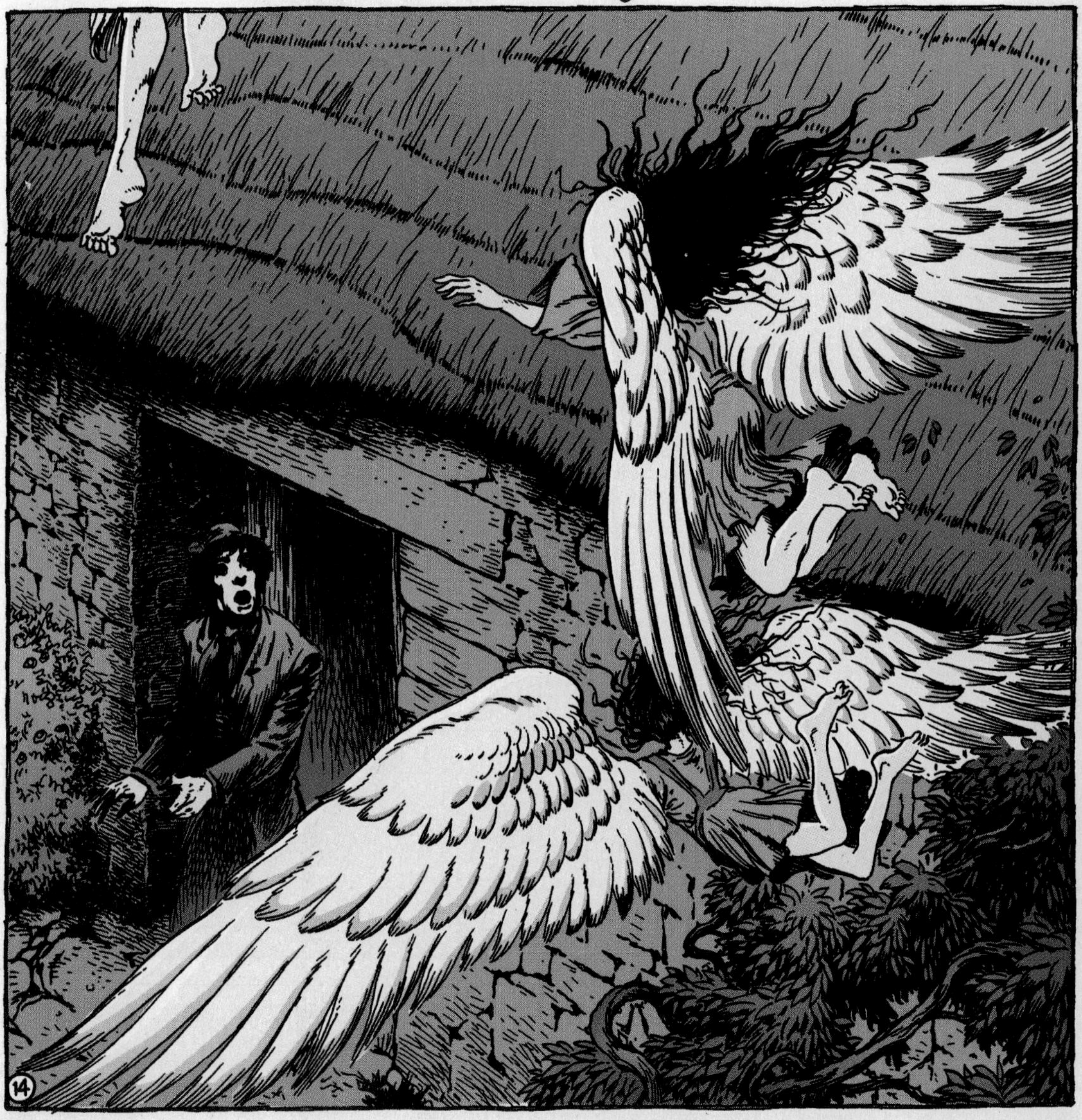

Where's our mam? they asked him.

She's out, picking berries, he tells them.

And what's all this blood on your hands and on the floor?

I was killing a pig, he says.

But the youngest girl she looks under the bed, and she sees her mother's dead face, staring out at them.

And they let out a wail deep and long and sad. Then they fell on him, all three of them, teeth and claw, and they killed him. They left his body there on the floor.

And they flew off into the sky, and nobody saw them again.

And as soon as he was sure that he was dead, he got up and shook himself, and looked around, and there waiting for him on the bed was his wife, with long claws out, and her eyes blazing like a green cat ready to spring.

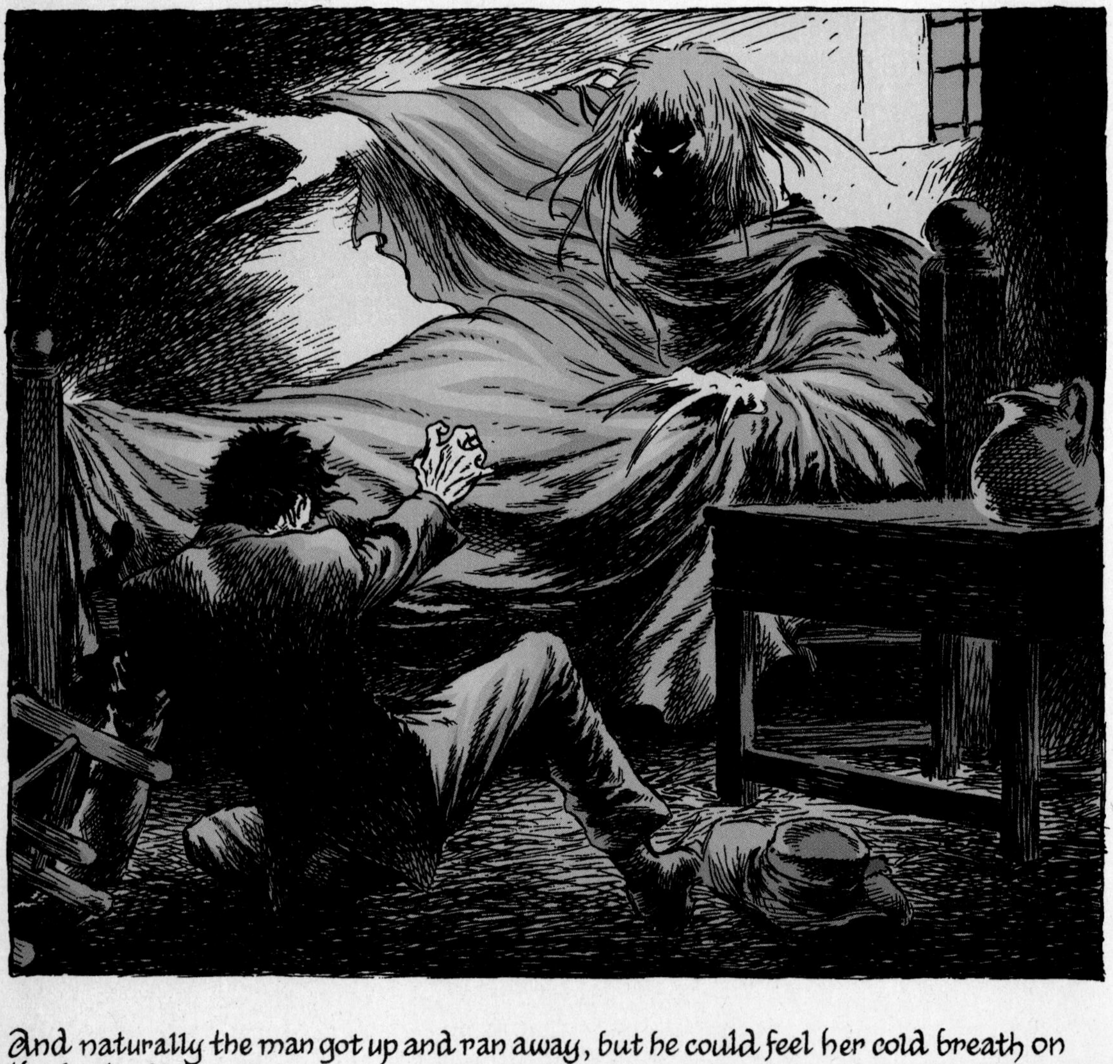

And naturally the man got up and ran away, but he could feel her cold breath on the back of his neck.

And he called out to the thunder, *Strike me dead*, but the thunder wouldn't, for he was dead already.

And he ran to the fire, and begged the fire to burn him up.

But the fire couldn't burn him, for the chill of death put it out...

And he threw himself in the water, and he screamed, *Drown me blue*, but the water wouldn't, for the death-color was coming into his face already, and the water tossed him out.

And last of all, he throws himself onto the ground, onto the midden-heap, and prays for the worms to come and eat him, so he could rest in his grave, and be quit of the woman.

He puts out one hand and he finds himself touching the skeleton hand of the old woman he'd killed for the cottage.

And he lies on the mud, his hand holding tight to that skeleton hand, waiting for his wife...

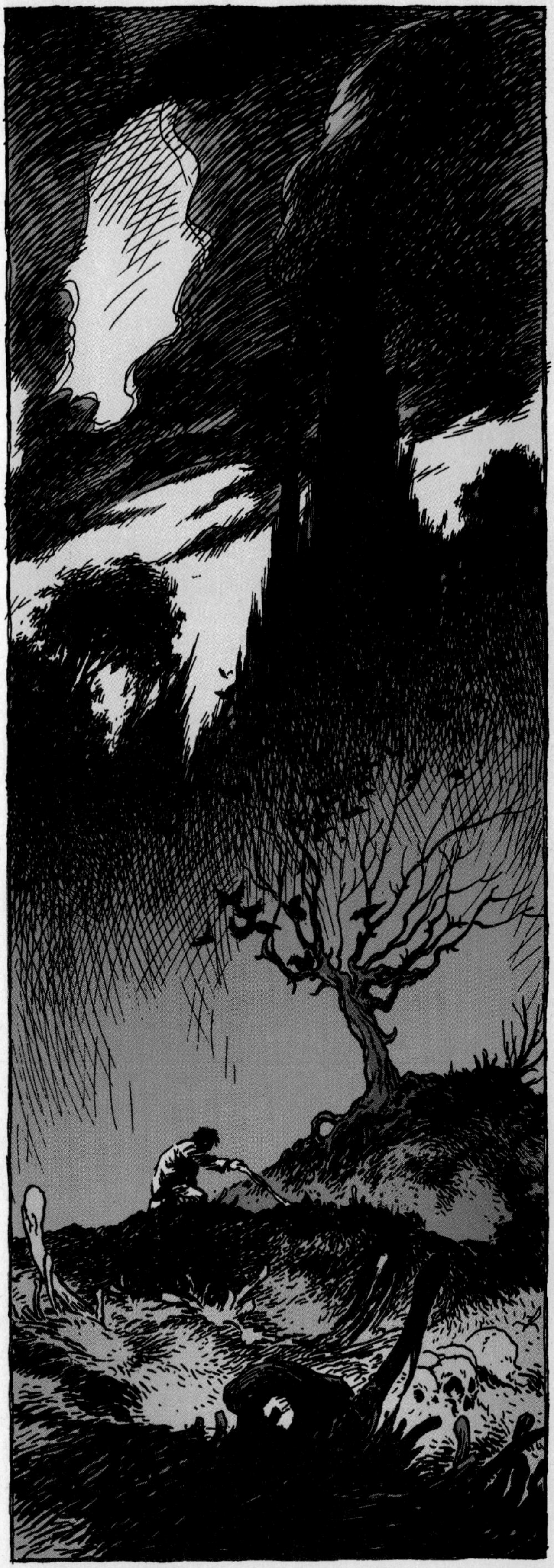

nd by and by along crept a great worm, and a strange thing it was, with his wife's face on the end of its long slimy body, and it crept up beside him and over him and all around him, and it druv all the other worms away. Her teeth were sharp and long.

And she wrapped her slimy worm body around his, and she whispered his name into his ear.

And he screams, Kill me, for god's sake, just get it over with. But she licks her lips with a long worm tongue, and she shakes her head.

A meal this good must never be hurried, she says. Just hold still, boy, and let me enjoy myself.

And she takes her first, gentle bite from his cheek with her sharp sharp teeth...

And that's the story, as my mother used to tell it.

17

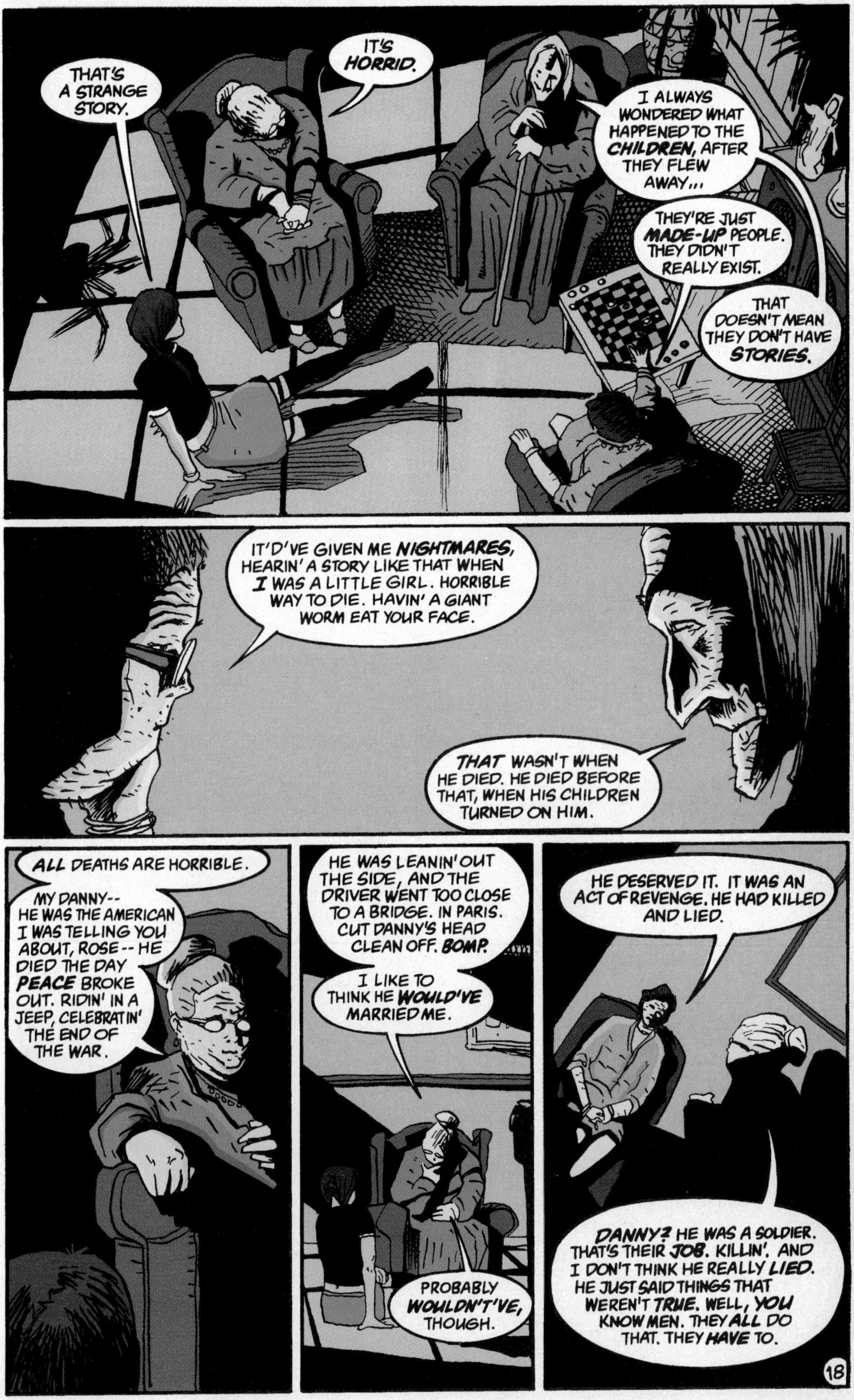

THAT'S A STRANGE STORY.
IT'S HORRID.
I ALWAYS WONDERED WHAT HAPPENED TO THE CHILDREN, AFTER THEY FLEW AWAY...
THEY'RE JUST MADE-UP PEOPLE. THEY DIDN'T REALLY EXIST.
THAT DOESN'T MEAN THEY DON'T HAVE STORIES.
IT'D'VE GIVEN ME NIGHTMARES, HEARIN' A STORY LIKE THAT WHEN I WAS A LITTLE GIRL. HORRIBLE WAY TO DIE. HAVIN' A GIANT WORM EAT YOUR FACE.
THAT WASN'T WHEN HE DIED. HE DIED BEFORE THAT, WHEN HIS CHILDREN TURNED ON HIM.
ALL DEATHS ARE HORRIBLE.
MY DANNY-- HE WAS THE AMERICAN I WAS TELLING YOU ABOUT, ROSE -- HE DIED THE DAY PEACE BROKE OUT. RIDIN' IN A JEEP, CELEBRATIN' THE END OF THE WAR.
HE WAS LEANIN' OUT THE SIDE, AND THE DRIVER WENT TOO CLOSE TO A BRIDGE. IN PARIS. CUT DANNY'S HEAD CLEAN OFF. BOMP.
I LIKE TO THINK HE WOULD'VE MARRIED ME.
PROBABLY WOULDN'T'VE, THOUGH.
HE DESERVED IT. IT WAS AN ACT OF REVENGE. HE HAD KILLED AND LIED.
DANNY? HE WAS A SOLDIER. THAT'S THEIR JOB. KILLIN'. AND I DON'T THINK HE REALLY LIED. HE JUST SAID THINGS THAT WEREN'T TRUE. WELL, YOU KNOW MEN. THEY ALL DO THAT. THEY HAVE TO.

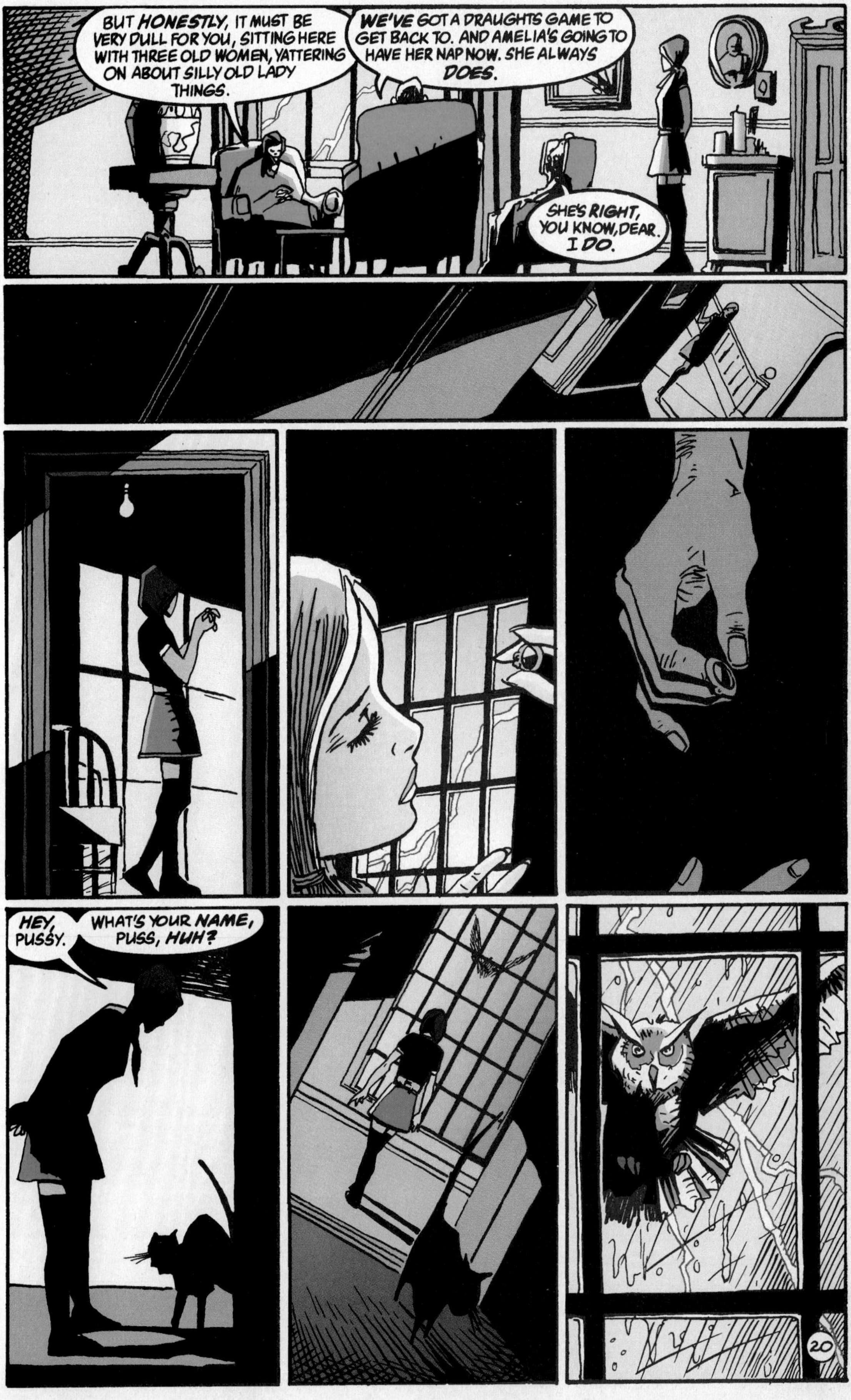
BUT HONESTLY, IT MUST BE VERY DULL FOR YOU, SITTING HERE WITH THREE OLD WOMEN, YATTERING ON ABOUT SILLY OLD LADY THINGS.
WE'VE GOT A DRAUGHTS GAME TO GET BACK TO. AND AMELIA'S GOING TO HAVE HER NAP NOW. SHE ALWAYS DOES.
SHE'S RIGHT, YOU KNOW, DEAR. I DO.
HEY, PUSSY.
WHAT'S YOUR NAME, PUSS, HUH?

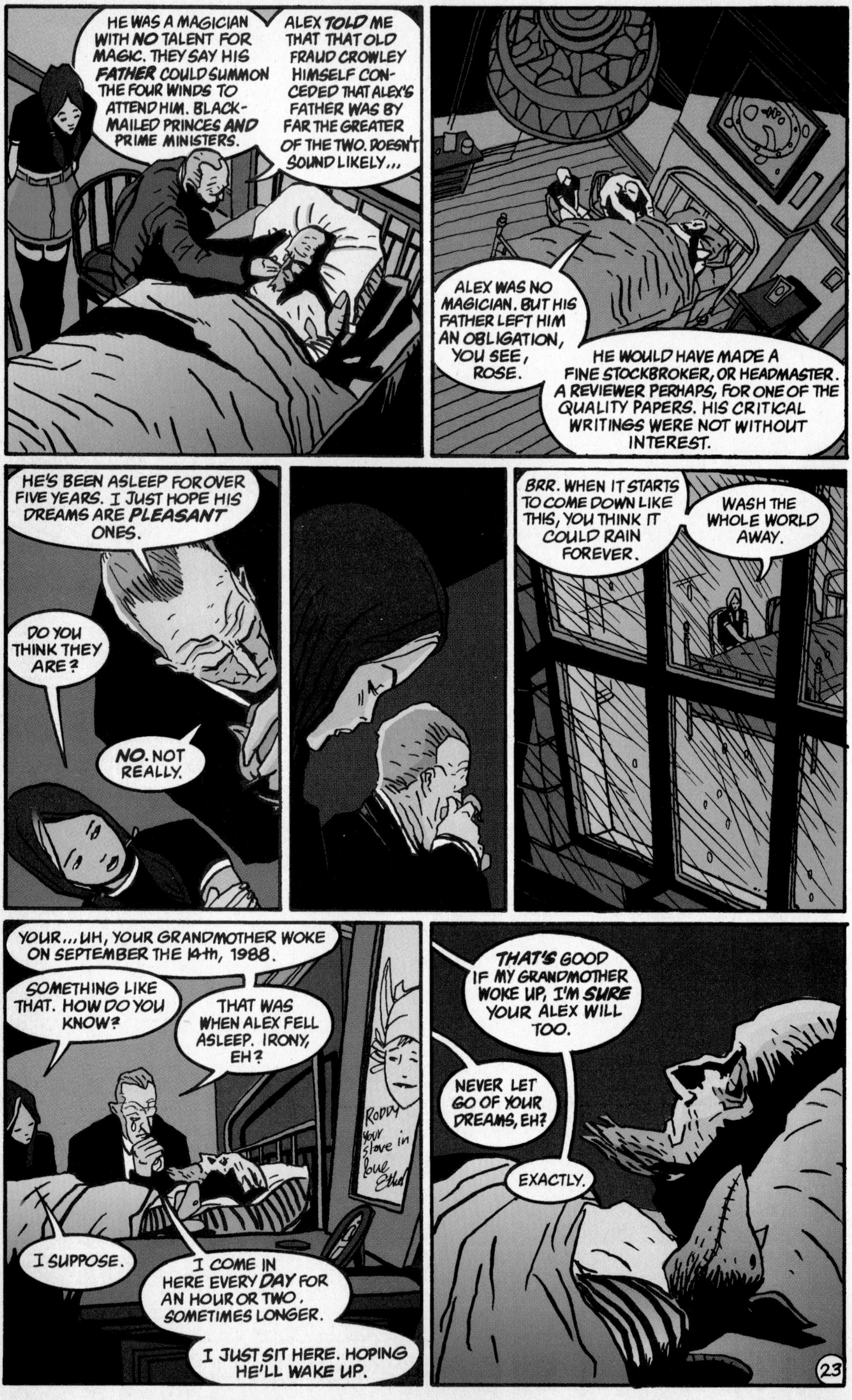
HE WAS A MAGICIAN WITH NO TALENT FOR MAGIC. THEY SAY HIS FATHER COULD SUMMON THE FOUR WINDS TO ATTEND HIM. BLACK-MAILED PRINCES AND PRIME MINISTERS.
ALEX TOLD ME THAT THAT OLD FRAUD CROWLEY HIMSELF CONCEDED THAT ALEX'S FATHER WAS BY FAR THE GREATER OF THE TWO. DOESN'T SOUND LIKELY...
ALEX WAS NO MAGICIAN. BUT HIS FATHER LEFT HIM AN OBLIGATION, YOU SEE, ROSE.
HE WOULD HAVE MADE A FINE STOCKBROKER, OR HEADMASTER. A REVIEWER PERHAPS, FOR ONE OF THE QUALITY PAPERS. HIS CRITICAL WRITINGS WERE NOT WITHOUT INTEREST.
HE'S BEEN ASLEEP FOR OVER FIVE YEARS. I JUST HOPE HIS DREAMS ARE PLEASANT ONES.
DO YOU THINK THEY ARE?
NO. NOT REALLY.
BRR. WHEN IT STARTS TO COME DOWN LIKE THIS, YOU THINK IT COULD RAIN FOREVER.
WASH THE WHOLE WORLD AWAY.
YOUR... UH, YOUR GRANDMOTHER WOKE ON SEPTEMBER THE 14th, 1988.
SOMETHING LIKE THAT. HOW DO YOU KNOW?
THAT WAS WHEN ALEX FELL ASLEEP. IRONY, EH?
RODDY your slave in love Ethel
I SUPPOSE.
I COME IN HERE EVERY DAY FOR AN HOUR OR TWO, SOMETIMES LONGER.
I JUST SIT HERE. HOPING HE'LL WAKE UP.
THAT'S GOOD IF MY GRANDMOTHER WOKE UP, I'M SURE YOUR ALEX WILL TOO.
NEVER LET GO OF YOUR DREAMS, EH?
EXACTLY.

part
SEVEN

tse   s   tse

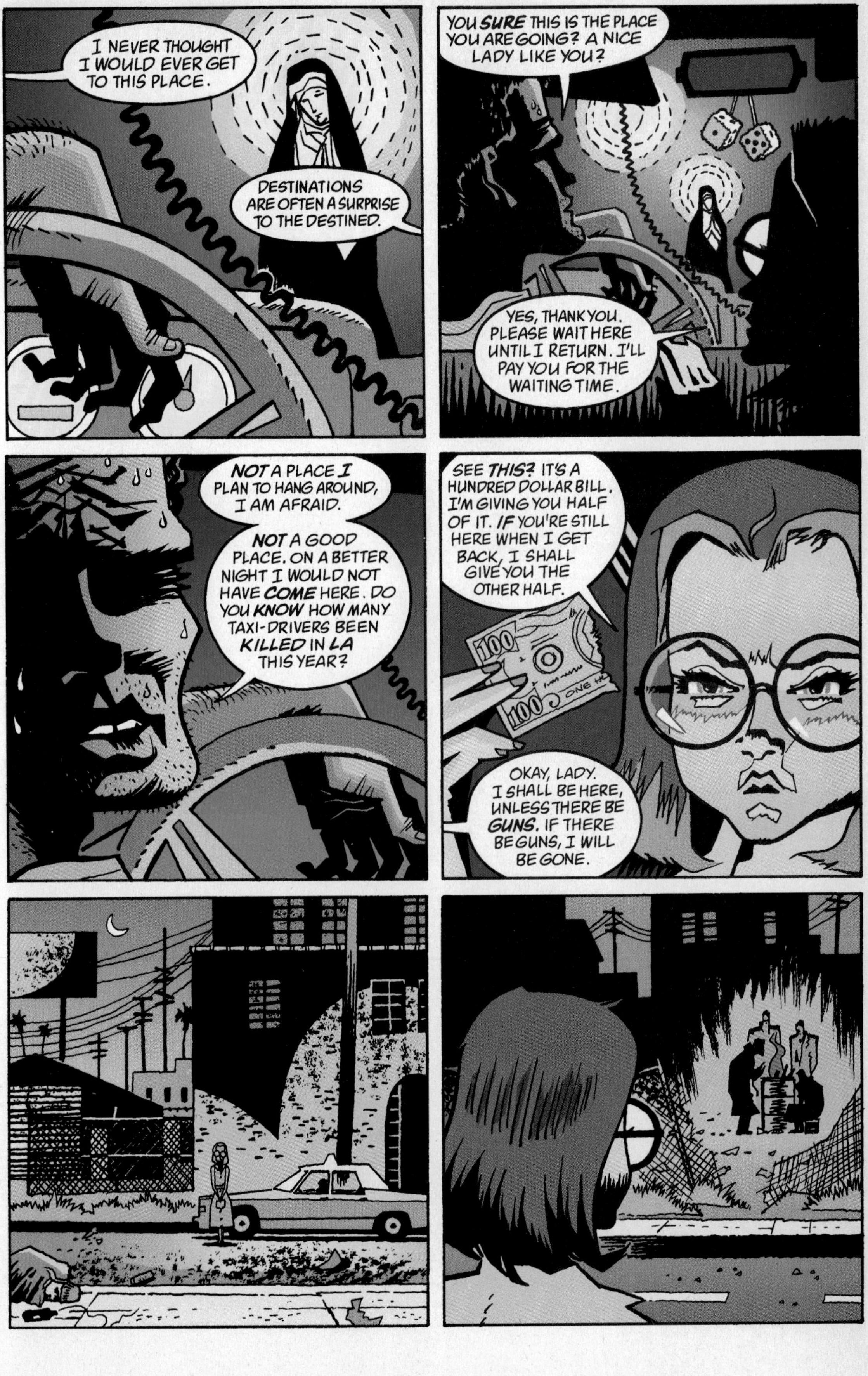
I NEVER THOUGHT I WOULD EVER GET TO THIS PLACE.
DESTINATIONS ARE OFTEN A SURPRISE TO THE DESTINED.
YOU SURE THIS IS THE PLACE YOU ARE GOING? A NICE LADY LIKE YOU?
YES, THANK YOU. PLEASE WAIT HERE UNTIL I RETURN. I'LL PAY YOU FOR THE WAITING TIME.
NOT A PLACE I PLAN TO HANG AROUND, I AM AFRAID.
NOT A GOOD PLACE. ON A BETTER NIGHT I WOULD NOT HAVE COME HERE. DO YOU KNOW HOW MANY TAXI-DRIVERS BEEN KILLED IN LA THIS YEAR?
SEE THIS? IT'S A HUNDRED DOLLAR BILL. I'M GIVING YOU HALF OF IT. IF YOU'RE STILL HERE WHEN I GET BACK, I SHALL GIVE YOU THE OTHER HALF.
OKAY, LADY. I SHALL BE HERE, UNLESS THERE BE GUNS. IF THERE BE GUNS, I WILL BE GONE.

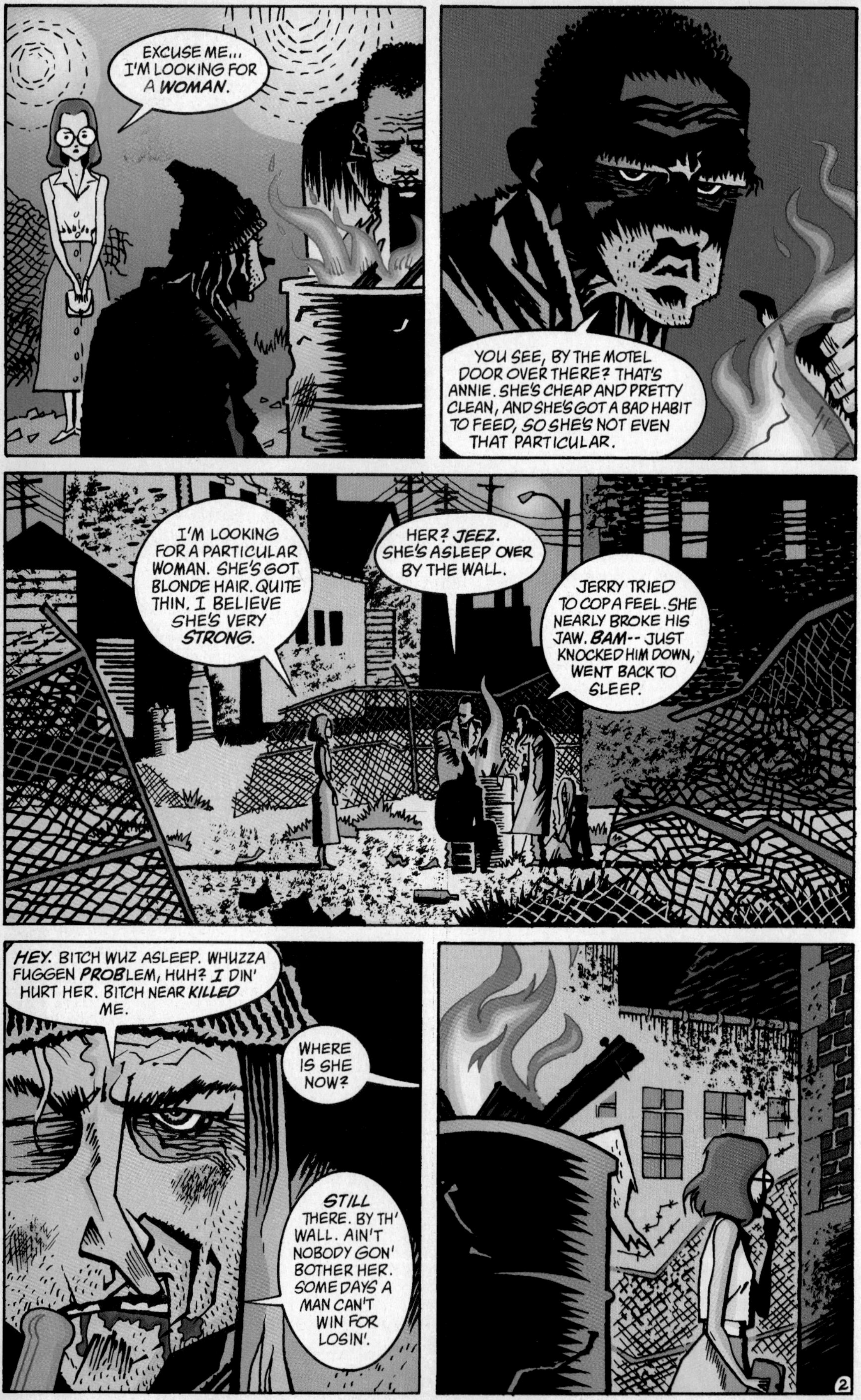

EXCUSE ME... I'M LOOKING FOR A WOMAN.
YOU SEE, BY THE MOTEL DOOR OVER THERE? THAT'S ANNIE. SHE'S CHEAP AND PRETTY CLEAN, AND SHE'S GOT A BAD HABIT TO FEED, SO SHE'S NOT EVEN THAT PARTICULAR.
I'M LOOKING FOR A PARTICULAR WOMAN. SHE'S GOT BLONDE HAIR. QUITE THIN. I BELIEVE SHE'S VERY STRONG.
HER? JEEZ. SHE'S ASLEEP OVER BY THE WALL.
JERRY TRIED TO COP A FEEL. SHE NEARLY BROKE HIS JAW. BAM-- JUST KNOCKED HIM DOWN, WENT BACK TO SLEEP.
HEY. BITCH WUZ ASLEEP. WHUZZA FUGGEN PROBLEM, HUH? I DIN' HURT HER. BITCH NEAR KILLED ME.
WHERE IS SHE NOW?
STILL THERE. BY TH' WALL. AIN'T NOBODY GON' BOTHER HER. SOME DAYS A MAN CAN'T WIN FOR LOSIN'.

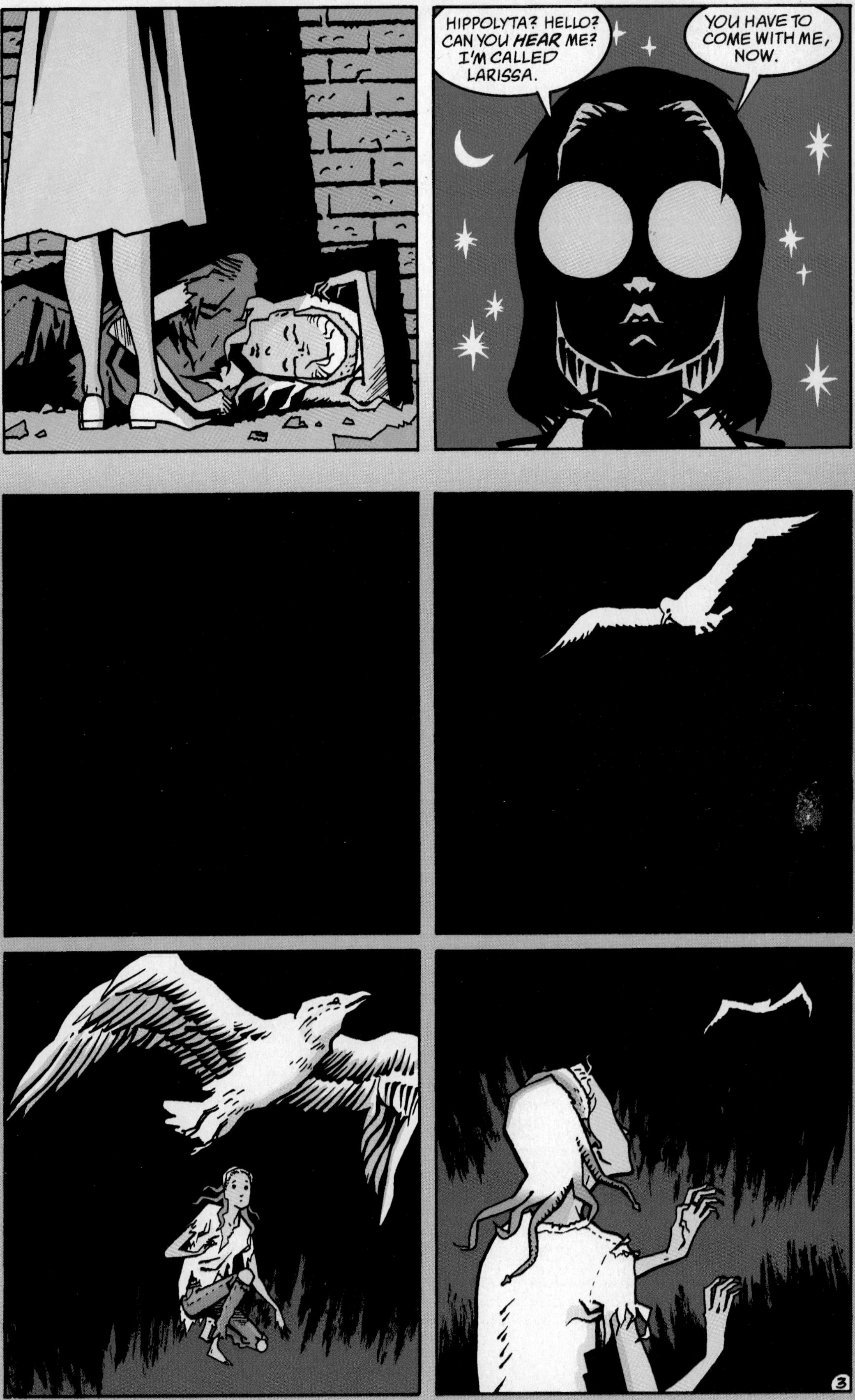
HIPPOLYTA? HELLO? CAN YOU *HEAR* ME? I'M CALLED LARISSA.
YOU HAVE TO COME WITH ME, NOW.

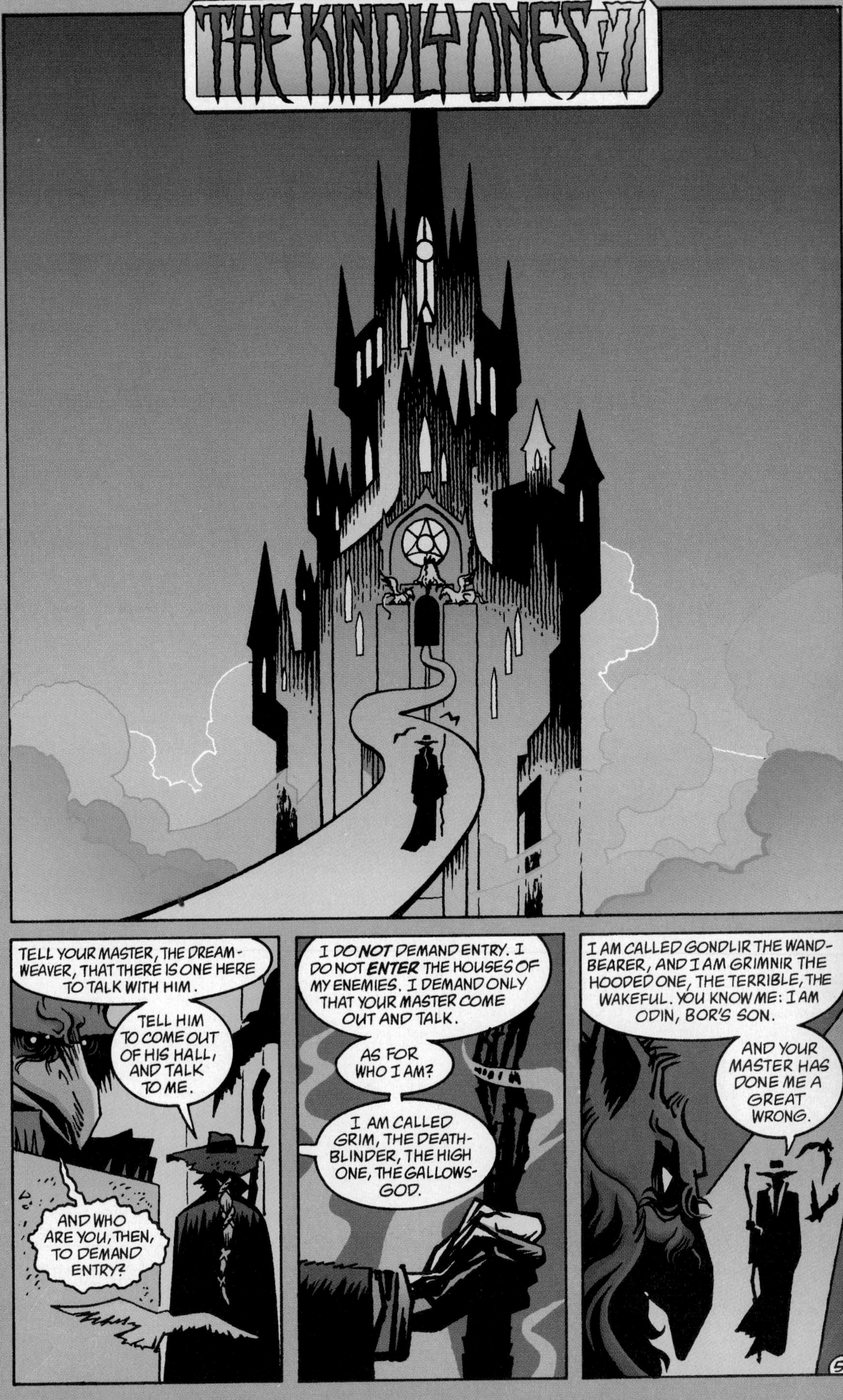
THE KINDLY ONES: 7
TELL YOUR MASTER, THE DREAM-WEAVER, THAT THERE IS ONE HERE TO TALK WITH HIM.
TELL HIM TO COME OUT OF HIS HALL, AND TALK TO ME.
AND WHO ARE YOU, THEN, TO DEMAND ENTRY?
I DO NOT DEMAND ENTRY. I DO NOT ENTER THE HOUSES OF MY ENEMIES. I DEMAND ONLY THAT YOUR MASTER COME OUT AND TALK.
AS FOR WHO I AM?
I AM CALLED GRIM, THE DEATH-BLINDER, THE HIGH ONE, THE GALLOWS-GOD.
I AM CALLED GONDLIR THE WAND-BEARER, AND I AM GRIMNIR THE HOODED ONE, THE TERRIBLE, THE WAKEFUL. YOU KNOW ME: I AM ODIN, BOR'S SON.
AND YOUR MASTER HAS DONE ME A GREAT WRONG.

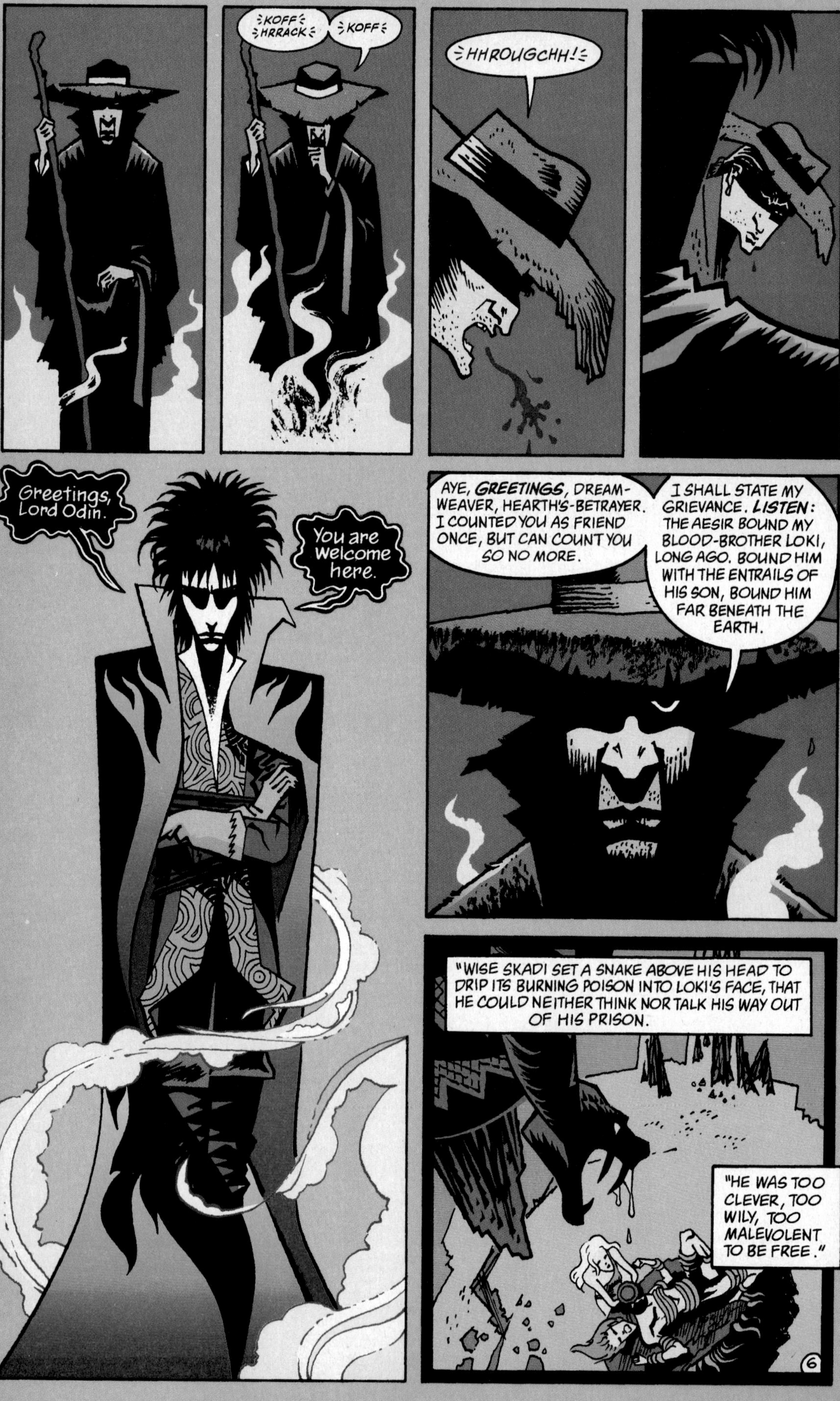
KOFF HRRACK
KOFF
HHROUGCHH!
Greetings, Lord Odin.
You are Welcome here.
AYE, GREETINGS, DREAM-WEAVER, HEARTH'S-BETRAYER. I COUNTED YOU AS FRIEND ONCE, BUT CAN COUNT YOU SO NO MORE.
I SHALL STATE MY GRIEVANCE. LISTEN: THE AESIR BOUND MY BLOOD-BROTHER LOKI, LONG AGO. BOUND HIM WITH THE ENTRAILS OF HIS SON, BOUND HIM FAR BENEATH THE EARTH.
"WISE SKADI SET A SNAKE ABOVE HIS HEAD TO DRIP ITS BURNING POISON INTO LOKI'S FACE, THAT HE COULD NEITHER THINK NOR TALK HIS WAY OUT OF HIS PRISON.
"HE WAS TOO CLEVER, TOO WILY, TOO MALEVOLENT TO BE FREE."
6

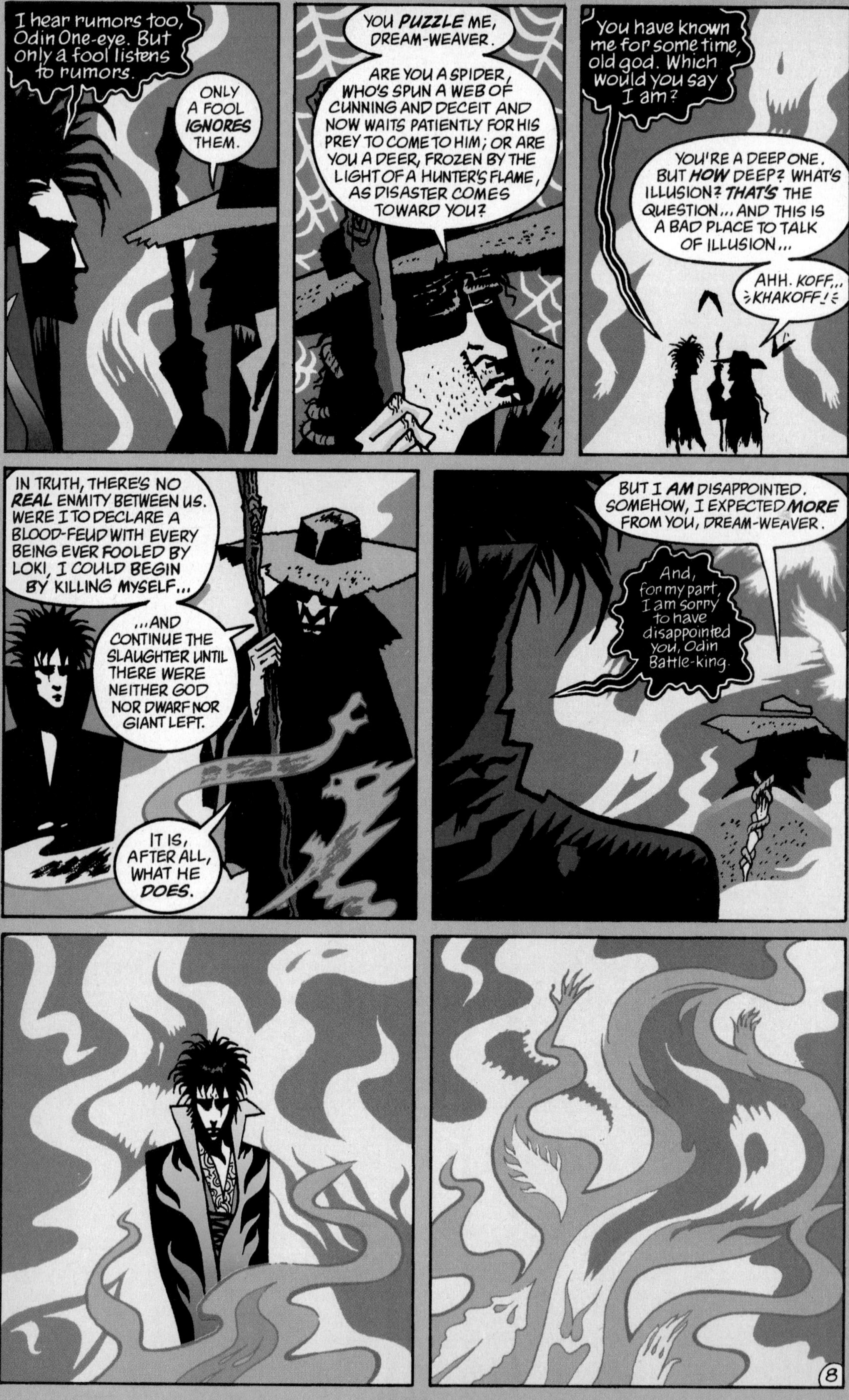
I hear rumors too, Odin One-eye. But only a fool listens to rumors.
ONLY A FOOL IGNORES THEM.
YOU PUZZLE ME, DREAM-WEAVER.
ARE YOU A SPIDER, WHO'S SPUN A WEB OF CUNNING AND DECEIT AND NOW WAITS PATIENTLY FOR HIS PREY TO COME TO HIM; OR ARE YOU A DEER, FROZEN BY THE LIGHT OF A HUNTER'S FLAME, AS DISASTER COMES TOWARD YOU?
You have known me for some time, old god. Which would you say I am?
YOU'RE A DEEP ONE. BUT HOW DEEP? WHAT'S ILLUSION? THAT'S THE QUESTION... AND THIS IS A BAD PLACE TO TALK OF ILLUSION...
AHH. KOFF,.. KHAKOFF!
IN TRUTH, THERE'S NO REAL ENMITY BETWEEN US. WERE I TO DECLARE A BLOOD-FEUD WITH EVERY BEING EVER FOOLED BY LOKI, I COULD BEGIN BY KILLING MYSELF...
...AND CONTINUE THE SLAUGHTER UNTIL THERE WERE NEITHER GOD NOR DWARF NOR GIANT LEFT.
IT IS, AFTER ALL, WHAT HE DOES.
BUT I AM DISAPPOINTED. SOMEHOW, I EXPECTED MORE FROM YOU, DREAM-WEAVER.
And, for my part, I am sorry to have disappointed you, Odin Battle-king.
8

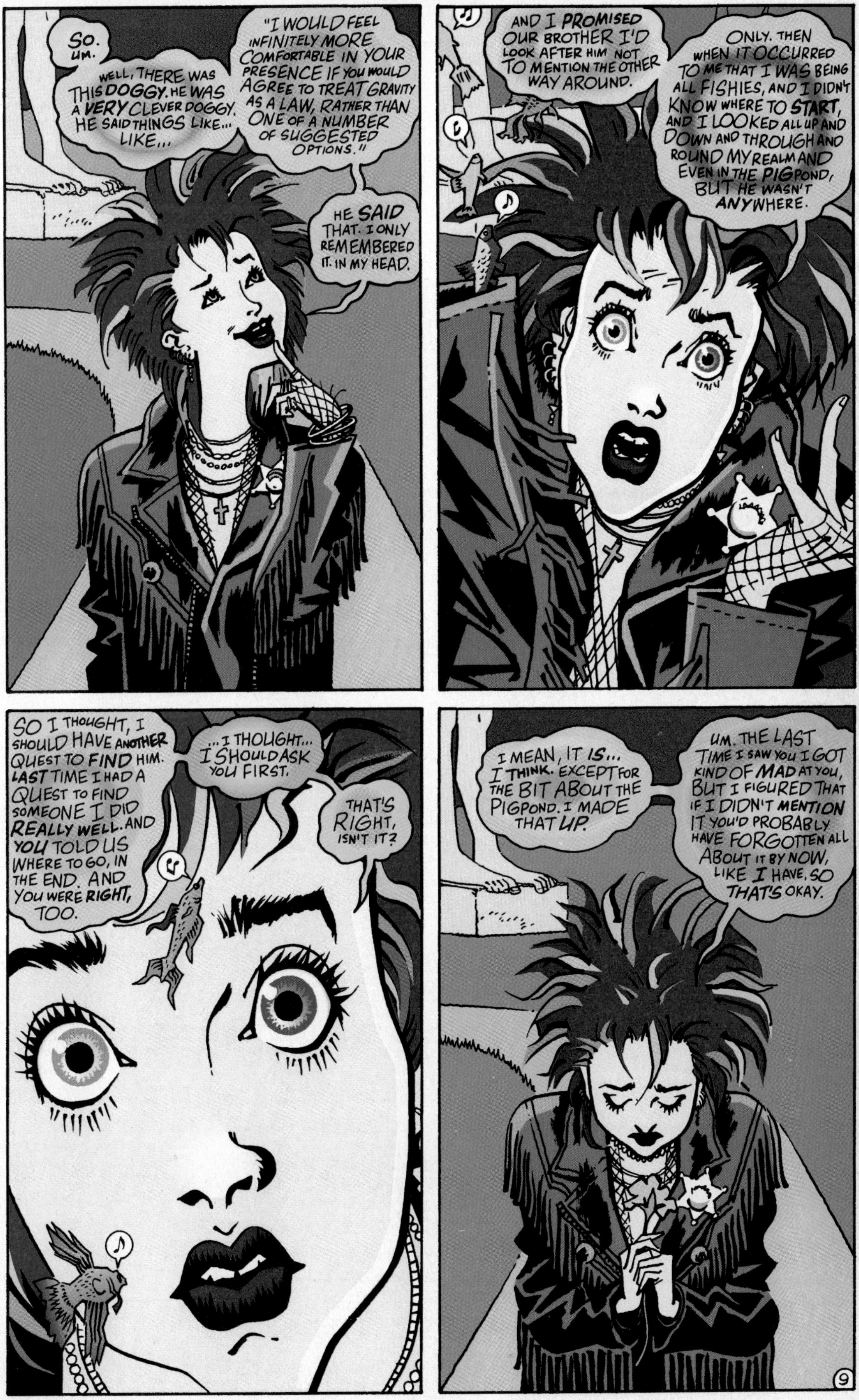

SO. UM.
WELL, THERE WAS THIS DOGGY. HE WAS A VERY CLEVER DOGGY. HE SAID THINGS LIKE... LIKE...
"I WOULD FEEL INFINITELY MORE COMFORTABLE IN YOUR PRESENCE IF YOU WOULD AGREE TO TREAT GRAVITY AS A LAW, RATHER THAN ONE OF A NUMBER OF SUGGESTED OPTIONS."
HE SAID THAT. I ONLY REMEMBERED IT. IN MY HEAD.
AND I PROMISED OUR BROTHER I'D LOOK AFTER HIM NOT TO MENTION THE OTHER WAY AROUND.
ONLY. THEN WHEN IT OCCURRED TO ME THAT I WAS BEING ALL FISHIES, AND I DIDN'T KNOW WHERE TO START, AND I LOOKED ALL UP AND DOWN AND THROUGH AND ROUND MY REALM AND EVEN IN THE PIGPOND, BUT HE WASN'T ANYWHERE.
SO I THOUGHT, I SHOULD HAVE ANOTHER QUEST TO FIND HIM. LAST TIME I HAD A QUEST TO FIND SOMEONE I DID REALLY WELL. AND YOU TOLD US WHERE TO GO, IN THE END. AND YOU WERE RIGHT, TOO.
...I THOUGHT... I SHOULD ASK YOU FIRST.
THAT'S RIGHT, ISN'T IT?
I MEAN, IT IS... I THINK. EXCEPT FOR THE BIT ABOUT THE PIGPOND. I MADE THAT UP.
UM. THE LAST TIME I SAW YOU I GOT KIND OF MAD AT YOU, BUT I FIGURED THAT IF I DIDN'T MENTION IT YOU'D PROBABLY HAVE FORGOTTEN ALL ABOUT IT BY NOW, LIKE I HAVE, SO THAT'S OKAY.
9

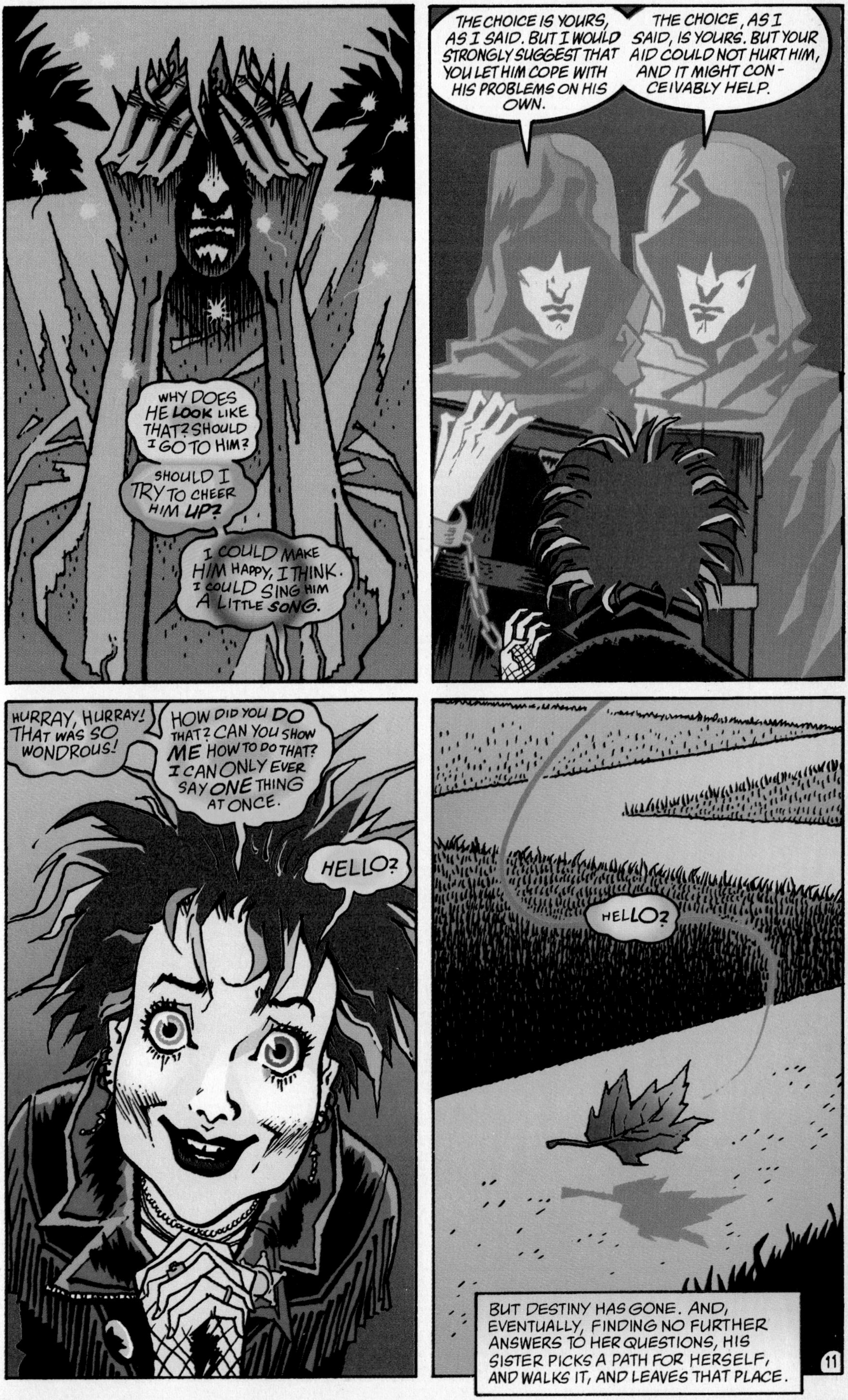
WHY DOES HE LOOK LIKE THAT? SHOULD I GO TO HIM?
SHOULD I TRY TO CHEER HIM UP?
I COULD MAKE HIM HAPPY, I THINK. I COULD SING HIM A LITTLE SONG.
THE CHOICE IS YOURS, AS I SAID. BUT I WOULD STRONGLY SUGGEST THAT YOU LET HIM COPE WITH HIS PROBLEMS ON HIS OWN.
THE CHOICE, AS I SAID, IS YOURS. BUT YOUR AID COULD NOT HURT HIM, AND IT MIGHT CON-CEIVABLY HELP.
HURRAY, HURRAY! THAT WAS SO WONDROUS!
HOW DID YOU DO THAT? CAN YOU SHOW ME HOW TO DO THAT? I CAN ONLY EVER SAY ONE THING AT ONCE.
HELLO?
HELLO?
BUT DESTINY HAS GONE. AND, EVENTUALLY, FINDING NO FURTHER ANSWERS TO HER QUESTIONS, HIS SISTER PICKS A PATH FOR HERSELF, AND WALKS IT, AND LEAVES THAT PLACE.
11

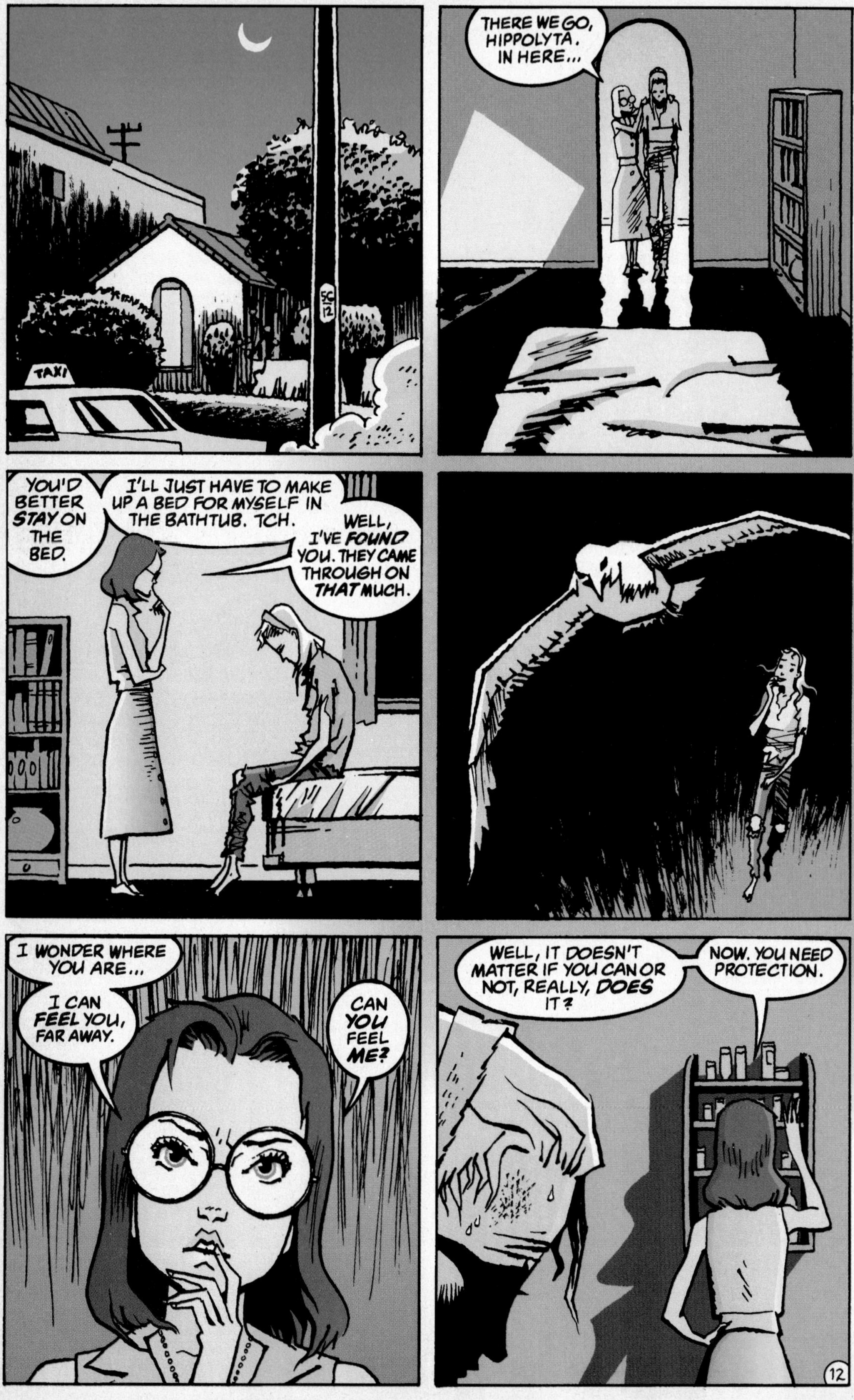
TAXI
5C 12
THERE WE GO, HIPPOLYTA. IN HERE...
YOU'D BETTER STAY ON THE BED.
I'LL JUST HAVE TO MAKE UP A BED FOR MYSELF IN THE BATHTUB. TCH.
WELL, I'VE FOUND YOU. THEY CAME THROUGH ON THAT MUCH.
I WONDER WHERE YOU ARE...
I CAN FEEL YOU, FAR AWAY.
CAN YOU FEEL ME?
WELL, IT DOESN'T MATTER IF YOU CAN OR NOT, REALLY, DOES IT?
NOW. YOU NEED PROTECTION.

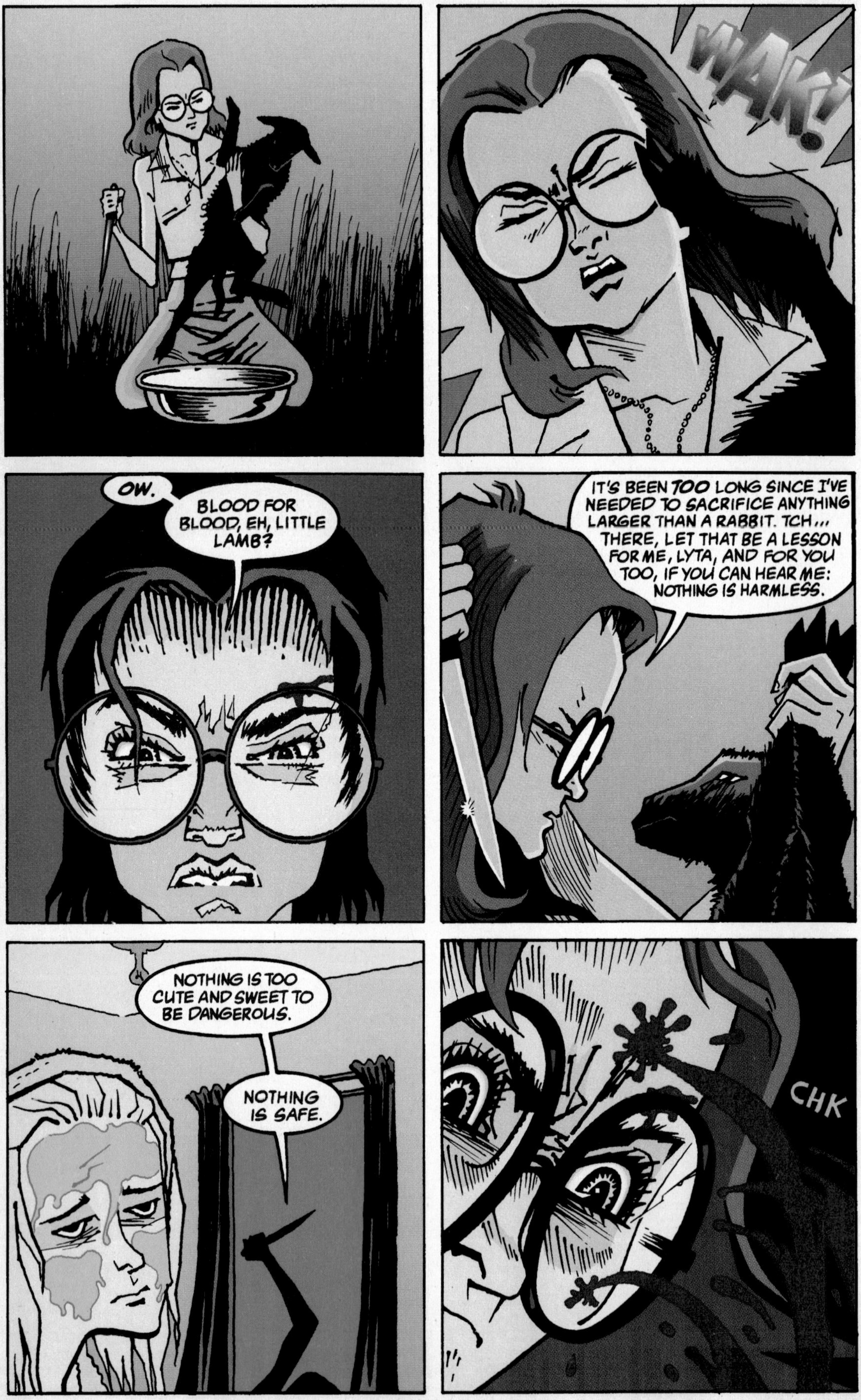
WAK!
OW.
BLOOD FOR BLOOD, EH, LITTLE LAMB?
IT'S BEEN TOO LONG SINCE I'VE NEEDED TO SACRIFICE ANYTHING LARGER THAN A RABBIT. TCH... THERE, LET THAT BE A LESSON FOR ME, LYTA, AND FOR YOU TOO, IF YOU CAN HEAR ME: NOTHING IS HARMLESS.
NOTHING IS TOO CUTE AND SWEET TO BE DANGEROUS.
NOTHING IS SAFE.
CHK

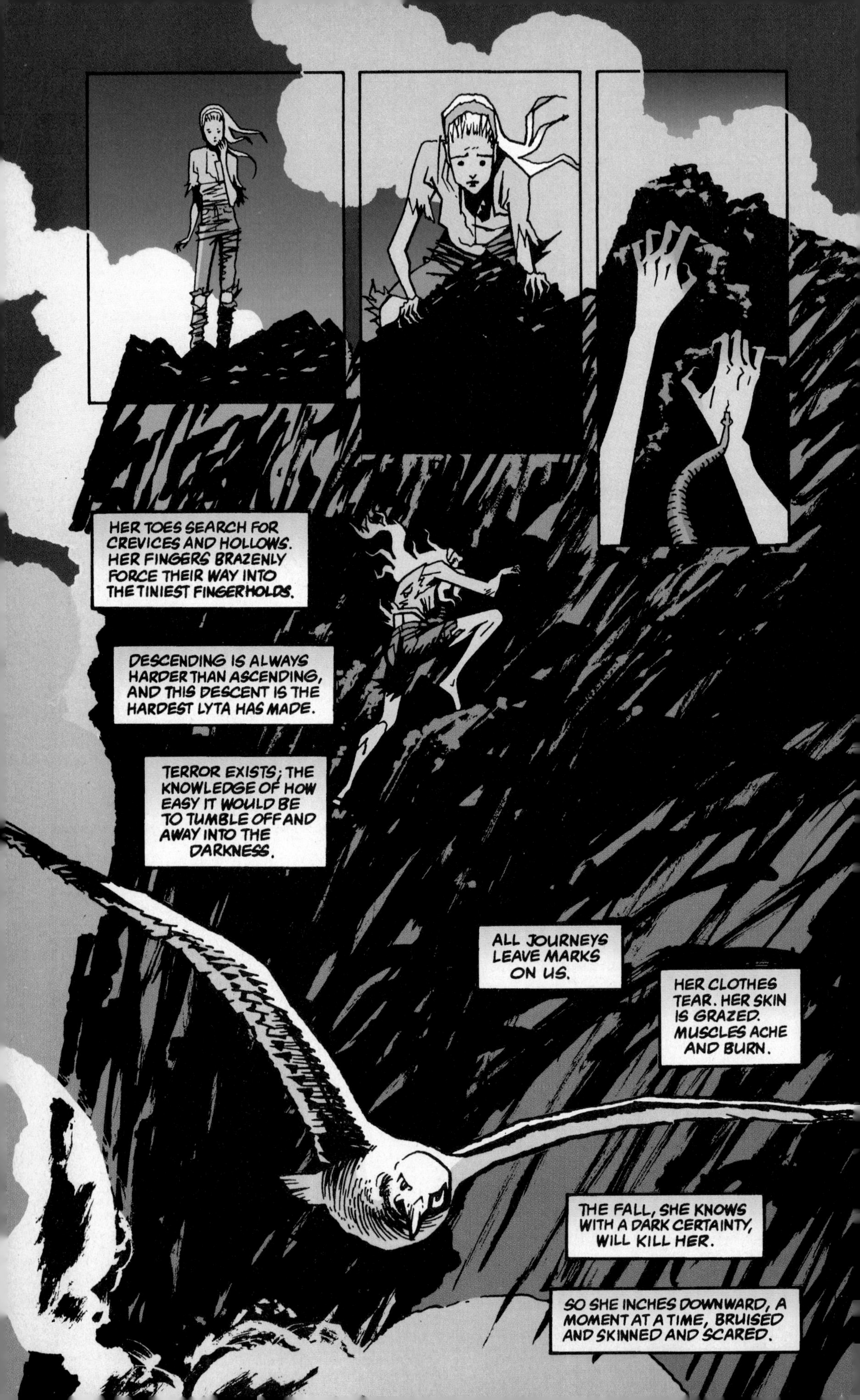
HER TOES SEARCH FOR CREVICES AND HOLLOWS. HER FINGERS BRAZENLY FORCE THEIR WAY INTO THE TINIEST FINGERHOLDS.
DESCENDING IS ALWAYS HARDER THAN ASCENDING, AND THIS DESCENT IS THE HARDEST LYTA HAS MADE.
TERROR EXISTS; THE KNOWLEDGE OF HOW EASY IT WOULD BE TO TUMBLE OFF AND AWAY INTO THE DARKNESS.
ALL JOURNEYS LEAVE MARKS ON US.
HER CLOTHES TEAR. HER SKIN IS GRAZED. MUSCLES ACHE AND BURN.
THE FALL, SHE KNOWS WITH A DARK CERTAINTY, WILL KILL HER.
SO SHE INCHES DOWNWARD, A MOMENT AT A TIME, BRUISED AND SKINNED AND SCARED.

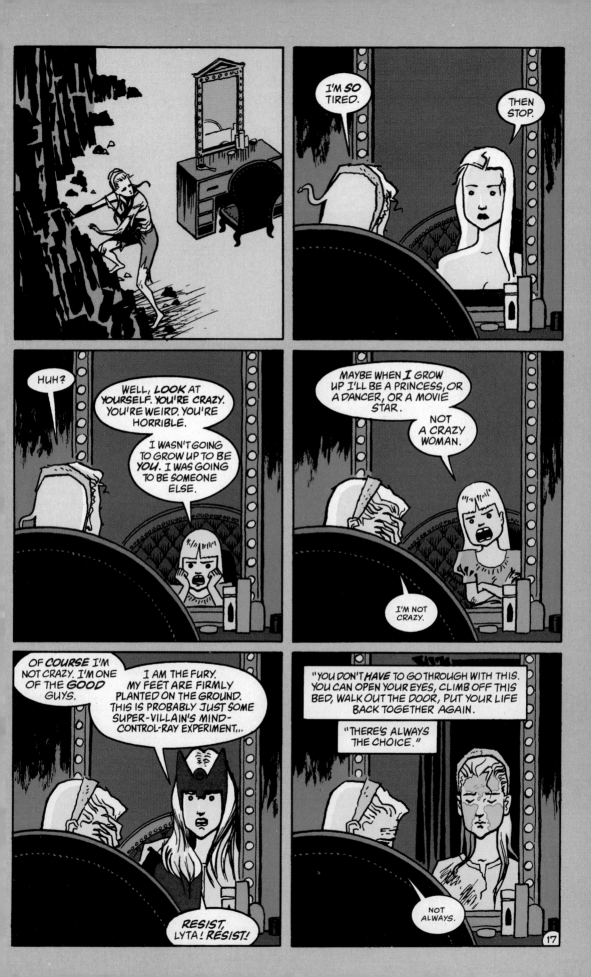

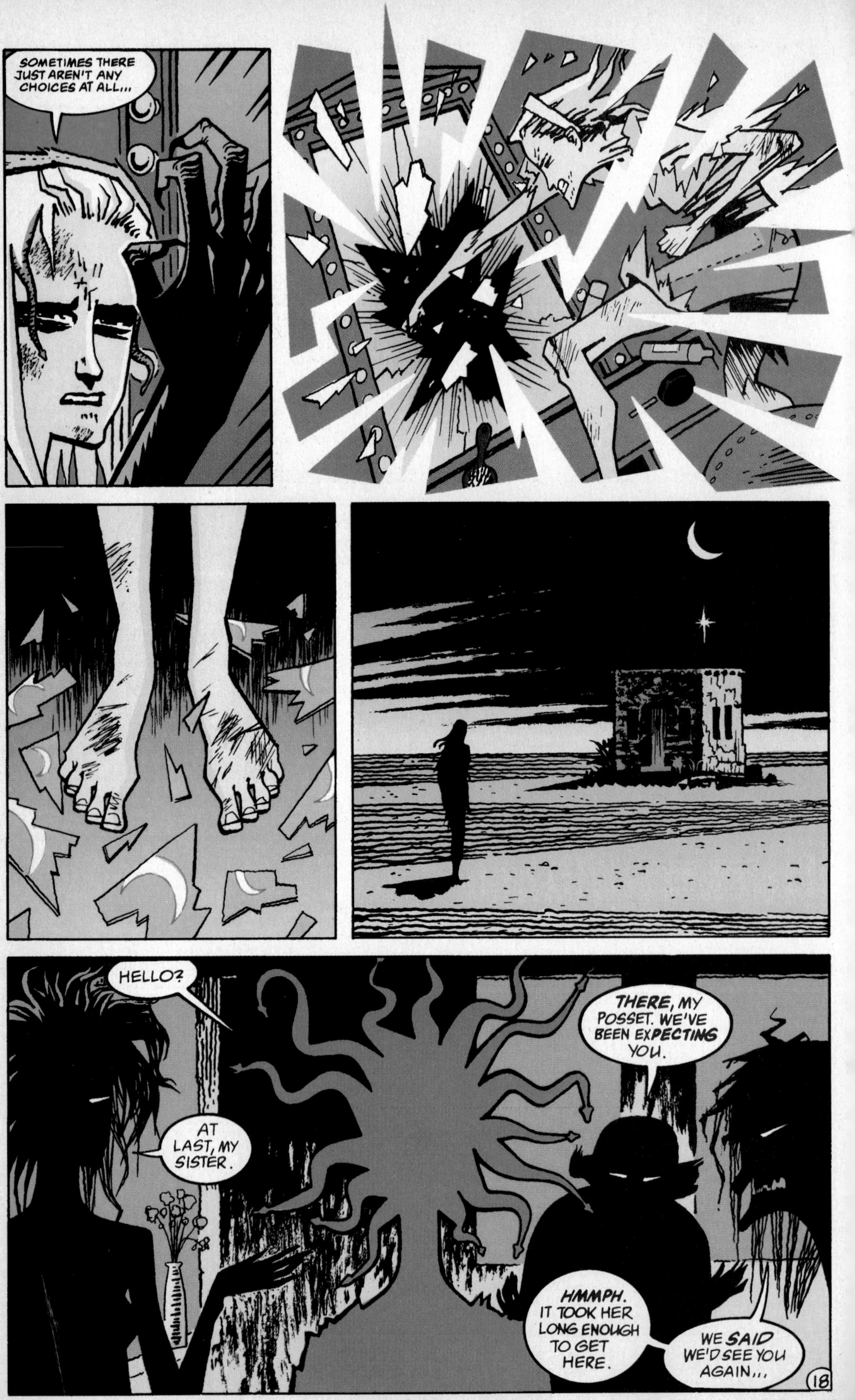
SOMETIMES THERE JUST AREN'T ANY CHOICES AT ALL...
HELLO?
AT LAST, MY SISTER.
THERE, MY POSSET. WE'VE BEEN EXPECTING YOU.
HMMPH. IT TOOK HER LONG ENOUGH TO GET HERE.
WE SAID WE'D SEE YOU AGAIN...
18

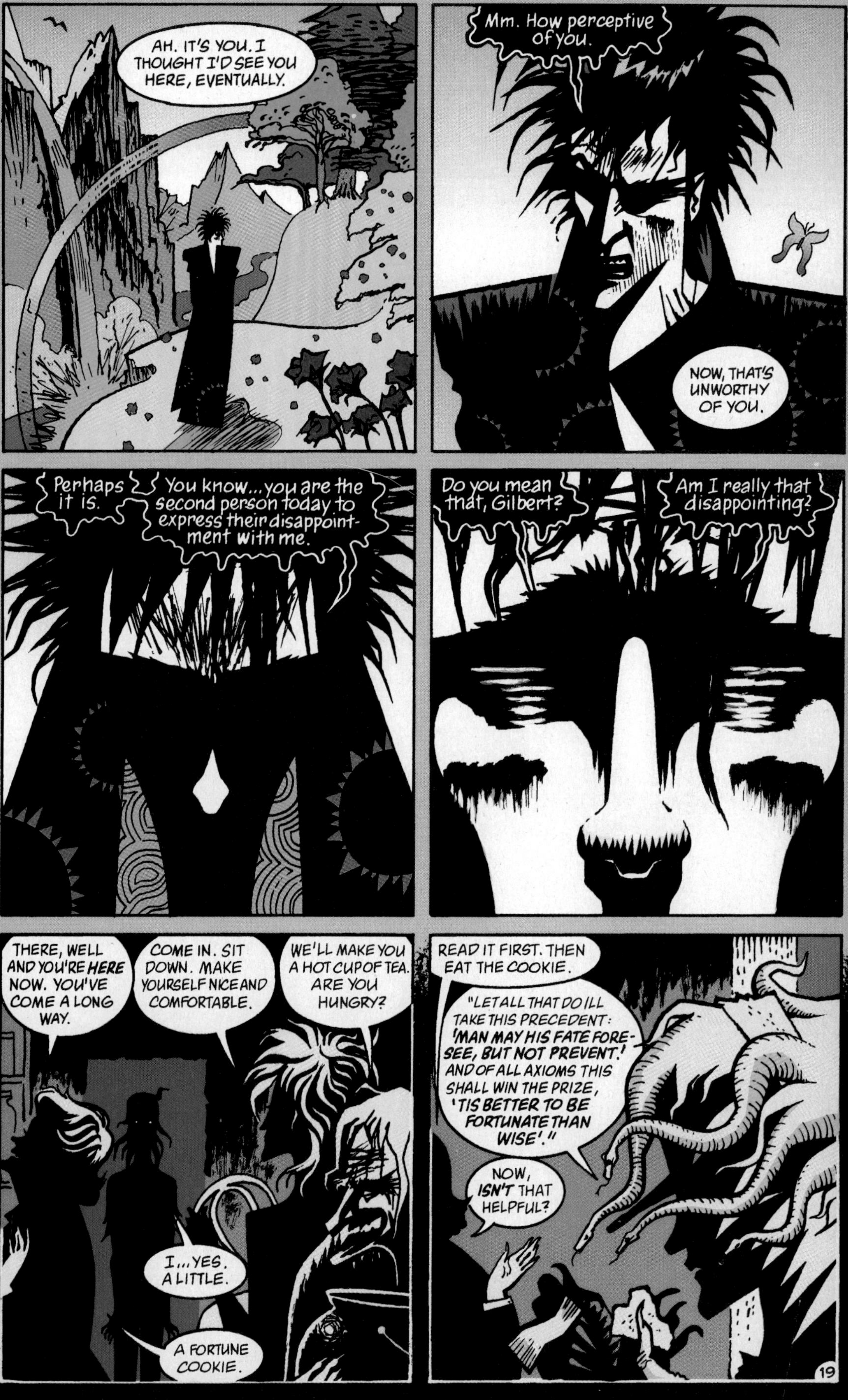
AH. IT'S YOU. I THOUGHT I'D SEE YOU HERE, EVENTUALLY.
Mm. How perceptive of you.
NOW, THAT'S UNWORTHY OF YOU.
Perhaps it is.
You know... you are the second person today to express their disappointment with me.
Do you mean that, Gilbert?
Am I really that disappointing?
THERE, WELL AND YOU'RE HERE NOW. YOU'VE COME A LONG WAY.
COME IN. SIT DOWN. MAKE YOURSELF NICE AND COMFORTABLE.
WE'LL MAKE YOU A HOT CUP OF TEA. ARE YOU HUNGRY?
I... YES. A LITTLE.
A FORTUNE COOKIE.
READ IT FIRST. THEN EAT THE COOKIE.
"LET ALL THAT DO ILL TAKE THIS PRECEDENT: 'MAN MAY HIS FATE FORESEE, BUT NOT PREVENT.' AND OF ALL AXIOMS THIS SHALL WIN THE PRIZE, 'TIS BETTER TO BE FORTUNATE THAN WISE'."
NOW, ISN'T THAT HELPFUL?
19

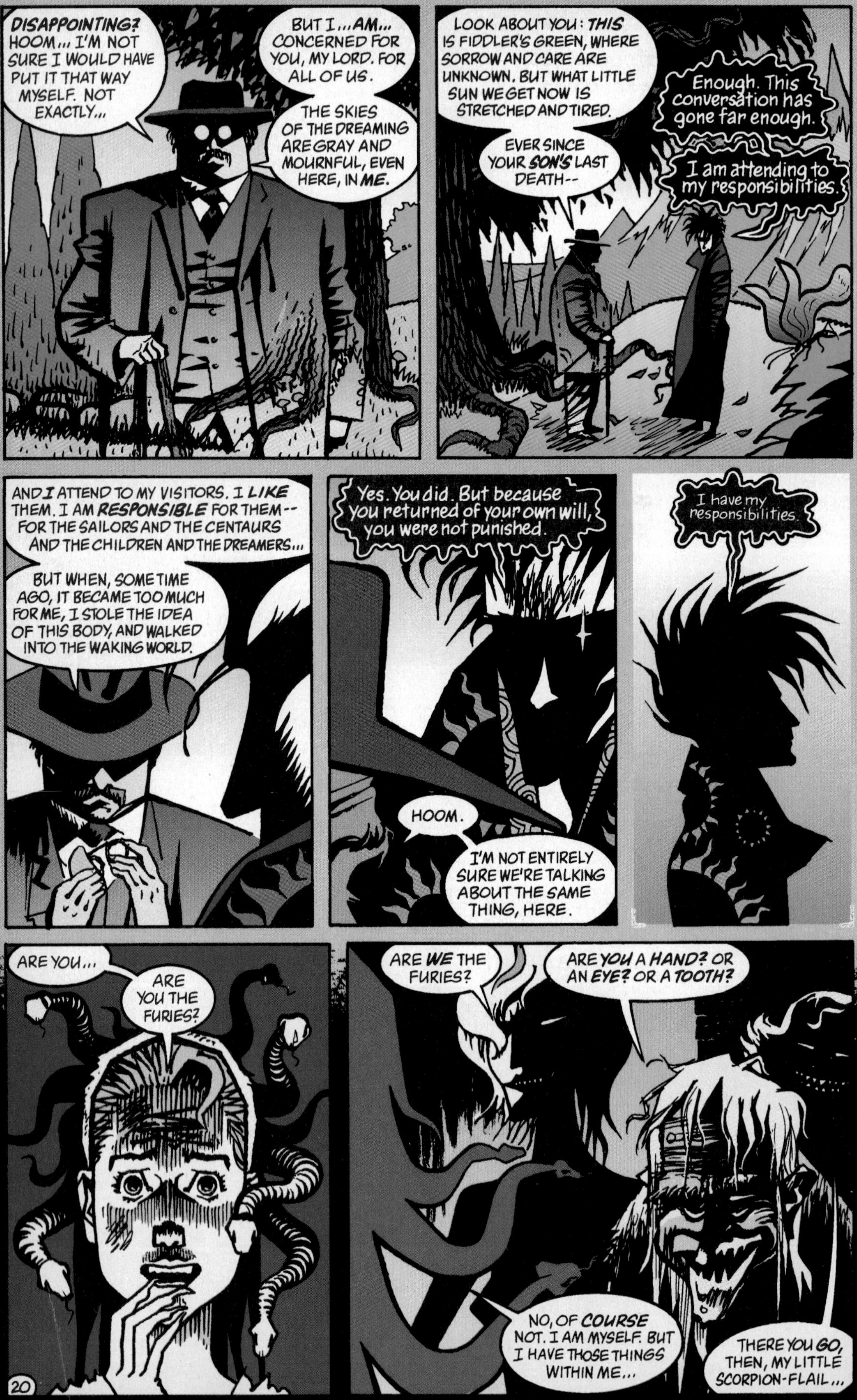
DISAPPOINTING? HOOM... I'M NOT SURE I WOULD HAVE PUT IT THAT WAY MYSELF. NOT EXACTLY...
BUT I...AM... CONCERNED FOR YOU, MY LORD. FOR ALL OF US.
THE SKIES OF THE DREAMING ARE GRAY AND MOURNFUL, EVEN HERE, IN ME.
LOOK ABOUT YOU: THIS IS FIDDLER'S GREEN, WHERE SORROW AND CARE ARE UNKNOWN. BUT WHAT LITTLE SUN WE GET NOW IS STRETCHED AND TIRED.
EVER SINCE YOUR SON'S LAST DEATH--
Enough. This conversation has gone far enough.
I am attending to my responsibilities.
AND I ATTEND TO MY VISITORS. I LIKE THEM. I AM RESPONSIBLE FOR THEM-- FOR THE SAILORS AND THE CENTAURS AND THE CHILDREN AND THE DREAMERS...
BUT WHEN, SOME TIME AGO, IT BECAME TOO MUCH FOR ME, I STOLE THE IDEA OF THIS BODY, AND WALKED INTO THE WAKING WORLD.
Yes. You did. But because you returned of your own will, you were not punished.
HOOM.
I'M NOT ENTIRELY SURE WE'RE TALKING ABOUT THE SAME THING, HERE.
I have my responsibilities.
ARE YOU...
ARE YOU THE FURIES?
ARE WE THE FURIES?
ARE YOU A HAND? OR AN EYE? OR A TOOTH?
NO, OF COURSE NOT. I AM MYSELF. BUT I HAVE THOSE THINGS WITHIN ME...
THERE YOU GO, THEN, MY LITTLE SCORPION-FLAIL...

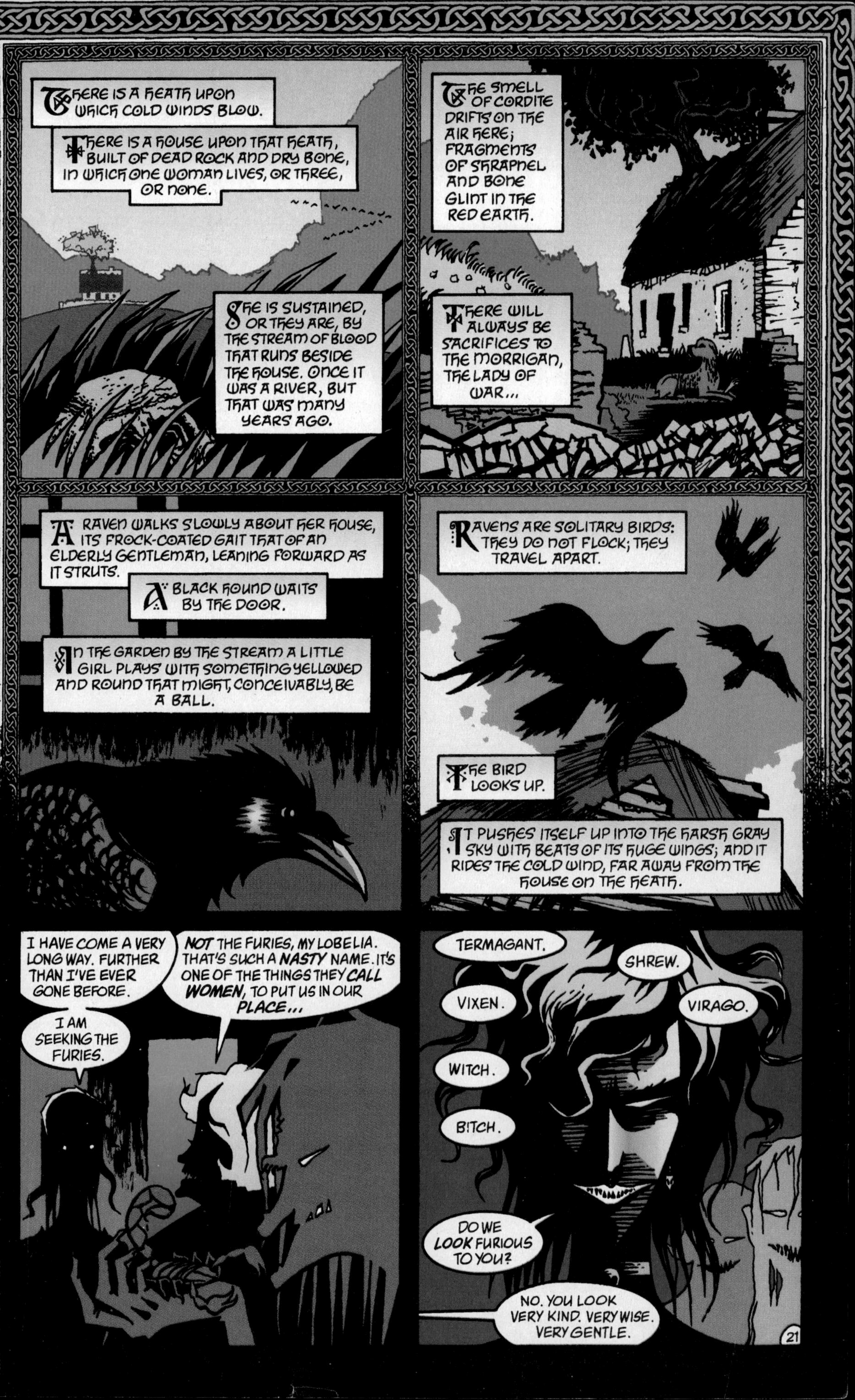
THERE IS A HEATH UPON WHICH COLD WINDS BLOW.
THERE IS A HOUSE UPON THAT HEATH, BUILT OF DEAD ROCK AND DRY BONE, IN WHICH ONE WOMAN LIVES, OR THREE, OR NONE.
SHE IS SUSTAINED, OR THEY ARE, BY THE STREAM OF BLOOD THAT RUNS BESIDE THE HOUSE. ONCE IT WAS A RIVER, BUT THAT WAS MANY YEARS AGO.
THE SMELL OF CORDITE DRIFTS ON THE AIR HERE; FRAGMENTS OF SHRAPNEL AND BONE GLINT IN THE RED EARTH.
THERE WILL ALWAYS BE SACRIFICES TO THE MORRIGAN, THE LADY OF WAR...
A RAVEN WALKS SLOWLY ABOUT HER HOUSE, ITS FROCK-COATED GAIT THAT OF AN ELDERLY GENTLEMAN, LEANING FORWARD AS IT STRUTS.
A BLACK HOUND WAITS BY THE DOOR.
IN THE GARDEN BY THE STREAM A LITTLE GIRL PLAYS WITH SOMETHING YELLOWED AND ROUND THAT MIGHT, CONCEIVABLY, BE A BALL.
RAVENS ARE SOLITARY BIRDS: THEY DO NOT FLOCK; THEY TRAVEL APART.
THE BIRD LOOKS UP.
IT PUSHES ITSELF UP INTO THE HARSH GRAY SKY WITH BEATS OF ITS HUGE WINGS; AND IT RIDES THE COLD WIND, FAR AWAY FROM THE HOUSE ON THE HEATH.
I HAVE COME A VERY LONG WAY. FURTHER THAN I'VE EVER GONE BEFORE.
I AM SEEKING THE FURIES.
NOT THE FURIES, MY LOBELIA. THAT'S SUCH A NASTY NAME. IT'S ONE OF THE THINGS THEY CALL WOMEN, TO PUT US IN OUR PLACE...
TERMAGANT.
SHREW.
VIXEN.
VIRAGO.
WITCH.
BITCH.
DO WE LOOK FURIOUS TO YOU?
NO. YOU LOOK VERY KIND. VERY WISE. VERY GENTLE.
21

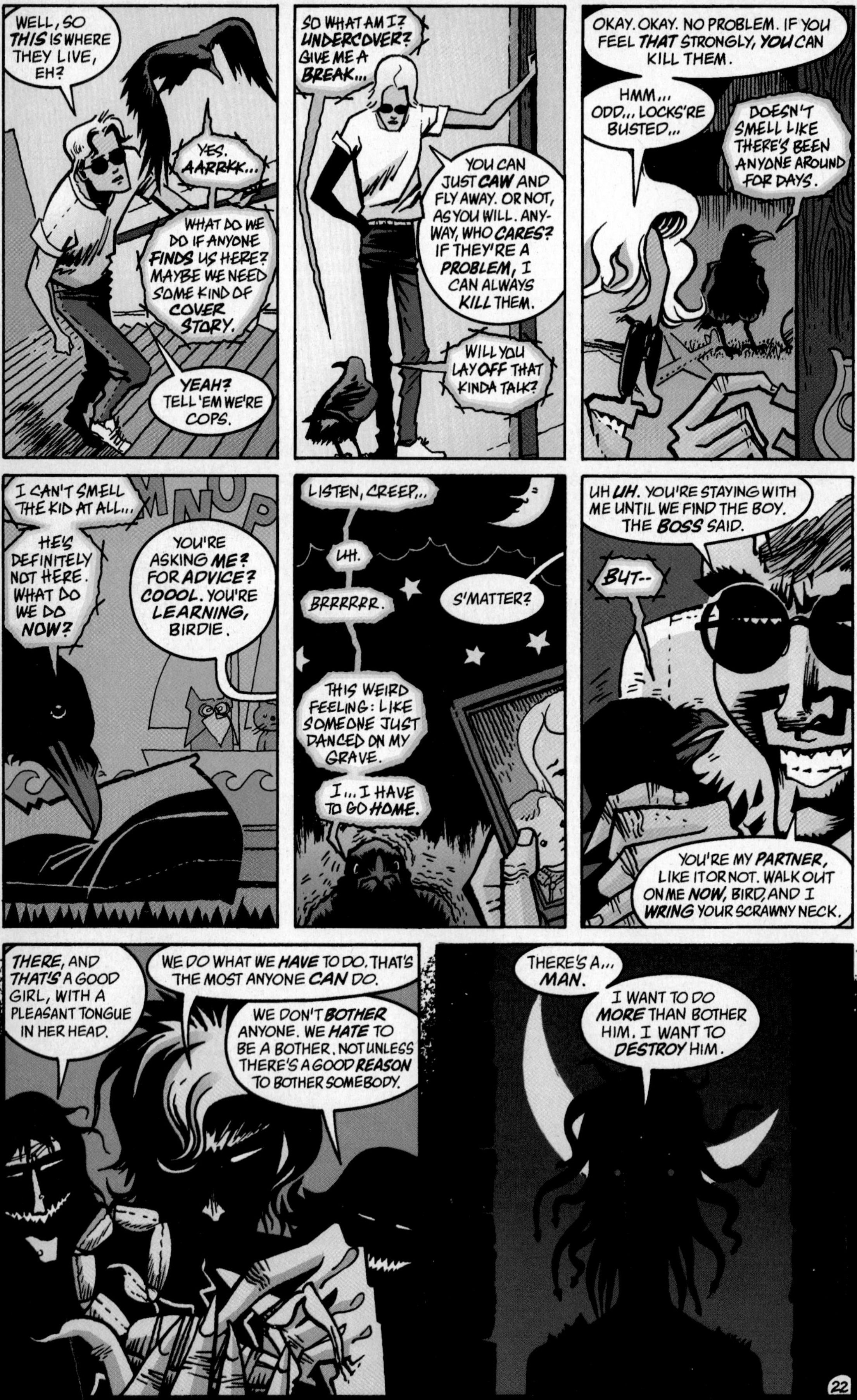
WELL, SO THIS IS WHERE THEY LIVE, EH?
YES. AARRKK...
WHAT DO WE DO IF ANYONE FINDS US HERE? MAYBE WE NEED SOME KIND OF COVER STORY.
YEAH? TELL 'EM WE'RE COPS.
SO WHAT AM I? UNDERCOVER? GIVE ME A BREAK...
YOU CAN JUST CAW AND FLY AWAY. OR NOT, AS YOU WILL. ANY-WAY, WHO CARES? IF THEY'RE A PROBLEM, I CAN ALWAYS KILL THEM.
WILL YOU LAY OFF THAT KINDA TALK?
OKAY. OKAY. NO PROBLEM. IF YOU FEEL THAT STRONGLY, YOU CAN KILL THEM.
HMM... ODD... LOCKS'RE BUSTED...
DOESN'T SMELL LIKE THERE'S BEEN ANYONE AROUND FOR DAYS.
I CAN'T SMELL THE KID AT ALL...
HE'S DEFINITELY NOT HERE. WHAT DO WE DO NOW?
YOU'RE ASKING ME? FOR ADVICE? COOOL. YOU'RE LEARNING, BIRDIE.
LISTEN, CREEP...
UH.
BRRRRRR.
S'MATTER?
THIS WEIRD FEELING: LIKE SOMEONE JUST DANCED ON MY GRAVE.
I... I HAVE TO GO HOME.
UH UH. YOU'RE STAYING WITH ME UNTIL WE FIND THE BOY. THE BOSS SAID.
BUT--
YOU'RE MY PARTNER, LIKE IT OR NOT. WALK OUT ON ME NOW, BIRD, AND I WRING YOUR SCRAWNY NECK.
THERE, AND THAT'S A GOOD GIRL, WITH A PLEASANT TONGUE IN HER HEAD.
WE DO WHAT WE HAVE TO DO. THAT'S THE MOST ANYONE CAN DO.
WE DON'T BOTHER ANYONE. WE HATE TO BE A BOTHER. NOT UNLESS THERE'S A GOOD REASON TO BOTHER SOMEBODY.
THERE'S A... MAN.
I WANT TO DO MORE THAN BOTHER HIM. I WANT TO DESTROY HIM.

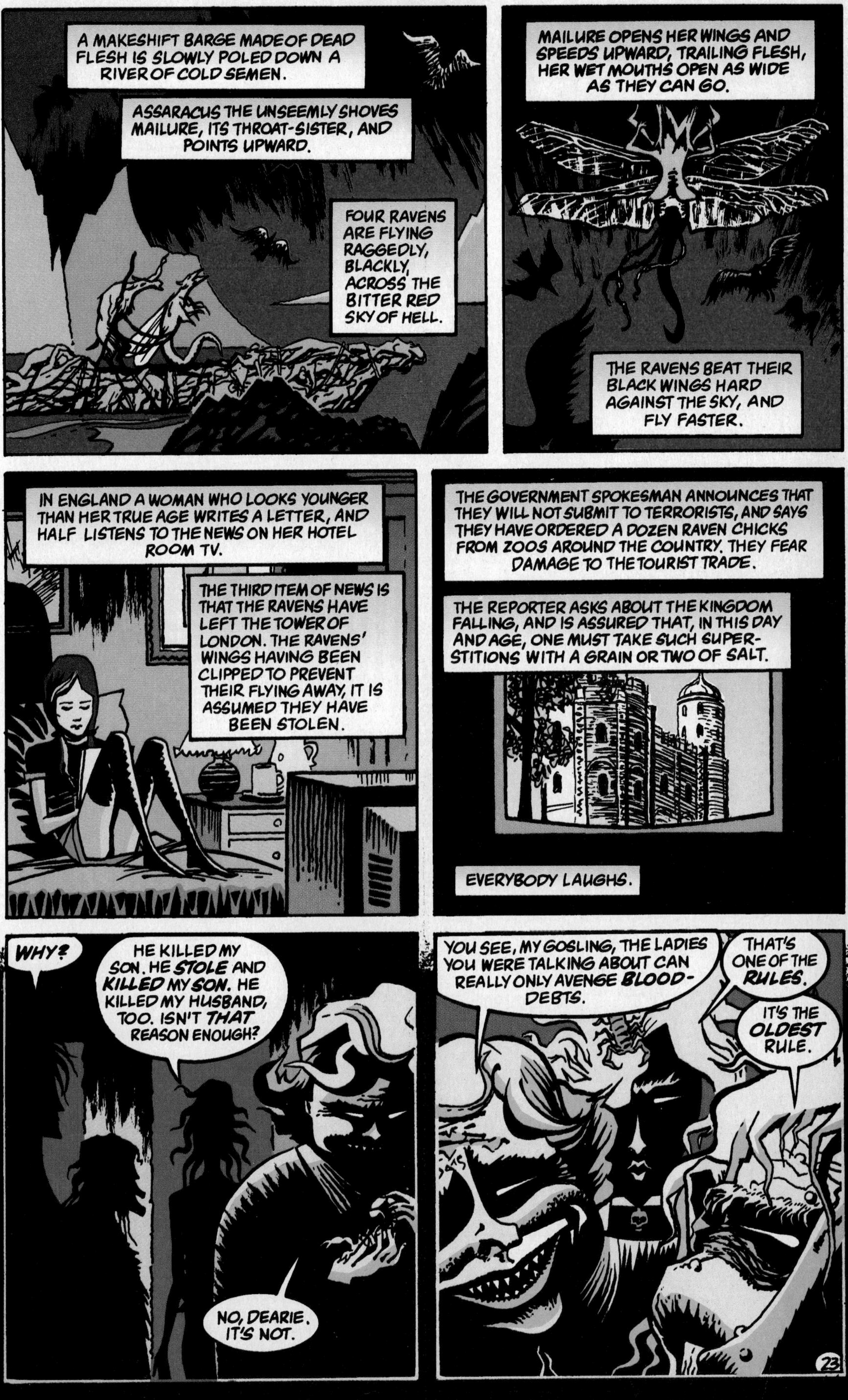
A MAKESHIFT BARGE MADE OF DEAD FLESH IS SLOWLY POLED DOWN A RIVER OF COLD SEMEN.
ASSARACUS THE UNSEEMLY SHOVES MAILURE, ITS THROAT-SISTER, AND POINTS UPWARD.
FOUR RAVENS ARE FLYING RAGGEDLY, BLACKLY, ACROSS THE BITTER RED SKY OF HELL.
MAILURE OPENS HER WINGS AND SPEEDS UPWARD, TRAILING FLESH, HER WET MOUTHS OPEN AS WIDE AS THEY CAN GO.
THE RAVENS BEAT THEIR BLACK WINGS HARD AGAINST THE SKY, AND FLY FASTER.
IN ENGLAND A WOMAN WHO LOOKS YOUNGER THAN HER TRUE AGE WRITES A LETTER, AND HALF LISTENS TO THE NEWS ON HER HOTEL ROOM TV.
THE THIRD ITEM OF NEWS IS THAT THE RAVENS HAVE LEFT THE TOWER OF LONDON. THE RAVENS' WINGS HAVING BEEN CLIPPED TO PREVENT THEIR FLYING AWAY, IT IS ASSUMED THEY HAVE BEEN STOLEN.
THE GOVERNMENT SPOKESMAN ANNOUNCES THAT THEY WILL NOT SUBMIT TO TERRORISTS, AND SAYS THEY HAVE ORDERED A DOZEN RAVEN CHICKS FROM ZOOS AROUND THE COUNTRY. THEY FEAR DAMAGE TO THE TOURIST TRADE.
THE REPORTER ASKS ABOUT THE KINGDOM FALLING, AND IS ASSURED THAT, IN THIS DAY AND AGE, ONE MUST TAKE SUCH SUPER-STITIONS WITH A GRAIN OR TWO OF SALT.
EVERYBODY LAUGHS.
WHY?
HE KILLED MY SON. HE STOLE AND KILLED MY SON. HE KILLED MY HUSBAND, TOO. ISN'T THAT REASON ENOUGH?
NO, DEARIE. IT'S NOT.
YOU SEE, MY GOSLING, THE LADIES YOU WERE TALKING ABOUT CAN REALLY ONLY AVENGE BLOOD-DEBTS.
THAT'S ONE OF THE RULES.
IT'S THE OLDEST RULE.
23

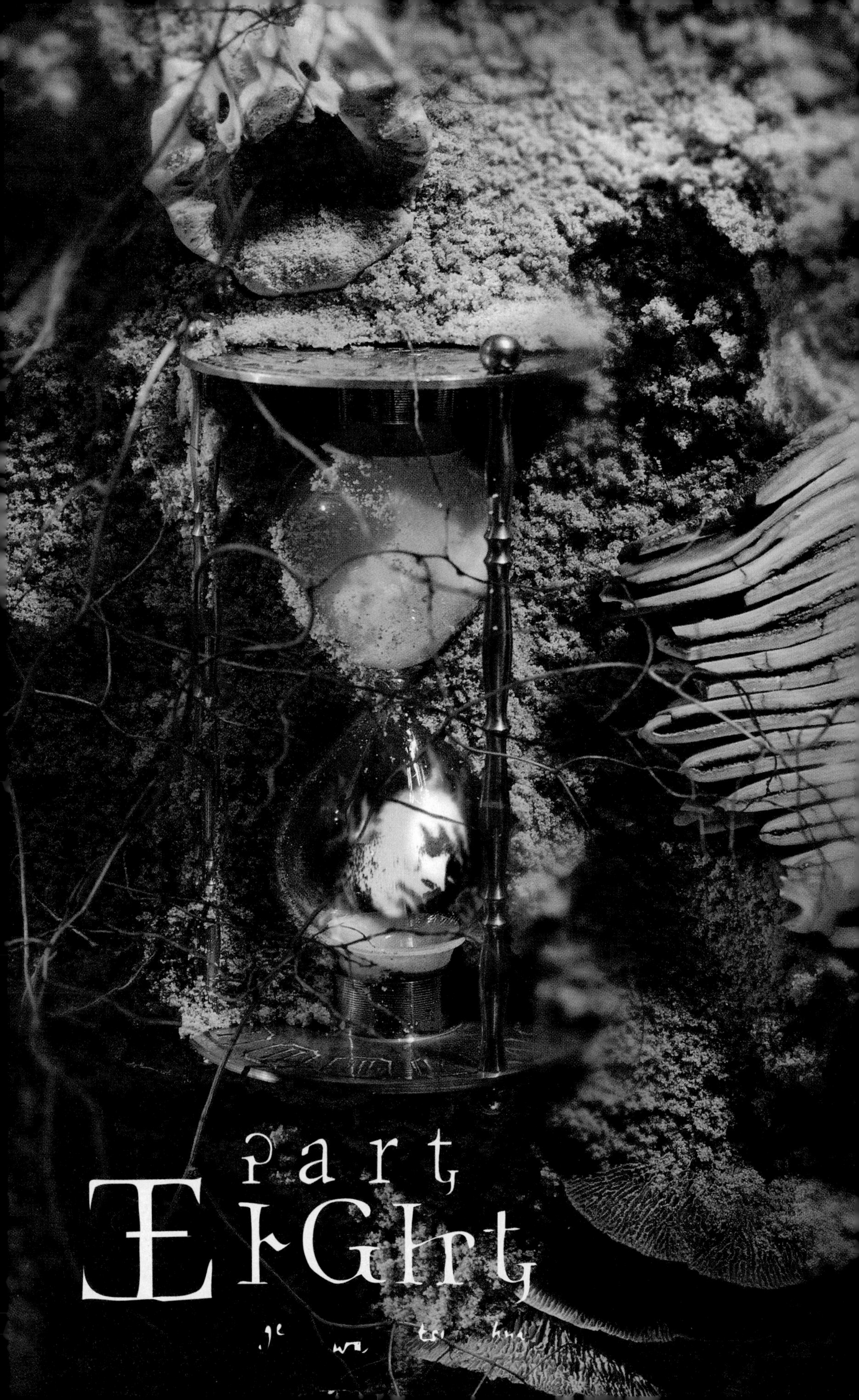
part
Eight

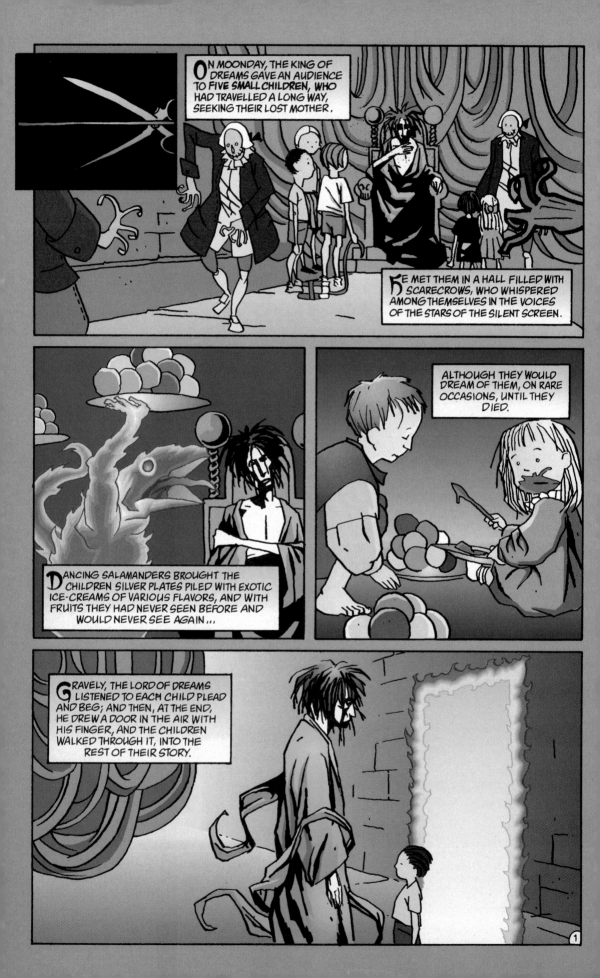

ON MOONDAY, THE KING OF DREAMS GAVE AN AUDIENCE TO FIVE SMALL CHILDREN, WHO HAD TRAVELLED A LONG WAY, SEEKING THEIR LOST MOTHER.

HE MET THEM IN A HALL FILLED WITH SCARECROWS, WHO WHISPERED AMONG THEMSELVES IN THE VOICES OF THE STARS OF THE SILENT SCREEN.

DANCING SALAMANDERS BROUGHT THE CHILDREN SILVER PLATES PILED WITH EXOTIC ICE-CREAMS OF VARIOUS FLAVORS, AND WITH FRUITS THEY HAD NEVER SEEN BEFORE AND WOULD NEVER SEE AGAIN ...

ALTHOUGH THEY WOULD DREAM OF THEM, ON RARE OCCASIONS, UNTIL THEY DIED.

GRAVELY, THE LORD OF DREAMS LISTENED TO EACH CHILD PLEAD AND BEG; AND THEN, AT THE END, HE DREW A DOOR IN THE AIR WITH HIS FINGER, AND THE CHILDREN WALKED THROUGH IT, INTO THE REST OF THEIR STORY.

1

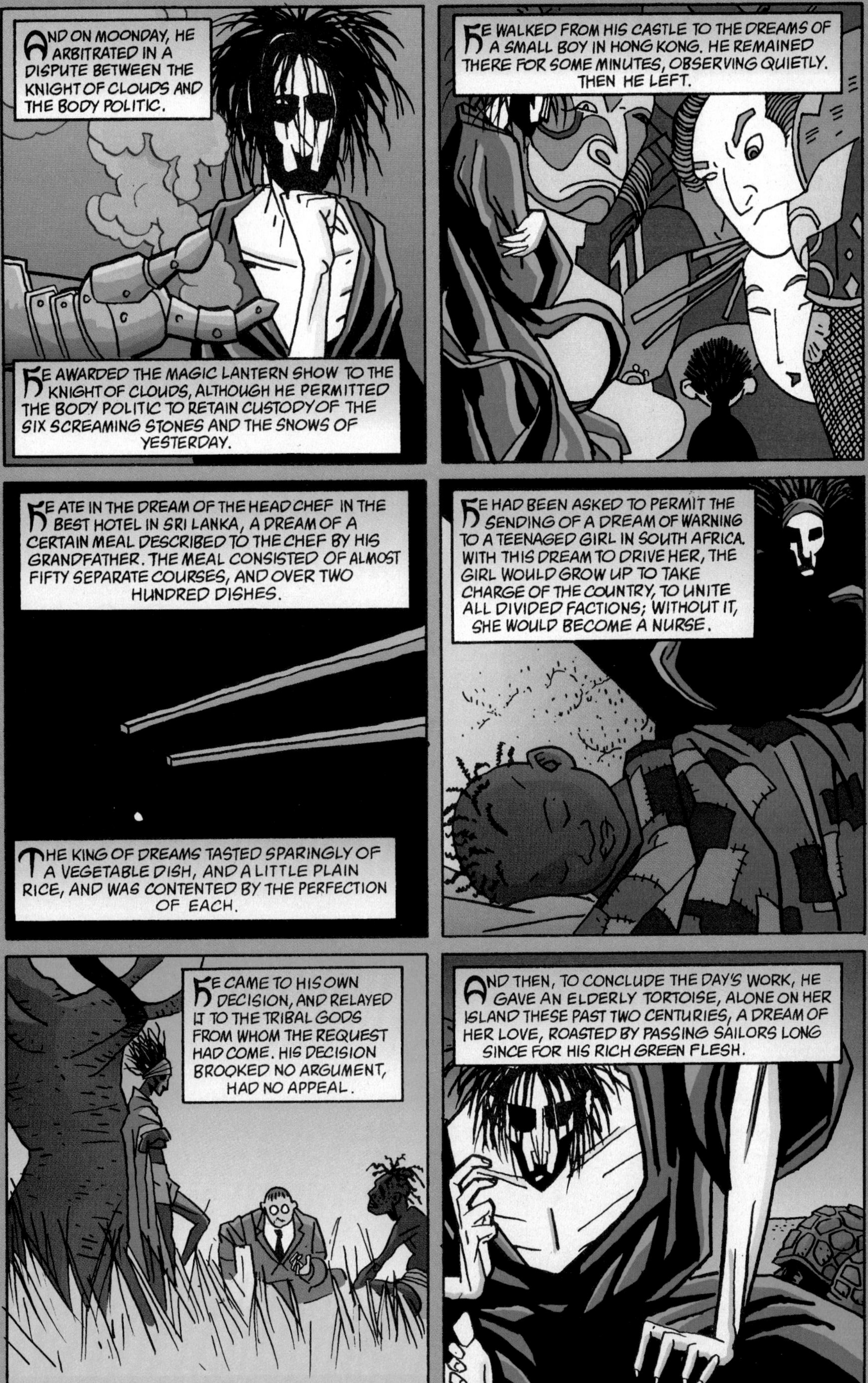
AND ON MOONDAY, HE ARBITRATED IN A DISPUTE BETWEEN THE KNIGHT OF CLOUDS AND THE BODY POLITIC.
HE AWARDED THE MAGIC LANTERN SHOW TO THE KNIGHT OF CLOUDS, ALTHOUGH HE PERMITTED THE BODY POLITIC TO RETAIN CUSTODY OF THE SIX SCREAMING STONES AND THE SNOWS OF YESTERDAY.
HE WALKED FROM HIS CASTLE TO THE DREAMS OF A SMALL BOY IN HONG KONG. HE REMAINED THERE FOR SOME MINUTES, OBSERVING QUIETLY. THEN HE LEFT.
HE ATE IN THE DREAM OF THE HEAD CHEF IN THE BEST HOTEL IN SRI LANKA, A DREAM OF A CERTAIN MEAL DESCRIBED TO THE CHEF BY HIS GRANDFATHER. THE MEAL CONSISTED OF ALMOST FIFTY SEPARATE COURSES, AND OVER TWO HUNDRED DISHES.
THE KING OF DREAMS TASTED SPARINGLY OF A VEGETABLE DISH, AND A LITTLE PLAIN RICE, AND WAS CONTENTED BY THE PERFECTION OF EACH.
HE HAD BEEN ASKED TO PERMIT THE SENDING OF A DREAM OF WARNING TO A TEENAGED GIRL IN SOUTH AFRICA. WITH THIS DREAM TO DRIVE HER, THE GIRL WOULD GROW UP TO TAKE CHARGE OF THE COUNTRY, TO UNITE ALL DIVIDED FACTIONS; WITHOUT IT, SHE WOULD BECOME A NURSE.
HE CAME TO HIS OWN DECISION, AND RELAYED IT TO THE TRIBAL GODS FROM WHOM THE REQUEST HAD COME. HIS DECISION BROOKED NO ARGUMENT, HAD NO APPEAL.
AND THEN, TO CONCLUDE THE DAY'S WORK, HE GAVE AN ELDERLY TORTOISE, ALONE ON HER ISLAND THESE PAST TWO CENTURIES, A DREAM OF HER LOVE, ROASTED BY PASSING SAILORS LONG SINCE FOR HIS RICH GREEN FLESH.
2

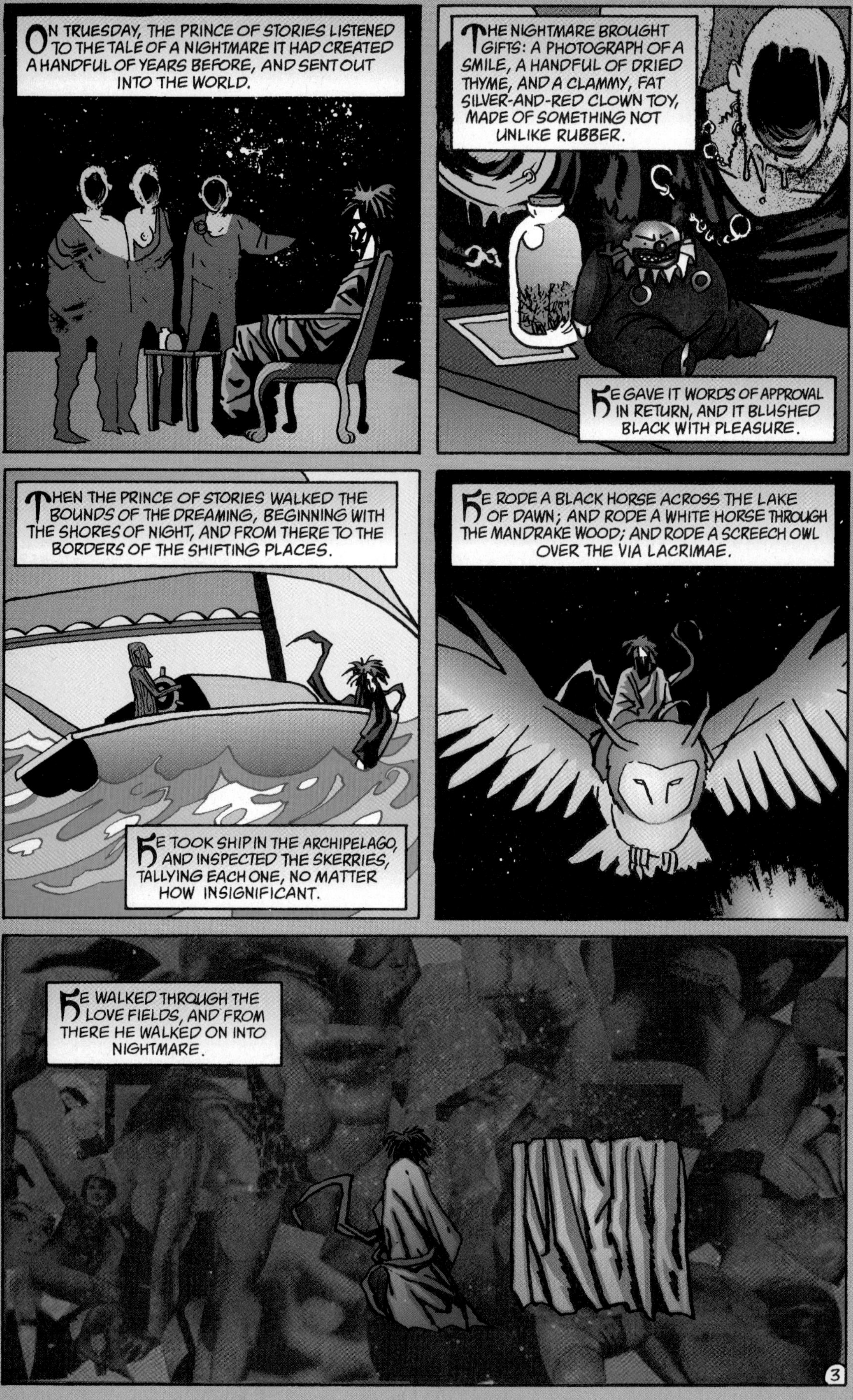

ON TRUESDAY, THE PRINCE OF STORIES LISTENED TO THE TALE OF A NIGHTMARE IT HAD CREATED A HANDFUL OF YEARS BEFORE, AND SENT OUT INTO THE WORLD.
THE NIGHTMARE BROUGHT GIFTS: A PHOTOGRAPH OF A SMILE, A HANDFUL OF DRIED THYME, AND A CLAMMY, FAT SILVER-AND-RED CLOWN TOY, MADE OF SOMETHING NOT UNLIKE RUBBER.
HE GAVE IT WORDS OF APPROVAL IN RETURN, AND IT BLUSHED BLACK WITH PLEASURE.
THEN THE PRINCE OF STORIES WALKED THE BOUNDS OF THE DREAMING, BEGINNING WITH THE SHORES OF NIGHT, AND FROM THERE TO THE BORDERS OF THE SHIFTING PLACES.
HE TOOK SHIP IN THE ARCHIPELAGO, AND INSPECTED THE SKERRIES, TALLYING EACH ONE, NO MATTER HOW INSIGNIFICANT.
HE RODE A BLACK HORSE ACROSS THE LAKE OF DAWN; AND RODE A WHITE HORSE THROUGH THE MANDRAKE WOOD; AND RODE A SCREECH OWL OVER THE VIA LACRIMAE.
HE WALKED THROUGH THE LOVE FIELDS, AND FROM THERE HE WALKED ON INTO NIGHTMARE.

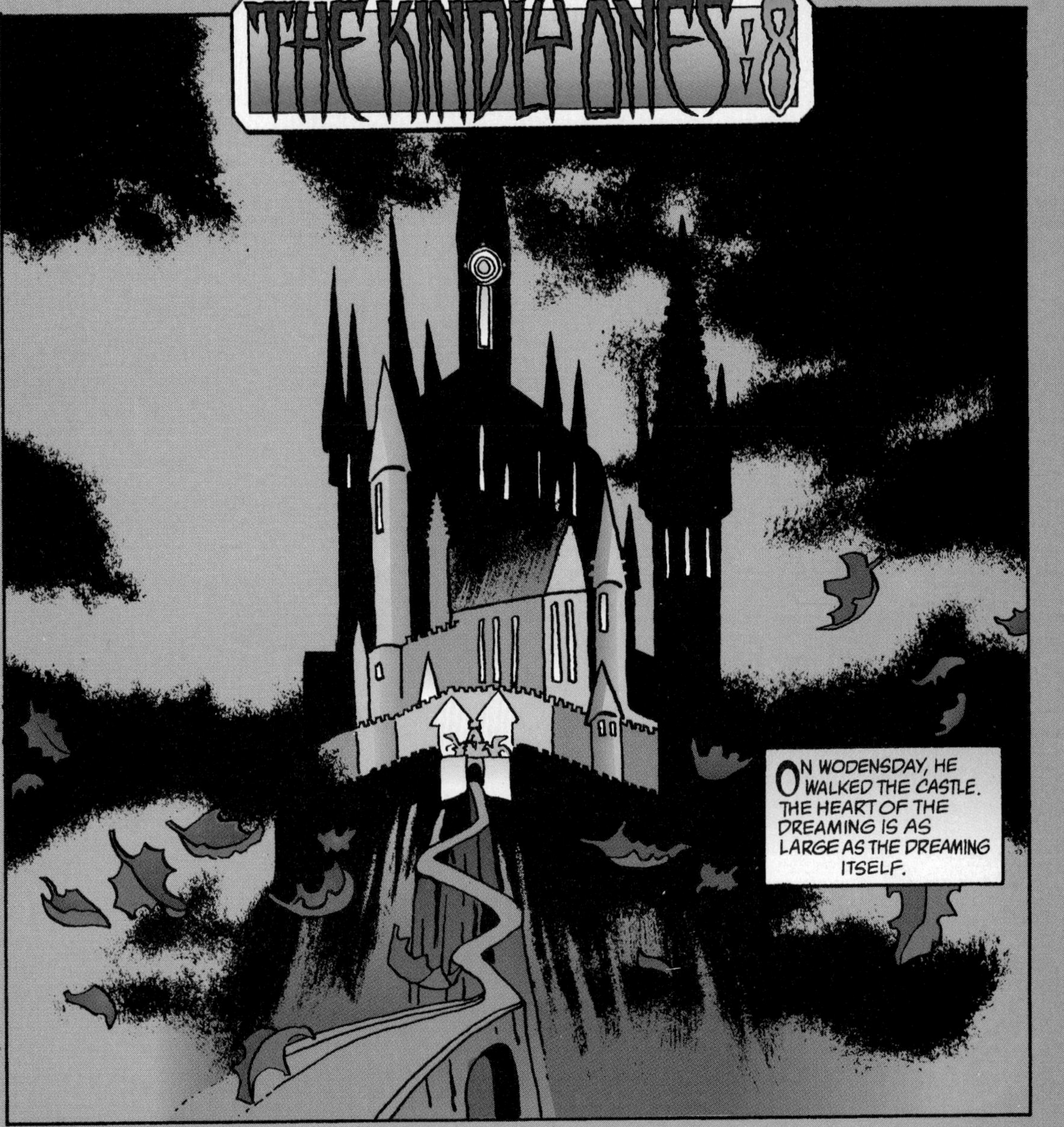
THE KINDLY ONES: 8
ON WODENSDAY, HE WALKED THE CASTLE. THE HEART OF THE DREAMING IS AS LARGE AS THE DREAMING ITSELF.

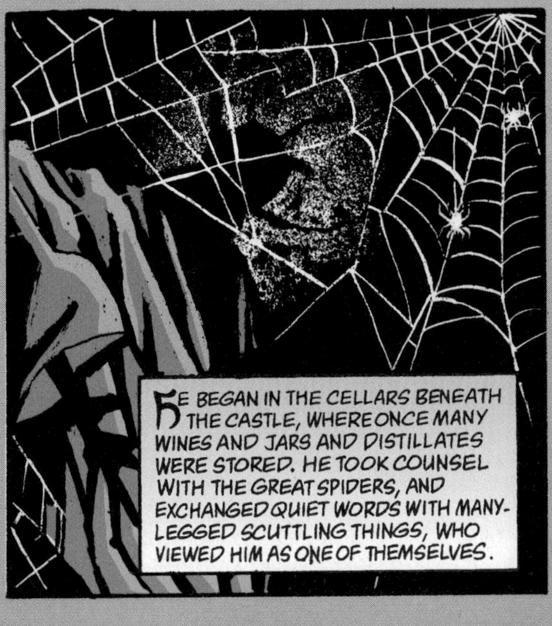
HE BEGAN IN THE CELLARS BENEATH THE CASTLE, WHERE ONCE MANY WINES AND JARS AND DISTILLATES WERE STORED. HE TOOK COUNSEL WITH THE GREAT SPIDERS, AND EXCHANGED QUIET WORDS WITH MANY-LEGGED SCUTTLING THINGS, WHO VIEWED HIM AS ONE OF THEMSELVES.

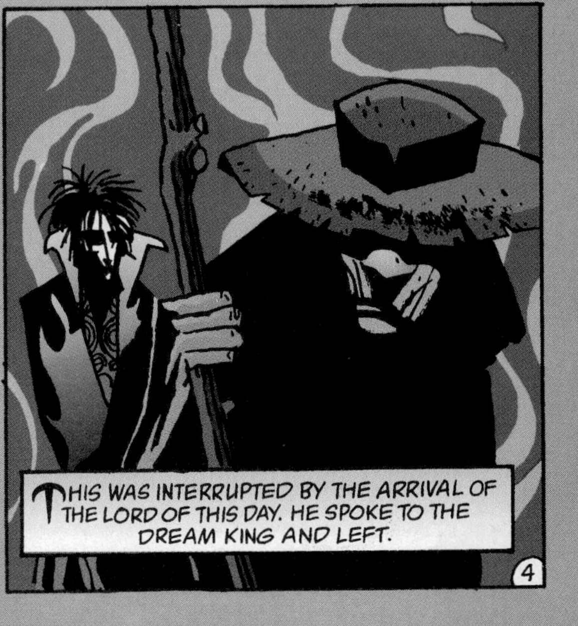
THIS WAS INTERRUPTED BY THE ARRIVAL OF THE LORD OF THIS DAY. HE SPOKE TO THE DREAM KING AND LEFT.

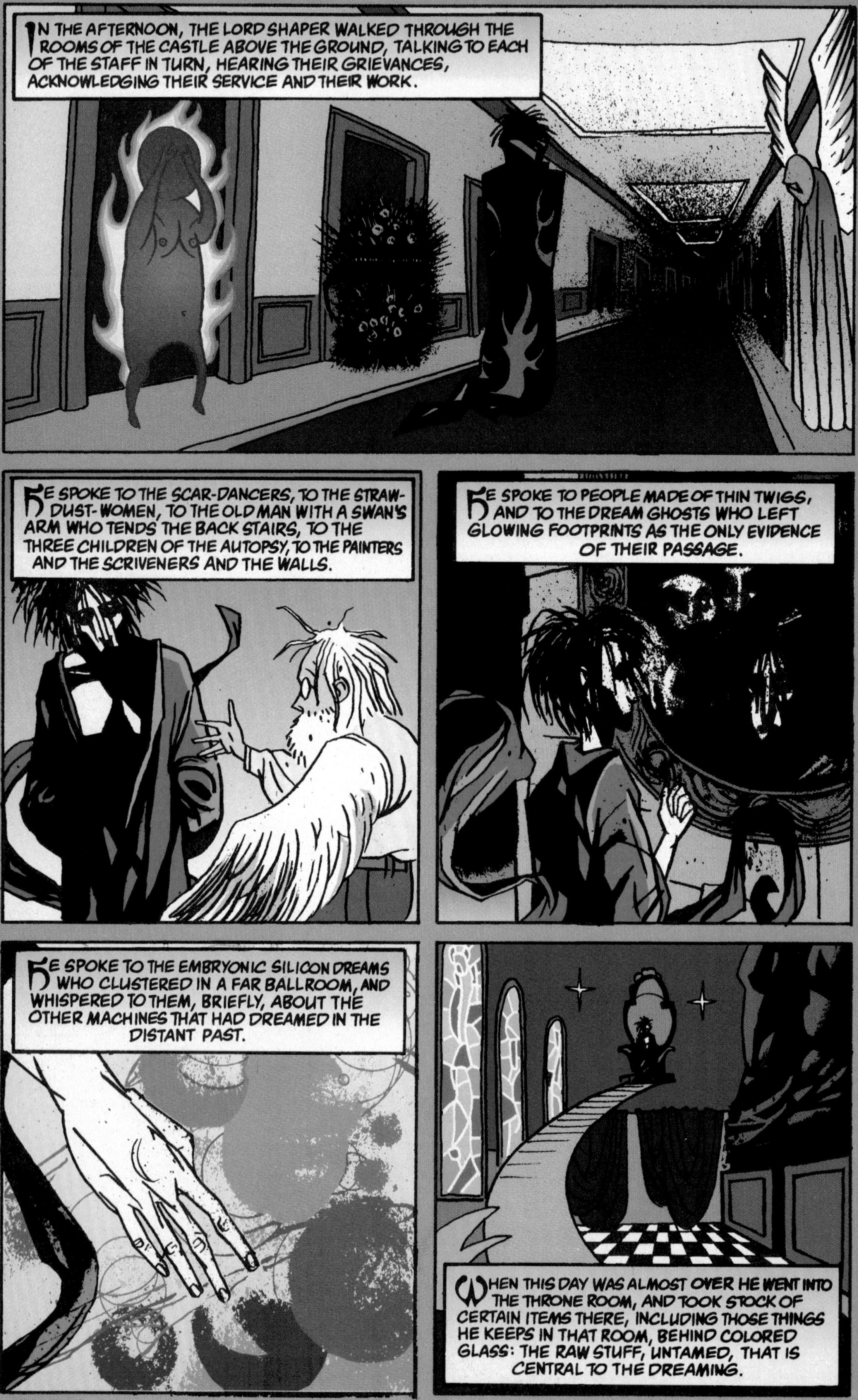
IN THE AFTERNOON, THE LORD SHAPER WALKED THROUGH THE ROOMS OF THE CASTLE ABOVE THE GROUND, TALKING TO EACH OF THE STAFF IN TURN, HEARING THEIR GRIEVANCES, ACKNOWLEDGING THEIR SERVICE AND THEIR WORK.
HE SPOKE TO THE SCAR-DANCERS, TO THE STRAW-DUST-WOMEN, TO THE OLD MAN WITH A SWAN'S ARM WHO TENDS THE BACK STAIRS, TO THE THREE CHILDREN OF THE AUTOPSY, TO THE PAINTERS AND THE SCRIVENERS AND THE WALLS.
HE SPOKE TO PEOPLE MADE OF THIN TWIGS, AND TO THE DREAM GHOSTS WHO LEFT GLOWING FOOTPRINTS AS THE ONLY EVIDENCE OF THEIR PASSAGE.
HE SPOKE TO THE EMBRYONIC SILICON DREAMS WHO CLUSTERED IN A FAR BALLROOM, AND WHISPERED TO THEM, BRIEFLY, ABOUT THE OTHER MACHINES THAT HAD DREAMED IN THE DISTANT PAST.
WHEN THIS DAY WAS ALMOST OVER HE WENT INTO THE THRONE ROOM, AND TOOK STOCK OF CERTAIN ITEMS THERE, INCLUDING THOSE THINGS HE KEEPS IN THAT ROOM, BEHIND COLORED GLASS: THE RAW STUFF, UNTAMED, THAT IS CENTRAL TO THE DREAMING.

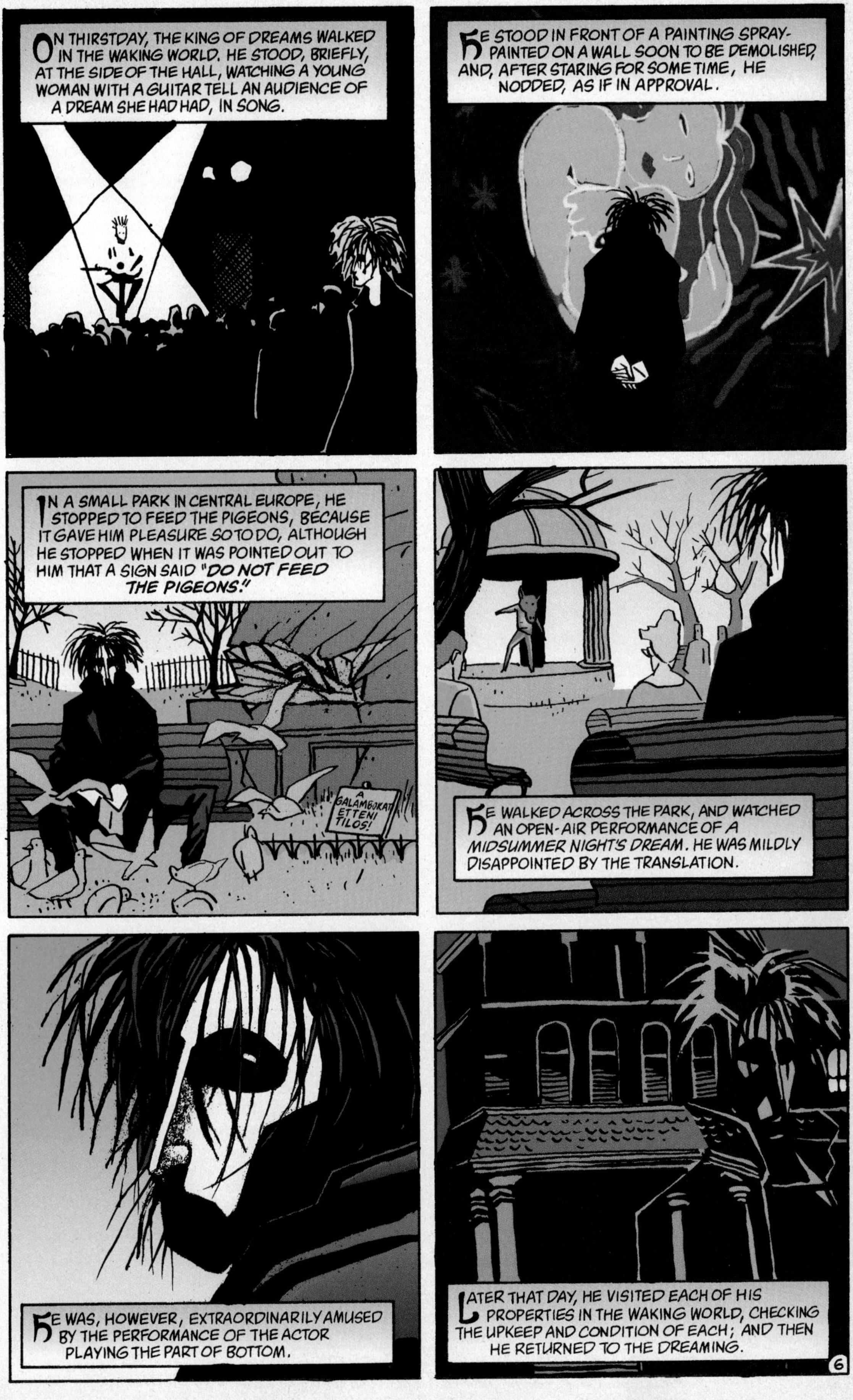
ON THIRSTDAY, THE KING OF DREAMS WALKED IN THE WAKING WORLD. HE STOOD, BRIEFLY, AT THE SIDE OF THE HALL, WATCHING A YOUNG WOMAN WITH A GUITAR TELL AN AUDIENCE OF A DREAM SHE HAD HAD, IN SONG.
HE STOOD IN FRONT OF A PAINTING SPRAY-PAINTED ON A WALL SOON TO BE DEMOLISHED, AND, AFTER STARING FOR SOME TIME, HE NODDED, AS IF IN APPROVAL.
IN A SMALL PARK IN CENTRAL EUROPE, HE STOPPED TO FEED THE PIGEONS, BECAUSE IT GAVE HIM PLEASURE SO TO DO, ALTHOUGH HE STOPPED WHEN IT WAS POINTED OUT TO HIM THAT A SIGN SAID "DO NOT FEED THE PIGEONS."
A GALAMBOKAT ETTENI TILOS!
HE WALKED ACROSS THE PARK, AND WATCHED AN OPEN-AIR PERFORMANCE OF A MIDSUMMER NIGHT'S DREAM. HE WAS MILDLY DISAPPOINTED BY THE TRANSLATION.
HE WAS, HOWEVER, EXTRAORDINARILY AMUSED BY THE PERFORMANCE OF THE ACTOR PLAYING THE PART OF BOTTOM.
LATER THAT DAY, HE VISITED EACH OF HIS PROPERTIES IN THE WAKING WORLD, CHECKING THE UPKEEP AND CONDITION OF EACH; AND THEN HE RETURNED TO THE DREAMING.

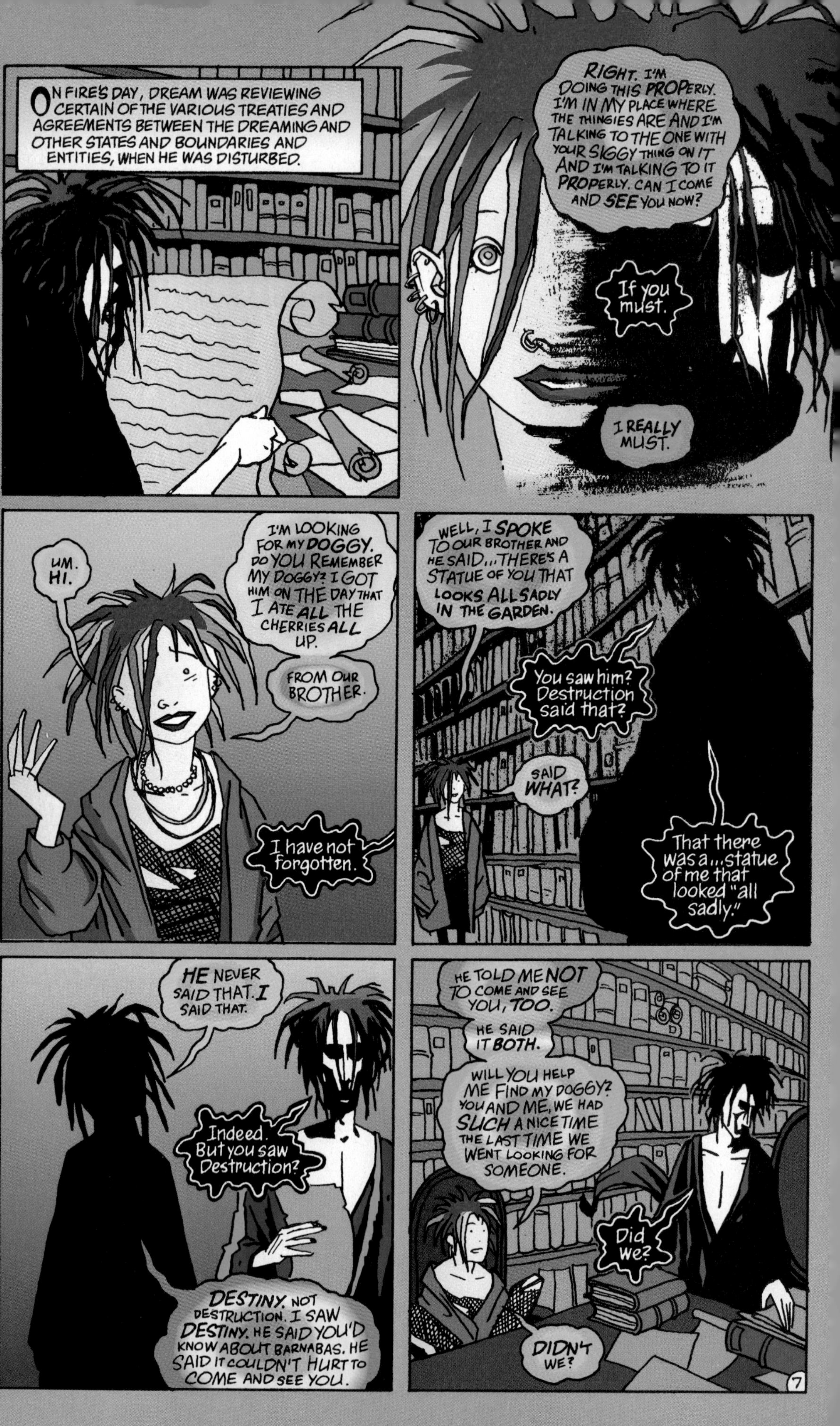

ON FIRE'S DAY, DREAM WAS REVIEWING CERTAIN OF THE VARIOUS TREATIES AND AGREEMENTS BETWEEN THE DREAMING AND OTHER STATES AND BOUNDARIES AND ENTITIES, WHEN HE WAS DISTURBED.
RIGHT. I'M DOING THIS PROPERLY. I'M IN MY PLACE WHERE THE THINGIES ARE AND I'M TALKING TO THE ONE WITH YOUR SIGGY THING ON IT AND I'M TALKING TO IT PROPERLY. CAN I COME AND SEE YOU NOW?
If you must.
I REALLY MUST.
UM. HI.
I'M LOOKING FOR MY DOGGY. DO YOU REMEMBER MY DOGGY? I GOT HIM ON THE DAY THAT I ATE ALL THE CHERRIES ALL UP.
FROM OUR BROTHER.
I have not forgotten.
WELL, I SPOKE TO OUR BROTHER AND HE SAID... THERE'S A STATUE OF YOU THAT LOOKS ALL SADLY IN THE GARDEN.
You saw him? Destruction said that?
SAID WHAT?
That there was a... statue of me that looked "all sadly."
HE NEVER SAID THAT. I SAID THAT.
Indeed. But you saw Destruction?
DESTINY. NOT DESTRUCTION. I SAW DESTINY. HE SAID YOU'D KNOW ABOUT BARNABAS. HE SAID IT COULDN'T HURT TO COME AND SEE YOU.
HE TOLD ME NOT TO COME AND SEE YOU, TOO.
HE SAID IT BOTH.
WILL YOU HELP ME FIND MY DOGGY? YOU AND ME, WE HAD SUCH A NICE TIME THE LAST TIME WE WENT LOOKING FOR SOMEONE.
Did we?
DIDN'T WE?

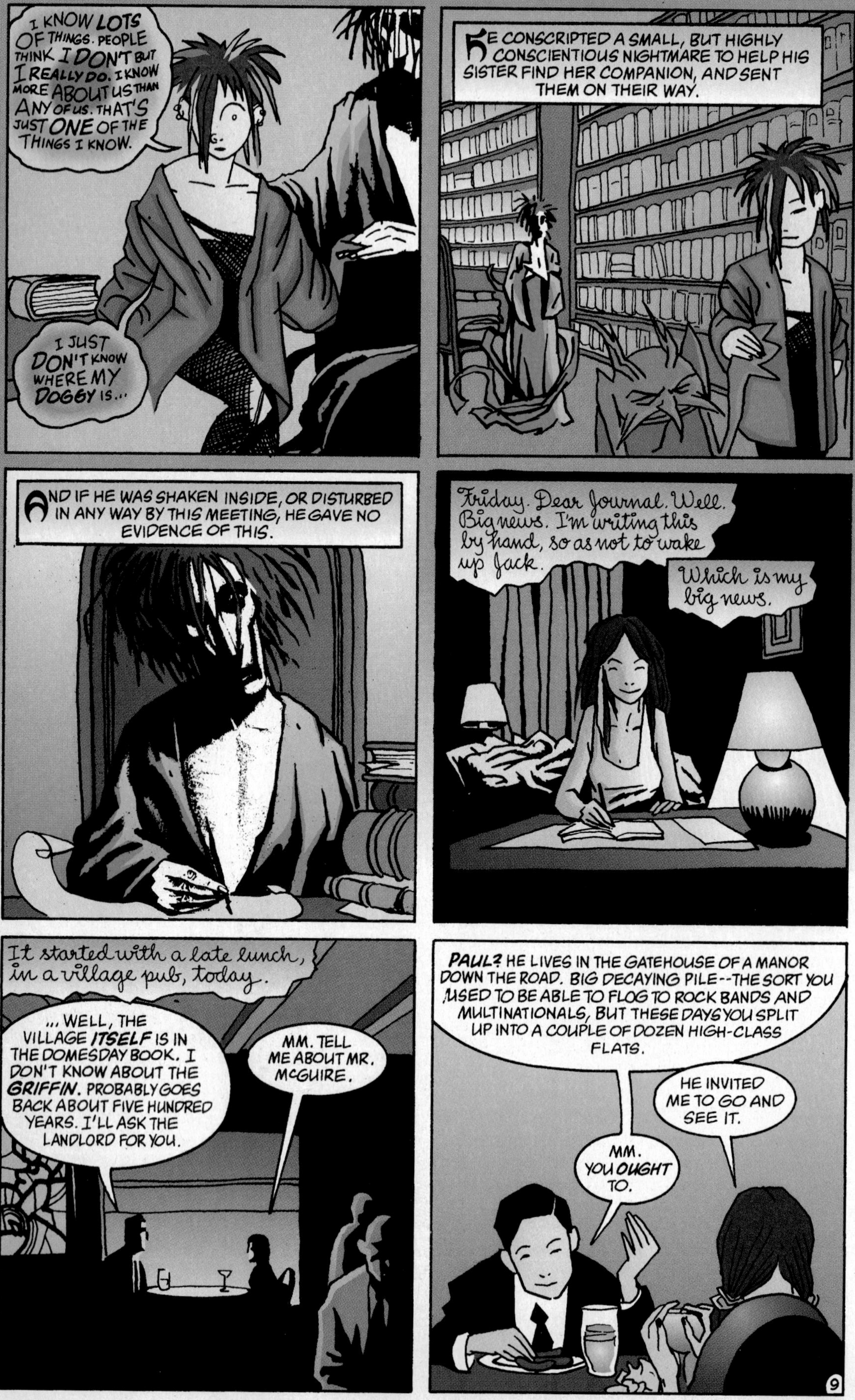
I KNOW LOTS OF THINGS. PEOPLE THINK I DON'T BUT I REALLY DO. I KNOW MORE ABOUT US THAN ANY OF US. THAT'S JUST ONE OF THE THINGS I KNOW.
I JUST DON'T KNOW WHERE MY DOGGY IS...
HE CONSCRIPTED A SMALL, BUT HIGHLY CONSCIENTIOUS NIGHTMARE TO HELP HIS SISTER FIND HER COMPANION, AND SENT THEM ON THEIR WAY.
AND IF HE WAS SHAKEN INSIDE, OR DISTURBED IN ANY WAY BY THIS MEETING, HE GAVE NO EVIDENCE OF THIS.
Friday. Dear Journal. Well. Big news. I'm writing this by hand, so as not to wake up Jack.
Which is my big news.
It started with a late lunch, in a village pub, today.
... WELL, THE VILLAGE ITSELF IS IN THE DOMESDAY BOOK. I DON'T KNOW ABOUT THE GRIFFIN. PROBABLY GOES BACK ABOUT FIVE HUNDRED YEARS. I'LL ASK THE LANDLORD FOR YOU.
MM. TELL ME ABOUT MR. McGUIRE.
PAUL? HE LIVES IN THE GATEHOUSE OF A MANOR DOWN THE ROAD. BIG DECAYING PILE--THE SORT YOU USED TO BE ABLE TO FLOG TO ROCK BANDS AND MULTINATIONALS, BUT THESE DAYS YOU SPLIT UP INTO A COUPLE OF DOZEN HIGH-CLASS FLATS.
HE INVITED ME TO GO AND SEE IT.
MM. YOU OUGHT TO.

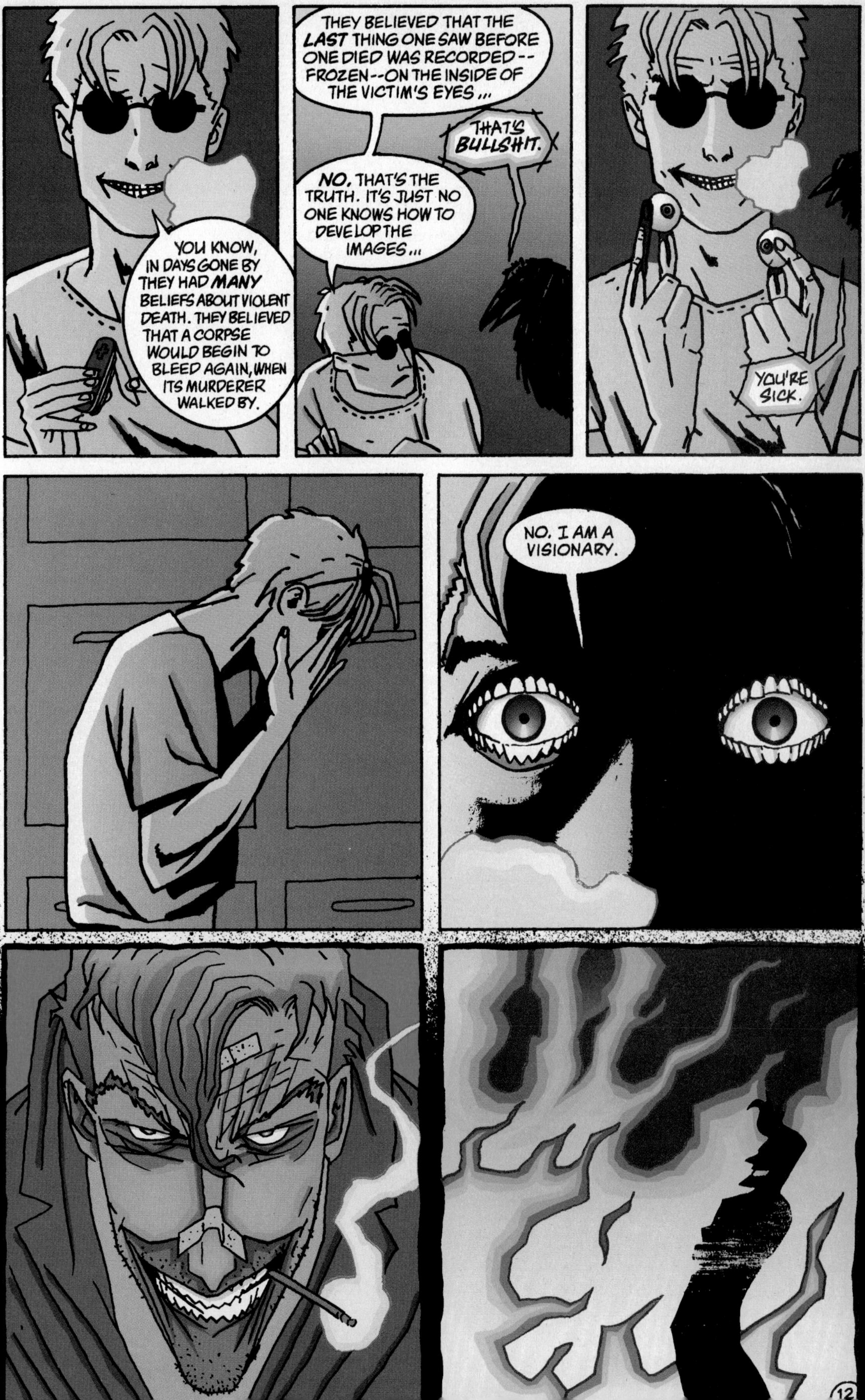
YOU KNOW, IN DAYS GONE BY THEY HAD MANY BELIEFS ABOUT VIOLENT DEATH. THEY BELIEVED THAT A CORPSE WOULD BEGIN TO BLEED AGAIN, WHEN ITS MURDERER WALKED BY.
THEY BELIEVED THAT THE LAST THING ONE SAW BEFORE ONE DIED WAS RECORDED--FROZEN--ON THE INSIDE OF THE VICTIM'S EYES...
THAT'S BULLSHIT.
NO. THAT'S THE TRUTH. IT'S JUST NO ONE KNOWS HOW TO DEVELOP THE IMAGES...
YOU'RE SICK.
NO. I AM A VISIONARY.

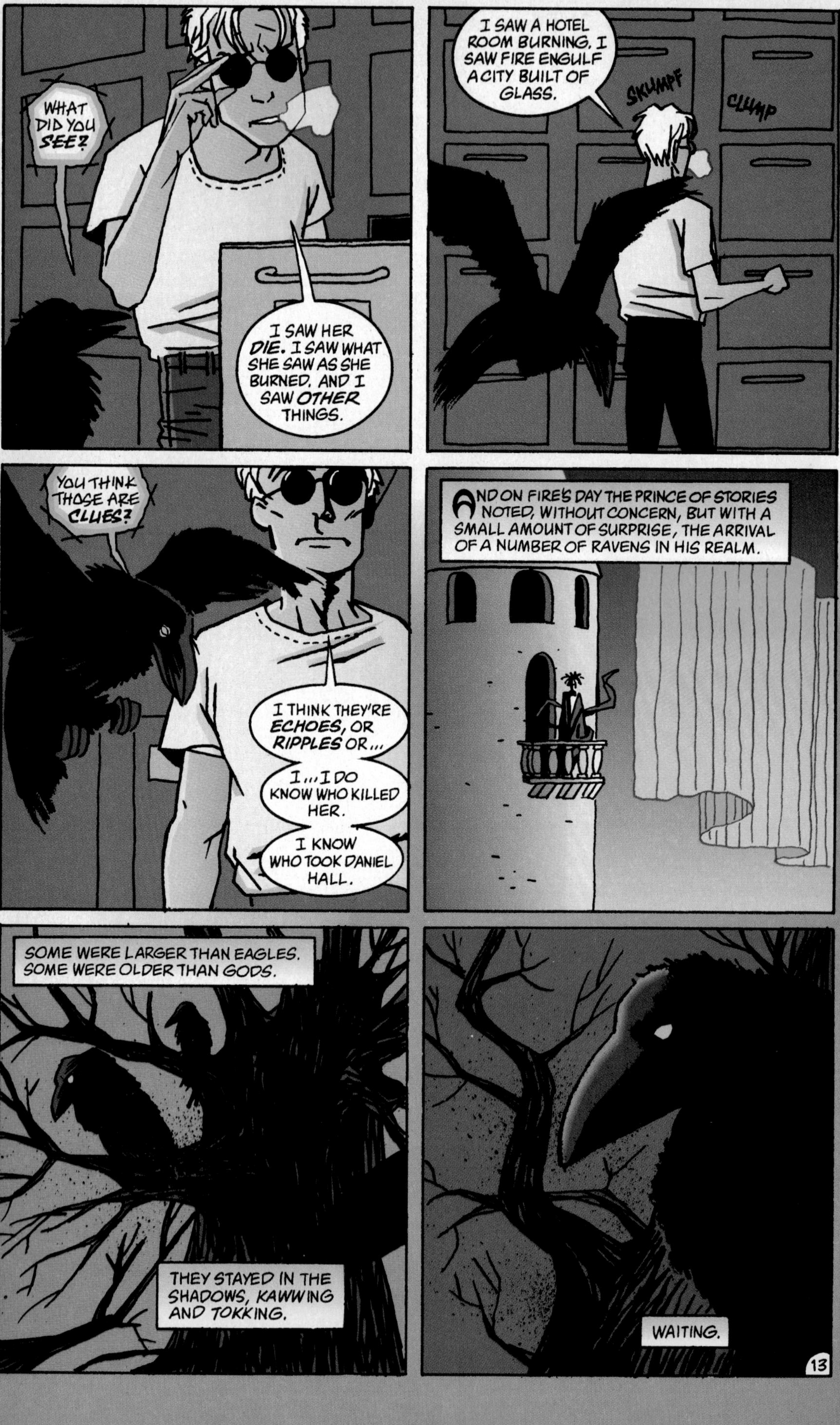
WHAT DID YOU SEE?
I SAW HER DIE. I SAW WHAT SHE SAW AS SHE BURNED, AND I SAW OTHER THINGS.
I SAW A HOTEL ROOM BURNING, I SAW FIRE ENGULF A CITY BUILT OF GLASS.
SKUMPF
CLUMP
YOU THINK THOSE ARE CLUES?
I THINK THEY'RE ECHOES, OR RIPPLES OR...
I... I DO KNOW WHO KILLED HER.
I KNOW WHO TOOK DANIEL HALL.
AND ON FIRE'S DAY THE PRINCE OF STORIES NOTED, WITHOUT CONCERN, BUT WITH A SMALL AMOUNT OF SURPRISE, THE ARRIVAL OF A NUMBER OF RAVENS IN HIS REALM.
SOME WERE LARGER THAN EAGLES. SOME WERE OLDER THAN GODS.
THEY STAYED IN THE SHADOWS, KAWWING AND TOKKING.
WAITING.

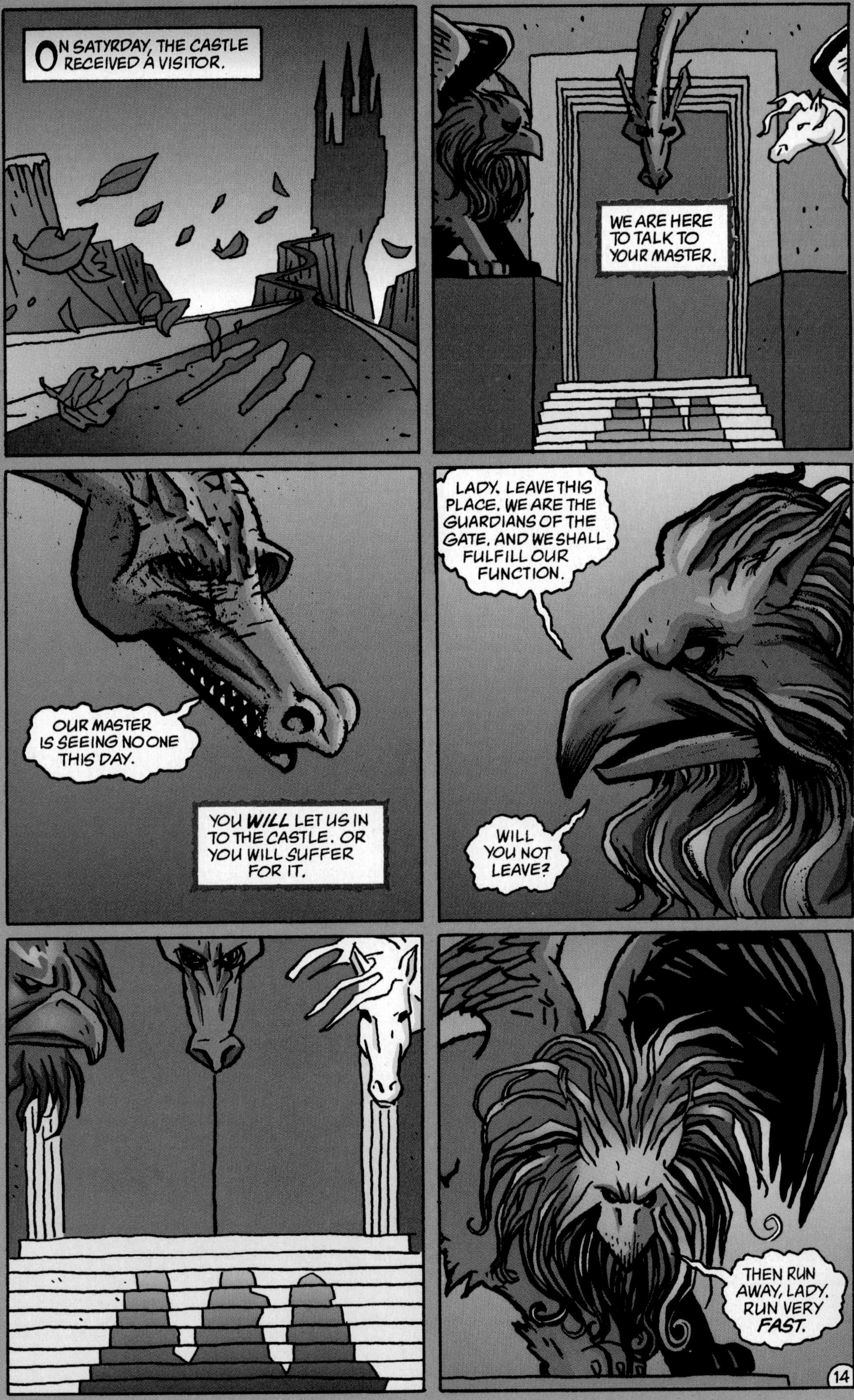
ON SATYRDAY, THE CASTLE RECEIVED A VISITOR.
WE ARE HERE TO TALK TO YOUR MASTER.
OUR MASTER IS SEEING NO ONE THIS DAY.
YOU *WILL* LET US IN TO THE CASTLE. OR YOU WILL SUFFER FOR IT.
LADY. LEAVE THIS PLACE. WE ARE THE GUARDIANS OF THE GATE. AND WE SHALL FULFILL OUR FUNCTION.
WILL YOU NOT LEAVE?
THEN RUN AWAY, LADY. RUN VERY *FAST*.
14

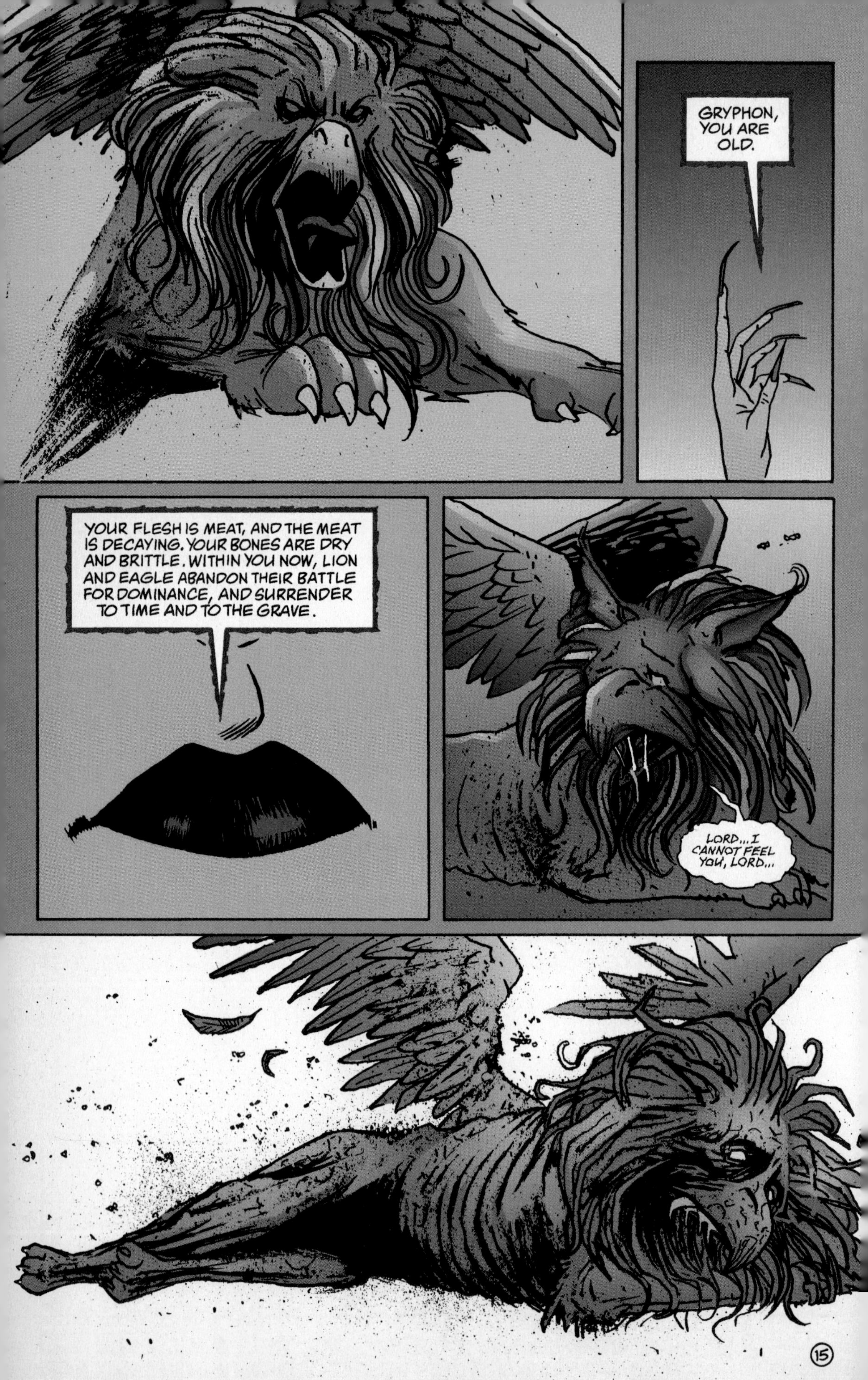
GRYPHON, YOU ARE OLD.
YOUR FLESH IS MEAT, AND THE MEAT IS DECAYING. YOUR BONES ARE DRY AND BRITTLE. WITHIN YOU NOW, LION AND EAGLE ABANDON THEIR BATTLE FOR DOMINANCE, AND SURRENDER TO TIME AND TO THE GRAVE.
LORD... I CANNOT FEEL YOU, LORD...

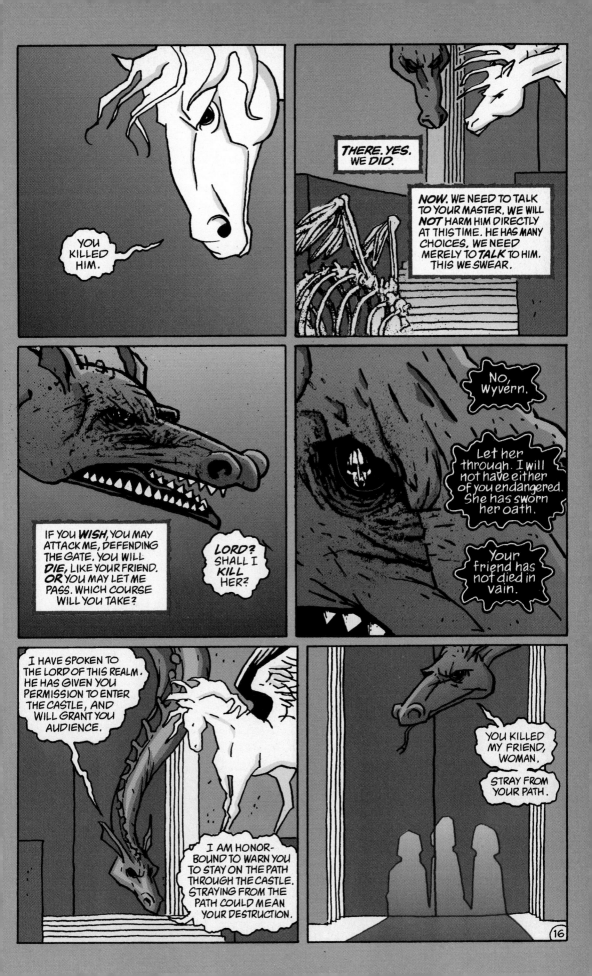

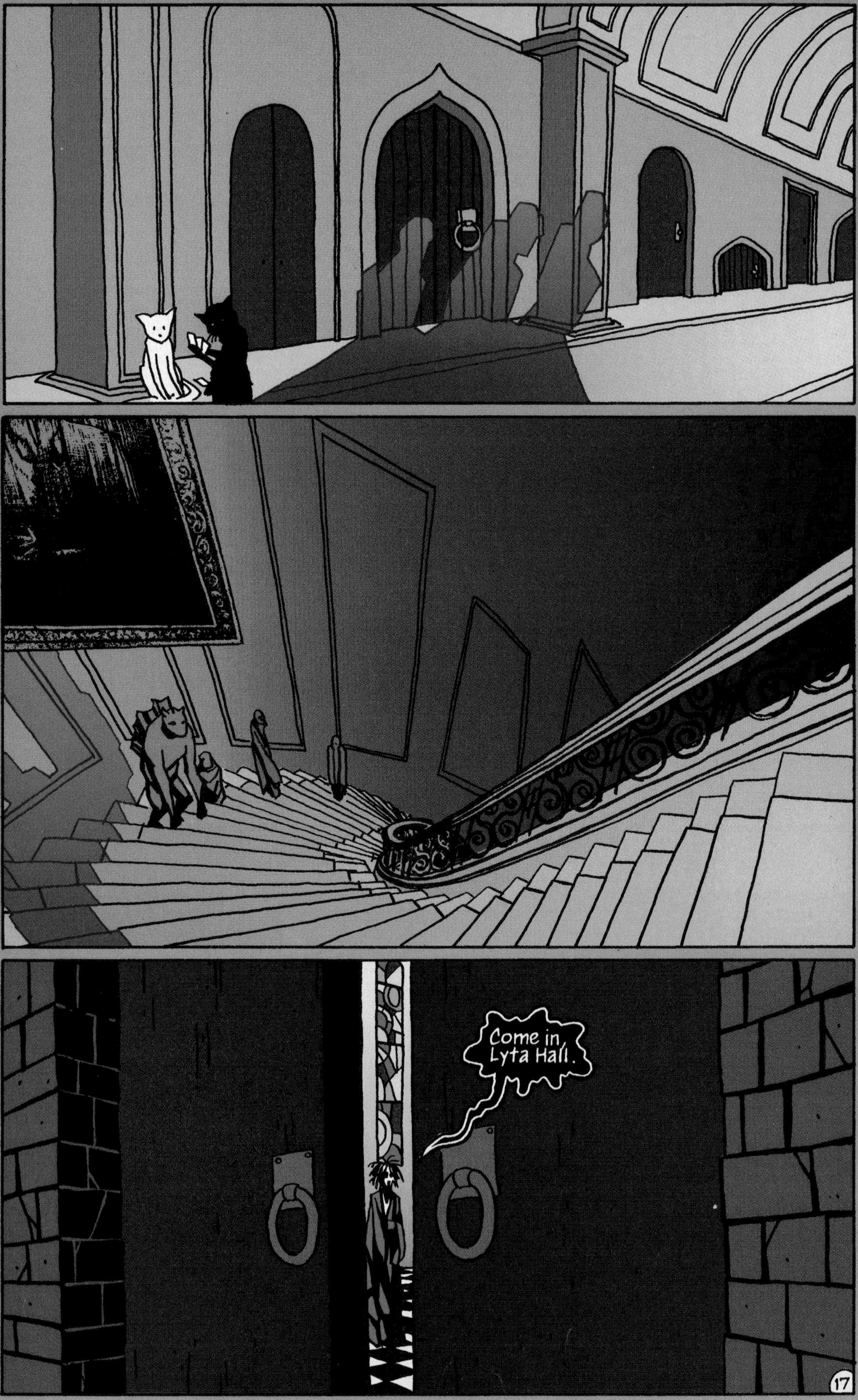
Come in, Lyta Hall.

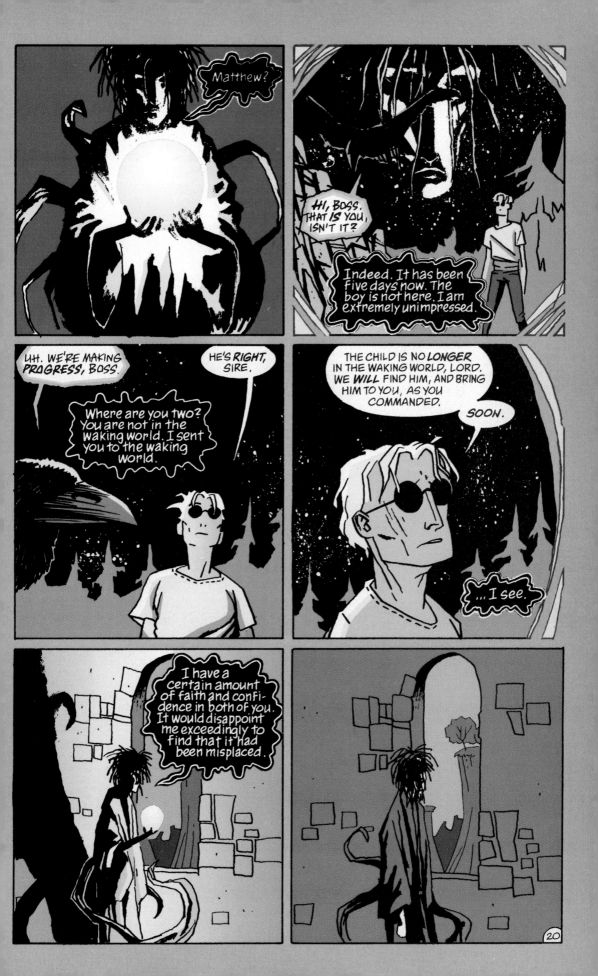

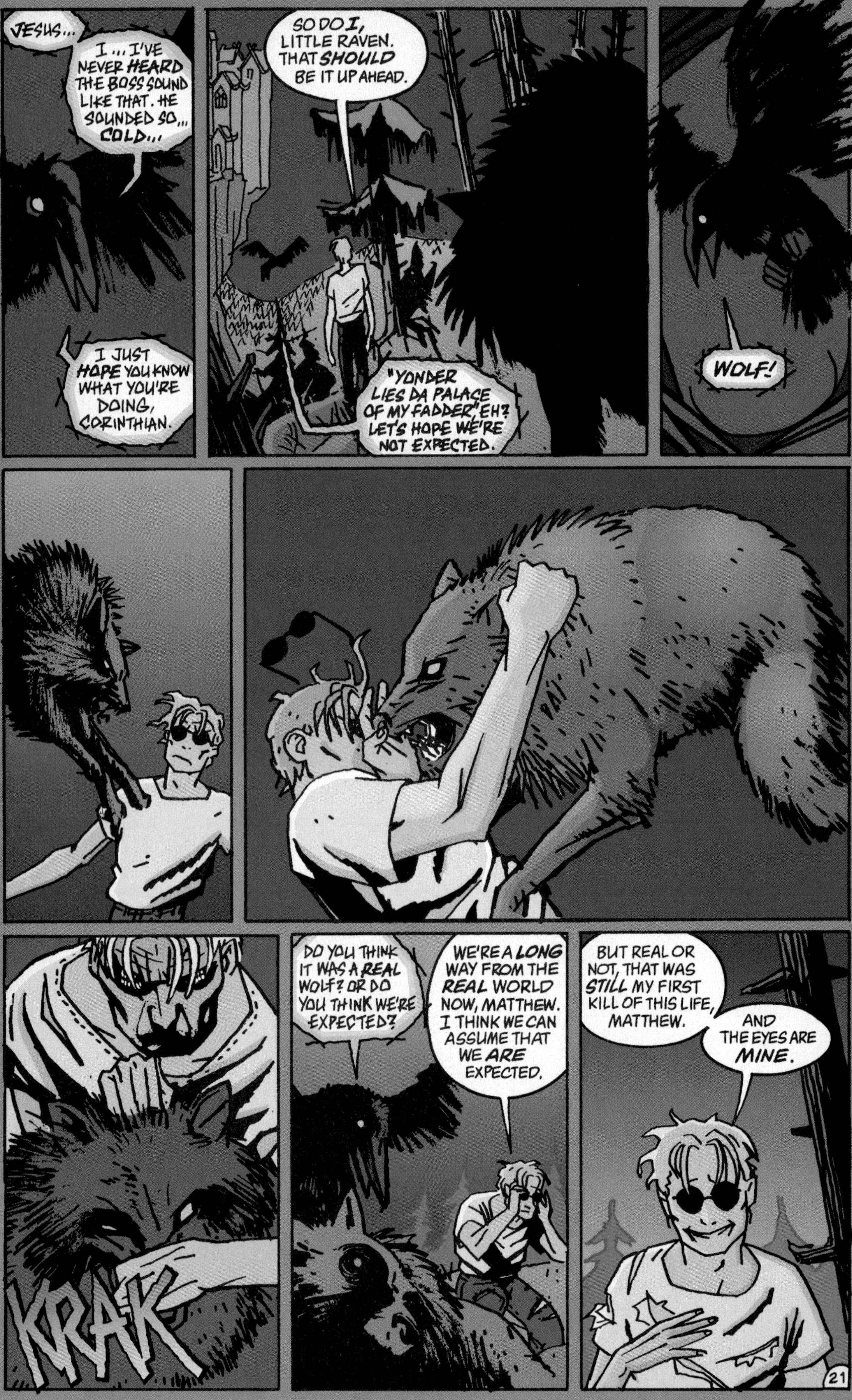
JESUS...
I... I'VE NEVER HEARD THE BOSS SOUND LIKE THAT. HE SOUNDED SO... COLD...
I JUST HOPE YOU KNOW WHAT YOU'RE DOING, CORINTHIAN.
SO DO I, LITTLE RAVEN. THAT SHOULD BE IT UP AHEAD.
"YONDER LIES DA PALACE OF MY FADDER," EH? LET'S HOPE WE'RE NOT EXPECTED.
WOLF!
KRAK
DO YOU THINK IT WAS A REAL WOLF? OR DO YOU THINK WE'RE EXPECTED?
WE'RE A LONG WAY FROM THE REAL WORLD NOW, MATTHEW. I THINK WE CAN ASSUME THAT WE ARE EXPECTED.
BUT REAL OR NOT, THAT WAS STILL MY FIRST KILL OF THIS LIFE, MATTHEW.
AND THE EYES ARE MINE.

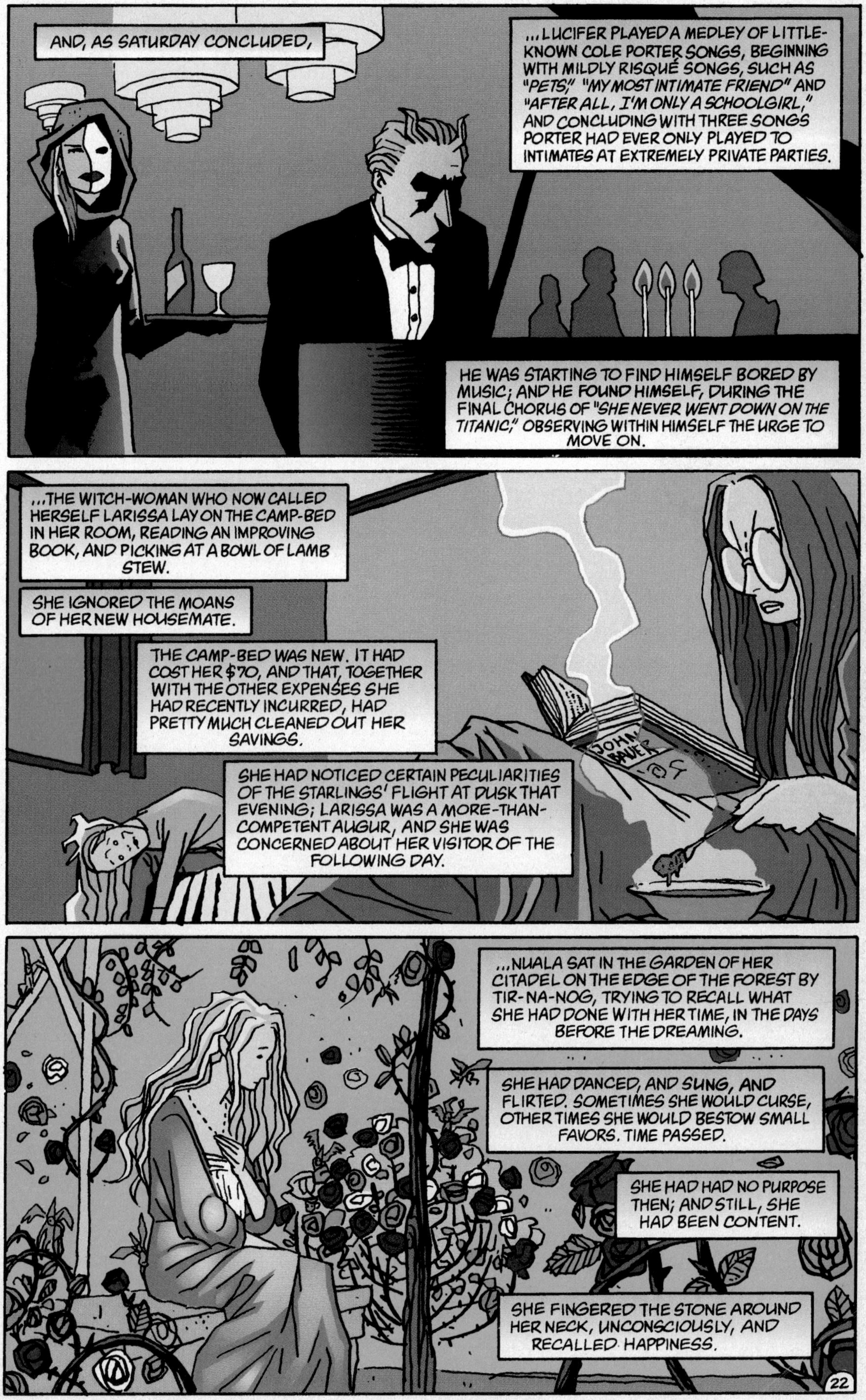
AND, AS SATURDAY CONCLUDED,
...LUCIFER PLAYED A MEDLEY OF LITTLE-KNOWN COLE PORTER SONGS, BEGINNING WITH MILDLY RISQUÉ SONGS, SUCH AS "PETS," "MY MOST INTIMATE FRIEND" AND "AFTER ALL, I'M ONLY A SCHOOLGIRL," AND CONCLUDING WITH THREE SONGS PORTER HAD EVER ONLY PLAYED TO INTIMATES AT EXTREMELY PRIVATE PARTIES.
HE WAS STARTING TO FIND HIMSELF BORED BY MUSIC; AND HE FOUND HIMSELF, DURING THE FINAL CHORUS OF "SHE NEVER WENT DOWN ON THE TITANIC," OBSERVING WITHIN HIMSELF THE URGE TO MOVE ON.
...THE WITCH-WOMAN WHO NOW CALLED HERSELF LARISSA LAY ON THE CAMP-BED IN HER ROOM, READING AN IMPROVING BOOK, AND PICKING AT A BOWL OF LAMB STEW.
SHE IGNORED THE MOANS OF HER NEW HOUSEMATE.
THE CAMP-BED WAS NEW. IT HAD COST HER $70, AND THAT, TOGETHER WITH THE OTHER EXPENSES SHE HAD RECENTLY INCURRED, HAD PRETTY MUCH CLEANED OUT HER SAVINGS.
SHE HAD NOTICED CERTAIN PECULIARITIES OF THE STARLINGS' FLIGHT AT DUSK THAT EVENING; LARISSA WAS A MORE-THAN-COMPETENT AUGUR, AND SHE WAS CONCERNED ABOUT HER VISITOR OF THE FOLLOWING DAY.
...NUALA SAT IN THE GARDEN OF HER CITADEL ON THE EDGE OF THE FOREST BY TIR-NA-NOG, TRYING TO RECALL WHAT SHE HAD DONE WITH HER TIME, IN THE DAYS BEFORE THE DREAMING.
SHE HAD DANCED, AND SUNG, AND FLIRTED. SOMETIMES SHE WOULD CURSE, OTHER TIMES SHE WOULD BESTOW SMALL FAVORS. TIME PASSED.
SHE HAD HAD NO PURPOSE THEN; AND STILL, SHE HAD BEEN CONTENT.
SHE FINGERED THE STONE AROUND HER NECK, UNCONSCIOUSLY, AND RECALLED HAPPINESS.
22

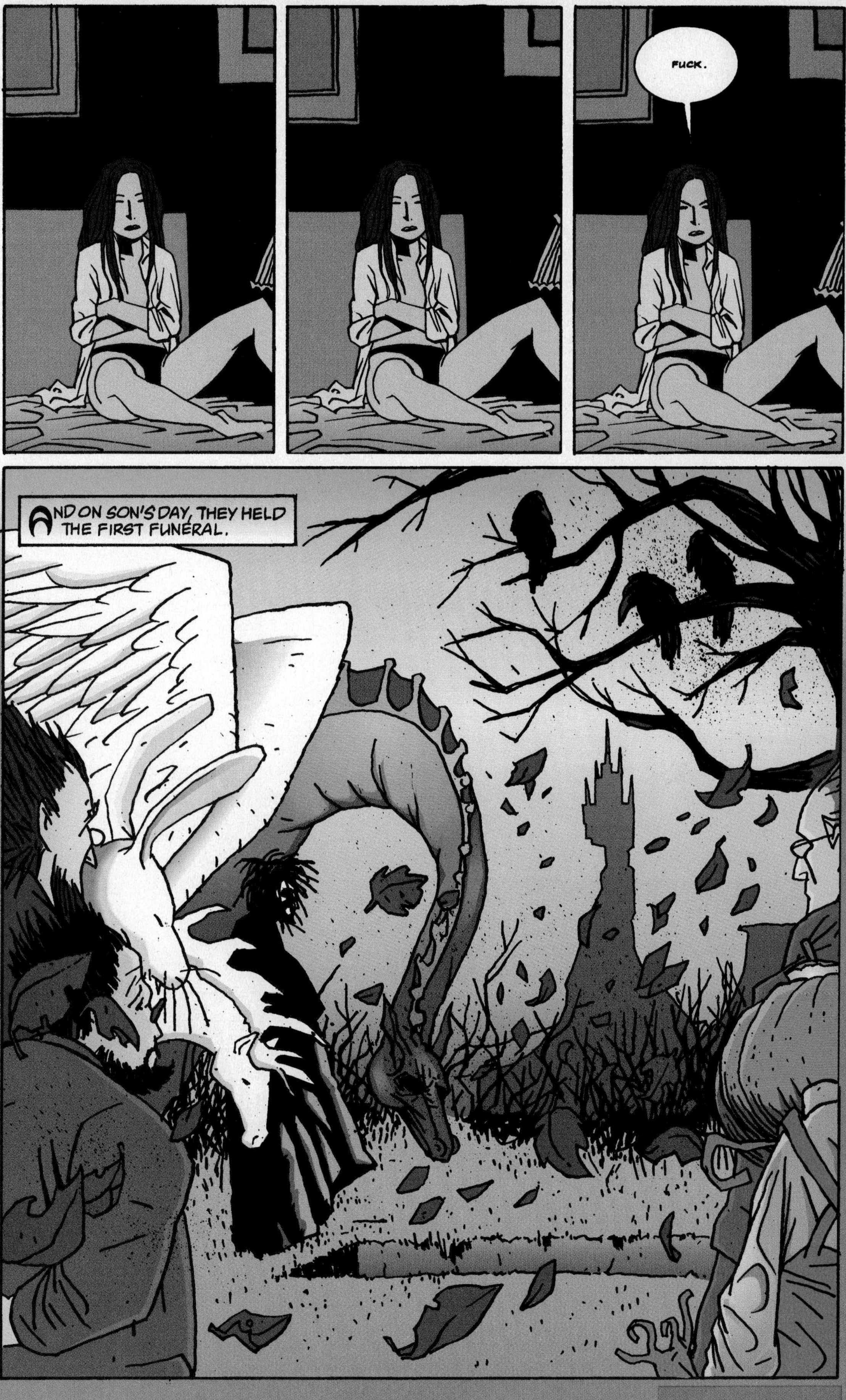
FUCK.
AND ON SON'S DAY, THEY HELD THE FIRST FUNERAL.

part
TIME

tse

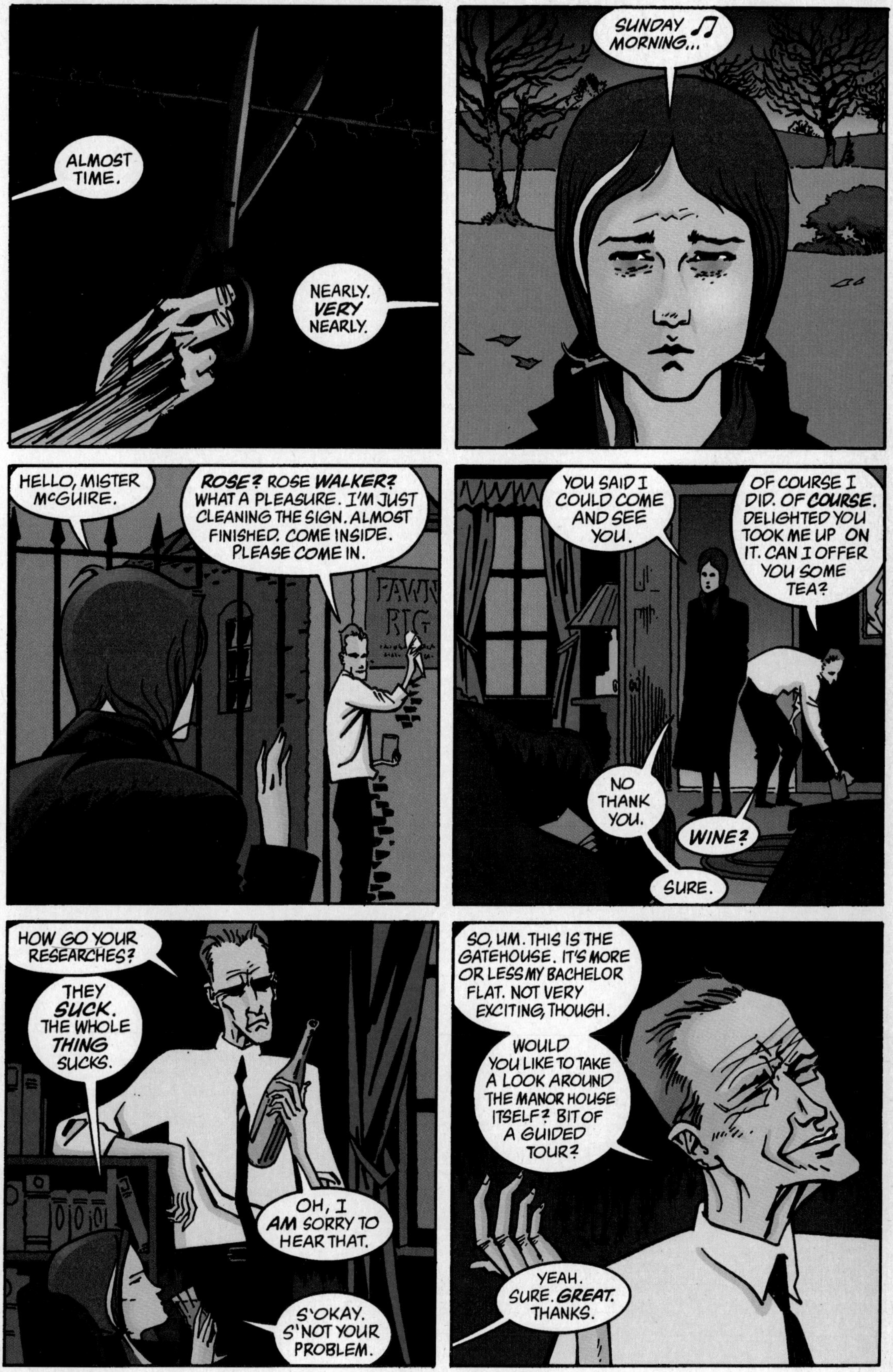
ALMOST TIME.
NEARLY. VERY NEARLY.
SUNDAY MORNING...
HELLO, MISTER McGUIRE.
ROSE? ROSE WALKER? WHAT A PLEASURE. I'M JUST CLEANING THE SIGN. ALMOST FINISHED. COME INSIDE. PLEASE COME IN.
FAWN RIG
YOU SAID I COULD COME AND SEE YOU.
OF COURSE I DID. OF COURSE. DELIGHTED YOU TOOK ME UP ON IT. CAN I OFFER YOU SOME TEA?
NO THANK YOU.
WINE?
SURE.
HOW GO YOUR RESEARCHES?
THEY SUCK. THE WHOLE THING SUCKS.
OH, I AM SORRY TO HEAR THAT.
S'OKAY. S'NOT YOUR PROBLEM.
SO, UM. THIS IS THE GATEHOUSE. IT'S MORE OR LESS MY BACHELOR FLAT. NOT VERY EXCITING, THOUGH.
WOULD YOU LIKE TO TAKE A LOOK AROUND THE MANOR HOUSE ITSELF? BIT OF A GUIDED TOUR?
YEAH. SURE. GREAT. THANKS.

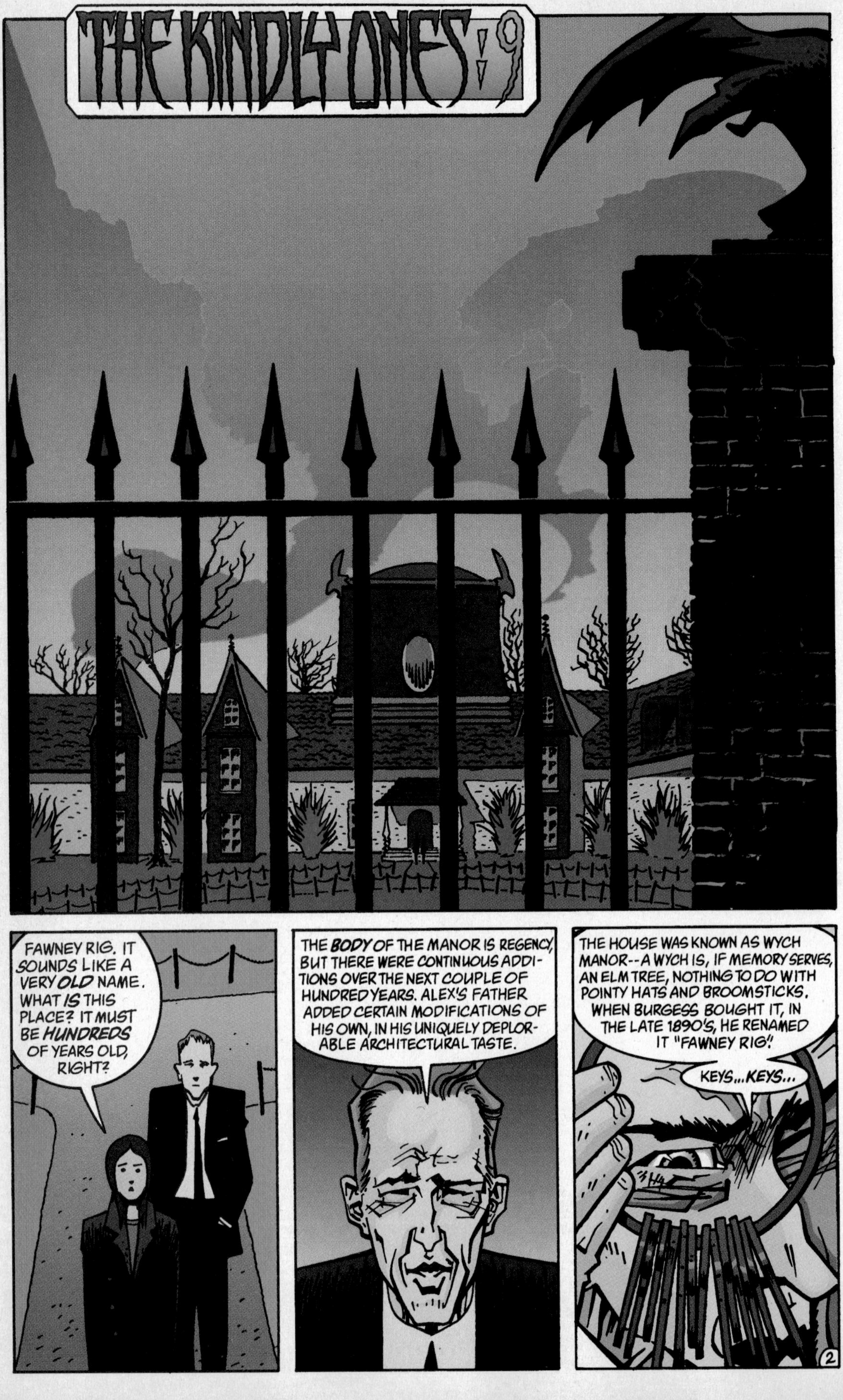
THE KINDLY ONES: 9
FAWNEY RIG. IT SOUNDS LIKE A VERY OLD NAME. WHAT IS THIS PLACE? IT MUST BE HUNDREDS OF YEARS OLD, RIGHT?
THE BODY OF THE MANOR IS REGENCY, BUT THERE WERE CONTINUOUS ADDITIONS OVER THE NEXT COUPLE OF HUNDRED YEARS. ALEX'S FATHER ADDED CERTAIN MODIFICATIONS OF HIS OWN, IN HIS UNIQUELY DEPLORABLE ARCHITECTURAL TASTE.
THE HOUSE WAS KNOWN AS WYCH MANOR--A WYCH IS, IF MEMORY SERVES, AN ELM TREE, NOTHING TO DO WITH POINTY HATS AND BROOMSTICKS. WHEN BURGESS BOUGHT IT, IN THE LATE 1890'S, HE RENAMED IT "FAWNEY RIG."
KEYS... KEYS...
2

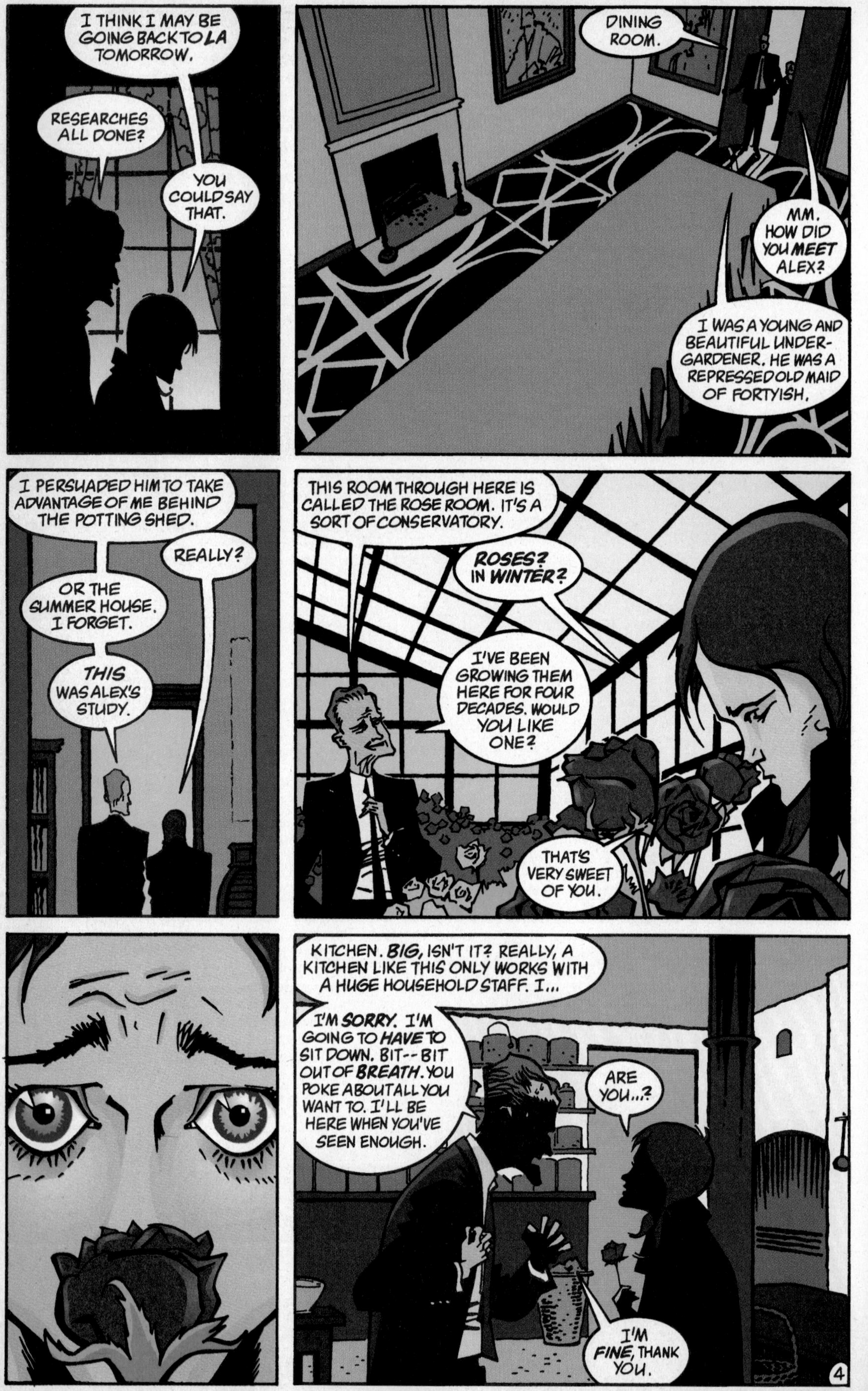
I THINK I MAY BE GOING BACK TO LA TOMORROW.
RESEARCHES ALL DONE?
YOU COULD SAY THAT.
DINING ROOM.
MM. HOW DID YOU MEET ALEX?
I WAS A YOUNG AND BEAUTIFUL UNDER-GARDENER. HE WAS A REPRESSED OLD MAID OF FORTYISH.
I PERSUADED HIM TO TAKE ADVANTAGE OF ME BEHIND THE POTTING SHED.
REALLY?
OR THE SUMMER HOUSE. I FORGET.
THIS WAS ALEX'S STUDY.
THIS ROOM THROUGH HERE IS CALLED THE ROSE ROOM. IT'S A SORT OF CONSERVATORY.
ROSES? IN WINTER?
I'VE BEEN GROWING THEM HERE FOR FOUR DECADES. WOULD YOU LIKE ONE?
THAT'S VERY SWEET OF YOU.
KITCHEN. BIG, ISN'T IT? REALLY, A KITCHEN LIKE THIS ONLY WORKS WITH A HUGE HOUSEHOLD STAFF. I...
I'M SORRY. I'M GOING TO HAVE TO SIT DOWN. BIT-- BIT OUT OF BREATH. YOU POKE ABOUT ALL YOU WANT TO. I'LL BE HERE WHEN YOU'VE SEEN ENOUGH.
ARE YOU...?
I'M FINE, THANK YOU.
4

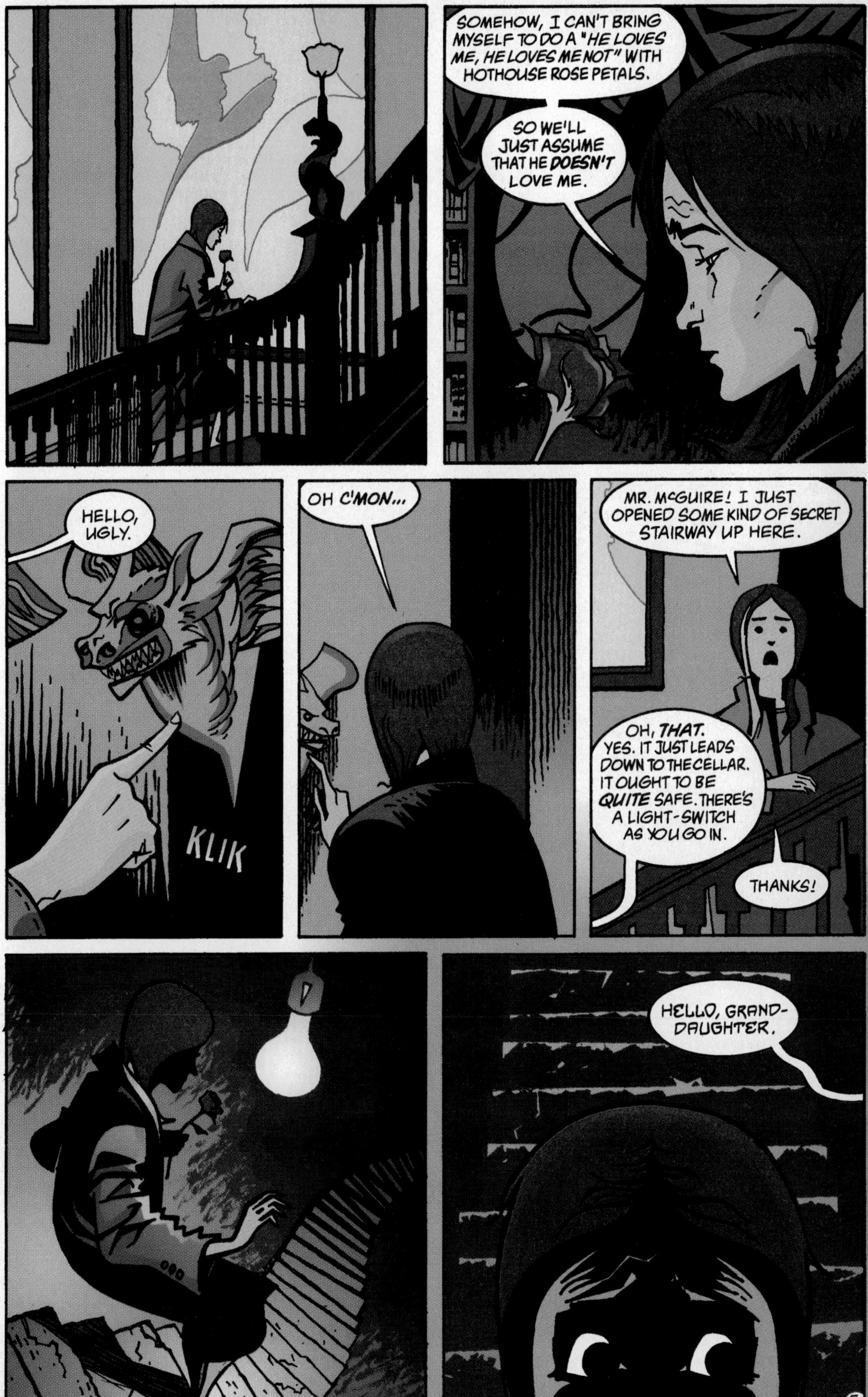
SOMEHOW, I CAN'T BRING MYSELF TO DO A "HE LOVES ME, HE LOVES ME NOT" WITH HOTHOUSE ROSE PETALS.
SO WE'LL JUST ASSUME THAT HE DOESN'T LOVE ME.
HELLO, UGLY.
KLIK
OH C'MON...
MR. McGUIRE! I JUST OPENED SOME KIND OF SECRET STAIRWAY UP HERE.
OH, THAT. YES. IT JUST LEADS DOWN TO THE CELLAR. IT OUGHT TO BE QUITE SAFE. THERE'S A LIGHT-SWITCH AS YOU GO IN.
THANKS!
HELLO, GRAND-DAUGHTER.

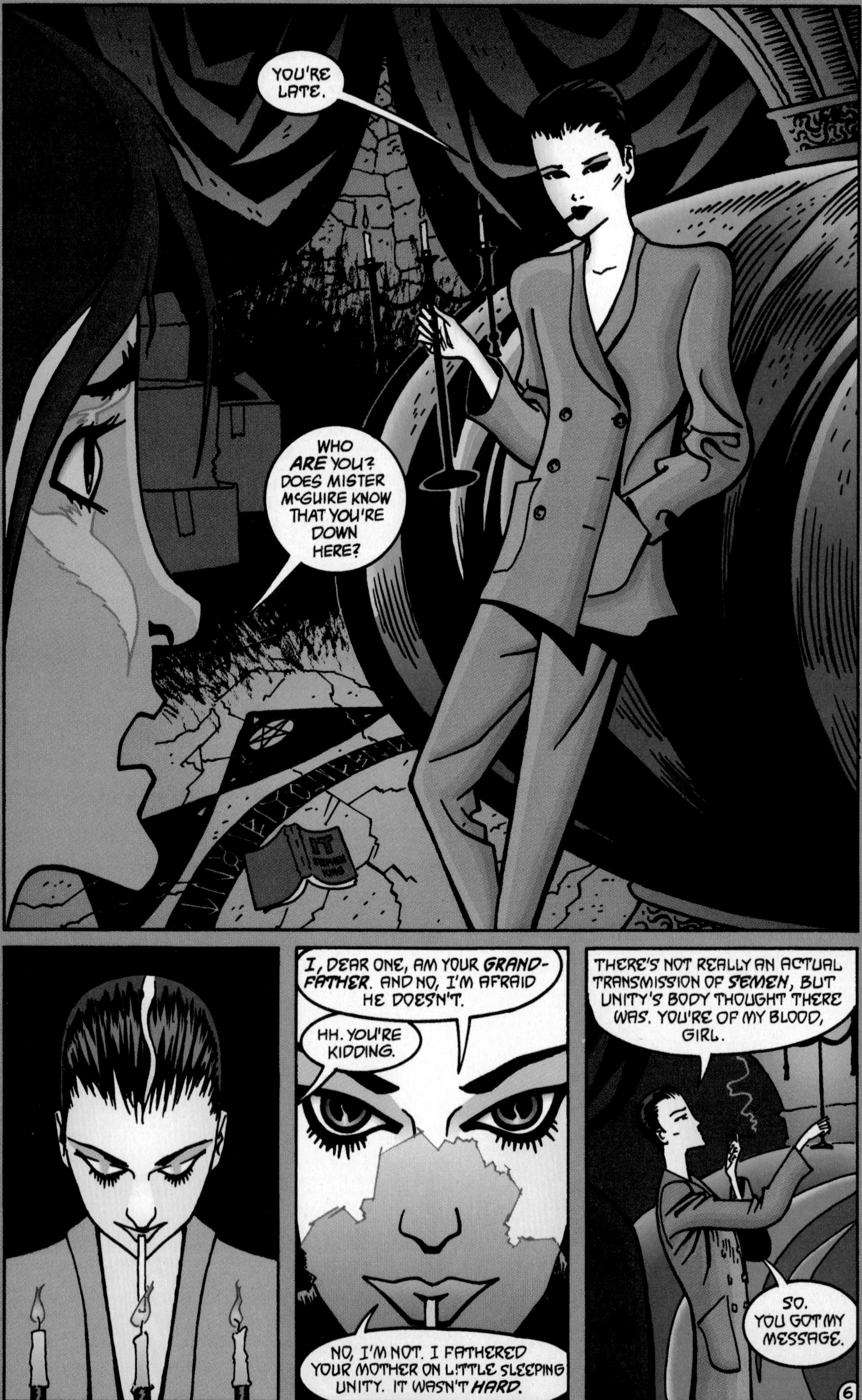
YOU'RE LATE.
WHO ARE YOU? DOES MISTER McGUIRE KNOW THAT YOU'RE DOWN HERE?
IT STEPHEN KING
I, DEAR ONE, AM YOUR GRAND-FATHER. AND NO, I'M AFRAID HE DOESN'T.
HH. YOU'RE KIDDING.
NO, I'M NOT. I FATHERED YOUR MOTHER ON LITTLE SLEEPING UNITY. IT WASN'T HARD.
THERE'S NOT REALLY AN ACTUAL TRANSMISSION OF SEMEN, BUT UNITY'S BODY THOUGHT THERE WAS. YOU'RE OF MY BLOOD, GIRL.
SO. YOU GOT MY MESSAGE.

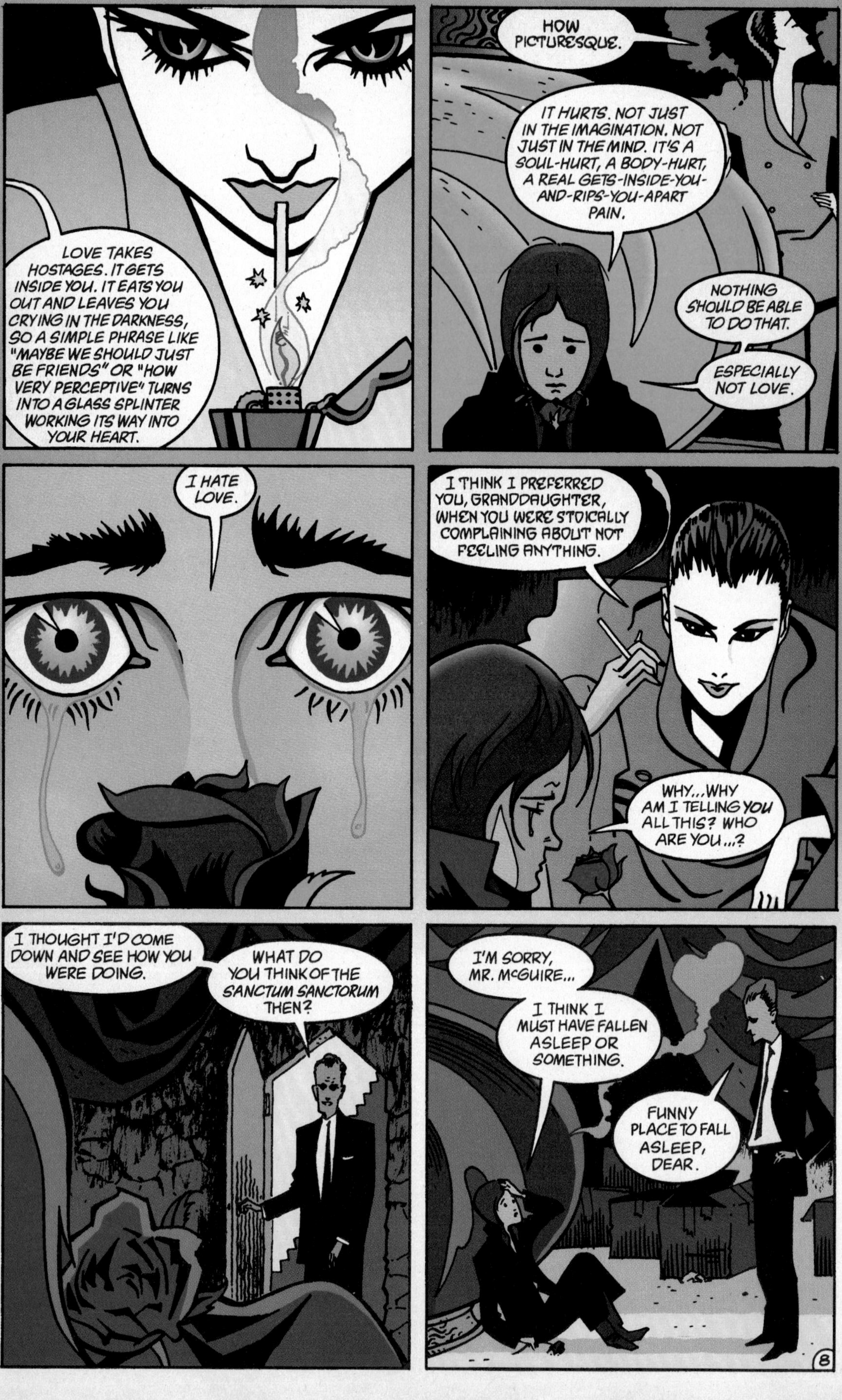
LOVE TAKES HOSTAGES. IT GETS INSIDE YOU. IT EATS YOU OUT AND LEAVES YOU CRYING IN THE DARKNESS, SO A SIMPLE PHRASE LIKE "MAYBE WE SHOULD JUST BE FRIENDS" OR "HOW VERY PERCEPTIVE" TURNS INTO A GLASS SPLINTER WORKING ITS WAY INTO YOUR HEART.
HOW PICTURESQUE.
IT HURTS. NOT JUST IN THE IMAGINATION. NOT JUST IN THE MIND. IT'S A SOUL-HURT, A BODY-HURT, A REAL GETS-INSIDE-YOU-AND-RIPS-YOU-APART PAIN.
NOTHING SHOULD BE ABLE TO DO THAT.
ESPECIALLY NOT LOVE.
I HATE LOVE.
I THINK I PREFERRED YOU, GRANDDAUGHTER, WHEN YOU WERE STOICALLY COMPLAINING ABOUT NOT FEELING ANYTHING.
WHY...WHY AM I TELLING YOU ALL THIS? WHO ARE YOU...?
I THOUGHT I'D COME DOWN AND SEE HOW YOU WERE DOING.
WHAT DO YOU THINK OF THE SANCTUM SANCTORUM THEN?
I'M SORRY, MR. McGUIRE...
I THINK I MUST HAVE FALLEN ASLEEP OR SOMETHING.
FUNNY PLACE TO FALL ASLEEP, DEAR.

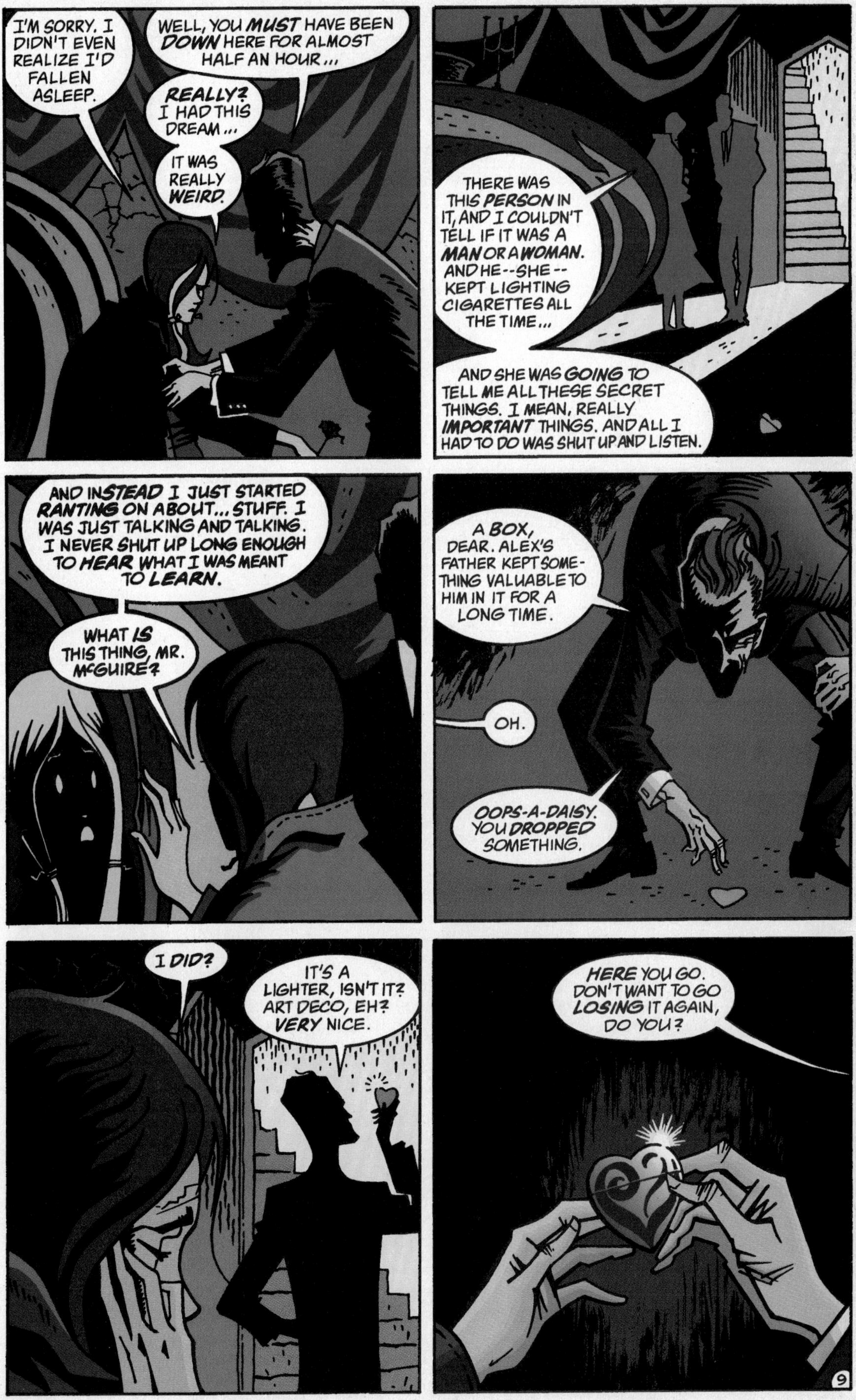
I'M SORRY. I DIDN'T EVEN REALIZE I'D FALLEN ASLEEP.
WELL, YOU MUST HAVE BEEN DOWN HERE FOR ALMOST HALF AN HOUR...
REALLY? I HAD THIS DREAM...
IT WAS REALLY WEIRD.
THERE WAS THIS PERSON IN IT, AND I COULDN'T TELL IF IT WAS A MAN OR A WOMAN. AND HE--SHE--KEPT LIGHTING CIGARETTES ALL THE TIME...
AND SHE WAS GOING TO TELL ME ALL THESE SECRET THINGS. I MEAN, REALLY IMPORTANT THINGS. AND ALL I HAD TO DO WAS SHUT UP AND LISTEN.
AND INSTEAD I JUST STARTED RANTING ON ABOUT... STUFF. I WAS JUST TALKING AND TALKING. I NEVER SHUT UP LONG ENOUGH TO HEAR WHAT I WAS MEANT TO LEARN.
WHAT IS THIS THING, MR. McGUIRE?
A BOX, DEAR. ALEX'S FATHER KEPT SOME-THING VALUABLE TO HIM IN IT FOR A LONG TIME.
OH.
OOPS-A-DAISY. YOU DROPPED SOMETHING.
I DID?
IT'S A LIGHTER, ISN'T IT? ART DECO, EH? VERY NICE.
HERE YOU GO. DON'T WANT TO GO LOSING IT AGAIN, DO YOU?
9

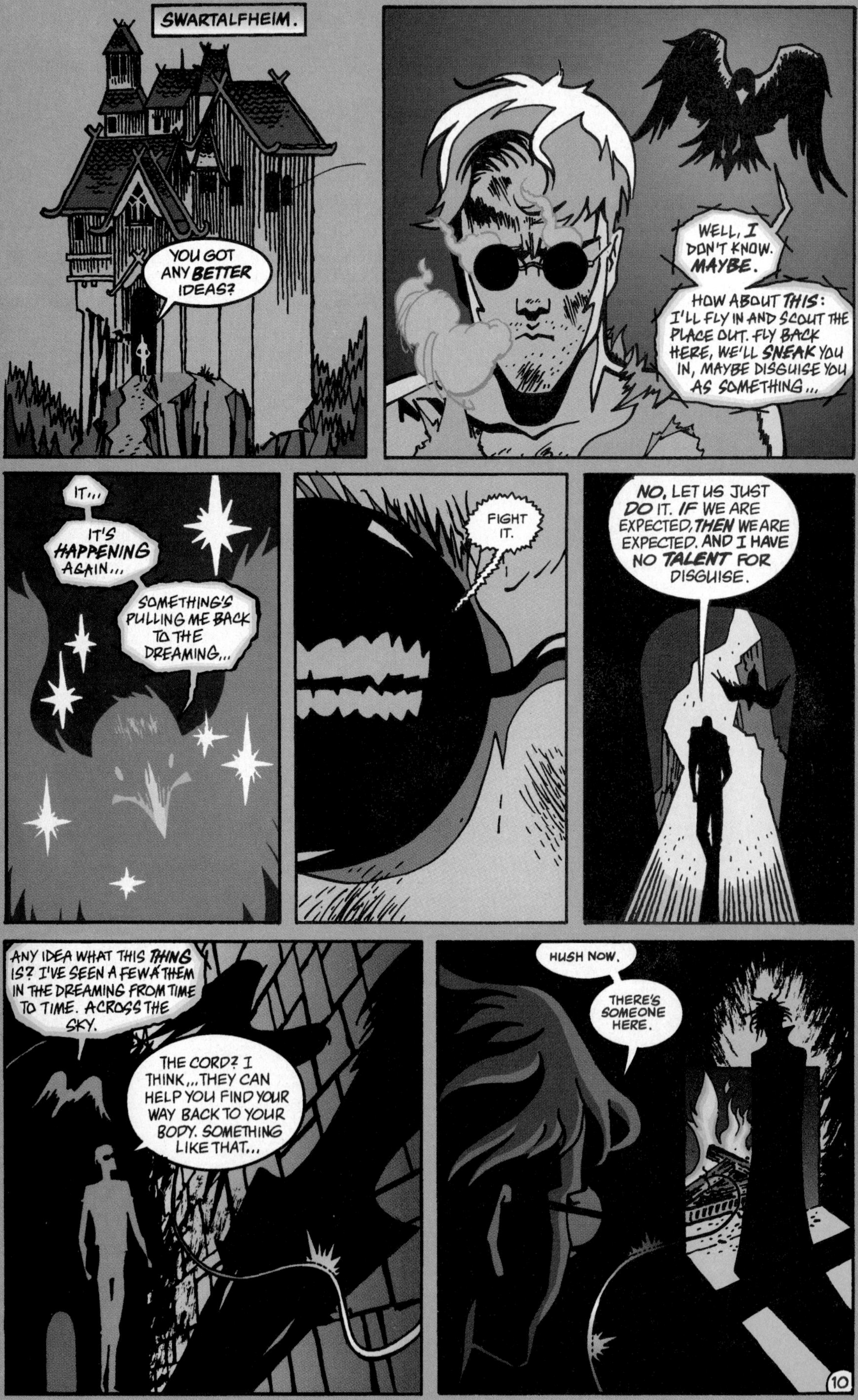
SWARTALFHEIM.
YOU GOT ANY BETTER IDEAS?
WELL, I DON'T KNOW. MAYBE.
HOW ABOUT THIS: I'LL FLY IN AND SCOUT THE PLACE OUT. FLY BACK HERE, WE'LL SNEAK YOU IN, MAYBE DISGUISE YOU AS SOMETHING...
IT...
IT'S HAPPENING AGAIN...
SOMETHING'S PULLING ME BACK TO THE DREAMING...
FIGHT IT.
NO, LET US JUST DO IT. IF WE ARE EXPECTED, THEN WE ARE EXPECTED. AND I HAVE NO TALENT FOR DISGUISE.
ANY IDEA WHAT THIS THING IS? I'VE SEEN A FEW A' THEM IN THE DREAMING FROM TIME TO TIME. ACROSS THE SKY.
THE CORD? I THINK... THEY CAN HELP YOU FIND YOUR WAY BACK TO YOUR BODY. SOMETHING LIKE THAT...
HUSH NOW.
THERE'S SOMEONE HERE.
10

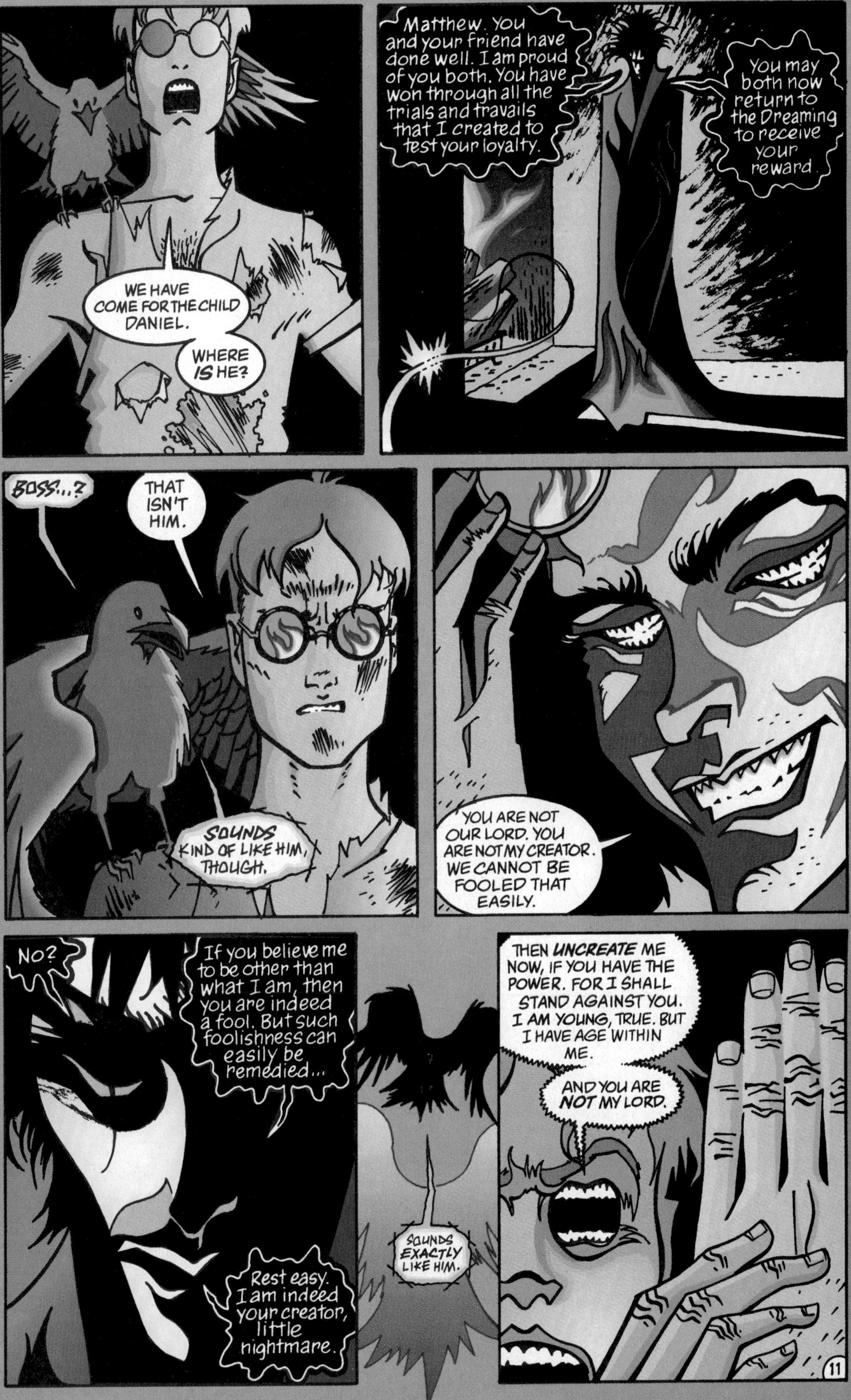
WE HAVE COME FOR THE CHILD DANIEL.
WHERE IS HE?
Matthew. You and your friend have done well. I am proud of you both. You have won through all the trials and travails that I created to test your loyalty.
You may both now return to the Dreaming to receive your reward.
BOSS...?
THAT ISN'T HIM.
SOUNDS KIND OF LIKE HIM, THOUGH.
YOU ARE NOT OUR LORD. YOU ARE NOT MY CREATOR. WE CANNOT BE FOOLED THAT EASILY.
No?
If you believe me to be other than what I am, then you are indeed a fool. But such foolishness can easily be remedied...
Rest easy. I am indeed your creator, little nightmare.
SOUNDS EXACTLY LIKE HIM.
THEN UNCREATE ME NOW, IF YOU HAVE THE POWER. FOR I SHALL STAND AGAINST YOU. I AM YOUNG, TRUE. BUT I HAVE AGE WITHIN ME.
AND YOU ARE NOT MY LORD.
11

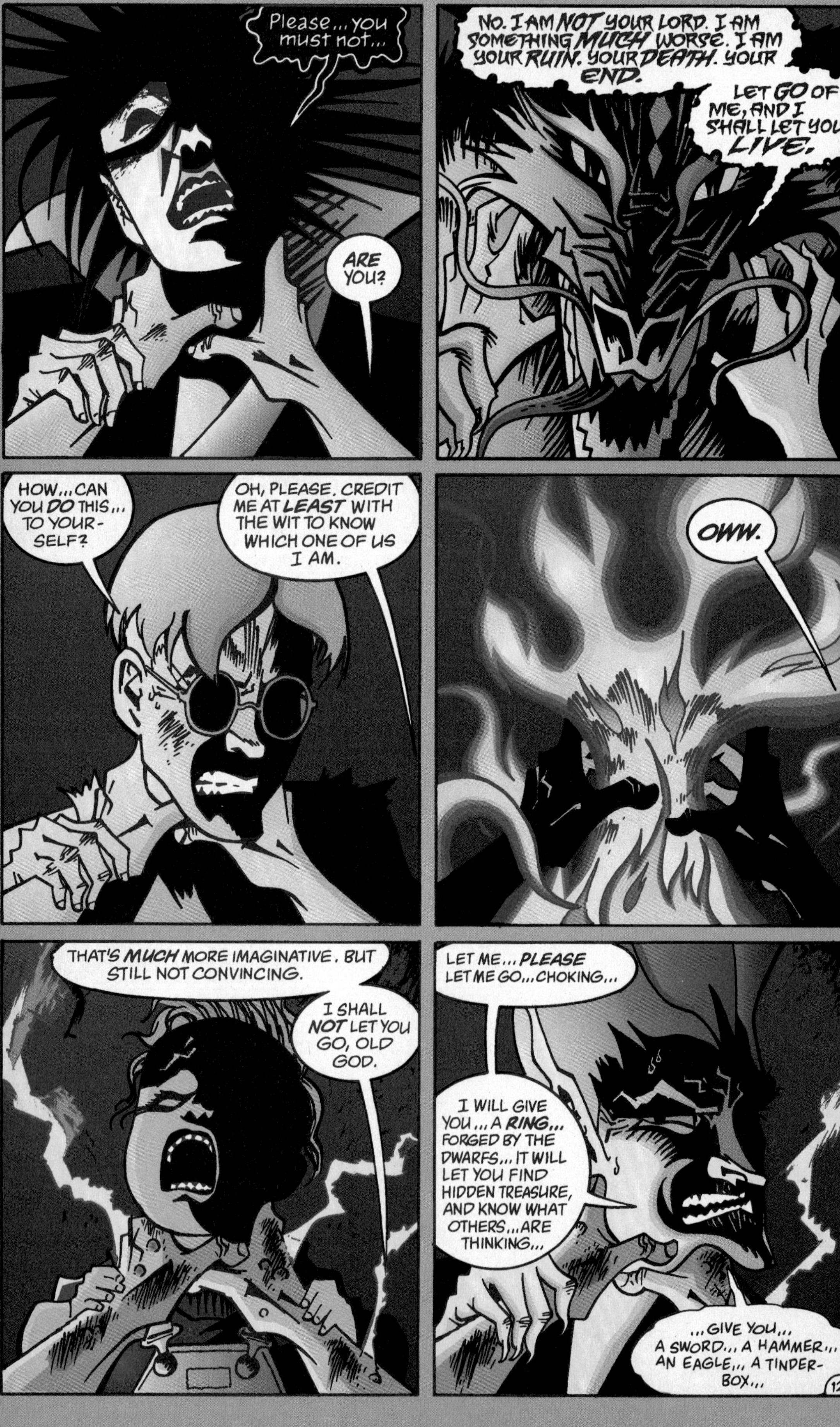
Please... you must not...
ARE YOU?
NO. I AM NOT YOUR LORD. I AM SOMETHING MUCH WORSE. I AM YOUR RUIN. YOUR DEATH. YOUR END.
LET GO OF ME, AND I SHALL LET YOU LIVE.
HOW... CAN YOU DO THIS... TO YOURSELF?
OH, PLEASE. CREDIT ME AT LEAST WITH THE WIT TO KNOW WHICH ONE OF US I AM.
OWW.
THAT'S MUCH MORE IMAGINATIVE. BUT STILL NOT CONVINCING.
I SHALL NOT LET YOU GO, OLD GOD.
LET ME... PLEASE LET ME GO... CHOKING...
I WILL GIVE YOU... A RING... FORGED BY THE DWARFS... IT WILL LET YOU FIND HIDDEN TREASURE, AND KNOW WHAT OTHERS... ARE THINKING...
...GIVE YOU... A SWORD... A HAMMER... AN EAGLE... A TINDER-BOX...

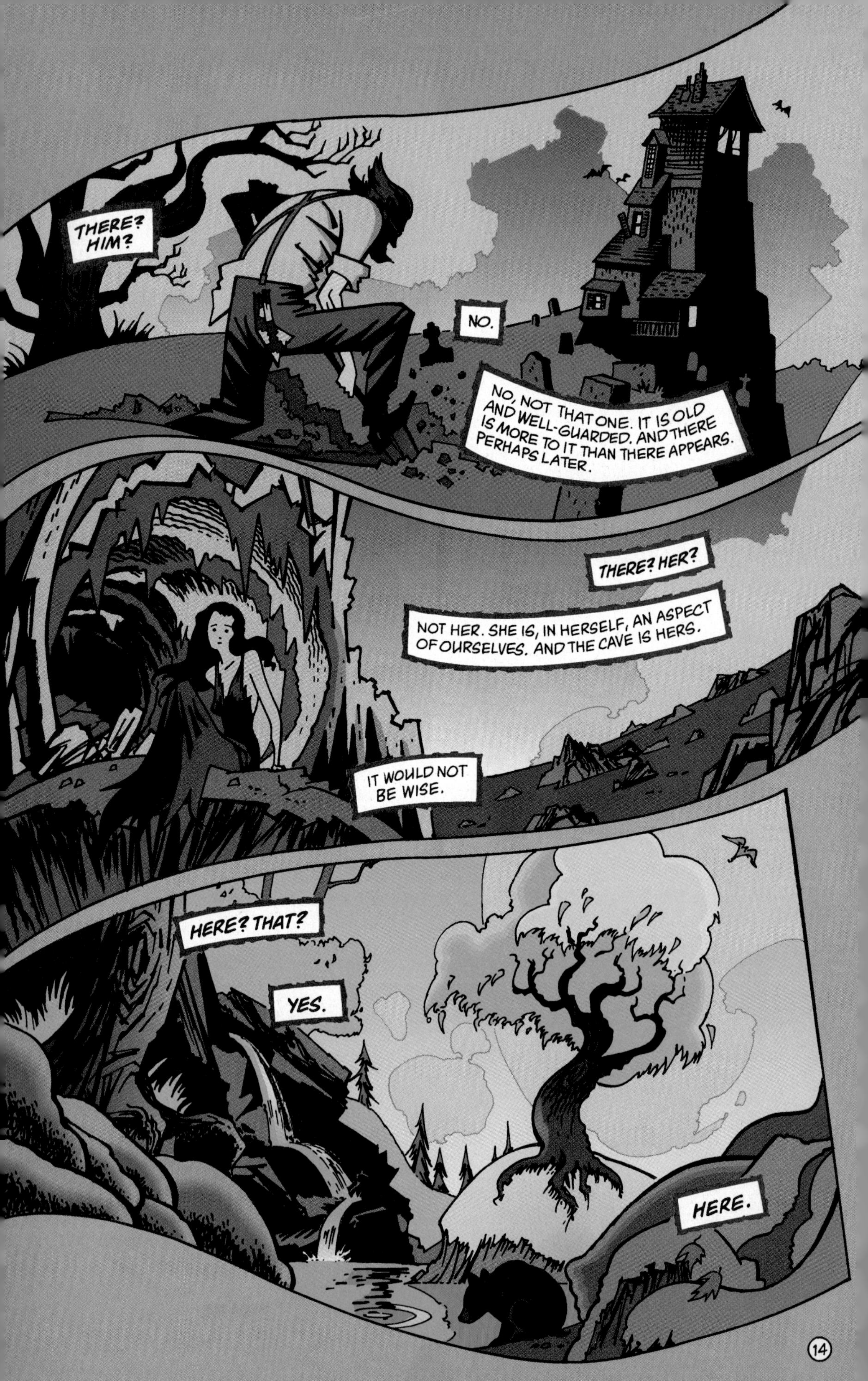
THERE? HIM?
NO.
NO, NOT THAT ONE. IT IS OLD AND WELL-GUARDED, AND THERE IS MORE TO IT THAN THERE APPEARS. PERHAPS LATER.
THERE? HER?
NOT HER. SHE IS, IN HERSELF, AN ASPECT OF OURSELVES. AND THE CAVE IS HERS.
IT WOULD NOT BE WISE.
HERE? THAT?
YES.
HERE.

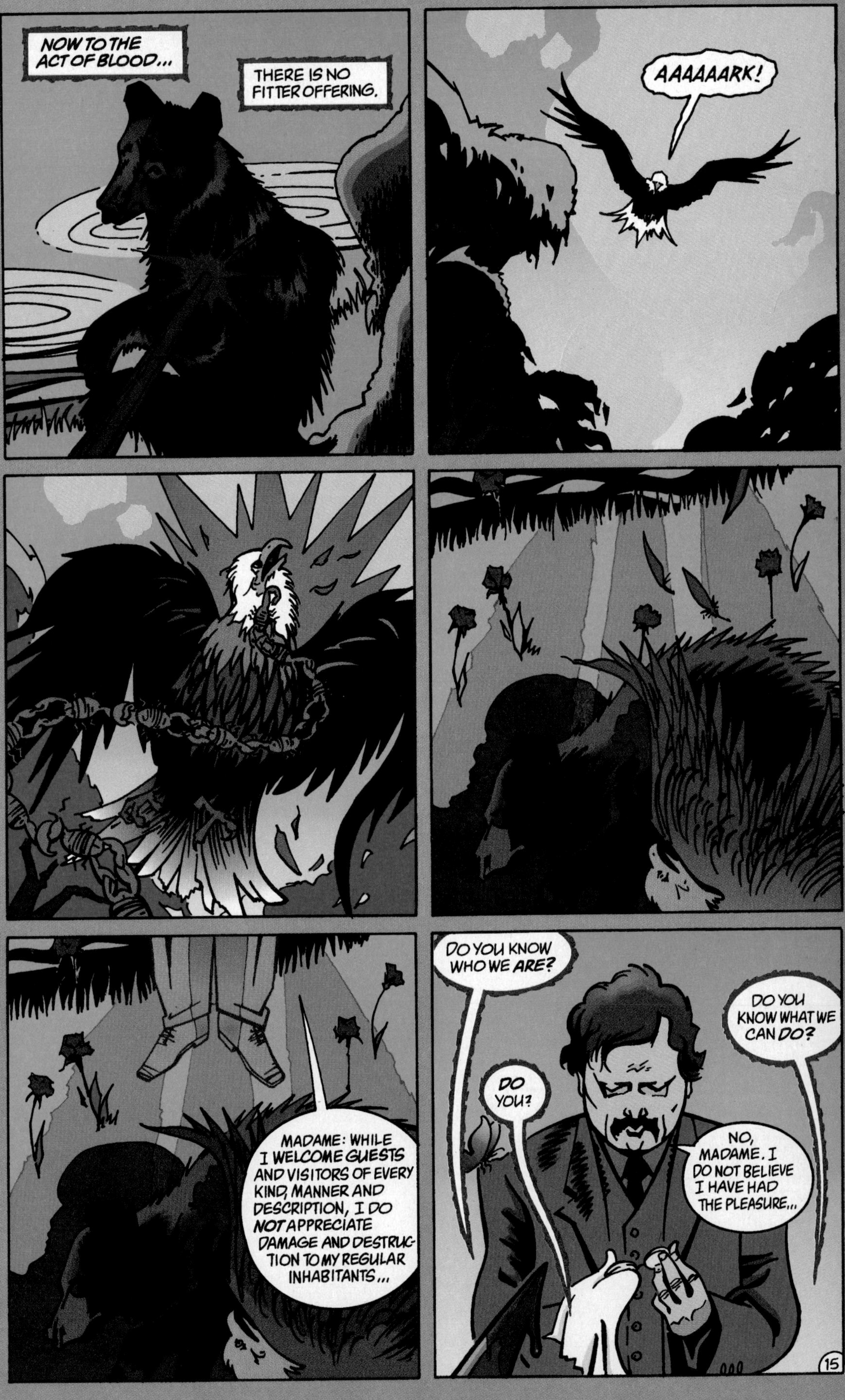
NOW TO THE ACT OF BLOOD...
THERE IS NO FITTER OFFERING.
AAAAAARK!
DO YOU KNOW WHO WE ARE?
DO YOU KNOW WHAT WE CAN DO?
DO YOU?
MADAME: WHILE I WELCOME GUESTS AND VISITORS OF EVERY KIND, MANNER AND DESCRIPTION, I DO NOT APPRECIATE DAMAGE AND DESTRUCTION TO MY REGULAR INHABITANTS...
NO, MADAME. I DO NOT BELIEVE I HAVE HAD THE PLEASURE...
15

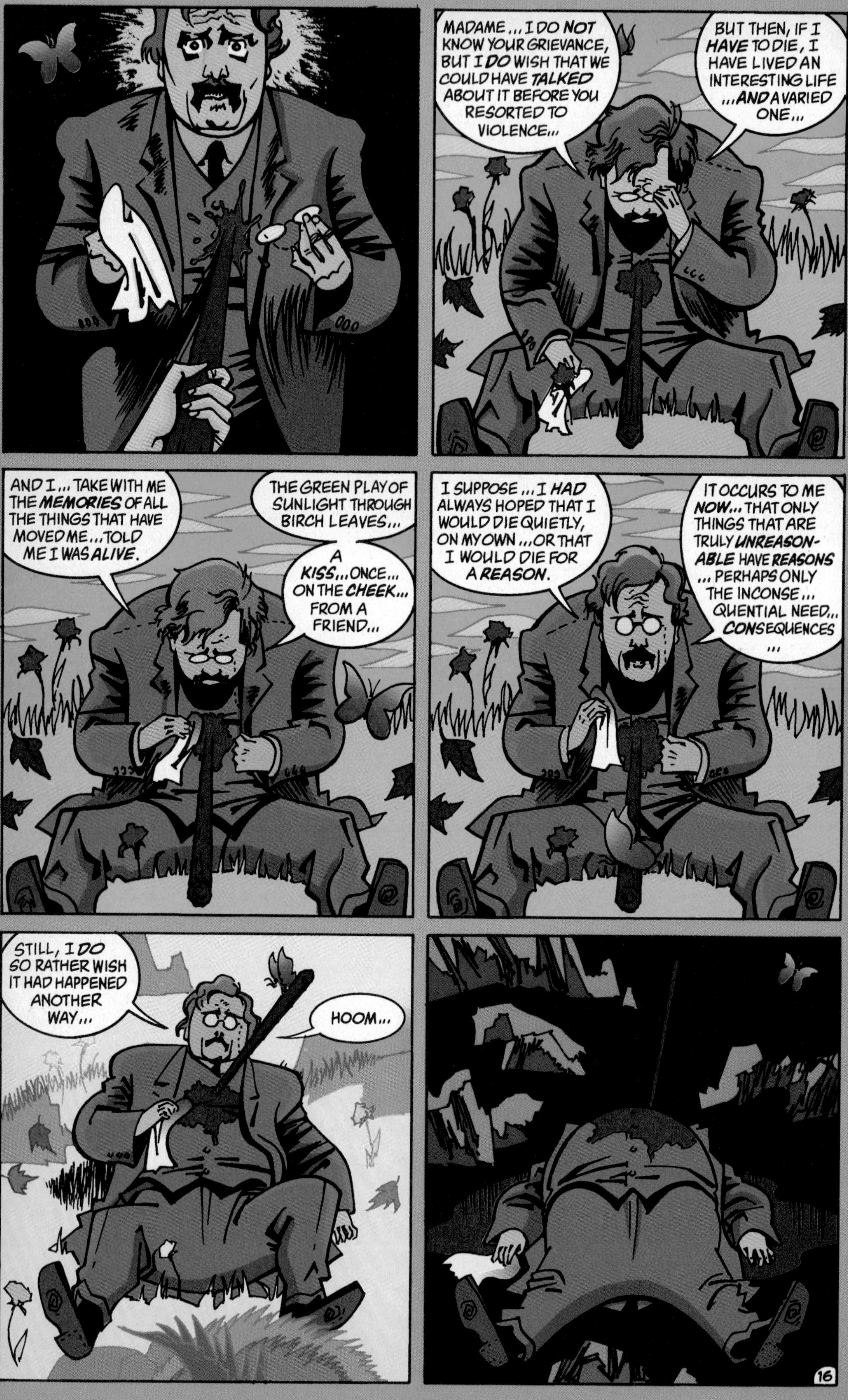
MADAME ... I DO NOT KNOW YOUR GRIEVANCE, BUT I DO WISH THAT WE COULD HAVE TALKED ABOUT IT BEFORE YOU RESORTED TO VIOLENCE...
BUT THEN, IF I HAVE TO DIE, I HAVE LIVED AN INTERESTING LIFE ...AND A VARIED ONE...
AND I... TAKE WITH ME THE MEMORIES OF ALL THE THINGS THAT HAVE MOVED ME... TOLD ME I WAS ALIVE.
THE GREEN PLAY OF SUNLIGHT THROUGH BIRCH LEAVES...
A KISS... ONCE... ON THE CHEEK... FROM A FRIEND...
I SUPPOSE ... I HAD ALWAYS HOPED THAT I WOULD DIE QUIETLY, ON MY OWN ... OR THAT I WOULD DIE FOR A REASON.
IT OCCURS TO ME NOW... THAT ONLY THINGS THAT ARE TRULY UNREASON-ABLE HAVE REASONS ... PERHAPS ONLY THE INCONSE... QUENTIAL NEED... CONSEQUENCES ...
STILL, I DO SO RATHER WISH IT HAD HAPPENED ANOTHER WAY...
HOOM...
16

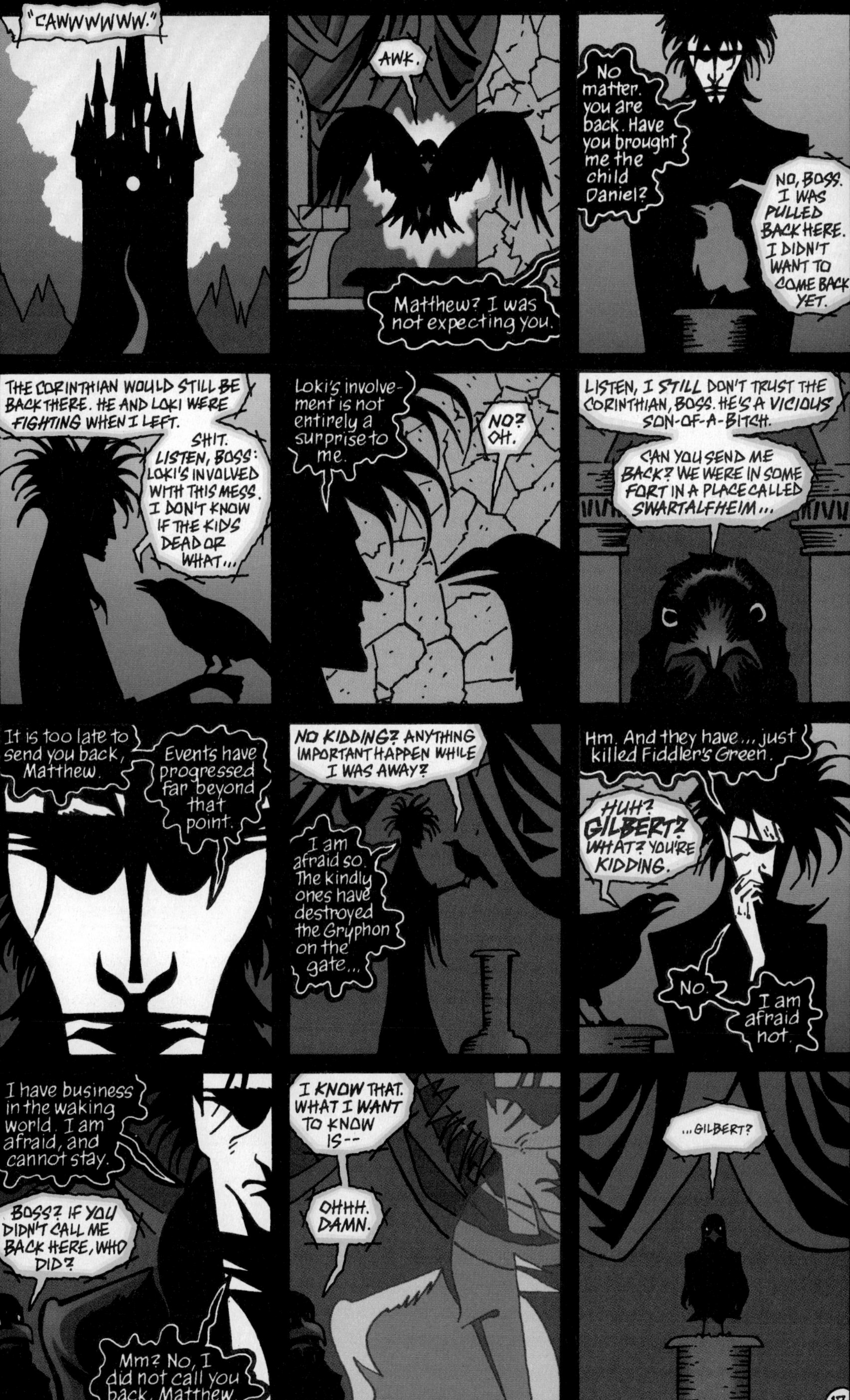
"CAWWWWWW."
AWK.
Matthew? I was not expecting you.
No matter. you are back. Have you brought me the child Daniel?
NO, BOSS. I WAS PULLED BACK HERE. I DIDN'T WANT TO COME BACK YET.
THE CORINTHIAN WOULD STILL BE BACK THERE. HE AND LOKI WERE FIGHTING WHEN I LEFT.
SHIT. LISTEN, BOSS: LOKI'S INVOLVED WITH THIS MESS. I DON'T KNOW IF THE KID'S DEAD OR WHAT...
Loki's involvement is not entirely a surprise to me.
NO? OH.
LISTEN, I STILL DON'T TRUST THE CORINTHIAN, BOSS. HE'S A VICIOUS SON-OF-A-BITCH.
CAN YOU SEND ME BACK? WE WERE IN SOME FORT IN A PLACE CALLED SWARTALFHEIM...
It is too late to send you back, Matthew.
Events have progressed far beyond that point.
NO KIDDING? ANYTHING IMPORTANT HAPPEN WHILE I WAS AWAY?
I am afraid so. The kindly ones have destroyed the Gryphon on the gate...
Hm. And they have... just killed Fiddler's Green.
HUH? GILBERT? WHAT? YOU'RE KIDDING.
No.
I am afraid not.
I have business in the waking world. I am afraid, and cannot stay.
BOSS? IF YOU DIDN'T CALL ME BACK HERE, WHO DID?
Mm? No, I did not call you back, Matthew.
I KNOW THAT. WHAT I WANT TO KNOW IS--
OHHH. DAMN.
...GILBERT?

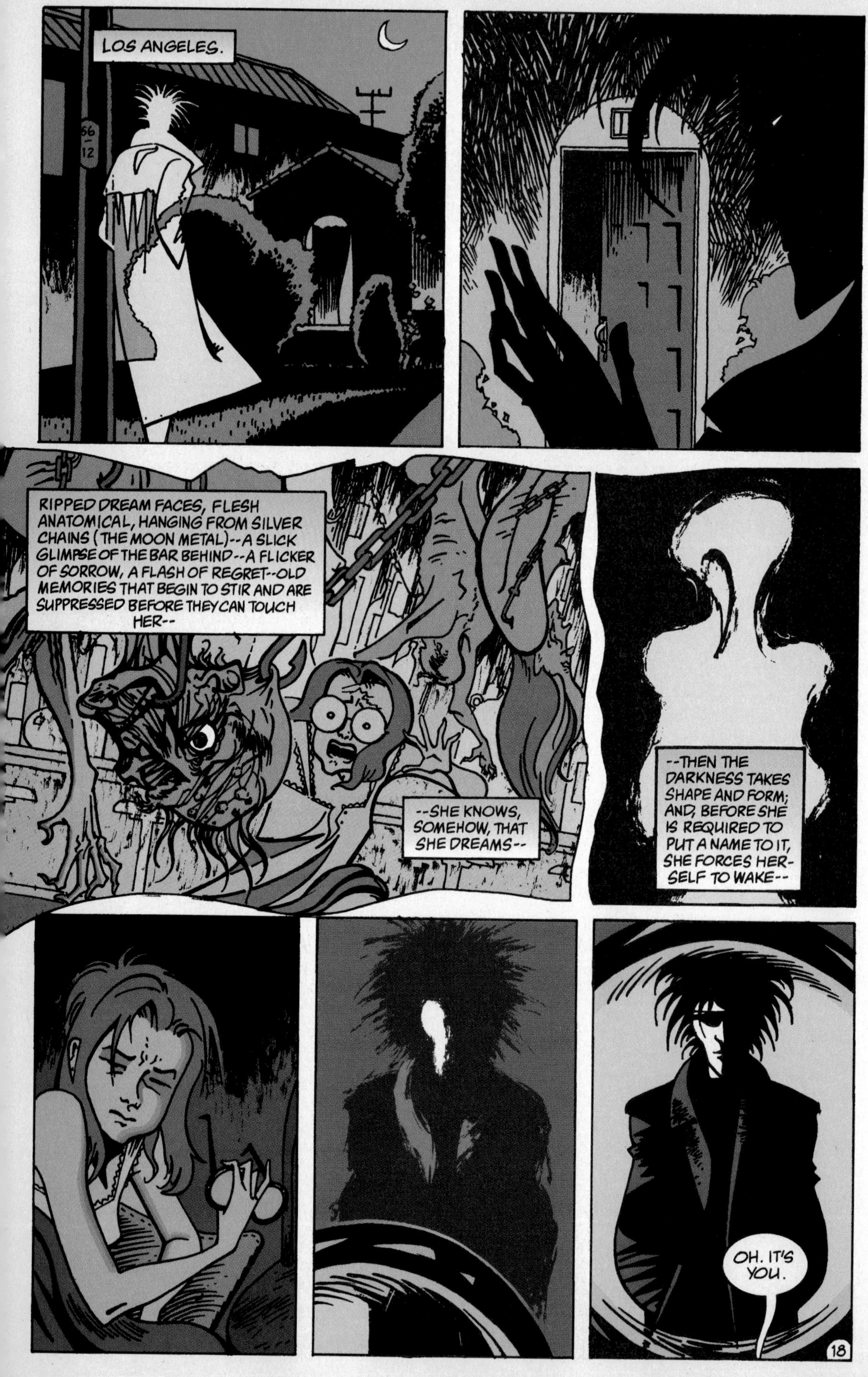
LOS ANGELES.
RIPPED DREAM FACES, FLESH ANATOMICAL, HANGING FROM SILVER CHAINS (THE MOON METAL)--A SLICK GLIMPSE OF THE BAR BEHIND--A FLICKER OF SORROW, A FLASH OF REGRET--OLD MEMORIES THAT BEGIN TO STIR AND ARE SUPPRESSED BEFORE THEY CAN TOUCH HER--
--SHE KNOWS, SOMEHOW, THAT SHE DREAMS--
--THEN THE DARKNESS TAKES SHAPE AND FORM; AND, BEFORE SHE IS REQUIRED TO PUT A NAME TO IT, SHE FORCES HER-SELF TO WAKE--
OH. IT'S YOU.
18

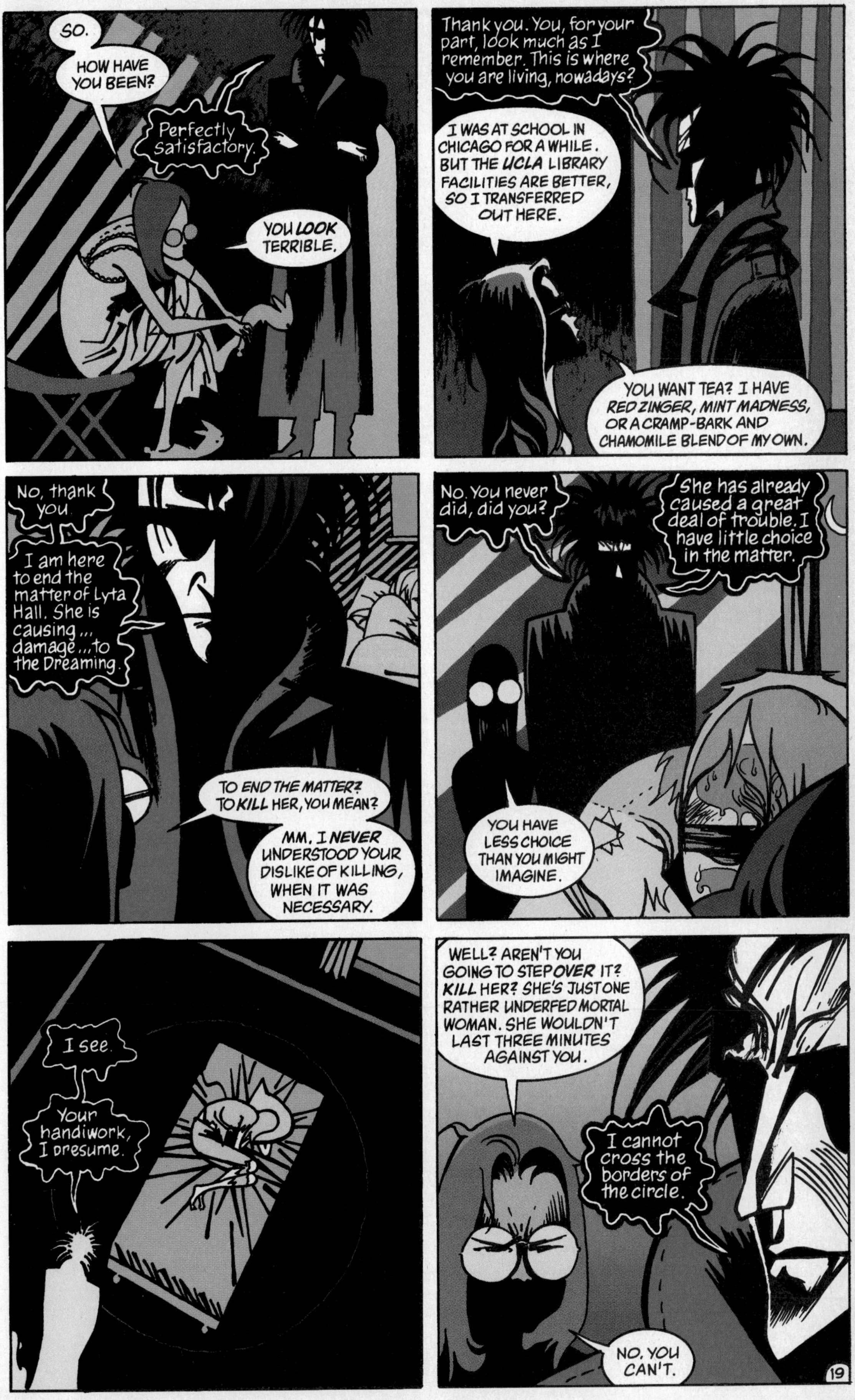
SO.
HOW HAVE YOU BEEN?
Perfectly satisfactory.
YOU LOOK TERRIBLE.
Thank you. You, for your part, look much as I remember. This is where you are living, nowadays?
I WAS AT SCHOOL IN CHICAGO FOR A WHILE. BUT THE UCLA LIBRARY FACILITIES ARE BETTER, SO I TRANSFERRED OUT HERE.
YOU WANT TEA? I HAVE RED ZINGER, MINT MADNESS, OR A CRAMP-BARK AND CHAMOMILE BLEND OF MY OWN.
No, thank you.
I am here to end the matter of Lyta Hall. She is causing... damage... to the Dreaming.
TO END THE MATTER? TO KILL HER, YOU MEAN?
MM. I NEVER UNDERSTOOD YOUR DISLIKE OF KILLING, WHEN IT WAS NECESSARY.
No. You never did, did you?
She has already caused a great deal of trouble. I have little choice in the matter.
YOU HAVE LESS CHOICE THAN YOU MIGHT IMAGINE.
I see.
Your handiwork, I presume.
WELL? AREN'T YOU GOING TO STEP OVER IT? KILL HER? SHE'S JUST ONE RATHER UNDERFED MORTAL WOMAN. SHE WOULDN'T LAST THREE MINUTES AGAINST YOU.
I cannot cross the borders of the circle.
NO, YOU CAN'T.

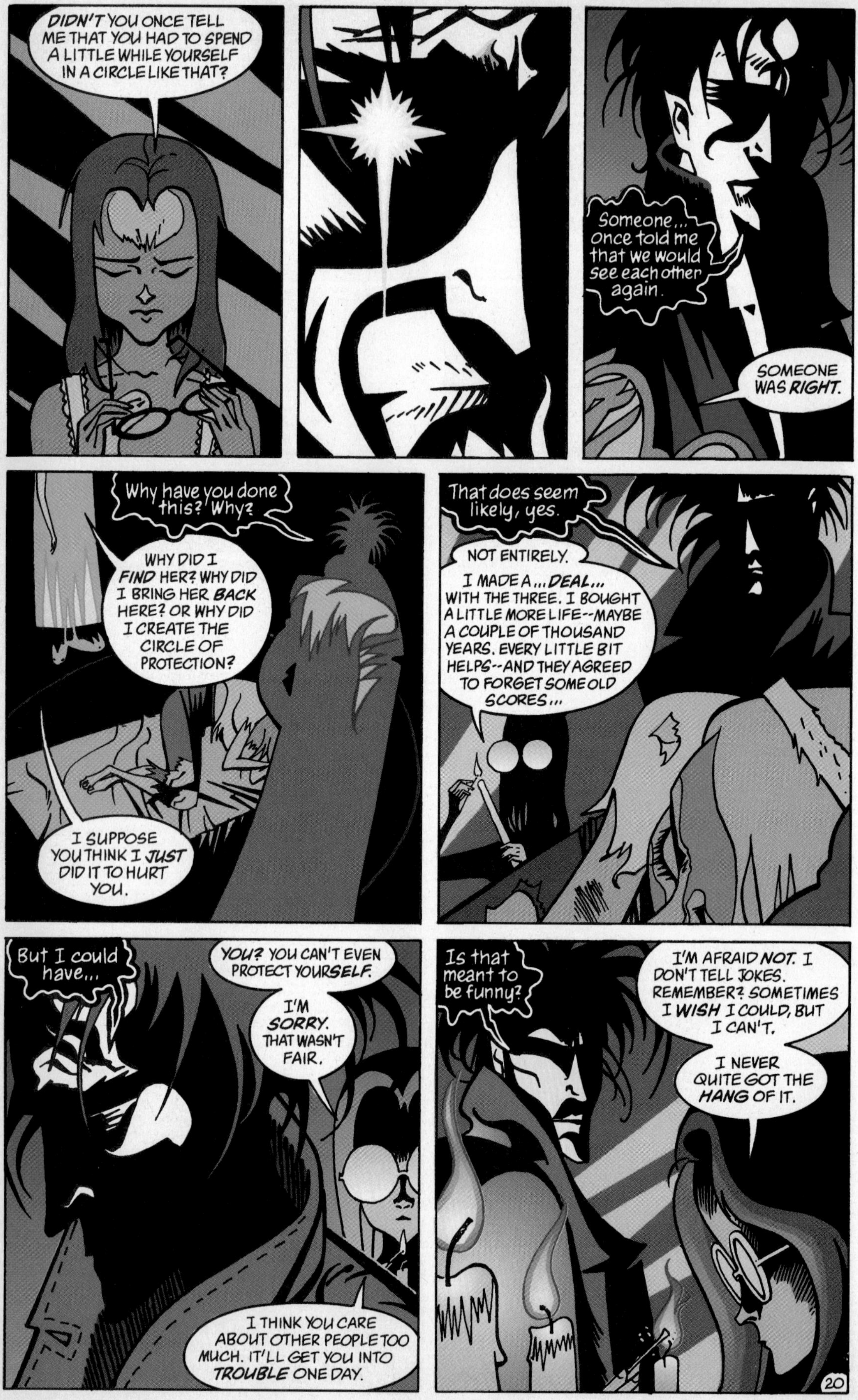
DIDN'T YOU ONCE TELL ME THAT YOU HAD TO SPEND A LITTLE WHILE YOURSELF IN A CIRCLE LIKE THAT?
Someone... once told me that we would see each other again.
SOMEONE WAS RIGHT.
Why have you done this? Why?
WHY DID I FIND HER? WHY DID I BRING HER BACK HERE? OR WHY DID I CREATE THE CIRCLE OF PROTECTION?
I SUPPOSE YOU THINK I JUST DID IT TO HURT YOU.
That does seem likely, yes.
NOT ENTIRELY.
I MADE A... DEAL... WITH THE THREE. I BOUGHT A LITTLE MORE LIFE--MAYBE A COUPLE OF THOUSAND YEARS. EVERY LITTLE BIT HELPS--AND THEY AGREED TO FORGET SOME OLD SCORES...
But I could have...
YOU? YOU CAN'T EVEN PROTECT YOURSELF.
I'M SORRY. THAT WASN'T FAIR.
I THINK YOU CARE ABOUT OTHER PEOPLE TOO MUCH. IT'LL GET YOU INTO TROUBLE ONE DAY.
Is that meant to be funny?
I'M AFRAID NOT. I DON'T TELL JOKES. REMEMBER? SOMETIMES I WISH I COULD, BUT I CAN'T.
I NEVER QUITE GOT THE HANG OF IT.
20

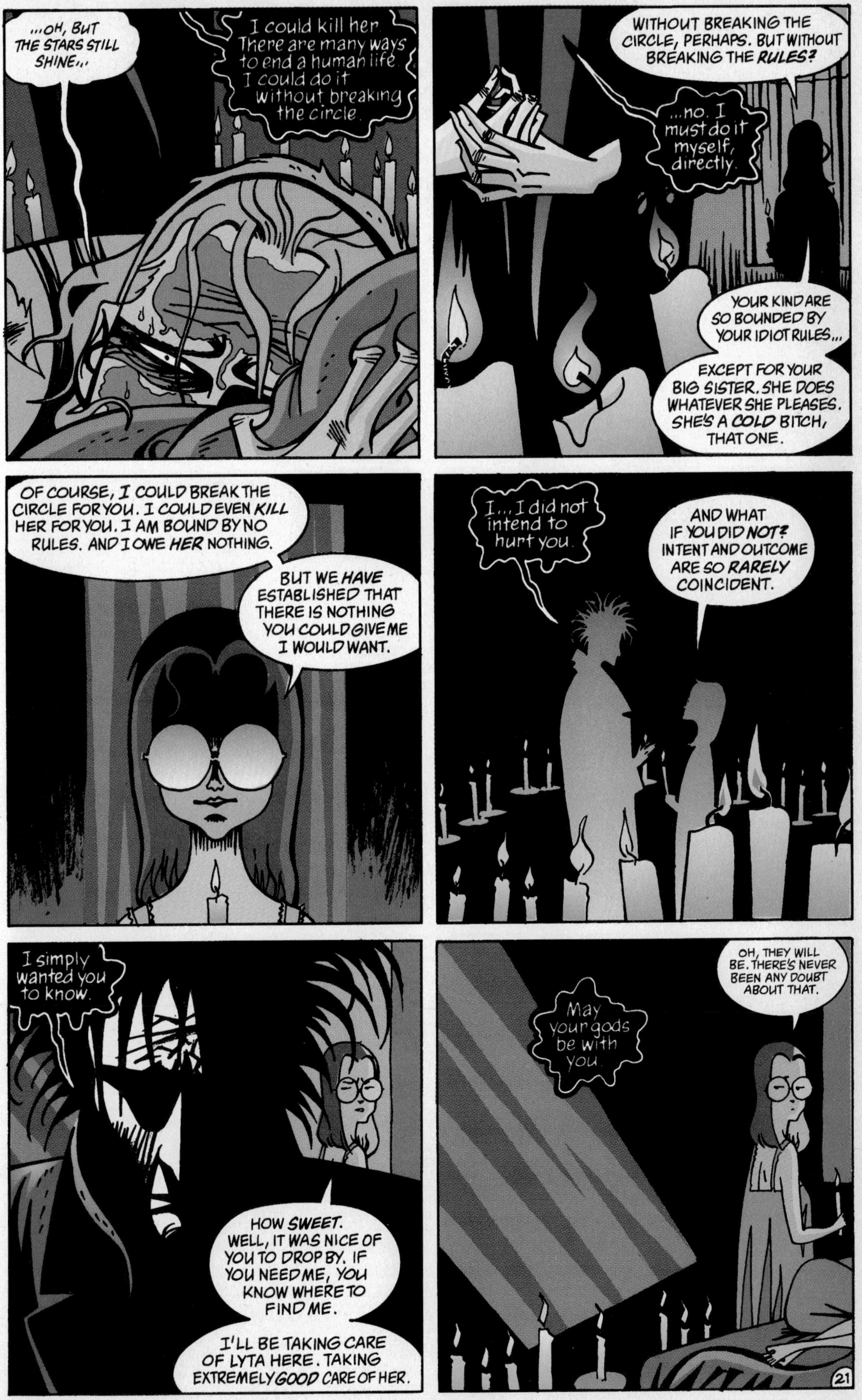

...OH, BUT THE STARS STILL SHINE...
I could kill her. There are many ways to end a human life. I could do it without breaking the circle.
WITHOUT BREAKING THE CIRCLE, PERHAPS. BUT WITHOUT BREAKING THE *RULES?*
...no. I must do it myself, directly.
YOUR KIND ARE SO BOUNDED BY YOUR IDIOT RULES...
EXCEPT FOR YOUR BIG SISTER. SHE DOES WHATEVER SHE PLEASES. SHE'S A *COLD* BITCH, THAT ONE.
OF COURSE, I COULD BREAK THE CIRCLE FOR YOU. I COULD EVEN *KILL* HER FOR YOU. I AM BOUND BY NO RULES. AND I OWE *HER* NOTHING.
BUT WE *HAVE* ESTABLISHED THAT THERE IS NOTHING YOU COULD GIVE ME I WOULD WANT.
I... I did not intend to hurt you.
AND WHAT IF YOU DID *NOT?* INTENT AND OUTCOME ARE SO *RARELY* COINCIDENT.
I simply wanted you to know.
HOW *SWEET*. WELL, IT WAS NICE OF YOU TO DROP BY. IF YOU NEED ME, YOU KNOW WHERE TO FIND ME.
I'LL BE TAKING CARE OF LYTA HERE. TAKING EXTREMELY *GOOD* CARE OF HER.
May your gods be with you.
OH, THEY WILL BE. THERE'S NEVER BEEN ANY DOUBT ABOUT THAT.

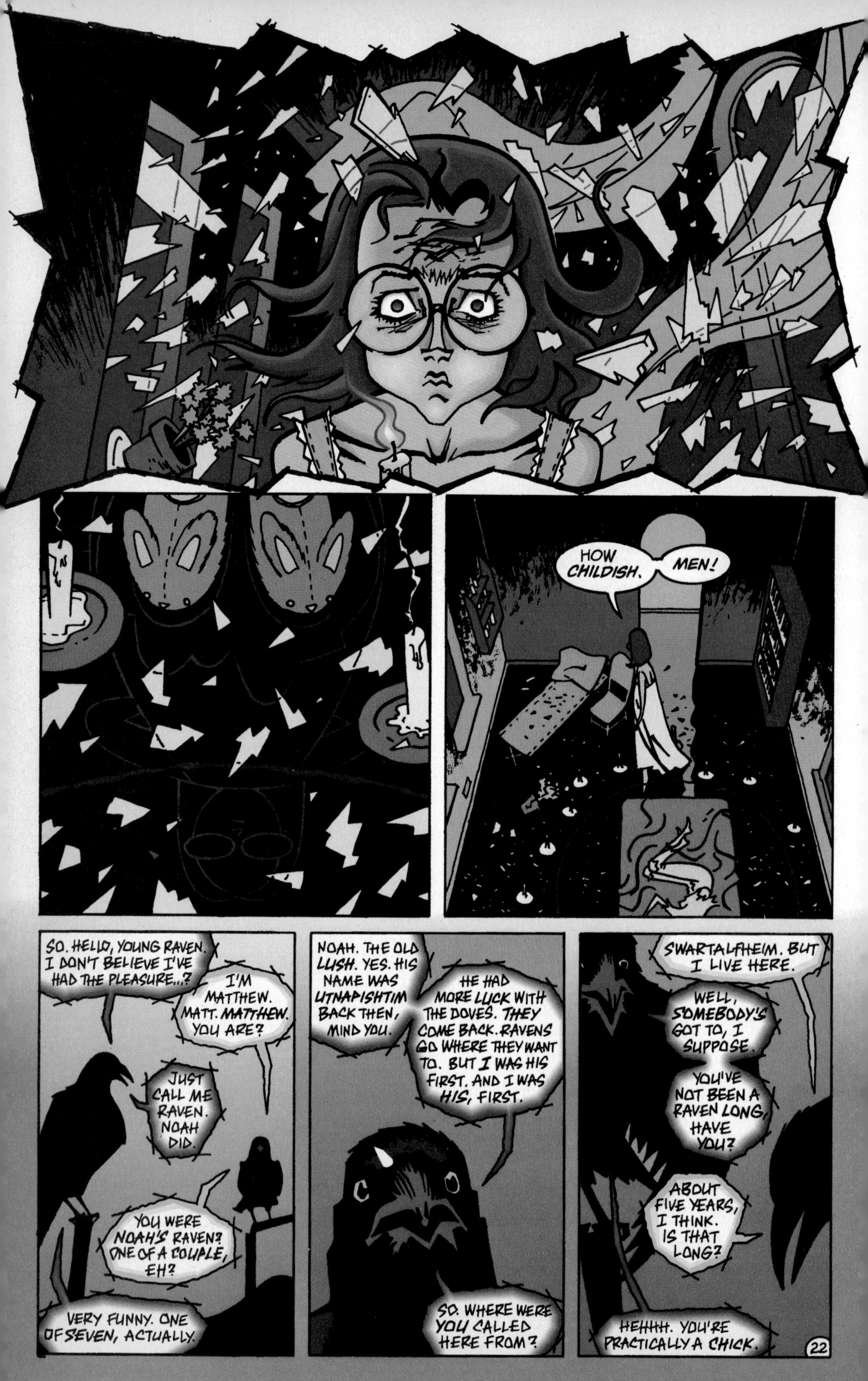
HOW CHILDISH.
MEN!
SO. HELLO, YOUNG RAVEN. I DON'T BELIEVE I'VE HAD THE PLEASURE...?
I'M MATTHEW. MATT. MATTHEW. YOU ARE?
JUST CALL ME RAVEN. NOAH DID.
YOU WERE NOAH'S RAVEN? ONE OF A COUPLE, EH?
VERY FUNNY. ONE OF SEVEN, ACTUALLY.
NOAH. THE OLD LUSH. YES. HIS NAME WAS UTNAPISHTIM BACK THEN, MIND YOU.
HE HAD MORE LUCK WITH THE DOVES. THEY COME BACK. RAVENS GO WHERE THEY WANT TO. BUT I WAS HIS FIRST. AND I WAS HIS, FIRST.
SO. WHERE WERE YOU CALLED HERE FROM?
SWARTALFHEIM. BUT I LIVE HERE.
WELL, SOMEBODY'S GOT TO, I SUPPOSE.
YOU'VE NOT BEEN A RAVEN LONG, HAVE YOU?
ABOUT FIVE YEARS, I THINK. IS THAT LONG?
HEHHHH. YOU'RE PRACTICALLY A CHICK.
22

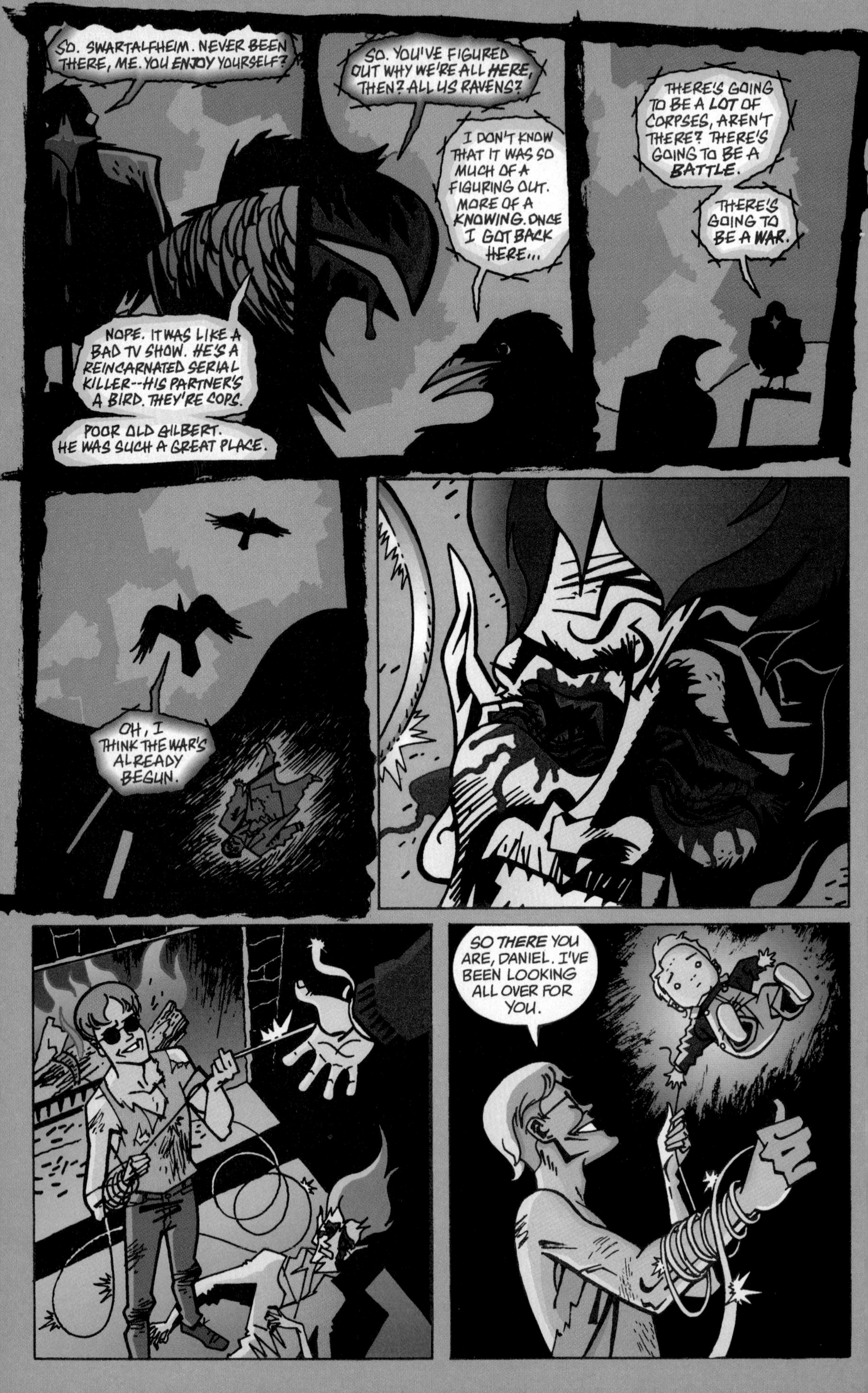

SO. SWARTALFHEIM. NEVER BEEN THERE, ME. YOU ENJOY YOURSELF?
NOPE. IT WAS LIKE A BAD TV SHOW. HE'S A REINCARNATED SERIAL KILLER--HIS PARTNER'S A BIRD. THEY'RE COPS.
POOR OLD GILBERT. HE WAS SUCH A GREAT PLACE.
SO. YOU'VE FIGURED OUT WHY WE'RE ALL HERE, THEN? ALL US RAVENS?
I DON'T KNOW THAT IT WAS SO MUCH OF A FIGURING OUT. MORE OF A KNOWING. ONCE I GOT BACK HERE...
THERE'S GOING TO BE A LOT OF CORPSES, AREN'T THERE? THERE'S GOING TO BE A BATTLE.
THERE'S GOING TO BE A WAR.
OH, I THINK THE WAR'S ALREADY BEGUN.
SO THERE YOU ARE, DANIEL. I'VE BEEN LOOKING ALL OVER FOR YOU.

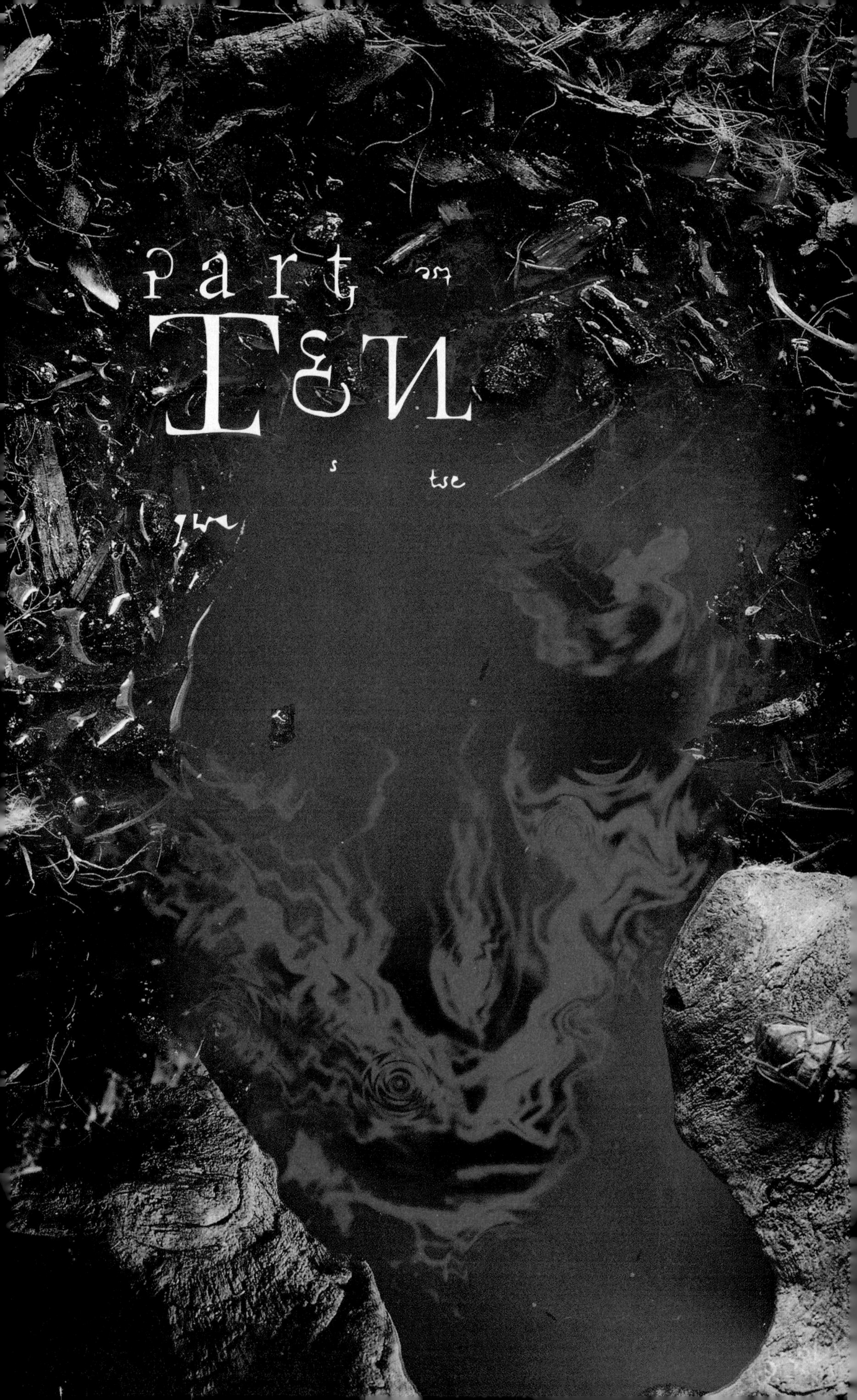
part
TEN

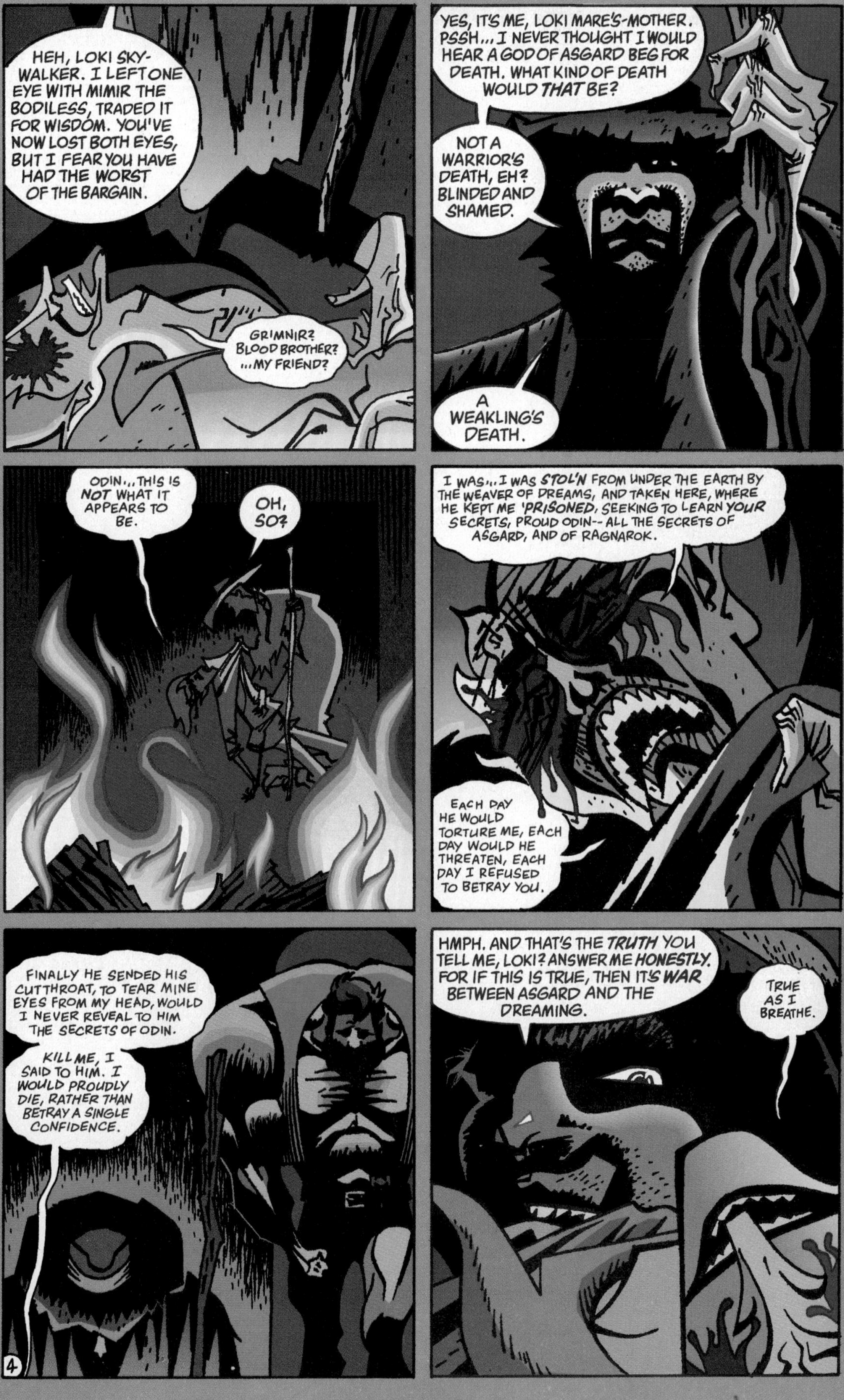
HEH, LOKI SKY-WALKER. I LEFT ONE EYE WITH MIMIR THE BODILESS, TRADED IT FOR WISDOM. YOU'VE NOW LOST BOTH EYES, BUT I FEAR YOU HAVE HAD THE WORST OF THE BARGAIN.
GRIMNIR? BLOOD BROTHER? ...MY FRIEND?
YES, IT'S ME, LOKI MARE'S-MOTHER. PSSH... I NEVER THOUGHT I WOULD HEAR A GOD OF ASGARD BEG FOR DEATH. WHAT KIND OF DEATH WOULD *THAT* BE?
NOT A WARRIOR'S DEATH, EH? BLINDED AND SHAMED.
A WEAKLING'S DEATH.
ODIN... THIS IS *NOT* WHAT IT APPEARS TO BE.
OH, SO?
I WAS... I WAS *STOL'N* FROM UNDER THE EARTH BY THE WEAVER OF DREAMS, AND TAKEN HERE, WHERE HE KEPT ME *'PRISONED*, SEEKING TO LEARN *YOUR* SECRETS, PROUD ODIN-- ALL THE SECRETS OF ASGARD, AND OF RAGNAROK.
EACH DAY HE WOULD TORTURE ME, EACH DAY WOULD HE THREATEN, EACH DAY I REFUSED TO BETRAY YOU.
FINALLY HE SENDED HIS CUTTHROAT, TO TEAR MINE EYES FROM MY HEAD, WOULD I NEVER REVEAL TO HIM THE SECRETS OF ODIN.
KILL ME, I SAID TO HIM. I WOULD PROUDLY DIE, RATHER THAN BETRAY A SINGLE CONFIDENCE.
HMPH. AND THAT'S THE *TRUTH* YOU TELL ME, LOKI? ANSWER ME *HONESTLY*. FOR IF THIS IS TRUE, THEN IT'S *WAR* BETWEEN ASGARD AND THE DREAMING.
TRUE AS I BREATHE.

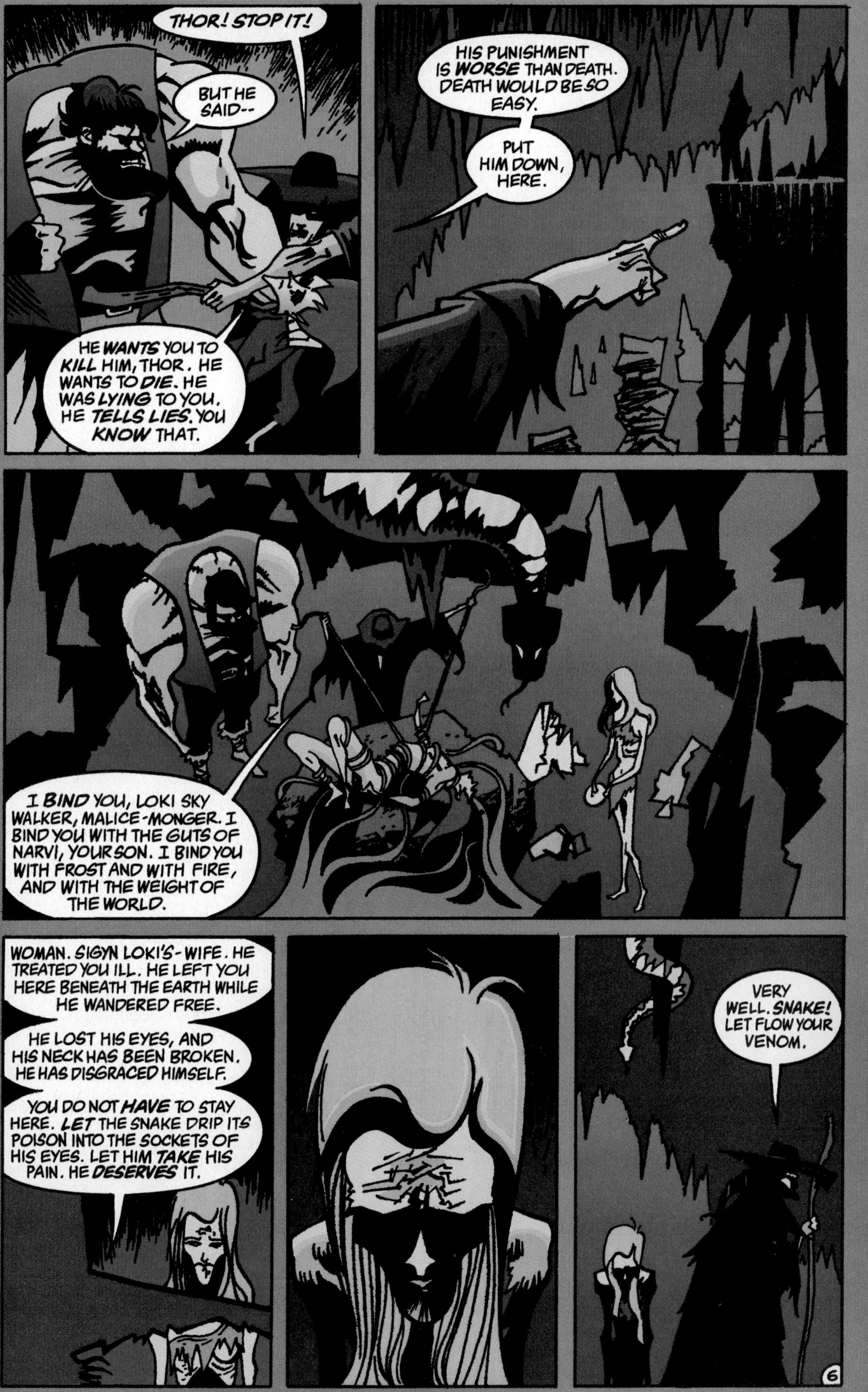
THOR! STOP IT!
BUT HE SAID--
HE WANTS YOU TO KILL HIM, THOR. HE WANTS TO DIE. HE WAS LYING TO YOU. HE TELLS LIES. YOU KNOW THAT.
HIS PUNISHMENT IS WORSE THAN DEATH. DEATH WOULD BE SO EASY.
PUT HIM DOWN, HERE.
I BIND YOU, LOKI SKY WALKER, MALICE-MONGER. I BIND YOU WITH THE GUTS OF NARVI, YOUR SON. I BIND YOU WITH FROST AND WITH FIRE, AND WITH THE WEIGHT OF THE WORLD.
WOMAN. SIGYN LOKI'S-WIFE. HE TREATED YOU ILL. HE LEFT YOU HERE BENEATH THE EARTH WHILE HE WANDERED FREE.
HE LOST HIS EYES, AND HIS NECK HAS BEEN BROKEN. HE HAS DISGRACED HIMSELF.
YOU DO NOT HAVE TO STAY HERE. LET THE SNAKE DRIP ITS POISON INTO THE SOCKETS OF HIS EYES. LET HIM TAKE HIS PAIN. HE DESERVES IT.
VERY WELL. SNAKE! LET FLOW YOUR VENOM.

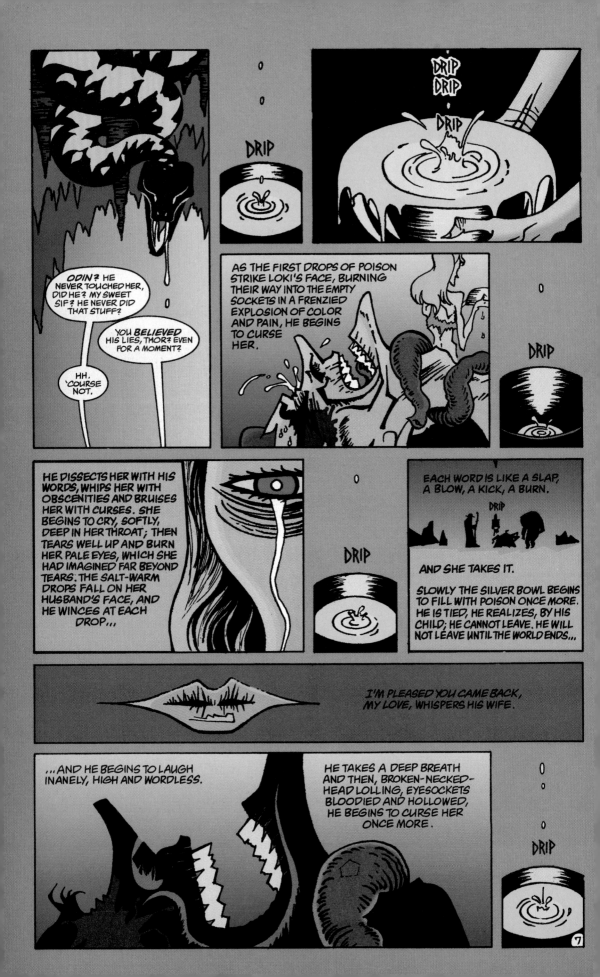

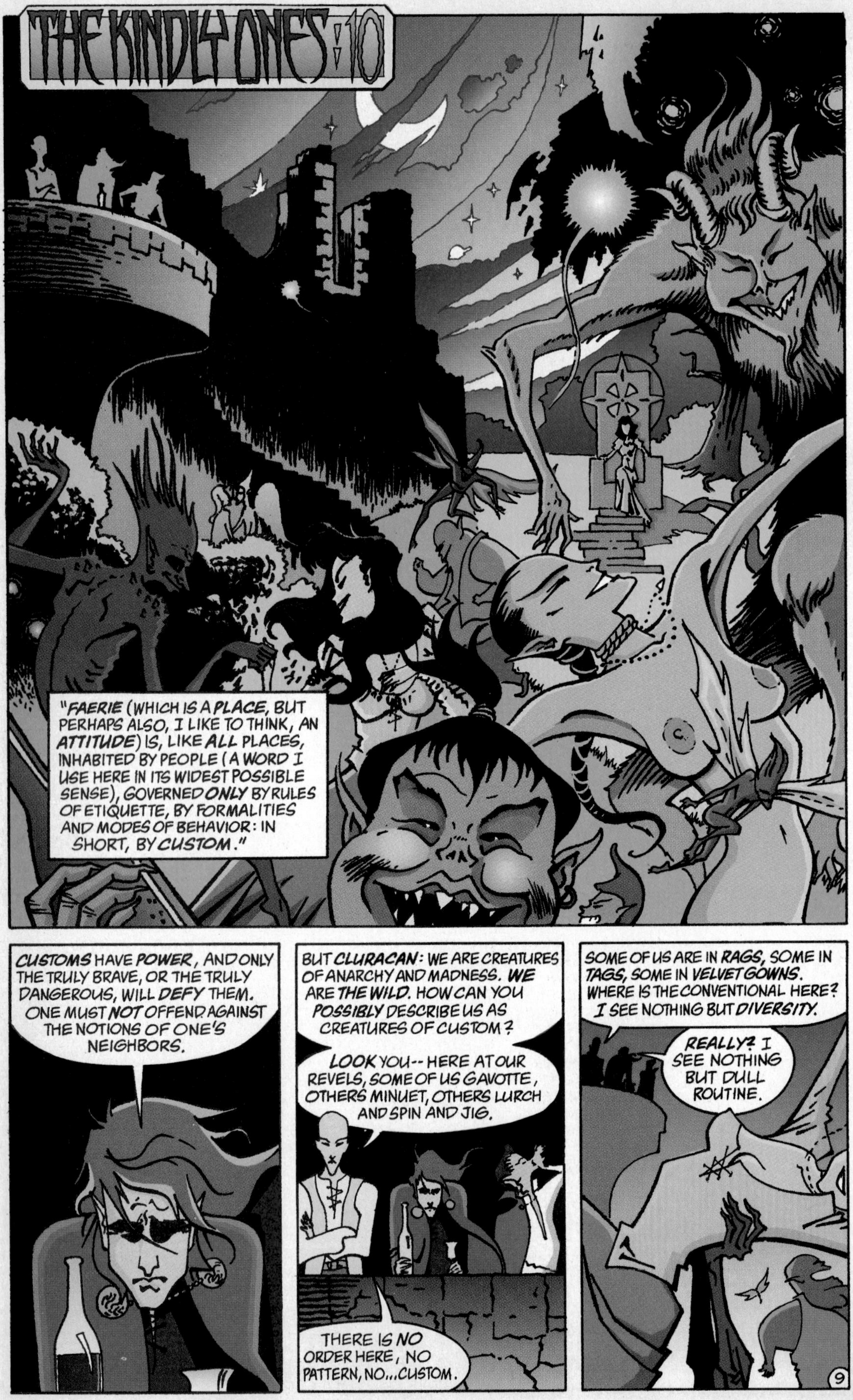
THE KINDLY ONES: 10
"FAERIE (WHICH IS A PLACE, BUT PERHAPS ALSO, I LIKE TO THINK, AN ATTITUDE) IS, LIKE ALL PLACES, INHABITED BY PEOPLE (A WORD I USE HERE IN ITS WIDEST POSSIBLE SENSE), GOVERNED ONLY BY RULES OF ETIQUETTE, BY FORMALITIES AND MODES OF BEHAVIOR: IN SHORT, BY CUSTOM."
CUSTOMS HAVE POWER, AND ONLY THE TRULY BRAVE, OR THE TRULY DANGEROUS, WILL DEFY THEM. ONE MUST NOT OFFEND AGAINST THE NOTIONS OF ONE'S NEIGHBORS.
BUT CLURACAN: WE ARE CREATURES OF ANARCHY AND MADNESS. WE ARE THE WILD. HOW CAN YOU POSSIBLY DESCRIBE US AS CREATURES OF CUSTOM?
LOOK YOU-- HERE AT OUR REVELS, SOME OF US GAVOTTE, OTHERS MINUET, OTHERS LURCH AND SPIN AND JIG.
THERE IS NO ORDER HERE, NO PATTERN, NO...CUSTOM.
SOME OF US ARE IN RAGS, SOME IN TAGS, SOME IN VELVET GOWNS. WHERE IS THE CONVENTIONAL HERE? I SEE NOTHING BUT DIVERSITY.
REALLY? I SEE NOTHING BUT DULL ROUTINE.
9

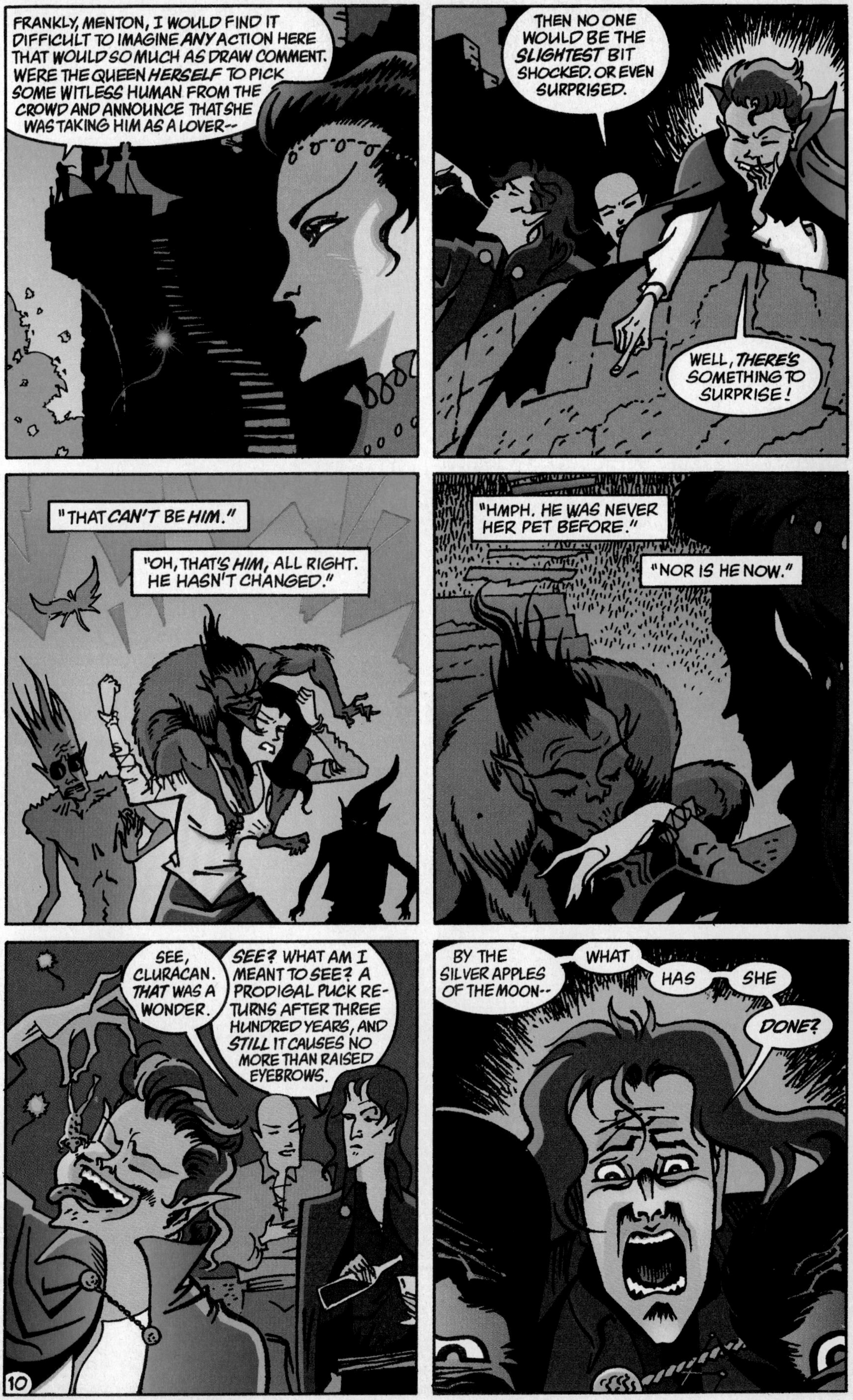

FRANKLY, MENTON, I WOULD FIND IT DIFFICULT TO IMAGINE ANY ACTION HERE THAT WOULD SO MUCH AS DRAW COMMENT. WERE THE QUEEN HERSELF TO PICK SOME WITLESS HUMAN FROM THE CROWD AND ANNOUNCE THAT SHE WAS TAKING HIM AS A LOVER--
THEN NO ONE WOULD BE THE SLIGHTEST BIT SHOCKED. OR EVEN SURPRISED.
WELL, THERE'S SOMETHING TO SURPRISE!
"THAT CAN'T BE HIM."
"OH, THAT'S HIM, ALL RIGHT. HE HASN'T CHANGED."
"HMPH. HE WAS NEVER HER PET BEFORE."
"NOR IS HE NOW."
SEE, CLURACAN. THAT WAS A WONDER.
SEE? WHAT AM I MEANT TO SEE? A PRODIGAL PUCK RETURNS AFTER THREE HUNDRED YEARS, AND STILL IT CAUSES NO MORE THAN RAISED EYEBROWS.
BY THE SILVER APPLES OF THE MOON--
WHAT
HAS
SHE
DONE?

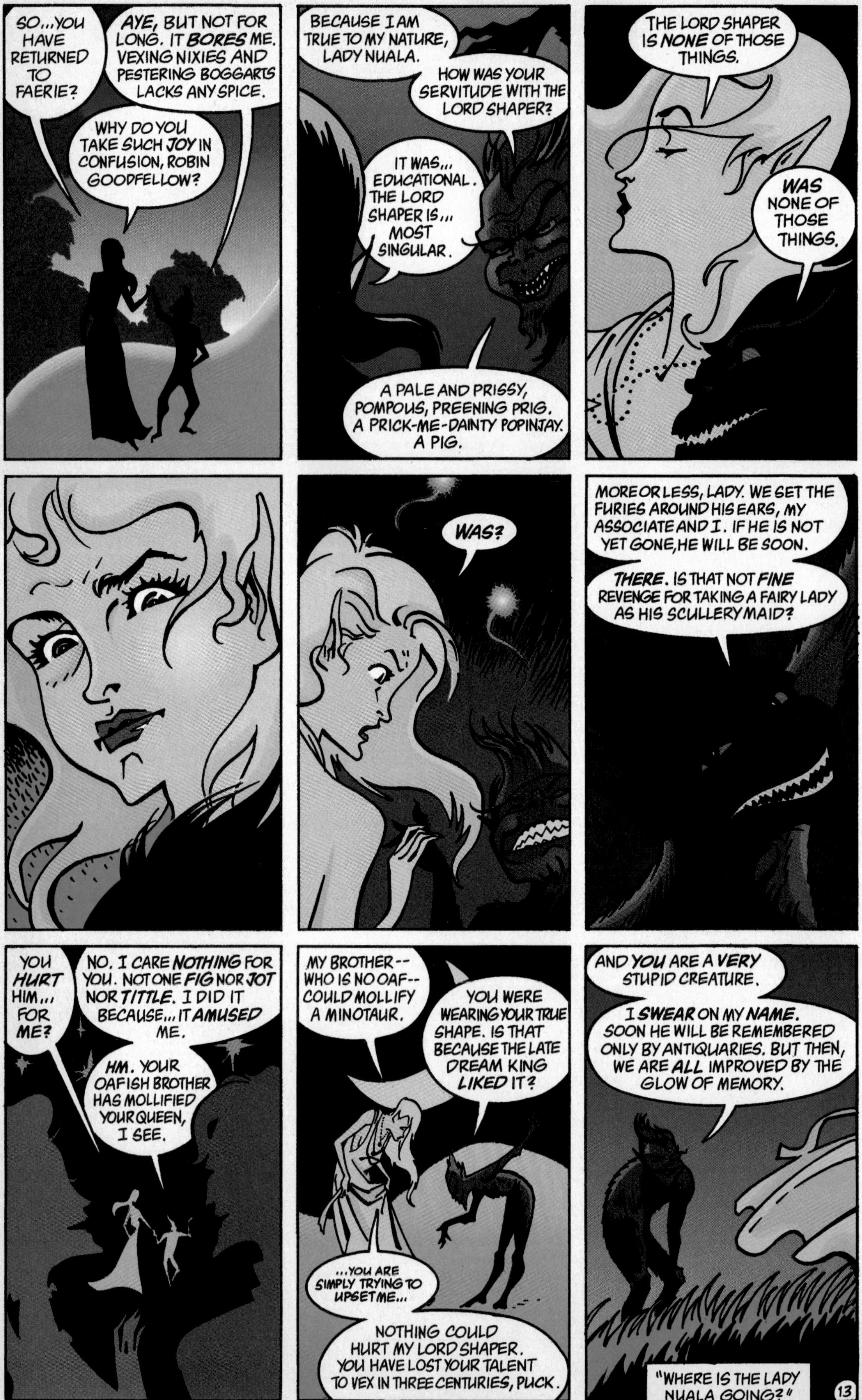
SO...YOU HAVE RETURNED TO FAERIE?
AYE, BUT NOT FOR LONG. IT BORES ME. VEXING NIXIES AND PESTERING BOGGARTS LACKS ANY SPICE.
WHY DO YOU TAKE SUCH JOY IN CONFUSION, ROBIN GOODFELLOW?
BECAUSE I AM TRUE TO MY NATURE, LADY NUALA.
HOW WAS YOUR SERVITUDE WITH THE LORD SHAPER?
IT WAS... EDUCATIONAL. THE LORD SHAPER IS... MOST SINGULAR.
A PALE AND PRISSY, POMPOUS, PREENING PRIG. A PRICK-ME-DAINTY POPINJAY. A PIG.
THE LORD SHAPER IS NONE OF THOSE THINGS.
WAS NONE OF THOSE THINGS.
WAS?
MORE OR LESS, LADY. WE SET THE FURIES AROUND HIS EARS, MY ASSOCIATE AND I. IF HE IS NOT YET GONE, HE WILL BE SOON.
THERE. IS THAT NOT FINE REVENGE FOR TAKING A FAIRY LADY AS HIS SCULLERY MAID?
YOU HURT HIM... FOR ME?
NO. I CARE NOTHING FOR YOU. NOT ONE FIG NOR JOT NOR TITTLE. I DID IT BECAUSE... IT AMUSED ME.
HM. YOUR OAFISH BROTHER HAS MOLLIFIED YOUR QUEEN, I SEE.
MY BROTHER -- WHO IS NO OAF -- COULD MOLLIFY A MINOTAUR.
YOU WERE WEARING YOUR TRUE SHAPE. IS THAT BECAUSE THE LATE DREAM KING LIKED IT?
...YOU ARE SIMPLY TRYING TO UPSET ME...
NOTHING COULD HURT MY LORD SHAPER. YOU HAVE LOST YOUR TALENT TO VEX IN THREE CENTURIES, PUCK.
AND YOU ARE A VERY STUPID CREATURE.
I SWEAR ON MY NAME. SOON HE WILL BE REMEMBERED ONLY BY ANTIQUARIES. BUT THEN, WE ARE ALL IMPROVED BY THE GLOW OF MEMORY.
"WHERE IS THE LADY NUALA GOING?"

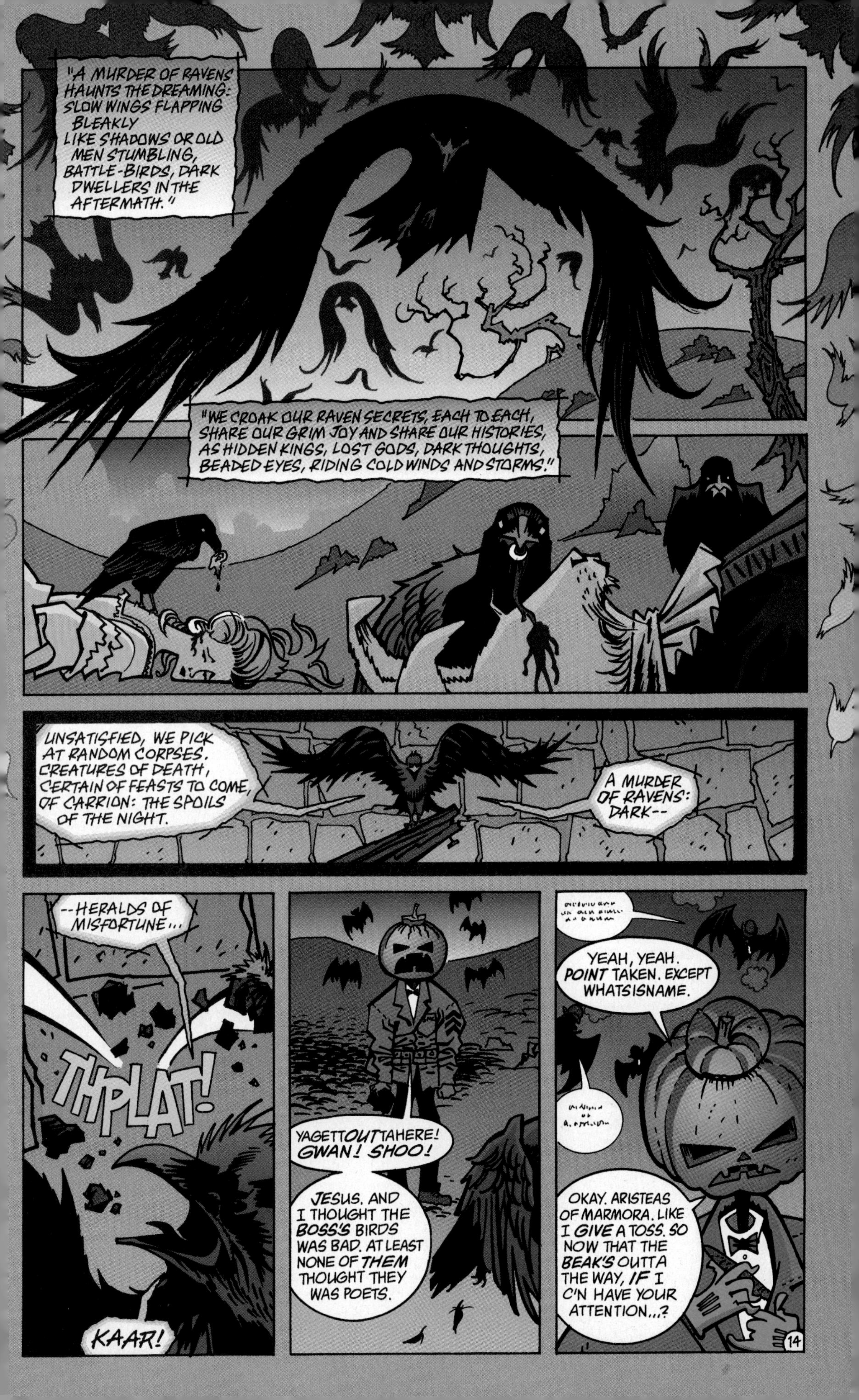
"A MURDER OF RAVENS HAUNTS THE DREAMING: SLOW WINGS FLAPPING BLEAKLY LIKE SHADOWS OR OLD MEN STUMBLING, BATTLE-BIRDS, DARK DWELLERS IN THE AFTERMATH."
"WE CROAK OUR RAVEN SECRETS, EACH TO EACH, SHARE OUR GRIM JOY AND SHARE OUR HISTORIES, AS HIDDEN KINGS, LOST GODS, DARK THOUGHTS, BEADED EYES, RIDING COLD WINDS AND STORMS."
UNSATISFIED, WE PICK AT RANDOM CORPSES. CREATURES OF DEATH, CERTAIN OF FEASTS TO COME, OF CARRION: THE SPOILS OF THE NIGHT.
A MURDER OF RAVENS: DARK--
--HERALDS OF MISFORTUNE...
THPLAT!
KAAR!
YAGETTOUTTAHERE! GWAN! SHOO!
JESUS. AND I THOUGHT THE BOSS'S BIRDS WAS BAD. AT LEAST NONE OF THEM THOUGHT THEY WAS POETS.
YEAH, YEAH. POINT TAKEN. EXCEPT WHATSISNAME.
OKAY. ARISTEAS OF MARMORA. LIKE I GIVE A TOSS. SO NOW THAT THE BEAK'S OUTTA THE WAY, IF I C'N HAVE YOUR ATTENTION...?

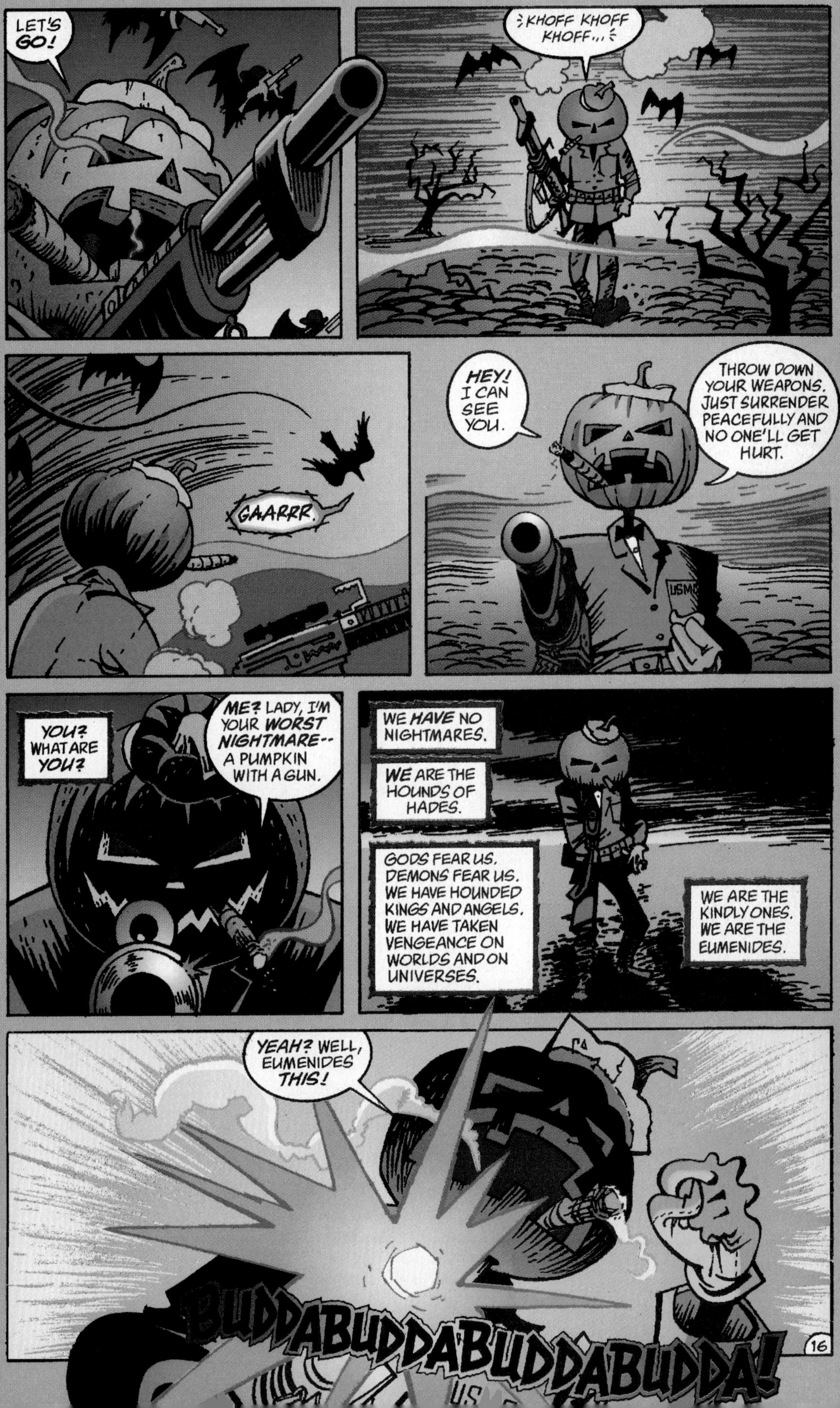

LET'S GO!
KHOFF KHOFF KHOFF...
GAARRR.
HEY! I CAN SEE YOU.
THROW DOWN YOUR WEAPONS. JUST SURRENDER PEACEFULLY AND NO ONE'LL GET HURT.
YOU? WHAT ARE YOU?
ME? LADY, I'M YOUR WORST NIGHTMARE-- A PUMPKIN WITH A GUN.
WE HAVE NO NIGHTMARES.
WE ARE THE HOUNDS OF HADES.
GODS FEAR US. DEMONS FEAR US. WE HAVE HOUNDED KINGS AND ANGELS. WE HAVE TAKEN VENGEANCE ON WORLDS AND ON UNIVERSES.
WE ARE THE KINDLY ONES. WE ARE THE EUMENIDES.
YEAH? WELL, EUMENIDES THIS!
BUDDABUDDABUDDABUDDA!

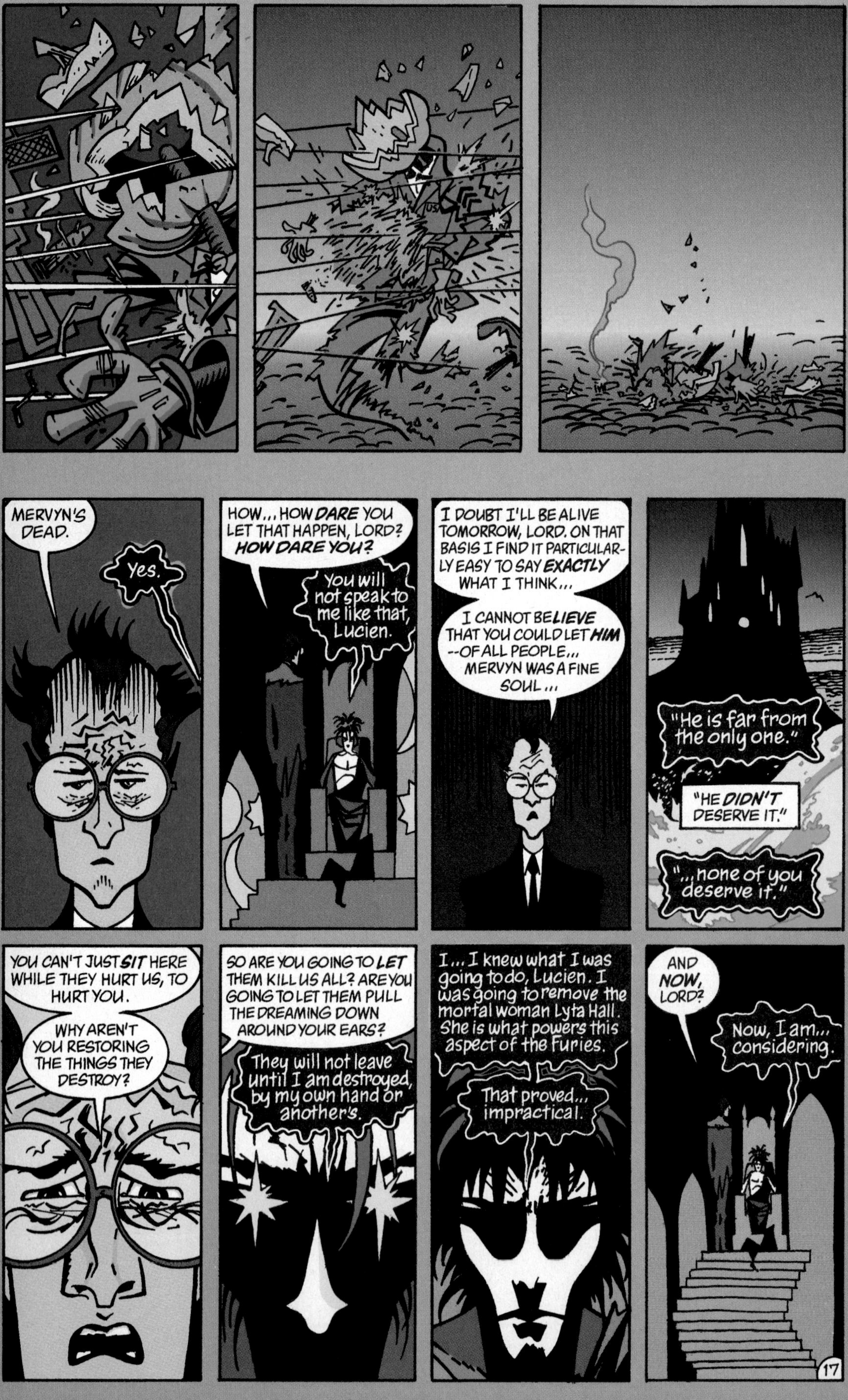

MERVYN'S DEAD.
Yes.
HOW... HOW DARE YOU LET THAT HAPPEN, LORD? HOW DARE YOU?
You will not speak to me like that, Lucien.
I DOUBT I'LL BE ALIVE TOMORROW, LORD. ON THAT BASIS I FIND IT PARTICULARLY EASY TO SAY EXACTLY WHAT I THINK...
I CANNOT BELIEVE THAT YOU COULD LET HIM --OF ALL PEOPLE... MERVYN WAS A FINE SOUL...
"He is far from the only one."
"HE DIDN'T DESERVE IT."
"...none of you deserve it."
YOU CAN'T JUST SIT HERE WHILE THEY HURT US, TO HURT YOU.
WHY AREN'T YOU RESTORING THE THINGS THEY DESTROY?
SO ARE YOU GOING TO LET THEM KILL US ALL? ARE YOU GOING TO LET THEM PULL THE DREAMING DOWN AROUND YOUR EARS?
They will not leave until I am destroyed, by my own hand or another's.
I... I knew what I was going to do, Lucien. I was going to remove the mortal woman Lyta Hall. She is what powers this aspect of the Furies.
That proved... impractical.
AND NOW, LORD?
Now, I am... considering.

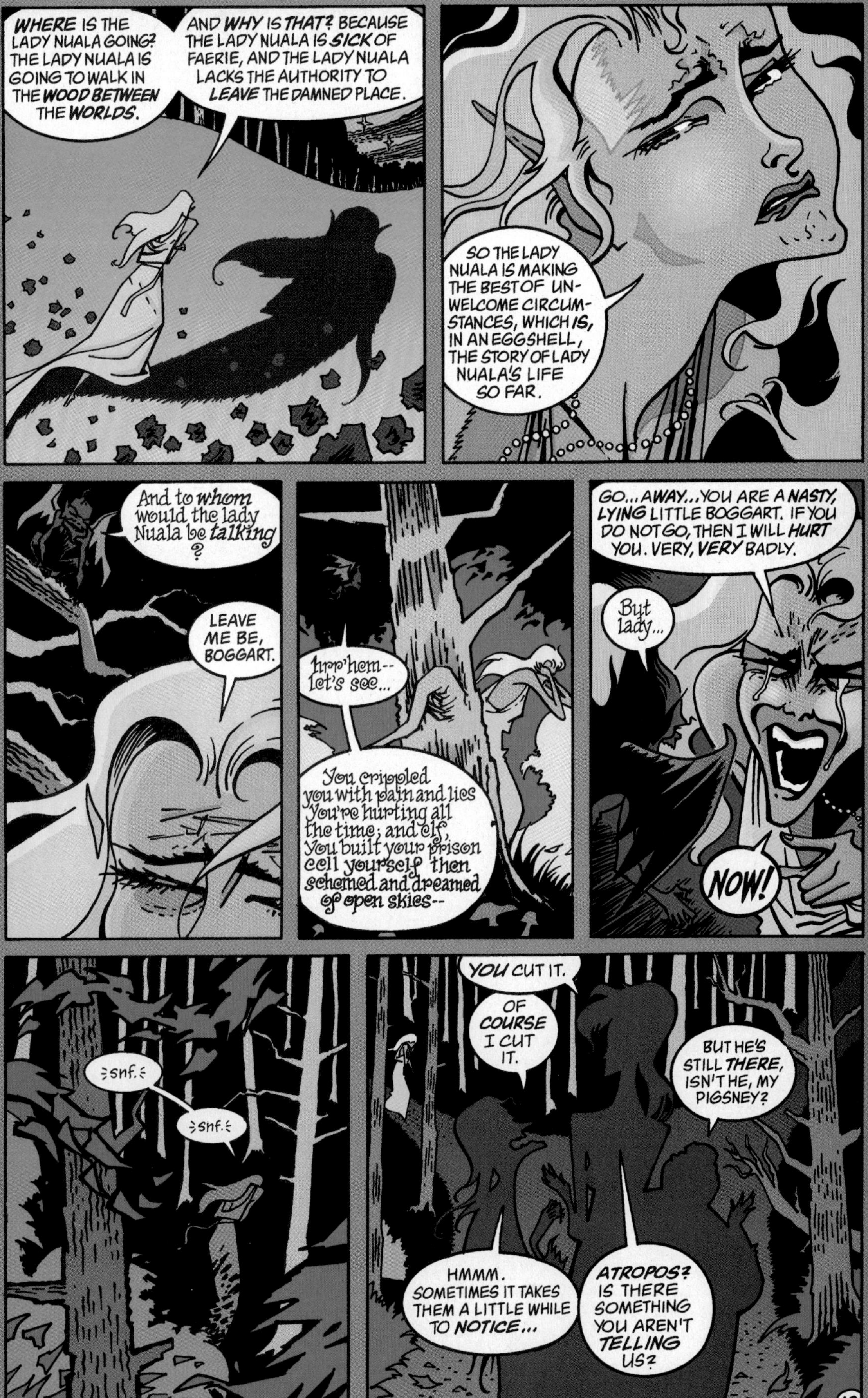
WHERE IS THE LADY NUALA GOING? THE LADY NUALA IS GOING TO WALK IN THE WOOD BETWEEN THE WORLDS.
AND WHY IS THAT? BECAUSE THE LADY NUALA IS SICK OF FAERIE, AND THE LADY NUALA LACKS THE AUTHORITY TO LEAVE THE DAMNED PLACE.
SO THE LADY NUALA IS MAKING THE BEST OF UNWELCOME CIRCUMSTANCES, WHICH IS, IN AN EGGSHELL, THE STORY OF LADY NUALA'S LIFE SO FAR.
And to whom would the lady Nuala be talking?
LEAVE ME BE, BOGGART.
hrr'hem--let's see...
You crippled you with pain and lies You're hurting all the time; and elf, You built your prison cell yourself then schemed and dreamed of open skies--
GO... AWAY... YOU ARE A NASTY, LYING LITTLE BOGGART. IF YOU DO NOT GO, THEN I WILL HURT YOU. VERY, VERY BADLY.
But lady...
NOW!
snf.
snf.
YOU CUT IT.
OF COURSE I CUT IT.
BUT HE'S STILL THERE, ISN'T HE, MY PIGSNEY?
HMMM. SOMETIMES IT TAKES THEM A LITTLE WHILE TO NOTICE...
ATROPOS? IS THERE SOMETHING YOU AREN'T TELLING US?
18

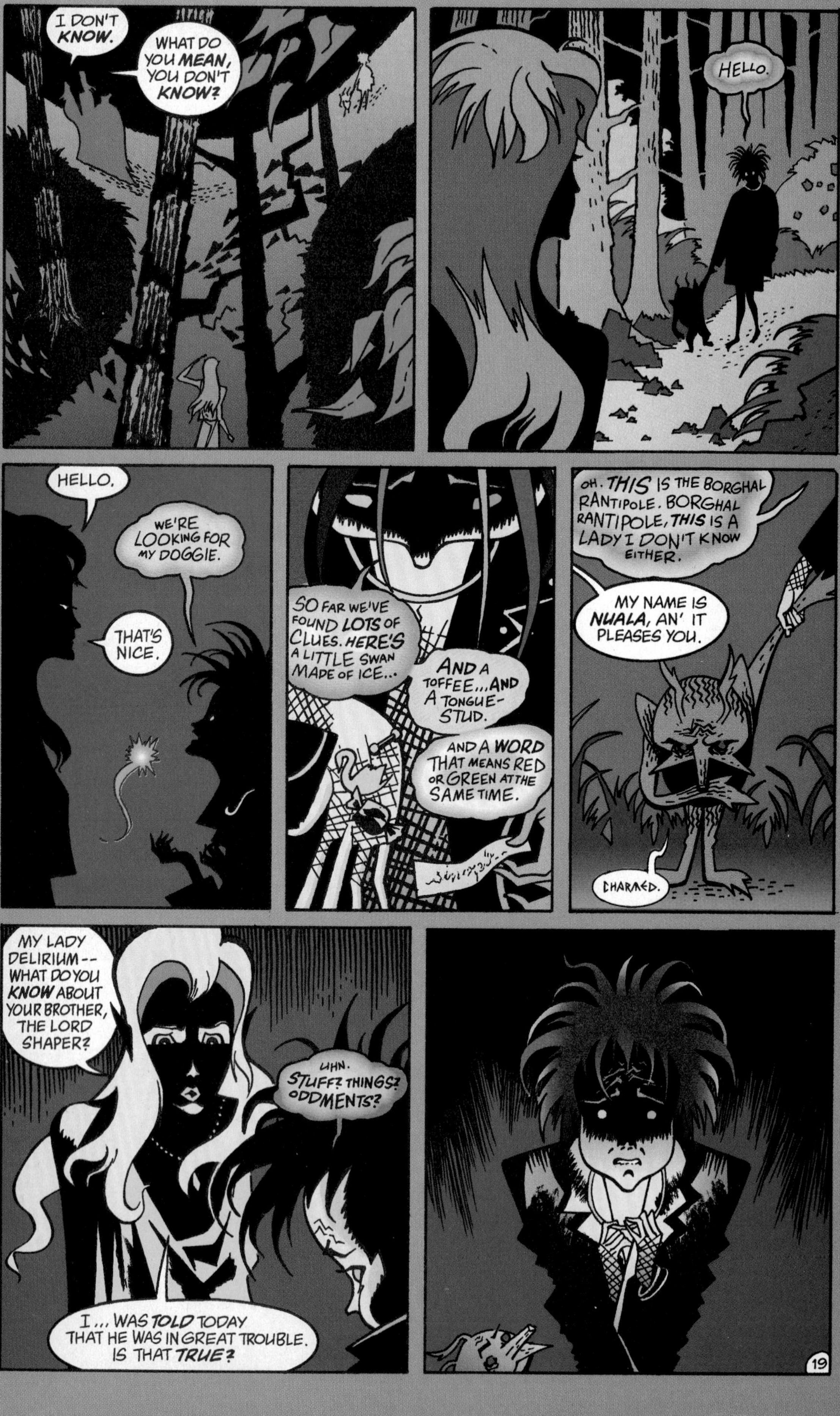
I DON'T KNOW.
WHAT DO YOU MEAN, YOU DON'T KNOW?
HELLO.
HELLO.
WE'RE LOOKING FOR MY DOGGIE.
THAT'S NICE.
SO FAR WE'VE FOUND LOTS OF CLUES. HERE'S A LITTLE SWAN MADE OF ICE...
AND A TOFFEE...AND A TONGUE-STUD.
AND A WORD THAT MEANS RED OR GREEN AT THE SAME TIME.
OH. THIS IS THE BORGHAL RANTIPOLE. BORGHAL RANTIPOLE, THIS IS A LADY I DON'T KNOW EITHER.
MY NAME IS NUALA, AN' IT PLEASES YOU.
CHARMED.
MY LADY DELIRIUM -- WHAT DO YOU KNOW ABOUT YOUR BROTHER, THE LORD SHAPER?
UHN. STUFF? THINGS? ODDMENTS?
I... WAS TOLD TODAY THAT HE WAS IN GREAT TROUBLE. IS THAT TRUE?

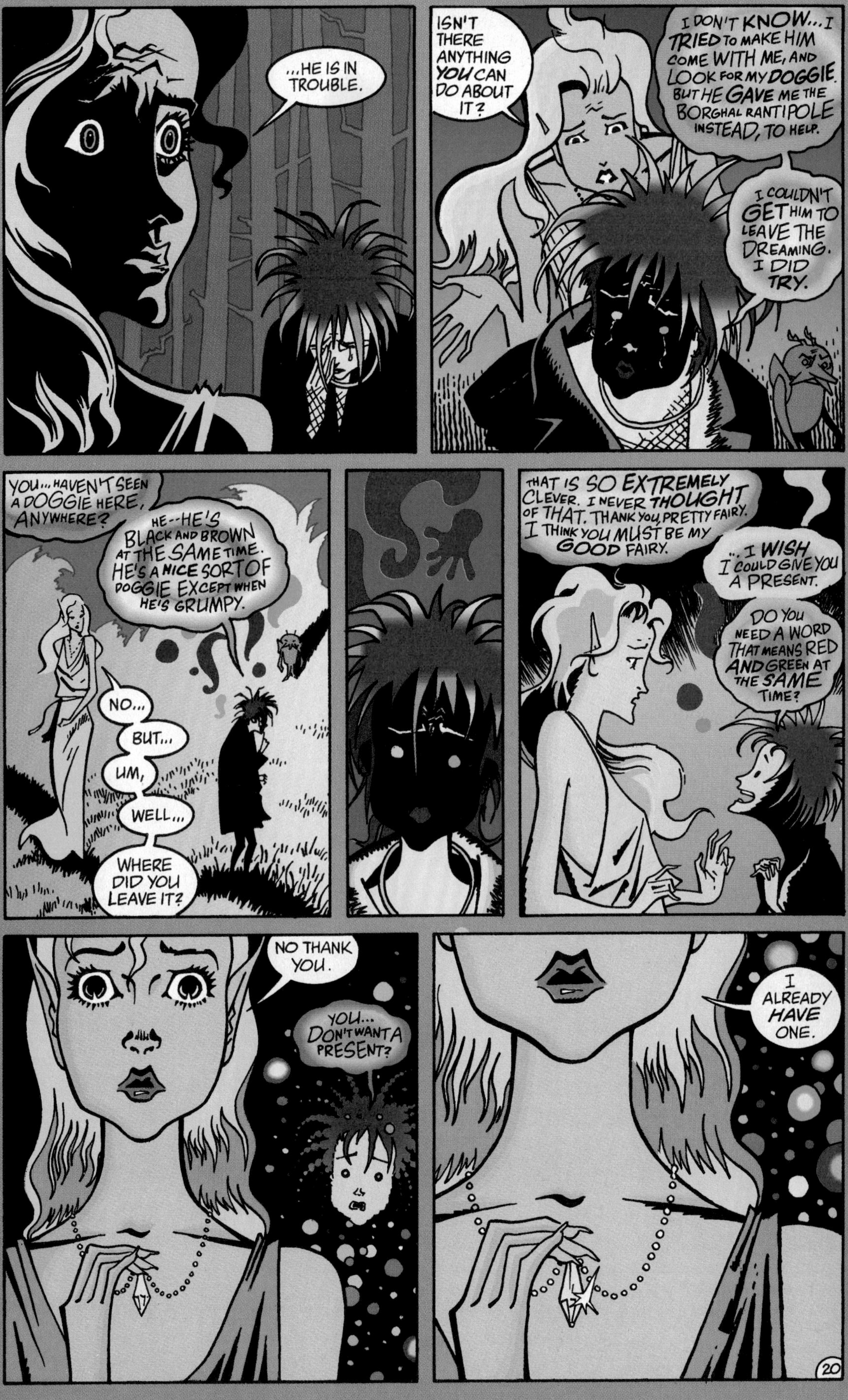
...HE IS IN TROUBLE.
ISN'T THERE ANYTHING YOU CAN DO ABOUT IT?
I DON'T KNOW... I TRIED TO MAKE HIM COME WITH ME, AND LOOK FOR MY DOGGIE. BUT HE GAVE ME THE BORGHAL RANTIPOLE INSTEAD, TO HELP.
I COULDN'T GET HIM TO LEAVE THE DREAMING. I DID TRY.
YOU... HAVEN'T SEEN A DOGGIE HERE, ANYWHERE?
HE--HE'S BLACK AND BROWN AT THE SAME TIME. HE'S A NICE SORT OF DOGGIE EXCEPT WHEN HE'S GRUMPY.
NO...
BUT...
UM,
WELL...
WHERE DID YOU LEAVE IT?
THAT IS SO EXTREMELY CLEVER. I NEVER THOUGHT OF THAT. THANK YOU, PRETTY FAIRY. I THINK YOU MUST BE MY GOOD FAIRY.
...I WISH I COULD GIVE YOU A PRESENT.
DO YOU NEED A WORD THAT MEANS RED AND GREEN AT THE SAME TIME?
NO THANK YOU.
YOU... DON'T WANT A PRESENT?
I ALREADY HAVE ONE.
20

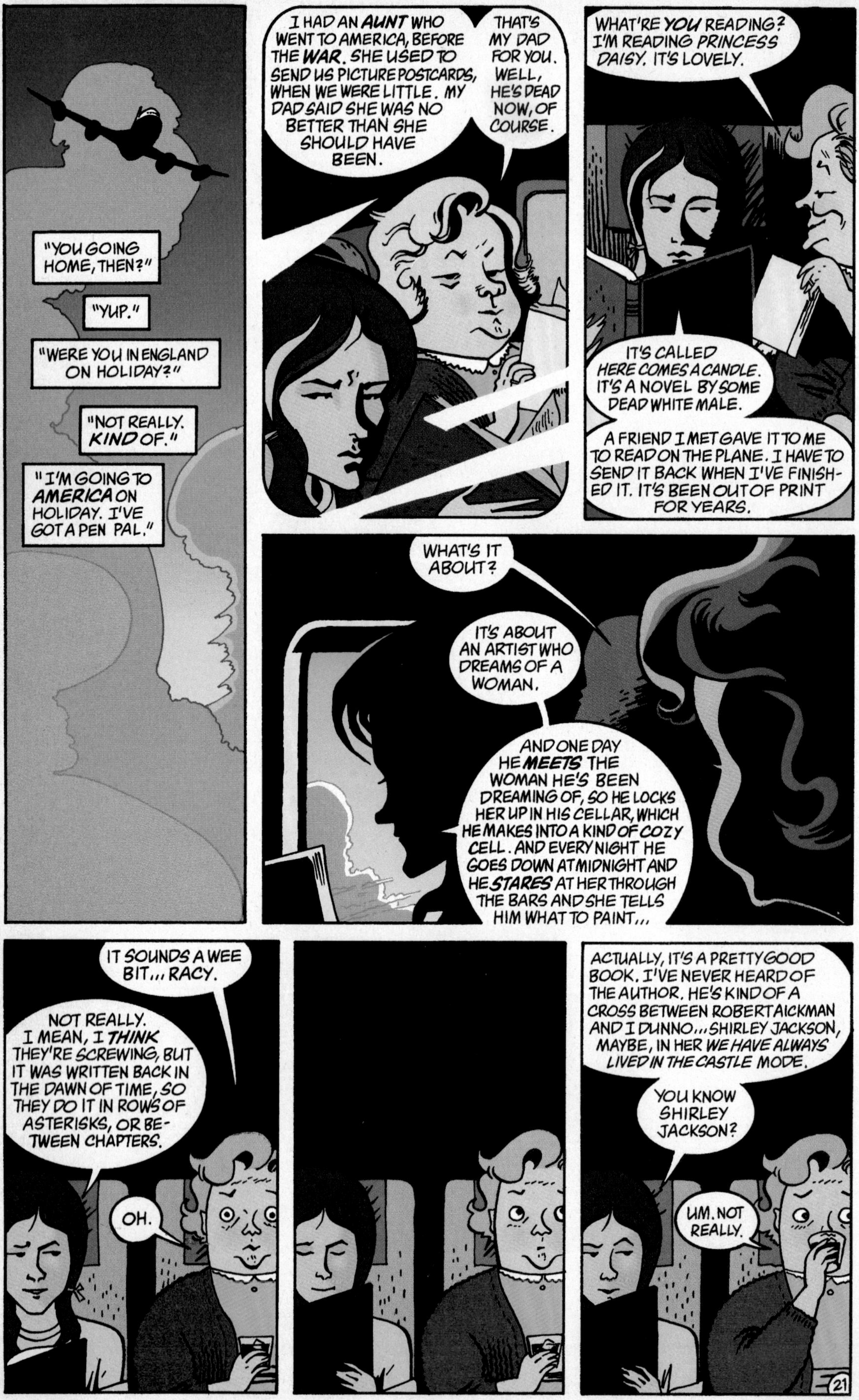
"YOU GOING HOME, THEN?"
"YUP."
"WERE YOU IN ENGLAND ON HOLIDAY?"
"NOT REALLY. KIND OF."
"I'M GOING TO AMERICA ON HOLIDAY. I'VE GOT A PEN PAL."
I HAD AN AUNT WHO WENT TO AMERICA, BEFORE THE WAR. SHE USED TO SEND US PICTURE POSTCARDS, WHEN WE WERE LITTLE. MY DAD SAID SHE WAS NO BETTER THAN SHE SHOULD HAVE BEEN.
THAT'S MY DAD FOR YOU. WELL, HE'S DEAD NOW, OF COURSE.
WHAT'RE YOU READING? I'M READING PRINCESS DAISY. IT'S LOVELY.
IT'S CALLED HERE COMES A CANDLE. IT'S A NOVEL BY SOME DEAD WHITE MALE.
A FRIEND I MET GAVE IT TO ME TO READ ON THE PLANE. I HAVE TO SEND IT BACK WHEN I'VE FINISHED IT. IT'S BEEN OUT OF PRINT FOR YEARS.
WHAT'S IT ABOUT?
IT'S ABOUT AN ARTIST WHO DREAMS OF A WOMAN.
AND ONE DAY HE MEETS THE WOMAN HE'S BEEN DREAMING OF, SO HE LOCKS HER UP IN HIS CELLAR, WHICH HE MAKES INTO A KIND OF COZY CELL. AND EVERY NIGHT HE GOES DOWN AT MIDNIGHT AND HE STARES AT HER THROUGH THE BARS AND SHE TELLS HIM WHAT TO PAINT...
IT SOUNDS A WEE BIT... RACY.
NOT REALLY. I MEAN, I THINK THEY'RE SCREWING, BUT IT WAS WRITTEN BACK IN THE DAWN OF TIME, SO THEY DO IT IN ROWS OF ASTERISKS, OR BETWEEN CHAPTERS.
OH.
ACTUALLY, IT'S A PRETTY GOOD BOOK. I'VE NEVER HEARD OF THE AUTHOR. HE'S KIND OF A CROSS BETWEEN ROBERT AICKMAN AND I DUNNO... SHIRLEY JACKSON, MAYBE, IN HER WE HAVE ALWAYS LIVED IN THE CASTLE MODE.
YOU KNOW SHIRLEY JACKSON?
UM. NOT REALLY.

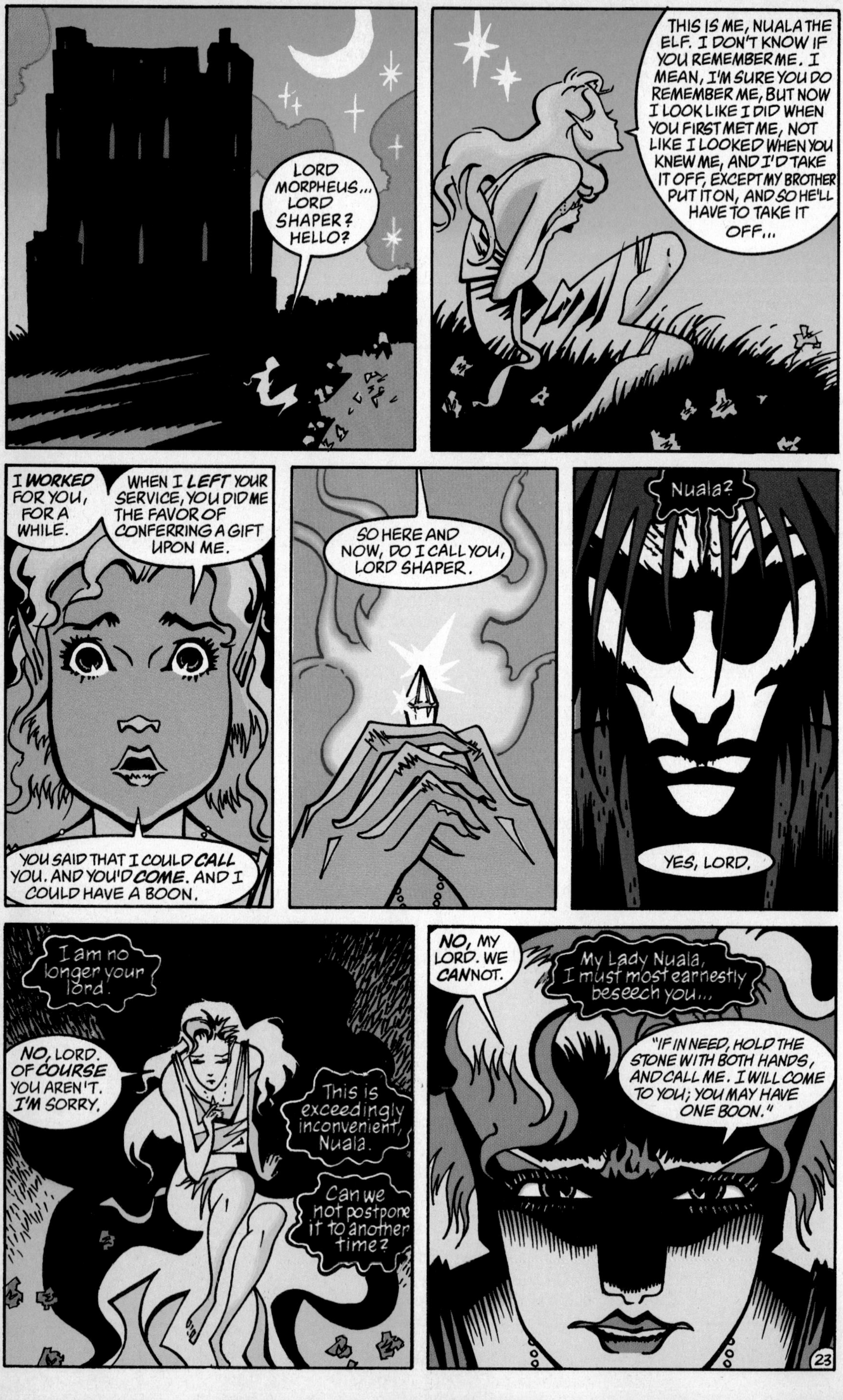
LORD MORPHEUS... LORD SHAPER? HELLO?
THIS IS ME, NUALA THE ELF. I DON'T KNOW IF YOU REMEMBER ME. I MEAN, I'M SURE YOU DO REMEMBER ME, BUT NOW I LOOK LIKE I DID WHEN YOU FIRST MET ME, NOT LIKE I LOOKED WHEN YOU KNEW ME, AND I'D TAKE IT OFF, EXCEPT MY BROTHER PUT IT ON, AND SO HE'LL HAVE TO TAKE IT OFF...
I WORKED FOR YOU, FOR A WHILE.
WHEN I LEFT YOUR SERVICE, YOU DID ME THE FAVOR OF CONFERRING A GIFT UPON ME.
YOU SAID THAT I COULD CALL YOU. AND YOU'D COME. AND I COULD HAVE A BOON.
SO HERE AND NOW, DO I CALL YOU, LORD SHAPER.
Nuala?
YES, LORD.
I am no longer your lord.
NO, LORD. OF COURSE YOU AREN'T. I'M SORRY.
This is exceedingly inconvenient, Nuala.
Can we not postpone it to another time?
NO, MY LORD. WE CANNOT.
My Lady Nuala, I must most earnestly beseech you...
"IF IN NEED, HOLD THE STONE WITH BOTH HANDS, AND CALL ME. I WILL COME TO YOU; YOU MAY HAVE ONE BOON."

Part Eleven

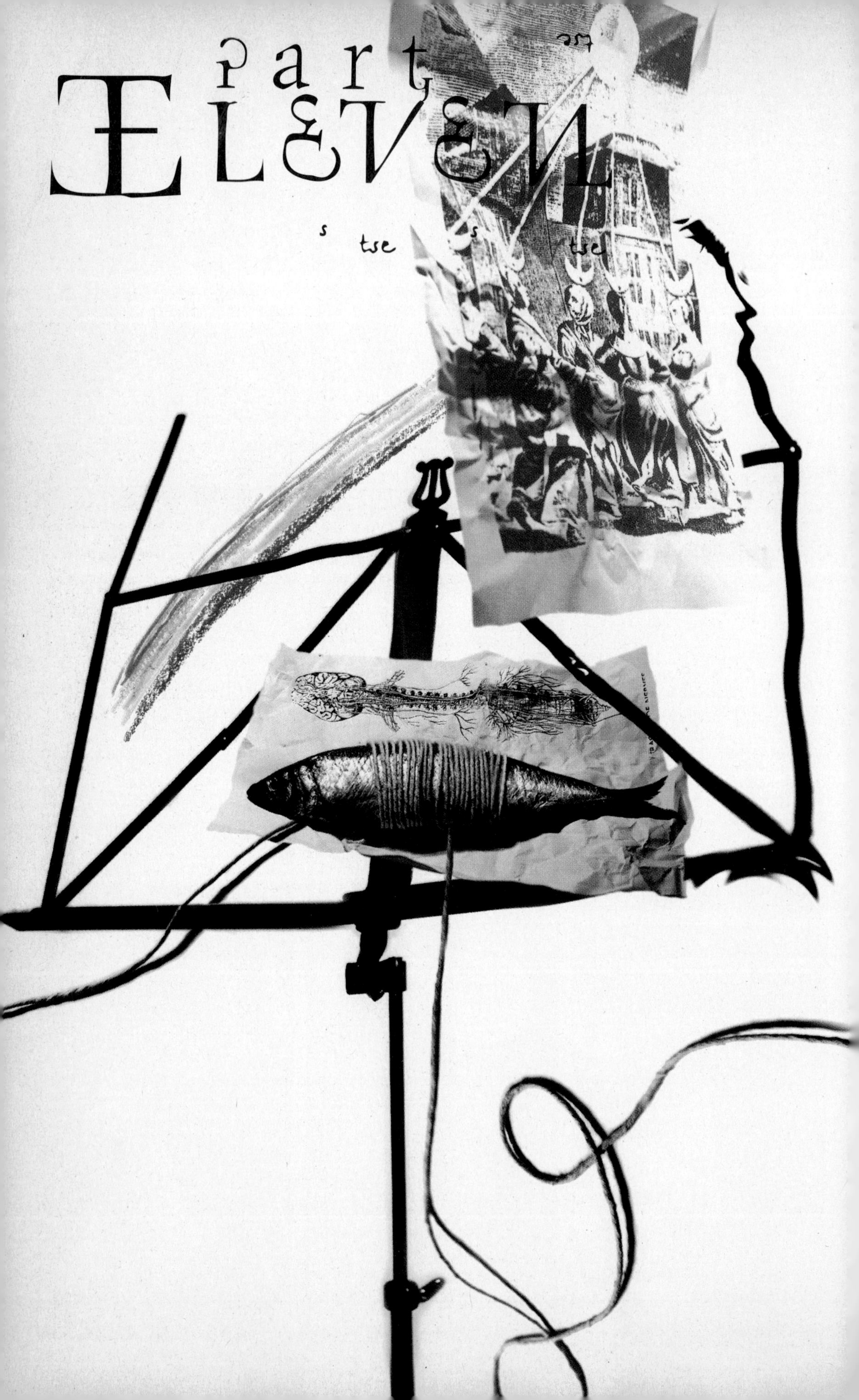
s tse s tse

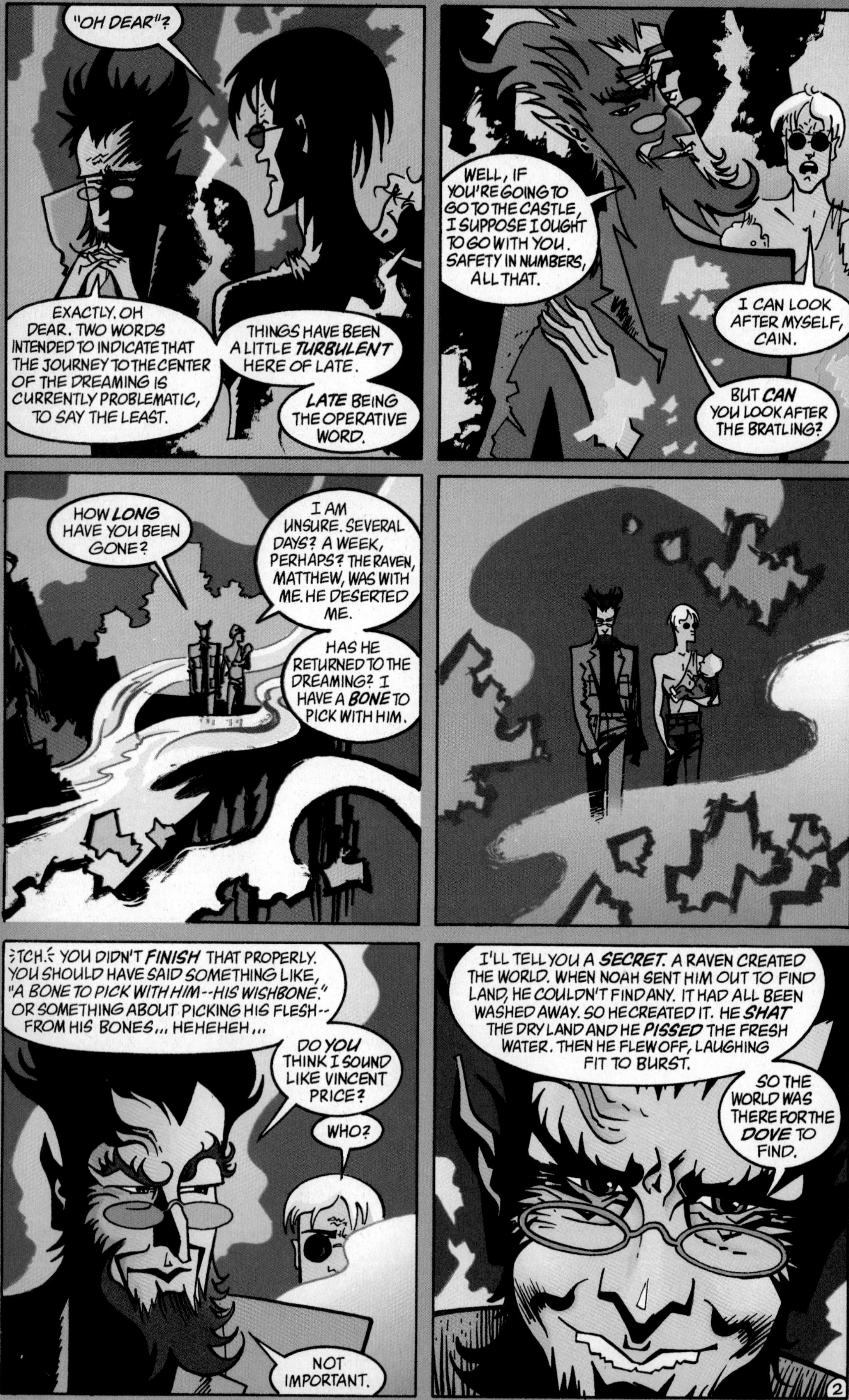
"OH DEAR"?
EXACTLY. OH DEAR. TWO WORDS INTENDED TO INDICATE THAT THE JOURNEY TO THE CENTER OF THE DREAMING IS CURRENTLY PROBLEMATIC, TO SAY THE LEAST.
THINGS HAVE BEEN A LITTLE TURBULENT HERE OF LATE.
LATE BEING THE OPERATIVE WORD.
WELL, IF YOU'RE GOING TO GO TO THE CASTLE, I SUPPOSE I OUGHT TO GO WITH YOU. SAFETY IN NUMBERS, ALL THAT.
I CAN LOOK AFTER MYSELF, CAIN.
BUT CAN YOU LOOK AFTER THE BRATLING?
HOW LONG HAVE YOU BEEN GONE?
I AM UNSURE. SEVERAL DAYS? A WEEK, PERHAPS? THE RAVEN, MATTHEW, WAS WITH ME. HE DESERTED ME.
HAS HE RETURNED TO THE DREAMING? I HAVE A BONE TO PICK WITH HIM.
TCH. YOU DIDN'T FINISH THAT PROPERLY. YOU SHOULD HAVE SAID SOMETHING LIKE, "A BONE TO PICK WITH HIM--HIS WISHBONE." OR SOMETHING ABOUT PICKING HIS FLESH--FROM HIS BONES... HEHEHEH...
DO YOU THINK I SOUND LIKE VINCENT PRICE?
WHO?
NOT IMPORTANT.
I'LL TELL YOU A SECRET. A RAVEN CREATED THE WORLD. WHEN NOAH SENT HIM OUT TO FIND LAND, HE COULDN'T FIND ANY. IT HAD ALL BEEN WASHED AWAY. SO HE CREATED IT. HE SHAT THE DRY LAND AND HE PISSED THE FRESH WATER. THEN HE FLEW OFF, LAUGHING FIT TO BURST.
SO THE WORLD WAS THERE FOR THE DOVE TO FIND.
2

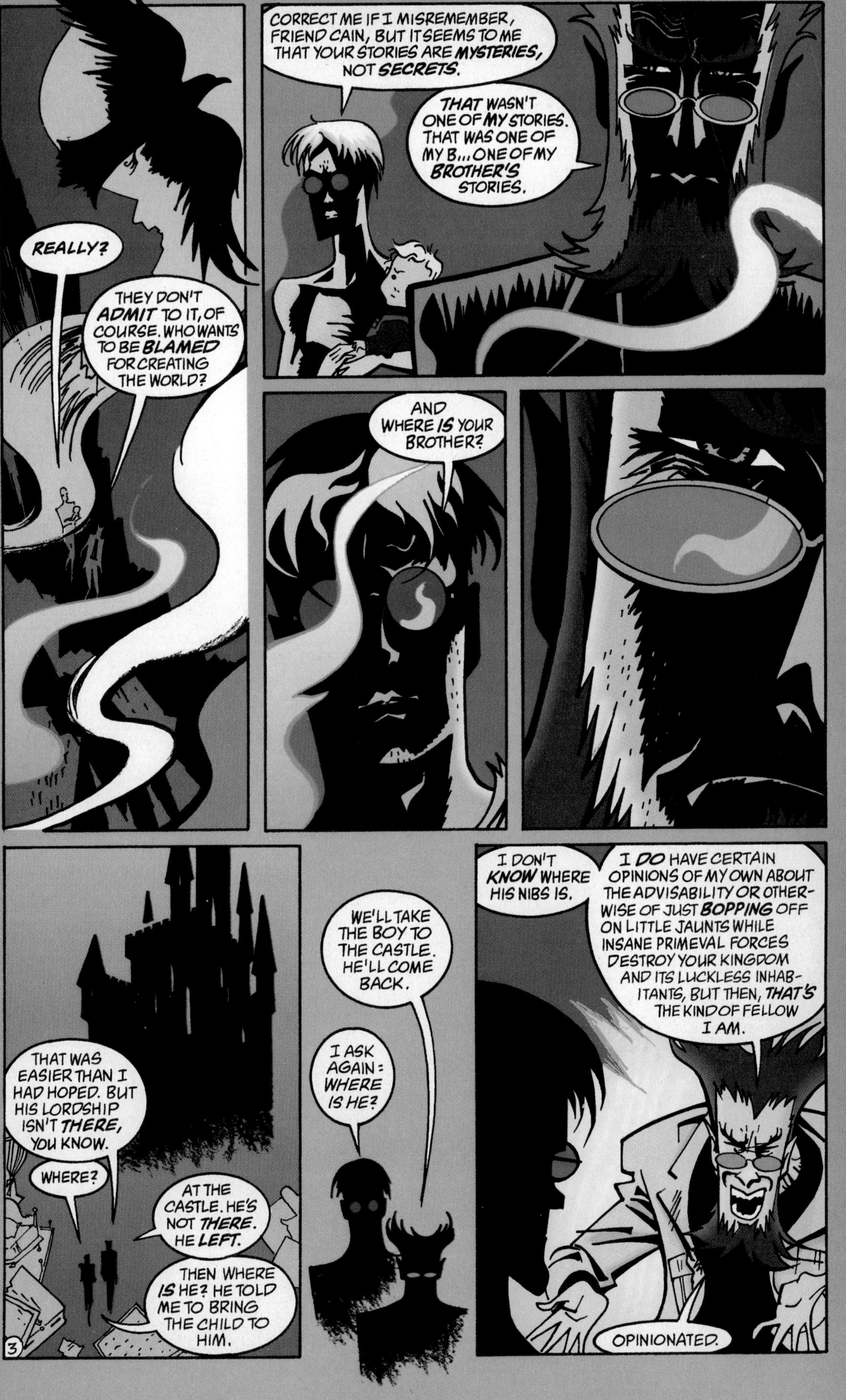

CORRECT ME IF I MISREMEMBER, FRIEND CAIN, BUT IT SEEMS TO ME THAT YOUR STORIES ARE MYSTERIES, NOT SECRETS.
THAT WASN'T ONE OF MY STORIES. THAT WAS ONE OF MY B... ONE OF MY BROTHER'S STORIES.
REALLY?
THEY DON'T ADMIT TO IT, OF COURSE. WHO WANTS TO BE BLAMED FOR CREATING THE WORLD?
AND WHERE IS YOUR BROTHER?
THAT WAS EASIER THAN I HAD HOPED. BUT HIS LORDSHIP ISN'T THERE, YOU KNOW.
WHERE?
AT THE CASTLE. HE'S NOT THERE. HE LEFT.
THEN WHERE IS HE? HE TOLD ME TO BRING THE CHILD TO HIM.
WE'LL TAKE THE BOY TO THE CASTLE. HE'LL COME BACK.
I ASK AGAIN: WHERE IS HE?
I DON'T KNOW WHERE HIS NIBS IS.
I DO HAVE CERTAIN OPINIONS OF MY OWN ABOUT THE ADVISABILITY OR OTHERWISE OF JUST BOPPING OFF ON LITTLE JAUNTS WHILE INSANE PRIMEVAL FORCES DESTROY YOUR KINGDOM AND ITS LUCKLESS INHABITANTS, BUT THEN, THAT'S THE KIND OF FELLOW I AM.
OPINIONATED.

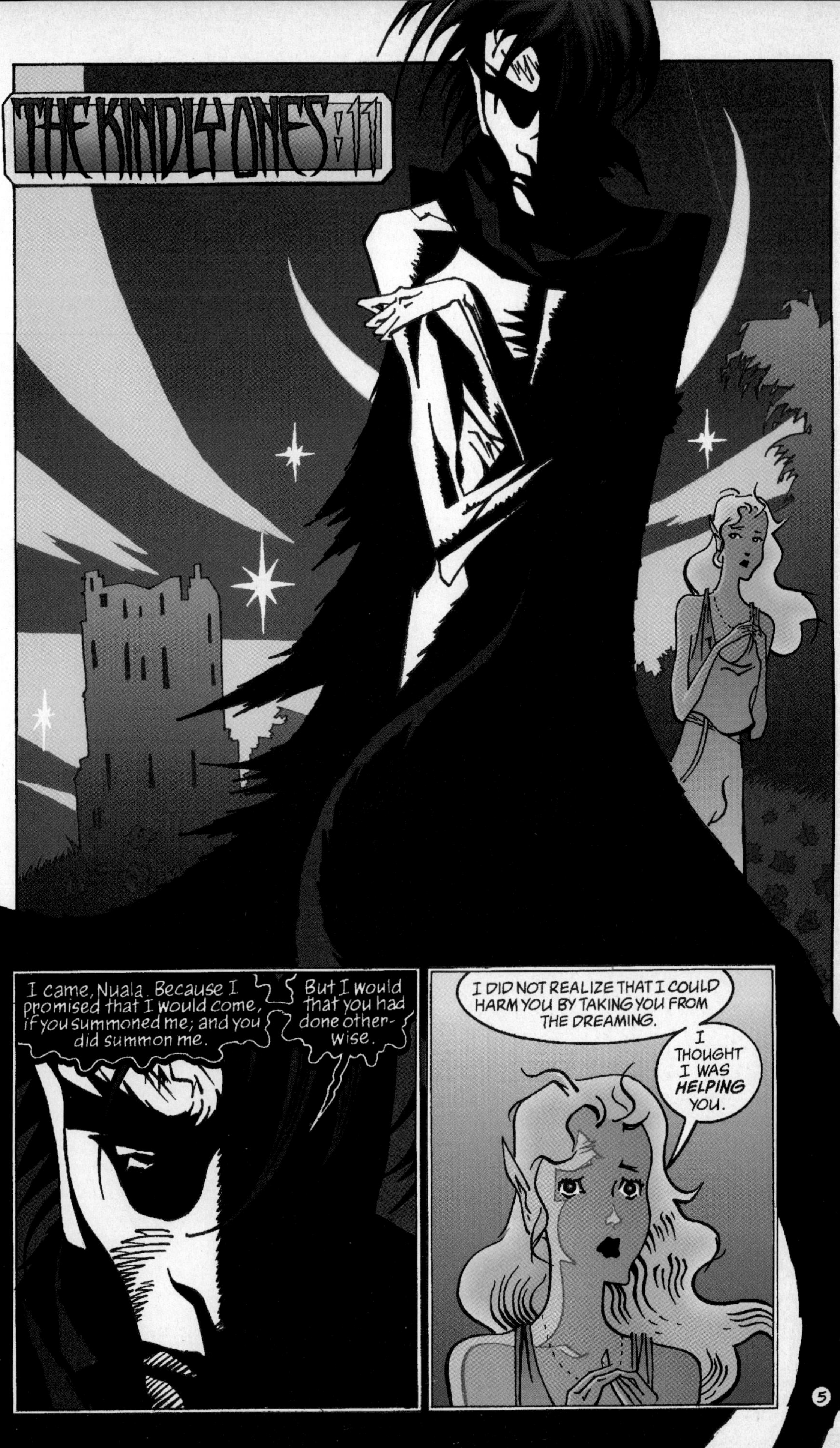
THE KINDLY ONES: 11
I came, Nuala. Because I promised that I would come, if you summoned me; and you did summon me.
But I would that you had done other-wise.
I DID NOT REALIZE THAT I COULD HARM YOU BY TAKING YOU FROM THE DREAMING.
I THOUGHT I WAS HELPING YOU.

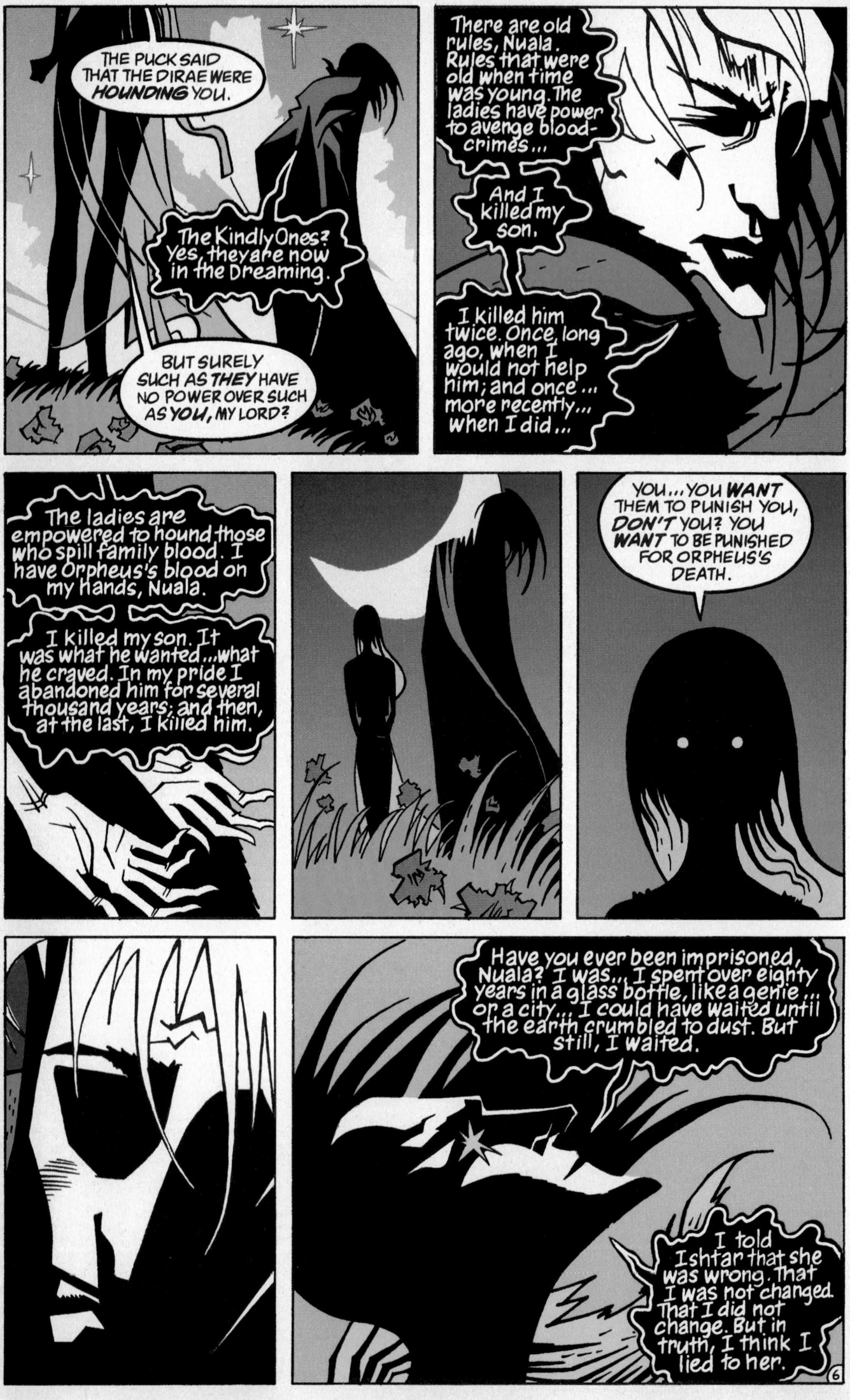

THE PUCK SAID THAT THE DIRAE WERE HOUNDING YOU.
The Kindly Ones? Yes, they are now in the Dreaming.
BUT SURELY SUCH AS THEY HAVE NO POWER OVER SUCH AS YOU, MY LORD?
There are old rules, Nuala. Rules that were old when time was young. The ladies have power to avenge blood-crimes...
And I killed my son.
I killed him twice. Once, long ago, when I would not help him; and once... more recently... when I did...
The ladies are empowered to hound those who spill family blood. I have Orpheus's blood on my hands, Nuala.
I killed my son. It was what he wanted...what he craved. In my pride I abandoned him for several thousand years; and then, at the last, I killed him.
YOU... YOU WANT THEM TO PUNISH YOU, DON'T YOU? YOU WANT TO BE PUNISHED FOR ORPHEUS'S DEATH.
Have you ever been imprisoned, Nuala? I was... I spent over eighty years in a glass bottle, like a genie... or a city... I could have waited until the earth crumbled to dust. But still, I waited.
I told Ishtar that she was wrong. That I was not changed. That I did not change. But in truth, I think I lied to her.
6

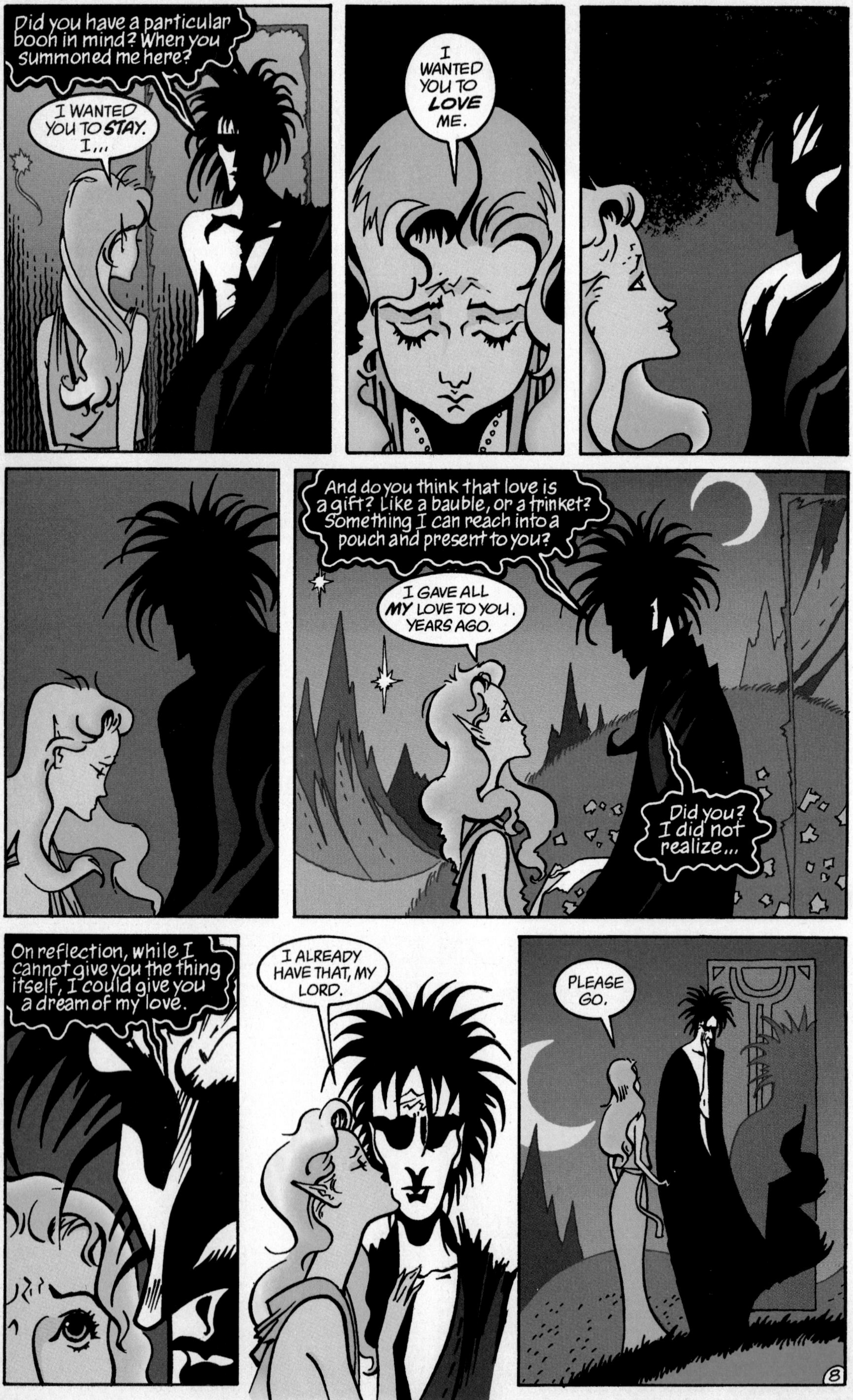
Did you have a particular boon in mind? When you summoned me here?
I WANTED YOU TO STAY. I,...
I WANTED YOU TO LOVE ME.
And do you think that love is a gift? Like a bauble, or a trinket? Something I can reach into a pouch and present to you?
I GAVE ALL MY LOVE TO YOU. YEARS AGO.
Did you? I did not realize...
On reflection, while I cannot give you the thing itself, I could give you a dream of my love.
I ALREADY HAVE THAT, MY LORD.
PLEASE GO.
8

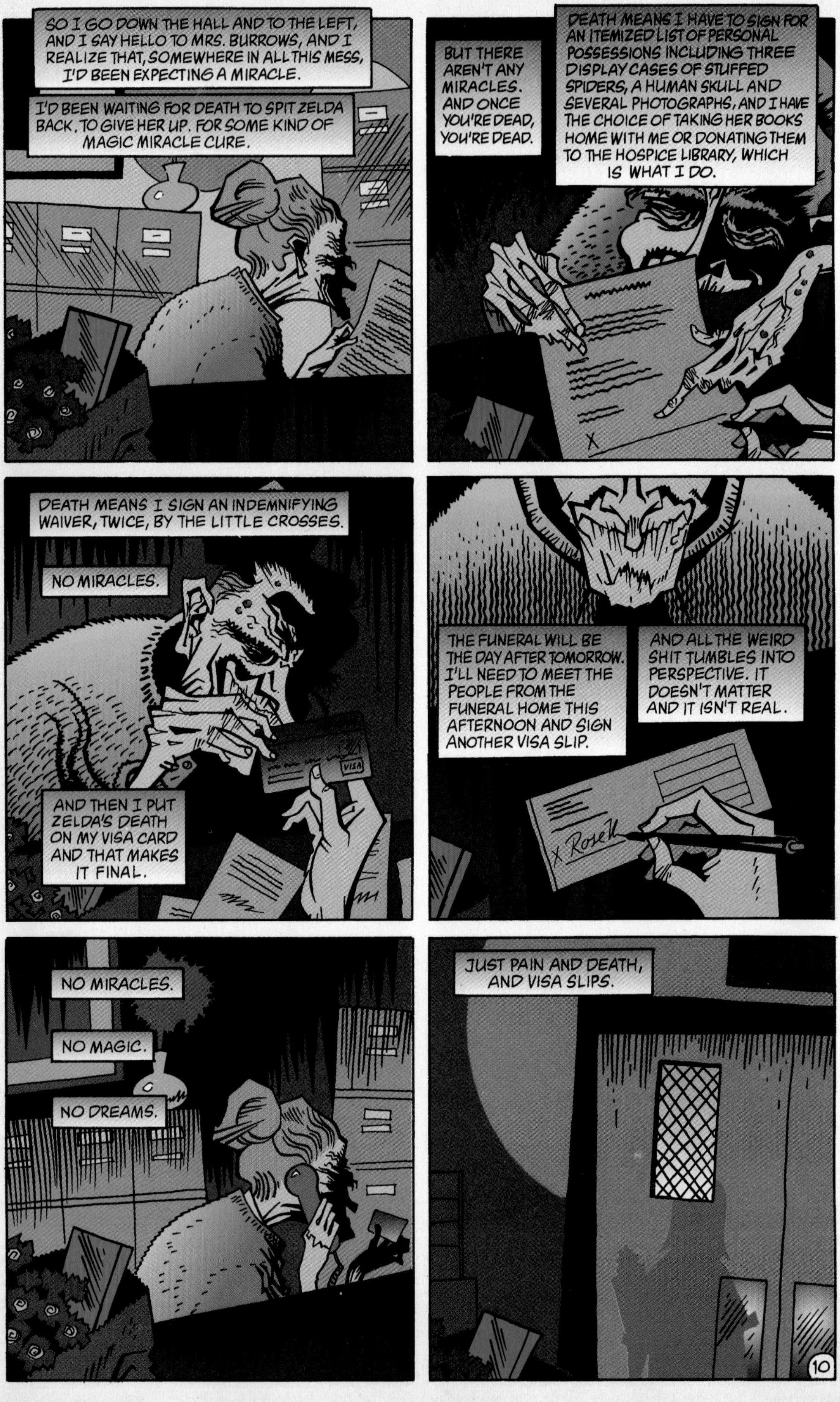
SO I GO DOWN THE HALL AND TO THE LEFT, AND I SAY HELLO TO MRS. BURROWS, AND I REALIZE THAT, SOMEWHERE IN ALL THIS MESS, I'D BEEN EXPECTING A MIRACLE.
I'D BEEN WAITING FOR DEATH TO SPIT ZELDA BACK. TO GIVE HER UP. FOR SOME KIND OF MAGIC MIRACLE CURE.
BUT THERE AREN'T ANY MIRACLES. AND ONCE YOU'RE DEAD, YOU'RE DEAD.
DEATH MEANS I HAVE TO SIGN FOR AN ITEMIZED LIST OF PERSONAL POSSESSIONS INCLUDING THREE DISPLAY CASES OF STUFFED SPIDERS, A HUMAN SKULL AND SEVERAL PHOTOGRAPHS, AND I HAVE THE CHOICE OF TAKING HER BOOKS HOME WITH ME OR DONATING THEM TO THE HOSPICE LIBRARY, WHICH IS WHAT I DO.
DEATH MEANS I SIGN AN INDEMNIFYING WAIVER, TWICE, BY THE LITTLE CROSSES.
NO MIRACLES.
VISA
AND THEN I PUT ZELDA'S DEATH ON MY VISA CARD AND THAT MAKES IT FINAL.
THE FUNERAL WILL BE THE DAY AFTER TOMORROW. I'LL NEED TO MEET THE PEOPLE FROM THE FUNERAL HOME THIS AFTERNOON AND SIGN ANOTHER VISA SLIP.
AND ALL THE WEIRD SHIT TUMBLES INTO PERSPECTIVE. IT DOESN'T MATTER AND IT ISN'T REAL.
NO MIRACLES.
NO MAGIC.
NO DREAMS.
JUST PAIN AND DEATH, AND VISA SLIPS.

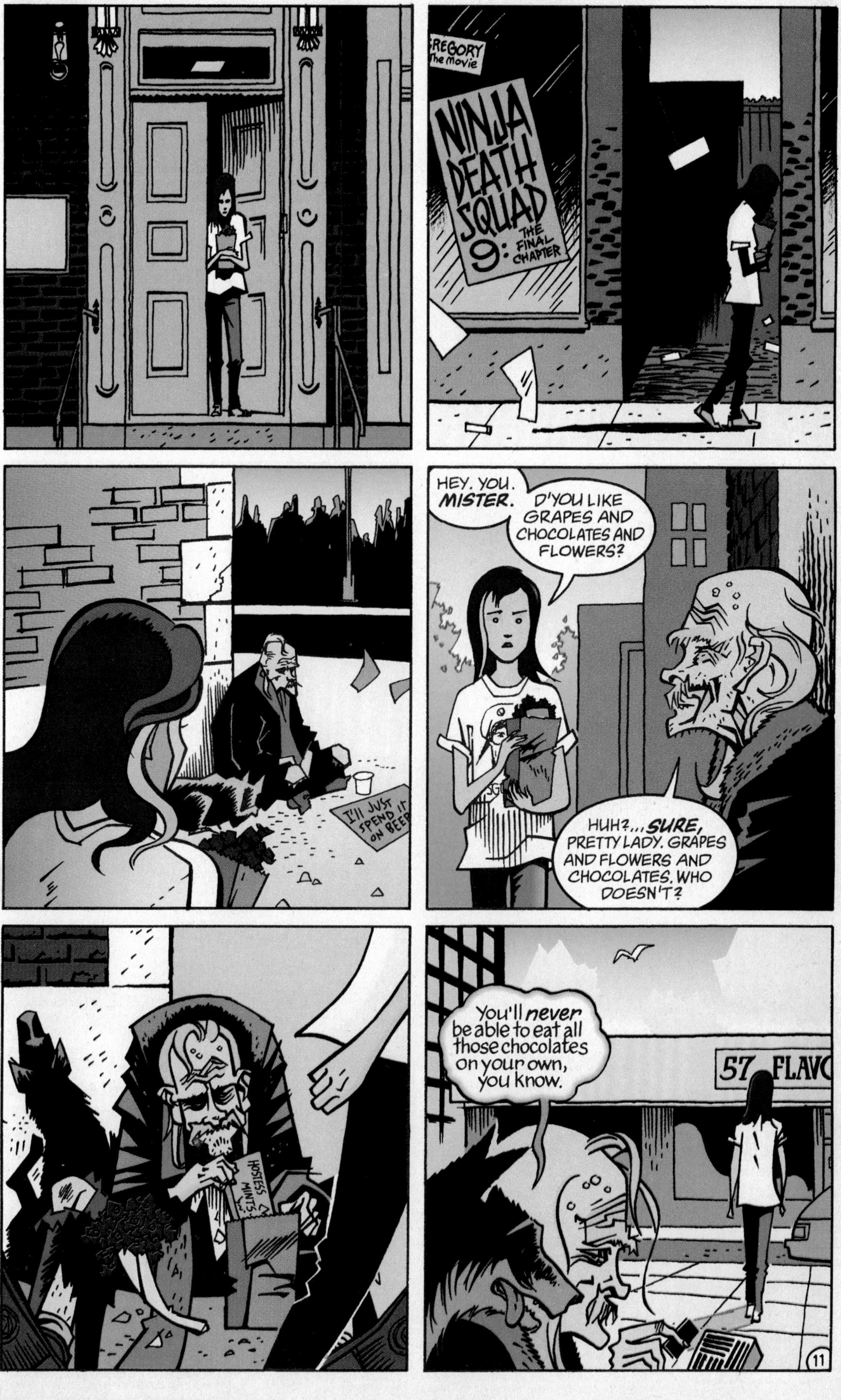
GREGORY The movie
NINJA DEATH SQUAD 9: THE FINAL CHAPTER
I'LL JUST SPEND IT ON BEER
HEY. YOU. **MISTER.**
D'YOU LIKE GRAPES AND CHOCOLATES AND FLOWERS?
HUH?... **SURE,** PRETTY LADY. GRAPES AND FLOWERS AND CHOCOLATES. WHO DOESN'T?
HOSTESS MINTS
You'll ***never*** be able to eat all those chocolates on your own, you know.
57 FLAVO

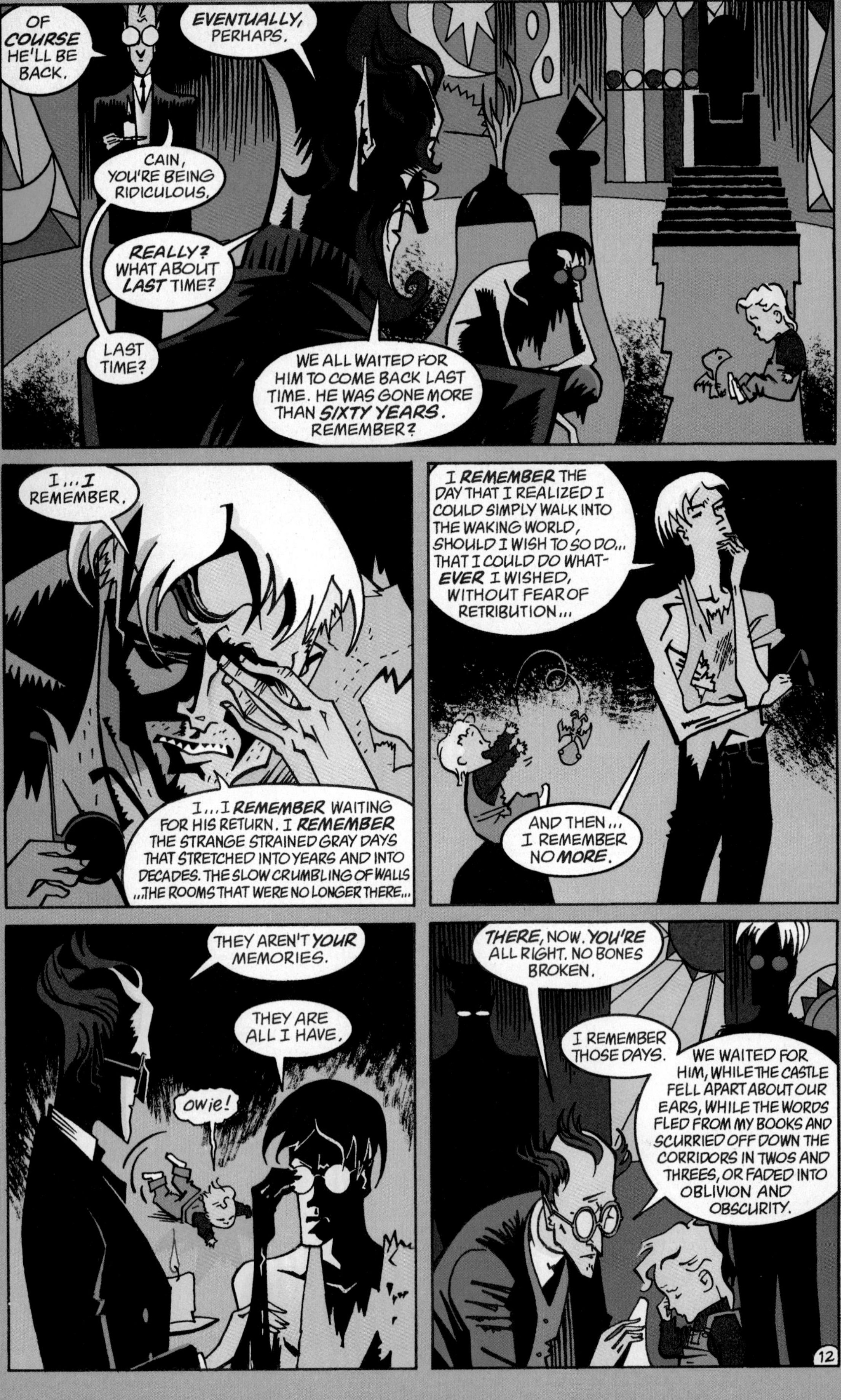
OF COURSE HE'LL BE BACK.
EVENTUALLY, PERHAPS.
CAIN, YOU'RE BEING RIDICULOUS.
REALLY? WHAT ABOUT LAST TIME?
LAST TIME?
WE ALL WAITED FOR HIM TO COME BACK LAST TIME. HE WAS GONE MORE THAN SIXTY YEARS. REMEMBER?
I...I REMEMBER.
I...I REMEMBER WAITING FOR HIS RETURN. I REMEMBER THE STRANGE STRAINED GRAY DAYS THAT STRETCHED INTO YEARS AND INTO DECADES. THE SLOW CRUMBLING OF WALLS ...THE ROOMS THAT WERE NO LONGER THERE...
I REMEMBER THE DAY THAT I REALIZED I COULD SIMPLY WALK INTO THE WAKING WORLD, SHOULD I WISH TO SO DO... THAT I COULD DO WHAT-EVER I WISHED, WITHOUT FEAR OF RETRIBUTION...
AND THEN... I REMEMBER NO MORE.
THEY AREN'T YOUR MEMORIES.
THEY ARE ALL I HAVE.
owie!
THERE, NOW. YOU'RE ALL RIGHT. NO BONES BROKEN.
I REMEMBER THOSE DAYS.
WE WAITED FOR HIM, WHILE THE CASTLE FELL APART ABOUT OUR EARS, WHILE THE WORDS FLED FROM MY BOOKS AND SCURRIED OFF DOWN THE CORRIDORS IN TWOS AND THREES, OR FADED INTO OBLIVION AND OBSCURITY.

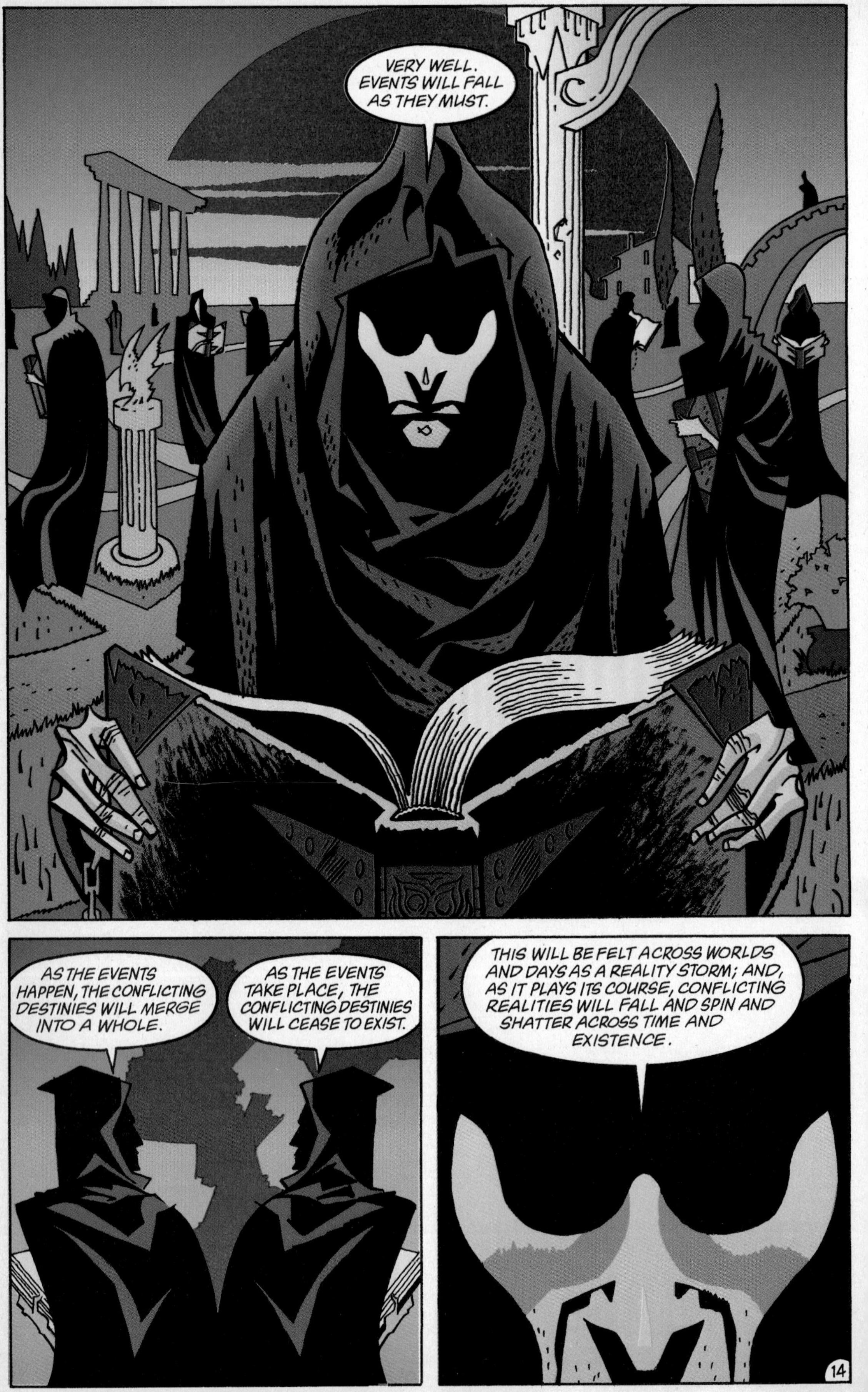
VERY WELL. EVENTS WILL FALL AS THEY MUST.
AS THE EVENTS HAPPEN, THE CONFLICTING DESTINIES WILL MERGE INTO A WHOLE.
AS THE EVENTS TAKE PLACE, THE CONFLICTING DESTINIES WILL CEASE TO EXIST.
THIS WILL BE FELT ACROSS WORLDS AND DAYS AS A REALITY STORM; AND, AS IT PLAYS ITS COURSE, CONFLICTING REALITIES WILL FALL AND SPIN AND SHATTER ACROSS TIME AND EXISTENCE.

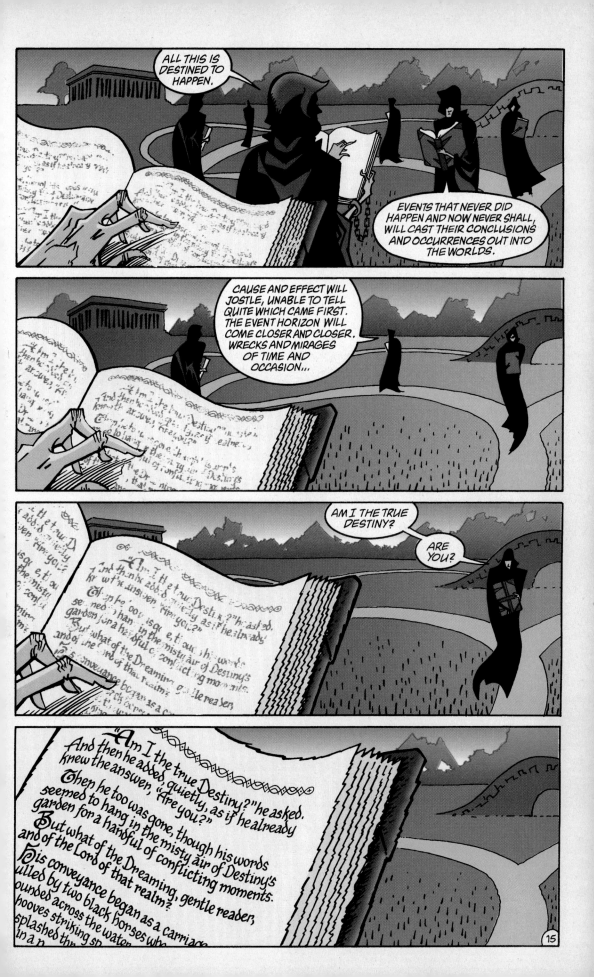

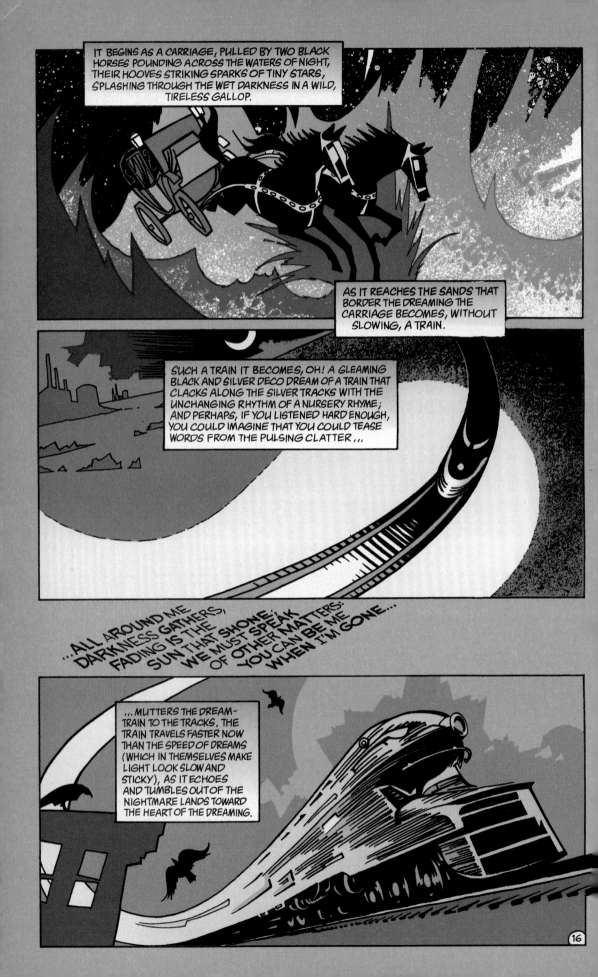

IT BEGINS AS A CARRIAGE, PULLED BY TWO BLACK HORSES POUNDING ACROSS THE WATERS OF NIGHT, THEIR HOOVES STRIKING SPARKS OF TINY STARS, SPLASHING THROUGH THE WET DARKNESS IN A WILD, TIRELESS GALLOP.

AS IT REACHES THE SANDS THAT BORDER THE DREAMING THE CARRIAGE BECOMES, WITHOUT SLOWING, A TRAIN.

SUCH A TRAIN IT BECOMES, OH! A GLEAMING BLACK AND SILVER DECO DREAM OF A TRAIN THAT CLACKS ALONG THE SILVER TRACKS WITH THE UNCHANGING RHYTHM OF A NURSERY RHYME; AND PERHAPS, IF YOU LISTENED HARD ENOUGH, YOU COULD IMAGINE THAT YOU COULD TEASE WORDS FROM THE PULSING CLATTER...

...ALL AROUND ME DARKNESS GATHERS, FADING IS THE SUN THAT SHONE; WE MUST SPEAK OF OTHER MATTERS: YOU CAN BE ME WHEN I'M GONE...

...MUTTERS THE DREAM-TRAIN TO THE TRACKS, THE TRAIN TRAVELS FASTER NOW THAN THE SPEED OF DREAMS (WHICH IN THEMSELVES MAKE LIGHT LOOK SLOW AND STICKY), AS IT ECHOES AND TUMBLES OUT OF THE NIGHTMARE LANDS TOWARD THE HEART OF THE DREAMING.

16

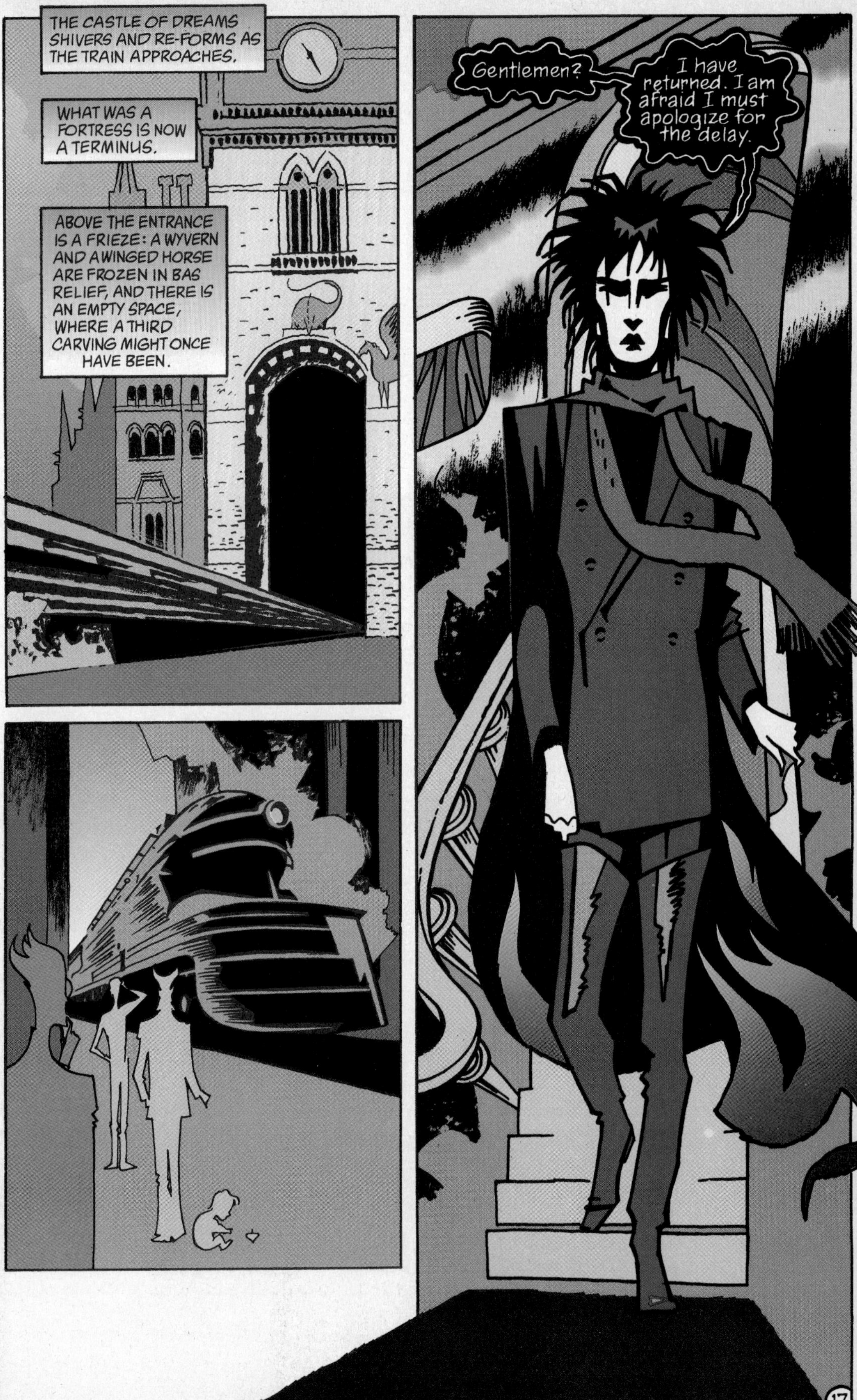
THE CASTLE OF DREAMS SHIVERS AND RE-FORMS AS THE TRAIN APPROACHES.
WHAT WAS A FORTRESS IS NOW A TERMINUS.
ABOVE THE ENTRANCE IS A FRIEZE: A WYVERN AND A WINGED HORSE ARE FROZEN IN BAS RELIEF, AND THERE IS AN EMPTY SPACE, WHERE A THIRD CARVING MIGHT ONCE HAVE BEEN.
Gentlemen?
I have returned. I am afraid I must apologize for the delay.

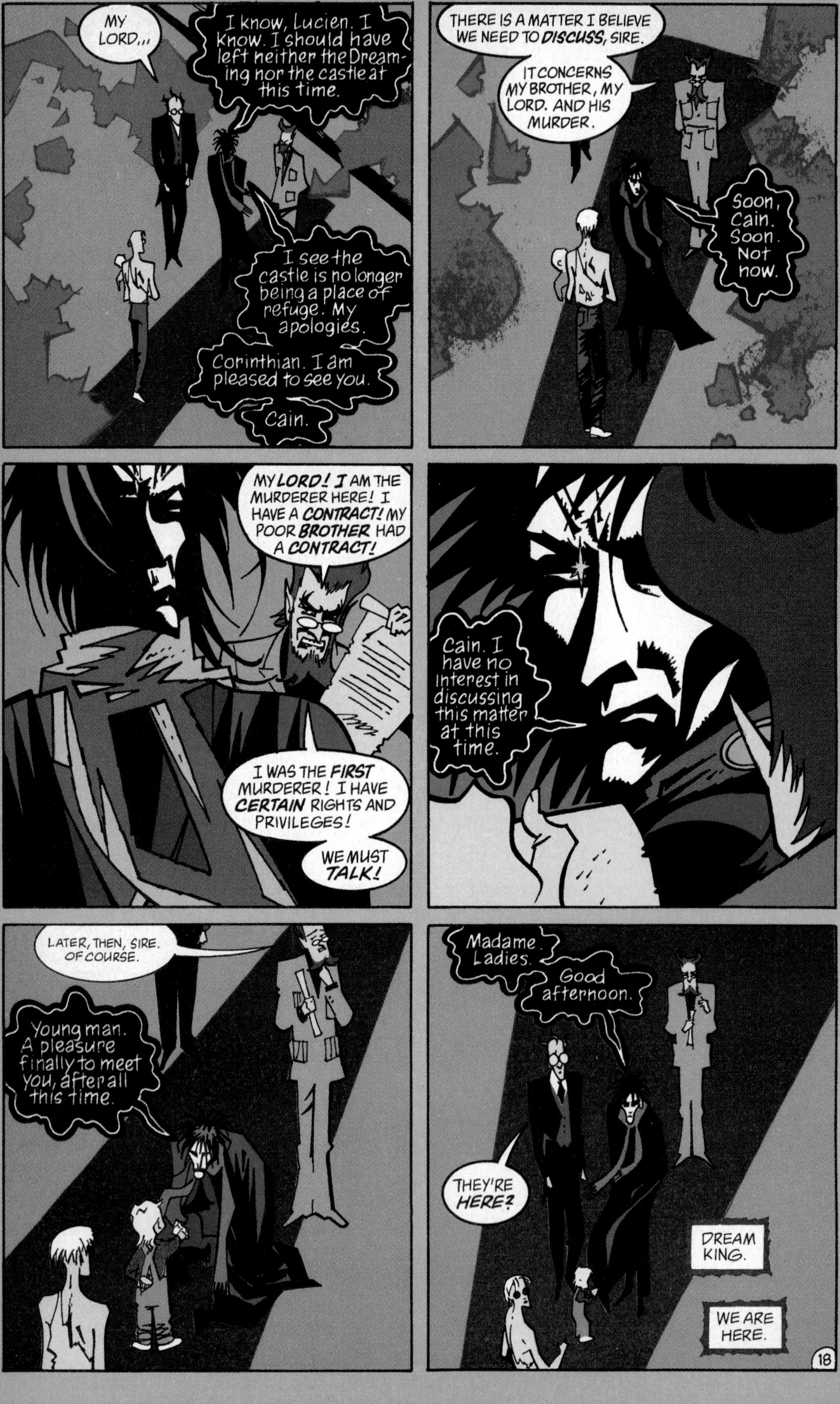
MY LORD,,,
I know, Lucien. I know. I should have left neither the Dreaming nor the castle at this time.
I see the castle is no longer being a place of refuge. My apologies.
Corinthian. I am pleased to see you.
Cain.
THERE IS A MATTER I BELIEVE WE NEED TO DISCUSS, SIRE.
IT CONCERNS MY BROTHER, MY LORD. AND HIS MURDER.
Soon, Cain. Soon. Not now.
MY LORD! I AM THE MURDERER HERE! I HAVE A CONTRACT! MY POOR BROTHER HAD A CONTRACT!
I WAS THE FIRST MURDERER! I HAVE CERTAIN RIGHTS AND PRIVILEGES!
WE MUST TALK!
Cain. I have no interest in discussing this matter at this time.
LATER, THEN, SIRE. OF COURSE.
Young man. A pleasure finally to meet you, after all this time.
Madame. Ladies.
Good afternoon.
THEY'RE HERE?
DREAM KING.
WE ARE HERE.

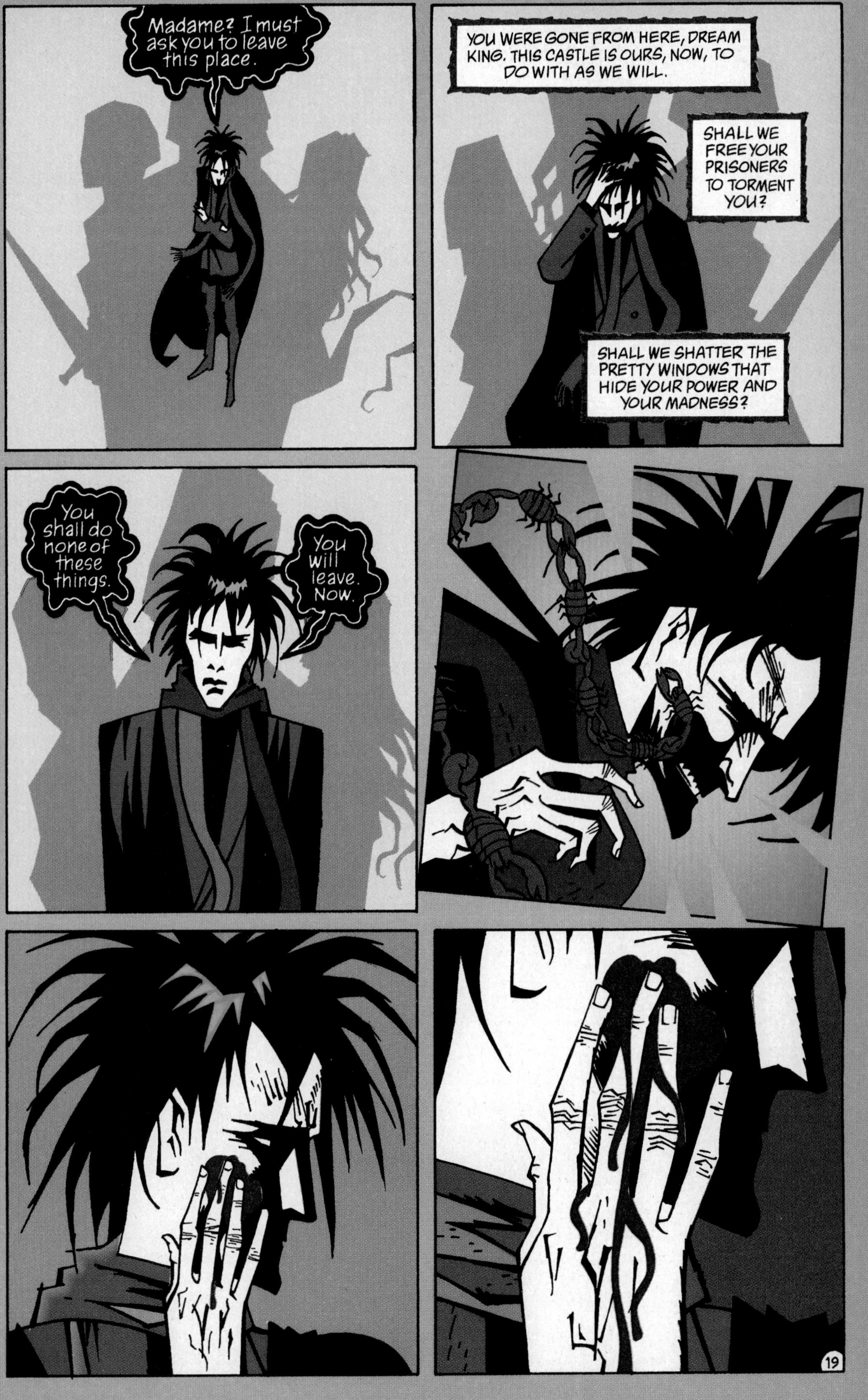

Madame? I must ask you to leave this place.
YOU WERE GONE FROM HERE, DREAM KING. THIS CASTLE IS OURS, NOW, TO DO WITH AS WE WILL.
SHALL WE FREE YOUR PRISONERS TO TORMENT YOU?
SHALL WE SHATTER THE PRETTY WINDOWS THAT HIDE YOUR POWER AND YOUR MADNESS?
You shall do none of these things.
You will leave. Now.

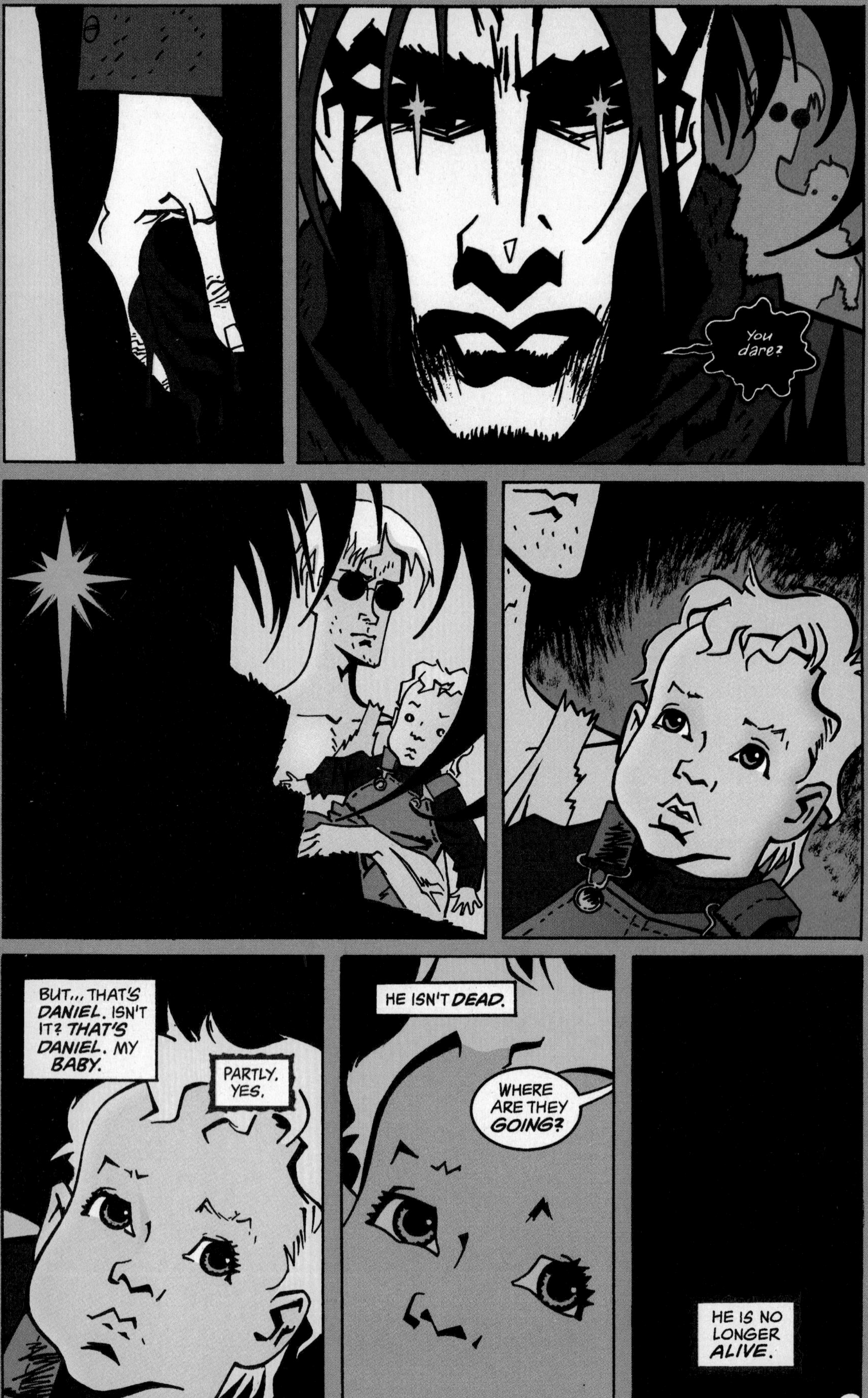
You dare?
BUT... THAT'S DANIEL. ISN'T IT? THAT'S DANIEL. MY BABY.
PARTLY. YES.
HE ISN'T DEAD.
WHERE ARE THEY GOING?
HE IS NO LONGER ALIVE.

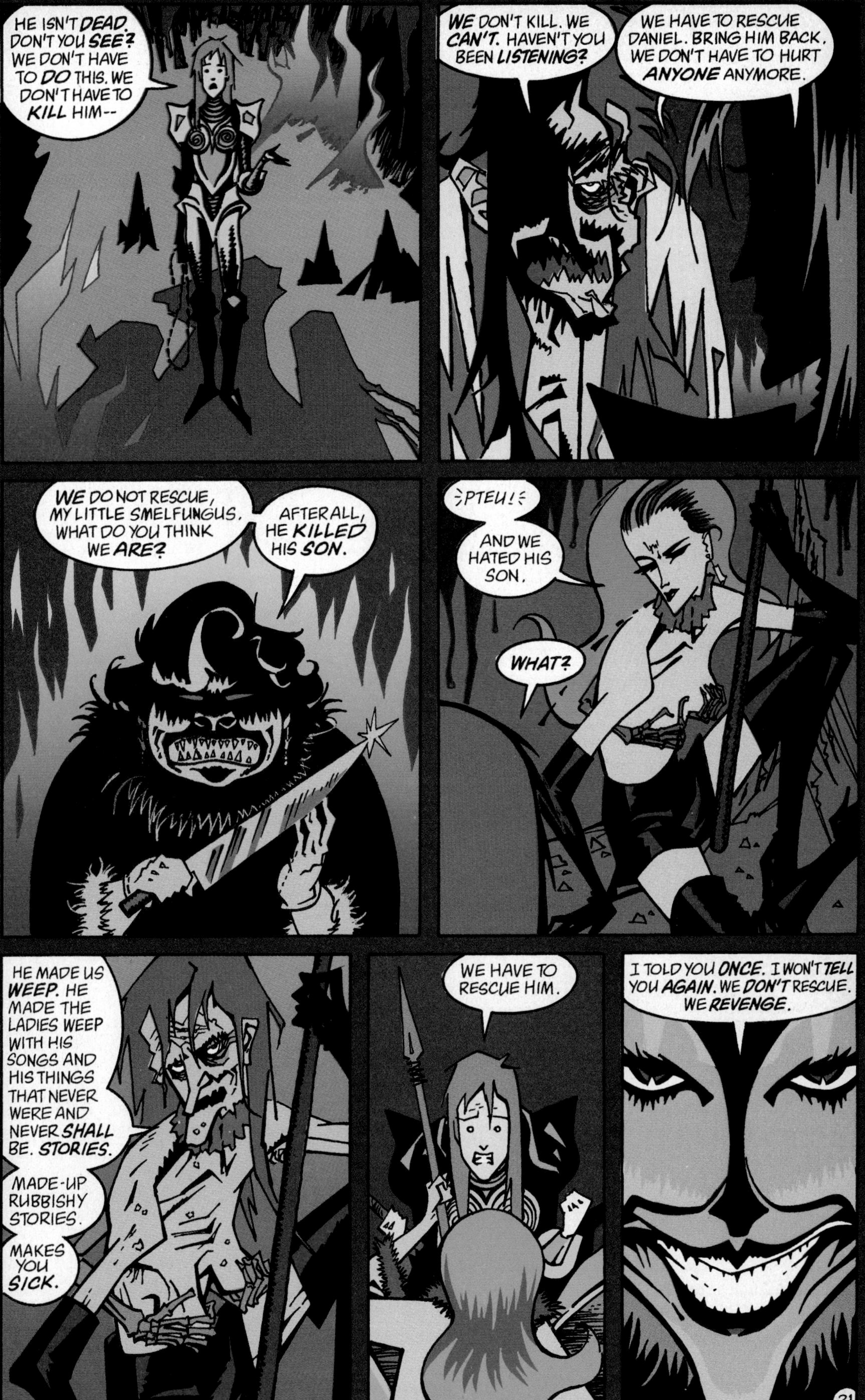
HE ISN'T **DEAD**. DON'T YOU **SEE?** WE DON'T HAVE TO **DO** THIS. WE DON'T HAVE TO **KILL** HIM--
WE DON'T KILL. WE **CAN'T**. HAVEN'T YOU BEEN **LISTENING?**
WE HAVE TO RESCUE DANIEL. BRING HIM BACK. WE DON'T HAVE TO HURT **ANYONE** ANYMORE.
WE DO NOT RESCUE, MY LITTLE SMELFUNGUS. WHAT DO YOU THINK WE **ARE?**
AFTER ALL, HE **KILLED** HIS **SON**.
PTEU!
AND WE HATED HIS SON.
WHAT?
HE MADE US **WEEP**. HE MADE THE LADIES WEEP WITH HIS SONGS AND HIS THINGS THAT NEVER WERE AND NEVER **SHALL** BE. **STORIES**.
MADE-UP RUBBISHY STORIES.
MAKES YOU **SICK**.
WE HAVE TO RESCUE HIM.
I TOLD YOU **ONCE**. I WON'T **TELL** YOU **AGAIN**. WE **DON'T** RESCUE. WE **REVENGE**.

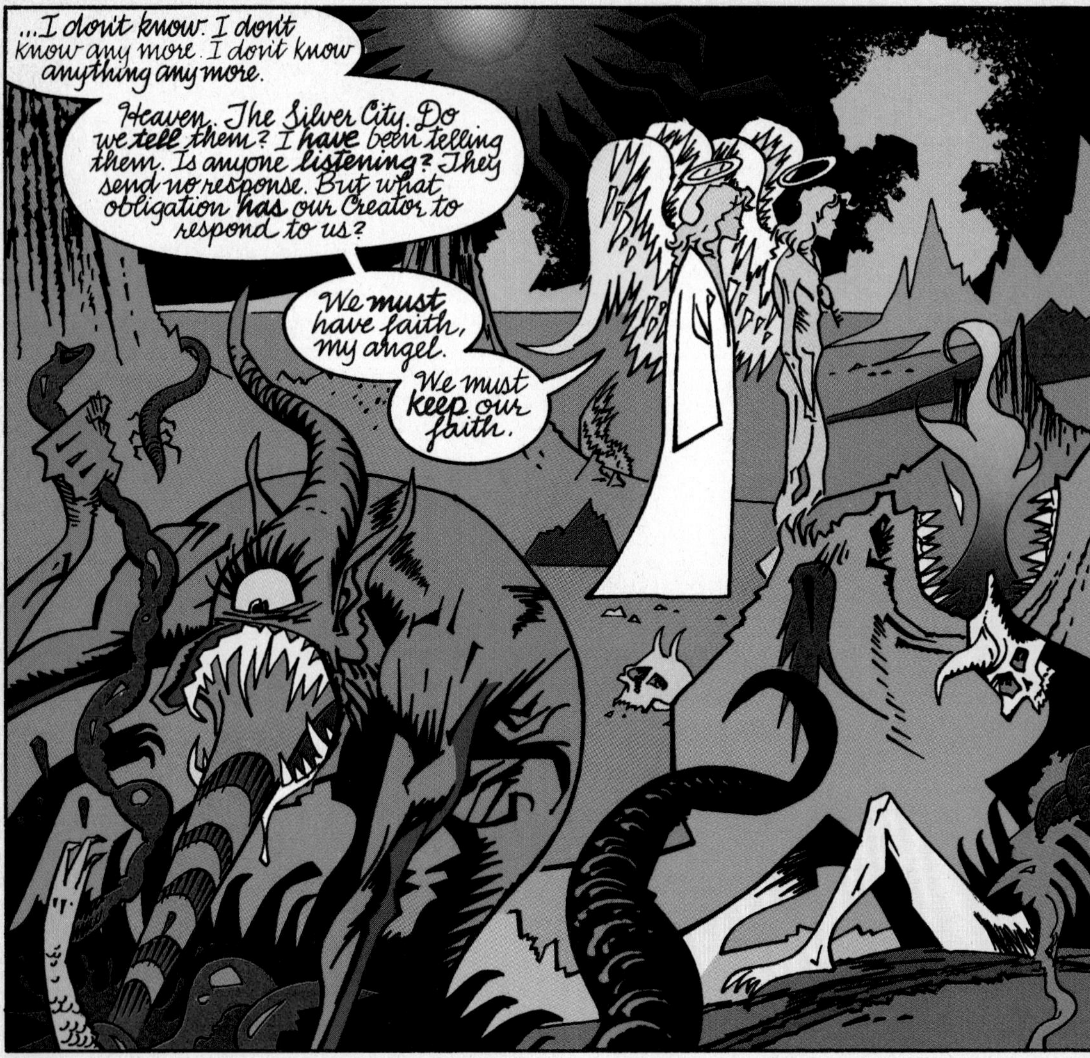
...I don't know. I don't know any more. I don't know anything any more.
Heaven. The Silver City. Do we **tell** them? I **have** been telling them. Is anyone **listening**? They send no response. But what obligation **has** our Creator to respond to us?
We **must** have faith, my angel.
We must **keep** our faith.

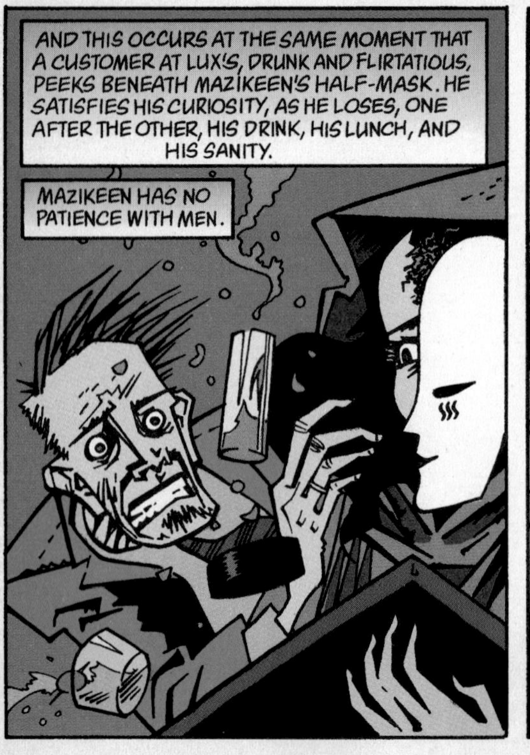
AND THIS OCCURS AT THE SAME MOMENT THAT A CUSTOMER AT LUX'S, DRUNK AND FLIRTATIOUS, PEEKS BENEATH MAZIKEEN'S HALF-MASK. HE SATISFIES HIS CURIOSITY, AS HE LOSES, ONE AFTER THE OTHER, HIS DRINK, HIS LUNCH, AND HIS SANITY.
MAZIKEEN HAS NO PATIENCE WITH MEN.

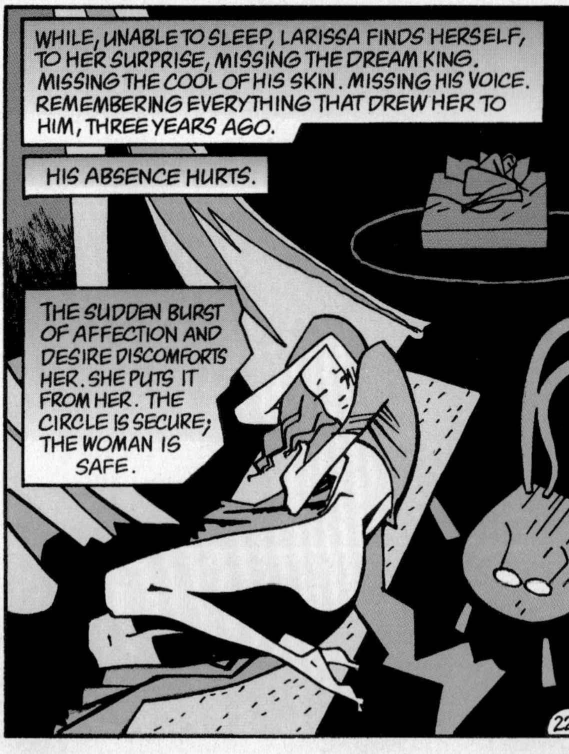
WHILE, UNABLE TO SLEEP, LARISSA FINDS HERSELF, TO HER SURPRISE, MISSING THE DREAM KING. MISSING THE COOL OF HIS SKIN. MISSING HIS VOICE. REMEMBERING EVERYTHING THAT DREW HER TO HIM, THREE YEARS AGO.
HIS ABSENCE HURTS.
THE SUDDEN BURST OF AFFECTION AND DESIRE DISCOMFORTS HER. SHE PUTS IT FROM HER. THE CIRCLE IS SECURE; THE WOMAN IS SAFE.
22

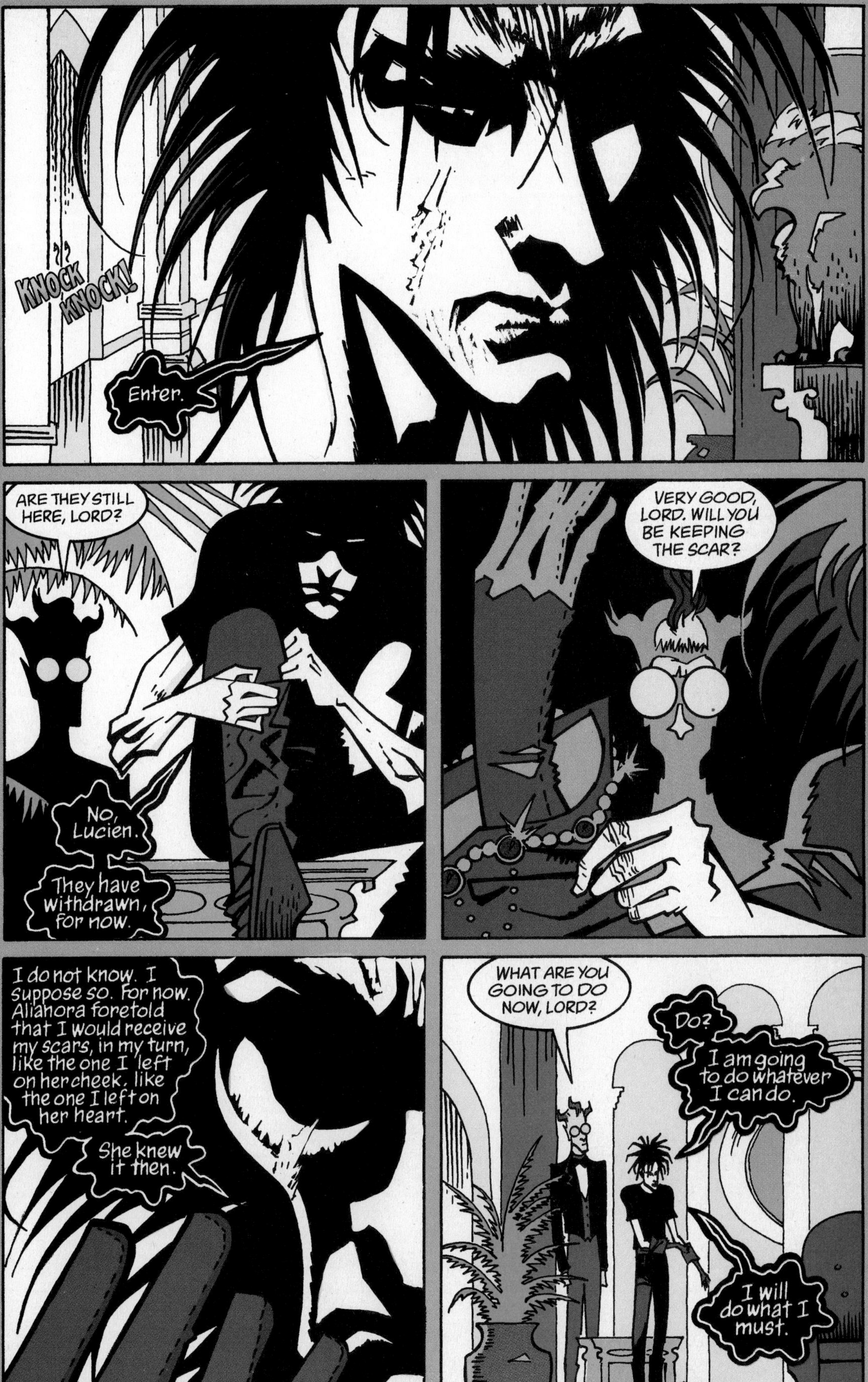
KNOCK KNOCK!
Enter.
ARE THEY STILL HERE, LORD?
No, Lucien.
They have withdrawn, for now.
VERY GOOD, LORD. WILL YOU BE KEEPING THE SCAR?
I do not know. I suppose so. For now. Alianora foretold that I would receive my scars, in my turn, like the one I left on her cheek, like the one I left on her heart.
She knew it then.
WHAT ARE YOU GOING TO DO NOW, LORD?
Do?
I am going to do whatever I can do.
I will do what I must.
23

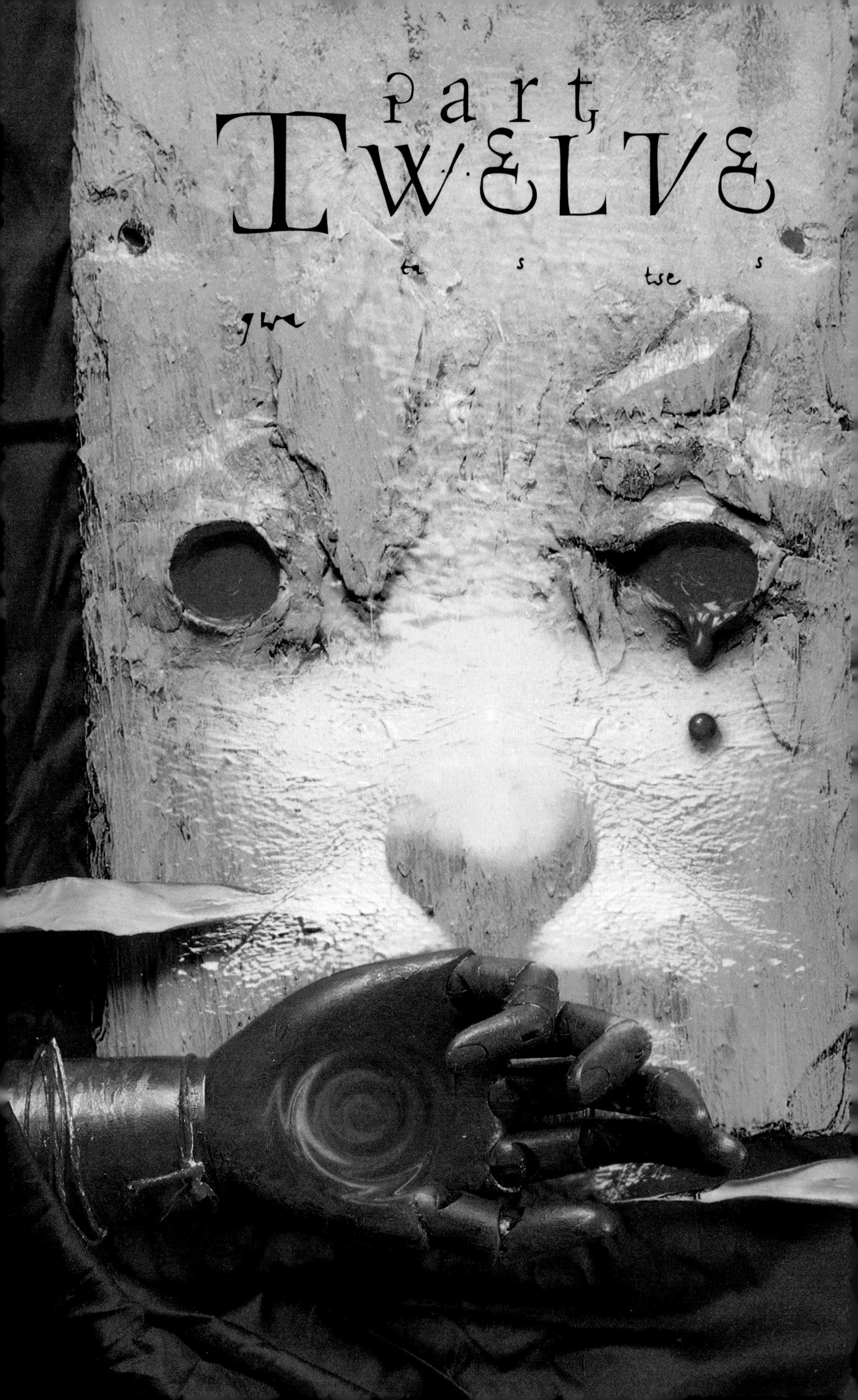
part
TWELVE

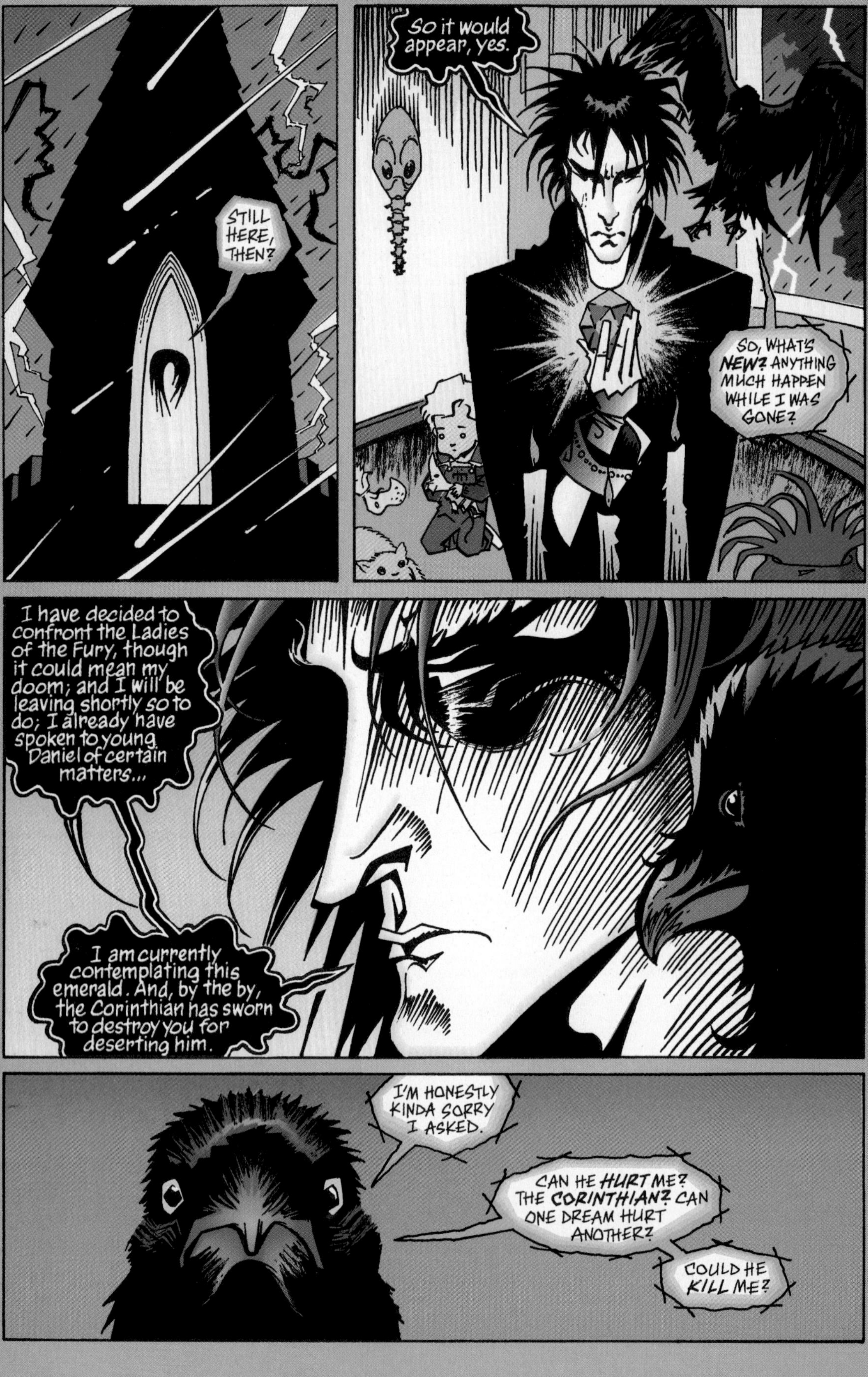
STILL HERE, THEN?
So it would appear, yes.
SO, WHAT'S NEW? ANYTHING MUCH HAPPEN WHILE I WAS GONE?
I have decided to confront the Ladies of the Fury, though it could mean my doom; and I will be leaving shortly so to do; I already have spoken to young Daniel of certain matters...
I am currently contemplating this emerald. And, by the by, the Corinthian has sworn to destroy you for deserting him.
I'M HONESTLY KINDA SORRY I ASKED.
CAN HE HURT ME? THE CORINTHIAN? CAN ONE DREAM HURT ANOTHER?
COULD HE KILL ME?

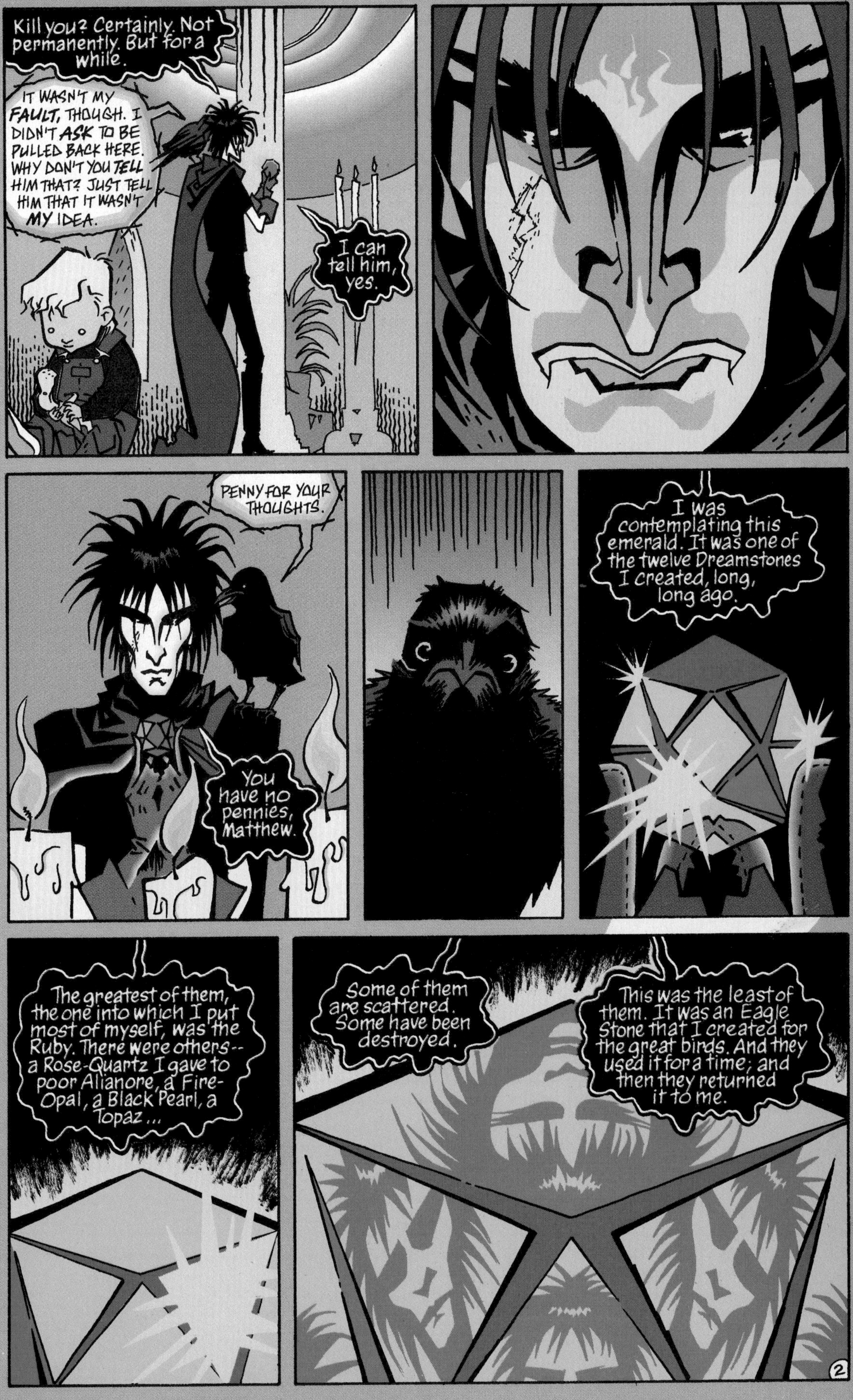

Kill you? Certainly. Not permanently. But for a while.
IT WASN'T MY FAULT, THOUGH. I DIDN'T ASK TO BE PULLED BACK HERE. WHY DON'T YOU TELL HIM THAT? JUST TELL HIM THAT IT WASN'T MY IDEA.
I can tell him, yes.
PENNY FOR YOUR THOUGHTS.
You have no pennies, Matthew.
I was contemplating this emerald. It was one of the twelve Dreamstones I created, long, long ago.
The greatest of them, the one into which I put most of myself, was the Ruby. There were others -- a Rose-Quartz I gave to poor Alianore, a Fire-Opal, a Black Pearl, a Topaz ...
Some of them are scattered. Some have been destroyed.
This was the least of them. It was an Eagle Stone that I created for the great birds. And they used it for a time; and then they returned it to me.
2

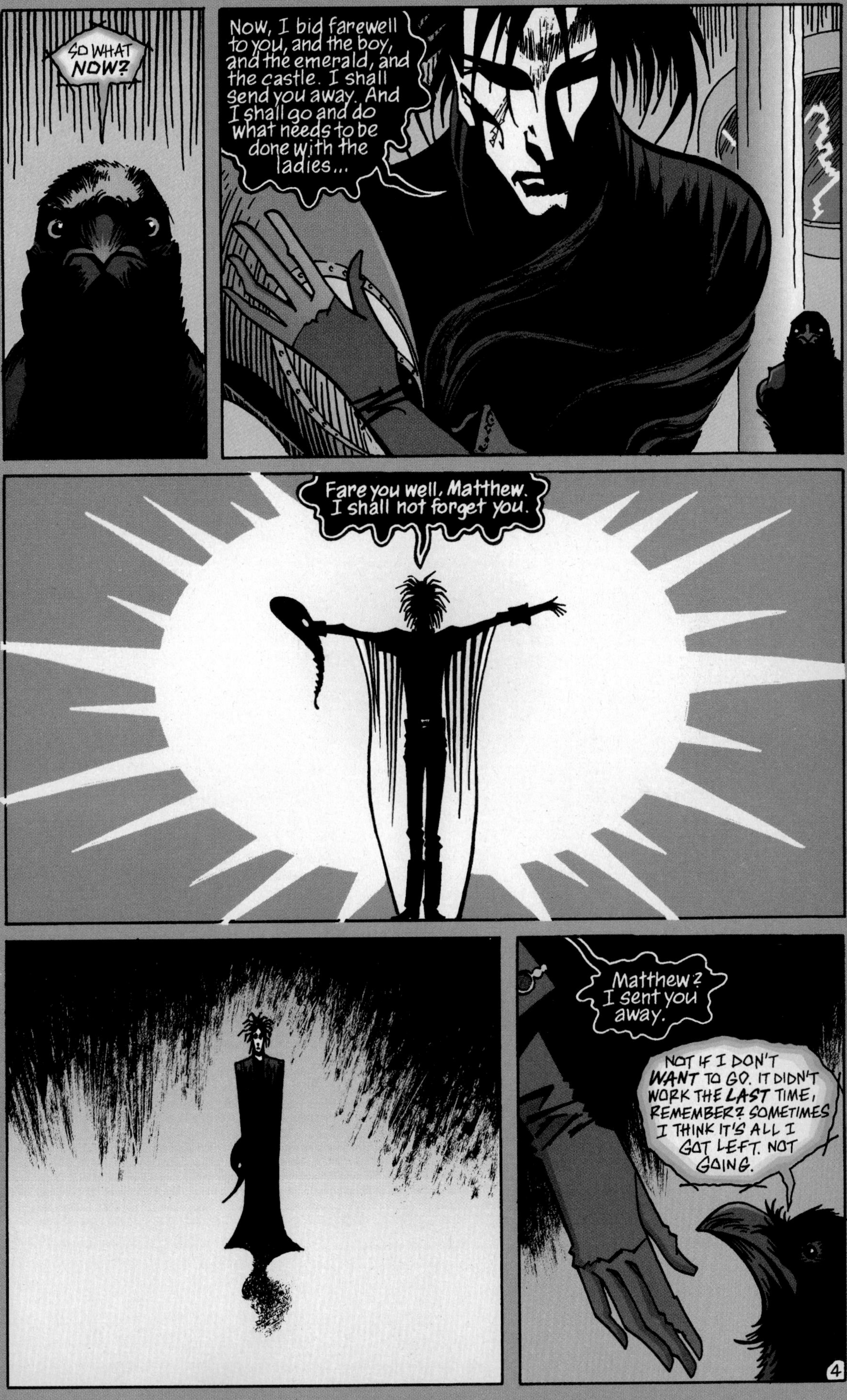
SO WHAT NOW?
Now, I bid farewell to you, and the boy, and the emerald, and the castle. I shall send you away. And I shall go and do what needs to be done with the ladies...
Fare you well, Matthew. I shall not forget you.
Matthew? I sent you away.
NOT IF I DON'T WANT TO GO. IT DIDN'T WORK THE LAST TIME, REMEMBER? SOMETIMES I THINK IT'S ALL I GOT LEFT. NOT GOING.
4

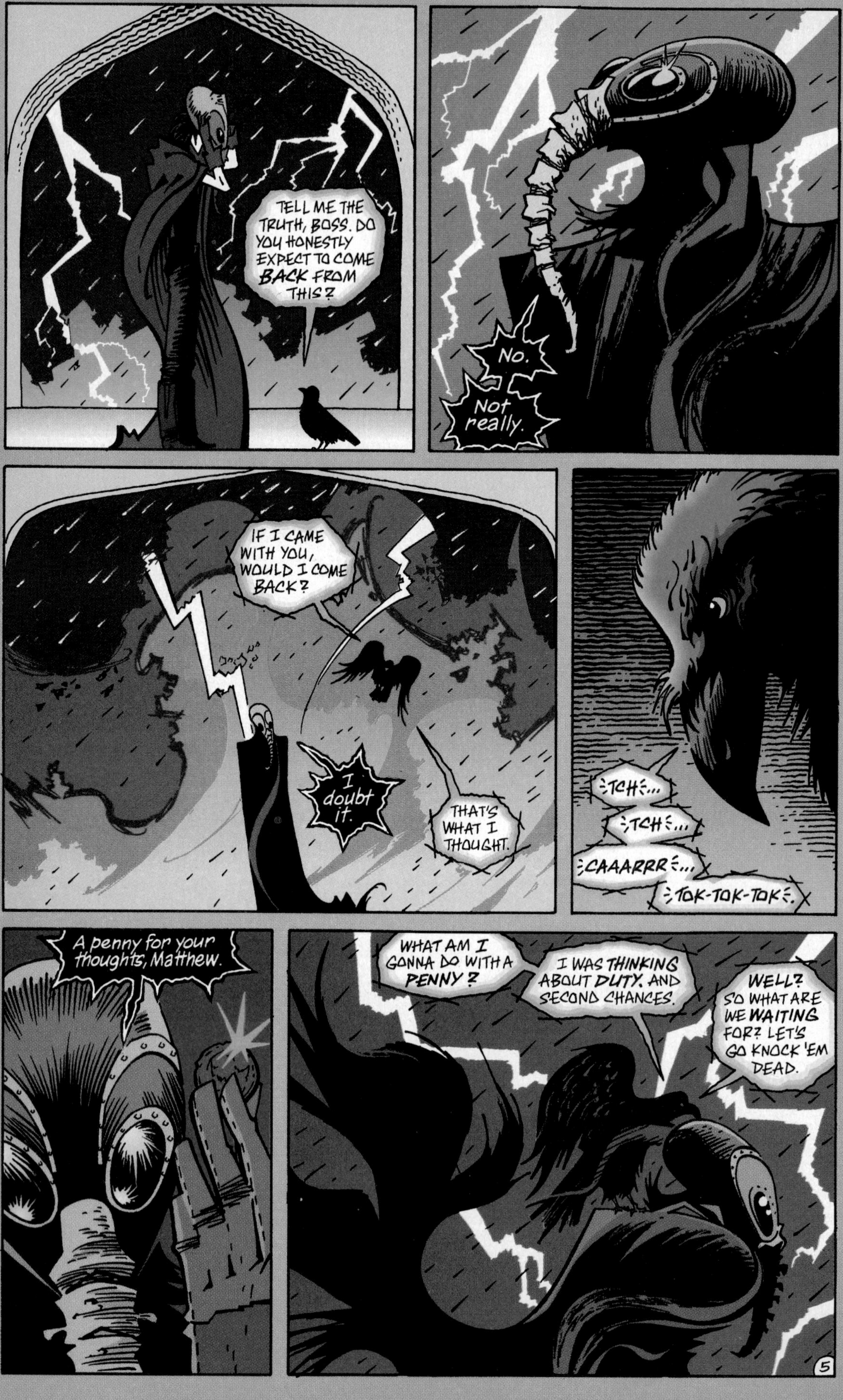

TELL ME THE TRUTH, BOSS. DO YOU HONESTLY EXPECT TO COME BACK FROM THIS?
No.
Not really.
IF I CAME WITH YOU, WOULD I COME BACK?
I doubt it.
THAT'S WHAT I THOUGHT.
TCH...
TCH...
CAAARRR...
TOK-TOK-TOK.
A penny for your thoughts, Matthew.
WHAT AM I GONNA DO WITH A PENNY?
I WAS THINKING ABOUT DUTY. AND SECOND CHANCES.
WELL? SO WHAT ARE WE WAITING FOR? LET'S GO KNOCK 'EM DEAD.

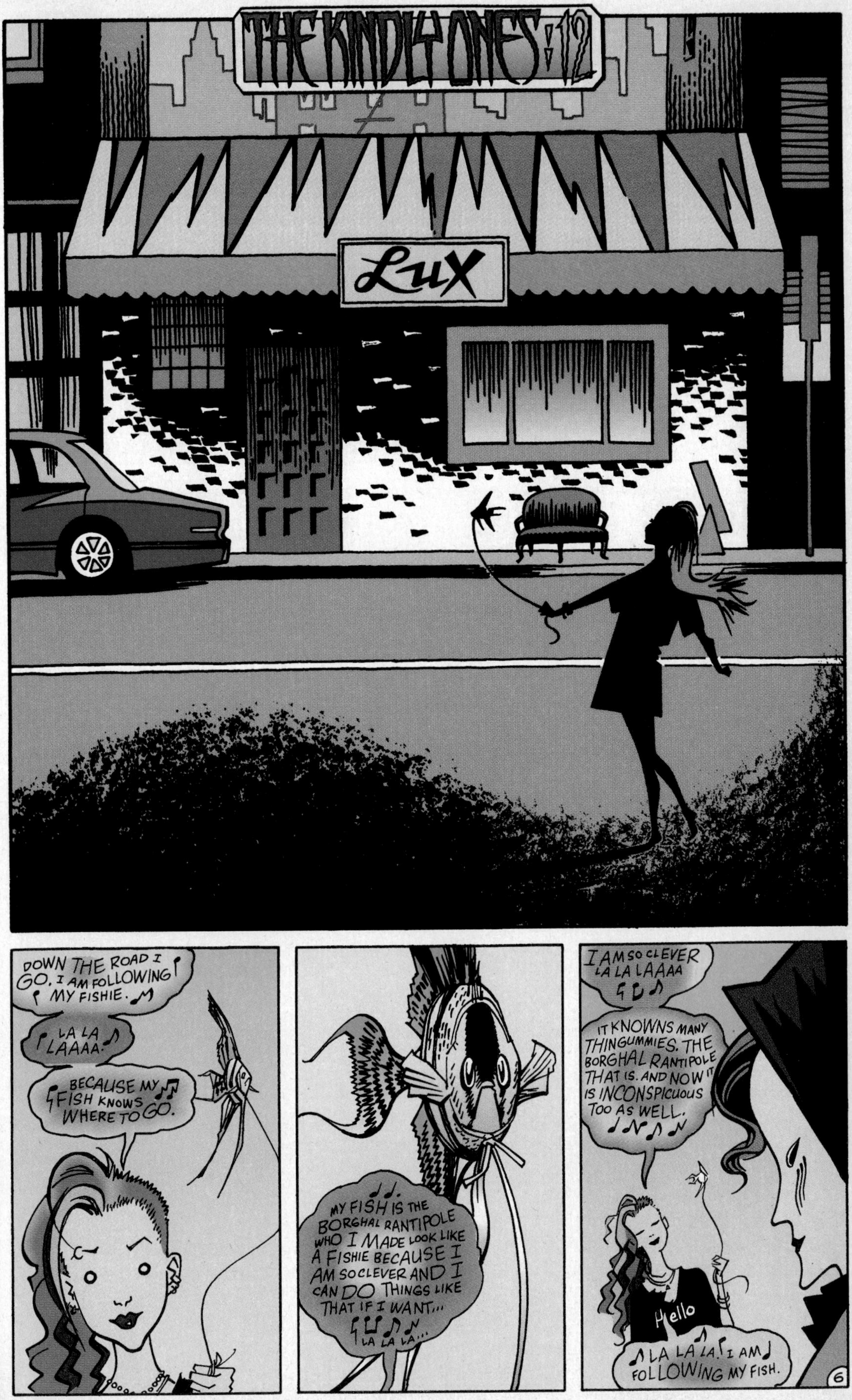
THE KINDLY ONES: 12
LUX
DOWN THE ROAD I GO. I AM FOLLOWING MY FISHIE.
LA LA LAAAA.
BECAUSE MY FISH KNOWS WHERE TO GO.
MY FISH IS THE BORGHAL RANTIPOLE WHO I MADE LOOK LIKE A FISHIE BECAUSE I AM SO CLEVER AND I CAN DO THINGS LIKE THAT IF I WANT...
LA LA LA...
I AM SO CLEVER LA LA LAAAAA
IT KNOWNS MANY THINGUMMIES. THE BORGHAL RANTIPOLE THAT IS. AND NOW IT IS INCONSPICUOUS TOO AS WELL.
Hello
LA LA LA. I AM FOLLOWING MY FISH.
6

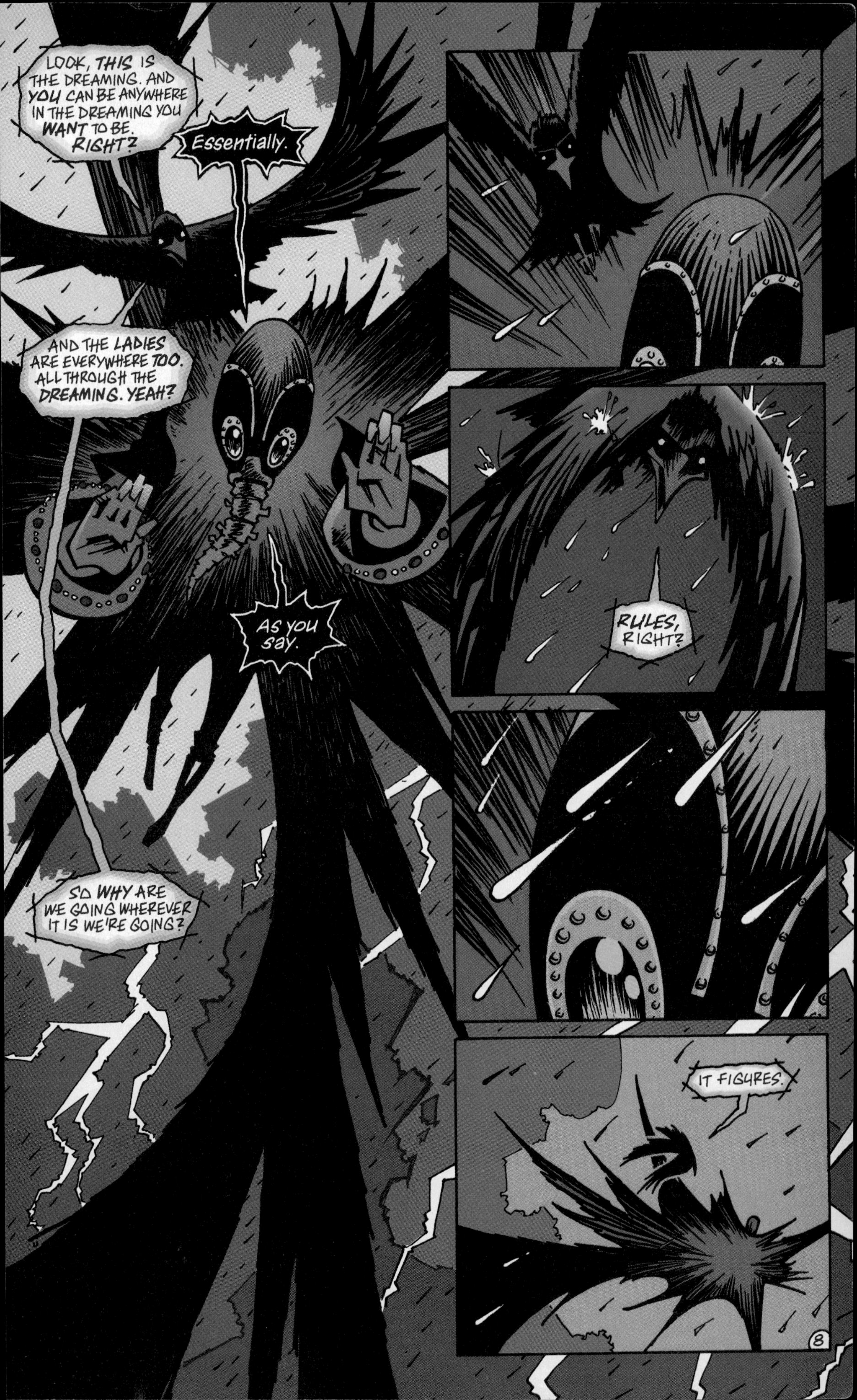

LOOK, THIS IS THE DREAMING. AND YOU CAN BE ANYWHERE IN THE DREAMING YOU WANT TO BE. RIGHT?
Essentially.
AND THE LADIES ARE EVERYWHERE TOO. ALL THROUGH THE DREAMING. YEAH?
As you say.
SO WHY ARE WE GOING WHEREVER IT IS WE'RE GOING?
RULES, RIGHT?
IT FIGURES.
8

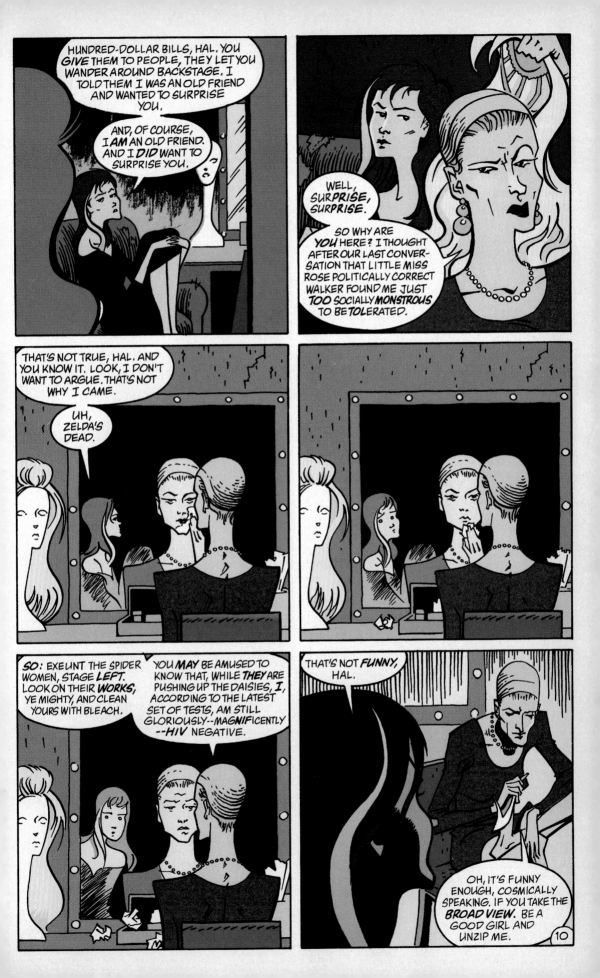

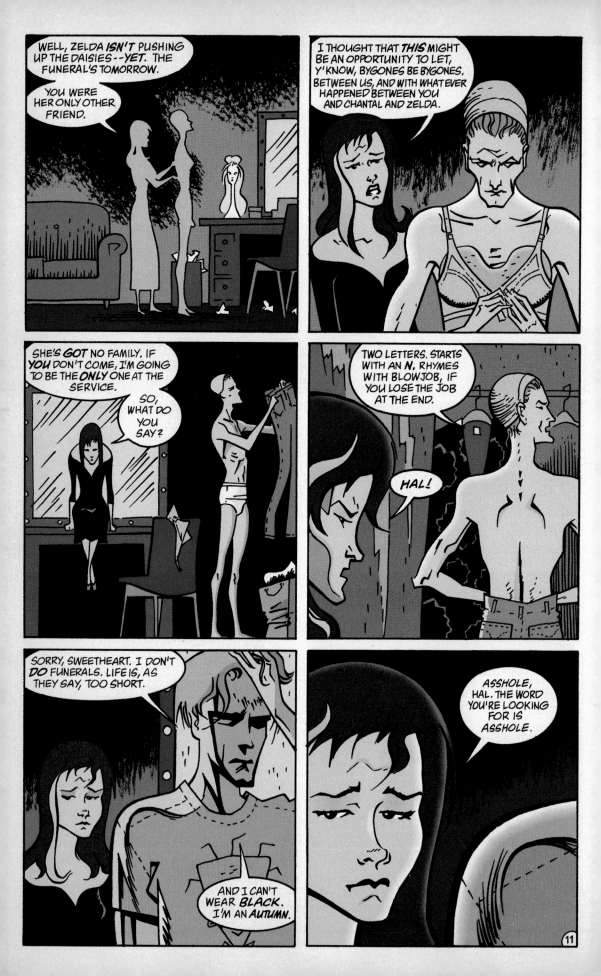

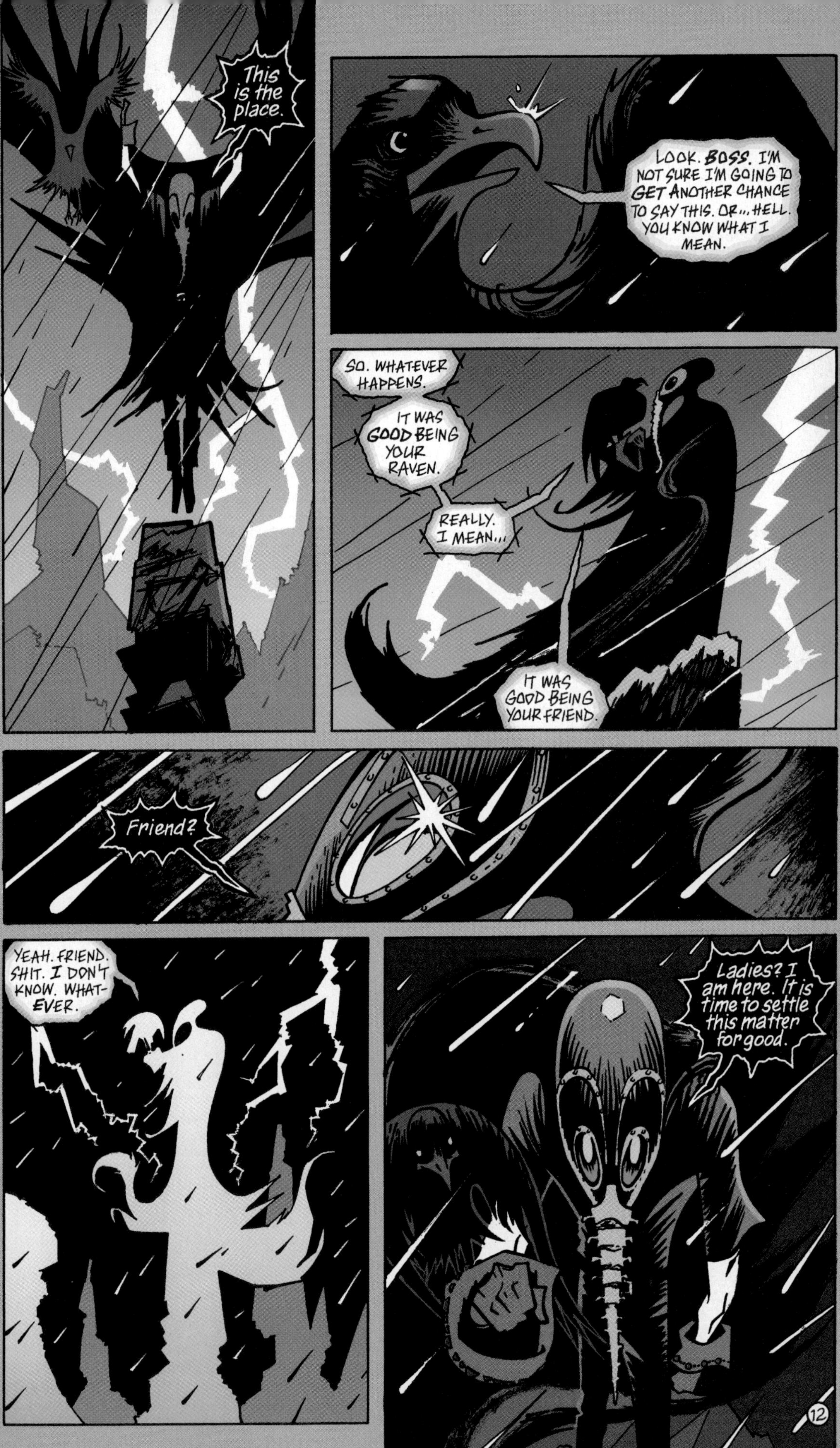

This is the place.
LOOK. BOSS. I'M NOT SURE I'M GOING TO GET ANOTHER CHANCE TO SAY THIS. OR... HELL. YOU KNOW WHAT I MEAN.
SO. WHATEVER HAPPENS.
IT WAS GOOD BEING YOUR RAVEN.
REALLY. I MEAN...
IT WAS GOOD BEING YOUR FRIEND.
Friend?
YEAH. FRIEND. SHIT. I DON'T KNOW. WHAT-EVER.
Ladies? I am here. It is time to settle this matter for good.

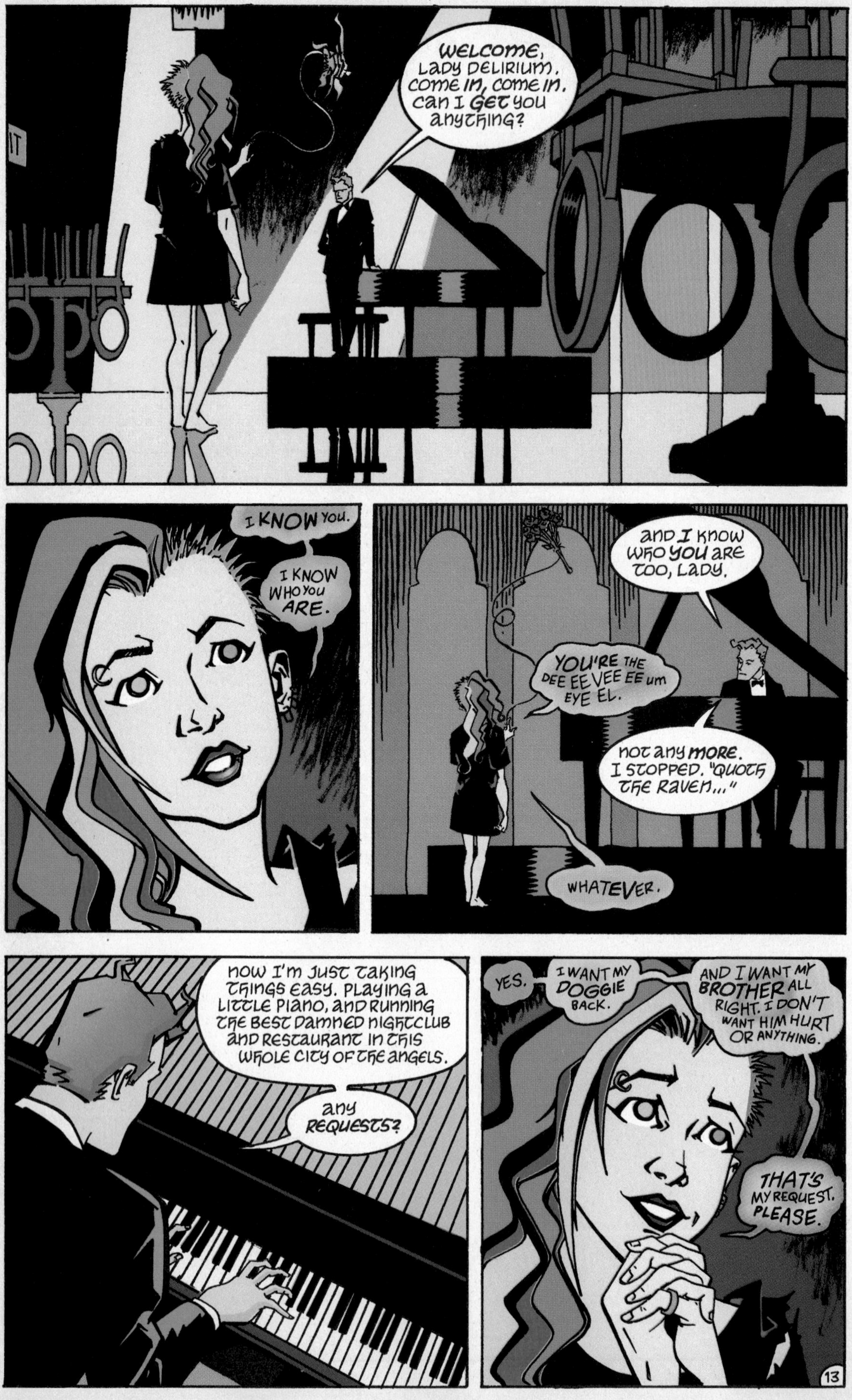
WELCOME, LADY DELIRIUM. COME IN, COME IN. CAN I GET YOU ANYTHING?
I KNOW YOU.
I KNOW WHO YOU ARE.
AND I KNOW WHO YOU ARE TOO, LADY.
YOU'RE THE DEE EE VEE EE um EYE EL.
NOT ANY MORE. I STOPPED. "QUOTH THE RAVEN..."
WHATEVER.
NOW I'M JUST TAKING THINGS EASY. PLAYING A LITTLE PIANO, AND RUNNING THE BEST DAMNED NIGHTCLUB AND RESTAURANT IN THIS WHOLE CITY OF THE ANGELS.
ANY REQUESTS?
YES.
I WANT MY DOGGIE BACK.
AND I WANT MY BROTHER ALL RIGHT. I DON'T WANT HIM HURT OR ANYTHING.
THAT'S MY REQUEST. PLEASE.
13

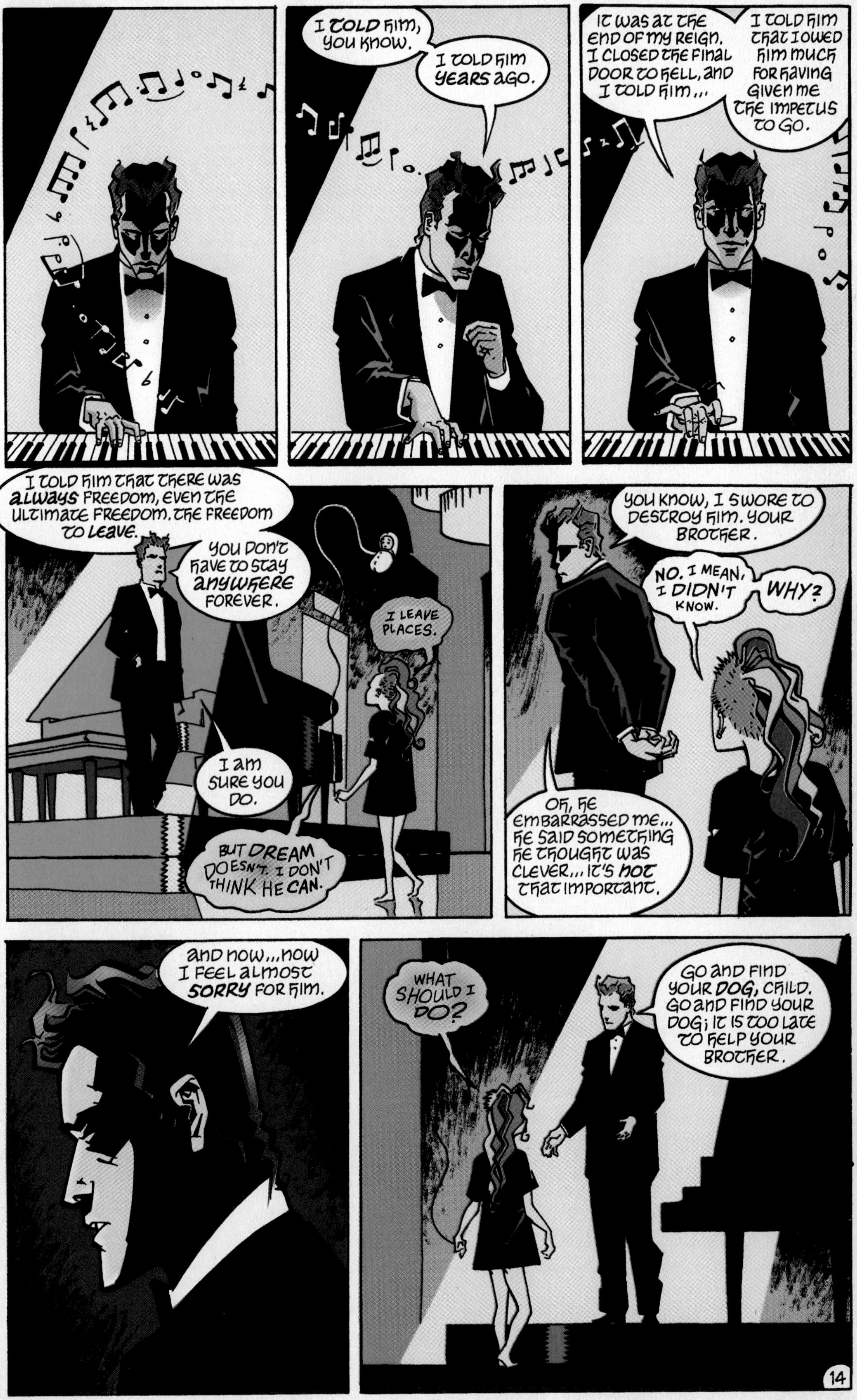
I TOLD HIM, YOU KNOW.
I TOLD HIM YEARS AGO.
IT WAS AT THE END OF MY REIGN. I CLOSED THE FINAL DOOR TO HELL, AND I TOLD HIM...
I TOLD HIM THAT I OWED HIM MUCH FOR HAVING GIVEN ME THE IMPETUS TO GO.
I TOLD HIM THAT THERE WAS ALWAYS FREEDOM, EVEN THE ULTIMATE FREEDOM. THE FREEDOM TO LEAVE.
YOU DON'T HAVE TO STAY ANYWHERE FOREVER.
I LEAVE PLACES.
I AM SURE YOU DO.
BUT DREAM DOESN'T. I DON'T THINK HE CAN.
YOU KNOW, I SWORE TO DESTROY HIM. YOUR BROTHER.
NO. I MEAN, I DIDN'T KNOW.
WHY?
OH, HE EMBARRASSED ME... HE SAID SOMETHING HE THOUGHT WAS CLEVER... IT'S NOT THAT IMPORTANT.
AND NOW... NOW I FEEL ALMOST SORRY FOR HIM.
WHAT SHOULD I DO?
GO AND FIND YOUR DOG, CHILD. GO AND FIND YOUR DOG; IT IS TOO LATE TO HELP YOUR BROTHER.
14

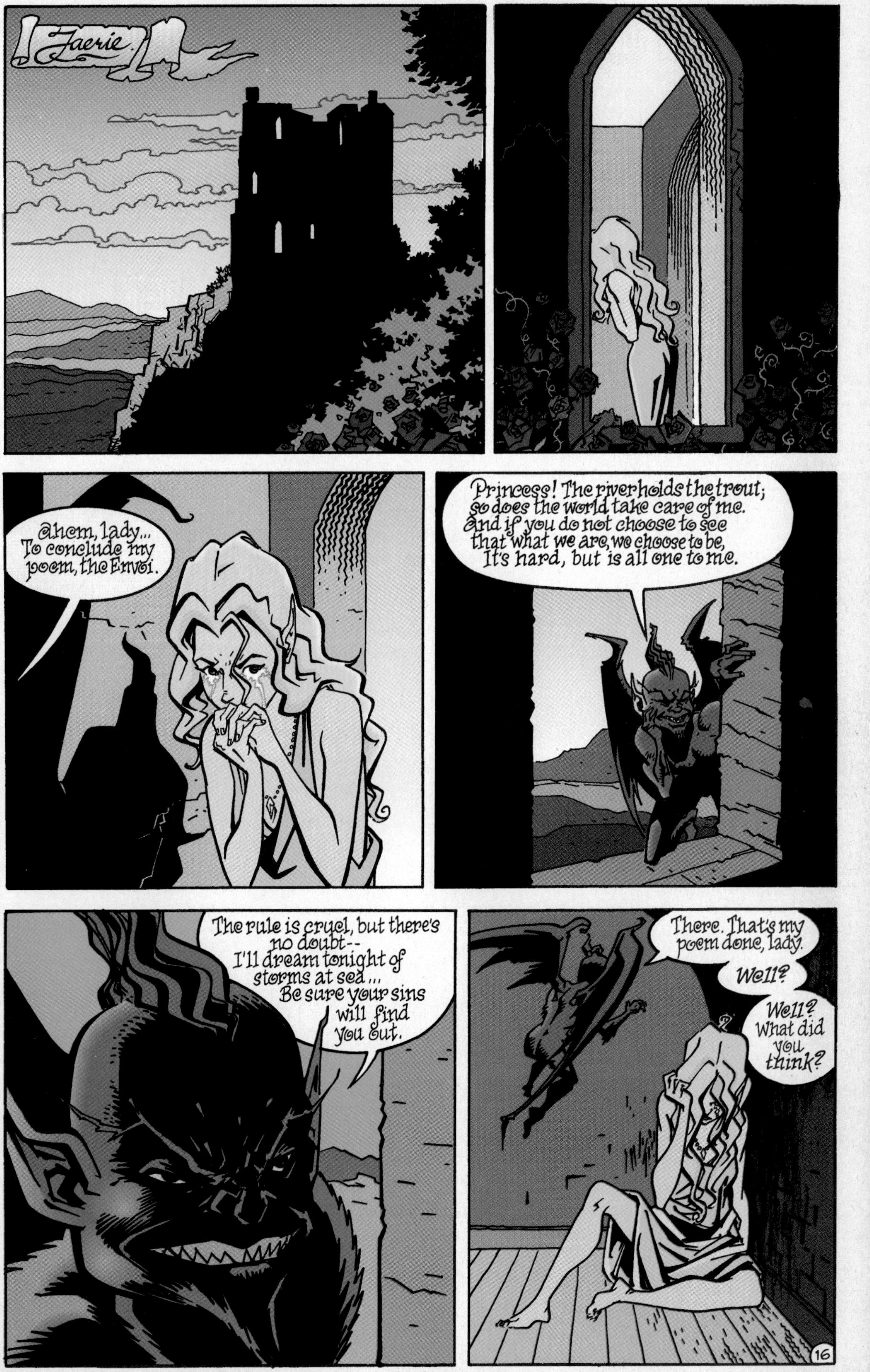
Faerie.
ahem, lady... To conclude my poem, the Envoi.
Princess! The river holds the trout; so does the world take care of me. And if you do not choose to see that what we are, we choose to be, It's hard, but is all one to me.
The rule is cruel, but there's no doubt-- I'll dream tonight of storms at sea... Be sure your sins will find you out.
There. That's my poem done, lady.
Well?
Well? What did you think?
16

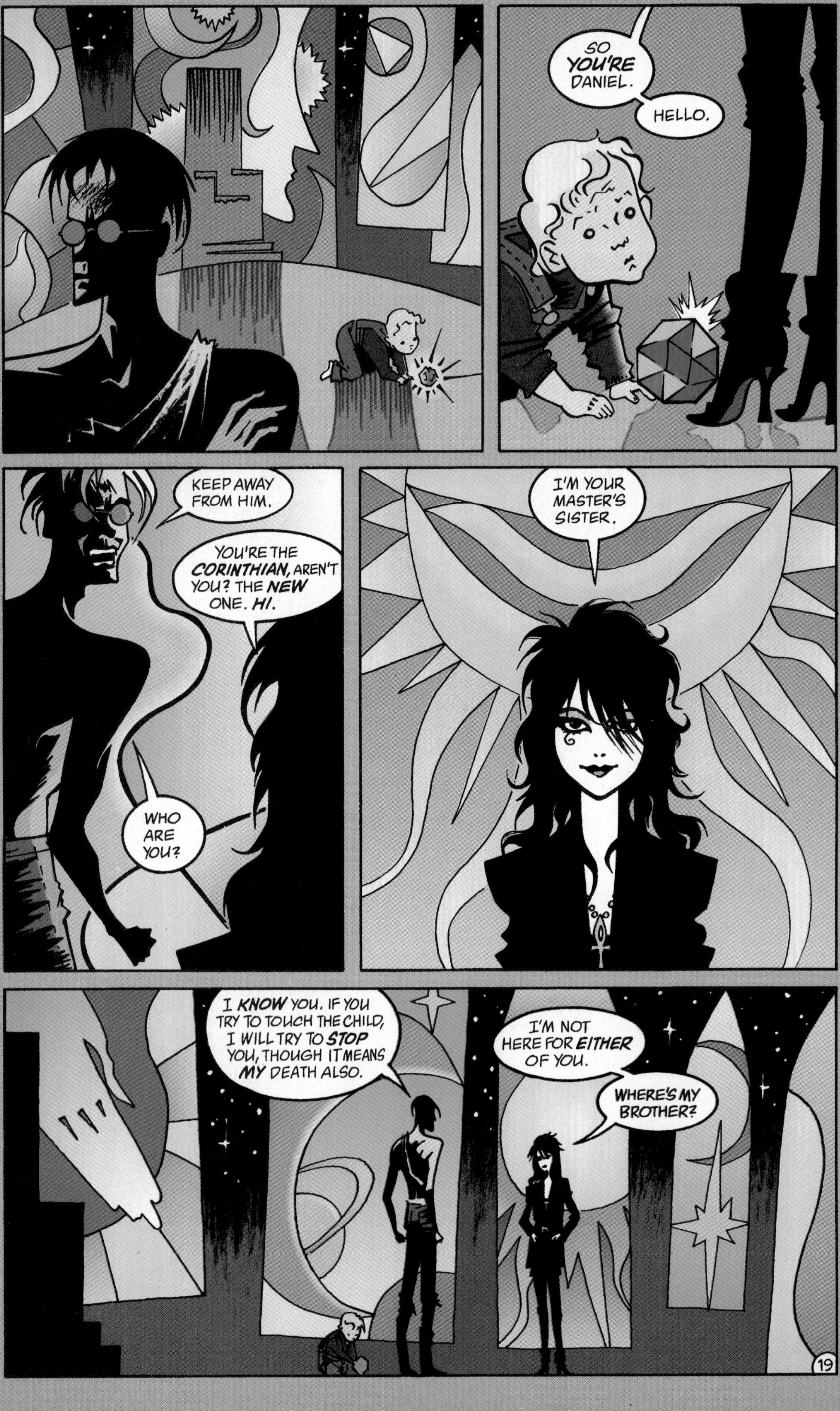

SO YOU'RE DANIEL.
HELLO.
KEEP AWAY FROM HIM.
YOU'RE THE CORINTHIAN, AREN'T YOU? THE NEW ONE. HI.
WHO ARE YOU?
I'M YOUR MASTER'S SISTER.
I KNOW YOU. IF YOU TRY TO TOUCH THE CHILD, I WILL TRY TO STOP YOU, THOUGH IT MEANS MY DEATH ALSO.
I'M NOT HERE FOR EITHER OF YOU.
WHERE'S MY BROTHER?
19

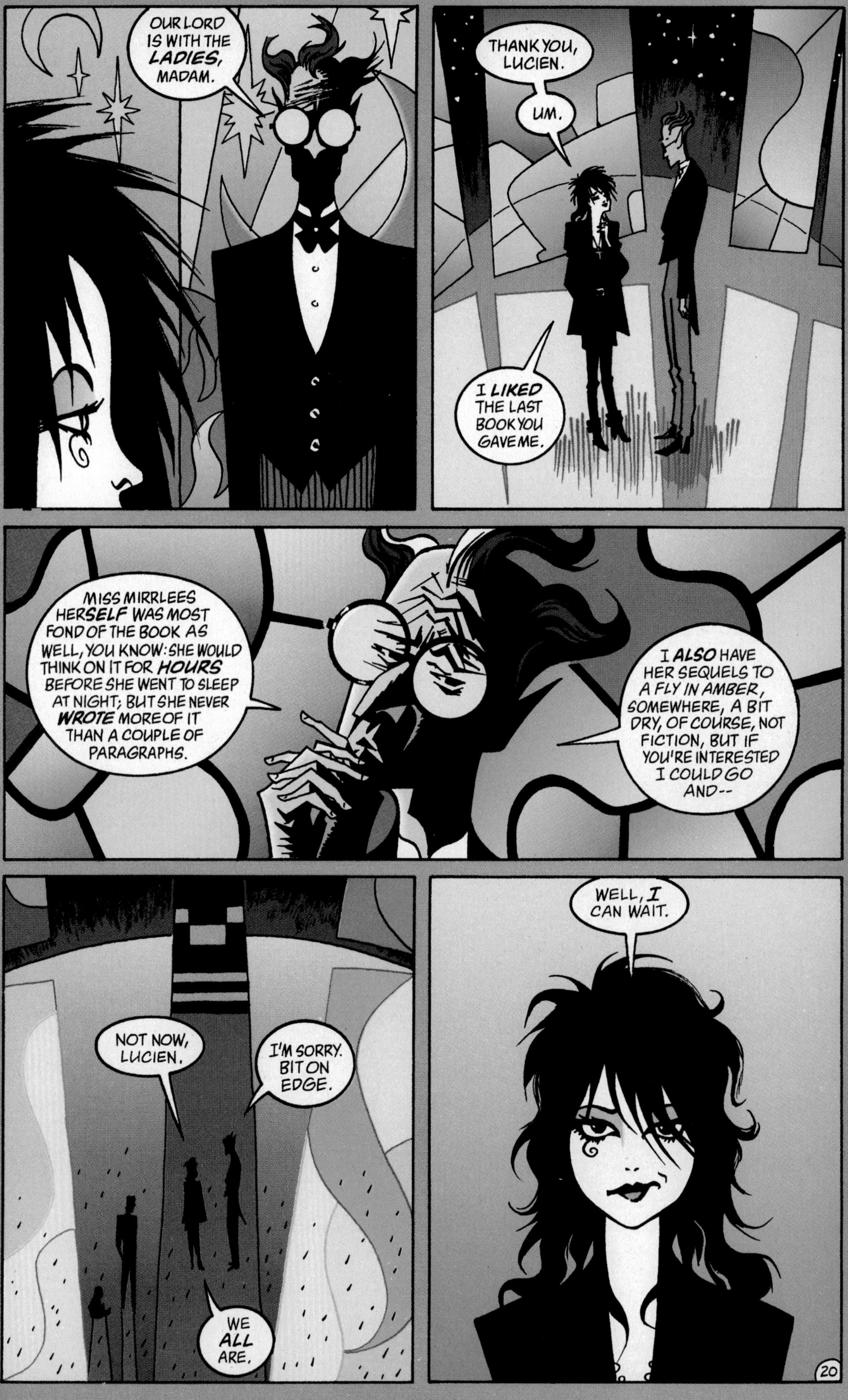
OUR LORD IS WITH THE LADIES, MADAM.
THANK YOU, LUCIEN.
UM.
I LIKED THE LAST BOOK YOU GAVE ME.
MISS MIRRLEES HERSELF WAS MOST FOND OF THE BOOK AS WELL, YOU KNOW: SHE WOULD THINK ON IT FOR HOURS BEFORE SHE WENT TO SLEEP AT NIGHT; BUT SHE NEVER WROTE MORE OF IT THAN A COUPLE OF PARAGRAPHS.
I ALSO HAVE HER SEQUELS TO A FLY IN AMBER, SOMEWHERE, A BIT DRY, OF COURSE, NOT FICTION, BUT IF YOU'RE INTERESTED I COULD GO AND--
NOT NOW, LUCIEN.
I'M SORRY. BIT ON EDGE.
WE ALL ARE.
WELL, I CAN WAIT.

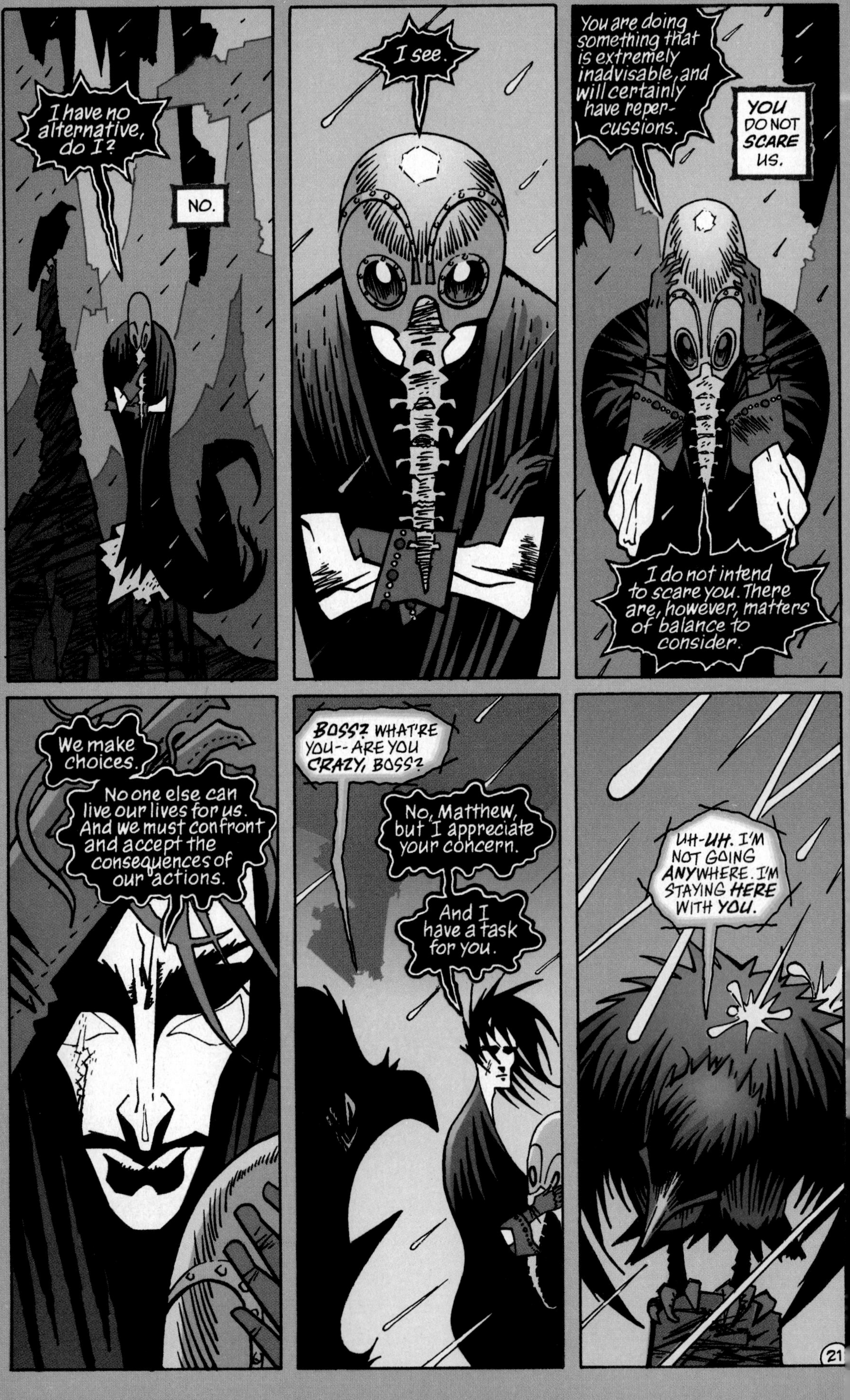
I have no alternative, do I?
NO.
I see.
You are doing something that is extremely inadvisable, and will certainly have repercussions.
YOU DO NOT SCARE US.
I do not intend to scare you. There are, however, matters of balance to consider.
We make choices.
No one else can live our lives for us. And we must confront and accept the consequences of our actions.
BOSS? WHAT'RE YOU-- ARE YOU CRAZY, BOSS?
No, Matthew, but I appreciate your concern.
And I have a task for you.
UH-UH. I'M NOT GOING ANYWHERE. I'M STAYING HERE WITH YOU.

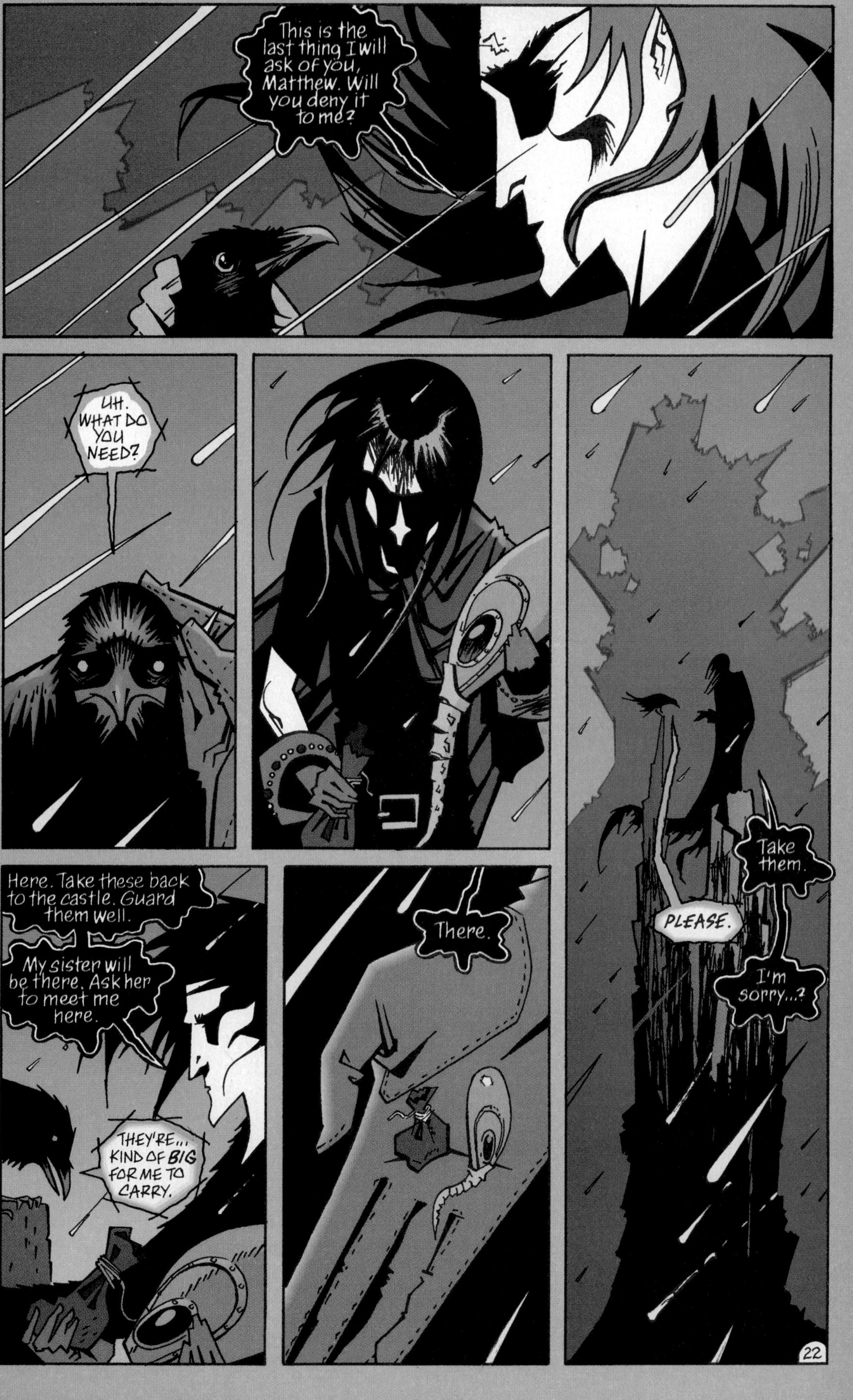
This is the last thing I will ask of you, Matthew. Will you deny it to me?
UH. WHAT DO YOU NEED?
Take them.
PLEASE.
I'm sorry...?
Here. Take these back to the castle. Guard them well.
My sister will be there. Ask her to meet me here.
THEY'RE... KIND OF BIG FOR ME TO CARRY.
There.

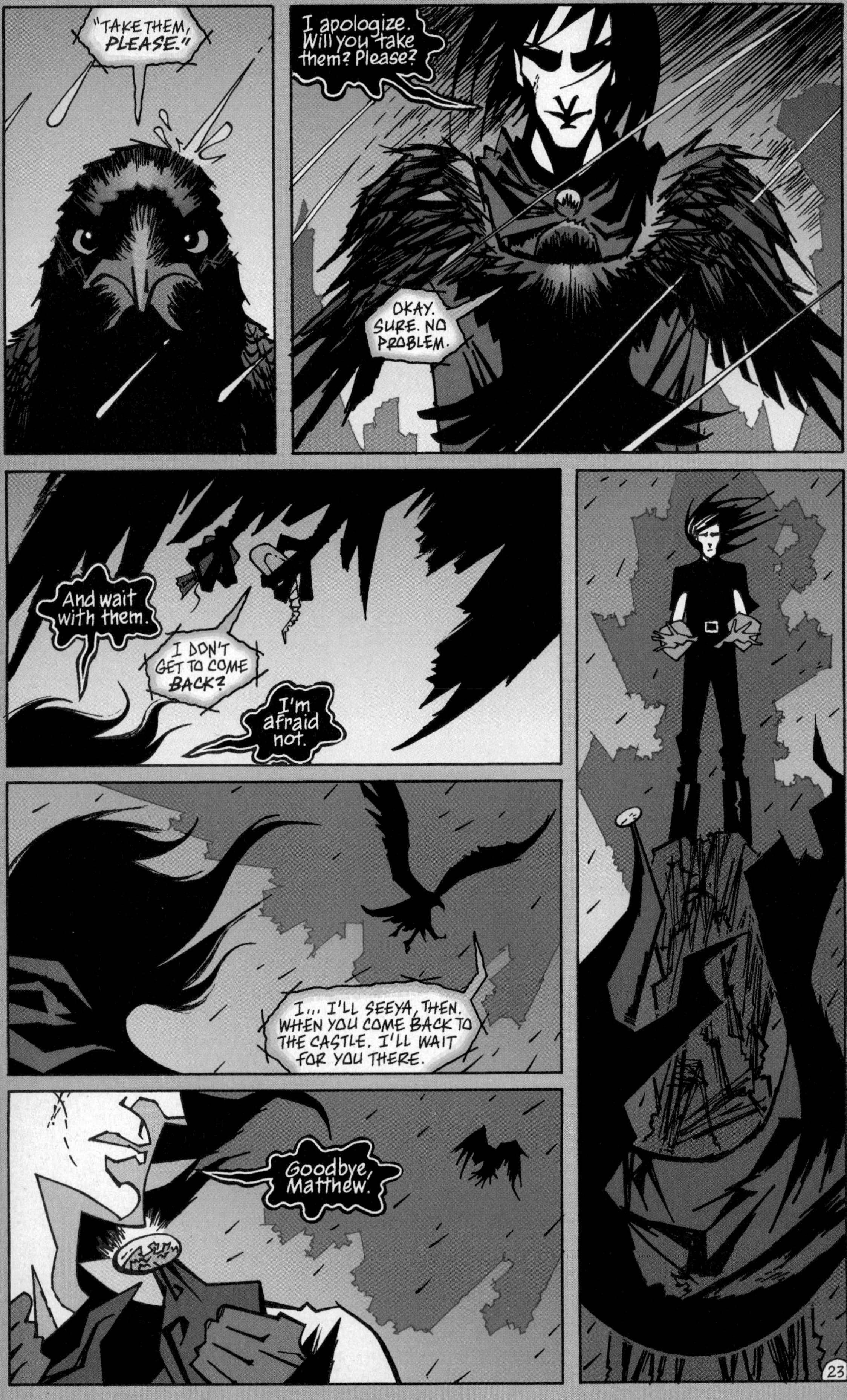
"TAKE THEM, PLEASE."
I apologize. Will you take them? Please?
OKAY. SURE. NO PROBLEM.
And wait with them.
I DON'T GET TO COME BACK?
I'm afraid not.
I... I'LL SEEYA, THEN. WHEN YOU COME BACK TO THE CASTLE. I'LL WAIT FOR YOU THERE.
Goodbye, Matthew.

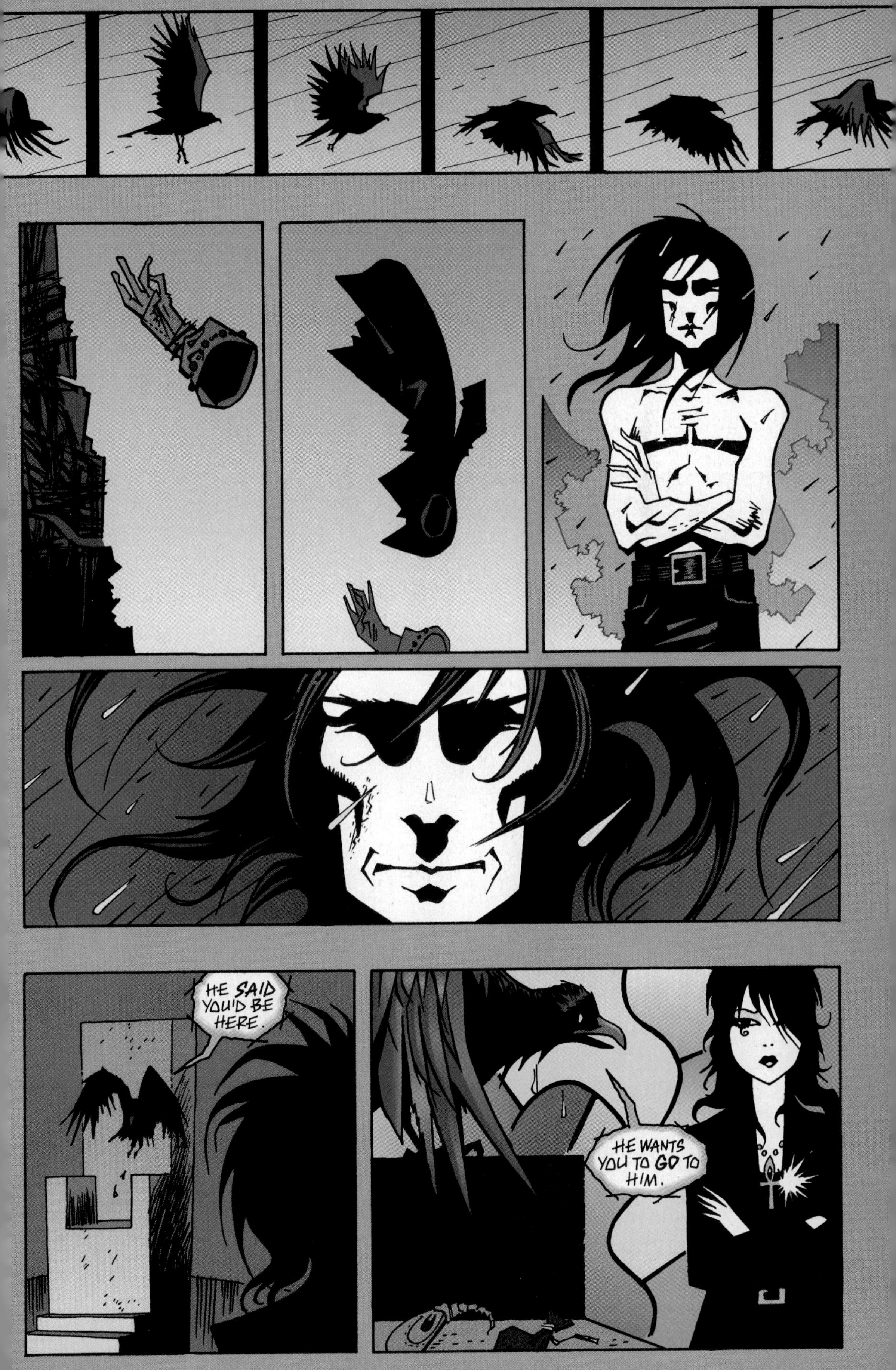
HE SAID YOU'D BE HERE.
HE WANTS YOU TO GO TO HIM.

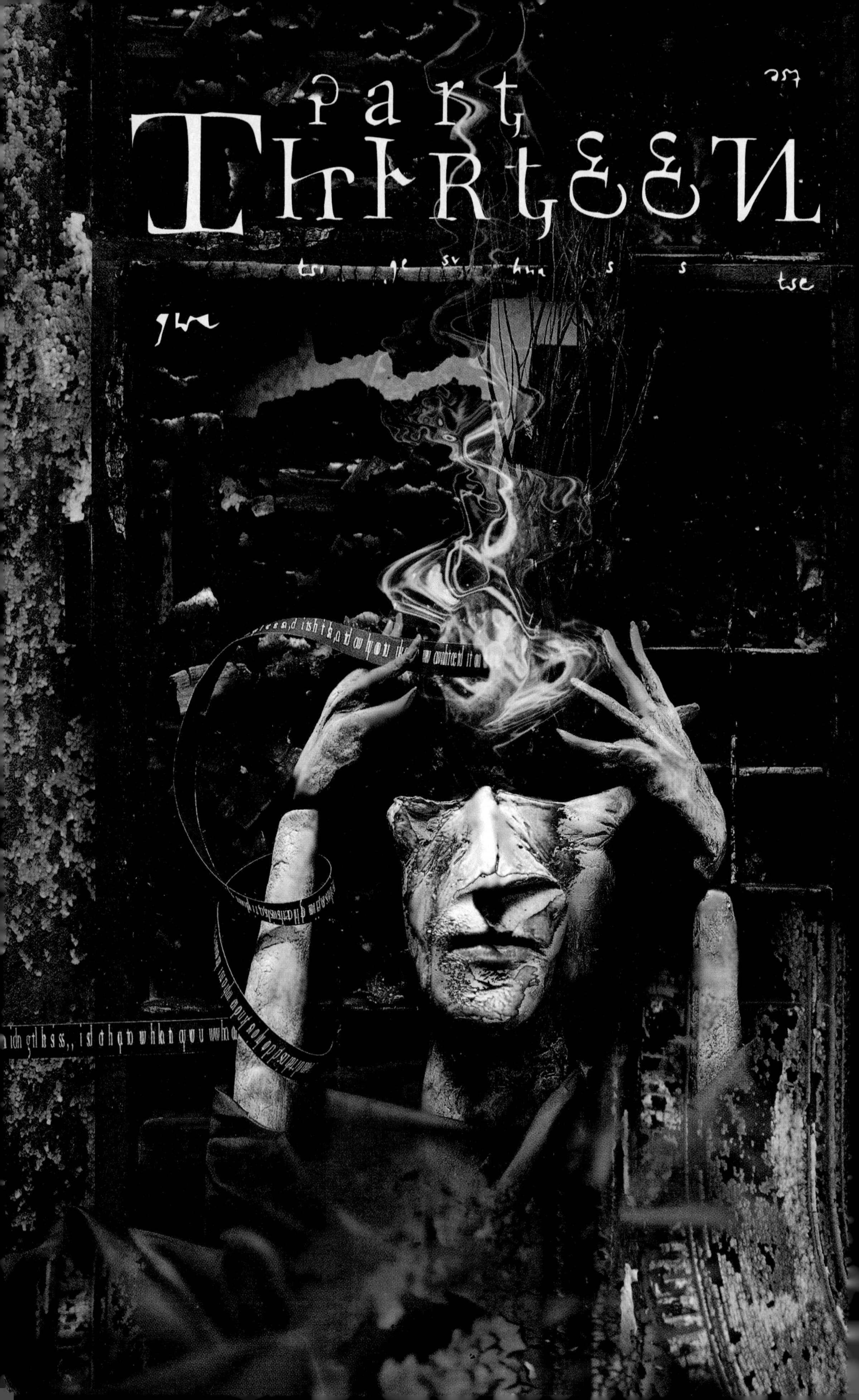
part
THIRTEEN

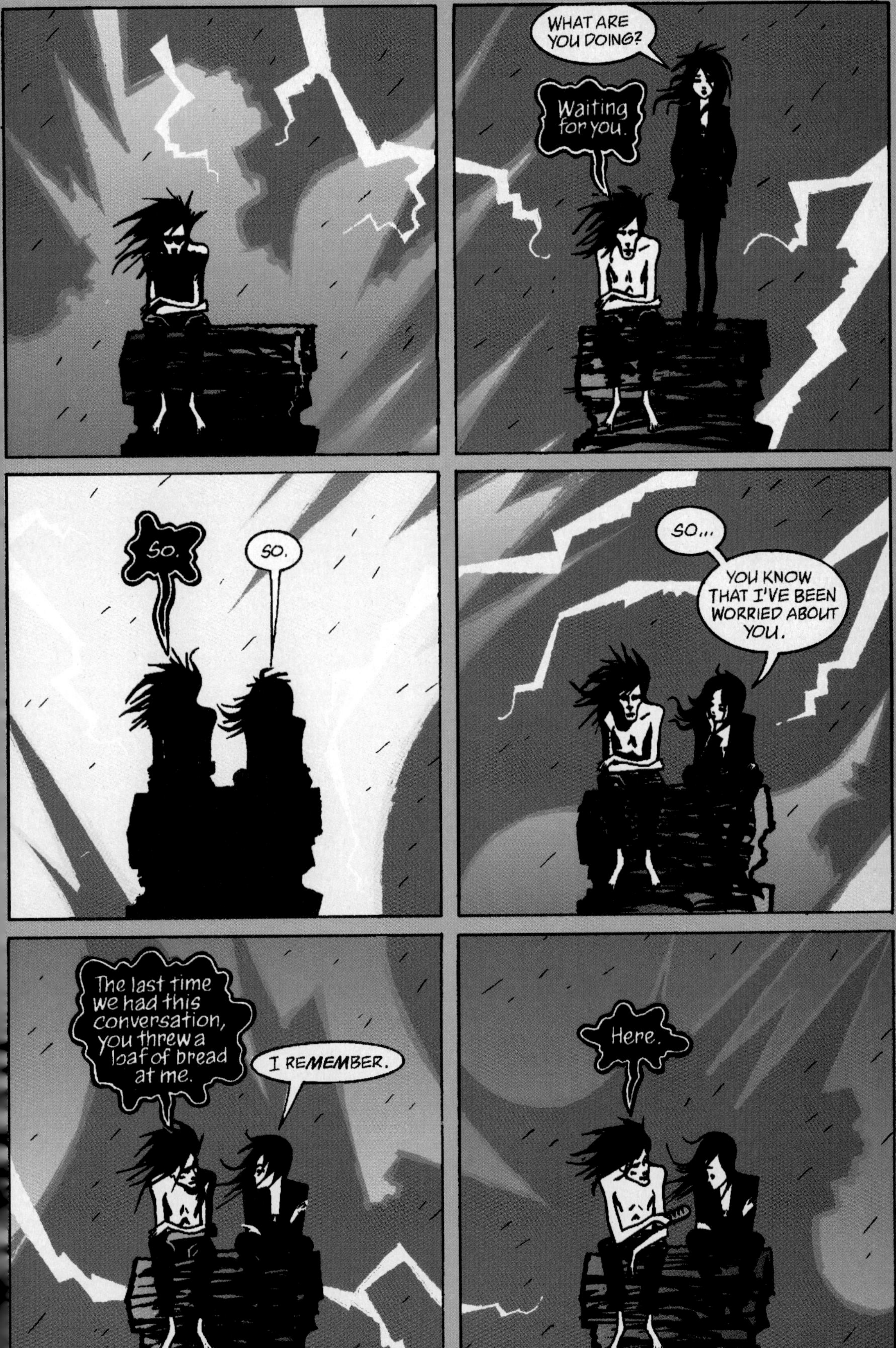
WHAT ARE YOU DOING?
Waiting for you.
So.
SO.
SO...
YOU KNOW THAT I'VE BEEN WORRIED ABOUT YOU.
The last time we had this conversation, you threw a loaf of bread at me.
I REMEMBER.
Here.

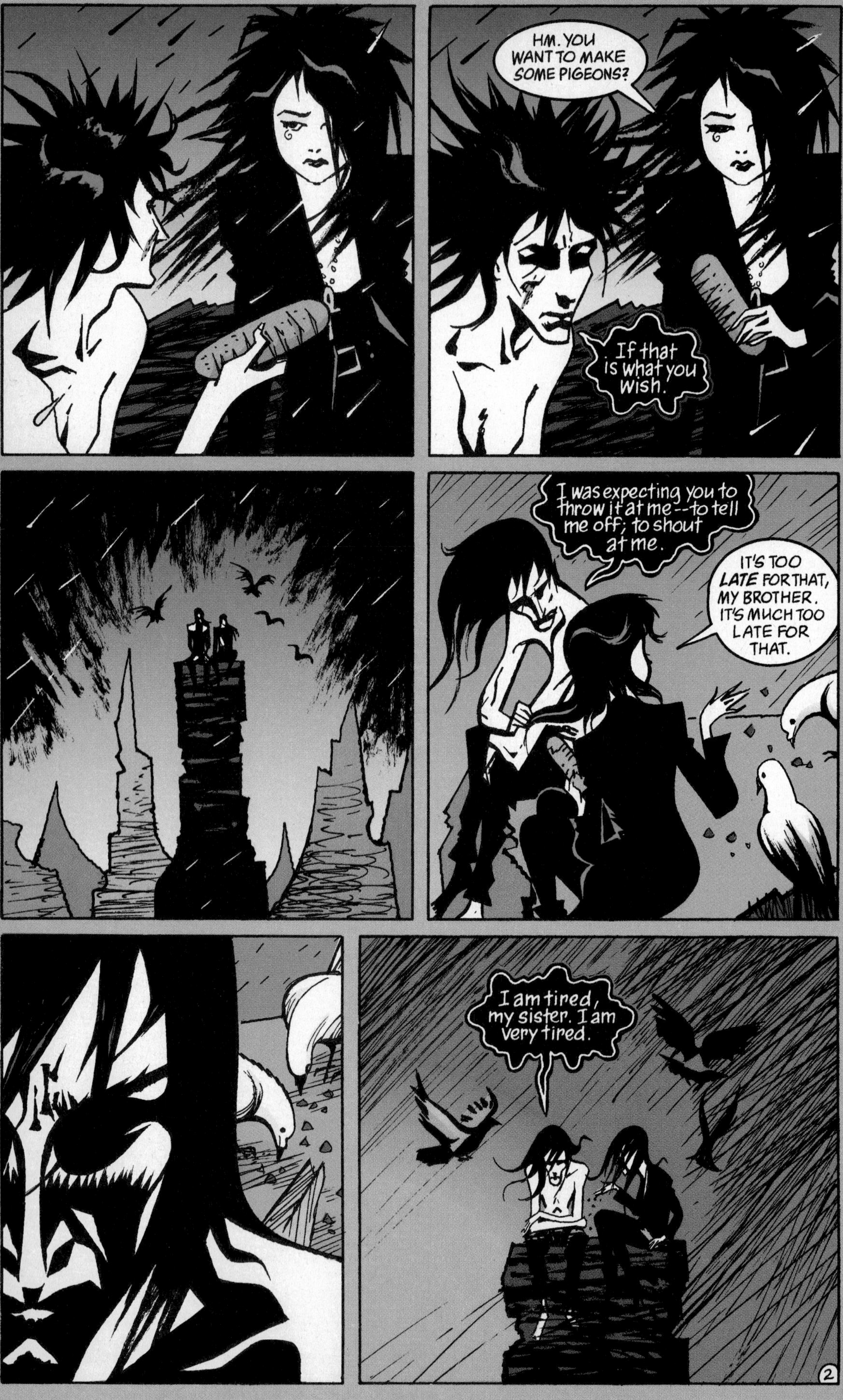
HM. YOU WANT TO MAKE SOME PIGEONS?
If that is what you wish.
I was expecting you to throw it at me--to tell me off; to shout at me.
IT'S TOO LATE FOR THAT, MY BROTHER. IT'S MUCH TOO LATE FOR THAT.
I am tired, my sister. I am very tired.
2

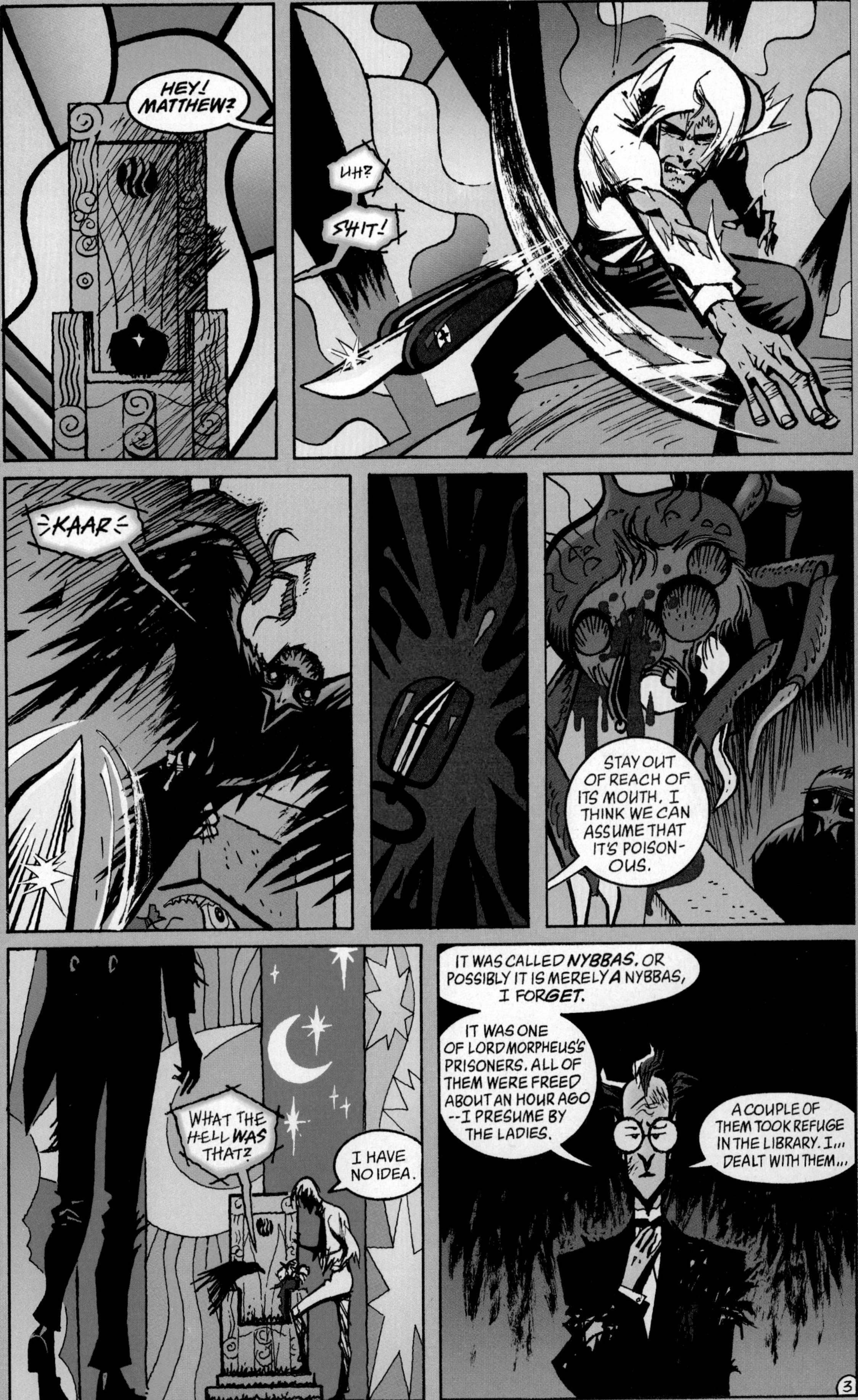
HEY! MATTHEW?
UH?
SHIT!
KAAR
STAY OUT OF REACH OF ITS MOUTH. I THINK WE CAN ASSUME THAT IT'S POISONOUS.
WHAT THE HELL WAS THAT?
I HAVE NO IDEA.
IT WAS CALLED NYBBAS. OR POSSIBLY IT IS MERELY A NYBBAS, I FORGET.
IT WAS ONE OF LORD MORPHEUS'S PRISONERS. ALL OF THEM WERE FREED ABOUT AN HOUR AGO --I PRESUME BY THE LADIES.
A COUPLE OF THEM TOOK REFUGE IN THE LIBRARY. I... DEALT WITH THEM...
3

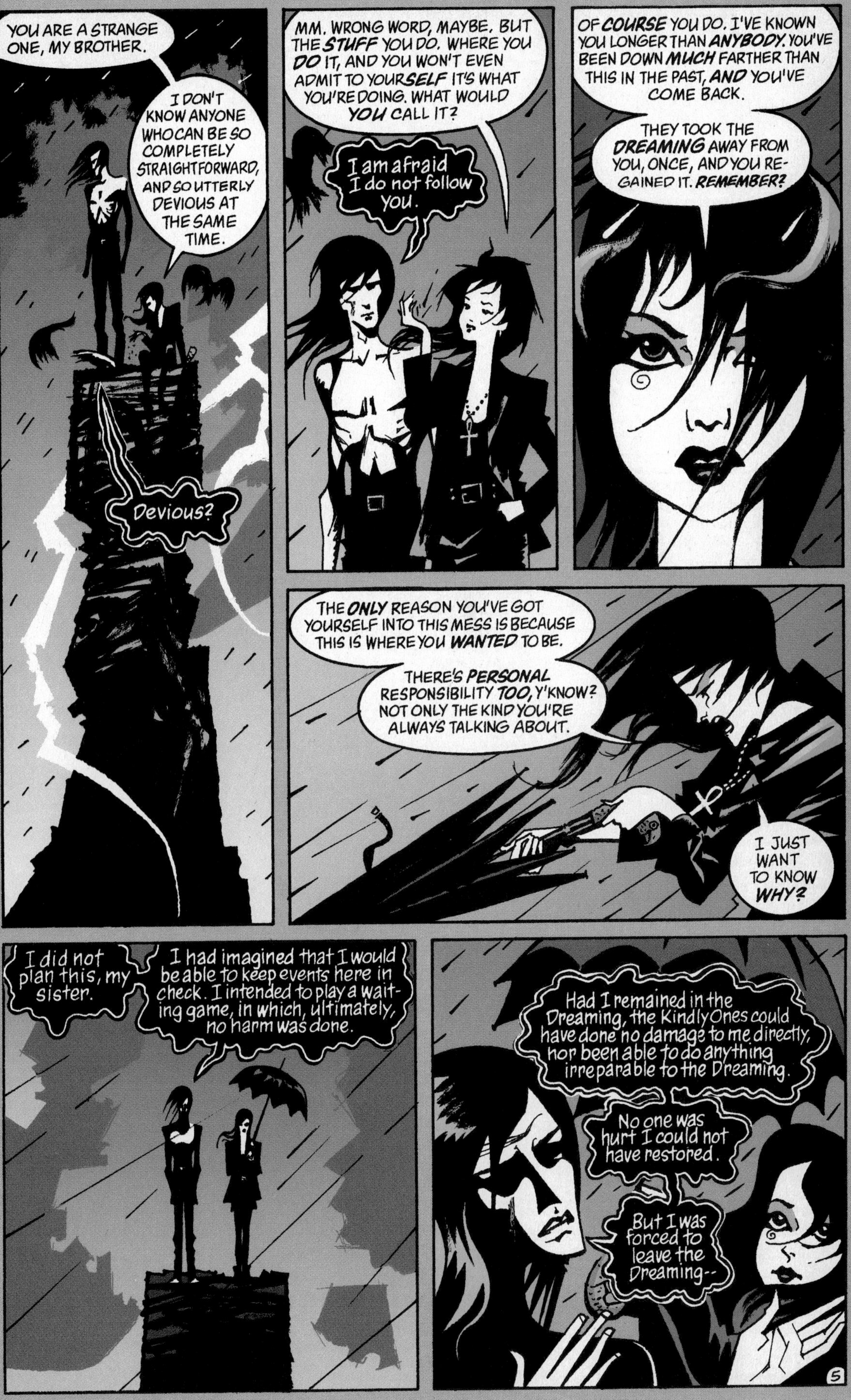
YOU ARE A STRANGE ONE, MY BROTHER.
I DON'T KNOW ANYONE WHOCAN BE SO COMPLETELY STRAIGHTFORWARD, AND SO UTTERLY DEVIOUS AT THE SAME TIME.
Devious?
MM. WRONG WORD, MAYBE. BUT THE STUFF YOU DO. WHERE YOU DO IT, AND YOU WON'T EVEN ADMIT TO YOURSELF IT'S WHAT YOU'RE DOING. WHAT WOULD YOU CALL IT?
I am afraid I do not follow you.
OF COURSE YOU DO. I'VE KNOWN YOU LONGER THAN ANYBODY. YOU'VE BEEN DOWN MUCH FARTHER THAN THIS IN THE PAST, AND YOU'VE COME BACK.
THEY TOOK THE DREAMING AWAY FROM YOU, ONCE, AND YOU RE-GAINED IT. REMEMBER?
THE ONLY REASON YOU'VE GOT YOURSELF INTO THIS MESS IS BECAUSE THIS IS WHERE YOU WANTED TO BE.
THERE'S PERSONAL RESPONSIBILITY TOO, Y'KNOW? NOT ONLY THE KIND YOU'RE ALWAYS TALKING ABOUT.
I JUST WANT TO KNOW WHY?
I did not plan this, my sister.
I had imagined that I would be able to keep events here in check. I intended to play a wait-ing game, in which, ultimately, no harm was done.
Had I remained in the Dreaming, the Kindly Ones could have done no damage to me directly, nor been able to do anything irreparable to the Dreaming.
No one was hurt I could not have restored.
But I was forced to leave the Dreaming--
5

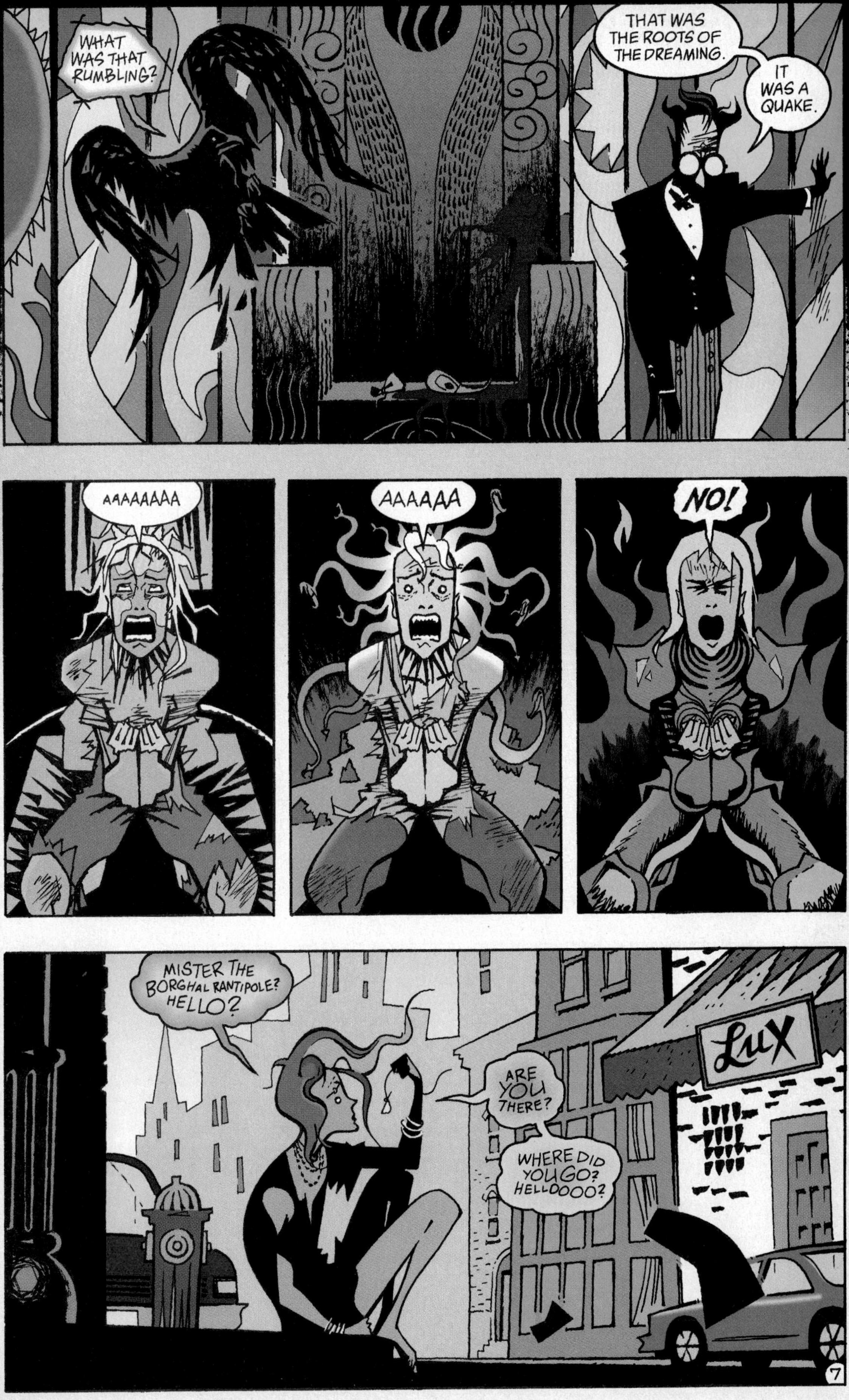
WHAT WAS THAT RUMBLING?
THAT WAS THE ROOTS OF THE DREAMING.
IT WAS A QUAKE.
AAAAAAAA
AAAAAA
NO!
MISTER THE BORGHAL RANTIPOLE? HELLO?
ARE YOU THERE?
WHERE DID YOU GO? HELLOOOO?
LUX

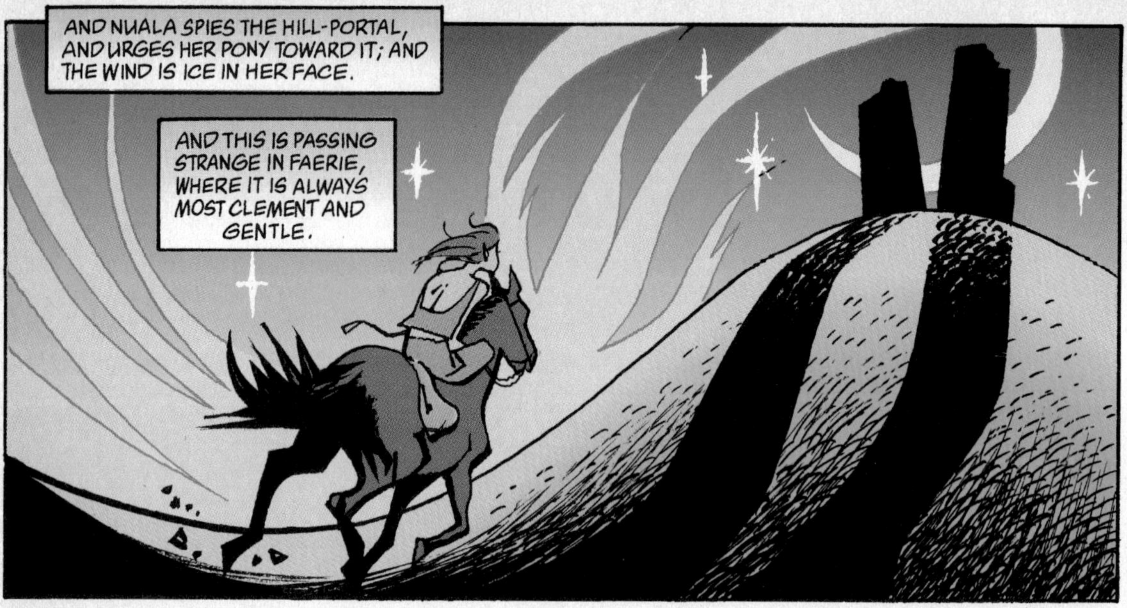

AND NUALA SPIES THE HILL-PORTAL, AND URGES HER PONY TOWARD IT; AND THE WIND IS ICE IN HER FACE.
AND THIS IS PASSING STRANGE IN FAERIE, WHERE IT IS ALWAYS MOST CLEMENT AND GENTLE.

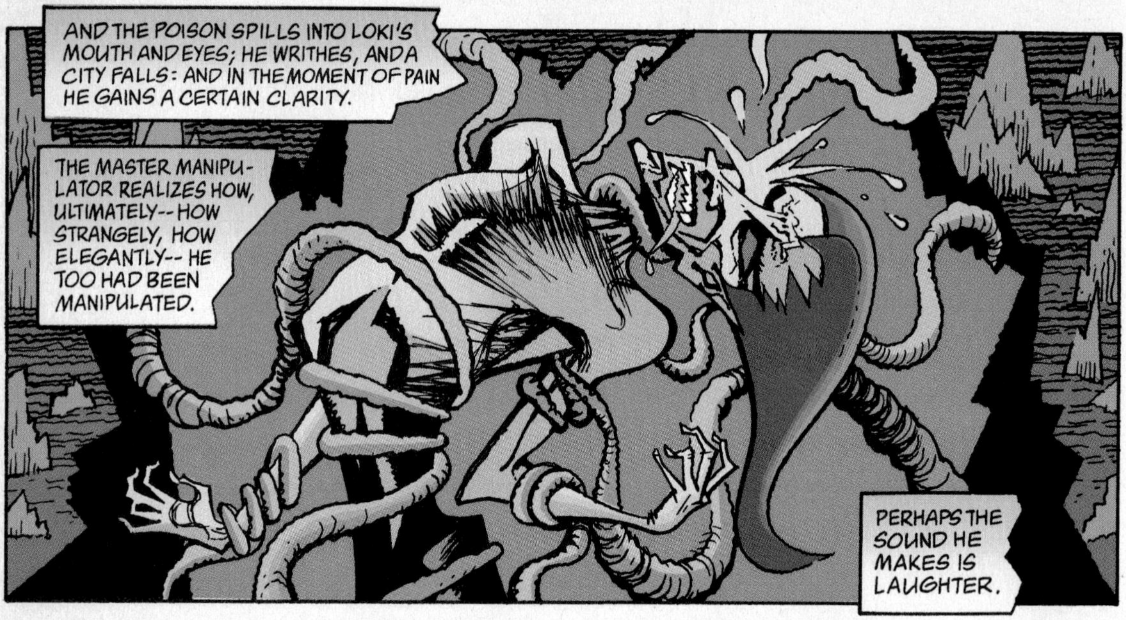

AND THE POISON SPILLS INTO LOKI'S MOUTH AND EYES; HE WRITHES, AND A CITY FALLS: AND IN THE MOMENT OF PAIN HE GAINS A CERTAIN CLARITY.
THE MASTER MANIPULATOR REALIZES HOW, ULTIMATELY-- HOW STRANGELY, HOW ELEGANTLY-- HE TOO HAD BEEN MANIPULATED.
PERHAPS THE SOUND HE MAKES IS LAUGHTER.

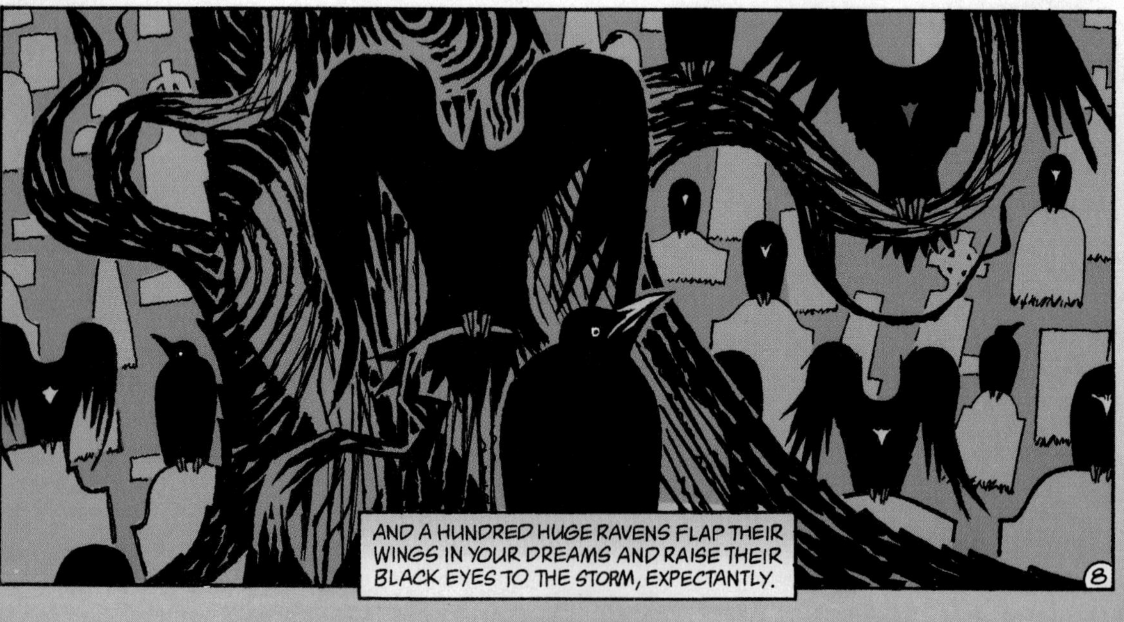

AND A HUNDRED HUGE RAVENS FLAP THEIR WINGS IN YOUR DREAMS AND RAISE THEIR BLACK EYES TO THE STORM, EXPECTANTLY.

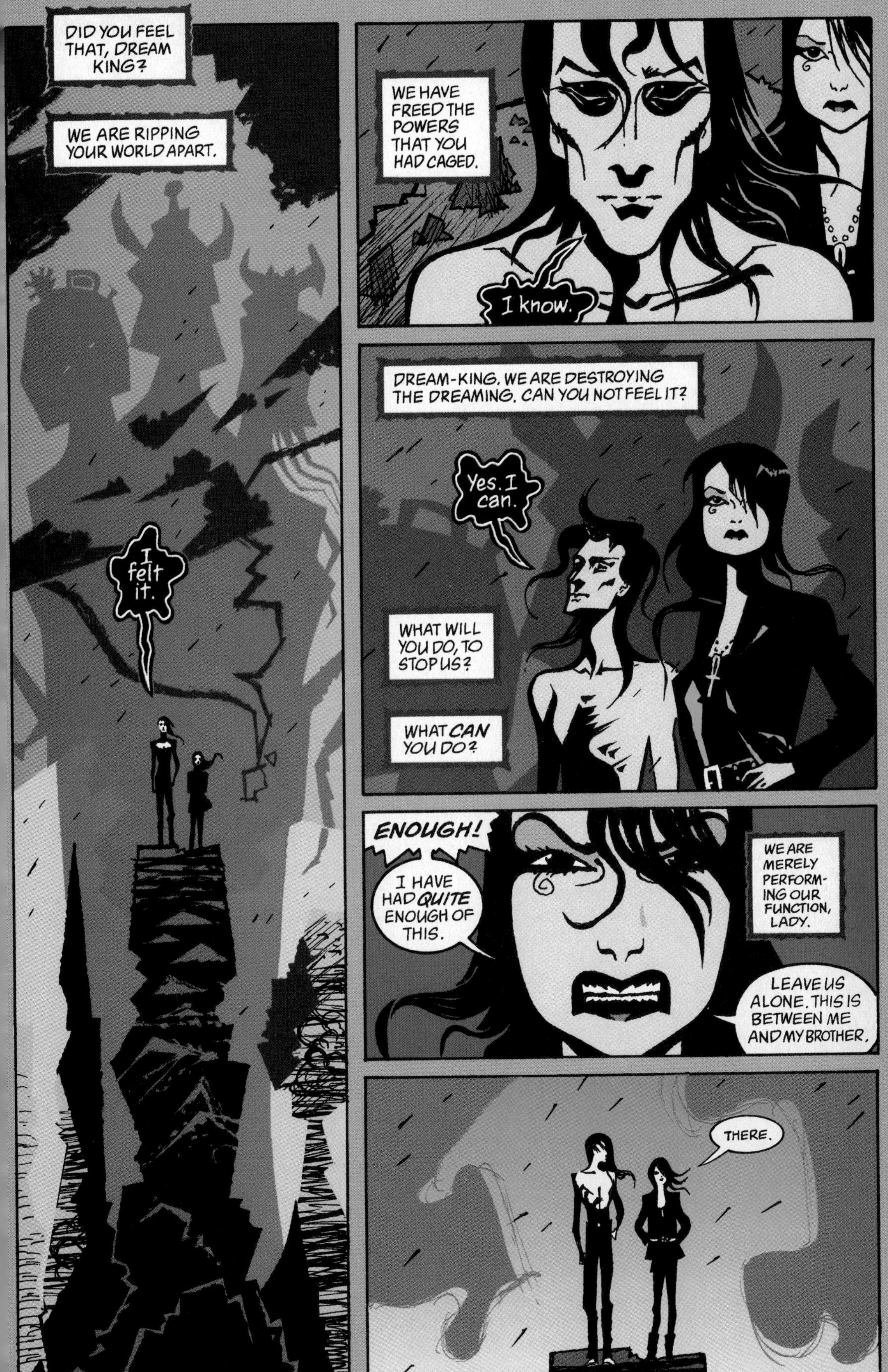
DID YOU FEEL THAT, DREAM KING?
WE ARE RIPPING YOUR WORLD APART.
I felt it.
WE HAVE FREED THE POWERS THAT YOU HAD CAGED.
I know.
DREAM-KING. WE ARE DESTROYING THE DREAMING. CAN YOU NOT FEEL IT?
Yes. I can.
WHAT WILL YOU DO, TO STOP US?
WHAT CAN YOU DO?
ENOUGH!
I HAVE HAD QUITE ENOUGH OF THIS.
WE ARE MERELY PERFORMING OUR FUNCTION, LADY.
LEAVE US ALONE. THIS IS BETWEEN ME AND MY BROTHER.
THERE.
9

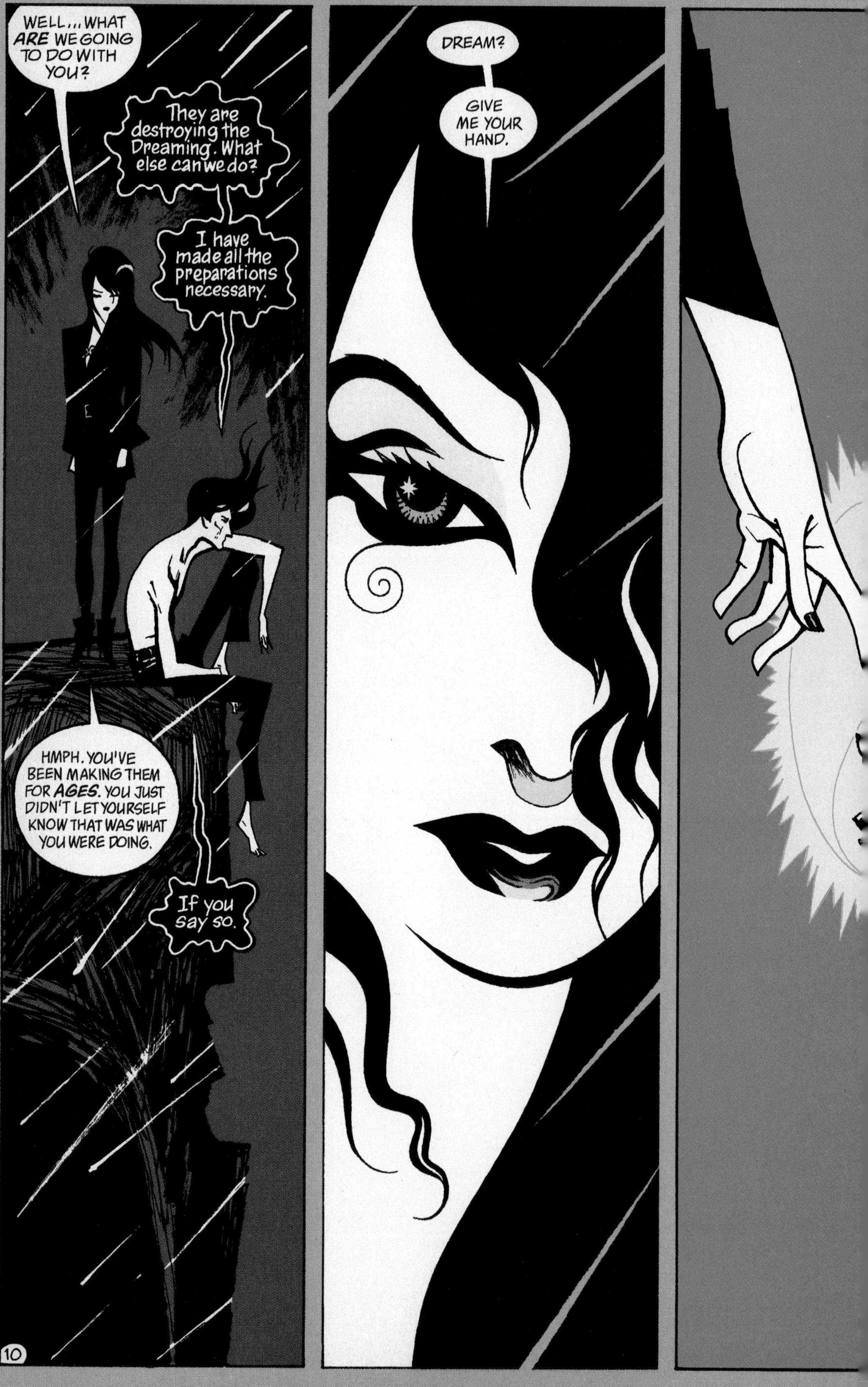
WELL... WHAT ARE WE GOING TO DO WITH YOU?
They are destroying the Dreaming. What else can we do?
I have made all the preparations necessary.
HMPH. YOU'VE BEEN MAKING THEM FOR AGES. YOU JUST DIDN'T LET YOURSELF KNOW THAT WAS WHAT YOU WERE DOING.
If you say so.
DREAM?
GIVE ME YOUR HAND.
10

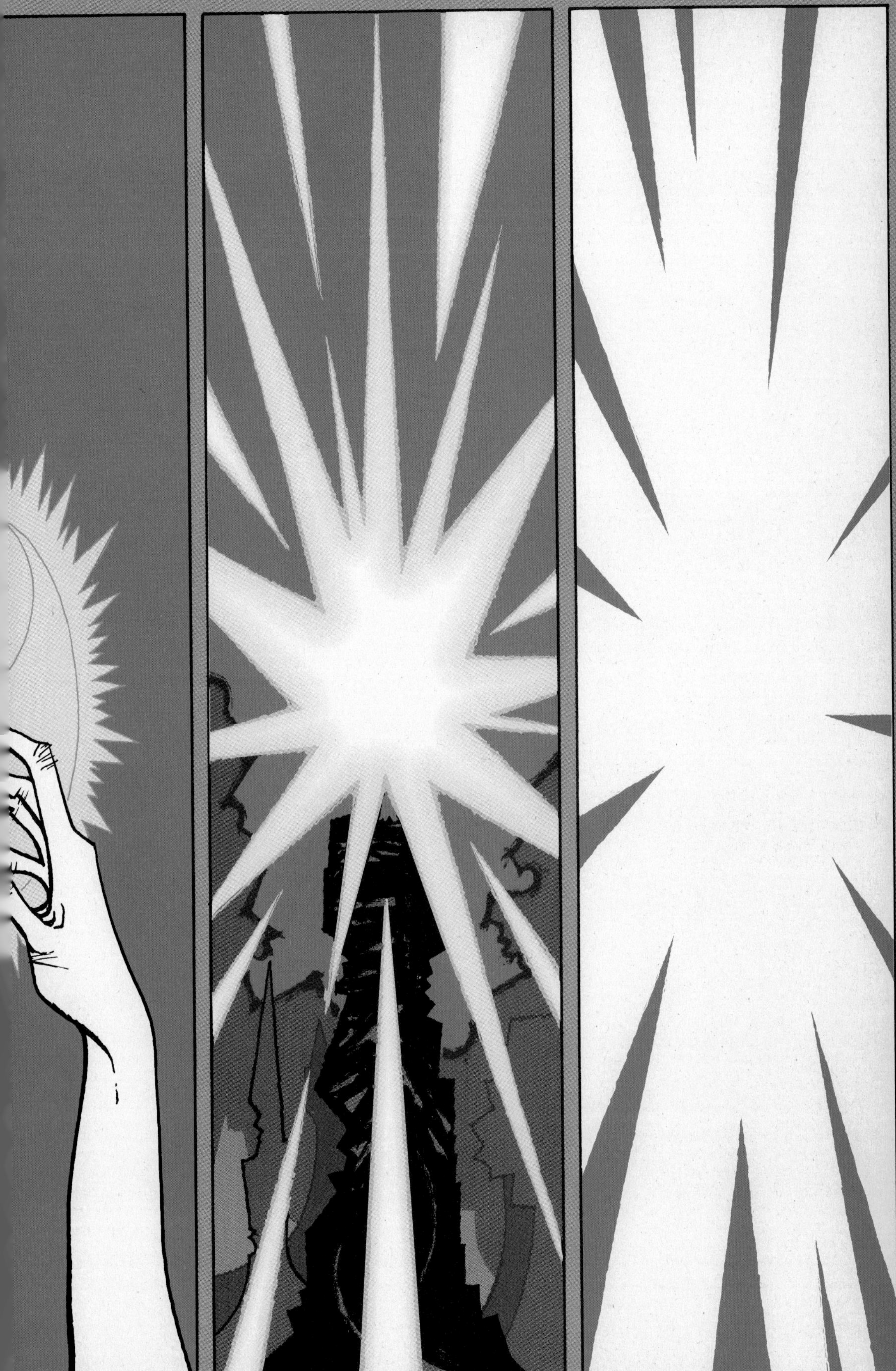

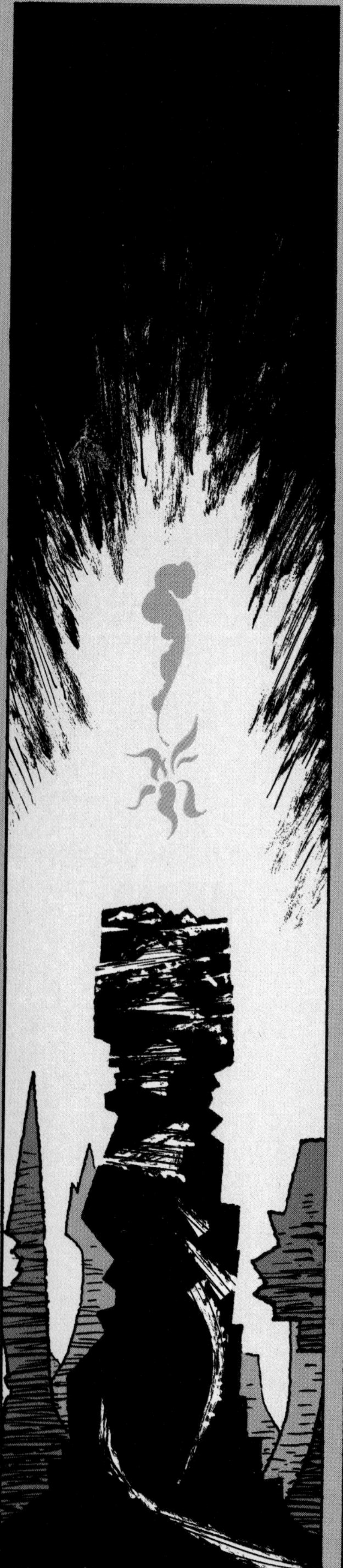
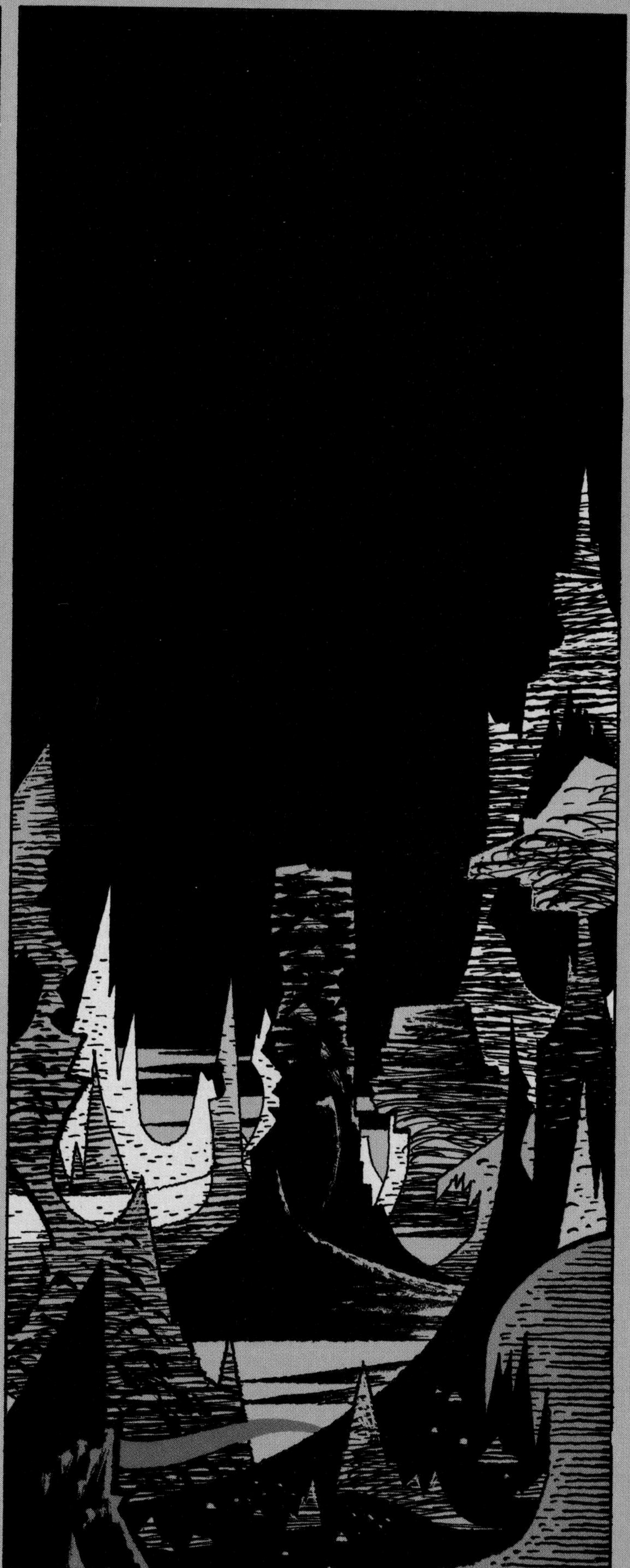

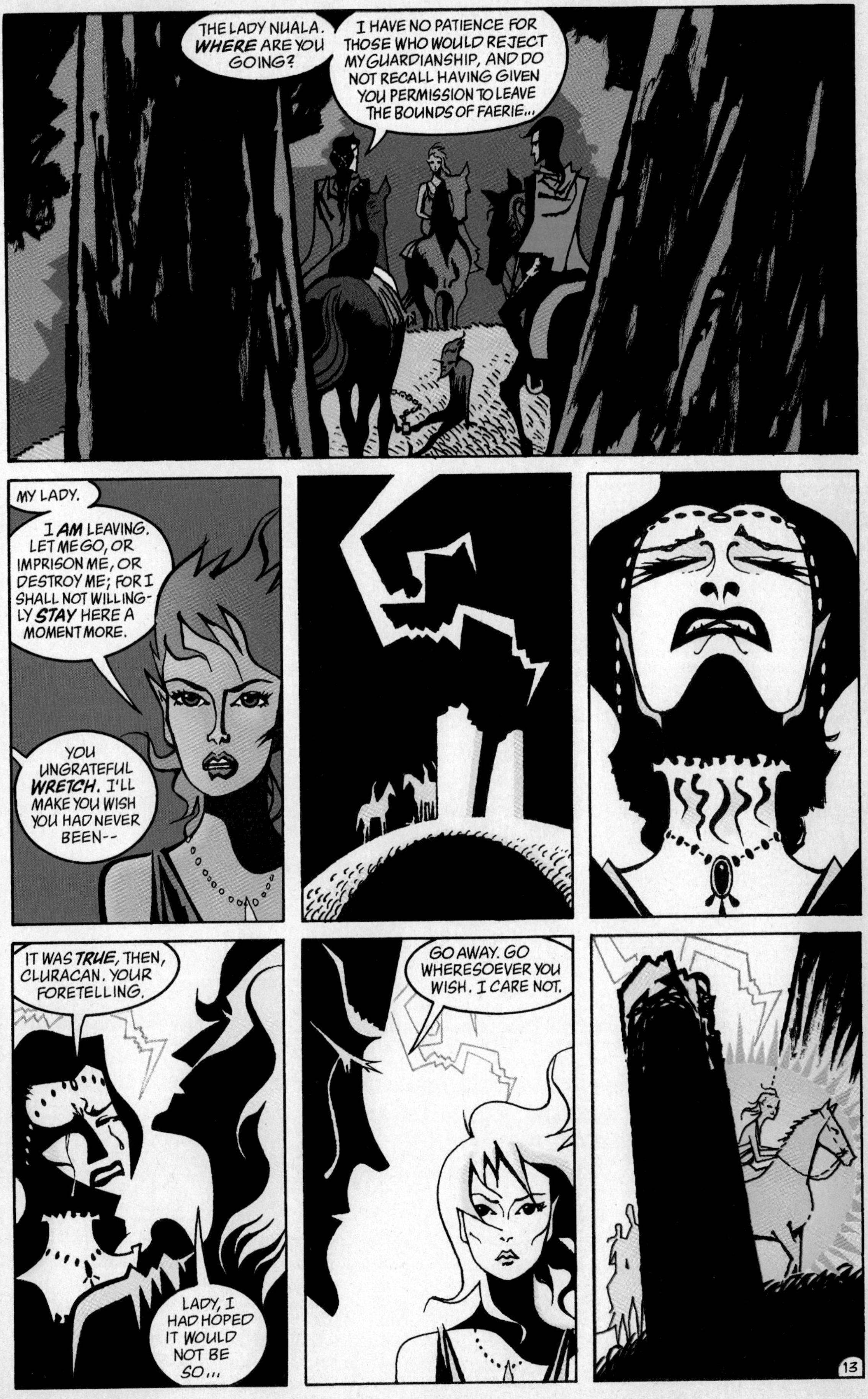
THE LADY NUALA. WHERE ARE YOU GOING?
I HAVE NO PATIENCE FOR THOSE WHO WOULD REJECT MY GUARDIANSHIP, AND DO NOT RECALL HAVING GIVEN YOU PERMISSION TO LEAVE THE BOUNDS OF FAERIE...
MY LADY.
I AM LEAVING. LET ME GO, OR IMPRISON ME, OR DESTROY ME; FOR I SHALL NOT WILLINGLY STAY HERE A MOMENT MORE.
YOU UNGRATEFUL WRETCH. I'LL MAKE YOU WISH YOU HAD NEVER BEEN--
IT WAS TRUE, THEN, CLURACAN. YOUR FORETELLING.
LADY, I HAD HOPED IT WOULD NOT BE SO...
GO AWAY. GO WHERESOEVER YOU WISH. I CARE NOT.

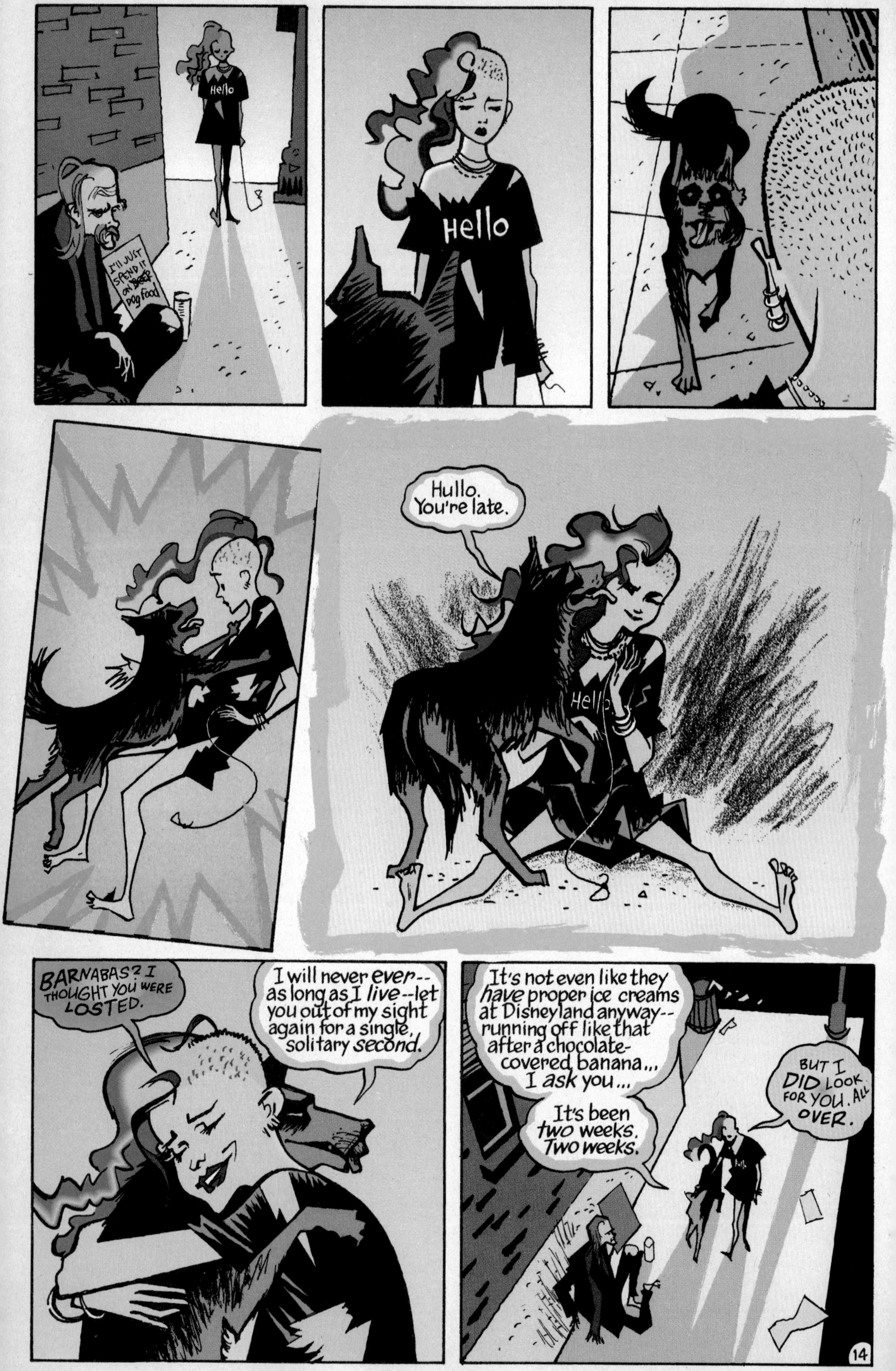
Hello
I'LL JUST SPEND IT ON ~~BEER~~ Dog Food
Hello
Hullo. You're late.
Hello
BARNABAS? I THOUGHT YOU WERE LOSTED.
I will never *ever*-- as long as I *live*--let you out of my sight again for a single, solitary *second*.
It's not even like they *have* proper ice creams at Disneyland anyway-- running off like that after a chocolate-covered banana... I *ask* you...
It's been *two* weeks. *Two* weeks.
BUT I DID LOOK FOR YOU. ALL OVER.

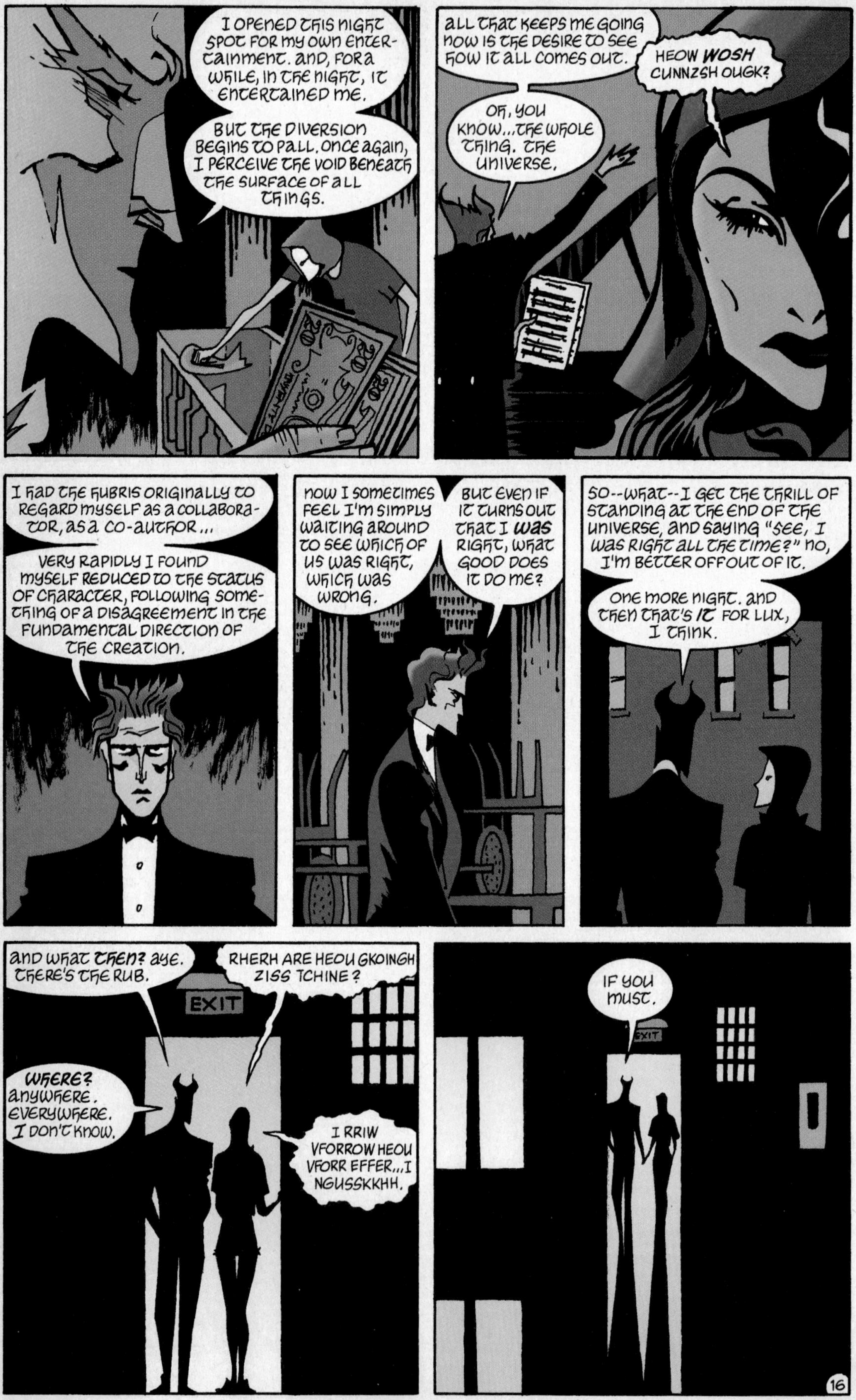
I OPENED THIS NIGHT SPOT FOR MY OWN ENTERTAINMENT. AND, FOR A WHILE, IN THE NIGHT, IT ENTERTAINED ME.
BUT THE DIVERSION BEGINS TO PALL. ONCE AGAIN, I PERCEIVE THE VOID BENEATH THE SURFACE OF ALL THINGS.
ALL THAT KEEPS ME GOING NOW IS THE DESIRE TO SEE HOW IT ALL COMES OUT.
HEOW WOSH CUNNZSH OUGK?
OH, YOU KNOW... THE WHOLE THING. THE UNIVERSE.
I HAD THE HUBRIS ORIGINALLY TO REGARD MYSELF AS A COLLABORATOR, AS A CO-AUTHOR...
VERY RAPIDLY I FOUND MYSELF REDUCED TO THE STATUS OF CHARACTER, FOLLOWING SOMETHING OF A DISAGREEMENT IN THE FUNDAMENTAL DIRECTION OF THE CREATION.
NOW I SOMETIMES FEEL I'M SIMPLY WAITING AROUND TO SEE WHICH OF US WAS RIGHT, WHICH WAS WRONG.
BUT EVEN IF IT TURNS OUT THAT I WAS RIGHT, WHAT GOOD DOES IT DO ME?
SO--WHAT--I GET THE THRILL OF STANDING AT THE END OF THE UNIVERSE, AND SAYING "SEE, I WAS RIGHT ALL THE TIME?" NO, I'M BETTER OFF OUT OF IT.
ONE MORE NIGHT. AND THEN THAT'S IT FOR LUX, I THINK.
AND WHAT THEN? AYE. THERE'S THE RUB.
EXIT
RHERH ARE HEOU GKOINGH ZISS TCHINE?
WHERE? ANYWHERE. EVERYWHERE. I DON'T KNOW.
I RRIW VFORROW HEOU VFORR EFFER... I NGUSSKKHH.
IF YOU MUST.
EXIT

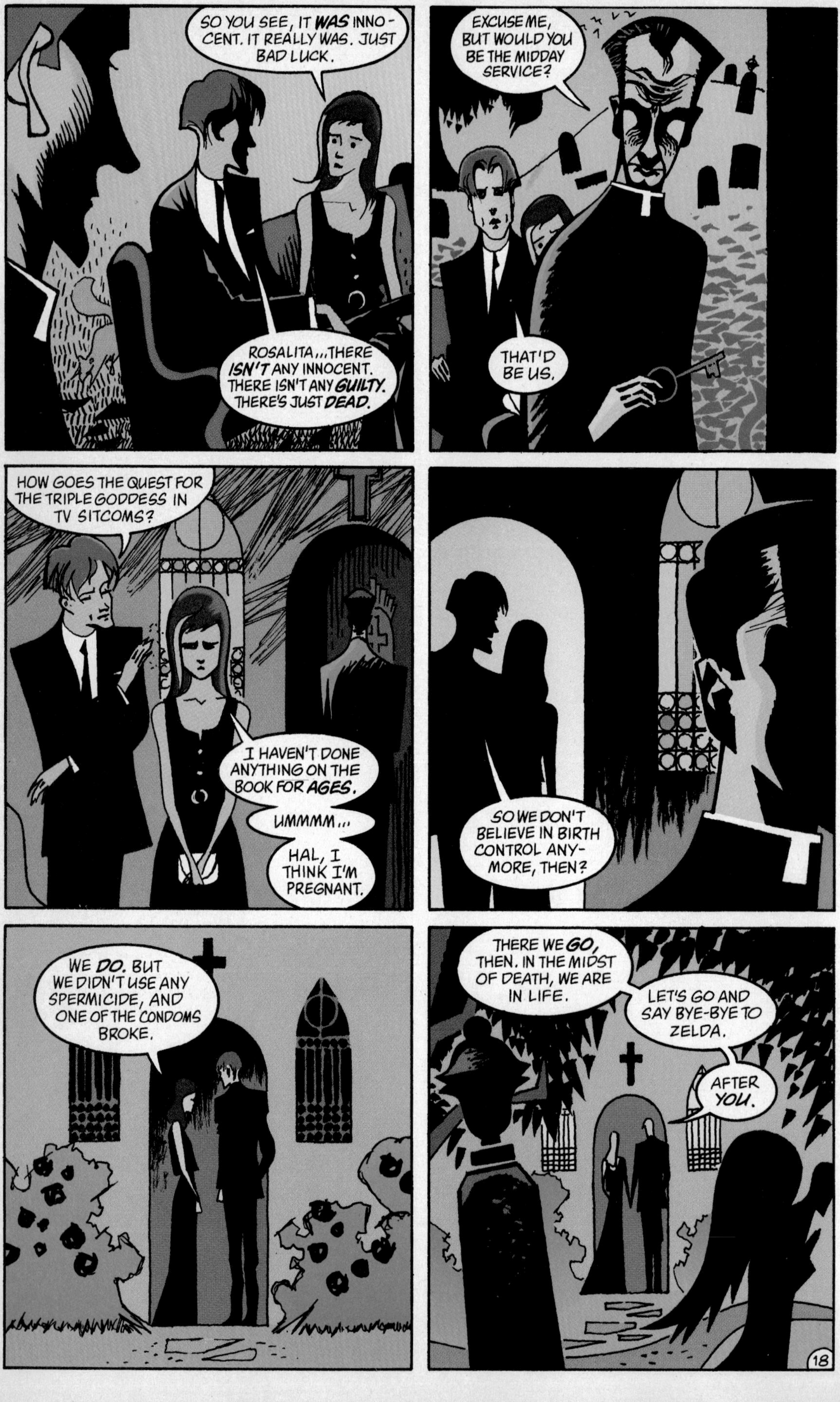
SO YOU SEE, IT WAS INNOCENT. IT REALLY WAS. JUST BAD LUCK.
ROSALITA...THERE ISN'T ANY INNOCENT. THERE ISN'T ANY GUILTY. THERE'S JUST DEAD.
EXCUSE ME, BUT WOULD YOU BE THE MIDDAY SERVICE?
THAT'D BE US.
HOW GOES THE QUEST FOR THE TRIPLE GODDESS IN TV SITCOMS?
I HAVEN'T DONE ANYTHING ON THE BOOK FOR AGES.
UMMMM...
HAL, I THINK I'M PREGNANT.
SO WE DON'T BELIEVE IN BIRTH CONTROL ANYMORE, THEN?
WE DO. BUT WE DIDN'T USE ANY SPERMICIDE, AND ONE OF THE CONDOMS BROKE.
THERE WE GO, THEN. IN THE MIDST OF DEATH, WE ARE IN LIFE.
LET'S GO AND SAY BYE-BYE TO ZELDA.
AFTER YOU.
18

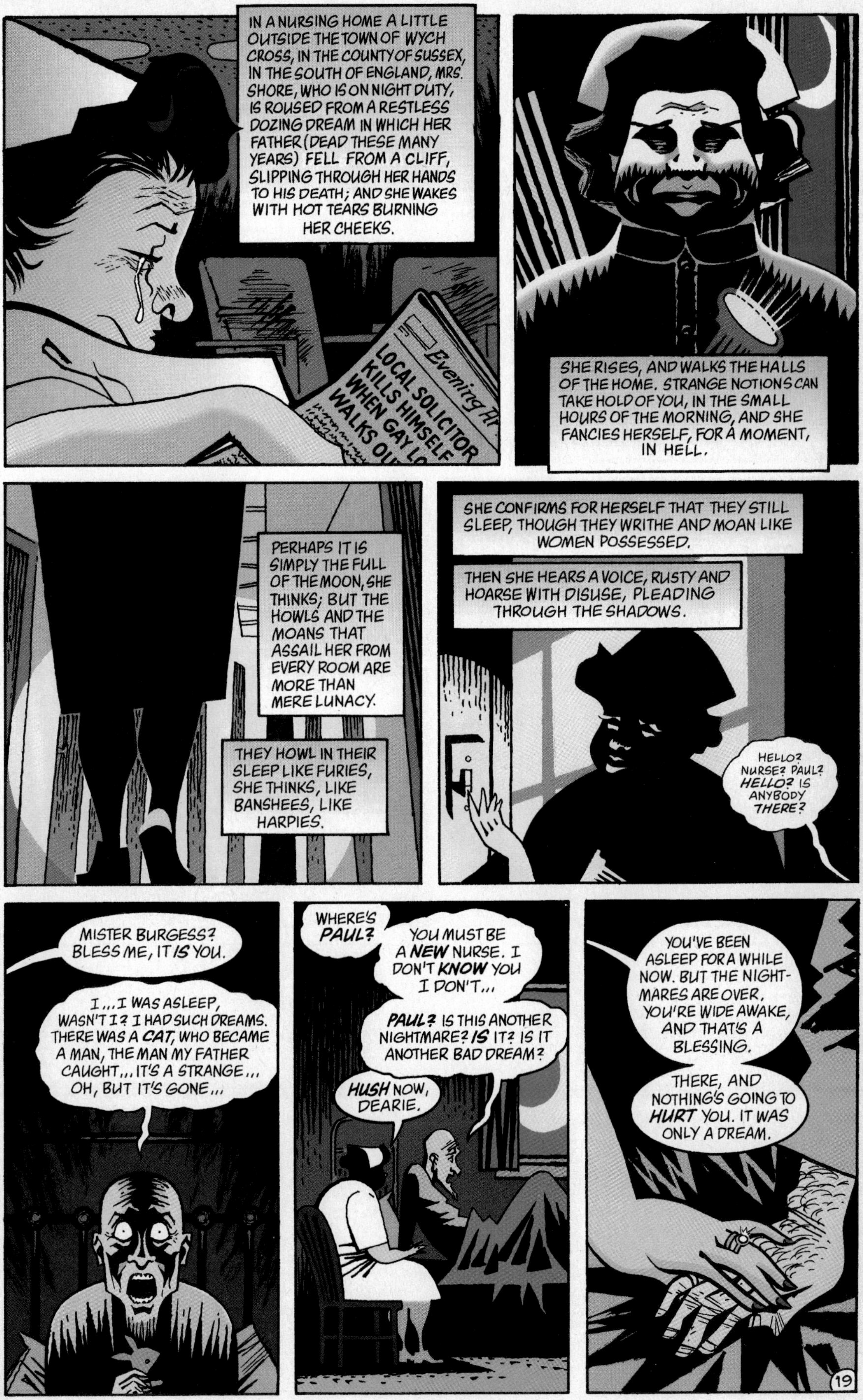

IN A NURSING HOME A LITTLE OUTSIDE THE TOWN OF WYCH CROSS, IN THE COUNTY OF SUSSEX, IN THE SOUTH OF ENGLAND, MRS. SHORE, WHO IS ON NIGHT DUTY, IS ROUSED FROM A RESTLESS DOZING DREAM IN WHICH HER FATHER (DEAD THESE MANY YEARS) FELL FROM A CLIFF, SLIPPING THROUGH HER HANDS TO HIS DEATH; AND SHE WAKES WITH HOT TEARS BURNING HER CHEEKS.
Evening
LOCAL SOLICITOR KILLS HIMSELF WHEN GAY LO WALKS OU
SHE RISES, AND WALKS THE HALLS OF THE HOME. STRANGE NOTIONS CAN TAKE HOLD OF YOU, IN THE SMALL HOURS OF THE MORNING, AND SHE FANCIES HERSELF, FOR A MOMENT, IN HELL.
PERHAPS IT IS SIMPLY THE FULL OF THE MOON, SHE THINKS; BUT THE HOWLS AND THE MOANS THAT ASSAIL HER FROM EVERY ROOM ARE MORE THAN MERE LUNACY.
THEY HOWL IN THEIR SLEEP LIKE FURIES, SHE THINKS, LIKE BANSHEES, LIKE HARPIES.
SHE CONFIRMS FOR HERSELF THAT THEY STILL SLEEP, THOUGH THEY WRITHE AND MOAN LIKE WOMEN POSSESSED.
THEN SHE HEARS A VOICE, RUSTY AND HOARSE WITH DISUSE, PLEADING THROUGH THE SHADOWS.
HELLO? NURSE? PAUL? HELLO? IS ANYBODY THERE?
MISTER BURGESS? BLESS ME, IT IS YOU.
I... I WAS ASLEEP, WASN'T I? I HAD SUCH DREAMS. THERE WAS A CAT, WHO BECAME A MAN, THE MAN MY FATHER CAUGHT... IT'S A STRANGE... OH, BUT IT'S GONE...
WHERE'S PAUL?
YOU MUST BE A NEW NURSE. I DON'T KNOW YOU I DON'T...
PAUL? IS THIS ANOTHER NIGHTMARE? IS IT? IS IT ANOTHER BAD DREAM?
HUSH NOW, DEARIE.
YOU'VE BEEN ASLEEP FOR A WHILE NOW. BUT THE NIGHTMARES ARE OVER, YOU'RE WIDE AWAKE, AND THAT'S A BLESSING.
THERE, AND NOTHING'S GOING TO HURT YOU. IT WAS ONLY A DREAM.

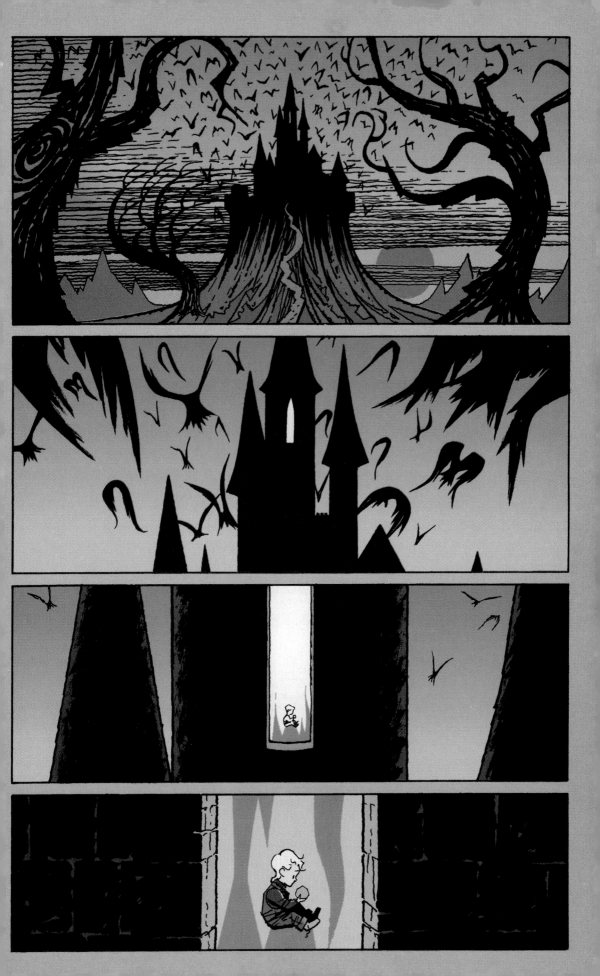

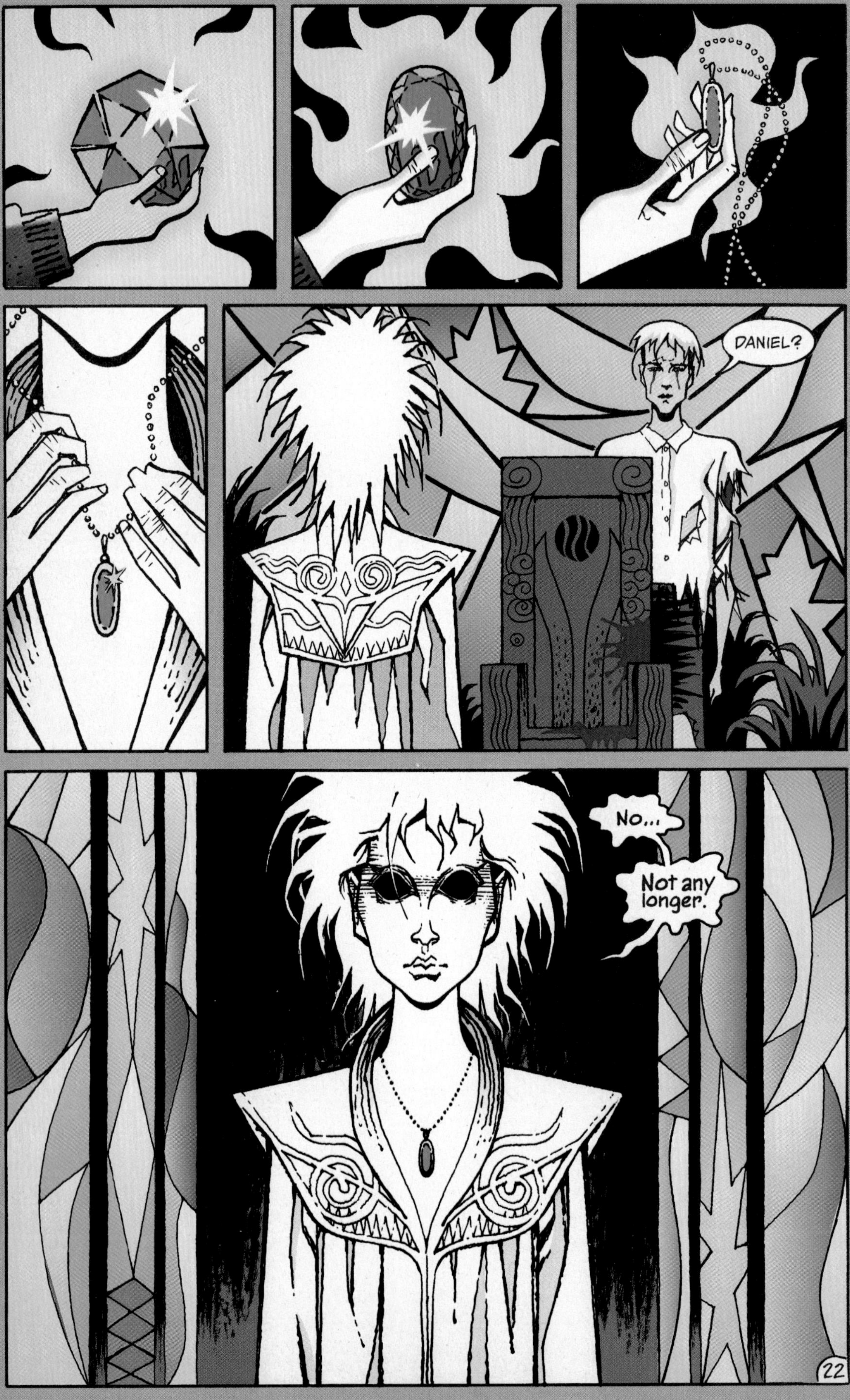
DANIEL?
No...
Not any longer.

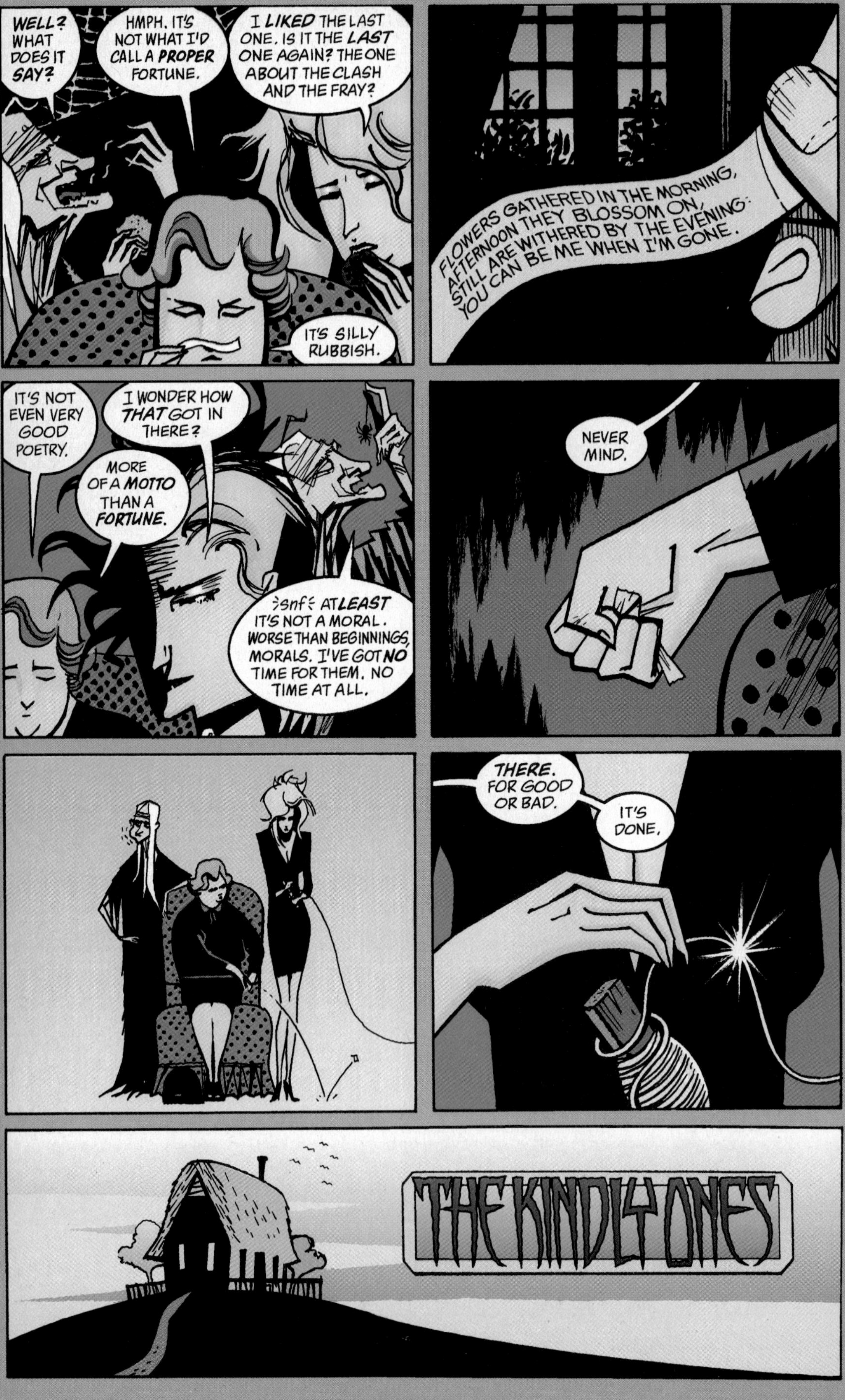
WELL? WHAT DOES IT SAY?
HMPH. IT'S NOT WHAT I'D CALL A PROPER FORTUNE.
I LIKED THE LAST ONE. IS IT THE LAST ONE AGAIN? THE ONE ABOUT THE CLASH AND THE FRAY?
IT'S SILLY RUBBISH.
FLOWERS GATHERED IN THE MORNING, AFTERNOON THEY BLOSSOM ON, STILL ARE WITHERED BY THE EVENING: YOU CAN BE ME WHEN I'M GONE.
IT'S NOT EVEN VERY GOOD POETRY.
I WONDER HOW THAT GOT IN THERE?
MORE OF A MOTTO THAN A FORTUNE.
snf AT LEAST IT'S NOT A MORAL. WORSE THAN BEGINNINGS, MORALS. I'VE GOT NO TIME FOR THEM. NO TIME AT ALL.
NEVER MIND.
THERE. FOR GOOD OR BAD.
IT'S DONE.
THE KINDLY ONES

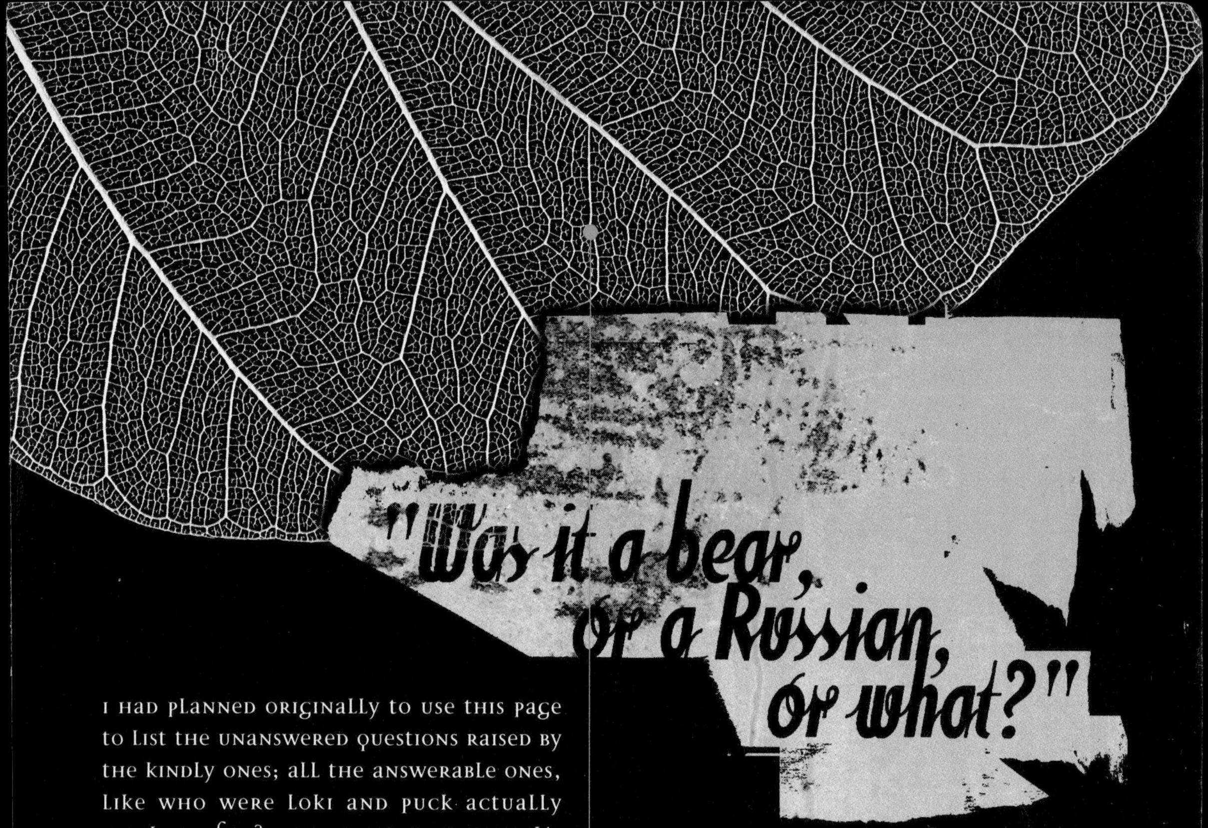
"Was it a bear, or a Russian, or what?"

i had planned originally to use this page to list the unanswered questions raised by the kindly ones; all the answerable ones, like who were loki and puck actually working for? and what was remiel's problem anyway? and the unanswerable, like how could anyone play, let alone win, mrs. crupp and mrs. treadgold's game of draughts (a.k.a. checkers)? or even so was that really piglet in the bed?

but you can make your own list.

some of your questions may be answered in the last sandman book, the wake, which follows this, and others may be answered in the earlier seven sandman collections. and for those that aren't answered anywhere, all i can do is quote cain, quoting robert aickman, quoting saccheverel sitwell. it is the mystery that lingers, they have all told us, at one time or another, and not the explanation.

this was the longest of all the sandman stories, and it was in many ways the hardest to write. through everything, shelly roeberg got pages out of me and out of the artists, and saw them through the production process. she was always there, and i cannot thank her enough.

thanks to the artists: marc hempel, richard case and d'israeli, glyn dillon, dean ormston, teddy kristiansen and charles vess. thanks to kevin nowlan.

thanks to danny vozzo for the colors, and to todd klein for making everyone talk, and over and above it all, thanks to dave mckean for the covers, the design, and being a sane friend in a delightfully crazy world.

karen berger reigns on high like juno, and bob kahan scuttles around in the depths like vulcan, hammering the thirteen episodes of the story into the correctly colored, relatively goof-free volume you hold in your hands; together they are our editors.

thanks to paul levitz and jenette kahn for letting the story end. thanks to john webster for seeing the skull beneath the skin, and to matthew the raven, for being the kind of fictional character one can rely on.

i still do not know how successful the kindly ones was, how close i got or how far i came from what i set out to say. still, it's the heaviest of all of these volumes, and thus, in hardback at least, could undoubtedly be used to stun a burglar; which has always been my definition of real art.

neil gaiman
out in the cold woods
november 1995

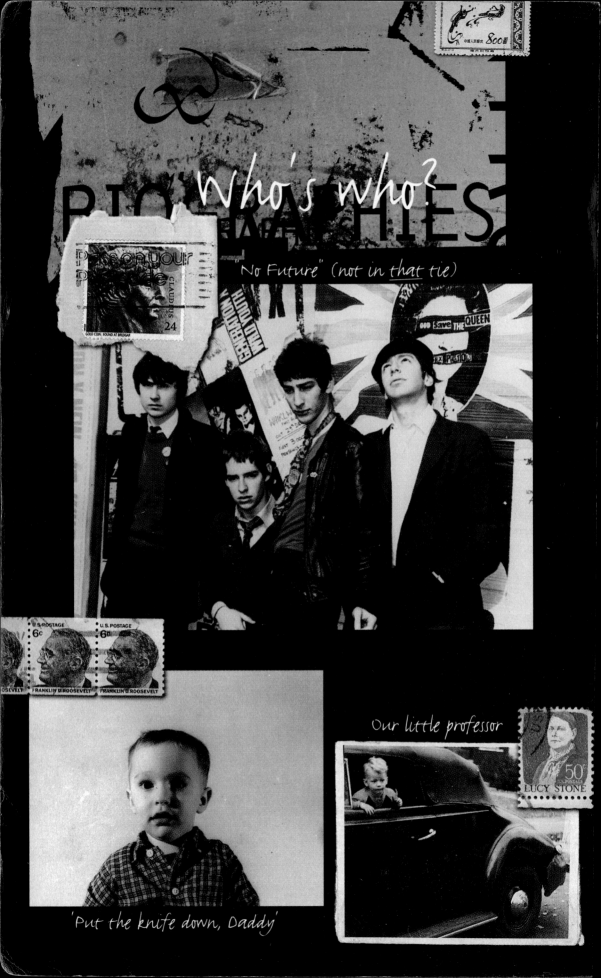

Who's who?

"No Future" (not in that tie)

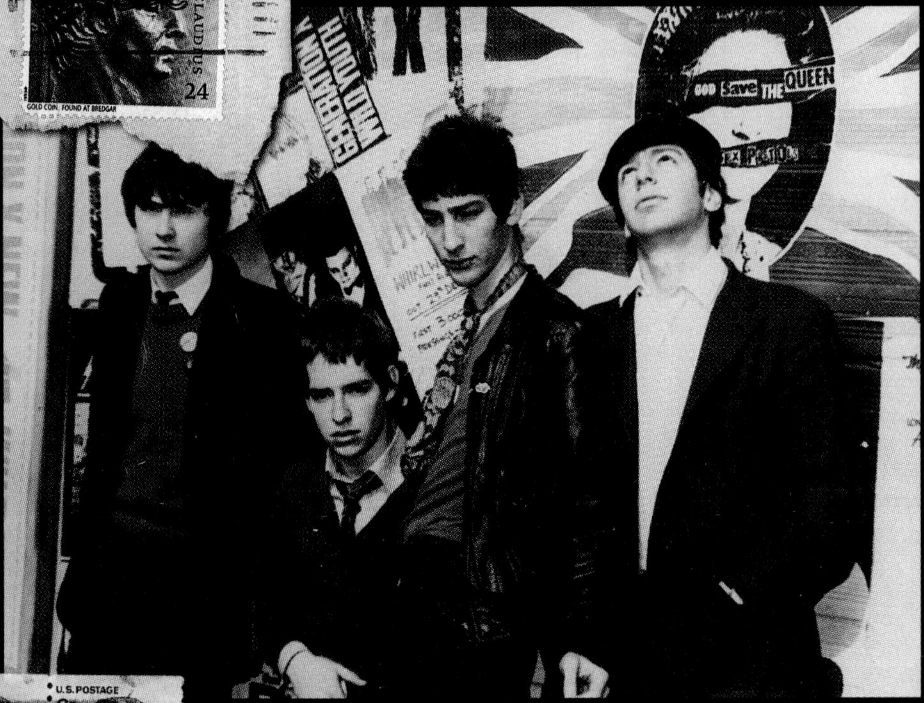
Save THE QUEEN

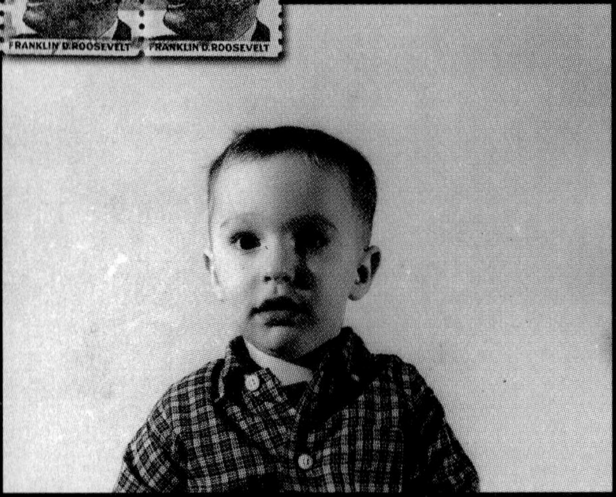

'Put the knife down, Daddy'

Our little professor

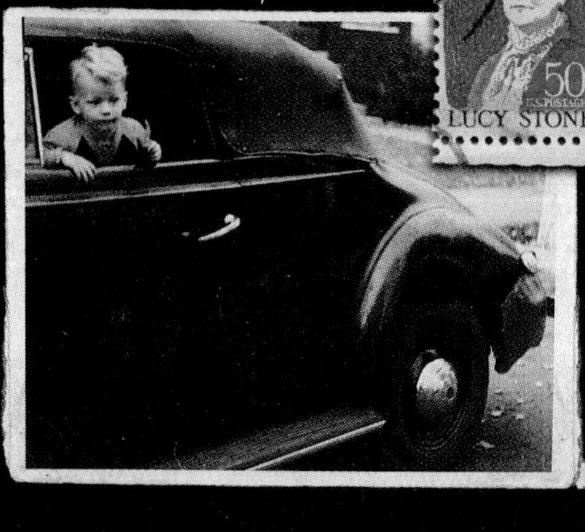

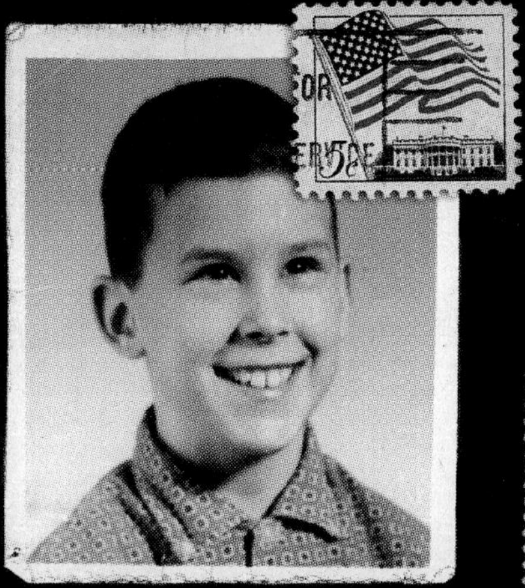

The Nice Vess boy.

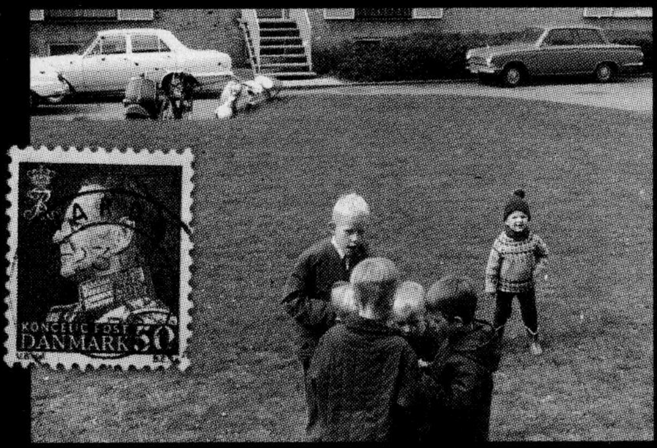
DANMARK 50

Small Dane with bobble hat

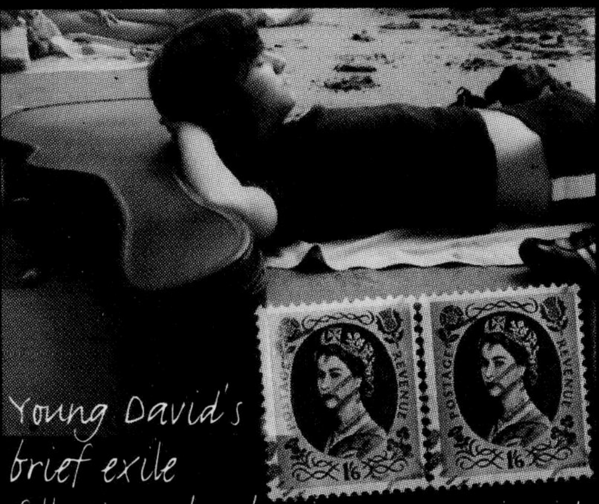

Young David's
brief exile
following the shaving cream incident.

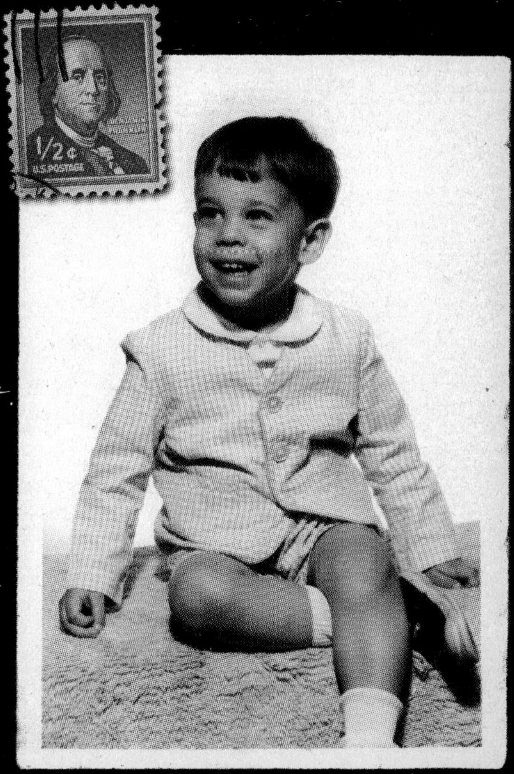
1/2¢
U.S.POSTAGE

Master Case could teach
Marc and Matt to smile!

"Ow! Glyn hurt his arm!"

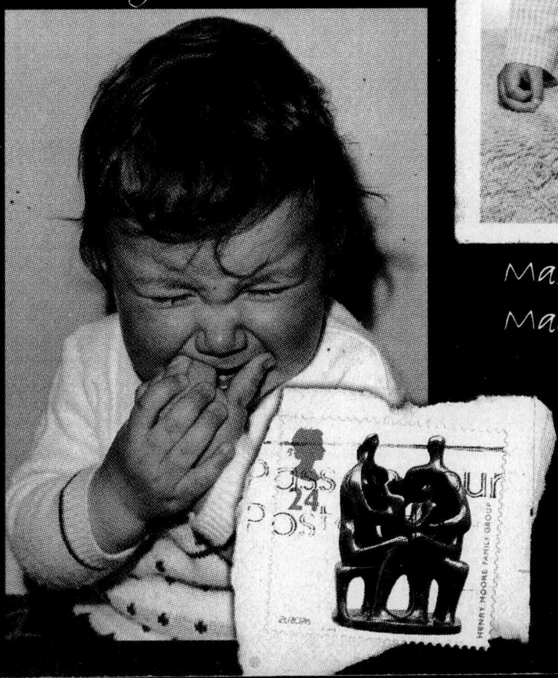
24

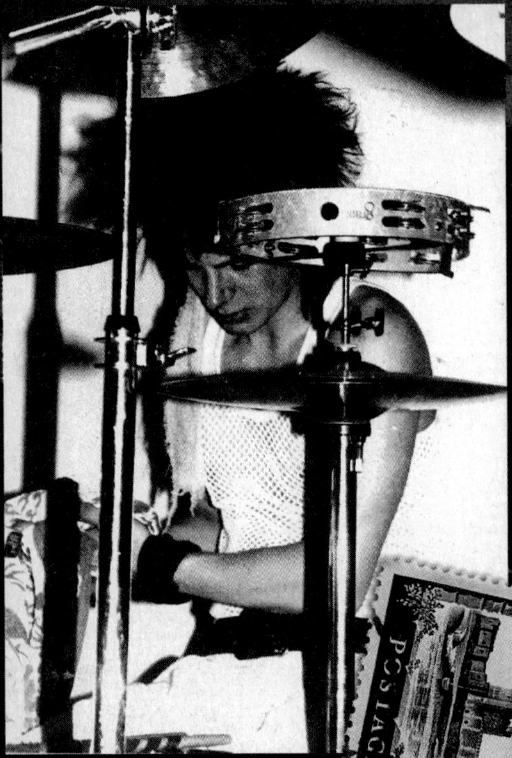
POSTAGE 2/6

Serious hair and drums, Dean.

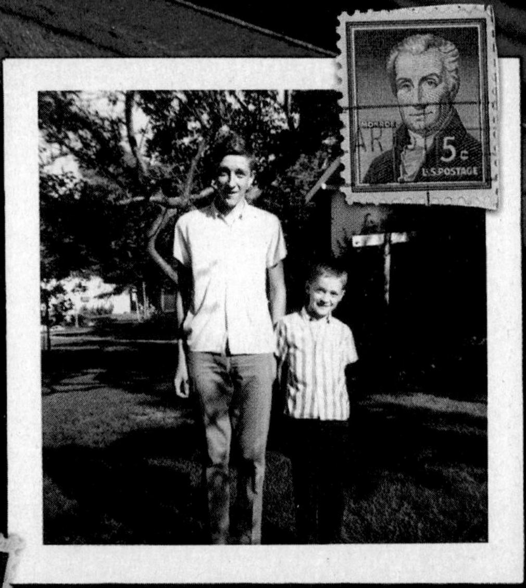
5¢
U.S. POSTAGE

Is that Kevin on the right?

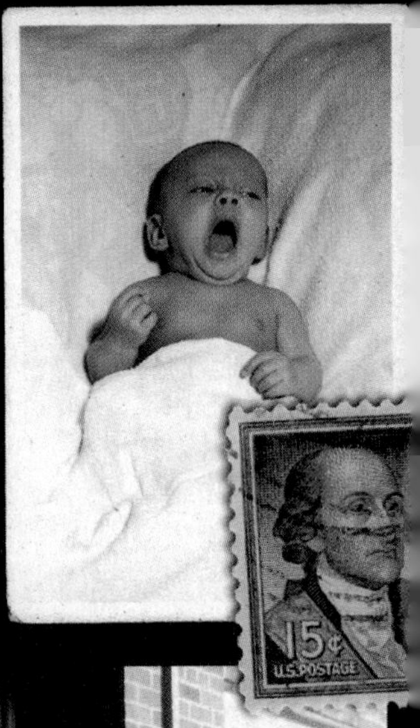
15¢
U.S. POSTAGE

mighty iron lungs!

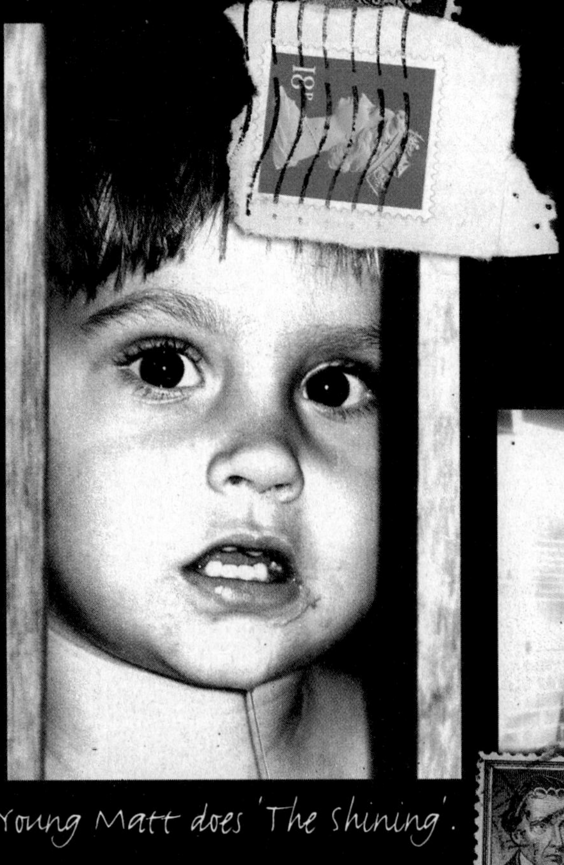
18p

Young Matt does 'The Shining'.

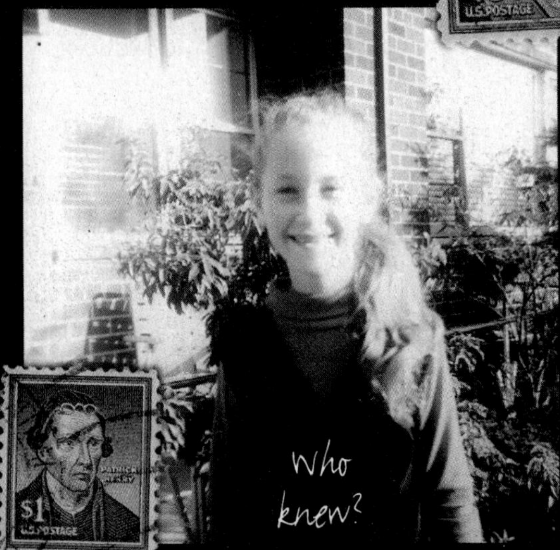
$1
U.S. POSTAGE

Who knew?

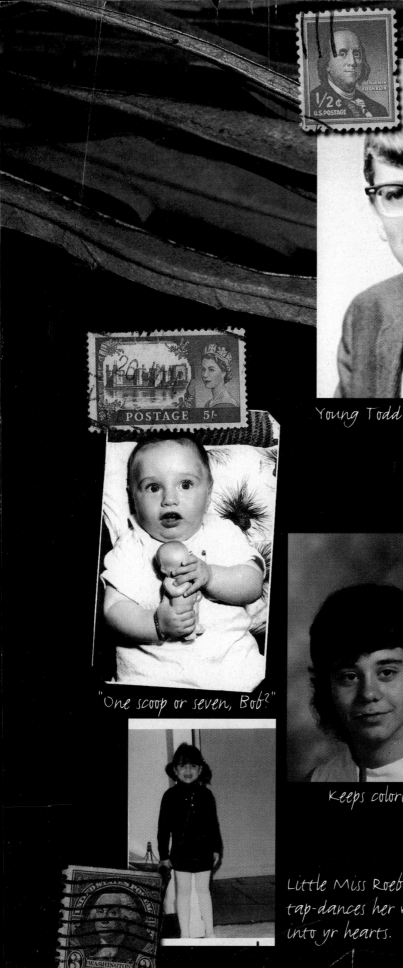

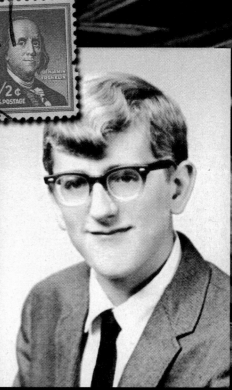

BENJAMIN FRANKLIN
1/2¢
U.S. POSTAGE
Young Todd - lovely penmanship.

POSTAGE 5/-
"One scoop or seven, Bob?"

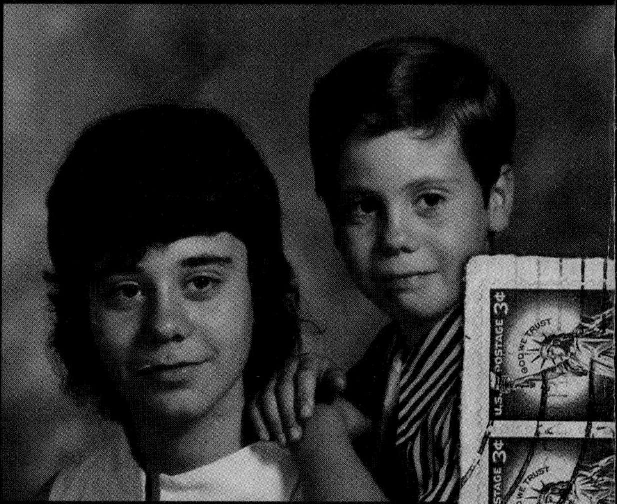

Keeps coloring things in.

U.S. POSTAGE 3¢
IN GOD WE TRUST

WASHINGTON

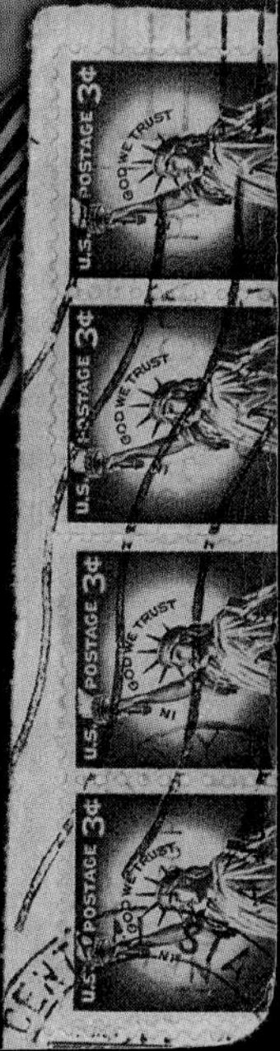

Little Miss Roeberg
tap-dances her way
into yr hearts.

THE SANDMAN LIBRARY

ELEVEN DEFINITIVE GRAPHIC NOVELS THAT REVEAL
THE STORY OF MORPHEUS AND THE ENDLESS,
HIS UNIQUELY DYSFUNCTIONAL FAMILY:

VOLUME 1: PRELUDES & NOCTURNES
Dream of the Endless, also known as the Sandman, had been
imprisoned for 70 years. After his escape, the Sandman must
reclaim his realm, The Dreaming, as well as his articles of power.

VOLUME 2: THE DOLL'S HOUSE
Rose Walker finds more than she bargained for — including
long lost relatives, a serial killers' convention and, ultimately,
her true identity — with the help of the Sandman.

VOLUME 3: DREAM COUNTRY
Four chilling and unique tales, including the World Fantasy Award-
winning story of the first performance of Shakespeare's *A Midsummer
Night's Dream* with art by Charles Vess. Also contains Gaiman's original
comic book script for *Calliope*.

VOLUME 4: SEASON OF MISTS
Ten thousand years ago, the Sandman condemned his one true love
to the pits of Hell. When his sister Death convinces him this was an
injustice, Dream journeys to Hell to rescue his lost lover — just as
Lucifer Morningstar decides to abdicate his throne, leaving the Key
to Hell in the hands of the Sandman.

VOLUME 5: A GAME OF YOU
Barbie used to dream of being a princess in a private kingdom with
strange animals as her subjects. But Barbie has stopped dreaming
and now her imaginary world and the real world entwine in a riveting
story about gender and identity.

VOLUME 6: FABLES & REFLECTIONS
From the mists of the past to the nightmares of the present, Dream
touches the lives of the king of ancient Baghdad and Lady Johanna
Constantine, among others, in nine remarkable self-contained stories.

VOLUME 7: BRIEF LIVES
Delirium, youngest of the Endless, prevails upon her brother Dream
to help find their missing brother, Destruction. Their odyssey through
the waking world also leads the Sandman to resolve his painful
relationship with his son, Orpheus.

VOLUME 8: WORLDS' END
Caught in the vortex of a reality storm, wayfarers from throughout
time, myth, and the imagination converge on a mysterious inn. In
the tradition of Chaucer's *Canterbury Tales*, the travelers wait out
the tempest that rages around them by sharing stories.

VOLUME 9: THE KINDLY ONES
Unstoppable in their mission of vengeance, the Kindly Ones will not
rest until the crime they seek to punish has been washed clean with
blood. Now Dream of the Endless, his acquaintances, and his family
find themselves caught up in this dark conspiracy.

VOLUME 10: THE WAKE
Ancient gods, old friends, and even enemies gather to remember and
pay tribute in the strangest wake ever held. And, at the end of his
life, William Shakespeare fulfills his side of a very strange bargain.

VOLUME 11: ENDLESS NIGHTS
Seven dark and beautiful tales — one each for the Sandman and his
siblings — are illustrated by an international dream team of artists.

FROM THE WORLD OF THE SANDMAN:

THE SANDMAN: THE DREAM HUNTERS
NEIL GAIMAN/YOSHITAKA AMANO
Set in Japan and told in illustrated prose, this adult fairy tale
featuring the Lord of Dreams is beautifully painted by legendary
artist Yoshitaka Amano.

DEATH: THE HIGH COST OF LIVING
NEIL GAIMAN/CHRIS BACHALO/MARK BUCKINGHAM
A solo story of Death, who, for one day every century, assumes
mortal form to learn more about the lives she must take.

DEATH: THE TIME OF YOUR LIFE
NEIL GAIMAN/CHRIS BACHALO/MARK BUCKINGHAM/MARK PENNINGTON
A young lesbian mother strikes a deal with Death for the life of her
son in a story about fame, relationships, and rock and roll.

DESTINY: A CHRONICLE OF DEATHS FORETOLD
ALISA KWITNEY/VARIOUS
In a doomed town in the year 2009, a handful of survivors awaiting
the final coming of the Plague are visited by a stranger claiming to
carry the Book of Destiny.

THE LITTLE ENDLESS STORYBOOK
JILL THOMPSON
This tale of a diminutive version of the Endless is written and painted
by acclaimed SANDMAN artist Jill Thompson.

DEATH: AT DEATH'S DOOR
JILL THOMPSON
It's the party from Hell — literally — in this fanciful retelling of
SEASON OF MISTS. Executed in a flawless *Manga* style by Jill Thompson.

DUST COVERS — THE COLLECTED SANDMAN COVERS 1989-1997
DAVE MCKEAN/NEIL GAIMAN
A complete portfolio of Dave McKean's celebrated SANDMAN cover art,
together with commentary by McKean and Gaiman.

THE QUOTABLE SANDMAN
NEIL GAIMAN/VARIOUS
A mini-hardcover of memorable quotations from THE SANDMAN
accompanied by a host of renditions of Morpheus and the Endless.

THE SANDMAN COMPANION
HY BENDER/VARIOUS
A treasury of artwork, essays, analysis, and interviews about
THE SANDMAN.

OTHER BOOKS BY NEIL GAIMAN FROM VERTIGO:

BLACK ORCHID
NEIL GAIMAN/DAVE MCKEAN
In the tradition of Alan Moore's SWAMP THING, Gaiman and McKean's
first comics collaboration reimagines the character of Black Orchid in
a lushly painted story of identity and betrayal.

THE BOOKS OF MAGIC
NEIL GAIMAN/JOHN BOLTON/SCOTT HAMPTON/CHARLES VESS/PAUL JOHNSON
A quartet of fallen mystics (John Constantine, the Phantom Stranger,
Dr. Occult, and Mister E) introduce the world of magic to young Tim
Hunter, who is destined to become the world's most powerful magician.

MR. PUNCH
NEIL GAIMAN/DAVE MCKEAN
Gaiman and McKean reunite to create a unique vision of nostalgia
and remembrance.

NEIL GAIMAN'S MIDNIGHT DAYS
NEIL GAIMAN/MATT WAGNER/TEDDY KRISTIANSEN/VARIOUS
A collection of Gaiman stories from other VERTIGO titles, featuring
Swamp Thing, John Constantine, and the Golden Age Sandman.

NEIL GAIMAN AND CHARLES VESS' STARDUST
NEIL GAIMAN/CHARLES VESS
A Victorian-era tale of the magic and romance between a young man
and a shooting star, told in prose with lavish painted illustrations.

Visit us at www.vertigocomics.com for more information on these
and many other titles from VERTIGO and DC Comics.
Call 1-888-COMIC BOOK for the ——s shop nearest you, or go to your local book store.

SND0011